W9-DBI-832
DISCARDED

THE CAMBRIDGE COMPANION TO ENGLISH NOVELISTS

In this Companion, leading scholars and critics address the work of the most celebrated and enduring novelists from the British Isles (excluding living writers), among them Defoe, Richardson, Sterne, Austen, Dickens, the Brontës, George Eliot, Hardy, James, Lawrence, Joyce, and Woolf. The significance of each writer in their own time is explained, the relation of their work to that of predecessors and successors explored, and their most important novels analysed. These essays do not aim to create a canon in a prescriptive way, but taken together they describe a strong, developing tradition of the writing of fictional prose over the past three hundred years. This volume is a helpful guide for those studying and teaching the novel, and will allow readers to consider the significance of less familiar authors such as Henry Green and Elizabeth Bowen alongside those with a more established place in literary history.

ADRIAN POOLE is Professor of English Literature and Fellow of Trinity College, Cambridge.

A complete list of books in the series is at the back of this book.

THE CAMBRIDGE
COMPANION TO

ENGLISH NOVELISTS

EDITED BY
ADRIAN POOLE

CAMBRIDGE UNIVERSITY PRESS
Cambridge, New York, Melbourne, Madrid, Cape Town, Singapore,
São Paulo, Delhi, Dubai, Tokyo

Cambridge University Press
The Edinburgh Building, Cambridge CB2 8RU, UK

Published in the United States of America by Cambridge University Press, New York

www.cambridge.org
Information on this title: www.cambridge.org/9780521691574

First published 2009

Printed in the United Kingdom at the University Press, Cambridge

A catalogue record for this publication is available from the British Library

Library of Congress Cataloguing in Publication data
The Cambridge companion to English novelists / [edited by] Adrian Poole.
p. cm. (Cambridge companions to)
Includes bibliographical references and index.
ISBN 978-0-521-87119-8 (hardback)
1. English fiction–History and criticism–Handbooks, manuals, etc.
I. Poole, Adrian. II. Title. III. Series.
PR821.C36 2010
823′.509–dc22
2009033923

ISBN 978-0-521-87119-8 Hardback
ISBN 978-0-521-69157-4 Paperback

CONTENTS

NOTES ON CONTRIBUTORS

DOROTHEA BARRETT teaches literature and writing at New York University at La Pietra and at Syracuse University in Florence. She is the author of *Vocation and Desire: George Eliot's Heroines* (1989) and various essays on nineteenth- and twentieth-century British and American literature. She has edited works by George Eliot, Oscar Wilde, E. M. Forster, James Joyce, Katherine Mansfield, and others.

MICHAEL BELL is Professor Emeritus in the Department of English and Comparative Literary Studies and Associate Fellow of the Centre for Research in Philosophy, Literature, and the Arts at the University of Warwick. He has written mainly on literary and philosophical themes, such as primitivism, sentiment, and education, from Enlightenment to modernity, as well as single-author studies on D. H. Lawrence and García Márquez.

PENNY BOUMELHA was Jury Professor of English Language and Literature at the University of Adelaide, South Australia, and a Fellow of the Academy of the Humanities in Australia; she is now Deputy Vice-Chancellor (Academic) at Victoria University of Wellington, New Zealand. She has published widely on nineteenth-century writers, realism, and issues of gender and narrative, including *Thomas Hardy and Women* (1982) and *Charlotte Brontë* (1990), and is the editor of a Casebook on *Jude the Obscure* (2000).

VICTORIA COULSON is a Lecturer in American Literature at the University of York. Her publications include *Henry James, Women and Realism* (2007) and essays on Austen, Charlotte Mary Yonge, and the poetics of material culture in nineteenth-century fiction. Her next book is about happiness in James.

NICHOLAS DAMES is Theodore Kahan Associate Professor in the Humanities at Columbia University. He is the author of *Amnesiac Selves: Nostalgia, Forgetting, and British Fiction, 1810–1870* (2001) and *The Physiology of the Novel: Reading, Neural Science, and the Form of Victorian Fiction* (2007).

SANTANU DAS teaches in the School of English and Drama at Queen Mary University of London and was formerly a research fellow at St John's College, Cambridge and at the British Academy, London. He is the author of *Touch and Intimacy in First World War Literature* (2006) and the editor of *Race, Empire and Writing the First World War* (2010). He is presently working on the Commonwealth literary and artistic responses to the First World War, with a focus on India.

MARIA DIBATTISTA, Professor of English and Comparative Literature at Princeton University, has written widely on modern literature and film. Her works include *Virginia Woolf: The Fables of Anon* (1980), *First Love: The Affections of Modern Fiction* (1991), and *Fast Talking Dames* (2001). Her most recent book is *Imagining Virginia Woolf: An Experiment in Critical Biography* (2009).

ROBERT DOUGLAS-FAIRHURST is Fellow and Tutor in English at Magdalen College, Oxford. He is the author of *Victorian Afterlives: The Shaping of Influence in Nineteenth-Century Literature* (2002) and has edited Dickens's *A Christmas Carol and Other Christmas Books* (2006) and *Great Expectations* (2008) for Oxford World's Classics.

MAUD ELLMANN is the Donald and Marilyn Keough Professor of Irish Studies and English at the University of Notre Dame. Her books include *The Hunger Artists: Starving, Writing, and Imprisonment* (1993) and *Elizabeth Bowen: The Shadow across the Page* (2004).

HEATHER GLEN is Professor of English Literature at the University of Cambridge and a Fellow of Murray Edwards College (formerly New Hall), Cambridge. Her publications include *Charlotte Brontë: The Imagination in History* (2002), *The Cambridge Companion to the Brontës* (ed., 2002), and an edition of Charlotte Brontë's *Tales of Angria* (2006).

ROBERT HAMPSON is Professor of Modern Literature and Head of the Department of English at Royal Holloway, University of London. He is the author of *Joseph Conrad: Betrayal and Identity* (1992) and

Cross-Cultural Encounters in Joseph Conrad's Malay Fiction (2000) and is currently working on *Conrad's Secrets*. He has edited various texts by Kipling, Haggard, and Conrad for Penguin.

JOCELYN HARRIS is an Emeritus Professor in the Department of English, University of Otago, New Zealand. She has edited Austen's favourite book, Samuel Richardson's *Sir Charles Grandison* (1979) and has written *Jane Austen's Art of Memory* (1989, repr. 2003). Her latest book is *A Revolution Almost beyond Expression: Jane Austen's Persuasion* (2007).

MICHIEL HEYNS is Professor Emeritus at the University of Stellenbosch, South Africa. He has written extensively on the nineteenth-century novel and on modern South African fiction. He is the author of *Expulsion and the Nineteenth-Century Novel: The Scapegoat in English Realist Fiction* (1994). He has published four novels and several translations.

VIVIEN JONES is Professor of Eighteenth-Century Gender and Culture in the School of English, University of Leeds. She has published widely on gender and writing in the period, including, as editor, *Women and Literature in Britain, 1700–1800* (2000) and *Evelina* (2002). She contributed an essay on 'Burney and Gender' to *The Cambridge Companion to Frances Burney* (2007).

THOMAS KEYMER is Chancellor Jackman Professor of English at the University of Toronto. His books include *Richardson's Clarissa and the Eighteenth-Century Reader* (1992), *Sterne, the Moderns, and the Novel* (2002), and the Oxford World's Classics editions of *Robinson Crusoe* (2007) and *Rasselas* (2009). He co-edits *Review of English Studies* and, with Peter Sabor, the Cambridge Edition of the Works and Correspondence of Samuel Richardson.

ANTHONY LANE is a film critic and staff writer on the *New Yorker* and author of *Nobody's Perfect* (2002), a collection of articles from the magazine. He is also an Academic Associate in English at Pembroke College, Cambridge.

BRIGID LOWE is a Fellow of Trinity College, Cambridge. She has published articles on Dickens and Hardy, as well as a book, *Victorian Fiction and the Insights of Sympathy: An Alternative to the Hermeneutics of Suspicion* (2007). She is currently enjoying research towards a study of the pleasures of realist fiction.

ALISON LUMSDEN is a Senior Lecturer in English and Scottish Literature at the University of Aberdeen. She is co-director of the Walter Scott Research Centre and a general editor of the Edinburgh Edition of the Waverley Novels. She has edited several volumes for the Edinburgh Edition including *The Heart of Mid-Lothian* and *The Pirate*. She is currently completing a monograph on Scott.

ROBERT MACFARLANE is a Fellow in English at Emmanuel College, Cambridge. He is the author of *Mountains of the Mind* (2003), *The Wild Places* (2007), and *Original Copy* (2007).

JILL L. MATUS is a Professor of English and Vice-Provost, Students at the University of Toronto. She has published a wide range of articles on Victorian fiction and is the author of *Unstable Bodies: Victorian Representations of Sexuality and Maternity* (1995) and editor of *The Cambridge Companion to Elizabeth Gaskell* (2007). Her forthcoming *Shock and the Victorian Psyche* explores the emergence of trauma as a concept in Victorian fiction and psychology.

MELVYN NEW Professor Emeritus of English, University of Florida, has been writing on Sterne for the past forty years. Volumes VII and VIII of the Florida Edition of the Works of Sterne, for which he is general editor, are now in press; co-edited with Peter de Voogd, they will contain the correspondence of Sterne.

ADRIAN POOLE is Professor of English Literature at the University of Cambridge and a Fellow of Trinity College, Cambridge. His monographs include *Gissing in Context* (1975), *Henry James* (1989), and *Shakespeare and the Victorians* (2003), and he has edited novels by Dickens, James, and Stevenson for Penguin and Oxford World's Classics. He is one of the general editors of the Complete Fiction of Henry James to be published by Cambridge University Press in thirty volumes.

PETER SABOR is Canada Research Chair in Eighteenth-Century Studies and Director of the Burney Centre at McGill University. His publications on Richardson include (with Thomas Keymer) *Pamela in the Marketplace: Literary Controversy and Print Culture in Eighteenth-Century Britain and Ireland* (2005). He is also, with Keymer, co-general editor of the Cambridge Edition of the Works and Correspondence of Samuel Richardson, to be published in twenty-five volumes.

DAVID SKILTON is Research Professor in English at Cardiff University. He has written extensively on Victorian literature and edited many of the novels of Trollope for various publishers. He is currently working on meaning production in illustrated texts and is a founding editor of the *Journal of Illustration Studies*.

JANE SPENCER is Professor of English at the University of Exeter. She has published widely on the eighteenth-century novel and on women's literary history from the Restoration to the nineteenth century. Her books include *The Rise of the Woman Novelist* (1986), *Aphra Behn's Afterlife* (2000), and *Literary Relations: Kinship and the Canon, 1660–1830* (2005). She is currently working on a book on animals in eighteenth-century writing.

PATSY STONEMAN is an Emeritus Reader in English at the University of Hull, where she taught for most of her academic life. She has published widely on the Brontës, including essays for both the *Oxford* and the *Cambridge Companions*. Her major monograph is *Brontë Transformations: The Cultural Dissemination of 'Jane Eyre' and 'Wuthering Heights'* (1996), and her most recent publication is *Jane Eyre on Stage, 1848–1898: An Illustrated Edition of Eight Plays with Contextual Notes* (2007).

BHARAT TANDON is Fellow and Tutor in English at St Anne's College, Oxford. He is the author of *Jane Austen and the Morality of Conversation* (2003); he is currently preparing an annotated edition of *Emma* for Harvard University Press and a book on echoing and haunting in Victorian fiction. He also reviews contemporary fiction for the *Times Literary Supplement*.

ADRIAN POOLE

Introduction

In 1706 Daniel Defoe was spying in Scotland. A year before the Union of England and Scotland, he wrote to his employer, Robert Harley, Queen Anne's Secretary of State, from Edinburgh:

> I have faithfull Emissaries in Every Company And I Talk to Everybody in Their Own way ... With the Glasgow Mutineers I am to be a fish Merchant, with the Aberdeen Men a woollen and with the Perth and western men a Linen Manufacturer, and still at the End of all Discourse the Union is the Essentiall and I am all to Every one that I may Gain some.[1]

Let us hope that Harley was amused as well as informed.

'I Talk to Everybody in Their Own way' – and everybody talks to me. This is good training for a writer of some sort, a dramatist perhaps and a journalist certainly. Not that Defoe was a novice: born in 1660, he was in his mid-forties, author of satirical poems and pamphlets including *The True-Born Englishman* and *The Shortest Way with Dissenters* (the latter landed him in jail). But a new – and safer – kind of writer was about to emerge. While the word 'novel' had been available throughout the seventeenth century to describe certain kinds of stories in print, especially in its later decades, the idea of 'the novelist' was about to leap into existence. The first date recorded by the *OED* of the word for an author of novels is 1728. The phenomenal success of Defoe's *Robinson Crusoe* (1719) had something to do with this.

Defoe boasts of his skills as an impersonator who can dance into people's confidence. Yet he could have been lying in bed and making the whole thing up. Did Robert Harley wonder whose side this secret agent was on? How could he be trusted? A hundred and fifty years or so later, one of Defoe's most brilliant successors, well trained as a journalist to listen to everybody in their own way, creates a character of whom it is said: 'He do the Police in different voices.'[2] Charles Dickens could do more than the police in different voices. Like Defoe, he could do outcasts, deviants, criminals, and their victims, all up and down the social scale, a seemingly unending performance. Whose side was *he* on?

In the novel with which Graham Greene's career began to take off, *Stamboul Train* (1932), a frantic female journalist pounces on a best-selling author named Mr Quin Savory and lures him into pompous fatuities. His views on modern literature – Joyce, Lawrence – for example: 'It will pass', he opines. As for himself:

> 'I'm not a poet. A poet's an individualist. He can dress as he likes; he depends only on himself. A novelist depends on other men; he's an average man with the power of expression. 'E's a spy,' Mr Savory added with confusing drama, dropping aitches right and left. ''E 'as to see everything and pass unnoticed. If people recognized 'im they wouldn't talk, they'd pose before 'im; 'e wouldn't find things out.'[3]

Greene is having fun at someone's expense – the novelist J. B. Priestley thought it was his. Mr Savory is not showing off to his interlocutor as brilliantly as Defoe to Harley or Dickens to his readers. He affects a more modest idea of the writer as nondescript, nearly anonymous, going about his business 'finding things out'. Yet however banal this way of putting it, there is a humdrum truth to the idea that a novelist depends on other men (and women) and tries to find things out. Greene, all his aitches in place, would sign up to it with zest and develop it with a good deal more verve (though no less success) than poor commonplace Mr Savory.

Not all twenty-seven novelists featured in this volume of essays led or depicted such adventurous lives as Defoe, Dickens, and Greene, out and about, on the road, at risk. Some preferred being around the house, not always their own, listening to gossip, to plots and plans about property, belongings, and dwellings, musing like Elizabeth Bennet that to be mistress of Pemberley, or wherever, might be something. More feminine interests, perhaps? But it would be wrong to gender this distinction between two kinds of novelist too neatly, or indeed to hold it too firmly at all. One of the contentions emerging from these essays is that novelists enjoy challenging distinctions of all kinds, between resident and vagrant, in-law and out-law, master and servant, domestic and exotic, loyalist and renegade, and so on. Outcasts and exiles are not always willing and male, as the creators of Clarissa Harlowe, Jane Eyre, and Tess Durbeyfield will testify, and even the most enthusiastic fugitive must find the occasional bed for the night. Novels have always been as interested in finding good lodgings as in taking long journeys, just as, to speak more largely, they have been no less intrigued and alarmed by the prospect of settlement, union, and closure, than appalled and excited by that of secession, divorce, and unending flight.

Nevertheless there is, up until the modernists among whom such distinctions more frankly collapse, a certain opposition between novelists who work mainly on the outside, as it were – Defoe, Fielding, Scott, Dickens, Stevenson – and those who dwell on the inside – Richardson, Burney, Austen, Eliot, James. Like all such distinctions, including that hoary old one between 'romance' and 'realism', this is too simple. Yet Scott recognised that the kind of fiction at which Jane Austen excelled with its 'minute fidelity of detail' (his phrase) was quite distinct from his own,[4] and George Eliot aspired to write novels radically different from Dickens's. Eliot was the first, so D. H. Lawrence thought, to 'put the action inside'.[5] An overstatement to be sure, but also a way of recognising that after Eliot, her successors would be more sharply uncertain where the action was – Forster and Woolf and Bowen, and even more drastically the Joyce of *Ulysses* and *Finnegans Wake*, the Golding of *The Inheritors* and *Pincher Martin*. Yet back in the eighteenth century this had also been true of Sterne's *Tristram Shandy*, that endless hopeless search, no less comical than tragical, for 'the action'.

Henry James memorably expressed the conviction that to render in words what goes on inside can be no less gripping than the most rampant adventure. He is reflecting here with pride on the chapter in his early masterpiece, *The Portrait of a Lady* (1881), 'the extraordinary meditative vigil', when his protagonist sits and thinks late at night by a dying fire. It shows, James says,

> what an 'exciting' inward life may do for the person leading it even while it remains perfectly normal ... It is a representation simply of her motionlessly *seeing*, and an attempt withal to make the mere still lucidity of her act as 'interesting' as the surprise of a caravan or the identification of a pirate.[6]

A quarter of a century separates James's comments from his first rendering of Isabel Archer; they are from the Preface to the revised version in the New York Edition of 1907–9. The intervening years had in fact seen an efflorescence of fiction involving caravans and pirates, spies, secret agents, anarchists, revolutionaries, all kinds of excitement in jungles at the margins of empire and back in its heart, the metropolis. Novelists cannot manage without violence of some sort, public or private, physical or verbal or psychological, the rape in *Clarissa*, the bomb-blast in Conrad's *Secret Agent*, Emma's rudeness to Miss Bates, or whatever happens to Adela Quested in Forster's Marabar Caves. And Gilbert Osmond's quiet torture of Isabel Archer.

Whatever form it takes, violence blows things and people apart, obliterating distinctions between them. Loyalties are hastily, fervently mustered. By the last page of James's *Portrait*, it is reasonably clear who has been loyal to Isabel and who has betrayed her. In this respect it resembles most of the preceding novels discussed in this volume – novels that take their last stand, as it seems, on issues of personal loyalty. Defoe wrote to Harley: 'still at the End of all Discourse the Union is the Essentiall'. A great many English novels would go on to pledge their support for 'the Union' of suitable partners, usually a man and a woman and with luck some surrounding supporters. Though there are flagrantly tragic exceptions, such as *Wuthering Heights*, and most of the novels by James's contemporary, Thomas Hardy, such unions remain, up until the later decades of the nineteenth century, a prime form of narrative closure. Yet the confidence with which the union is achieved is rarely unshadowed by doubts, regrets, guilts, anxieties, wounds. Scott's novels would be negligible without them. The wavering protagonist of his first novel may pass with breathtaking innocence from one side to another of the first (and so far greatest) crisis of the Union for which Defoe and others had laboured. But the sensitive reader is not as unscathed as Edward Waverley, nor of course are the glamorous doomed Highlanders by whom he is enchanted, Fergus and Flora Mac-Ivor.

Isabel Archer is scarred by the pain of betrayals and loyalties, her own and others, as Waverley is not, but she shares them with her readers. The reader of James's last major completed novel, *The Golden Bowl* (1904), is likely to be much less confident about who has been loyal and treacherous to whom. An adulterous couple has been separated; husbands and wives have returned to each other; somebody, or everybody, has been betrayed. In this respect the novel looks forward as *The Portrait* looks back. It is notable, in the later essays of the current volume, how prominent are questions of loyalty, betrayal, and treachery, from Conrad through Greene, Waugh and Bowen to Golding. Forster too, who declared that if he had to choose between betraying his country and betraying his friend, he hoped he should have the guts to betray his country.[7] But such bravura statements do not do justice, as novels can, to the traumatic reality of these choices. The wonderful ending of Forster's own *A Passage to India* (1924) ponders the depth of the forces that pull the closest of friends and loved ones apart.

Greene too was capable of making such public statements. In 1969 he gave a speech in Hamburg, entitled 'The Virtue of Disloyalty', in which he castigated Shakespeare as a servant of the Establishment, and lauded by contrast the brave outspoken victims of political oppression in contemporary Russia and elsewhere. By 'loyalty' here Greene meant collaboration or complicity with the power of the State; 'disloyalty' meant dissident identification with those on its receiving end. It is a naïve position that fails to discriminate between different states and the uses to which their power is put, and assumes it all to be equally brutal. But Greene was speaking as a writer. He was giving a shocking new twist to an old understanding, that for the novelist the licence to stray across everyday borders and limits is essential. 'If we enlarge the bounds of sympathy in our readers we succeed in making the work of the State a degree more difficult. That is a genuine duty we owe society, to be a piece of grit in the State machinery', he asserted.[8] Given that the University of Hamburg was trying to award Greene its Shakespeare Prize, the organisers may well have thought a piece of grit in the machinery was an apt description of their honorand.

Enlarging the bounds of sympathy is an ambition with which many novelists have found it easy to concur from the eighteenth century onwards, when modern notions of this mysterious passion get formed. George Eliot said something similar when she proposed that '[T]he greatest benefit we owe to the artist, whether painter, poet, or novelist, is the extension of our sympathies.'[9] We look to novelists to help us imagine what life looks and sounds and feels like to other people. Yet enlarge the bounds as we may, the empire must still have its limits. What is this 'sympathy' to which so many novelists and readers appeal? Or what, to use another familiar formulation, does it mean for readers to 'identify' with a character? Reading through these essays, one is struck by the ebb and flow of confidence they express, prompted by their particular authors, not only about the ability we have to know other people, to enter their worlds, to imagine their experience, but further, about its desirability. Is there not something in its turn tyrannical, colonising, at the least presumptive in supposing 'we' can enter 'them'? With whose permission? Who is this 'we'? Greene avers that the disloyalty of which he's in favour 'encourages you to roam through any human mind'. How would we like strangers or even loved ones roaming at large through our minds, rummaging in our drawers, ransacking our closets? (Elizabeth Bowen's *The Death of the Heart* (1938) begins with an elder half-sister-in-law reading her teenage ward's diary, and discovering what the girl thinks of her.) Novels are animated by a conflict between the desire to know other people's secrets and the anxiety that this is illicit, intrusive, an act of aggression, and dangerous for all concerned. One of the striking developments in the group of twentieth-century novelists featured here is a sense, more robust than amongst their Victorian forebears, that other people constitute a mystery to be respected and even honoured.

The authors represented in this volume held as many different political views as one would expect, even if these did not neatly correspond to official party lines in their own time, let alone ours. Most of them would have rebutted, some with indignation, the charge that they were in any sense spies, rather than virtuous witnesses, whether for the defence, the prosecution, or both. What's the opposite of a spy? A Holy Fool perhaps, like some of Dickens's or Golding's Matty in *Darkness Visible* (1979). Or a visionary like

Eliot's Mordecai in *Daniel Deronda* (1876) – a prophet, a mystic, a psychic, who can see straight through to the heart of the matter, or even the heart of darkness like Conrad's Kurtz, or remotely intuit it like Forster's Mrs Moore. Such figures are tempting to a novelist, yet they rarely occupy a central position. Dickens gives voice to the need we all feel, perplexed down here in the labyrinth, for the aerial viewpoint from which the secrets would all be visible: 'Oh for a good spirit who would take the house-tops off ... and show a Christian people what dark shapes issue from amidst their homes, to swell the retinue of the Destroying Angel as he moved forth among them.'[10] A Good Angel to match the Destroyer.

Spy, secret agent, correspondent, reporter, witness, angel: these are more and less dignified models for the act of relation, for finding things out and passing them on. Yet always there are the questions: on whose authority, at whose behest, and to whom? Defoe was being paid by Harley and reported back to him. Novelists are less constrained, more mysteriously spurred, and if they are lucky their words are dispersed to the four corners of the earth.

God's side would be a good one to be on. Throughout these essays there is a persistent reference to religious beliefs, values, and perspectives. These indicate the yearning for certitudes that the world, inside and outside the novels themselves, can no longer provide. If the idea of a literal or figurative journey is somehow essential to novels (even or especially when such movement is thwarted), then it is important to recognise the huge shadow cast over the English novel by John Bunyan's *Pilgrim's Progress* (1678–84), at least up until the second half of the nineteenth century.

One of the religious works that made an influential impression on the young Bunyan was Arthur Dent's best-selling guide from early in the seventeenth century, *The Plain Man's Path-way to Heaven*. No novelist would be tempted to adopt such a title, except in heaviest irony, nor many readers now to pull it off the shelf. (*The Plain Man's Pathway to Hell* is another matter.) Novelists and readers are certainly interested in pathways, but only if they lead through storms, tempests, wrecks, ruins, mazes, and labyrinths, the recurrent metaphors on which novels depend for their sense of space, along with the attendant states of perplexity, bewilderment, and ecstasy that they induce.

Among these spaces, however, is one to which many of the following essays pay particular attention: that of the human body itself and the experience of 'embodiment' that it entails – the primal needs for shelter from the elements and predators, for physical and spiritual nourishment, for intimate passion. It would seem too blunt to call these housing, food, and sex, and yet good novelists remain in touch with these base needs even as they explore the superstructures elaborated over them. They conduct experiments in what it might mean to be happy for these particular characters in these circumstances, within this realm of the possible and probable. As for example, for this individual the bliss of surrender to the elements, and for that escape into solitude. For the novelist, the risk of ruin is never far away (his or her own, as well as their characters'). The whereabouts of our daily bread are not normally as alluring as the prospect of unions, sexual and otherwise, but they press on us unforgivingly. To put it like this may simply be another way of acknowledging the permanent dispute on which the novel is founded, between 'romance' – the good future, the better world – and 'realism': or, to use William Hazlitt's unforgettable phrase, 'the mortifying standard of reality'.[11]

Let us come back to the issues about identity raised by the opening quotation by Defoe and turn them on the English novel itself. Defoe was writing at a moment in history when many questions of identity were focused in the union of the Kingdoms of England and Scotland. They continued after the official Act of Union in 1707, as they did after the other Act of Union with the third sister, the Kingdom of Ireland in 1801, and as they do of course to this day. Nor are these questions limited to the matter of how we name ourselves and each other and the countries where we were born, now reside, hope to die. Novels are particularly hospitable vehicles for exploring *all* kinds of question about identity. Who are you, who am I, who are we? Where and to what do we belong in a world so rapidly changing that we run the risk of not recognising it and therefore each other, ourselves? Who are all these Other People?

What is a novel? What is an *English* novel? Much critical capital or mere heavy weather can be made out of the questions raised by these terms 'English' and 'Novel'. There are occasions, even whole books, that can be profitably devoted to them. This introduction does not propose to do so at length. To take 'the novel' first. It is clear that in England and the anglophone world, novels established themselves as a durable way of making money from telling stories when Defoe late in life turned his brilliant hand to *Robinson Crusoe* and its successors. There had always been other ways of telling stories in writing, both in verse and prose – epic, romance, allegory, fable – and these older genres could be raided, adapted, and parodied in all sorts of ways by the shameless new upstart. There were pickings to be had from the ruins of classical antiquity, from Greek and Latin epic poetry and Alexandrian romance, and from other European vernaculars, from Boccaccio, Cervantes, Rabelais. Before Defoe there were some classics in English prose from the late Middle Ages, Malory's (and Caxton's) Arthurian romances, More's *Utopia* and Sidney's *Arcadia*. More promising perhaps, or less intimidating, were the examples of Elizabethan prose fiction in the lively rambunctious works of Thomas Nashe (*The Unfortunate Traveller*, 1594), Thomas Deloney (*Jack of Newbury*, 1597), and others. Nearer Defoe's own time, there were Bunyan's puritan allegories, most notably *Pilgrim's Progress*, and the more worldly commercial and erotic adventures of Aphra Behn, *Love-Letters between a Nobleman and His Sister* (1684–7) and *Oroonoko* (1688). Whether it is helpful to think of *Pilgrim's Progress* itself as 'a novel' is dubious; so too with Swift's *Gulliver's Travels* (1726) and Johnson's *Rasselas* (1759). Yet the boundaries that separate the novel from other prose fictions are ill-defined, porous, and permeable – constructs as artificial as those designed to keep people in their place, one side or the other of checkpoint or wall.

There are several points to be made about the intrinsic instabilities on which novels are founded and which they are designed to explore. The first is that writers have themselves often expressed anxiety about the appropriate terms for what they are up to. Frances Burney wrote of *Camilla*: 'I own I do not like calling it a *Novel* ...'.[12] Others have relished the multiplication of terms: Stevenson preferred words like tale, romance, epic, panorama. Then there's the matter of length or extent: how short can a novel be before it needs to be called something else – a novella, short story, or tale? This is an issue that only really arises around the end of the nineteenth century, with the downfall of the three-volume novel as the publishing norm and new opportunities for shorter fictional forms, eagerly seized by Stevenson, Kipling, James, Conrad, Joyce, Mansfield, and others. Thirdly: there is a vague and uneasy consensus that for a novel, 'realism' of some kind or degree may be a prerequisite. But this does not amount to much. If the novel exploits and corrupts in the interests of realism some of the allegedly purer genres of romance, allegory, fable, or satire, rooting and grounding them in time, place and circumstance, then they in turn continue to infect the novel with their own ambitions and designs, pulling it towards higher truths or other worlds.

This is not a *Companion to the English Novel*; if it were, its organising principles would probably have been quite different. A *Companion to English Novelists* promises something less concerted and more dishevelled or at least dispersed in its attention to the twenty-seven particular writers selected. It could be accused of a permissive attitude to what it means, in this context, to be 'English'. This has come to mean more than the language in which the novels are written. Nevertheless the consideration persists that there is no such thing as the British language any more than there is the American or Australian language, though of course there is comedy to be made from the mutual incomprehensibility of people who allegedly 'speak the same language'. There may be something it would be useful to think of as the British novel, as there are certainly university courses on British literature, but this should entail asking questions no less hard than those posed by historians about what it means and has meant to be 'British'. The tests that a work of literature should undergo to determine its affiliations are more complex than those employed by immigration officers checking our passports. It is salutary and a shade depressing to recall how few of the novelists included in this volume would have needed a passport or known what one was. The term 'British' is no less vexed than 'English' and probably more so. It has been known to cause offence to suggest that James Joyce might feel at home in a volume devoted to English novelists. But not as much as it would if the title were 'British novelists'.

For an 'English novel', the language itself would have seemed a sufficient condition until the emergence in the nineteenth century of 'the American novel', followed of course by the Irish novel, the Scottish, the Canadian, Australian, and so on. As the relevant essay in the current volume justly contends, there was in the early years of the nineteenth century no tradition or idea of the Scottish novel to which Walter Scott could think of himself as contributing.[13] By the 1880s, when Robert Louis Stevenson was making a name for himself, this was much less true, and when Lewis Grassic Gibbon (pen-name of James Leslie Mitchell) was producing the three novels subsequently collected as *A Scots Quair* (1946), he was part of a fully fledged project. The first of the trilogy, *Sunset Song* (1932), 'was hailed as the first really Scottish novel since Galt', so the *Oxford Companion to English Literature* tells us.[14] (John Galt (1779–1839) was Scott's contemporary, author of *Annals of the Parish* (1821) and others.) In the later nineteenth century questions about a writer's national identity or affiliation were not unknown. Henry James suffered a good deal of abuse from American friends and enemies alike for his settlement in England; writing loftily about poor Nathaniel Hawthorne and the vacancy of the American cultural scene didn't help. But James had it easy by comparison with his most obvious American successor, T. S. Eliot.

These questions of where writers really belong, to whom and what they owe allegiance, have come to seem increasingly important, at least to those involved in projects of cultural nationalism. Major writers represent precious capital; for the tourist trade too, as Ellmann's essay on Joyce here reminds us. Clearly a selection of English novelists that includes writers born in Edinburgh, Dublin, New York, and Berdyczów (in Russian Ukraine) – to take only the most blatant instances of Scott and Stevenson, Joyce, James, and Conrad – is making some claim of its own. This is not the foolish one that James is 'really' an English novelist, nor even that he is more English than American. Scott and Stevenson certainly belong in any *Companion to Scottish Literature*, as James does in the American, and Joyce in the Irish equivalents.[15] (Conrad is another matter, because of the language.) But there are other kinds of membership, in the European novel for instance, and beyond that, with increasing vacuity – though the Nobel Prize judges, like the UN, do their best – World Literature. Many of the writers included here drew inspiration from novels (and other writings) in other languages, from Cervantes of course, from Goethe, from Rabelais, Balzac, Flaubert, and Proust, from Turgenev, Tolstoy, Dostoevsky, and Chekhov. Writers as different from each other as James, Conrad, Lawrence, and Woolf all looked abroad at least as vigorously as they viewed their colleagues and rivals at home. Many of them in turn have been widely read beyond the anglophone world.

The claim made by the current selection therefore is for a permissive and inclusive idea of the English novel, one that readily acknowledges the contribution made by its chosen authors to other ideas, traditions, communities, and readerships. According to this idea the borders of what constitutes the English novel should be no more heavily policed than those surrounding the genre of the novel itself. To ask whether a novelist belongs here or there, to this country, nation, culture, club, or tribe, is to misprise and demean the whole nature of the writer's project, the good or great ones at least. Which is to contest those certitudes about identity both personal and collective on which authorities of all kinds seek to take their stand.

This *Companion* then celebrates the plurality and diversity of the English novel. Yet however enlarged the bounds of sympathy, limits have had to be drawn and choices made. These twenty-seven writers are those whose work currently seems of most enduring value; they are those whom most readers now are likely to wish to reread and whom they should therefore read first. All enthusiasts of the eighteenth-century novel will want to read Sarah Fielding's *The Adventures of David Simple* (1744) and Henry Mackenzie's *The Man of Feeling* (1771), as will admirers of the Victorian novel Sheridan Le Fanu's *Uncle Silas* (1864) and Margaret Oliphant's *Hester* (1883). But it would require a special or specialist loyalty to recommend reading any of these before *Tom Jones* and *Middlemarch*. A further way of justifying this selection is to claim that these are the figures who have seemed most important to their novelist peers, the richest and most fertile models against whom contemporary and subsequent writers have sought to measure themselves, from whom to draw strength: the most valuable to emulate. Let us avoid the depressing word 'canon'.

The number of authors included here is certainly a good deal larger than the handful admitted by F. R. Leavis to *The Great Tradition* (1948), a predictably recurrent point of reference for several contributors. The novelists featured here include several on whom Leavis specifically cast his anathema, such as Laurence Sterne. Nevertheless the Salon des Refusés to this volume is thronged by an impressive company of very good novelists. At the risk of causing further offence by omitting favoured names and thereby consigning them to even more remote ante-chambers, let me mention the following who have pressed, with varying degrees of urgency and conviction, towards the entrance threshold: Tobias Smollett, Maria Edgeworth, James Hogg, Wilkie Collins, George Meredith, George Gissing, H. G. Wells, Arnold Bennett, Ford Madox Ford, John Cowper Powys, Jean Rhys, Aldous Huxley, George Orwell, Joyce Cary, Anthony Powell, Elizabeth Taylor, Angus Wilson, Anthony Burgess, Iris Murdoch, Kingsley Amis, B. S. Johnson, Penelope Fitzgerald, Muriel Spark, and Angela Carter.

Of these, it may be worth singling out as cause for special regret the absences of Maria Edgeworth, Wilkie Collins, and Ford Madox Ford. Also Samuel Beckett, save that his ties to the world of the *English* novel, however loosely defined, seem distinctly weaker than those of his great Irish forebear, James Joyce. A generation or so ago, there would have been astonishment at the absence of Smollett and Meredith (whose reputation has suffered a remarkable decline since the heady days when his contemporaries looked up to him as the modern prose Shakespeare). Mention should also be made of the one-offs that have attained for themselves and their authors a special status: Mary Shelley's *Frankenstein* (1818) and Bram Stoker's *Dracula* (1897). To these could be added Aldous Huxley's *Brave New World* (1932) and George Orwell's *1984* (1949).

It will be noticed that the most recent novelists included here died in the early 1990s (Graham Greene in 1991 and William Golding in 1993). A decision was taken to exclude the living, and therefore to skirt questions about the stature of V. S. Naipaul and Doris Lessing, let alone those of a younger generation or generations, including Graham Swift, Salman Rushdie, Ian McEwan, Jonathan Coe, Jeanette Winterson, Pat Barker, Zadie Smith, Sarah Waters, and many others still to be sifted by time. It seemed advisable to draw a line in the mud somewhere in the 1970s and to conclude with William Golding. For the stories this volume tells draw to a close in the two decades after the Second World War. Four of the final five writers rose to prominence in the inter-war years. Bowen, Waugh, Green, and Greene all thrived through the war years themselves and their immediate aftermath, and some of them continued to produce important and distinctive work, including Bowen's *The Little Girls* (1964) and *Eva Trout* (1968) and Waugh's *Sword of Honour* trilogy (started in the Fifties and concluded in revised form in 1965),[16] while Graham Greene went on and on at the top of his bent. Born in 1911, a few years later than Waugh, Greene, and Green (1903, 1904, 1905), Golding presents a slightly different case. He was twenty-eight when the Second World War broke out, and of course therefore old enough to serve in it, as he did (in the Royal Navy). But unlike the others it was not until the 1950s that he burst into prominence with *Lord of the Flies* (1954). Golding's heyday seems now to have been mainly the 1950s and 60s, even if, like the others, he continued to issue arresting work such as *Darkness Visible* (1979). He was honoured with the Nobel Prize in 1983.

The experience of that war marks the lives and works of the last half-dozen novelists accounted for here. And it helps to draw a line that separates them from writers too young to have lived through it as adults (or in Woolf's case, died in the thick of it). By the 1970s the post-war world was dissolving into new shapes under pressure from the end of empire abroad, the stirring and eruption of nationalisms at home. Whatever it had once meant to be English (or British), or to be an 'English novelist', in the 1970s new kinds of hybrid were flexing their muscles and baring their teeth, even if they would continue ministering to something still worth thinking of as the English novel, amongst other things.

But that is another continuing story, including of course the future of the Union with which Defoe had been so gleefully embroiled at its inception, some three hundred years ago.

NOTES

1 *The Letters of Daniel Defoe*, ed. G. H. Healey (Oxford: Clarendon Press, 1955), pp. 158–9. I am indebted to John Kerrigan's 'Defoe, Scotland, and Union', in *Archipelagic English: Literature, History, and Politics 1603–1707* (Oxford: Oxford University Press, 2008), pp. 326–49.

2 This is Sloppy in *Our Mutual Friend* (1865), ed. Adrian Poole (London: Penguin, 1997), p. 198. The line appealed to T. S. Eliot, who considered it as a possible epigraph for *The Waste Land*.

3 *Stamboul Train* (Vintage Classics, 2004), p. 51.

4 See Alison Lumsden's essay on Scott, p. 119, this volume.

5 See Jill L. Matus's essay on George Eliot, p. 231, this volume.

6 Preface to *The Portrait of a Lady*, in *Literary Criticism: French Writers, Other European Writers, the Prefaces to the New York Edition*, ed. Leon Edel with the assistance of Mark Wilson (New York: Library of America, 1984), p. 1084.

7 E. M. Forster, 'What I Believe', in *Two Cheers for Democracy* (1951), ed. Oliver Stallybrass (London: Edward Arnold, 1972), p. 66.

8 'The Virtue of Disloyalty' (1969), in *The Portable Graham Greene*, ed. Philip Stratford (Harmondsworth: Penguin Books, 1977), p. 610.

9 'The Natural History of German Life', in *Selected Essays, Poems and Other Writings*, ed. A. S. Byatt and Nicholas Warren (London: Penguin, 1990), p. 110.

10 This is from *Dombey and Son*, chapter 47. See Robert Douglas-Fairhurst's essay in this volume, p. 146.

11 'Standard Novels and Romances', in *Complete Works*, ed. P. P. Howe (London and Toronto: Dent, 1933), XVI, p. 6. I am indebted to Patrick Parrinder's

Nation and Novel: The English Novel from Its Origins to the Present Day (Oxford: Oxford University Press, 2006), for reminding me what a fine early critic of the English novel Hazlitt was.

12 See Vivien Jones's essay in this volume, p. 86.

13 See Lumsden, p. 119, this volume.

14 *The Oxford Companion to English Literature*, 6th edn, ed. Margaret Drabble (Oxford: Oxford University Press, 2006), p. 406.

15 Joyce is indeed to be found, along with Maria Edgeworth, George Moore, Flann O'Brien, Samuel Beckett, and others, in *The Cambridge Companion to the Irish Novel*, ed. John Wilson Foster (Cambridge: Cambridge University Press, 2006).

16 See Anthony Lane's essay, p. 417, this volume.

I

THOMAS KEYMER

Daniel Defoe

Confronted by calamity on a scale 'impossible to describe, or indeed conceive',[1] the narrator of Defoe's fictionalised memoir of the Great Plague, *A Journal of the Plague Year* (1722), zooms in on an individual case: that of two brothers who flee the city to maximise their chances of survival. Shunned by wary villagers, and shunning their fellow refugees, the brothers typify the indigent, solitary state of displaced Londoners who scatter themselves across the fields in isolated, improvised shacks. 'Nor is it unlikely', adds Defoe's narrator (whom we know only by his initials, H.F.),

> but that some of the unhappy Wanderers might die so all alone, even sometimes for want of Help, as particularly in one Tent or Hutt, was found a Man dead, and on the Gate of a Field just by, was cut with his Knife in uneven Letters, the following Words, by which it may be suppos'd the other Man escap'd, or that one dying first, the other bury'd him as well as he could;
>
> O mIsErY!
> We BoTH ShaLL DyE,
> WoE, WoE.
>
> (*JPY*, 151)

With its faithful, even fussy transcription of an utterance pitched somewhere between elemental cry and grunting bathos, the passage flirts with absurdity in ways already acknowledged by Defoe's narrator. As he uneasily recognises, there are comic as well as tragic aspects to the incongruous condition of these early modern urbanites, torn by catastrophe from their humdrum world, 'who liv'd like wandring Pilgrims in the Desarts' (*JPY*, 57). Yet this enigmatic inscription on the gate, and H.F.'s painstaking treatment of it, also encapsulate some key features, both thematic and formal, of Defoe's fiction as a whole. This is a fiction of personal hardship, extreme conditions, and abrupt lurches into disaster, and a fiction in which the struggle to survive in unstable or hostile circumstances involves the individual in crises that are moral and spiritual as well as urgently practical. It is a fiction, above all, of solitary struggle, in which the isolation of Defoe's first and most famous hero, stranded for decades on a desert island, merely literalises a predicament he shares with the protagonists of later novels, all of whom are forced to negotiate treacherous environments of their own. Beyond Crusoe's far-flung island and H.F.'s infected streets, the hazardous and alienating worlds of Defoe's fiction range from the war-torn nation of *Memoirs of a Cavalier* (1720) and the uncharted wastes of *Captain Singleton* (1720) to the desperate criminal underworlds of *Moll Flanders* (1722) and *Colonel Jack* (1722) and the viperous Eurotrash playgrounds of Defoe's last major novel, *Roxana* (1724).

Accompanying this thematic focus is a relentless concentration on the state of the individual mind, isolated in outlook and usually in time, as it strives to understand, control, and document experience, subjecting its hostility to the tenuous order of explanatory language and first-person narrative form. This is never quite the same thing as introspection, and Defoe's narrators reveal themselves more by their responses to events, circumstances, and things than by direct or full self-analysis. But all are driven as much by the urge to articulate as by the need to survive, and the drive is such that even the most basic utterance or perception is seriously pondered and precisely recorded, as having enduring value. Crusoe too cuts improvised memorials in wood and gives cries of plangent simplicity: '*Poor* Robin Crusoe, *Where are you?*', as his parrot learns to repeat.[2] There is a sense in which his whole narrative is only a richer and more complex elaboration of the same message – a cry of self-assertion in the teeth of disaster – that H.F. finds in the field.

To readers of the nineteenth century, the last-gasp memorial on H.F.'s gate would probably have indicated something more fundamental still about Defoe's art. It was his patient attentiveness to just this kind of tangential detail that marked him out as a significant innovator and – in the classic period of the realist novel – an exemplary precursor. Walter Scott, who with Coleridge was the most perceptive reader of Defoe in the Romantic period, applauded his ability to 'select, in a fictitious narrative, such an enumeration of minute incidents as might strike the beholder of a real fact'. For Scott, this meticulous accumulation of circumstantial data gave the novels an illusion of reality that still remained unmatched a century later. In a move that looks forward to modern theories of narrative, in which excess or redundancy of concrete detail is central to the effect of reality, Scott identifies Defoe's focus on otherwise negligible 'petty particulars' as the basic technique through which he 'carried the air of authenticity to the highest pitch of perfection'.[3]

When similar techniques were applied in early Victorian fiction, it was of Defoe that readers were reminded. The vivid prison scene in Charles

Dickens's *Pickwick Papers* (1836–7), as one influential reviewer put it, was 'pictured throughout with the minute reality of a Defoe'.[4] By the second half of the century, Defoe's 'wonderful power in making a narrative seem real' had become almost proverbial, and could be used by Thomas Hardy as a shorthand way of indicating the mimetic project at its most direct. In *The Hand of Ethelberta* (1876), an upwardly mobile heroine with literary ambitions selects Defoe as her technical model, and is applauded in her choice by Hardy's narrator, for whom the forceful verisimilitude achieved by 'that master of delusion' derived not only from circumstantial detail but also from the low colloquialism of his narrating voices. 'A modern critic has well observed of Defoe that he had the most amazing talent on record for telling lies', Hardy adds; the critic in question is Leslie Stephen, who in an influential essay of 1868 drew a direct line, with mingled admiration and distaste, between Defoe's genius for fictional representation and the scandalous duplicity of his prior career as a political journalist and agent.[5]

Stephen's judgement set the tone of criticism for a generation, and was exuberantly expanded in a popular monograph of 1879 by William Minto, for whom Defoe's personal cynicism and his artistic brilliance were two sides of a single coin. 'He was a great, a truly great liar, perhaps the greatest liar that ever lived', Minto famously concluded, and critics still sometimes speak of Defoe's 'art of mendacity'.[6] This approach is less limiting than it sounds, for all Defoe's novels were anonymously published as real-life memoirs (though he was rapidly outed as the author of *Robinson Crusoe*), and each invited direct engagement, uncomplicated by authorial intervention, with a plausible first-person narrator. But what made this lie most persuasive, or best encouraged suspension of disbelief? At a time when the most innovative new fiction was concerning itself more with internal states of consciousness than with external or material reality, readers began to question whether Defoe's particularised facts were really the important thing. In a teasingly brief aside, Oscar Wilde identified *A Journal of the Plague Year* as a masterpiece of lying (by which he meant imaginative creativity) precisely because 'facts are either kept in their proper subordinate position, or else entirely excluded on the general ground of dulness'. For another *fin de siècle* critic, the 'air of truth' that characterised the novels flowed not from authenticating particulars but from their proto-Jamesian presentation of experience as discontinuous and complex: 'what Mr. Henry James calls "the strange, irregular rhythm of life"'. In this context, it becomes easy to see why several leading modernists were drawn to Defoe, including James Joyce, though Joyce's now celebrated Trieste lecture of 1912 is original only in its critique of *Robinson Crusoe* as a prophecy of empire, and relies heavily on Victorian orthodoxy for its talk of Defoe as 'the great precursor of the realist movement'.[7]

Appropriately enough, it was Virginia Woolf, the daughter of Leslie Stephen, who decisively broke with the Victorian account of Defoe as an objective realist. In two key discussions, the first of them a bicentennial essay of 1919 on *Robinson Crusoe*, she reinvented him for modernism as a novelist of subjective perception. With Sterne, Defoe was one of the key eighteenth-century sources co-opted by Woolf in her campaign for a mode of narrative attuned to the flux of consciousness as opposed to the material world, and to this end she was determined to contest his reputation as 'a mere journalist and literal recorder of facts with no conception of the nature of psychology'.[8] Solidity of specification remained a factor, and at the heart of Woolf's reading of *Robinson Crusoe* she places the earthenware pot he toils to create, which in its stark simplicity 'persuades us to see remote islands and the solitudes of the human soul'. But Woolf also insisted that Defoe's facts were secondary to his psychology, and only accessible through it; the important thing about the earthenware pot was its presentation within, and mediation through, the perception of Crusoe himself. Everything in a novel by Defoe was shaped and coloured by this first-person perspective, the effect being to represent not an independent world but a mind perceiving the world. In this sense, even – or perhaps especially – when most meticulous in their verbal description of things, Defoe's narratives rendered nothing so much as consciousness itself, and with an effect Woolf found 'as deep as pages of analysis could have made it'. In the case of Crusoe in particular, 'There is no escaping him. Everything appears as it would appear to that naturally cautious, apprehensive, conventional, and solidly matter-of-fact intelligence.'[9]

Defoe's first novel of 1719, written at the age of almost sixty after a prolific career in journalism and political writing,[10] lay at the heart of all these accounts. His enduring reputation as a one-hit wonder – 'Defoe wrote several stupid stories, and one masterpiece', as Charles Reade bluntly asserted in 1873[11] – was of course misplaced, but *Robinson Crusoe* certainly created a template for the small avalanche of follow-up novels that Defoe then produced, and this template, though ingeniously varied and transformed, was never entirely discarded. That is not to say that no existing fictional models stood before Defoe as he wrote, and innovative earlier examples range in style from Aphra Behn's trenchant narrative of colonial misgovernment in *Oroonoko* (1689) to the witty generic self-consciousness of William Congreve's *Incognita* (1691). But the impact of works like these on *Robinson Crusoe* is at best diffused, and Defoe drew more obviously on a rich blend of non-fictional genres, from voyage, captivity, and castaway narrative to the religious traditions of casuistry and spiritual autobiography.

Casuistry, a mode of ethical analysis in which questions of conscience or duty are debated and resolved in light of their distinctive circumstances, comes more conspicuously to the fore in the complex urban environments of the later novels, though Crusoe's agonised debates with himself about his entitlement to shoot the cannibals who imperil him make moves in this direction. More important at the outset is spiritual autobiography, a predominantly puritan mode of recording and analysing the progress of the soul from reprobacy to grace and salvation – though a term like progress fails to catch the anxious drama of ongoing struggle and repeated backsliding that typifies the genre. With its unflinching focus on the turbulent state of the inward soul, often expressed in images of storm or shipwreck, this is a genre with little place for the irrelevant contingencies of the material world. Its presentation of individuals cut off from community by their lonely quests for salvation is typified by John Bunyan's fraught account, in *Grace Abounding to the Chief of Sinners* (1666), of the battle within him between spiritual duties and carnal ties. As Bunyan writes on leaving his family to pursue his calling (and thus certain imprisonment) as an unlicensed preacher, 'the parting with my Wife and poor Children hath oft been to me in this place, as the pulling the flesh from my bones ... yet thought I, I must do it, I must do it'.[12]

Consciously or otherwise, *Robinson Crusoe* renders these patterns literal as a matter of plot. Storm and shipwreck are the inevitable hazards of his various voyages, and they elicit some of his most rigorous efforts at description, as when, washed half-drowned onto his island, he seeks to control the chaos in his prose with careful substitutions and qualifications: 'the Sea having hurried me along as before, landed me, or rather dash'd me against a Piece of a Rock, and that with such Force, as it left me senseless, and indeed helpless, as to my own Deliverance' (*RC*, 40). (Defoe was already expert at this kind of writing, and when a freak hurricane lashed southern England in 1703 he was inspired to compile *The Storm* (1704), a classic of meteorology that is still cited by climate historians.) Thereafter, Crusoe's island life is punctuated by near-fatal forays in improvised crafts and, eventually, the shipwreck of other Europeans; perhaps the novel's most desolate moment comes when a drowned boy is washed ashore, and Crusoe retrieves from the corpse a tobacco pipe, leaving some useless coins: 'In all the Time of my solitary Life, I never felt so earnest, so strong a Desire after the Society of my Fellow-Creatures, or so deep a Regret at the want of it' (*RC*, 158). He lives alone on his island for twenty-five years until his rescue of Friday, and even the events of his previous life presage this literal isolation. Captured by pirates while embarked on a slaving voyage, the young Crusoe is himself enslaved in the North African port of Sallee (the ironies associated with slavery in the novel are only now being disentangled), and he finds in the experience an anticipation of his island ordeal: 'a Taste of the Misery I was to go thro' (*RC*, 18). Later, settled in prosperity on his Brazilian plantation, 'I liv'd just like a Man cast away upon some desolate Island, that had no body there but himself' (*RC*, 32).

Storm and isolation also serve as indices of Crusoe's inward state. Even the earthquake he experiences on the island affects him 'like one that was toss'd at Sea' (*RC*, 69), and his spiritual life – we might call it mental, or even, with Woolf, psychological, for spiritual autobiography expands here into secular realms – involves the same oceanic forces. The effect is very deliberate when, having prayed for deliverance in an early tempest, Crusoe 'drowned all my Repentance' on the calming of the seas, 'and the Current of my former Desires return'd' (*RC*, 10); later he laments that 'in the midst of the greatest Composures of my Mind, [Anguish] would break out upon me like a Storm, and make me wring my Hands, and weep like a Child' (*RC*, 96); the pattern persists in the uneasy reflections 'rowling upon my Mind' which 'sometimes sunk my very Soul' (*RC*, 132, 147). In his lonely struggles to survive in practice and be redeemed in spirit (from sins that include, the text implies, his sins as a slaver), Crusoe's castaway condition also comes to express an inward state of reprobacy, solitude, and alienation. The island itself becomes a state of mind, or, as Crusoe puts it in a phrase more reminiscent of *The Pilgrim's Progress* than *Grace Abounding*, 'this dismal unfortunate Island, which I call'd *the Island of Despair*' (*RC*, 60).

Dickens's hero in *David Copperfield* (1849–50) catches something, though not all, of the bleakness of this atmosphere when he pities himself as 'more solitary than Robinson Crusoe, who had nobody to look at him and see that he was solitary'.[13] For nothing renders Crusoe more truly alone than the strength, and then the inevitable frustration or involution, of his impulse to communicate and express. The narrative that constitutes the text of the novel is the last and fullest stage of a long process in which Crusoe at first bewails, and then seeks to document and understand, his predicament, which he finally shapes into consoling and providentially meaningful narrative form. His first desperate exclamations on the island, 'crying out, I was undone, undone' (*RC*, 60), are vocalised back to him for years by his parrot, and these give way to the more dispassionate, though little more expansive, textual record that he carves on a post: 'viz., *I came on Shore here on the 30th of* Sept. 1659' (*RC*, 55). In a move heralding the statistical as well as verbal 'telling' that always accompanies the efforts of Defoe's narrators to make sense of experience (from Moll's financial balance sheets to H.F.'s bills of mortality, narrative 'Accounts' are punctuated by numerical 'Accompts') he cuts notches into the post to record the passing days. He also draws up a balance sheet of material and spiritual profit and loss, 'very impartially, like Debtor and Creditor, the Comforts I enjoy'd, against the Miseries I suffer'd' (*RC*, 57). It is as though all these methods are necessary, sequentially or in combination, to impose bearable structures of order and meaning on what he otherwise calls 'my unaccountable Life' (*RC*, 153).

The next stage in the process is Crusoe's journal, which, in one of the most technically interesting features of the novel, predominates for part of the text, offering a perspective similar in kind to Richardsonian 'writing to the moment' and significantly at variance with the retrospective stability that Crusoe finally achieves as he shapes his ordeal into a coherent progress from sin, through punishment and atonement, to eventual redemption. Even late in the novel, however, Crusoe's narrative falls back into a painful oscillation of disturbed and agitated thoughts, and the sheer impossibility of converting articulation to communication gives his writing a quarantined air of forced introspection. By composing the novel's text of 'secret Disputes with my self, and ... great Perplexities', as Crusoe puts it in one of his later moments of crisis (*RC*, 168), the novel creates an absolute match between solitude of theme and solipsism of form.

For the first published commentator on *Robinson Crusoe*, a wily rival journalist named Charles Gildon, the real isolation here was Defoe's own. The novel was not the factual traveller's tale it affected to be, Gildon alleged in a pamphlet that closely burlesqued Defoe's extended title, so that *The Life and Strange Surprizing Adventures of Robinson Crusoe, of York, Mariner: Who Lived Eight and Twenty Years, All Alone* ... becomes *The Life and Strange Surprizing Adventures of Mr. D - - - - De F - - , of London, Hosier, Who Has Liv'd above Fifty Years by Himself* .... Instead, Gildon proposes, Defoe had represented his own personality in that of Crusoe, and the novel was essentially a work of displaced autobiography: a narrative of Defoe's own loner status throughout his chequered and protean career as a failed hosiery merchant and then a scribbler and political hireling.

Far from rejecting this charge, Defoe enigmatically embraced it in a second sequel to the novel – Crusoe's *Farther Adventures* (1719) had already appeared when Gildon wrote – which he called *Serious Reflections During the Life and Surprising Adventures of Robinson Crusoe* (1720). With wonderful obfuscation, Defoe now assumed a voice poised indistinctly between that of imagined narrator and imagining author, to declare that the novel was true in both historical and allegorical senses, that it alluded to the life and actions of a well-known individual, and that its fictional episodes added up to

> one whole Scheme of a real Life of eight and twenty Years, spent in the most wandring desolate and afflicting Circumstances that ever Man went through,

> and in which I have liv'd so long in a Life of Wonders in continu'd Storms, fought with the worst kind of Savages and Man-eaters ... suffered all Manner of Violences and Oppressions, injurious Reproaches, contempt of Men, attacks of Devils, Corrections from Heaven, and Oppositions on Earth; have had innumerable Ups and Downs in Matters of Fortune, been in Slavery worse than *Turkish* ... been taken up at Sea in Distress, rais'd again and depress'd again, and that oftner perhaps in one Man's Life than ever was known before; Shipwreck'd often, tho' more by Land than by Sea: In a Word, there's not a Circumstance in the imaginary Story, but has its just Allusion to a real Story, and chimes Part for Part, and Step for Step with the inimitable Life of *Robinson Crusoe*.[14]

Defoe was toying with his audience here, and it would be wrong-headed to attempt to map *Robinson Crusoe* onto its author's life in a series of direct correspondences. Yet Defoe's play with intersecting identities at this point also has a serious aspect, and it is interesting to find him drawn to the same metaphors of disaster and deliverance in the directly autobiographical context of his political apologia *An Appeal to Honour and Justice* (1715) and in several of his plaintive letters to political patrons: 'The Gulph is too Large for me to Get ashore again', he laments in one such letter.[15] With his recurrent crises of personal bankruptcy and political prosecution, his arrests for debt and seditious libel, Defoe's life has the same character of precarious instability, of constant vulnerability to unforeseen disaster, that afflicts his protagonists; and he turns on all these lives, factual and fictional, a shared imagery of overwhelming elemental turmoil.

In *Robinson Crusoe*, persistent additional metaphors of tyranny, rebellion, captivity, and execution, alongside marked coincidences between dates in the novel's plot and the nation's history (Crusoe's exile begins just before the collapse of the Commonwealth in 1660 and ends just before the Glorious Revolution of 1688), have encouraged attempts at political as well as biographical decoding. As a young republican firebrand, Defoe had joined the first and disastrously unsuccessful attempt to overthrow James II, the Monmouth rebellion of 1685, and was lucky to escape the subsequent 'Bloody Assizes' with his life. (He later secured, through mechanisms that remain unclear, a full pardon.) The Victorian critic Arthur Quiller-Couch was the first to argue that deep structures of political allusion pervaded the text in this regard and that the specific date of the shipwreck (at which point Crusoe likens himself to a reprieved malefactor) commemorated the hanging of several fellow rebels in Somerset on 30 September 1685: 'your *Western* Martyrs, that, had they liv'd, would have been extraordinary Men', Defoe elsewhere calls the youths concerned.[16] For J. Paul Hunter, at least an element of political allusion accompanies the spiritual allegory, and 'Crusoe's twenty-eight years of isolation and suffering ... parallel the Puritan alienation between the Restoration and the accession of William and Mary.' For Tom Paulin, *Robinson Crusoe* is 'crucially defined by a type of Dissenting anxiety rooted in Stuart persecution, and particularly in Sedgemoor and the Bloody Assizes'; it also embodies a profound personal sense of survivor's guilt, arising from enduring identification on Defoe's part with the martyred friends and comrades whose fate he had escaped.[17]

There is enough in *Robinson Crusoe* to encourage, if not quite confirm, this kind of analysis, and it may be because of the novel's implicit radicalism that the leading poet and satirist of the period, Alexander Pope, persisted in portraying Defoe as an active dissident long after his withdrawal from political engagement. 'Ear-less on high, stood pillory'd *D*———', sneered Pope in 1728, belatedly invoking Defoe's spectacular punishment for seditious libel a quarter of a century beforehand.[18] But perhaps the most relevant feature to the novels of Defoe's earlier political journalism, and especially of the work that landed him in the pillory, *The Shortest Way with the Dissenters* (1702), is the expertise this kind of writing gave him in the arts of impersonation and irony. At one level, the anonymously published *Shortest Way* was a brilliant hoax, an exaggerated imitation or forgery of the rhetoric of Tory extremism at the time, arguing for bloody suppression – 'gallows and gallies' is the repeated phrase[19] – of the religious minority to which Defoe himself belonged. By tipping the rabble-rousing insinuations of his political adversaries into the realm of outright statement, and by tricking unwary readers into embracing and endorsing an almost genocidal proposal, Defoe aimed to expose and discredit a dangerously influential faction. 'The Case the Book pointed at', he later explained, 'was to speak in the first Person of the *Party*, and then, thereby, not only speak their Language, but make them acknowledge it to be theirs, which they did so openly, that confounded all their Attempts afterwards to deny it' (*PS*, 24). In his long-running newspaper the *Review*, Defoe even claimed to have received via his bookseller the letter of an unnamed Tory backwoodsman who valued *The Shortest Way* alongside his Bible and hoped Queen Anne would 'put all that is there prescribed into Execution'.[20]

There was even more to the pamphlet than this, however. As well as superbly impersonating his Tory persona (modelled on the incendiary preacher Henry Sacheverell), Defoe also laced *The Shortest Way* with quiet but devastating ironies: ironies imperceptible on casual reading but all too evident on reperusal after the hoax had taken effect. The ironies become increasingly intensive as the pamphlet nears it close, and in a masterly concluding move Defoe has his persona hysterically compare the established Church with the persecuted Christ in such a way as to subvert his own case from within:

> Alas the Church of England! What with Popery on one hand, and schismatics on the other, how has she been crucified between two thieves.
>
> Now let us crucify the thieves. Let her foundations be established upon the destruction of her enemies ... (*TBE*, 144)

Here and in the surrounding paragraphs, the peroration of *The Shortest Way* is a riot of uncontrolled contradiction. Beyond the absurdity of simultaneously claiming to suffer oppression while also proposing to inflict it, and of unselfconsciously switching from identification with the crucified Christ to identification with the crucifying authorities, Defoe's persona forgets here what his wording prompts us to remember: that in fact Christ blessed and saved the thief, and that he founded his Church not on the destruction of enemies but on the rock of faith.

Defoe repeated this kind of exercise on several later occasions, and in an impressive range of ventriloquised voices, from high-flying Jacobite to zealous Quaker. The gambit continued to get him into trouble, however, and in an abject petition to the throne of 1713 he was forced to improvise a whole theory of functional irony following his arrest for a group of pamphlets imagining the queen's death and inflaming public sentiment about the succession: 'In all which books', Defoe nervously explained,

> Altho' ... Sundry Expressions, as in all Ironicall Writeing it must be, may be Wrested Against the True Design of the whole; and Turned to a meaning quite different from ye Intention of the Author: yet yor Petitioner Humbly Assures yor Maj:^ty^ in The Solemnest manner Possible, That his True and Onely Design in all ye said books, was by an Ironicall Discourse of Recommending the Pretender, In the strongest and most forcible manner to Expose his designs, and the Ruinous Consequences of his Succeeding therein.[21]

There is an important conclusion about the novels to be drawn from these episodes, and from Defoe's self-consciousness here about first-person writing, ironic discourse, and the openness of literary meaning. Though clearly able to immerse himself with complete conviction in the voices he impersonated, each of which doubtless also reflects an aspect of his protean personality, Defoe was more than capable of operating as a systematic ironist: of writing, in other words, at the expense of the voices he assumes. But he also understood that implied meanings are inherently unstable, and that first-person discourse, written with whatever degree of ironic detachment, will be understood in different ways by different readers. The still widespread view of Defoe as an unconscious artist who operates through unreserved imaginative identification with, and hence total endorsement of, his protagonists and narrators is hard to defend. But it would be equally problematic to read his novels against the grain as implicit critiques of their narrators, rather than as the repertoire of interpretative possibilities that Defoe recognised, irrespective of conscious intention, as the inherent property of first-person irony. 'This Work is chiefly recommended to those who know how to Read it', he went on to write of *Moll Flanders*:[22] a cryptic recommendation, perhaps, but one that perfectly catches the effort of imaginative involvement and understanding he demands. Perhaps it is this engagement, more than anything else, that allows the novels to seem real.

Irony was not the only feature of Defoe's writing that tempted him to theorise. In a remarkable essay entitled 'Of Solitude' and included in *Serious Reflections*, he drew from Crusoe's drama of abandonment and exile a melancholy general account of the human condition. Here solitude is not the exceptional state of the forgotten castaway but the norm of modern life, paradoxically most acute in urban settings. Confined within his own perceptions, 'Man may be properly said to be *alone* in the Midst of the Crowds and Hurry of Men and Business', while Crusoe himself (or Defoe himself – again the voice is ambiguously pitched) now experiences 'much more Solitude in the Middle of the greatest Collection of Mankind in the World, I mean, at *London*, while I am writing this, than ever I could say I enjoy'd in eight and twenty Years Confinement to a desolate Island' (*SR*, 2, 4). The reason is to do with the inescapable subjectivity of human perspectives, and there emerges from the essay a view of life, or at least of consciousness of life, as to do not with public engagement but with private reflection. 'Every Thing revolves in our Minds by innumerable circular Motions, all centring in our selves', Defoe explains, and it is in this sense of centripetal self-absorption that 'we love, we hate, we covet, we enjoy, all in Privacy and Solitude' (*SR*, 2, 3). This is not exactly the kind of solitude that Woolf had in mind when she wrote of Defoe in general as a novelist of 'unfriended misery', and one for whom 'the unsheltered life, exposed to circumstances and forced to shift for itself, appealed to him imaginatively as the right matter for his art'.[23] But it perfectly matches her sense of Defoe as also, in his rudimentary way, a novelist of the inner life and does much to explain the claustrophobic effect, the sense of entrapment in a limited and often very blinkered perspective, that characterises his fiction.

In the novels that followed *Robinson Crusoe*, Defoe went on to combine desolate environments and brutal action with flintily egotistical narrative perspectives. The mercenary hero of *Memoirs of a Cavalier* (which remains an uncertain attribution and is partly put together from historical sources, sometimes merely replicated) is something of a cipher, and he passes with cool detachment through the murderous battlefields of the plot. But other novels present more artful visions of dire extremity and human anaesthesia. In *Captain Singleton*, the aptly named hero traverses Africa in pursuit of ivory and gold (this novel fascinated Victorian readers more than any after *Robinson Crusoe*), and the analogy with Crusoe's island becomes clear when he passes a wooden cross bearing, in Portuguese, the legend: '*Point Desperation. Jesus have Mercy!*' Determined progress leads Singleton further into 'a desolate, disconsolate Wilderness' (the transferred epithet is inspired), but what dominates this novel of survival and ruthless self-advancement is really the desert within, and in a grimly comic short-circuiting of Crusoe's dilemma Singleton barely speaks in jest when noting of this wilderness that, 'as to the Inhabitants being Cannibals, I believed we should be more likely to eat them, than they us, if we could but get at them'.[24] The protagonist of *Colonel Jack* remains entirely impervious, through a series of brutal escapades in London and America, to the bonds of fellow feeling and sympathetic identification that were to dominate the novel genre half a century later. Here the touch of comedy – unless this is a Freudian slip by a domestically troubled typesetter – comes on the extended title-page of the novel's first edition, which tells us that the emotionally disengaged Jack 'married Four Wives, and Five of them prov'd Whores'.

Defoe's later narrators are not all as unsympathetic as Jack, and some go out of their way to court the sympathy of their reader – or, in H.F.'s case, to arouse it for others. *A Journal of the Plague Year* presents a crisis so extreme that normal emotions and relations are in collapse, 'and this was a Time when every one's private Safety lay so near them, that they had no Room to pity the Distresses of others' (*JPY*, 115). But H.F. undertakes a compensatory effort here, and an effort which, though he speaks at one point of adopting 'such moving Accents as should alarm the very Soul of the Reader' (*JPY*, 104), involves a rigorous avoidance of emotive hyperbole or rhetorical overkill. Surrounded as he is by inarticulate despair and otherwise unrecorded mass extinction – 'Persons falling dead in the Streets, terrible Shrieks and Skreekings of Women, who in their Agonies would ... cry out in a dismal surprising Manner' (*JPY*, 80) – he writes with countervailing restraint, a less-is-more aesthetic that minimises adjectival and adverbial colouring in pursuit of truly serious verbalisation of an experience that would be trivialised by undisciplined language. What disturbs H.F. above all is the silence of sudden annihilation – not only the curtailment of individual lives but also the evisceration of those traces that normally survive – and his narrative is a sustained attempt to supply a collective memorial. 'They died by Heaps, and were buried by Heaps, that is to say without Account', as he writes of the anonymous mass graves gouged into the city churchyards (*JPY*, 237); even statistically, the victims vanish (and here the link between narration and numbering returns) because the grim work of the parish officers 'was not of a Nature to allow them Leisure, to take an exact Tale of the dead Bodies, which were all huddled together in the Dark into a Pit; which Pit, or Trench, no Man could come nigh, but at the utmost Peril' (*JPY*, 99). In a city where the circulation of rumour and panic is as worrying a contagion as the plague itself, the pared-down austerity and linguistic control of H.F.'s own 'Tale' become a source of sanity and affirmation, and even his occasional flourish of style is studiously acknowledged as such: 'London might well be said to be all in Tears.'

Even after all his efforts of empirical observation and literal description, of course, H.F. continues to recognise his text as something inevitably ill seen and ill said.[25] But the rigour with which he attempts his task remains an extraordinary effect, not least in its rejection of the idea that adequate description can attempt to transcend the limits of subjectivity. At the end of one dour and studied account of a parish plague-pit – a 'Gulph', H.F. meticulously notes, 'for such it was rather than a Pit' (*JPY*, 59) – he emphatically returns to the impossibility of getting outside, in practice or in language, the impressions of the perceiving mind: 'This may serve a little to describe the dreadful Condition of that Day, tho' it is impossible to say any Thing that is able to give a true Idea of it to those who did not see it, other than this; that it was indeed *very*, *very*, *very* dreadful, and such as no Tongue can express' (*JPY*, 60). The laconic eloquence of this passage is hard to appreciate out of context, but two 'dreadfuls' are exactly what H.F. means here, and three italicised 'verys', not one or two.

After the shipwreck (for this is another), the traumatised city returns to its ways, and 'the People harden'd by the Danger they had been in, like Seamen after a Storm is over, were … more bold and hardened in their Vices' (*JPY*, 229). This is the vicious world portrayed in *Moll Flanders*: the world in which, as Moll writes in a premature moment of complacency and repose, 'now I seem'd landed in a safe Harbour' (*MF*, 188). Much is different, however, both in this novel and *Roxana*, which combine prose styles superficially like H.F.'s with different and more teasingly ironic narrative stances. Both heroines are mysterious about identities that they veil as much as disclose, and they make themselves known to the reader only by pseudonyms; both pride themselves on using language not just to persuade but to beguile. Moll poses a radical discrepancy between competing personal identities, between narrating and narrated selves, in the early distinction she makes between 'who I have been, as well as who I am', and throughout the narrative she plays artfully on those around her, whether representing circumstances 'in the most moving Terms that I was able' or deploying with her explanations 'that known Womans Rhetorick … I mean that of Tears' (*MF*, 7, 125, 302). She turns the same rhetorical skills on the reader of her text, brilliantly converting what she at one point confesses to be 'a past life of a most wretched kind to account for' into a morally air-brushed simulacrum: 'a smooth Story to tell of myself' (*MF*, 187, 19). In *Roxana*, the memoir of a guilt-ridden adventuress who is apparently complicit in the murder of her own daughter, Defoe creates the voice of a virtuoso exponent of dissociation and extenuation who, in a deft appropriation of casuistical process, pleads poverty as the source of her actions 'not ... as a Justification of my Conduct, but that it may move the Pity, even of those that abhor the Crime'.[26]

Yet both these heroines have to navigate impossible conditions, and for Woolf it was the capacity of *Moll Flanders* and *Roxana* to make readers admire two deeply blameworthy protagonists that placed these works 'among the few English novels which we can call indisputably great'.[27] Casuistry is at the centre of this startling effect, but it functions in contrary ways. On one hand, casuistical methodology enables Moll and Roxana to undertake serious analysis of the urgent and peculiarly circumstanced cases of conscience with which the extreme environments they inhabit repeatedly confront them. On the other, it can tip into fraudulent special pleading, as in the superbly ironic set piece in which Moll narrates the theft of a child's necklace as though she, not the girl, is the horrified victim: she steals in the passive mood here, with the devil pulling the strings. Rounding off the episode, she glibly justifies it as a salutary lesson for delinquent parents, 'a just Reproof for their Negligence in leaving the poor little Lamb to come home by it self' (*MF*, 194): the seamless drift from 'poor little Lamb' to objectified 'it' catches her insincerity to perfection. The ethics of survival in an urban jungle are finely balanced overall, and Moll has a compelling argument to make when quoting a scriptural text – '*Give me not Poverty least I Steal*'[28] – to which Defoe was repeatedly drawn elsewhere, always with the implication that self-preservation is an unanswerable imperative. As he provocatively tells respectable readers of his journalism (pulling out his favourite metaphorical stops in the process), '*I tell you, Sir*, you would not Eat your Neighbours Bread only, but your Neighbour himself, rather than Starve, and your Honesty would all Shipwrack in the Storm of Necessity.'[29]

But Moll and Roxana typically lay these arguments on too thick for simple legitimacy, and they do so in cases where the sin or crime in question seems to enter not through what Moll at one point calls 'the Door of Necessity' but instead 'at the Door of Inclination' (*MF*, 129). Cases of conscience shade here into studies of bad conscience, and though the first of these leaves Moll in a state of questionable but comfortable penitence, the second drops Roxana into a living hell. Cynically aware that 'Death-bed Repentance, or Storm-Repentance' is typically self-serving and fleeting (*R*, 128), she reaches a state of spiritual paralysis reminiscent of *Hamlet*'s Claudius: 'brought so low', in her grim concluding words, 'that my Repentance seem'd to be only the Consequence of my Misery, as my Misery was of my Crime' (*R*, 330).

The trajectories are different, but from the common focus on cases of conscience in these novels, as G. A. Starr suggests, complexity of novelistic consciousness begins to emerge, and a practice of characterisation in which outward conduct gives way as the all-important factor to analysis of consciousness.[30] In Defoe's hands, this consciousness turns out to be a lonely thing, and it comes not in streams but in storms.

NOTE ON EDITIONS

The best textbook editions of Defoe's novels are in the Oxford World's Classics series; good alternatives are available from Penguin and Norton. *The Novels of Daniel Defoe*, 10 vols. (London: Pickering and Chatto 2007–8) has now been published under the general editorship of P. N. Furbank and W. R. Owens.

NOTES

1 Daniel Defoe, *A Journal of the Plague Year*, ed. Louis Landa, introduction by David Roberts (Oxford: Oxford University Press, 1990), p. 201. Hereafter *JPY*.

2 Daniel Defoe, *Robinson Crusoe*, ed. Thomas Keymer and James Kelly, introduction by Thomas Keymer (Oxford: Oxford University Press, 2007), p. 121. Hereafter *RC*.

3 *Sir Walter Scott on Novelists and Fiction*, ed. Ioan Williams (London: Routledge, 1968), pp. 154, 157, quoting editorial matter from Scott's 1814 edition of Swift; see also Roland Barthes's classic essay 'The Reality Effect' (1968), reprinted in Barthes, *The Rustle of Language*, trans. Richard Howard (Oxford: Blackwell, 1986), pp. 141–8.

4 John Forster in the *Examiner* for 2 July 1837, reviewing the fifteenth instalment of *Pickwick Papers*.

5 Thomas Hardy, *The Hand of Ethelberta*, ed. Tim Dolin (London: Penguin, 1998), pp. 107, 119. Hardy is quoting Stephen's essay 'De Foe's Novels', first published in the *Cornhill Magazine* (March 1868) and still an influence on his thinking decades later: see Thomas Hardy, *The Life and Work of Thomas Hardy*, ed. Michael Millgate (London: Macmillan, 1984), pp. 63, 424.

6 William Minto, *Daniel Defoe* (London: Macmillan, 1879), p. 169. On fiction and mendacity, see G. A. Starr, *Defoe and Casuistry* (Princeton: Princeton University Press, 1971), pp. 190–211; P. N. Furbank, 'Defoe's *Minutes of Mesnager*: The Art of Mendacity', *Eighteenth-Century Fiction*, 16.1 (2003), 1–12.

7 Oscar Wilde, 'The Decay of Lying' (1889), in *The Complete Works of Oscar Wilde*, vol. IV, *Criticism*, ed. Josephine M. Guy (Oxford: Oxford University Press, 2006), p. 87; A. B. Walkley, 'Unabashed Defoe', *Daily Chronicle* (17 February 1892); James Joyce, 'Daniel Defoe', ed. and trans. Joseph Prescott, *Buffalo Studies*, 1.1 (1964), 5–25, p. 12.

8 Virginia Woolf, *Collected Essays*, 4 vols. (London: Hogarth Press, 1966–7), I, p. 66.

9 Woolf, *Collected Essays*, I, pp. 74–5; I, p. 74; I, p. 73.

10 No record survives of Defoe's birth or baptism. He was probably born in London in autumn 1660, a few months after the Restoration; biographers sometimes assume a date of 30 September, the day of the fictional Crusoe's birth (in 1632) and also his shipwreck (in 1659).

11 Charles Reade in *Once a Week* for 25 January–8 February 1873. Reade's own *œuvre* was gloriously masterpiece-free; his best-known novel is *The Cloister and the Hearth* (1861).

12 John Bunyan, *Grace Abounding*, ed. John Stachniewski with Anita Pacheco (Oxford: Oxford University Press, 1998), pp. 89–90.

13 Charles Dickens, *David Copperfield*, ed. Nina Burgis (Oxford: Oxford University Press, 1983), p. 57.

14 Daniel Defoe, *Serious Reflections During the Life and Surprising Adventures of Robinson Crusoe* (1720), A4v (misprints corrected). Hereafter *SR*.

15 *The Letters of Daniel Defoe*, ed. G. H. Healey (Oxford: Clarendon Press, 1955), p. 16 (to Robert Harley, May/June 1704?).

16 A. H. Quiller-Couch, *Adventures in Criticism* (London: Cassell, 1896), pp. 90–2; Daniel Defoe, *The Present State of the Parties in Great Britain* (1712), p. 319. Hereafter *PS*.

17 J. Paul Hunter, *The Reluctant Pilgrim: Defoe's Emblematic Method and Quest for Form in Robinson Crusoe* (Baltimore: Johns Hopkins Press, 1966), p. 204; Tom Paulin, *Crusoe's Secret: The Aesthetics of Dissent* (London: Faber, 2005), p. 86.

18 *The Poems of Alexander Pope*, vol. III, *The Dunciad (1728) and The Dunciad Variorum (1729)*, ed. Valerie Rumbold (Harlow: Longman, 2007), p. 55 (ii.127). For the implications of Pope's slur (which compares Defoe with dissidents under Charles I whose ears were actually severed), see my 'Defoe's Ears: *The Dunciad*, the Pillory, and Seditious Libel', in *The Eighteenth-Century Novel* 7 6–7 (2009); Special Double Volume; *Essays in Honor of John Richetti*.

19 Daniel Defoe, *The True-Born Englishman and Other Writings* (hereafter *TBE*), ed. P. N. Furbank and W. R. Owens (London: Penguin, 1997), p. 142.

20 Daniel Defoe, *Review*, 2.69 (11 August 1705), p. 277.

21 Defoe's manuscript petition (The National Archives, SP 34/37/11) is photographically reproduced in Paula Backscheider, *Daniel Defoe: His Life* (Baltimore: Johns Hopkins University Press, 1989), p. 327.

22 Daniel Defoe, *Moll Flanders*, ed. G. A. Starr (Oxford: Oxford University Press, 1981), p. 2. Hereafter *MF*.

23 Woolf, *Collected Essays*, I, p. 64.

24 Daniel Defoe, *Captain Singleton*, ed. Shiv K. Kumar, introduction by Penelope Wilson (Oxford: Oxford University Press, 1990), pp. 33, 126, 13. The uneasy paradoxes of Montaigne's essay 'Of Cannibals' underlie Defoe's thinking in both places.

25 It has been argued that Samuel Beckett drew on Defoe for his focus 'on a narrator who is isolated, tenuously recording his life, appealing periodically to an unresponsive deity' (Frederik N. Smith, *Beckett's Eighteenth Century* (Basingstoke: Palgrave, 2002), p. 49). In *Ill Seen Ill Said* (1981) Beckett plays more obviously on Pope, but he frequently invokes Defoe elsewhere, beginning when, in his early poem 'Serena I' (1935), the poet surveys London from the top of Wren's Monument to the Great Fire, cursing 'I was not born Defoe'.

26 *Roxana*, ed. John Mullan (Oxford: Oxford University Press, 1998), p. 39. Hereafter *R*.
27 Woolf, *Collected Essays*, I, p. 63.
28 *MF*, p. 191, quoting Proverbs 30:9.
29 *Review*, 3.28 (5 March 1706), pp. 109–10.
30 Starr, *Defoe and Casuistry*, p. ix.

FURTHER READING

Alkon, Paul K., *Defoe and Fictional Time*, Athens, GA, University of Georgia Press, 1979

Backscheider, P. R., *Daniel Defoe: His Life*, Baltimore, Johns Hopkins University Press, 1989

Blewett, David, *Defoe and the Art of Fiction*, Toronto, University of Toronto Press, 1979

Faller, L. B., *Crime and Defoe: A New Kind of Writing*, Cambridge, Cambridge University Press, 1993

Furbank, P. N. and W. R. Owens, *A Critical Bibliography of Daniel Defoe*, London, Pickering and Chatto, 1998

Maniquis, R., and C. Fisher (eds.), *Defoe's Footprints: Essays in Honour of Maximillian E. Novak*, Toronto, University of Toronto Press, 2009

Novak, M. E., *Daniel Defoe, Master of Fictions: His Life and Ideas*, Oxford, Oxford University Press, 2001

Realism, Myth, and History in Defoe's Fiction, Lincoln, University of Nebraska Press, 1983

Richetti, J. J., *Defoe's Narratives: Situations and Structures*, Oxford, Clarendon Press, 1975

The Life of Daniel Defoe, Oxford, Blackwell, 2005

Richetti, J. J. (ed.), *The Cambridge Companion to Daniel Defoe*, Cambridge, Cambridge University Press, 2009

Starr, G. A., *Defoe and Spiritual Autobiography*, Princeton, Princeton University Press, 1965

Defoe and Casuistry, Princeton, Princeton University Press, 1971

Vickers, I., *Defoe and the New Sciences*, Cambridge, Cambridge University Press, 1996

Zimmerman, Everett, *Defoe and the Novel*, Berkeley, University of California Press, 1975

2

PETER SABOR

Samuel Richardson

In February 1751, Samuel Richardson (1689–1761) contributed an essay to Samuel Johnson's periodical *The Rambler*. Johnson, in introducing Richardson's piece, described his friend as one 'who has enlarged the knowledge of human nature, and taught the passions to move at the command of virtue'.[1] As a lexicographer, Johnson exempted Richardson from his general policy of not citing contemporaries and quoted him in his *Dictionary* on over one hundred occasions, far more than any other living author. By 1761, the year of his death, Richardson occupied a commanding position among European writers and was celebrated in a famous eulogy by Denis Diderot. Both Johnson and Diderot were struck by Richardson's profound insights into human psychology, and Diderot regarded him as a worthy successor to Homer. Richardson had achieved his reputation as the originator of a new kind of novel-writing on the strength of three works published over the two previous decades: *Pamela* (1740–1), *Clarissa* (1747–8), and *Sir Charles Grandison* (1753–4). *Pamela* created a sensation on its first publication and was the best-selling novel of its time. Richardson's masterpiece, *Clarissa*, is among the greatest (and longest) of all English novels; its protagonists, Clarissa and Lovelace, are archetypal figures. Frances Burney, writing to her son, declared that *Clarissa* 'has the deepest tragic powers that the pen can address to the heart'.[2] Angus Wilson, another of the many English novelists to have recorded a debt to Richardson, describes *Clarissa* as a work 'about the refusal of one human being (the heroine) to be treated as a thing by another (her pursuer, Lovelace)' and as 'the most complete and powerful account of that terrible battle against power to be found in literature'.[3] *Sir Charles Grandison*, a key work in the novel-of-manners tradition, fell out of favour in the twentieth century but is now becoming the subject of renewed critical interest.

Richardson began writing *Pamela* in November 1739. He was already a prominent figure in London's literary circles, but as a printer, rather than an author. In 1706, at the age of seventeen, he was apprenticed to the printer

John Wilde; in 1720, he established his own printing-house in Salisbury Court, off Fleet Street. He would maintain both his principal residence and his business in this area, the commercial district where the book trade continued to be based, for the remainder of his life. Unlike his great rival Henry Fielding, Richardson received no university education, knew no language (ancient or modern) other than English, and never left England, even for journeys to Scotland or Wales. He wrote novels for only fourteen years, but he was a printer for his entire adult life. In 1733, he became the first official printer for the House of Commons, a position he never relinquished. As he emphasised in a revealing autobiographical letter to his Dutch correspondent, Johannes Stinstra: 'My business, Sir, has ever been my chief Concern. My Writing-time has been at such times of Leisure as have not interfered with that' (2 June 1753).[4]

The main records of Richardson's printing-house have not survived, and the full extent of his massive output as a printer, over a forty-year period, has only recently come to light.[5] His work includes about a thousand books and pamphlets, a huge quantity of parliamentary printing (consisting of private and local bills, public bills, accounts and papers, and twenty-eight retrospective volumes of the House of Commons *Journal*), and a very large body of newspaper and magazine printing. In the 1720s, he printed Tory opposition papers such as the Duke of Wharton's *True Briton* and *Mist's Daily Journal*, both crypto-Jacobite and thus anathema to the Whig government of the day, and in 1728 he came close to arrest and imprisonment for his involvement with Nathaniel Mist's journal; Mist had his own press broken up and fled to France to avoid detention. In the 1730s, however, Richardson was printing works such as William Webster's religiously orientated *Weekly Miscellany* and the pro-government *Daily Gazetteer*. His early oppositional political views were tempered, in his later years, by business exigencies.

It is intriguing to consider what Richardson the future novelist was learning from the vast and diverse body of works that he printed before writing *Pamela*. From the private parliamentary bills, he gained the extensive legal knowledge of matters such as wills, estate settlements, and marriage contracts that he began to put to use in *Pamela* and exploited more fully in *Clarissa* and *Sir Charles Grandison*. The numerous works of poetry, drama, and prose fiction that he printed provided important literary models. Among the fiction was Philip Sidney's *Arcadia*, in which the Princess Pamela furnished Richardson with the then uncommon name of his servant-maid heroine. Richardson was also responsible for part of a reprinting of Delarivier Manley's scandalous *Adventures of Rivella*; two of the four volumes of Eliza Haywood's collection, *Secret Histories*; part of Elizabeth Rowe's *Miscellaneous Works in Prose and Verse*; and several works by

Jonathan Swift, including *Gulliver's Travels*. Richardson's debt to writers of amatory fiction such as Manley and Haywood is striking, although he refused to acknowledge their influence. Richardson was equally reluctant to acknowledge his obvious debt to Swift, to whose poetry and prose he alludes repeatedly in each of his novels.[6] In his observations on his own fiction, made in prefaces, postscripts, newspaper advertisements, and remarks to correspondents, Richardson presented his work as a loftier enterprise than that of his predecessors.

During his early years as a printer Richardson was also a miscellaneous writer, producing, at the behest of booksellers, 'Indexes, Prefaces, and sometimes for their minor Authors, *honest* Dedications; abstracting, abridging, compiling', as well as writing 'a few other little things of the Pamphlet kind' (letter to Stinstra, 2 June 1753). His editorial work included extensive revisions to Daniel Defoe's *Complete English Tradesman* (1737) and his *Tour thro' the Whole Island of Great Britain* (1738), in which he turned Defoe's idiosyncratic guidebook into a more methodical, orderly, and comprehensive work. He also published a new version of Sir Roger L'Estrange's edition of *Aesop's Fables* (1739), reducing the number of fables by over half. In *Pamela*, the heroine alludes to Richardson's edition of the *Fables* on several occasions, as do characters in both of his later novels. Richardson's *Aesop* also contains a Preface, explaining how and why he had condensed L'Estrange's text: he had given 'the *exceptionable Reflections* a more *general* and *useful* Turn' and 'put a stronger Point to several of the Fables' (pp. x, xi).[7] In the same year, he prepared a Preface and a massive table of contents for the diplomatic correspondence of Sir Thomas Roe. Richardson doubtless undertook other such projects that have not been identified. One of these undertakings may be the abridged edition of *Gulliver's Travels* that he printed in 1727 which, like his *Aesop*, is about half the length of the original. It too contains a Preface in which the editor explains and justifies the abridgement. Whether or not this editor was Richardson, the Preface manifests the same attitude to Swift that he later displayed in his novels and correspondence: a combination of fascination and disgust that impelled him at once to immerse himself in Swift's writings and to recoil from what he read. Another Preface by Richardson, to Penelope Aubin's *Collection of Entertaining Histories and Novels* (1739), has been persuasively attributed. Written shortly before he began work on *Pamela*, the Preface throws some interesting light on Richardson's didactic views of prose fiction, which should, he asserted, instil the minds of its youthful readers with 'the Principles of Virtue and Honour'.[8]

In January 1736, Edward Cave, the editor of the *Gentleman's Magazine*, observed that 'the Publick is often agreeably entertain'd' with Richardson's

'Elegant Disquisitions in Prose' (vol. 6, p. 51), corroborating his own later reference to publications 'of the Pamphlet kind'. The earliest of these elusive items to be identified is *The Apprentice's Vade Mecum; or, Young Man's Pocket-Companion* (1733), a conduct manual for apprentices that grew out of a long letter of advice written by Richardson to a nephew whom he had taken on as an apprentice. Another anonymous pamphlet identified as Richardson's is *A Seasonable Examination of the Pleas and Pretensions of the Proprietors of, and Subscribers to, Play-houses* (1735). This polemical piece develops arguments against playgoing made in the *Vade Mecum*, deploring the harm done to apprentices and tradesmen by too frequent attendance at the theatre. Later in life, Richardson became more tolerant towards the stage; in *Pamela*, the heroine concedes that 'the Stage, by proper Regulations, might be made a profitable Amusement' (IV, 81). His novels display an extensive knowledge of English drama, from Shakespeare to the works of his playwriting friends, such as Aaron Hill, David Garrick and Edward Moore, and he excelled in writing passages of sustained dialogue that have something of the dramatic force of a stage play.

In one of his own accounts of the origins of *Pamela*, Richardson describes its relationship to another of his publications, a collection of model letters. He had been asked to compile this work, dealing with 'useful concerns in common life' (letter to Aaron Hill, *c.* 1 February 1741), before turning to his novel, and it was duly published in January 1741, only two months after *Pamela*, as *Letters Written to and for Particular Friends, on the most Important Occasions*. It is no surprise that Richardson should have been asked to compile *Familiar Letters*, as it is usually known; he had long taken pride in his letter-writing skills. In his autobiographical letter to Stinstra, he refers to his youthful epistolary productions: a reproachful letter to a fifty-year-old widow that he wrote at the age of ten, pretending to be a 'Person in Years' but failing to disguise his hand; love-letters written on behalf of three young women at the age of thirteen; and what he terms 'Multitudes of Letters' exchanged with a mysterious 'Gentleman greatly my Superior in Degree', who was a 'Master of the Epistolary Style' but at whose urging Richardson had long since burned all of their correspondence. Two of the model letters are especially relevant to *Pamela*: number 138, 'A Father to a Daughter in Service, on hearing of her Master's attempting her Virtue', and number 139, 'The Daughter's Answer'. In Richardson's account these letters, giving 'cautions to young folks circumstanced as Pamela was', formed the basis of the novel: he 'gave way to enlargement: and so Pamela became as you see her' (letter to Hill, *c.* 1 February 1741). But *Pamela* does far more than merely 'enlarge' his model letters. In *Familiar Letters*, the servant-girl tells her father that she is entirely convinced by his advice: 'I have this Day left the House; and hope to be with you soon after you will have received this Letter' (p. 182). As Thomas Keymer observes, this is a far cry from what he terms the 'agonized hesitancies' of *Pamela*.[9]

It took Richardson only two months to complete *Pamela*, between November 1739 and January 1740. The novel is narrated in the heroine's epistolary voice; its first hundred pages consist of numbered letters, but the remainder is an extended journal-letter that concludes abruptly when Pamela's parents visit the household of their newly married daughter and the need for her journal supposedly ends. Technically, it is a tour de force: the fifty-year-old male author mimics, with astonishing plausibility, the characteristic tone and diction of his fifteen-year-old heroine, with no formal education or first-hand knowledge of the world. Having set himself the challenge, as a ten-year-old boy, of writing an admonitory letter in the voice of a 'Person in Years', Richardson, forty years later, took on the much greater challenge of sustaining the voice of his adolescent heroine over two substantial volumes.

In a letter of 1754, written after he had completed his three novels and was dwelling on their reception, Richardson suggested to his correspondent, Lady Bradshaigh, that the world was 'not enough used to this way of writing, to the moment' (14 February 1754). The phrase 'writing, to the moment' has since become a staple of Richardson criticism. It captures to perfection, as Keymer remarks, two associated qualities of his novels' epistolary form: 'not just its capacity to register the flux of consciousness over time, but more particularly its dramatic synchronizations of narration and crisis'.[10] Elsewhere, alluding to Henry Fielding's narrative technique, Richardson contrasts the monotony of third-person narration with the dramatic immediacy of his own epistolary fiction: the former resembles 'the dead Tolling of a single Bell', while epistolary fiction is akin to 'the wonderful Variety of Sounds, which constitute the Harmony of a Handel'.[11]

Despite Richardson's claims, however, 'writing, to the moment' is far from a straightforward process. When Pamela tells her master, Mr B., that her letters are transparent – 'I don't remember all I wrote, yet know I wrote my Heart; and that is not deceitful' (II, 14) – she is endorsing the idea that letters, in epistolary fiction, afford direct access to their writer's consciousness as the action unfolds. But letters, of course, also serve as manipulative devices. In *Shamela* (1741), Fielding's brilliant parodic reduction of Richardson's novel, the eponymous heroine purports to be writing to the moment, as she describes Squire Booby's entering her bedchamber, the door of which she has cagily left unlocked: 'if my Master should come – Odsbobs! I hear him just coming in at the Door. You see I write in the present Tense, as Parson *Williams* says.'[12] Here and elsewhere in *Shamela*, Fielding seizes on the artificiality of epistolary fiction: there is nothing spontaneous about Shamela's devious manipulations of the present moment, and there is, at least arguably, something devious about Pamela's self-presentation. In *Memoirs of a Woman of Pleasure* (1748–9), similarly, John Cleland parodies Richardson's prized technique with a passage in which his heroine, Fanny Hill, uses it to describe the act of penetration after her reunion with Charles, her lover and husband to be, at the end of the novel: 'I see! I feel! the delicious velvet tip! – he enters might and main with – oh! – my pen drops from me here in the extasy now present to my faithful memory!'[13] Early in Richardson's novel, when Pamela hopes to escape Mr B.'s predatory advances by returning to her parents, she records one of his complaints against her:

> I find she is a mighty Letter-writer! to her Father and Mother, and others, as far as I know; in which she makes herself an Angel of Light, and me, her kind Master and Benefactor, a Devil incarnate! – (O how People will sometimes, thought I, call themselves by the right Names!) (I.36–7)

But Mr B. is no more the 'Devil incarnate' than Pamela is an 'Angel of Light', and his charge has some foundation; Richardson uses his heroine's letters to provide insights into her consciousness, but there is no immediate, unmediated access into the workings of her mind.

Pamela's subtitle, 'Virtue Rewarded', glosses over the fact that there is a protracted debate within the novel over the morality of the heroine's conduct. Among her principal detractors are Mr B. himself, who complains repeatedly that she is using her charms to seduce him, his coarse housekeeper Mrs Jewkes, his aristocratic sister Lady Davers, and Lady Davers's oafish nephew Jackey. Lady Davers and Jackey are at the opposite end of the hierarchy of rank from Mrs Jewkes, but all three at first believe that Pamela's resistance to her master's sexual advances is a sham. After Mr B. is at length convinced of Pamela's virtue, and marries her, her fictive detractors are converted and Lady Davers becomes one of her numerous admirers. Readers of the novel took up the debate with a vengeance, and *Pamela* became an astonishingly successful best-seller. Five editions were called for in less than a year, together with a French translation (published in London) and piracies in both London and Dublin. As early as January 1741, before the publication of the later editions, the *Gentleman's Magazine* declared that it was 'as great a Sign of Want of Curiosity not to have read *Pamela*, as not to have seen the *French* and *Italian* Dancers' (vol. 11, p. 56).

Unlike her fictive critics, however, readers were sharply divided over the heroine's, and the novel's, merits. The controversy soon spread to continental Europe, where the Danish dramatist Ludvig Holberg characterised the debate as one between 'two different Parties, *Pamelists* and *Antipamelists*'.[14] One of the many charges made by the Antipamelists was that Richardson's ostensibly didactic novel was merely pornography in disguise, and that the various scenes in which Mr B. sexually assaults, or attempts to assault, the heroine are lubricious in design. Fielding's *Shamela*, published less than five months after Richardson's novel, in April 1741, was the first work to depict it in such terms. But *Shamela* was followed by a plethora of other responses – including counter-fictions, spurious continuations, parodies, dramatic and operatic adaptations, verses, and visual images. Some of these works took the form of panegyrics while others were dull recastings of the *Pamela* story, but many took a Shamelian view of Richardson's novel. Among the numerous participants in what has become known as the *Pamela* controversy, or the *Pamela* media event,[15] were Eliza Haywood, whose lapsed career as a novelist took off again with her follow-up to Fielding's *Shamela*, *Anti-Pamela: Or, Feign'd Innocence Detected* (1741); David Garrick, who took the role of Jack Smatter in Henry Giffard's dramatic adaptation of *Pamela* (1741), one of the young actor's first roles on the London stage; and Joseph Highmore, whose series of twelve paintings based on the novel (1742–4) was also made into prints sold in England and abroad with captions in English and French.

In the face of this remarkably sustained response to his first novel, Richardson took extraordinary measures to justify what he termed his 'new species of writing' (letter to Hill, *c.* 1 February 1741) and to defend *Pamela* from its critics. After equipping the first edition with a Preface, ostensibly by the editor of Pamela's letters, and with two sycophantic commendatory letters, one by the French translator Jean Baptiste de Freval and a second probably by the Revd William Webster, Richardson went much further in the second edition, published in February 1741. A new Introduction, in which he avowed that his aim was to make the work 'as unexceptionable as possible', supplemented the existing commendations with still more fulsome panegyrics by Aaron Hill, which provided Fielding and others with an easy target for their satires. At the same time Richardson began the laborious process of revising the text of the novel, which he would continue to undertake in each of the subsequent lifetime editions. One of these, the octavo sixth edition of 1742, replaced the ill-judged Introduction with an elaborate, thirty-six-page table of contents, although subsequent editions restored the introductory material, albeit in revised form. Also unique to the expensive octavo edition, 'beautifully printed on a Writing-Paper' according to Richardson's newspaper advertisements, were twenty-nine illustrations to the novel by Hubert Gravelot and Francis Hayman, designed to counter various unauthorised illustrations already in circulation and to help reinforce his own interpretation of the text.

Among the works exploiting the astonishing popularity of *Pamela* were three spurious continuations, all published in 1741: John Kelly's *Pamela's Conduct in High Life*, the anonymous *Pamela in High Life*, and *The Life of Pamela*, an anonymous third-person retelling of both Richardson's original novel and Kelly's continuation, first published in weekly instalments. Richardson's response was to publish a two-volume continuation of his own, displaying the heroine, according to the title-page, 'in her Exalted Condition' and dealing with 'the most Important and Entertaining Subjects, in Genteel Life'. As the emphasis here on gentility suggests (Richardson avoids the phrase 'High Life' associated with two of the spurious sequels), the continuation is a far blander affair than the original work: with Mr B. now reformed, there would be no occasion, as Richardson told one of his correspondents, for the quasi-pornographic 'deep Scenes' that had caused so much controversy. The 'Storms, the Stratagems, and all that could indanger Virtue' would now, he declared, give way to episodes 'more calm, serene, and instructive' (letter to George Cheyne, early January 1742). By refining both the language and conduct of Pamela and Mr B., Richardson answered critics who saw them as hypocrite and rake, while their fertile and generally harmonious union counters those who regarded the marriage as a regrettable misalliance. Controversial episodes from the first two volumes are rehearsed and explained, while obscure ones are given greater prominence: *Pamela II* is designed to show how *Pamela* should be read. In addition, a thicket of footnotes guides the reader to particular passages in both parts of the novel that support Richardson's authorial interpretation of the text.

Pamela II does have its share of vulgar characters: Sir Jacob Swynford, for example, whose porcine surname is a signpost to his character and who declares, 'I must have a boil'd Chicken, and shall eat it all myself' (III, 309). But Pamela and Mr B. converse in quite different tones. In their debate over the advantages and disadvantages of breast-feeding for infants, Pamela speaks authoritatively about colostrum and meconium ('a pitchy Substance' that the newborn 'wants to be purged off'), while Mr B. rejects her pro-nursing arguments by appealing to his fondness for her 'easy, genteel Form, which every body admires' (IV, 35, 38). The debate is conducted decorously, with none of the coarse language that Fielding had parodied relentlessly in *Shamela*. The distance between the two parts of *Pamela* is especially pronounced in the final volume of *Pamela II*, which contains the heroine's protracted analysis of John Locke's *Some Thoughts Concerning Education*. Both servant-maid and country squire are transformed. In a postscript to the novel, Richardson tells his readers that Mr B. lived in Europe for three years 'in the Service of the State' and distinguished himself 'in such a manner, as might be expected from his Qualifications, and Knowledge of the World'

(IV, 469); the apparent irony here is surely unintended. No longer the blundering booby satirised by Fielding, this is Mr B. the seasoned statesman and much-travelled man of affairs.

Like the pair of sequels that followed an earlier bestseller, Defoe's *Robinson Crusoe* (1719), *Pamela II* has always been eclipsed by its precursor. Aaron Hill, the most enthusiastic of Richardson's readers, heralded it as 'God's Rainbow, for the Comfort of a drowning World!' and saluted its author as the 'all-excelling, all-instructing, Humanizer of a People' (letter to Richardson, 8 December 1741), but this was a distinctly minority view. Yet for all its arid patches, *Pamela II* marks an important stage in Richardson's development as an epistolary novelist. Here, for the first time, there are exchanges of correspondence between masculine characters, such as Mr B. and Sir Simon Darnford, and there are many more letters in a variety of registers by minor characters, such as Lady Davers, Jackey, and Polly Darnford, than in the original novel. The polyphonic range of voices that Richardson created in *Clarissa*, first published in three instalments in 1747–8, grew out of his experiments with epistolary form in his sequel to *Pamela*. But *Clarissa* works on a much larger scale, with its elaborately orchestrated parallel series of letters between Clarissa and her confidante, Anna Howe, and Lovelace and his friend, John Belford. There is a cast of over two hundred characters, with even the most minor ones possessing a distinctive voice and manner. As the novelist Sarah Fielding, Henry Fielding's sister, observed in her treatise *Remarks on Clarissa* (1749), the 'various Stiles adapted to the many different Characters ... make so great a Variety, as would ... answer any Objection that might otherwise fairly be raised to the Length of the Story' (p. 41).

Clarissa aroused the admiration even of Richardson's critics and rivals. Henry Fielding, who had exposed what he regarded as the moral and technical deficiencies of *Pamela* first with *Shamela* and then with *Joseph Andrews* (1742), his demonstration of how a novel should be written, revised his opinion of Richardson when the first instalment of *Clarissa* appeared. The novel, he declared, was written with 'such Simplicity, such Manners, such deep Penetration into Nature; such Power to raise and alarm the Passions', that 'few Writers, either ancient or modern, have been possessed of'.[16] In a letter to Richardson on the fifth volume, in which Clarissa is imprisoned, drugged, and raped by Lovelace but indignantly refuses his proposal of marriage, Fielding records the intensity of the reading experience: 'Here my Terror ends and my Grief begins which the Cause of all my Tumultuous Passions soon changes into Raptures of Admiration and Astonishment' (15 October 1748). Tobias Smollett, who rightly admitted in a letter to Richardson that he was 'not much addicted to Compliment', commended his 'surprizing Intimacy with the human Heart' (10 August 1756). *Clarissa* had a hypnotic effect on its early readers, such as the poet and critic Thomas Edwards, author of books on textual editing and spelling reform, who read the seven volumes (eight in the third edition of 1751) on at least five occasions. Lady Bradshaigh was one of several correspondents who implored Richardson to spare Clarissa's life before the final volume was published, while her sister, Lady Echlin, went so far as to write her own conclusion to the novel, in which Lovelace does not rape Clarissa but dies a convert, shortly after Clarissa dies of a broken heart. As early as 1745, reading the novel in manuscript, the dramatist Colley Cibber reacted violently when he learned that Clarissa must die, reportedly swearing: 'God damn him, if she should, and that he should no longer believe Providence, or eternal Wisdom, or Goodness governed the world, if merit, innocence, and beauty were to be so destroyed' (Laetitia Pilkington to Richardson, 29 June 1745).

For Richardson, however, the death of Clarissa was an essential part of a specifically Christian tragedy: one which displays 'an overflow of divine grace upon the human mind' (William Warburton to Richardson, 25 April 1748). Richardson develops this concept of the novel both in his correspondence and in his Postscript to the final, three-volume instalment. Here, as part of his depiction of *Clarissa* as Christian tragedy, Richardson called, in a footnote, for a staged revival of Shakespeare's *King Lear*, in preference to Nahum Tate's sentimental version, *The History of King Lear*, which permits Cordelia to live. Richardson finds the 'Modern Taste' for Tate's revised *Lear* as misplaced as the cry for a happy ending to *Clarissa*, 'whether this *strange* preference be owing to the false Delicacy or affected Tenderness of the Players, or to that of the Audience' (*Clarissa*, VII, 428). Richardson lost this particular skirmish: Tate's *Lear* continued to hold the stage during his lifetime, and he removed the note in revising the Postscript for the third edition of 1751.[17] He also lost some of his potential readers, with protestors such as Lady Bradshaigh threatening not to read, or purchase, the final volumes. But just as Shakespeare's *Lear* was restored to the stage later in the century, the moral necessity for *Clarissa*'s tragic ending was widely accepted; if Richardson had lost the battle, he won the war.

Over a year before the first instalment of *Clarissa* was published, in a letter to Aaron Hill, Richardson announced his intention to create an ethically impeccable heroine; he 'intended to make her so faultless, that a Reader should find no way to account for the Calamities she met with, and to justify Moral Equity but by looking up to a future Reward' (29 October 1746). But the idea of human faultlessness is hard for other humans to swallow, and not all of Richardson's readers have taken him at his word. In a review of the novel first published in French before being translated in the *Gentleman's*

Magazine (vol. 19, 1749), the Swiss scientist and man of letters Albrecht von Haller objects that Clarissa 'shews too scrupulous a delicacy after she has suffered herself to be carry'd off by *Lovelace*: It then became expedient for her to marry *Lovelace*, who, more than once, offer'd her his hand, in the involuntary transports of his passion' (p. 348). Some of Richardson's extensive revisions to the second and third editions respond to this objection. Before the rape, Clarissa now poses a question about Lovelace's puzzling behaviour to her: 'Why, why will he take pains to make a heart wrap itself up in Reserve, that wishes only, and that for his sake as well as my own, to observe due decorum?' (2nd edn, IV, 64). And with the rape, Lovelace's reasons for making Clarissa's heart 'wrap itself up in Reserve' become clearly apparent. Von Haller had been deceived by what he took to be the rake's 'involuntary transports'; Lovelace couches his proposals of marriage in a form that he knew Clarissa would have to refuse.

The sympathy for Lovelace that von Haller displays in his review was symptomatic of a general trend in the contemporary reception of *Clarissa*; Richardson was thought to have made his libertine too attractive a figure. In *Pamela* he had created a hero, Mr B., who lacked even a surname and whose many obvious shortcomings make his transformation in *Pamela II* hard to swallow. In *Clarissa*, Richardson faced a different problem; here his readers were given to sympathising with Lovelace, for all his iniquities. Fielding's famous letter of praise is typical in this respect, terming the character 'Lovelass' and relishing his gifts for black humour. Fielding goes on to declare that the libertine's 'former Admirers must lose all Regard for him on his Perseverance, and as this Regard ceases, Compassion for Clarissa rises in the same Proportion'. Richardson's aim, in contrast, was for readers to have such compassion for Clarissa from the start, and for Lovelace to elicit not admiration but abhorrence.

Richardson's later editions of *Clarissa* attempted to counter his readers' sympathy for Lovelace in various ways. Among these is a forty-three-page table of contents, which, he complained to Aaron Hill, 'has cost me infinite Trouble' (10 May 1749), allowing him to guide his readers towards his own interpretation of the novel. Thus a letter from Clarissa to Anna Howe containing a portrait of Lovelace is, we are told, '*necessary to be attended to; especially by those who have thought favourably of him for some of his liberal actions,* and *hardly of her for the distance she at first kept him at*' (2nd edn, I, xxiv). In case this isn't clear enough, Richardson further directs his readers through a prefatory note to the contents, which will, he declares, 'not only point out the principal Facts, and shew the Connexion of the Whole; but will enable the *youthful Readers* of both Sexes to form a judgment as well of the *blameable* as of the *laudable* Conduct of the principal persons' (2nd edn, I, iii–iv). Richardson also buttressed the contents with a tissue of tendentious editorial footnotes, several of which explain Lovelace's machinations to inattentive readers. One footnote observes that despite his proposal to Anna Howe that her mother could assume the protection of Clarissa, Lovelace '*had artfully taken care, by means of his agent in the Harlowe family, not only to inflame the family against her, but to deprive her of Mrs. Howe's, and of every other protection*' (2nd edn, II, 21). Other notes chide readers for the slovenly reading that has occasioned the note's insertion. After expounding Lovelace's motives for his ostensible generosity towards the innocent country girl Rosebud, Richardson adds: '*This explanation is the more necessary to be given, as several of our Readers (thro' want of due attention) have attributed to Mr. Lovelace, on his behaviour to his Rosebud, a greater merit than was due to him*' (2nd edn, II, 146).

Despite his impatience with his readers, not all of Richardson's revisions to the depiction of Lovelace in later editions of *Clarissa* are designed to increase his culpability. Many of the revised passages emphasise the mordant wit and dazzling ingenuity that make Lovelace a consummate libertine in the Don Giovanni tradition. In one of the inserted passages in the second edition, Lovelace writes to Belford about a sexual encounter with 'the daughter of an old Epicure, who had taught the girl, without the least remorse, to roast Lobsters alive; to cause a poor Pig to be whipt to death; to scrape Carp the contrary way of the scales, making them leap in the stew-pan, and dressing them in their own blood for sawce' (2nd edn, III, 359–60). Richardson himself, in a manuscript memorandum on the second-edition changes, describes this passage as one about 'Pity, Cruelty, &c.'. The cruelty, however, is not that of Lovelace, but of the epicure and his daughter. Lovelace goes on to contrast their gormandising with his own sexual appetite, which needs no artificial stimulation, and contends that his carnality is, at worst, no more culpable than that of his sexual partners.

In revising *Clarissa*, Richardson also complicated his original conception of the heroine. Several of the altered passages respond to his critics by presenting her in a more favourable light, and extensive additions to Anna Howe's already long-winded eulogy, in particular, make her a relentlessly perfect figure. But to his credit, Richardson made his heroine more self-critical, acknowledging what she terms her 'most secret failings': 'What a pride did I take in the applause of every one! – What a pride even in supposing I had *not* that pride ... So desirous, in short, to be considered as an *Example!* ... And so secure in my own virtue!' (3rd edn, IV, 196–7). This accords with Richardson's changing depiction of Clarissa in his correspondence. In a letter to Frances Grainger, for example, Richardson clearly acknowledges that his heroine 'was not perfect. But Clarissa could accuse her self in Instances where she thought she ought not to be acquitted' (29 March 1750). Here Richardson addresses an issue taken up by some of some of his most perceptive modern readers, such as J. M. Coetzee, who notes that Clarissa 'does not fully know herself', but also knows that she does not fully know herself.[18]

While Richardson was undertaking his massive revisions of *Clarissa*, in the late 1740s and early 1750s, he was also at work on his final novel, *Sir Charles Grandison*. Published, like *Clarissa*, in three instalments, from November 1753 to March 1754, it was almost as long as its predecessor, but it is a novel of a very different kind. Richardson regarded his eponymous hero as both a male counterpart to Clarissa and the antithesis of Lovelace, possessing all of his attractive qualities but none of his vices; in his pre-publication correspondence on the novel, Richardson refers to him repeatedly as the 'good man'. The heroine, Harriet Byron, was designed 'to keep the middle course, between Pamela and Clarissa; and between Clarissa and Miss Howe; or rather, to make her what I would have supposed Clarissa to be, had she not met with such persecutions at home, and with such a tormentor as Lovelace' (Richardson to Lady Bradshaigh, 24 March 1751). In writing *Clarissa*, Richardson had resolved not merely to reproduce his success with *Pamela*; he was now determined to produce a novel taking a new direction again. As he boasted to a correspondent: 'I borrow not from any body, no, not from myself' (Richardson to Anne Dewes, 21 June 1752).

Sir Charles Grandison also afforded Richardson a way of turning the tables on his old rival Fielding, whose finest novel, *Tom Jones*, published only two months after the final instalment of *Clarissa*, had easily outsold its competitor. Fielding's final novel, *Amelia* (1751), however, had been less well received. Richardson belittled it repeatedly to his correspondents, and claimed, implausibly, to have read only the first volume; with its 'characters and situations so wretchedly low and dirty' (Richardson to Anne Donnellan, 22 February 1752), he had no incentive to proceed. *Sir Charles Grandison*, in contrast, would work on a higher plane. Among the many problems that its hero must resolve, the largest concerns his own complex love life: he is equally beloved by Harriet Byron, an English Protestant, and by Clementina della Porretta, an Italian Catholic from a family of high rank, and must somehow choose one without unduly distressing the other. His involvement with the della Porrettas compels Sir Charles to travel to and from Italy at a moment's notice, and he does so with ease. His appetite for arduous journeys across England and Europe is inexhaustible and he is indifferent to the hazards he must encounter. As one of his many admirers in the novel declares: 'Seas are nothing to him ... he considers all nations as joined on the same continent; and ... if he had a call, he would undertake a journey to Constantinople or Pekin, with as little difficulty, as some others would … to the Land's-end' (III, 43). These words are echoed in Sir Charles's valediction near the end of the novel, in the presence of Harriet, to the assembled della Porretta family: 'Friendship, dearest creatures, will make at pleasure a safe bridge over the narrow seas; it will cut an easy passage thro' rocks and mountains, and make England and Italy one country' (VII, 287). This is a far cry from the fastnesses of the Bedfordshire and Lincolnshire country houses in which Richardson had set his first novel.

Richardson's observations on his fellow novelists, with the exception of the unthreatening Penelope Aubin and Sarah Fielding, were largely negative. In addition to his obsessive attacks on Henry Fielding, he belittled the works of Aphra Behn, Delarivier Manley, and Eliza Haywood, and, at the very end of his life, Laurence Sterne; after reading the first two volumes of *Tristram Shandy*, he described it as a 'little book', filled with 'unaccountable wildness; whimsical digressions; comical incoherencies; uncommon indecencies; all with an air of novelty' (Richardson to Bishop Hildesley, *c.* March 1761). But novelists from Charlotte Lennox, Frances Burney, Maria Edgeworth, and George Eliot in the late eighteenth and nineteenth century to Ford Madox Ford, Virginia Woolf, Angus Wilson, and J. M. Coetzee in the twentieth century have been more generous towards Richardson. Among the most fervent of his admirers was Jane Austen, who alludes repeatedly to his novels in both her juvenilia and her published works and who collaborated with one of her nieces on a comic adaptation of *Sir Charles Grandison* as a miniature play. In 1818, a year after her death, Austen's brother Henry remarked that 'Richardson's power of creating and preserving the consistency of his characters, as particularly exemplified in "Sir Charles Grandison," gratified the natural discrimination of her mind'. In his *Memoir of Jane Austen* (1870), her nephew James Edward Austen-Leigh claimed that 'her knowledge of Richardson's works was such as no one is likely again to acquire', and, like Henry Austen, suggested that his final novel was her favourite:

> Every circumstance narrated in Sir Charles Grandison, all that was ever said or done in the cedar parlour, was familiar to her; and the wedding days of Lady L. and Lady G. were as well remembered as if they had been living friends.[19]

After the publication of *Sir Charles Grandison*, Richardson continued to dwell on his own art of fiction. In the letter to Lady Bradshaigh that describes his preferred 'writing, to the moment' technique, he also explains how his characters come to life on the page as their author recedes:

> Here I sit down to form characters. One I intend to be all goodness; All goodness he is. Another I intend to be all gravity; All gravity he is … I am all the while absorbed in the character. It is not fair to say – I, identically, am anywhere, while I keep within the character. (14 February 1754)

But there was another side to Richardson: the abstracting, compiling, editorialising side, which feared to give his characters free rein. This is the Richardson who compulsively solicited critical comments from his readers, who anxiously hedged his novels with rebarbative prefatory material, footnotes, and concluding remarks, and who continued rewriting them from the moment of their first publication. Even his death could not end the process: his daughters inherited revised copies of all of his novels, which they eventually saw through the press until as late as 1810.

The same compiling and editorialising Richardson produced, in 1755, a volume of 'moral and instructive sentiments' digested from his three novels: a dreary compilation that drains all the vitality from his fiction. In his *Collection of … Moral and Instructive Sentiments, Maxims, Cautions, and Reflexions*, Richardson's novels, each of which had troubled and provoked its readers in various ways, are combined into a single bloodless enterprise. But in the novels themselves, where Pamela, Clarissa, Lovelace, Sir Charles Grandison, Harriet Byron, and a multitude of lesser creations are given their own distinctive voices, Richardson demonstrated the extraordinary power over its readers that epistolary fiction, with its author absorbed in the character, can hold.

NOTE ON EDITIONS

No standard edition of Richardson's novels or letters has yet been published. There are useful paperback editions of *Pamela*, ed. Thomas Keymer and Alice Wakely (Oxford: Oxford University Press, 2001), and of *Clarissa*, ed. Angus Ross (Harmondsworth: Penguin, 1985). The Works and Correspondence of Samuel Richardson, published by Cambridge University Press under the general editorship of Thomas Keymer and Peter Sabor, is in progress.

NOTES

1 *The Rambler*, 97, in *The Yale Edition of the Works of Samuel Johnson*, ed. W. J. Bate and Albrecht B. Strauss (New Haven: Yale University Press, 1969), IV, p. 153.

2 Frances Burney to Alexander d'Arblay, 10 October 1822, in *The Journals and Letters of Fanny Burney*, ed. Joyce Hemlow (Oxford: Clarendon Press, 1972–84), XI, p. 376.

3 Angus Wilson, *Diversity and Depth in Fiction: Selected Critical Writings of Angus Wilson*, ed. Kerry McSweeney (London: Secker & Warburg, 1983), p. 28.

4 Quotations from Richardson's correspondence are from the surviving manuscripts, which will all be published in the forthcoming Cambridge Edition of the Works and Correspondence of Samuel Richardson.

5 See Keith Maslen, *Samuel Richardson of London, Printer* (Dunedin: University of Otago, 2001).

6 See Peter Sabor, '"A large portion of our etherial fire": Swift and Samuel Richardson', in *Reading Swift: Papers from the Fourth Münster Symposium on Jonathan Swift*, ed. Hermann J. Real and Helgard Stöver-Leidig (Munich: Wilhelm Fink, 2003), pp. 387–401.

7 References to Richardson's novels and other writings are, unless otherwise noted, to first-edition texts, which will also form the basis of the forthcoming Cambridge Edition of the Works and Correspondence of Samuel Richardson.

8 See Wolfgang Zach, 'Mrs Aubin and Richardson's Earliest Literary Manifesto (1739)', *English Studies*, 62 (1981), p. 282.

9 Thomas Keymer, introduction to *Pamela*, ed. Keymer and Alice Wakely (Oxford: Oxford University Press, 2001), p. xv.

10 Thomas Keymer, introduction to Henry Fielding, *Joseph Andrews and Shamela*, ed. Douglas Brooks-Davies (Oxford: Oxford University Press, 1999), pp. ix–x.

11 Richardson's manuscript 'Hints of Prefaces for Clarissa', in *Samuel Richardson's Published Commentary on Clarissa 1747–65* (London: Pickering and Chatto, 1998), vol. I, introduction by Jocelyn Harris, ed. Thomas Keymer, p. 334.

12 *Shamela*, ed. Brooks-Davies, p. 318.

13 *Memoirs of a Woman of Pleasure*, ed. Peter Sabor (Oxford: Oxford University Press, 1985), p. 183.

14 Peter Shaw, *The Reflector* (1750), p. 14, adapting Ludvig Holberg's introduction to *Moralske Tanker* (1744).

15 See William B. Warner's chapter on 'The *Pamela* Media Event' in his *Licensing Entertainment: The Elevation of Novel Reading in Britain, 1684–1750* (Berkeley: University of California Press, 1998).

16 *The Jacobite's Journal and Related Writings*, ed. W. B. Coley (Oxford: Clarendon Press, 1974), p. 119 (2 January 1748).

17 See Keymer, Headnote, in *Richardson's Published Commentary*, I, p. 48.

18 J. M. Coetzee, 'Samuel Richardson, *Clarissa*', in *Stranger Shores: Literary Essays 1986–1999* (New York: Viking, 2001), p. 26.

19 J. E. Austen-Leigh, *A Memoir of Jane Austen and Other Family Recollections*, ed. Kathryn Sutherland (Oxford: Oxford University Press, 2002), pp. 141, 71.

FURTHER READING

Blewett, David (ed.), *Passion and Virtue: Essays on the Novels of Samuel Richardson*, Toronto, University of Toronto Press, 2001

Doody, Margaret Anne, *A Natural Passion: A Study of the Novels of Samuel Richardson*, Oxford, Clarendon Press, 1974

Doody, Margaret Anne, and Peter Sabor (eds.), *Samuel Richardson: Tercentenary Essays*, Cambridge, Cambridge University Press, 1989

Eaves, T. C. Duncan, and Ben D. Kimpel, *Samuel Richardson: A Biography*, Oxford, Clarendon Press, 1971

Flynn, Carol Houlihan, *Samuel Richardson: A Man of Letters*, Princeton, Princeton University Press, 1982

Gwilliam, Tassie, *Samuel Richardson's Fictions of Gender*, Stanford, Stanford University Press, 1993

Harris, Jocelyn, *Samuel Richardson*, Cambridge, Cambridge University Press, 1987

Keymer, Thomas, *Richardson's Clarissa and the Eighteenth-Century Reader*, Cambridge, Cambridge University Press, 1992

Keymer, Thomas, and Peter Sabor, *Pamela in the Marketplace: Literary Controversy and Print Culture in Eighteenth-Century Britain and Ireland*, Cambridge, Cambridge University Press, 2005

Kinkead-Weekes, Mark, *Samuel Richardson: Dramatic Novelist*, London, Methuen, 1973

Maslen, Keith, *Samuel Richardson of London, Printer*, Dunedin, University of Otago, 2001

Michie, Allen, *Richardson and Fielding: The Dynamics of a Critical Rivalry*, Lewisburg, PA, Bucknell University Press, 1999

Rivero, Albert J. (ed.), *New Essays on Samuel Richardson*, New York, St. Martin's Press, 1996

Zunshine, Lisa, and Jocelyn Harris (eds.), *Approaches to Teaching the Novels of Samuel Richardson*, New York, The Modern Language Association of America, 2006

3

JANE SPENCER

Henry Fielding

Henry Fielding (1707–54) gave the English novel a new breadth. In his masterpiece, *The History of Tom Jones, a Foundling* (1748), the title-page promise of the story of a low-life individual leads instead to an epic treatment of a contemporary society peopled by a vividly varied set of characters whose entertaining differences nevertheless add up, the narrator insists, to one fundamental article: human nature, that subject of endless Enlightenment fascination. Authors before and after Fielding looked for ways to create an epic poem for a modern age. Milton, in *Paradise Lost*, found in the Christian story a heroic argument to surpass classical heroism; Pope, in his darkly comic attack on modern civilisation, thought it worthy only of the mock-heroic epic that is *The Dunciad*; and Wordsworth took the epic quest within the self, making the subject of *The Prelude* the growth of the poet's mind. Fielding transferred epic ambition from poetry to novel. Prose narrative, he thought, could become the medium for a new human comedy: his work, as he famously put it in *Joseph Andrews*, was to produce 'a comic Epic-Poem in Prose'.[1]

Writing novels was not Fielding's first choice of literary career. During the 1730s he was England's foremost dramatist, writing five-act comedies and short, uproarious farces. His opinion at that time of the novel as a form can be gauged from his caricature of the popular novelist Eliza Haywood as 'Mrs Novel' in *The Author's Farce*: one of a medley of representatives of silly, modern, commercial entertainments, she lives in the style of her own erotic fictions, and has an affair with the equally ridiculous Signior Opera. Fielding's own activities as a dramatist were partly responsible for far-reaching changes in the theatrical world, which ultimately sent him back to rethink the potential of modern fiction. His satirical attacks on the government were part of a highly politicised theatrical culture that attracted persistent ministry efforts to suppress it, culminating in the Licensing Act of 1737, which put an end to Fielding's dramatic career. After that, he trained as a lawyer, wrote political journalism and miscellaneous essays, and experimented with various kinds of fiction, including imitations of the Greek *Dialogues of the Dead* by the second-century satirist Lucian in *Journey from This World to the Next* and a continuation of satire on the prime minister, Robert Walpole, ironically styled a 'Great Man', in *The History of Jonathan Wild the Great*, both published in 1743.

In 1741 Fielding published *Shamela*, a short, anonymous, and hilarious parody of Samuel Richardson's first novel, *Pamela* (1740). From that point on, the making of the English novel in the middle of the eighteenth century became a dance of rivalry between these two great and very different writers, their relationship triangulated by another Fielding novelist, Henry's sister Sarah, whose work each of the male authors praised and claimed as belonging to his own style of fiction. Out of this rivalry emerged a tradition of fiction in some ways deeply divided, between Fielding's satiric and comic mode of external presentation of human character through a third-person narrator, and Richardson's attempts to immerse the reader in the characters' internal experiences through the epistolary mode. The division is real, but can be exaggerated, and a critical tendency to polarise the two novelists has led to alternating swings of fashion between them. Fielding, who fifty years ago tended to be preferred to Richardson on the grounds of his wide panorama, air of openness, his humour, and his greater perceived masculinity, has more recently lost favour in comparison to a rival whose acute psychological insight and interest in the rendition of human consciousness have been increasingly recognised. Yet Fielding, too, is interested in trying to understand what the narrator of *Jonathan Wild* calls the 'secret Springs, various Windings, and perplexed Mazes' of humanity, though his methods of revealing them are very different from Richardson's.[2]

Fielding's methods as lawyer and novelist intertwined: he invited his readers to judge the merits of fictional cases on the evidence he supplied. That evidence could be incomplete and testimony unreliable was part of the point. Right judgement, he insisted, was as difficult as it was important, and for all the air of authority adopted by the narrator of *Tom Jones*, he leaves the reader in the lurch many times, refusing to take the responsibility of omniscient narration and tell us what to believe. 'Whether [Dr Blifil's] Religion was real, or consisted only in Appearance, I shall not presume to say, as I am not possessed of any Touchstone, which can distinguish the true from the false', he explains.[3] The joke here is that the narrator himself is being both false and true: in the immediate context, his words are ironic, for straight after this he gives the reader quite enough information about Dr Blifil's thoughts to warrant the conclusion that he would have married Bridget Allworthy for her money if he could, that he is only deterred from attempting bigamy with her because Mr Allworthy knows he is already married, and that he promotes Bridget's marriage with his brother for selfish motives. This seems more than enough of a touchstone to the falsity of his religious professions. In the wider context of the narrative, though, we are being given fair warning here, close to the outset, that not all cases will be so clear-cut, and that our narrative guide does not propose to do our thinking for us.

Crucial to Fielding's courtroom approach is that plaintiff, witness, and defendant may all have reasons to lie; and that even where there is no conscious intent to deceive, people telling their own story are not to be trusted. When Tom Jones, dismissed from Paradise Hall, tells his story to Benjamin, the latter cannot understand how Mr Allworthy could have been so unjust as to cast him out, which is not surprising since he had not heard from Tom

> one single Circumstance upon which he was condemned ... For let a Man be never so honest, the Account of his own Conduct will, in Spite of himself, be so very favourable, that his Vices will come purified through his Lips ... For tho' the Facts themselves may appear, yet so different will be the Motives, Circumstances, and Consequences, when a Man tells his own Story, and when his Enemy tells it, that we scarce can recognize the Facts to be one and the same. (*TJ*, 370)

And where a man may not be honest at all, readers had better beware. In *Joseph Andrews*, the thief locked up overnight under a constable's guard has disappeared by morning. Indirect narrative purports to give us access to the constable's mind when he is left alone with the prisoner: 'It came into the Constable's Head, that the Prisoner might leap on him by surprise ... He wisely therefore, to prevent this Inconvenience, slipt out of the Room himself and locked the Door', but 'most unhappily forgot the Window', through which the thief soon disappeared (*JA*, 63). The narrator then lays the facts before us: the constable had no hope of reward from the thief's capture; his story about why he left the room was absurd and he was unlikely to have forgotten, as he claims, to close the window; the thief had the means to bribe him, and the constable was well known for selling his vote to both parties at elections. We are invited to judge the constable on the evidence of motive, opportunity, previous character, and the plausibility of the story about why he left the room – a story which, it is now clear, came not from direct access to his head but from his own report, indirectly and ironically absorbed into the third-person narrative. In another twist, the narrator then claims:

> But notwithstanding these and many other such Allegations, I am sufficiently convinced of [the constable's] Innocence; having been positively assured of it, by those who received their Information from his own Mouth; which, in the Opinion of some Moderns, is the best and indeed only Evidence. (*JA*, 63–4)

Here the main target of Fielding's narrative irony is made clear: the 'Modern' trust to the evidence of people's own words for the story of their innocence.

This misplaced trust, Fielding considered, was found in the success of the emergent genre of autobiography, as practised by his one-time rival in the theatre, the actor and manager Colley Cibber, whose *Apology for the Life of Colley Cibber, Esq*. came out in 1740. In the same year, the popularity of the autobiographical tendency was confirmed when Richardson's *Pamela; or, Virtue Rewarded* appeared, rapidly becoming a publishing sensation: the story of a servant-girl whose virtuous resistance to her master's propositions is eventually rewarded by marriage to him, told through her own letters describing her experiences and prefaced by letters to the 'editor', praising the heroine and the moral tendency of her writing. Though Richardson's epistolary method was more sophisticated than his critics thought, allowing for distance between reader and character and an awareness of Pamela's moments of self-deception, it was premised on the reader's acceptance of the heroine's basic truth and sincerity. Refusing to take part in that autobiographical pact, Fielding turned Pamela into Shamela. His heroine, as introduced by Parson Oliver, is the real person behind the pretence: Shamela's letters are the originals, the letters in *Pamela* deliberate deceptions, cooked up after her marriage in a deal between her husband, Mr B., and Parson Williams. Richardson's virtuous heroine is replaced by Fielding's calculating hussy, who has already had a baby by Parson Williams and now resolves to make the most of Mr Booby's infatuation, vowing 'nothing under a regular taking into Keeping, a settled Settlement, for me, and all my Heirs, all my whole Life-time, shall do the Business – or else cross-legged, is the Word, faith, with *Sham*', and then deciding to hold out for marriage: 'I once thought of making a little Fortune by my Person. I now intend to make a great one by my Vartue.'[4]

His sham heroine, who owes a good deal to the brisk, pert young female characters Fielding the dramatist had created for the actress Kitty Clive, gives the narrative its life. Though we know she is a hypocrite to Mr Booby, she is not so to the reader: she is gloriously unashamed, letting us into all her schemes, rejoicing in her tricks, relaying the farcical details of her knockabout courtship. In fact, she runs away with the narrative: the first-person voice that Fielding wants readers to distrust ends up working its magic, making Shamela perversely likeable. In the end the charge of hypocrisy is levelled not so much at her as at the author of the false Pamela and her letters – Parson Williams, inside the fiction, but outside it, of course, Richardson.

When Shamela gathers up her belongings to leave the Hall, she includes a famous book of religious guidance, significantly mutilated: '*The Whole*

Duty of Man, with only the Duty to one's Neighbour, torn out' (*S*, 344). This encapsulates Fielding's critique of the kind of morality he saw embodied in Calvinist doctrine in general and *Pamela* in particular: an egotistical morality that sees duty in relation to one's own purity and salvation, ignoring the needs of others. In his subsequent novels he explored that 'Duty to one's Neighbour' without which he thought the whole duty was as nothing. Fielding's central concept of benevolence shaped his development of fiction: his novels explore social existence, the relation with the neighbour, as fundamental to human duty.

In *Joseph Andrews*, he sets out explicitly to judge the competing claims of charity and chastity within the comic panorama of an England that displays little of either virtue. The narrative's starting-point is parodic: the footman Joseph Andrews invokes the virtue of Richardson's heroine as he fends off advances from the waiting-woman Mrs Slipslop and her mistress, Lady Booby. '"Madam," says *Joseph*, "that Boy is the Brother of *Pamela*, and would be ashamed, that the Chastity of his Family, which is preserved in her, should be stained in him"' (*JA*, 36). Joseph, instead of being imprisoned like Pamela, is cast out of the house, delivered to the open life of the public road. It is in this active life, rather than in the reflection encouraged by confinement, that Fielding locates the possibility for moral good. Setting out from London to Lady Booby's country house to find his true love, Fanny, Joseph soon meets up with Parson Adams, the Quixotic clergyman who serves both as the novel's moral guide for his championship of warm goodness, and its comic butt for his unworldliness. On his way to London to publish his sermons, Adams soon realises that he has left them behind and joins forces with Joseph instead. Losing himself on the road in a typical fit of absent-mindedness, Adams rescues from violent attack a young woman who turns out to be Fanny. Soon all three are together, innocents abroad undergoing various adventures and misunderstandings on their journey home.

It is a corrupt, unjust, and violent world they travel through, where the hero is set upon by footpads and the heroine is abducted and threatened with rape; where lawyers twist the law to please rich patrons; and where even those who are not actively malignant are usually out for themselves. The kindest characters are often low-born or outcasts. When a coachful of passengers refuses to help a wounded Joseph because he is naked, only the postilion '(a Lad who hath since been transported for robbing a Hen-roost)' offers a coat (*JA*, 47). When Joseph, Fanny, and Adams have no money to pay their bill at the inn, Parson Trulliber, who only preaches of charity, refuses to help, and so do all his parishioners; it is a poor pedlar who lends them all he has. The novel's evidence would appear to support the conclusion reached by Mr Wilson, who tells his story of misspent youth and later repentance to Adams: 'the Pleasures of the World are chiefly Folly, and the business of it mostly Knavery; and both, nothing better than Vanity' (*JA*, 199).

Yet for all Fielding's satiric attacks on the ways of the world, his vision in this novel is emphatically comic. The lawyer in the stage-coach, who advises his companions to help Joseph entirely out of concern for their legal liability ('he wished they had past by without taking any Notice: But that now they might be proved to have been *last in his Company*'), or Mrs Tow-wouse, who wants to throw the wounded and penniless man out of her inn ('Common Charity, a F – t!'), are described with delighted gusto (*JA*, 46, 50). The narrator is more pleased with himself for finding and anatomising such characters than he is indignant with them. They prove his claim to have described a general human nature, whose faults he so enjoys exposing that he almost celebrates them: 'I describe not Men, but Manners; not an Individual, but a Species … I have writ little more than I have seen. The Lawyer is not only alive, but hath been so these 4000 Years, and I hope G – will indulge his Life as many yet to come' (*JA*, 168). Meanwhile, his good-hearted protagonists are as often as not figures of fun. Joseph's resistance to Lady Booby's embraces may be admirable but his professions of chastity sound ridiculous; and even when he becomes a spokesman for the more important virtue of charity he is mocked: his solemn speech on the subject sends Parson Adams to sleep. Adams himself, the good clergyman, is subjected to all manner of comic indignities: thrown into Parson Trulliber's pig-pen, attacked by hounds who tear his cassock and wig, or forgetting to put on his breeches when he runs out in the night to save Fanny from ravishers, he is always the object of laughter. Whatever misfortunes the hero and heroine suffer occur within a comic providential order that the reader never has cause to doubt. We know all will turn out right, so when Fanny has been abducted by three men who leave Joseph and Adams tied to bed-posts and carry her away 'without any more Consideration of her Cries than a Butcher hath of those of a Lamb' (*JA*, 231), her lover may lament with 'Groans, which would have pierced any Heart but those which are possessed by some People, and are made of a certain composition not unlike Flint' (*JA*, 235), but we remain, if not quite stony-hearted, spectators sympathising from an amused distance.

The novel is both a modern *Odyssey*, in which Penelope, instead of waiting at home for her Odysseus, comes out to meet him, and an imitation of Cervantes, with Don Quixote transformed into a good clergyman with a foolish trust not in romances but in learning and sermons. Fielding's Quixote, however, unlike the original, is finally vindicated: sermons and learning may be useless but good does triumph. In the final volume, the journey ends in Adams's parish, on which all the main characters converge, the protagonists being joined by Lady Booby, Pamela and Mr Booby, Wilson, the pedlar, and Gammer and Gaffer Andrews. In a parody of the recognition-scenes of romance, we get not one but two far-fetched revelations of identity: Joseph and Fanny, briefly threatened with turning out to be brother and sister, are eventually free to marry, and Joseph is not Pamela's brother after all, just as his story disclaims any real kinship with hers.[5]

Jonathan Wild, probably drafted before the publication of *Joseph Andrews*, though not printed till 1743,[6] is sustained satire rather than comic narrative, taking the life of the notorious thief-taker and dealer in stolen goods as a paradigm for the hypocrisy, self-aggrandisement, and manipulation of others that Fielding saw in the public life of 'great' men, most notably the prime minister, Robert Walpole. The parallels between low-life criminal and powerful politician run like an ironic thread through the narrative. Wild, like Shamela, is a boastful hypocrite: his eloquent speech against honour undermines all notions of the virtue with nominalist vigour. 'A Man of Honour is he that is called a Man of Honour; and while he is so called, he so remains, and no longer' (*JW*, 40). As the protagonist swindles, cheats, rules his gang and betrays them, the reader knows from the real-life outcome (Wild was hanged in 1725) that he will get his punishment, but we are never allowed to forget that greater criminals go free. The narrator warns ironically that fortune is inescapable, 'whether she hath determined you shall be hanged or be a Prime Minister' (*JW*, 174), and Wild's execution is 'a Sight much more rare in popular Cities than one would reasonably imagine it should be, *viz.* the proper Catastrophe of a GREAT MAN' (*JW*, 175). Brilliant as satire, the narrative falters when it tries to balance its account of villainy with tales of goodness. It is not just that Wild has all the energy, while the virtuous Mr and Mrs Heartfree remain limp and unattractive. The satiric attitude held so firmly against Wild seems suspended when Mrs Heartfree relates her adventures: resolutely defending her honour while being captured, rescued, and taken to Africa, she finally gets home after hitching a lift on a slave-ship bound for America. Rejoicing that she has managed to retain her chastity, she concludes in capitals 'THAT PROVIDENCE WILL, SOONER OR LATER, PROCURE THE FELICITY OF THE VIRTUOUS AND INNOCENT' (*JW*, 163). Mrs Heartfree makes no mention of the infelicity of the innocent slaves who share part of her journey – and the narrator makes no explicit mention of her omission. Perhaps he intends us to note it, but he provides none of the clear signals that, elsewhere in the text, ensure the reader's suspicious scrutiny of Wild.

Jonathan Wild's trouble with representing goodness throws into relief Fielding's much greater success in *Tom Jones*, which explores virtue more critically and laughs at the notion that it will be rewarded in this world even while its providential ending suggests that, within a fiction, it may be. *Tom Jones* picks up many of the themes of *Joseph Andrews* and explores them more fully, against a richer and more detailed background. The epic journey has both deeper mythic resonance, encompassing expulsion from Paradise Hall, a wandering journey to the corrupt city and a final return to the country on new terms, and greater realism, closely tying character to action and setting them against the contemporary background of the Jacobite uprising of 1745, which occurred during the novel's composition. A fiercely committed Hanoverian who spent some of his time in the late 1740s writing anti-Jacobite journalism, Fielding wove into his novel a series of connections between the characters and fortunes of his private protagonists and the great public question of the day. Tom, the foundling, whose illegitimacy pointedly remains even after the last-act revelation of his true identity, is in moral terms the right person to take over Western's place as country squire and to stand as heir to Paradise Hall, just as the technically illegitimate Hanoverian dynasty is better fitted to rule Britain than the true royal line. The Jacobite Squire Western attempts to assert the powers of paternal absolutism over his daughter Sophia, but paternal tyranny is no more justified in Fielding's England than an absolute monarchy. Even the narrator, who cheerfully compares himself to a monarch and his readers to his subjects, limits his own authority just as the monarch's powers were limited in the post-1688 settlement: 'For I do not', he assures his readers, 'like a *jure divino* Tyrant, imagine that they are my Slaves, or my Commodity. I am, indeed, set over them for their own Good only, and was created for their Use, and not they for mine' (*TJ*, 75). Tom, fittingly, supports the Hanoverian cause and even joins the army to fight the Jacobite invaders, but this thread of the narrative is quietly dropped as he heads for London and Sophia instead. The emphasis is on comic reconciliation. Autocratic Squire Western is a very ineffective tyrant, and at the end is heartily reconciled to his daughter and to Jones, allowing the narrative to end with the hopeful vision of a newly united country.

The themes of parental despotism and a daughter's rebellion echo those of Richardson's great second novel, *Clarissa* (1747–8), parts of which Fielding read before publication. Recognising the complex power of its narrative exploration of different viewpoints and touched by its evocation of the heroine's distress, Fielding, who had so scorned *Pamela*, admired *Clarissa* and defended it in print. But his own vision remains very different. The family conflict that turns to tragedy in *Clarissa* is kept firmly comic here. When Clarissa flees from her father's house the action, however excused by circumstances, is a prelude to inevitable tragedy; when Sophia does the same thing it is a spirited and practical measure that leads to comic complications but no lasting harm. The darkest moment, when she is threatened with rape by Lord Fellamar, is happily interrupted by the arrival of her boisterously angry father. Fielding envied Richardson his ability to touch the reader's heart, as can be discerned from his letter of somewhat barbed congratulation on the fifth volume of *Clarissa*.[7] After praising Richardson's ability to touch his feelings as a reader he adds that 'nothing but my Heart can force me to say Half of what I think of *the* Book [i.e. *Clarissa*]', implying that his head wanted to withhold the encomium. He certainly hoped to rouse feeling himself: in *Tom Jones* one of the muses he calls on for assistance is 'Humanity', whom he asks to provide the 'tender Sensations' he needs to paint the 'tender Scene' (*TJ*, 603). But Fielding's tender scenes are generally tempered by comedy. In Tom's worst moments, when he lies in prison with every prospect of being hanged for his duel with Fitzpatrick, or receives Sophia's letter saying that she knows of his affair with Lady Bellaston, or is told that his affair with Mrs Waters was incestuous, readers remain aware of the larger comic framework that will somehow resolve these difficulties. When the narrative approaches an emotional climax, such as Allworthy's eventual reconciliation with Tom, the narrator frankly bows out: 'It is impossible to conceive a more tender or moving Scene, than the Meeting between Uncle and nephew ... The first Agonies of Joy which were felt on both Sides, are indeed beyond my Power to describe: I shall not therefore attempt it' (*TJ*, 853).

When Fielding draws back like this from the empathetic rendering of even his favourite characters' sensations, it is hard to avoid the contrast with Richardson, whose epistolary narrative aroused its readers' feelings through its close charting of those of the characters. 'When I read of her, I am all sensation', reported Fielding's sister Sarah of his rival's tragic heroine (*Corr.*, 123). This difference fuelled the understanding of Fielding as a novelist of externals only, 'a man who could tell the time by looking on the dial-plate', in Samuel Johnson's famous phrase, while Richardson 'knew how a watch was made'.[8] Fielding certainly brings externals to life: scenic description is sparing but vivid; his characters are memorable physical presences; their speeches are relayed with dramatic gusto, and their actions described in detail and with verve. But he is not confined to the surface of life. He is very much interested in what goes on in human minds, though he aims to access them not through empathy, but through analysis. The narrator implores Genius:

> kindly take me by the Hand, and lead me through all the Mazes, the winding Labyrinths, of Nature ...Teach me, which to thee is no difficult Task, to know Mankind better than they know themselves. Remove that Mist which dims the Intellects of Mortals, and causes them to adore men for their Art, or to detest them for their Cunning in deceiving others, when they are, in Reality, the Objects only of Ridicule, for deceiving themselves. (*TJ*, 602)

Throughout the novel, the narrator enjoys exposing the self-deceptions of his worst and best characters; to do so, he moves periodically from the colourful description of external action to the interior analysis of motive.

Analysing Blifil, whose detestable cunning so contrasts with Tom's goodness, the narrator employs a favourite method of ironically disclaiming any knowledge of the character's mind and then subjecting it to a range of interpretations which culminate in a clear revelation. 'I have often thought it wonderful', he claims, that Blifil did not suspect that Tom and Sophia were in love: but 'perhaps' he thought a modest woman could not love such a wild fellow, or was deceived by their careful behaviour when together (both possibilities indicating how little Blifil knows of people); and 'Lastly, and indeed principally, he was well assured there was not another Self in the Case' (*TJ*, 263). Blifil is blind to Tom's feelings not only because he thinks Tom's affair with Molly Seagrim is still continuing but because he is so bad at recognising any feelings with good in them, having none himself. For Fielding, the benevolent may be easily deceived by the cunning, as the long-standing deception of Allworthy by Thwackum, Square, and Blifil himself indicates; but the wicked also deceive themselves when they judge others' motives by their own. Meanwhile, Sophia, Blifil's opposite in goodness and with a name that means 'wisdom', is also subject to narrative ridicule, though of a much gentler kind. In thrall to the social requirement for female delicacy, she formulates her feelings for Tom in obfuscatory rhetoric until the narrator interrupts his indirect mimicry of her thoughts with a plain statement of the fact: 'she soon felt for him all those gentle Sensations which are consistent with a virtuous and elevated female Mind – In short, all which Esteem, Gratitude and Pity, can inspire in such, towards an agreeable Man – Indeed, all which the nicest Delicacy can allow. – In a Word, – she was in Love with him to Distraction' (*TJ*, 211).

Fielding's approach to his characters' minds does not always involve ironic exposure. At times he describes their thoughts in a psycho-narration that combines sympathy and detachment, as when he shows Tom struggling between his new love for Sophia and his sense of obligation to Molly. Doubts about Sophia's feelings, the certainty of her father's opposition, guilt in relation to Allworthy, and compassion for Molly aided by continuing desire for her, combine to give Tom a sleepless night that ends with the decision to stick by Molly (*TJ*, 196–7). That this 'virtuous Resolution' lasts only till he has some reason to think Sophia returns his feelings may prompt some humour at his expense, but the narrative attitude to Tom's mixed feelings and motives is not in essence satiric. Indeed, it has often been pointed out that Fielding is very indulgent towards his hero here, giving him all the credit for his remorse at seducing an innocent young girl, then letting him off the hook by the handy revelation that Molly had been seduced before by Will Barnes and is now enjoying a farcical affair with the philosopher Square.

Throughout the novel, Fielding juggles the requirements of intellectual judgement and benevolent mercy. The problems of a good man in a corrupt world, comically treated in Parson Adams, are approached more seriously in Allworthy, whose blind trust in the wrong people has serious consequences when he banishes Tom. Still, the large gap between the reader's understanding and Allworthy's maintains the comic tone: we are never in danger of misreading Thwackum and Square. We are encouraged to be suspicious readers, as unlike Allworthy as possible. Sophia's shrewd surmise that Mrs Fitzpatrick is no better than she should be is our assurance that suspicion need not be mean. That 'quick-sighted Penetration into Evil' that comes from a heart inclined to find it is to be condemned, but the suspicion that comes from the head is another matter: it is 'indeed no other than the Faculty of seeing what is before your Eyes, and of drawing Conclusions from what you see. The former of these is unavoidable by those who have any Eyes, and the latter is perhaps no less certain and necessary a Consequence of our having any Brains' (*TJ*, 542). If the juggling act ever falters, it is when readers become suspicious in matters where Fielding does not want them to look too closely. The comic ending depends on passing lightly over matters that in other hands would have been serious psychological issues. There appear to be no lasting emotional consequences for the characters from Blifil's long betrayal, Tom's discovery that he has lived with his mother till her death and never known her, Sophia's discovery of Tom's amour with Lady Bellaston, or Western's harsh treatment of his daughter. All is right with the world once the truth is known and Tom and Sophia are united. Fielding holds disturbing emotions at bay and keeps a social, moral, and religious order together by virtue of an all-seeing eye and benign laughter. If readers today are unlikely to respond to such order as the reflection of providential reality, we can all the more admire the power of Fielding's writing to turn human messiness into a beautifully balanced, if precarious, comic construct.

In *Amelia* (1751), in Paul Hunter's phrase, 'the tenuous balance is gone',[9] and contemporary London, with its corrupt systems of patronage and badly administered law, provides a dark and confused background. Fielding's work as a judge, in Ronald Paulson's view, helped change his attitude as a novelist: 'If in *Tom Jones* he assumed the role of an advocate ... here he is a stern and realistic magistrate' (*Life*, 289). The novel is serious, ambitious, and innovative, examining life after marriage and the difficulties of trying to live in a corrupt world as opposed to moving through it on a rite of passage. Tom Jones can get away with mistakes and grow out of them, but Booth has taken his follies into marriage and brought poverty on his wife and children. The story of his love for Amelia is tainted by the effect it has on Miss Mathews, who seduces him into adultery partly because she is so bewitched by her vision of him as a loving husband. Fielding had been criticised for creating a faulty hero in Tom, but Tom had gallantry and an attractive spirit; Booth is well-meaning but weak. He is Fielding's attempt to create an ordinary protagonist for an imperfect world, a man whose real life lies in his domestic ties, since the world outside the home holds so little moral worth; it is because of this focus on home and family that his adultery is so serious a matter. At times he becomes a kind of new man, staying with his wife during childbirth and supporting her in his arms.[10] But his gaming, vices, weakness, and general lack of heroic qualities meant he had little appeal. Women, especially, wondered what his wife saw in him. 'I can't help despising him, and wondering that Amelia did not do so too', wrote Sarah Chapone.[11]

Heroism here is reserved for the woman, and this novel, with its concentration on the trials of a virtuous heroine, has been seen as Fielding's attempt to enter Richardson's territory. His dark vision of public corruption places a great burden on domestic life, seen here as society's only refuge. Booth, with his scepticism about religion and his sins against the family, needs to be converted to Christianity and domesticity in a narrative that allows plain didacticism a role Fielding had never given it before. Dr Harrison is one guide to morality (without being funny like Parson Adams), but Amelia, the good wife and mother, carries the main burden of virtue, not only bearing with her husband's adultery, gambling, and extravagance, but contending with sexual advances from a man who holds power over her husband. The importance of Amelia's sexual virtue is highlighted by contrast with Miss Mathews and Mrs Bennet. The novel has a melodramatic sense of the dangers to social order of female sexual transgression. Miss Mathews stabs her unfaithful lover, while Mrs Bennet's story indicates that even with mitigating circumstances (conspiracy and the use of drugs make her more a victim of ravishment than seduction) a wife's infidelity kills her husband: infected by her with a sexually transmitted disease, he flies into a rage and accidentally injures himself. Weeks later, he dies.

Whether women's adultery kills literally or symbolically is not entirely clear. Mrs Bennet assures Amelia that the 'Surgeon, a Man of the highest Eminence' told her that Mr Bennet died not of disease or injury but from 'what they called a Polypus in his Heart, and that nothing which had happened on Account of me was in the least the Occasion of it' (*A*, 302). No teasing narrator intervenes here to direct our views while pretending not to, and we are left to make what we can of the story. Given Fielding's views on the unreliability of autobiographical narrative, his tendency to satirise physicians, and the internal evidence of Mr Bennet's injuries and disease, we may well conclude that Mrs Bennet is wrong to acquit herself; but the point is not so much the accuracy of the diagnosis as our view of her mind, caught (whatever the medical truth of the matter) in a cycle of guilty feeling and anxious self-exculpation. This offers a finer psychological insight than that provided by the exuberant ironies of *Tom Jones* and is typical of *Amelia*'s odd combination of crude overall moral scheme with a new subtlety, at the local level, in the approach to psychology. Amelia herself, lacking the sharp voice that always gives an edge to Richardson's most saintly women, is often less than engaging, and sentimental scenes of her weeping with her poor bewildered children fail to move; yet even in her there are some newly subtle touches, where Fielding reaches beyond conventional ideas of female virtue. After resisting all manner of temptations to her chastity, she is roused to tenderness by Serjeant Atkinson's honest declaration of his hopeless love, and a moment of emotional infidelity gives her 'a Confusion on her Mind that she had never felt before' (*A*, 483).

Amelia insists on curing Booth's scepticism about religion and reinstating a providential order, but the happy ending seems contrived, where the multiple contrivances of *Tom Jones* had seemed like a benign universe at work. What remains convincing about *Amelia* is its earlier, sour, world-weary picture of a venal society. Fielding's last novel is a bold experiment that does not quite work and has never had wide appeal. Richardson responded to it with a sneer: 'Who can care for any of his people?'[12] Biased though he always was against his rival, he had a point. Fielding was at his best teasing his readers to think, not rousing them to feel. We can care for the characters in *Tom Jones*, quite as much as we need to, through understanding and laughing at them. As Mary Delany reported, however, *Amelia* 'neither makes one laugh or cry, though there are some very dismal scenes described, but there is something wanting to make them touching' (*CH*, 313). The novel's darkened view of society influenced the later course of the genre, and Fielding's admirer Thackeray created, in *Vanity Fair*, a much more successful treatment of similar themes.

It is *Tom Jones*, though, for which Fielding is best remembered and rightly so. Its pleasing plot symmetries, its colourful gallery of characters, its ability to give an individual story social and historical significance, its humour, its ironic insight into motive, and above all the narrator who brings all these together demonstrate the extraordinary power of the novel in the mid-eighteenth century.

NOTE ON EDITIONS

The Wesleyan Edition of the Works of Henry Fielding published by Oxford University Press contains editions of all of the novels (1967–2008). The Wesleyan Edition is drawn on by the editors of the highly recommended Oxford World's Classics and Penguin editions of the novels, which come with good notes and introductions. OWC publishes *Joseph Andrews and Shamela*, *Jonathan Wild*, and *Tom Jones*; Penguin publishes *Joseph Andrews and Shamela* and *Tom Jones*. A new edition of *Amelia* is forthcoming from Broadview Press.

NOTES

1 Henry Fielding, *The History of the Adventures of Joseph Andrews* (hereafter *JA*), in *Joseph Andrews and Shamela*, ed. Douglas Brooks (London: Oxford University Press, 1970), p. 4.

2 Henry Fielding, *The History of the Life of the Late Jonathan Wild the Great*, ed. Hugh Amory (Oxford: Oxford University Press, 2003), p. 7. Hereafter *JW*.

3 Henry Fielding, *The History of Tom Jones, a Foundling*, ed. Thomas Keymer and Alice Wakely (London: Penguin Classics, 2005), p. 60. Hereafter *TJ*.

4 Henry Fielding, *An Apology for the Life of Mrs. Shamela Andrews*, in *Joseph Andrews and Shamela*, ed. Douglas Brooks (London: Oxford University Press, 1970), pp. 330, 342. Hereafter *S*.

5 Jill Campbell, *Natural Masques: Gender and Identity in Fielding's Plays and Novels* (Stanford: Stanford University Press, 1995), p. 71.

6 Ronald Paulson, *The Life of Henry Fielding: A Critical Biography* (Oxford: Blackwell, 2000), p. 121. Hereafter *Life*.

7 Henry Fielding, in *The Correspondence of Henry and Sarah Fielding*, ed. Martin C. Battestin and Clive T. Probyn (Oxford: Clarendon Press, 1993), pp. 71–2. Hereafter *Corr*.

8 James Boswell, *Life of Johnson*, ed. R. W. Chapman, corr. J. D. Fleeman (Oxford: Oxford University Press, 1970), p. 389.

9 J. Paul Hunter, *Occasional Form: Henry Fielding and the Chains of Circumstance* (Baltimore and London: Johns Hopkins University Press, 1975), p. 193.

10 Henry Fielding, *Amelia*, ed. Martin C. Battestin (Oxford: Clarendon Press, 1993), p. 128. Hereafter *A*.

11 Ronald Paulson and Thomas Lockwood, *Henry Fielding: The Critical Heritage* (London: Routledge & Kegan Paul, 1969), p. 351. Hereafter *CH*.

12 Samuel Richardson, *Selected Letters of Samuel Richardson*, ed. John Carroll (Oxford: Clarendon Press, 1964), p. 199.

FURTHER READING

Battestin, Martin C. (ed.), *Twentieth Century Interpretations of Tom Jones: A Collection of Critical Essays*, Englewood Cliffs, NJ, Prentice-Hall, 1968

Battestin, Martin C. *The Providence of Wit: Aspects of Form in Augustan Literature and the Arts*, Oxford, Clarendon Press, 1974

Bender, John, *Imagining the Penitentiary: Fiction and the Architecture of the Mind in Eighteenth-Century England*, Chicago, University of Chicago Press, 1987

Bertelsen, Lance, *Henry Fielding at Work: Magistrate, Businessman, Writer*, Basingstoke, Palgrave, 2000

Braudy, Leo, *Narrative Form in History and Fiction: Hume, Fielding and Gibbon*, Princeton, Princeton University Press, 1970

Campbell, Jill, *Natural Masques: Gender and Identity in Fielding's Plays and Novels*, Stanford, Stanford University Press, 1995

Hunter, J. Paul, *Occasional Form: Henry Fielding and the Chains of Circumstance*, Baltimore and London, Johns Hopkins University Press, 1975

Lamb, Jonathan, 'Exemplarity and Excess in Fielding's Fiction', *Eighteenth-Century Fiction*, 1 (1989), 187–207

Miller, Henry Knight, *Henry Fielding's Tom Jones and the Romance Tradition*, Victoria, BC, English Literary Studies, 1976

Rawson, Claude J., *Henry Fielding and the Augustan Ideal under Stress*, London, Routledge & Kegan Paul, 1972

Rawson, Claude J. (ed.), *The Cambridge Companion to Henry Fielding*, Cambridge, Cambridge University Press, 2007

Richetti, John, 'The Old Order and the New Novel of the Mid-Eighteenth Century: Narrative Authority in Fielding and Smollett', *Eighteenth-Century Fiction*, 2 (1990), 183–96

Smallwood, Angela J., *Fielding and the Woman Question: The Novels of Henry Fielding and the Feminist Debate 1700–1750*, Hemel Hempstead, Harvester Wheatsheaf, 1989

4

MELVYN NEW

Laurence Sterne

> So Hills amid the Air encounter'd Hills
> Hurl'd to and fro with jaculation dire ...
> *Paradise Lost*, VI, 664–5

Laurence Sterne (1713–68) spent the first twenty-five years of his adult life in obscurity as the functioning clergyman of a Yorkshire village. The closest contacts he had with fame were the opportunities to participate in the ecclesiastical pursuits of the York Minster establishment, second only to Canterbury in the Anglican hierarchy, and the local publication of two of his sermons (1747, 1750). Neither brought advancement. If anything else distinguishes Sterne's life prior to 1758, it would be his long bout with ill-health, a lingering consumption that seems to have first appeared during his time at Jesus College, Cambridge; it would eventually kill him.

In 1758, a squabble within the York church concerning preferments triggered in Sterne a short satiric pamphlet reducing the arguments from the minster to the parish; *A Political Romance* was published in December 1758, and immediately suppressed by Sterne's superiors – only six copies are known to have survived. Immediately thereafter, Sterne started a satiric account of sermon-writing, apparently modelled on Pope's satire targeting bad poetry, *Peri Bathous* (i.e. *On the Bathetic*, a play on Longinus's famous first-century work of literary criticism, *Peri Hupsous*, i.e. *On the Sublime*). Thus the narrator's name, Longinus Rabelaicus, ties the work to both Pope and Rabelais; only two chapters survive of this so-called 'Rabelaisian Fragment'. Despite abandoning the project, Sterne worked passages from it into the first four volumes of his new work, *The Life and Opinions of Tristram Shandy, Gentleman*, published in instalments over the next eight years (vols. I–II, December, 1759; vols. III–IV, 1761; vols.V–VI, 1762; vols. VII–VIII, 1765; vol. IX, 1767).[1] If we could ever fully reconstruct the creative process that raised this obscure cleric to the literary lion of the London of 1760, we would perhaps have a better understanding of the mysteries of genius. Short of that, we can only struggle with the fact that had Sterne died in 1758 he would have remained unknown; by February 1760, he was on his way to becoming a figure who could be mentioned in the same sentence with Rabelais, Cervantes, and Swift, on the one hand, James Joyce, Virginia Woolf, and Salman Rushdie, on the other.

Among the twenty-seven distinguished authors in this volume, Sterne offers one of the slimmest canons; after *Tristram Shandy*, he wrote two volumes of *A Sentimental Journey through France and Italy*, published just months before his death on 18 March 1768. Though his fiction-writing career spanned only nine years, it produced two titles that have cemented his place in the Western literary tradition, an author of the world perhaps better known and better appreciated since the nineteenth century in every country but his own; however, having survived the disapproval of Thackeray and the Victorians, and F. R. Leavis's dismissal of *Tristram* as 'irresponsible (and nasty) trifling',[2] Sterne's fortunes in the second half of the twentieth century have particularly waxed under the dual illuminations of metafiction and postmodernism.

It has become fashionable in the past two decades for Sterne's critics to talk about a 'long-standing' division among commentators on his masterpiece, *Tristram Shandy*, between those who believe Sterne looked backward to the Renaissance tradition of learned wit, embodied in Rabelais, Montaigne, Robert Burton (*Anatomy of Melancholy*), and Cervantes, and, in the generation before Sterne, in the Augustan satirists, Pope and Swift; and those who believe, conversely, that *Tristram* looks forward, Sterne being the first 'modern' novelist, the explorer of novelistic conventions even prior to the establishment of the novel tradition, precursor of modernism, postmodernism, the world of fiction from Proust, Joyce, and Woolf to Rushdie, Milan Kundera, Georges Perec, and B. S. Johnson, and now, in the twenty-first century, to the next evolutions of the narrative art.

All authors borrow from the past, and all authors, those who are read at any rate, influence the future. Critical arguments that emphasise tradition at the expense of innovation, or innovation at the expense of tradition are always partial arguments, unable to encompass the full range of a great writer's art. What particularly complicates these approaches in the instance of Sterne, however, is that questions of past and future take on special significance because they can produce markedly different – indeed opposed – commentaries.

At the beginning of the nineteenth century Sir Walter Scott and others began the process of canonising the novelists; by the 1930s, the eighteenth-century English novel tradition was defined in one word: Defoe-Richardson-Fielding-Sterne-Smollett, usually pronounced very quickly so that the enormous differences between each were lost in their one similarity: they all wrote long fictions. Needless to say, this canonisation has been reviled in recent years for its gender bias, its 'exclusion' of Behn, Haywood, Burney, and Sarah Fielding; as the present volume indicates, Burney has now replaced Smollett, although whether this corrects a bias or introduces a new one will remain for future generations to decide. There is a genre bias in the list as well, however, and perhaps no author has been more affected by it than Sterne. *A Sentimental Journey*, only a hundred pages in any textbook edition, does not appear to be a 'novel' if length defines the genre; and while *Tristram Shandy* is lengthy, it is always the work *not* discussed by 'rise of the novel' scholars, even if they glance in puzzlement at Viktor Shklovsky's famous comment that *Tristram Shandy* is 'the most typical novel in world literature'.[3] Still, both works continue to be taught in eighteenth-century 'novel' courses, after students, proceeding chronologically, have read Defoe, Richardson, and Fielding, perhaps also Behn or Haywood; Sterne is too often made to conform to – or is measured against – these novelists who preceded him. The concomitant scholarship has consisted of uncovering the plot of *Tristram Shandy*, or showing that its characters are well-rounded, or that its themes of narrative time, detailed observation, and autonomous selfhood (usually lodged in Sterne's interest in Locke and sensibility) are those of the other earlier novelists as well; *A Sentimental Journey*, on the other hand, is seen as a series of autobiographical vignettes, acute moments of detailed observation of character, basically an unfinished travelogue in which Sterne's journeys to France were chronicled under the thin veil of his narrator, Yorick. In these lights, I believe, Sterne's best achievements as a writer can easily be overlooked.

In the 1950s, the genre criticism of Northrop Frye began the process of liberating Sterne from this tradition. Frye attacked 'the novel-centered' Ptolemaic universe of prose fiction, suggesting instead a more Copernican orientation where various modes of fiction circled around the concept of prose – the novel was one planet, but biography was another, history a third, and so forth.[4] In this schema, *Tristram Shandy* seemed best defined by what Frye labelled the 'anatomy' (defined as 'a form of prose fiction ... characterized by a great variety of subject-matter [and forms, and styles] and a strong interest in ideas'; modern examples might include *Moby-Dick*, *Ulysses*, and Thomas Pynchon's *Gravity's Rainbow*), but as we moved into the 1960s and 70s, one found most discussions equated anatomy with satire, and the notion slowly emerged that Sterne's art could better be understood in relation to the prose tradition of Rabelais, Cervantes, and Swift, rather than the novel tradition of Defoe and Fielding. Still, when I published *Laurence Sterne as Satirist* in 1969, it seemed unwelcome news to most Sterneans – one suggested, typically enough, that no sensible reader could think of *poor* Uncle Toby in satiric terms. To be sure, my work had been anticipated by D. W. Jefferson, Wayne Booth, and John Stedmond, among others,[5] but I added to their work the notion that satire and novel were antithetical in certain significant ways, and that we needed to read Sterne in courses that included Dryden, Swift, and Pope, in order to grasp the antipathy between the two genres. It is rewarding – if a bit depressing as well – to have written about Sterne for so long that what once seemed an innovative reading of *Tristram Shandy* is now seen as one of two traditional approaches; indeed, most recent studies of Sterne, following Tom Keymer's study,[6] have been suggesting that while it is obvious that the work is a satire, it is a satire on, or parodic imitation of, novelistic writing in his own day; Fielding and Richardson – and a swarm of lesser lights – are thus restored to importance while Pope and Swift are again diminished.

To suggest that Sterne is best understood within the eighteenth-century satiric tradition is not to argue that he is a mere imitator of Pope or Swift. Indeed, since today I need no longer defend what is now traditional thinking on the subject, I am willing to make concessions to those who want to read Sterne in the light of Richardson and Fielding, and the many lesser novelists of the 1750s and 1760s whose 'fame' was on Sterne's own mind as he sought to become the 'author' of the moment. Without doubt, Sterne read some modern literature (although not as often, I suspect, as he read the older works); without doubt, he wrote not to be fed but to be famous, reversing, significantly enough, a sentence borrowed from Pope's great *bête noire*, Colley Cibber. Still, Sterne could teach very little about self-promotion to either Pope or Richardson; the argument that he uniquely shaped his conduct or book to the *new* demands of the market-place in mid-century seems to me far less likely than recent commentaries (all branded with excessive use of the word *commodification*) have suggested. I will also concede what is obvious to anyone who reads both of Sterne's fictions, namely, that the serial nature of *Tristram Shandy* allowed him to alter aspects of the work over the years in response both to the critics and to his own altered existence. This response ultimately emerges in a seemingly new direction, *A Sentimental Journey.* These are, however, simply common-sense concessions to positions never in dispute. My argument has never been that Sterne was not a writer of his own time and his own place, and, most significantly, his own genius; what I did suggest, and what I will here again argue, is that Sterne's response to his age and our appreciation of his *genius* (both in intent and in execution) is best understood within the tradition to which his work pays most homage – and that is the satiric tradition as he received it from the hands of Pope and Swift.

I emphasise the word 'genius' because the notion that some writers possess genius has been universally frowned on by postmodernists as a culturally determined homage, the unacceptable privileging of literature over commentary as separate modes of discourse. Derrida, Habermas, and Benjamin may themselves be geniuses, but to apply that term to Fielding or Sterne meets with scorn as the naïve ploy of cultural hegemony. In Sterne's brilliant absorption of Swift's *Tale of a Tub*, however, as in Joyce's absorption of *Tristram Shandy* in his own work, I see genius paying homage to genius, the first and most essential lesson, I believe, of our appreciation of artistic achievement. Homage, of course, takes many forms, of which verbal echoes are only the most overt; much more telling, I would suggest, is this remark by Joyce, when asked to explain *Finnegans Wake*:

> Time and the river and the mountain are the real heroes of my book. Yet the elements are exactly what every novelist might use: man and woman, birth, childhood, night, sleep, marriage, prayer, death. There is nothing paradoxical about this. Only I am trying to build as many planes of narrative with a single esthetic purpose. Did you ever read Laurence Sterne?[7]

Whatever refinements we might attach to the word 'genius', in the broadest sense it is the capacity to include this sweep of human experience within a single conceptual framework, whether the canvas be large or small, the subject-matter local or cosmopolitan. I realise that my definition has no theoretical standing; as a practical exercise, however, one might weigh the authors in this volume against this notion of genius and deduce its pragmatic validity. If nothing else, I would suggest that when we talk about Sterne it does not behove us to diminish him by considering his fictions as failed or emergent or haphazard novels (as was the tendency after Scott until mid-twentieth-century commentary), or, as in more recent commentary, to suggest a difference in degree but not in kind from the most commonplace writers of his own few decades, governed, as they were, solely by the market-place.

Tristram Shandy is indeed about birth and death and the life we lead between the two. A work that literally begins with an act of conception, and is occupied for the first three volumes with birthing, certainly signals an interest in procreation; and a work that chronicles the deaths of its major characters; that has two funeral orations and a volume chronicling a flight from death (vol. VII); that everywhere recalls the deaths of thousands of human beings in the wars we conduct; and that is pervaded by injury, impotency, and sterility, certainly signals its interest in death. *A Sentimental Journey* eschews these beginnings and endings to concentrate on the journey in-between. Conception requires two people, but we die by ourselves (as Sterne understood at least as well as Heidegger, who famously made the point the cornerstone of the most important philosophical treatise of the twentieth century, *Being and Time*). Life then may be defined by our relationships with other people, the unions we seek and the separations that are thrust on us, including that final separation poignantly chronicled in a touching passage in *Tristram Shandy*, one that also contains the essence of the *Journey*, written, quite literally, during Sterne's final illness:

> I will not argue the matter: Time wastes too fast: every letter I trace tells me with what rapidity Life follows my pen; the days and hours of it, more precious, my dear Jenny! than the rubies about thy neck, are flying over our heads like light clouds of a windy day, never to return more——every thing presses on——whilst thou art twisting that lock,——see! it grows grey; and every time I kiss thy hand to bid adieu, and every absence which follows it, are preludes to that eternal separation which we are shortly to make.——
>
> ——Heaven have mercy upon us both! (*TS*, IX, viii, 754)

Immediately after this heartfelt passage, Sterne pens a one-sentence paragraph: 'Now, for what the world thinks of that ejaculation——I would not give a groat' (IX, ix, 755). This quick turn is an ironic strategy that pervades both works. In *Journey*, for example, the episode closest to the evocative nostalgia of the Jenny passage is the meeting with the peasant family and its celebration of life by feasting and dancing, the beautiful chapter entitled 'The Grace'. Good authors would have ended the work here, justifiably satisfied with their literary skills; the genius goes on to a final chapter, in which Yorick finds himself in a 'case of delicacy'. Forced to share a room at the inn with an attractive fellow traveller, he finds himself protesting that he has not, in his restlessness, broken their oath of silence with his 'O my God!' It was, he insists, 'no more than an ejaculation' and, stretching his arm across the space between them by way of emphasis, he succeeds in catching hold of the in-rushing 'Fille de Chambre's / END OF VOL. II' (*ASJ*, 164–5).

Sterne's punning use of 'ejaculation' in these two passages can help us understand why reading him as a satiric rather than novelistic writer best exhibits his genius to us. We might begin with the obvious: Sterne intertwines the religious ('ejaculation' as short prayer) with the bawdy ('ejaculation' as male sexual discharge). We might also keep in mind that the first definition provided by the *OED-Online* is: 'The action of hurling (missiles)', and thus the word seems to have had a military bearing as well; and 'ejaculation' has yet another definition, 'the hasty utterance of words expressing emotion', and so we can tie it to language in general, perhaps specifically to the language of all those who speak and write before they think – the world of the putative narrator of *Tristram Shandy*, who tells us early on that his writing is characterised by 'rash jerks, and hare-brain'd squirts': 'spurting thy ink about thy table and thy books' (*TS*, III, xxviii, 254; compare Toby's wonderful question, a few chapters earlier: '*are children brought into the world with a squirt?*' (III, xv, 219)). Put another way, life begins with an *ejaculation*, continues by means of human exchange, some of it thoughtful, most of it by way of *ejaculations* that result, in far too many instances, with both sides *ejaculating* missiles at one another, and concludes, if one dies as one should live (at least in the eyes of the Christian world Sterne inhabited), with an *ejaculation* to God for the salvation of one's soul at the final judgement, at which time, as Sterne wrote, may 'Heaven have mercy upon us'.

The imposition of a very narrow notion (here, obviously, a bit of verbal play) to a vastly more complicated work than such reductiveness can possibly account for is the human way with words and the world. In his portrait of Walter Shandy, Sterne personifies those who thus reduce the length and breadth of existence to their own dimensions, patterns, designs – words: 'he was systematical, and, like all systematick reasoners, he would move both heaven and earth, and twist and torture every thing in nature to support his hypothesis' (*TS*, I, xix, 61). Sterne's vision here clearly echoes that of Jonathan Swift in his great satire on religious enthusiasm and literary ignorance, *Tale of a Tub* (1696; 1704); what is at stake for both is not merely a campaign against the 'cant of criticism' or the reductiveness of human 'solutions', but a satiric posture toward the entire process by which human beings ejaculate their notions to the world, possessed by the desire to publish them and convert the world to what is, after all, only an ejaculation. Some have argued that Walter is merely the starting-point for a satire that turned into a novel. I would suggest instead that he represents Sterne's consistent portrayal of the aggressiveness of the human mind; thus, we can again see the same 'ejaculating mind' in the opening pages of *Sentimental Journey*, where Yorick denies charity to the begging monk: 'we distinguish, my good Father! betwixt those who wish only to eat the bread of their own labour – and those who eat the bread of other people's, and have no other plan in life, but to get through it in sloth and ignorance, *for the love of God*' (*ASJ*, 9–10). Underwriting this hasty utterance one finds centuries of religious and ethnic bigotry and warfare in Europe, that is, I would suggest, Sterne's primary target in all his writing. It is a purpose, moreover, far better revealed when we approach his work through the satiric writings of, say, Rabelais, Burton, Erasmus, and Swift, all of whom confronted, with a variety of satiric strategies, the incipient violence that inheres in the opinions of mankind.

Many years ago when I first started writing on *Tristram Shandy*, at the height of the anti-war movement in America, my suggestion that Sterne satirises the militarism of Uncle Toby fell, nonetheless, on hostile ears; how could anyone not love a man who would not hurt a fly? Now, almost a half century later, when it has become sufficiently apparent that nothing was learned from the Viet Nam experience (at least by politicians), there seems to be more sympathy for the fact, carefully documented in the Florida *Notes* to *Tristram Shandy*, that every one of the battles enacted on the bowling green meant the deaths of thousands of human beings. Then as now, and keeping in mind Sterne's own sentimental ties to the military (his father was a career soldier), it is certainly possible to support the poor souls who fight wars, while deploring the human folly that brings them about. At the heart of *Tristram Shandy* we find this complication – too complicated for many who think in ejaculations (called 'sound bites' today) – and it mirrors what is again and again Sterne's cosmology of human thought: if Nietzsche, a Sterne enthusiast, is correct in opining (as I believe he is) that 'truth has never yet clung to the arm of an inflexible man',[8] Sterne's great genius was in seeking truth always (as did Nietzsche, we might note), but being willing at the same time to hold it lightly, always caressing rather than grasping the insights that he momentarily reached. Much has been made by those reading Sterne as a novelist of his absorption with time, but the satirical approach to the work is again more revealing: transitoriness is, for Sterne, an ethical condition more than a narrative problem. That we exist in time, that our time is limited, that we will run out of time into judgement and eternity, these are the more useful contexts with which to approach Sterne's many allusions to the passing of time. And certainly ejaculations and time are, by definition, related; the rapidity of our ideas is a function of their momentariness and vice versa; because we can never completely work through the infinitely complex problems that confront us, all our human 'truths' are always premature ejaculations.

We often mask this fugacity or transitoriness of ideas by the invocation of deep study, logical consideration, and, above all else, long-standing and absolute conviction: in short, what begins in jest ends in downright earnest and becomes the hobby-horse, Sterne's device (echoing Pope's 'ruling passion', the dominating drive, as he thought, behind each person's individuality) for indicating how our half-baked notions become our obsessions (truths). As readers of *Tristram Shandy* quickly discover, the hobby-horse pervades the work, most particularly in Walter's obsession with theorising, Toby's with militarism, and Tristram's with writing his book. There is, however, an interesting moment near the beginning of *Sentimental Journey* that usefully embodies the same idea, although not often considered in that light. When Yorick decides to buy a post-chaise from Monsieur Dessein ('In the Street. Calais.') he exposes his thoughts to us:

> It must needs be a hostile kind of a world, when the buyer ... cannot go forth with the seller ... to terminate the difference betwixt them, but he instantly falls into the same frame of mind ... as if he was going along with him to Hyde-park corner to fight a duel ... I looked at Monsieur *Dessein* through and through – ey'd him as he walked along in profile – then, *en face* – thought he look'd like a Jew – then a Turk – disliked his wig – cursed him by my gods – wished him at the devil. (*ASJ*, 20)

Represented in this brief passage is as profound an account of the human condition as one can find in literature, the necessity we all have to enter into exchange transactions with other people, and the wariness and desire for advantage that seem always to accompany it. As so often in Sterne's writings, moments of particular significance are signalled by scriptural allusion, here Yorick's lament that his 'hand is against every man, and every man's hand against' him (*ASJ*, 20; see Genesis 16:12). Verbal intercourse, the language by which we communicate and hence interchange with the world around us, is fraught with violence, whether in bargaining for a 'good' price for the wares (and ideas) of others, or selling our own, by persuasion if possible (Walter), by warfare if necessary (Toby); only when the world buys and sells at the price we demand can there be peace in the world. Sterne's writings suggest that such amity is possible, but not probable, given our incessant need for superiority; in the space between the possible and the probable one locates the ethical.

Significantly enough, however, Yorick's invocation of the scriptural hand against hand turns immediately into a very different 'hand': 'heaven forbid! said she, raising her hand up to her forehead' (*ASJ* 20). Yorick's encounter with his fellow traveller in Calais opens the search for a responding woman that climaxes in the 'case of delicacy', but also continues a dominant aspect of *Tristram*, the pervasiveness of the sexual in all our intercourse. This is, obviously, the meaning of 'ejaculation' that Sterne particularly plays on, its sexual denotation as male emission, the means by which life continues. If so many of our verbal ejaculations indicate life's rampant triumphalism, what are we to make of this other usage, which has resulted in Sterne's reputation for bad taste in the past, sexism in the present, and a lack of good sense among the *tartuffes* (Tartuffe is the eponymous hero of Molière's comedy (1664) satirising religious hypocrites) of every generation. Nor should we deny the *tartuffery* in ourselves, the twinge I sense in writing an essay dominated by the word 'ejaculation', and that readers will feel as they read it. Sterne has anticipated our response in a splendid passage at the very end of *Tristram Shandy*:

> and wherefore, when we go about to make and plant a man, do we put out the candle? and for what reason is it, that all the parts thereof – the congredients – the preparations – the instruments, and whatever serves thereto, are so held as to be conveyed to a cleanly mind by no language, translation, or periphrasis whatever? (*TS*, IX, xxxiii, 806)

And then Sterne ties together, by way of contrast, the various aspects of ejaculation that we have been discussing; as opposed to the act of conceiving life, 'the act of killing and destroying a man, continued my father ... is glorious – and the weapons by which we do it are honourable——We march with them upon our shoulders——We strut with them by our sides ...' (806–7). It is no accident that the entire passage is borrowed directly from Pierre Charron's *Of Wisdome* (1612); Charron was a student and populariser of Montaigne, one of Sterne's favourite authors, particularly, we may suspect, because of the frankness with which Montaigne approached questions of his own body. Everywhere in Sterne's fictions, the body demands recognition. The classic division of the past between body, mind, and soul had become in Sterne's day the dichotomy of head and heart. There is nothing dreadfully erroneous about this formulation, except that neither head nor heart was deemed to be bodily in nature; hence Sterne's desire to retriangulate (and recomplicate) the wisdom of his day by an insistent demand that every human equation take into account our bodily (sexual) existence.

For Yorick, a heterosexual male, his accounting takes the form of a quest for a reciprocating woman, one who will offer her hand to be caressed, her forearm so that her pulse may be taken, her purse so that he may insert a crown, herself so that he may experience, as in Italy with the appropriately named Marquesina di F***, a connection that gives him 'more pleasure than any one [he] had the honour to make in Italy' (*ASJ*, 78). For Tristram, invocations of dear Jenny indicate the same quest, as does Don Diego's journey to the promontory of noses, Trim's pursuit of the female Shandy housemaids, and, from the other side, Widow Wadman's open and frank pursuit of a suitably fit sexual partner. Even more pervasive than these couplings (or aborted couplings) is Sterne's play with sexual innuendo throughout *Tristram*, a game that has led careless critics to suggest that he believes language is a failed system of communication, that ambivalence and ambiguity are infinite, and hence that all language is penetrated by postmodernist indeterminacy. Actually, nothing is further from the truth. The hobby-horse and other modes of expectancy can obviously change the meaning of words in transit from speaker to hearer ('bridge', 'thing', 'crack', 'stick', 'trench', 'covered way', and on and on), but the point of Sterne's insistence on sexual punning is that we will always know the two (or three or four) possibilities of misapprehension. When, for example, Toby stares at the crack in the chimney-piece we do not think of a wind chariot as the *double entendre* behind the joke; always, we know the denotation in the mind of the speaker, the different denotation in the mind of the auditor – that is what makes the joke. If anything, Sterne shows us that language is overdetermined in its sexual underpinnings; when teaching *Tristram Shandy* in a modern classroom, one need only suggest that the work is pregnant with meaning but anticlimactic in narrative to provide students with an obvious illustration of how difficult it is *not* to find determinate sexual allusion in our everyday words.

The more meaningful problem for Sterne, and perhaps for the Christian world in general, is that the English vocabulary offers the same single word, 'love', as both religious and sexual imperative. 'Love thy neighbour', Sterne the parson intoned from his pulpit hundreds of times during his career as an Anglican priest; 'Love thy neighbour', Mrs Wadman might say, as she peers over her hedge into Toby's bowling green. Perhaps because of this shared vocabulary, the Church found itself again and again trying to (re-)establish a distinction between the 'two loves', but as Yorick argues when Walter confronts him with the division between a 'love' for the vulgar and another for the learned, 'I think ONE LOVE might have served both of them very well' (*TS*, VIII, xxxiii, 720), and, this normative voice goes on, 'the procreation of children [is] as beneficial to the world, said Yorick, as the finding out the longitude', to which Mrs Shandy chimes in, 'To be sure ... *love* keeps peace in the world'. In *Sentimental Journey* the town of Abdera embodies the same difficulty: 'nothing but "Cupid! Cupid! prince of God and men"—The fire caught—and the whole city, like the heart of one man, open'd itself to Love ... 'Twas only in the power ... of the God whose empire extendeth from heaven to earth, and even to the depths of the sea, to have done this' (*ASJ*, 45–6).

Sterne's interest in the power of love is, as one might expect, multifaceted. Clearly he has the satirist's inclination to remind us of those things we want to forget, in this case our physical bodies and their embarrassments. From ancients like Aristophanes and Petronius to modernists like Milan Kundera and Juan Goytisolo, writers have been intent on deflating the spiritual and mental aspirations of human beings by recalling our bodily functions, fluids, and facts. Moreover, although we all share the tendency to forget our bodies in pursuit of 'higher' things ('for to say a man is *fallen* in love ... carries an idiomatical kind of implication that love is a thing *below* a man' (*TS*, VI, xxxvii, 565)), Sterne singles out the *tartuffes* of the world as his particular target, the hypocrites who decried, from pulpit and press, his openness and delight in bawdry. Almost from the beginning of his literary career, voices are heard warning him to rein in his bawdiness in the interest of religion and society; mine his 'sentimental' vein, as the reviewers told him, and stop soiling his cassock. It is surely one of the marks of Sterne's genius that he never heeded half this advice, although he certainly increased his sentimental content, not as a sop to his critics but to heighten the contrast between the two loves that became his primary ejaculatory concern once he left Walter Shandy behind (the head) and turned to Toby (the heart) and beyond *Tristram Shandy*, to Yorick's quest for communion. Later volumes of *Tristram Shandy* remain as bawdy as ever (see, e.g., chapter xi of volume VIII), and, as indicated above, the most poignant moment of religious sentimentalism in *Journey* is followed by a bawdy *conte*. Whatever else we may say of Sterne, he never changed the overarching vision of the world that generated his fictions, a vision that included an ethical imperative to include our sexuality in every consideration of what it might mean to be human.

Sterne's interest in 'love' had a second source, however, having to do with his own conduct and appetites. His interest in women not his wife, and outside the sacrament of marriage, to which, as husband and clergyman he would seem to have committed himself, is a fact of his life that cannot be ignored. It is telling that Sterne entrusted his locally published first two volumes of *Tristram* to a young actress (Catherine Fourmantel) with whom he was then enamoured, to deliver to David Garrick in London; and equally telling, that when writing *Sentimental Journey* he was simultaneously writing his *Bramine's Journal* for Eliza Draper, an Anglo-Indian, thirty-one years his junior, with whom he fell in love in the last year of his life. As Yorick says, echoing sentiments in Sterne's own correspondence, 'having been in love with one princess or another almost all my life ... I hope I shall go on so, till I die, being firmly persuaded, that if ever I do a mean action, it must be in some interval betwixt one passion and another' (*ASJ*, 44).

Like Swift, like Richardson, perhaps like most men, Sterne enjoyed the company of women. We can argue that adultery was more heinous in his day than ours, or less heinous, and probably make a good case on either side, whether we consider Sterne as a husband or a cleric. What really matters, however, is Sterne's own ambivalence about his wanderings, and our evidence of that is in his fictions, one long attempt to justify those dalliances that weighed heavily on him as his illness increased (*Tristram Shandy* was begun in the illness that killed him a few months after completing *Sentimental Journey*), and his mind turned, as I believe would any mind after preaching Christian doctrine for thirty years, to the four last things: Death, Judgement, Heaven, Hell. Again, I find this aspect of Sterne far more evident in a satiric reading of his work than in any other approach. The modern secular world, announced but never fully realised by the novel tradition, has at its core the concept of an autonomous human character; in fact, one might suggest the novel entered its decline when modernist authors recognised, as did Joyce and Woolf, that they could image that autonomy only by eschewing realism, since, realistically speaking, we and our literary characters are not self-creating entities.[9] Autonomy is as much a psychic fiction as dependency myths and has been a target of satirists at least since the Lord spoke to Job.

Sterne's writings, then, can be seen, at least in part, as a hopeful petition before the seat of Judgement; as such, they return us once again to 'ejaculation', but the pertinency now changes from the broadly defined 'short hasty emotional utterance' to the more specific definition, 'A short prayer "darted up to God"'. It is not, however, a single defence, a single prayer. Quite the opposite, Sterne tests several defences, all of which seem less than sufficient. For example, Yorick seems to make a cogent argument for putting all the blame on Divinity for human fallibilities: 'for thou hast made us – and not we ourselves' (*ASJ*, 124), but Sterne, significantly enough, marks this speech with those little hints of bawdiness ('let me feel the movements ... I will trust the issues') that evoke the other meaning of 'ejaculation' and we remain in the dark as to what 'The Conquest' refers to. Nor is he suggesting, as with Yorick's observing copulating sparrows on his window-sill and lamenting the shame he feels in reporting it, that we should simply accept our natural instincts and be at home with them. Again, a familiarity with the satiric tradition is helpful for reading Sterne because it alerts us to the fact that, as Tristram phrases it, '☞A dwarf who brings a standard along with him to measure his own size——take my word, is a dwarf in more articles than one' (*TS*, IV, xxv, 375). The essence of satire is measurement or judgement, and unlike novels, which are attempts to tell the story of our lives here on earth, satires are written under the sign of Heaven; 'Heaven have mercy upon us both!' is, in this light, a most meaningful ejaculation.

From the beginning of *Tristram Shandy*, the question of satiric judgement is prominent in Sterne's mind, lodged in his *alter ego*, Yorick (York), *Hamlet*'s jester/*memento mori*, a dual function he also serves in Sterne's writings. His conversation with Eugenius (*TS*, I, xi–xii) about the dire consequences of his satiric tongue is imitative of the traditional satiric *apologia*, from Horace's *Satire* II.i, to Pope's *Epistle to Dr. Arbuthnot*. His death ('Alas, poor YORICK!') signals entrance into a brave new world where satire (judgement) is no longer relevant, the world of the Shandys (crack-brained, in Yorkshire dialect); because of Sterne's digressive progressive chronology, however, Yorick reappears again and again, always in the role of a normative presence. We might point, for example, to Sterne's inclusion of his quite serious 'Abuses of Conscience' sermon (published ten years earlier in York) in volume II as Yorick's composition; the subject of this Assize sermon is clear: we are severely limited by our passions in both self-judgement and our judgement of others.

However, in light of my previous discussion of our love-affair with our own opinions, our own voices, and the way in which our dogmatisms lead to warfare, we might best point to that moment in the work where Yorick's normative judgement seems most Heaven-sent, his evaluation of his own sermon-writing, characterised by excessive modesty so that even the complimentary 'Bravo!' on his favourite sermon is lined through and written so faintly that it is 'more like a *ritratto* of the shadow of vanity, than vanity itself' (*TS*, VI, xi, 516). Sterne's celebration here of modesty and self-abnegation, the very opposite qualities of his other persona, Tristram, suggests to us one possible way to avoid the rush of absoluteness, certainty, and violence that defines our usual way with ideas. It is important to keep in mind that Sterne presents himself as both Yorick and Tristram; as with Swift's brilliantly portrayed hack-writer in *Tale of a Tub*, one of the most salient qualities of satiric genius is the willingness to confront the mote in one's own eye, before turning the eye of God on to the human scene. Most of us live, as do Tristram and Sterne, without measurement and certainly without a pervasive sense of impending death and judgement; the satirist, however, rather like the minister (when in the pulpit), consistently weighs his own and other human activity against the judgement of Heaven. Satire and sermon alike convince us that we can only pray for mercy in the face of an audit that will, without doubt, find us all lacking.

Yorick in *Sentimental Journey* is still on this journey toward judgement, although now, closer to his author's own impending death, he can no longer think in terms of forty more volumes to write and a flight from Death as in volume VII of *Tristram*. The journey of life has become the final pilgrimage, the destination predetermined and constantly in mind. The time is short, and every encounter a preparation for offering oneself to judgement. Yorick sets out to learn how to think differently ('I have only just set out upon my travels; and shall learn better manners as I get along' (*ASJ*, 11)); an essential part of that learning, Sterne suggests, has to do with that 'ejaculation' that returns Yorick to his own sexuality.

Again and again in this final work, Love and Heaven are brought together in both easy and uneasy conjunction. Hence, when Yorick tries to talk about love to the woman in Calais, he notes

> That grave people hate Love for the name's sake –
> That selfish people hate it for their own –
> Hypocrites for heaven's – (*ASJ*, 34)

And again, a few pages later, he condemns Smelfungus and Mundungus (in words borrowed from one of his sermons, which, in turn, was borrowed from the Christian Platonist John Norris of Bemerton) for their inability to prepare themselves for Heaven because they are rooted in worldliness, so that neither 'Love or Pity should seduce' them out of their road. Heaven comes 'upon the wings of Love', it offers 'fresh raptures of love' but they have 'brought up no faculties' able to absorb Heaven's love, and so will do 'penance there to all eternity' (38). Yorick's journey is a preparation to accept that love and be found worthy of it; his inability to separate the two loves will be his offering to final judgement, and he seems convinced that such an offering will do better than what *tartuffery*, the archbishops and arch-critics of the world, has to offer. There are, he says, 'worse occupations in this world *than feeling a woman's pulse*' (71), and welcoming the depths of that insight into our moral system (Toby's occupation, 'answering the great ends of our creation' comes to mind (*TS*, VI, xxxii, 557)) turns us in the right direction on our own pilgrimage.

We return to a chapter mentioned earlier, 'The Grace', in which Yorick sees '*Religion* mixing in the dance', an observation validated by the old peasant's remark that 'a chearful and contented mind was the best sort of thanks to heaven' that we can offer (*ASJ*, 159). Tristram had reported a similar scene in volume VII of *Tristram*, where he encounters a group of harvesters celebrating the fecundity of the season. There the encounter begins with bawdiness: 'They are running at the ring of pleasure, said I, giving him [his mule] a prick——By saint Boogar, and all the saints at the backside of the door of purgatory, said he ... I'll not go a step further' (*TS*, VII, xliii, 649). Tristram then decides to dance with the peasants, including Nannette, who entices him with a 'cursed slit' in her petticoat: 'Just disposer of our joys and sorrows, cried I, why could not a man sit down in the lap of content here —and dance, and sing, and say his prayers, and go to heaven with this nut brown maid ...' (650–1). But then, in one of those rare moments in which literary genius most displays itself, Sterne does not allow finality, but instead has Tristram dance away, much as Yorick cannot end his journey with the peasant dance, but only with his hand reaching towards the woman in the bed next to his own. Pope, one of the most significant if unspecified presences in Sterne's writings, tells us why: 'Hope springs eternal in the human breast: / Man never Is, but always To be blest'. To this sentiment, Sterne could only ejaculate: 'Heaven have mercy upon us' all!

NOTE ON EDITIONS

The definitive edition is the University Press of Florida Works of Laurence Sterne: vols. I–II, *The Life and Opinions of Tristram Shandy: Text*, ed. M. New and J. New (1978); vol. III, *Notes*, ed. M. New, with R. Davies and W. G. Day (1984); vol. IV, *The Sermons: Text* (1996); vol. V, *The Sermons: Notes*, ed. M. New (1996); vol. VI, *A Sentimental Journey and Continuation of the Bramine's Journal*, ed. M. New and W. G. Day (2002); vols. VII–VIII, *The Letters*, ed. M. New and P. de Voogd (2009).

NOTES

1 All citations to Sterne's works – volume, chapter, and page – are from the Florida Edition of the Works of Laurence Sterne (Gainesville: University Press of Florida,

1978–): see 'Note on Editions' above. The following abbreviations are used: *TS* for *Tristram Shandy* and *ASJ* for *A Sentimental Journey*.

2 F. R. Leavis, *The Great Tradition: George Eliot, Henry James, Joseph Conrad* (London: Chatto & Windus, 1948), p. 2.

3 Shklovsky was a Russian formalist who made this comment in 1929; see *Theory of Prose*, trans. Benjamin Sher (Elmwood Park, IL: Dalkey Archive Press, 1990), p. 170.

4 *Anatomy of Criticism: Four Essays* (Princeton: Princeton University Press, 1957).

5 Jefferson, '*Tristram Shandy* and the Tradition of Learned Wit', *Essays in Criticism*, 1 (1951), 225–48; Booth, 'The Self-Conscious Narrator in Comic Fiction before *Tristram Shandy*', *PMLA*, 67 (1952), 163–85; Stedmond, *The Comic Art of Laurence Sterne* (Toronto: Toronto University Press, 1967).

6 *Sterne, The Moderns, and the Novel* (Oxford: Oxford University Press, 2002).

7 *James Joyce: Two Decades of Criticism*, ed. Seon Givens (New York: Vanguard Press, 1948), pp. 11–12.

8 *Thus Spoke Zarathustra*, trans. R. J. Hollingdale (Harmondsworth: Penguin, 1961), p. 79. For a reading of *Tristram Shandy* within a Nietzschean ambience, see New, '*Tristram Shandy*': *A Book for Free Spirits* (New York: Twayne, 1994).

9 See Virginia Woolf's 'Modern Fiction', especially her dramatic assertion that, unlike nineteenth-century realists, 'Mr Joyce is spiritual', after which she concludes with a tribute to Sterne (and Thackeray): 'did not the reading of *Ulysses* suggest how much of life is excluded or ignored, and did it not come with a shock to open *Tristram Shandy* or even *Pendennis* and be by them convinced that there are not only other aspects of life, but more important ones into the bargain' (*The Common Reader* (1925) (New York: Harvest-Harcourt, 1984), pp. 151–2).

FURTHER READING

Cash, A.H., *Laurence Sterne: The Early and Middle Years*, London, Methuen, 1975

Laurence Sterne: The Later Years, London, Methuen, 1986

de Voogd, P. (ed.), *The Shandean: An Annual Volume Devoted to Laurence Sterne and His Works*, Coxwold, The Laurence Sterne Trust, 1989–

de Voogd, P. and J. Neubauer (eds.), *The Reception of Laurence Sterne in Europe*, London, Thoemmes Continuum, 2004

Gerard, W. B., *Laurence Sterne and the Visual Imagination*, Aldershot, Ashgate, 2006

Howes, A.B. (ed.), *Sterne: The Critical Heritage*, London, Routledge & Kegan Paul, 1974

Keymer, T., *Sterne, the Moderns, and the Novel*, Oxford, Oxford University Press, 2002

The Cambridge Companion to Laurence Sterne, Cambridge, Cambridge University Press, in press

Keymer, T., (ed.), *Laurence Sterne's 'Tristram Shandy': A Casebook*, Oxford, Oxford University Press, 2006

Kraft, E., *Laurence Sterne Revisited*, New York: Twayne, 1996

New, M., *Laurence Sterne as Satirist: A Reading of 'Tristram Shandy'*, Gainesville, University of Florida Press, 1969

'Tristram Shandy': A Book for Free Spirits, New York, Twayne, 1994
New, M. (ed.), *Critical Essays on Laurence Sterne*, New York, G. K. Hall, 1998
The Life and Opinions of Tristram Shandy, Gentleman, *New Casebooks*, New York, St Martin's Press, 1992
Walsh, M. (ed.), *Laurence Sterne*, *Longman Critical Readers*, London, Longman, 2002

5

VIVIEN JONES

Frances Burney

Had this collection of essays been produced only a decade – certainly two decades – ago, it is by no means certain that Frances Burney would have been included. To her contemporaries and immediate successors, Burney (1752–1840) was a major figure: an innovative pioneer in the development of the novel and a significant contributor to its rapid growth in status and respectability at the end of the eighteenth century. Following the publication of her first two novels, *Evelina* (1778) and *Cecilia* (1782), critics and influential cultural commentators such as Samuel Johnson and Elizabeth Montagu hailed Burney as successor to the already highly respected male novelists of the mid-century. Her fiction was seen to combine 'the dignity and pathos of Richardson' with 'the acuteness and ingenuity of Fielding'. Jane Austen's well-known defence of novels in *Northanger Abbey* cites *Cecilia*, together with Burney's third novel, *Camilla* (1796), as exemplars of the form 'in which the greatest powers of the mind are displayed, in which the most thorough knowledge of human nature, the happiest delineation of its varieties, the liveliest effusions of wit and humour are conveyed to the world in the best chosen language'. And Anna Letitia Barbauld included all three novels in her monumental canon-making collection, *The British Novelists* (1810), prefacing them with the by then established judgement that: 'Scarcely any name, if any, stands higher in the list of novel-writers than that of Miss BURNEY.'[1] But with the publication in 1814 of Burney's fourth and final novel, *The Wanderer*, her canonical status began to look more precarious – and it remained so, until feminist and historicist critics at the end of the twentieth century (re)discovered how to read her fiction in ways which have begun to restore her to a deservedly more secure position.

In an influential, and now notorious, review of *The Wanderer*, William Hazlitt dismissed Burney's last novel as outmoded and its author as 'quite of the old school, a mere common observer of manners, – and a very woman'.[2] Exacerbated by responses to the posthumous publication of Burney's journals and correspondence, which appeared under her married name as the

Diary and Letters of Madame d'Arblay (1842), Hazlitt's objections anticipate several of the dominant strands in subsequent critical assessments of Burney. The elevation of Burney the diarist and the view that her later novels, most particularly *The Wanderer*, represent a serious falling-off from the achievement of *Evelina* and *Cecilia* quickly became critical orthodoxies. And Hazlitt's dismissive suggestion that Burney's fiction ultimately fails to transcend either the conventions of its time or the sex of its author was echoed in various guises by openly negative as well as ostensibly positive commentators throughout the nineteenth century and into the twentieth.

Very often, such judgements say far more about the gendered nature of criticism and taste than they do about the distinctiveness and quality of Burney's achievement, but they nevertheless point up an issue – about the relationship of the 'woman's novel' to the novel more generally – which remains key for any attempt to define Burney's particular significance within the history of the form. Thus while Thomas Babington Macaulay concludes, in his essentially supportive review of the *Diary and Letters*, that Burney is not in the 'highest rank' of writers, he is eager to praise her for a feminine decorum which 'took away the reproach which lay on a most useful and delightful species of composition' and which 'vindicated the right of her sex to an equal share in a fair and noble province of letters'. It is because of Burney and her female successors – notably Maria Edgeworth (disappointingly not included in this *Companion*) and, of course, Jane Austen – that the novel, according to Macaulay, is 'honourably distinguished by fine observation, by grace, by delicate wit, by pure moral feeling'.[3] A century later, in 1957, this mid-nineteenth-century view is still recognisable, in less moralising form, in Ian Watt's seminal study, *The Rise of the Novel*. Austen, Watt notes, 'completed the work that Fanny Burney had begun', demonstrating that 'the feminine sensibility was in some ways better equipped to reveal the intricacies of personal relationships and was therefore at a real advantage in the realm of the novel'.[4] But the ambivalence remains. Burney is presented as preparing the way for Jane Austen, whose supposedly superior skill allows her the status of representative female writer, and this feminine influence on fiction also has its downside: a 'tendency to restrict the field on which [the novel's] psychological and intellectual discriminations operate to a small and arbitrary selection of human situations'.[5]

Within this fraught narrative of the novel as (feminised) psycho-social realism, Burney's reputation suffered from teleological comparisons with Austen, as well as from the growing critical identification of her as primarily a diarist. The combined effect was to categorise Burney the novelist as above all a comedienne of manners, to dismiss her as the recorder of the quaint eccentricities and caricatures of a bygone era, and to downgrade her later novels, *Camilla* and particularly *The Wanderer*, because, unlike *Evelina* or even *Cecilia*, they seemed to aspire less successfully to that condition. Burney, it was conceded, provided the bridge between Fielding or Richardson and Austen. But, having been allowed the distinction of recovering the novel's respectability by lending it the feminine touch, and in spite of the social breadth which distinguishes all her novels, Burney was subjected to the accusation that her subject-matter was necessarily, and increasingly, limited by her gender. Such arguments are already evident at the beginning of the nineteenth century with the reception of *The Wanderer; or, Female Difficulties*. Picking up on this subtitle, it was Hazlitt, again, who dismissed '[t]he difficulties in which [Burney] involves her heroines [as] indeed "Female Difficulties;" – they are difficulties created out of nothing'.[6] Of course Austen, too, has been criticised for addressing a narrow range of experience. Unlike Austen, however, Burney's gendered limitations are seen as issues of style and sensibility as much as subject-matter. Her fiction came to represent an outmoded feminine discourse – a 'prudish refinement of sentiment', as another review of *The Wanderer* put it[7] – transcended by the forensic precision and sceptical irony of Austen's more modern narrative voice.

The slow process of rediscovering how to read Burney independently of Austen began in the latter part of the twentieth century, as the history of the novel was rewritten and recontextualised. Feminist critics exposed the gendered assumptions governing language and culture, recuperated women writers, and questioned the traditional canon; historicist critics examined fiction's commodity status and its interrelationship with other popular genres in a rapidly expanding print market; and, even more recently, groundbreaking bibliographies have for the first time exhaustively mapped shifting patterns of novel publication, including the numbers of novels written by women and men.[8] The effect is a much more precise understanding of the complexities of gender, genre, and taste which Burney's fiction reflects and which she herself negotiated as a female novelist in the literary marketplace. In the discussions which follow, of Burney's reception and of the novels themselves, I want to trace something of that complexity in order to define Frances Burney's distinctive role, so obvious to her contemporaries (including, of course, Jane Austen), in the inescapably gendered early history of the English novel.

A female novelist's entrance into the world: realism and reputation

Burney's early success was established both because of and in spite of her gender. Acutely aware of the ambiguous status of both the female author and of fiction, Burney was a consummate professional, strategically exploiting her femininity to the benefit of her chosen form. In 1778, she published her first novel, *Evelina*, anonymously and played teasingly in the Preface with her readers' ignorance of its author's identity. With Burney's characteristic mixture of professional confidence and feminine diffidence, the Preface places this latest addition to the ranks of the novel within a tradition of highly respected male fiction-writers:

> while in the annals of those few of our predecessors, to whom this species of writing is indebted for being saved from contempt, and rescued from depravity, we can trace such names as Rousseau, Johnson, Marivaux, Fielding, Richardson, and Smollet [*sic*], no man need blush at starting from the same post.[9]

The passage invokes, and thus reinforces, an emerging canon of internationally respected writers, all of whom are men. It deliberately chooses not to name such highly acclaimed contemporary female novelists as Sarah Fielding, Frances Brooke, or Elizabeth Griffith, working instead with a stark distinction between these 'few' (male) predecessors, who represent quality, and, by implication, the majority of fiction writers whose publications threaten the form with 'contempt' and 'depravity'. The invited inference, of course, is that, like *Clarissa* or *Amelia*, this new feminocentric narrative is written by a man and can therefore claim a degree of critical respect and attention untainted by gallantry or prejudice. As is well known, the critics were indeed respectful. *Evelina* was an instant success. Its epistolary form prompted the view that it 'would have disgraced neither the head nor the heart of Richardson'; and it was assumed by many of its first readers, including members of Burney's family, to be the work of a man.[10] When the truth about its authorship was revealed, Burney – and with her the woman novelist more generally – couldn't lose. The critical and popular success of *Evelina* guaranteed Burney's personal literary celebrity; the fact that its author was a woman also revealed the serious joke at work in the Preface, undermining any simplistic identification of fictional excellence and respectability with male writers.

Evelina, along with its Preface, was a crucial intervention at a key moment in the entangled histories of the novel and the female writer. In 1778 novel production was undergoing 'a steep decline'. A decade later, its recovery was assured, and, as James Raven notes, a 'remarkable feature' of that recovery is 'a flock of imitators of Frances Burney'.[11] In 1778, too, English literary culture was already predisposed to celebrate its female artists and intellectuals – though not yet those who identified themselves simply as novelists. The quality of British female education, epitomised in the Bluestocking circle, was seen as incontrovertible evidence of the quality of British civilisation, and print culture helped reinforce the Bluestockings' social prominence. Richard Samuel's much-reproduced group portrait, *The Nine Living Muses of Great Britain*, for example, or the roll-call of prominent women in Mary Scott's celebratory poem *The Female Advocate* (1774) extended the visibility and cultural authority of the female intellectual well beyond literary London. But that cultural authority was heavily dependent on its subjects adhering to principles of feminine decorum. In an atmosphere where the reputation of novels and lady novelists was always precarious, Burney's achievement was not simply to revitalise the ailing novel, but to establish fiction-writing as a legitimate means by which a woman might achieve intellectual respect and respectability.

The Burney imitators of the 1780s identified by Raven had not just *Evelina*, but also Burney's second novel, *Cecilia* (1782), as their model. *Cecilia* further consolidated the reputation established by its predecessor. Unlike the epistolary *Evelina*, *Cecilia* uses an authoritative and flexible third-person narrative voice, encouraging contemporary critics to identify Burney as heir to not only 'the dignity and pathos of Richardson', but also 'the acuteness and ingenuity of Fielding'. Now fully aware of her identity, critical opinion conceded that she 'stands on firmer ground' than needing to 'plead any privilege of her sex': 'with a spirit superior to solicitation or fear, [she] may meet the decision of impartial criticism'.[12] Given this avowed readiness to accept Burney on equal terms with her male precursors, the key concern in a study such as this, which seeks to define her role in the development of the novel form, must be to identify the criteria against which such avowedly 'impartial' contemporary criticism was judging fictional quality. What are the aesthetic principles and expectations underpinning the critical acclaim for Burney's distinctive and influential achievement, and to what extent do they actually succeed in transcending questions of gender?

The critics took their cue from Burney herself. In spite of feminine diffidence, she was in little doubt about the originality of her writing. In part, this is a question of subject-matter. In a letter to her eventual publisher, Thomas Lowndes, for example, Burney persuades him to take *Evelina* on the grounds that the novel's scenario and setting, familiar enough to Londoners, were still a novelty in the realms of fiction:

> The plan of the first Volume, is the Introduction of a well educated, but inexperienced young woman into public company, and a round of the most fashionable Spring Diversions of London. I believe it has not before been executed, though it seems a fair field open for the Novelist, as it offers a fund inexhaustible for Conversation, observations, and probable Incidents.[13]

Evelina's subtitle is 'a Young Lady's Entrance into the World', and in the next section I shall discuss in more detail the wider significance of Burney's distinctive plot, repeated across all her fiction, in which the young female protagonist negotiates her social and economic survival in the face of the 'probable Incidents' thrown up by 'public company'. But Burney's originality is a matter not just of subject but of technique, and I want first to focus on her attempts to articulate her realist methodology and the critical endorsement – or otherwise – of that claim.

In the *Evelina* Preface, Burney's concern is to distinguish her fiction from what she dismissively calls 'the fantastic regions of Romance' (*E*, 10). Initially, at least, she describes her 'attempted plan' in comparatively modest and conventional terms: 'to draw characters from nature, though not from life, and to mark the manners of the times' (*E*, 9). By appropriating the familiar neo-classical eighteenth-century ideal of art as aspiring to the condition of nature, Burney seeks critical authority for the new form which, unlike the romance, can claim only a very recent pedigree. In the opening chapter of *Tom Jones*, Fielding had similarly defined what he called his 'history' as dealing with 'no other than HUMAN NATURE', and he invoked Pope's *An Essay on Criticism*: 'True wit is nature to advantage drest / What oft' was thought, but ne'er so well exprest.' Burney's self-justification is less flamboyant, but no less concerned to define the degree to which art, or novels in particular, might legitimately shape or embellish 'nature'. Invoking the allegorical landscape of romance to argue against romance's excess, Burney warns that her novel will disappoint any reader expecting 'Fiction ... coloured by all the gay tints of luxurious Imagination, where Reason is an outcast, and where the sublimity of the *Marvellous* rejects all aid from sober Probability' (*E*, 10). Instead, Burney claims to offer the satisfactions of a restrained (and, incidentally, more decorously feminine) aesthetic based on Enlightenment principles: 'Reason' and 'sober Probability'. Thus, in *Evelina*, as we shall see, the heroine learns to defend herself against the all too probable irritations of everyday harassment, rather than submitting to the full melodrama of seduction; and 'the sublimity of the *Marvellous*' appears only in burlesque form, in the entertainments to be enjoyed at London's popular pleasure gardens.

Cecilia was published unprefaced by such methodological self-justification. Wisely, Burney chose not to include the anxious, rambling introduction which she had initially drafted, preferring a very brief and conventionally self-deprecating 'Advertisement'.[14] But in a letter to her mentor, Samuel Crisp, she is confident enough to claim her second novel as again 'somewhat original', and her explanation throws more detailed light on her commitment to 'real life':

> I think the book, in its present conclusion, somewhat original, for the hero and heroine are neither plunged in the depths of misery, nor exalted to UN*human*

> happiness. Is not such a middle state more natural, more according to real life, and less resembling every other book of fiction?[15]

Burney's defence here of her more 'natural' ending, on the grounds that it keeps faith with recognisable experience rather than the 'UN*human*', is entirely consistent both with the 'sober Probability' invoked in the Preface to *Evelina* and with the way in which she defines her subject in the opening paragraph of her third novel, *Camilla*. There, she rejects the Fieldingesque title of 'historian of human life', the recorder of 'accidents and adventures', preferring the more exacting (and more Richardsonian) role of 'investigator of the human heart in its feelings and changes'.[16] And in a letter written during the composition of *Camilla*, she is even unwilling to commit herself to the idea that she is writing a 'novel' at all: 'I own I do not like calling it a *Novel*: it gives so simply the notion of a mere love story, that I recoil a little from it. I mean it to be *sketches of Characters & morals, put in action*, not a Romance.'[17] Consistent though they are in their commitment to (human) nature, these statements nevertheless show Burney carefully refining and redefining her terms as she describes her technique and subject-matter. Distancing herself from the excesses and repetitions of popular fiction, she seeks a vocabulary for what would come to be called psychological realism, and, in the process, offers an increasingly complex challenge to a critical orthodoxy which still expected fiction, and particularly women's fiction, to moderate verisimilitude in the interests of moral certainty and/or unambiguous closure.

The reviews of *Cecilia* were almost exclusively positive, endorsing Burney's sense of her own achievement in their emphasis on her 'natural, well drawn, and well supported' characters, on 'the force and extent of [the Writer's] understanding', and on the fact that the quality of her work ensures that she need 'not plead any privilege of her sex'.[18] As she had anticipated, however, readers were uncertain about the 'sober Probability' of the novel's ending, in which the heroine's personal happiness in marriage is secured only by agreeing to sacrifice her fortune. Edmund Burke, for example, complained to Burney that 'he wished the conclusion either more happy or more miserable; "for in a work of imagination … there is no medium"'.[19] And the *Critical* reviewer was indignant: 'nor do we entirely approve of the conclusion, as we are of the opinion that the pride and ostentation of old Delvile ought, in justice, to have been punished'.[20] This is a position derived from Samuel Johnson's influential warning, in the fourth number of *The Rambler*, that, in the interests of moral clarity, the novelist's responsible imitation of nature requires them 'to distinguish those parts of nature, which are most proper for imitation: greater care is still required in representing life, which is so often discoloured by passion, or deformed by wickedness'.[21] Burney's statement of principle at the beginning of *Camilla* can be seen as a direct, but more sophisticated, response to these pervasive anxieties about mixed characters and equivocal endings. Burney was a friend and a fan of Johnson. But in defiance of a Johnsonian, mechanistic concern about novelists who 'so mingle good and bad qualities in their principal personages, that they are both equally conspicuous',[22] her no less seriously moral subject is, precisely, the 'difficulty and intricacy' of representing 'that amazing assemblage of all possible contrarieties' which constitutes the human – including, even more daringly, the 'perverseness of spirit which grafts desire on what is denied' (*Camilla*, 7).

Probability; intricacy; contrariety: these are the key terms to emerge from Burney's effort to articulate her character-based realist aesthetic. Unsurprising and unexceptionable though they might appear to the modern reader, a recognition of their hard-fought provenance is crucial to understanding Burney's very particular contribution to the novel. Burney's self-assessment is reflected in the vocabulary of contemporary critical opinion. *Camilla*'s 'extensive acquaintance with human nature, ... acute discernment, and exact discrimination of characters' were hailed as exemplary of the modern novel. And, in a telling phrase, the *Monthly*'s review of *Cecilia* approvingly defined Burney's narrative voice as 'peculiarly nervous and perspicuous'.[23] Its terms drawn from the discourse of sensibility, this striking formulation struggles to capture Burney's pioneering mode of narration – what later criticism, referring particularly to Austen's mature realisation of the method, would call 'free indirect discourse'. Burney's narrative method reinvigorates the language and fiction of sensibility; mediating constantly between omniscient narration and the heroine's consciousness, it re-establishes the difficult and intricate connection between feelings and moral reason.

I shall be defining the 'nervousness' and 'perspicuity' of Burney's innovative narrative method more closely in the following section. What I want to emphasise here is the way in which an acceptably feminine novelistic sensibility, supported by the impeccable decorum of Burney's public persona, established and enhanced not only Burney's reputation, but that of the novel more generally. In the fraught atmosphere of the 1790s, Burney consciously avoided any overt political reference in *Camilla*, opining that politics were 'not a *feminine* subject for discussion, & that ... should the little work sufficiently succeed to be at all generally read, it would be a better office to general Readers to carry them wide of all politics, to their domestic fire sides'.[24] And the anti-Revolutionary Madame d'Arblay, wife of a French *émigré* and former keeper of the queen's robes, was preferred over her popular but more politically partisan contemporaries – most notably, Charlotte Smith. Some doubts remained. Intricacy might result in over-elaboration – both *Cecilia* and *Camilla* were accused of being too long – and concerns at being 'tantalized with imperfect happiness' persisted, still echoing in Barbauld's celebratory essay in *The British Novelists*.[25] But at the turn of the nineteenth century, Burney's feminised and comparatively apolitical brand of realism, her 'command of the language of character' across an 'inexhaustible fund of … personages', was established as the touchstone of fictional excellence.[26]

By 1814 and the publication of Burney's final novel, *The Wanderer*, 'command of the language of character' had passed, by popular critical consent, to Maria Edgeworth and to the as yet less high-profile author of *Sense and Sensibility* and *Pride and Prejudice*. In the work of Edgeworth and Austen, the narrative technique they learned from Burney was refined and developed, and the reviews of *The Wanderer* reflect this subtly changed fictional aesthetic, as well as a different cultural moment. The reviews are characterised by a brisk confidence that social mores have moved on, leaving Burney's 'agreeably intricate and busy' novel, begun and set in the 1790s, out of touch and out of time, not just in its subject-matter, but in its narrative method:

> the interest of her story arises out of the violent and unnatural state of things produced by revolution … the sympathy excited by this order of incident has gone by … The great defects of the tale we are considering, is [*sic*] its want of development … The adventures of the heroine, while under a cloud, furnish scenes of passion and pathos, and supply opportunities for whimsical sketching, and amusing caricature; but they neither advance nor retard the final catastrophe.[27]

Such judgements begin to construe Burney's erstwhile strengths – her detailed delineation of feeling; the breadth of her social canvas – as unserious and unimportant, mere 'whimsical sketching' or 'amusing caricature'. But there is more going on here than simply a shift in taste. Presenting themselves as progressive, symptomatic of 'the great march of civilisation', these reviews of *The Wanderer* are in fact representative of the fraught conservative consensus of the early nineteenth century.[28] They reflect a process of personal and social privatisation, one result of which was a narrowing in the terms of acceptability of the female novel, creating a taste eminently suited to the talents of Austen, though not of Burney. Thus, the reviewers can claim 'an alteration insensibly progressive' in sexual relationships and offer 'common sense' as a bracing antidote to 'high-wrought misery', whilst at the same time acknowledging that 'the different classes of society and of character intermingle less'. In this defensive climate, *The Wanderer*'s relentless exposure of the economic vulnerability of an unprotected woman represented an uncomfortable challenge, with Hazlitt's essay in *The Edinburgh Review*, from which I have already quoted, just the most virulent example of the novel's distinctly mixed reception.

The politics of gender is at the heart of Hazlitt's attack: not simply the obvious point of his dismissal of female difficulties as 'created out of nothing', but also his characterisation of Burney's breadth of canvas as somehow symptomatic of the 'superficial and confined' nature of the female imagination, more suited to 'immediate observation' than 'general reasonings on causes or consequences'.[29] As taste shifts, Burney's gender takes on a more negative prominence. *The Wanderer*'s post-French Revolutionary setting makes it her most explicitly political novel. Its subtitle, 'Female Difficulties', could as easily be attached to any of her other novels, however. Arguably, the earlier critical eagerness to celebrate an accomplished female writer served to downplay some of the more challenging aspects of Burney's technique and subject-matter – features which came under greater scrutiny with changes in taste and politics during the Napoleonic period. *The Wanderer* sold much less well than expected, and Burney's reputation began the decline from which, happily, it has now largely recovered.

Young ladies' entrances into the world: Burney's novels

Burney's career, spanning almost four decades, was crucial to a late eighteenth-century understanding of what the novel, including novels written by women, might do. With the subtitle of her first novel, 'A Young Lady's Entrance into the World', Burney established her characteristic subject-matter: the engagement of an individualised female consciousness with the contemporary public world which tests, frustrates, misrepresents, but also shapes it. She has not yet developed her innovative narrative method, however, content in her first publication to represent the heroine's consciousness through the Richardsonian epistolary form also deployed by such respected contemporary female novelists as Elizabeth Griffith in *The History of Lady Barton* (1771) and *The Story of Lady Juliana Harley* (1776). Burney's basic scenario is not new, of course. The entrance of young ladies into the world was an established fictional trope, and Burney's subtitle might as easily describe Charlotte Lennox's *Female Quixote* (1752), or, more pertinently, Eliza Haywood's *History of Miss Betsy Thoughtless* (1751), in which, as in *Evelina*, a fatherless heroine excitedly and successfully confronts the pleasures and dangers of the metropolis. For Haywood, inescapably identified with the barely respectable seduction narratives which gained her notoriety in the 1720s, the city in *Betsy Thoughtless* remains primarily a place of sexual threat. Burney, however, uses her intelligent female ingénue to offer a much broader social critique of London's pleasure-seeking culture. And unlike Griffith's post-Richardsonian narratives of female suffering and renunciation, *Evelina* presents a heroine whose practical as well as simply moral resilience helps ensure her survival.

Refusing to be trammelled by the limited paradigms of established feminocentric fiction – whether the tragedy of sexual ruin or the comic resolution of marriage – *Evelina* exploits to the full the generic elasticity of Burney's chosen form. *Evelina* is about the moral and social education of its heroine, but it is at least as interested in the variety and relative value of the pleasures offered by the 1770s entertainment industry. Indeed, Evelina's worth is in part measured by her ability to negotiate and assess the diversions the city has to offer. The effect is to make a bold case for the superiority of fiction as a form of (moral) entertainment as Burney demonstrates the novel's capacity not simply to absorb and replicate other literary genres, most notably satire and drama, but also to act as a discriminating guide to a whole range of popular as well as polite amusements which competed for its readers' attention. The result is a work which moves between the exigencies of decorum required at fashionable balls and incidents of cruel physical satire more suited to Smollett. Feminine propriety and the rules of politeness exemplified by Evelina and her dull suitor, Lord Orville, are constantly challenged and disturbed by the entertainment afforded by the rather less respectable members of Evelina's family, her embarrassing nouveau-riche grandmother, Madame Duval, her cousins the Branghtons, and the irrepressible Captain Mirvan, the instigator of many of the novel's slapstick episodes. This unusual range of setting, character, and incident, more reminiscent of Fielding than the female novel, disturbed some contemporary commentators. Elizabeth Montagu, 'Queen' of the Bluestockings, for example 'c[ould] not bear' *Evelina* and was 'amazed that so delicate a Girl could write so *boisterous* a Book'.[30] But, as we have seen, most critics were delighted, and from the start of her career Burney was identified with fiction in its most socially panoramic form. London's famous pleasure-gardens, Vauxhall and Marylebone, the settings for two of *Evelina*'s most important scenes, are paradigmatic here. Popular with a broad clientele, from peers to prostitutes, the gardens' attractions catered for a wide variety of tastes, and they consequently became a byword, among those worried about such things, for the dangers of indiscriminate social mixing. Burney's novel acknowledges but transcends that attitude. At Marylebone, Evelina survives being mistaken for a prostitute and retains textual and rational control through her discriminating epistolary reports to her anxious guardian; whilst for her author, the serendipity of Marylebone's social mix provides a romantic plot device through which Evelina, visiting her lower-class cousins, can be reunited with her aristocratic suitor.

In *Evelina*, this social panorama is mediated by the heroine's first-person epistolary consciousness. In *Cecilia*, Burney abandons the immediacy, but also the interpretative uncertainties, of letters for the more directive third-person narrative mode which she used for each of her succeeding novels. But the narrator's Johnsonian authority is balanced always by the extensive use of dialogue. Burney was a playwright *manqué*, denied the opportunity to see her plays produced on the London stage by the interventions of her father and her mentor, Samuel Crisp, who feared that such public exposure would be improper for a young woman. In all Burney's fiction, her characters are distinguished and defined by their idiom. In *Evelina*, in keeping with the novel's essentially comic mode, this often takes the form of the familiar idiolects of conventional satirical types: the predatory Sir Clement, for example, or the crude nautical jargon of Captain Mirvan. But in *Cecilia*, Burney's darkly complex vision produces 'mixed' characters whose distinctive speech does not necessarily mean that they are susceptible to easy categorisation or judgement. In this, Burney typifies and contributes to the late eighteenth-century shift in understanding of what 'character' might mean: from a representative moral or social type to the individuated consciousness of psychological realism.

Evelina's entrance into the world involves discovering which entertainments she prefers, learning the rules of politeness, finding a father and securing a husband. But, as Austen might have put it, *Cecilia* is rather less 'light & bright & sparkling'.[31] In the world depicted in this novel, the treachery and violence held precariously at bay in *Evelina* begin to dominate, and the heroine's entrance as a young, independent heiress precipitates a near-fatal trajectory of disillusion and abandonment in which guardians and friends prove unreliable and, at times, unfathomable. Evelina enters the world penniless and ignorant of her paternity. Her happy ending involves not simply finding her father, her patronymic, and thus her social identity, but also, as many commentators have pointed out, securing the protection of no less than three father-figures: her birth-father, her guardian, and her husband. In the darker world of *Cecilia*, by contrast, the name of the father becomes a curse, as Burney exposes the helplessness of unprotected women within a patrilinear system. The heroine, 'only survivor of the Beverley family' (*Cecilia*, 5), confident of her identity and heir to a substantial fortune, enters the world apparently free to choose her destiny. The constraints are the requirement that her husband take her (father's) name and, more predictably, the greed and corruptibility of those around her. The consequences are absolute social isolation as she is betrayed by even her most trusted allies, and loss of self as she descends, Clarissa-like, into temporary madness.

That Cecilia should be betrayed by her three male guardians, the very different but equally monstrous trustees of her fortune, is comparatively unsurprising. As she moves from one of their houses to another, across another broad social landscape, her growing disillusionment structures the novel's satirical exposure of the pride, prejudice, and self-interest endemic in a society Cecilia initially thinks of as 'abounding with opulence, hospitality, and splendour, and of which the principal inhabitants ... were now almost universally rising in elegance and liberality' (374). Like Fielding before and Austen after her, Burney probes the moral reality behind that social aesthetic. She does so most tellingly, however, through Cecilia's much more unexpected betrayal by her friend and mentor, Mrs Delvile, mother of the novel's genial but ineffectual hero, Mortimer Delvile. Burney's innovative intention here was 'to draw a great, but not a perfect character; I meant ... to blend upon paper, as I have frequently seen blended in life, noble and rare qualities with striking and incurable defects'.[32] Part of Mrs Delvile's 'greatness' is her capacity for moral subtlety and firm principle. Most prominent among her defects is her readiness, as Cecilia puts it, 'to sacrifice to her sense of duty the happiness of a son' (701), where 'duty' means the stubborn upholding of patriarchal convention. In spite of her love and admiration for Cecilia, Mrs Delvile insists that continuing the family name (her husband's, of course, rather than her own) take precedence over marriage for love – or, in the case of Cecilia and Mortimer, love and fortune. Burney's technical originality – the authentically mixed character, and the compromised rather than unmitigatedly happy ending, 'more according to real life' – exposes the actualities which bear down on individuals', and particularly women's, freedom of choice. Cecilia chooses security and personal happiness, but the price is independence, the woman's sacrifice of name and fortune as she enters her husband's family.

It was *Cecilia* that the *Monthly*'s reviewer described as 'related in a style peculiarly nervous and perspicuous'. The comment helpfully captures Burney's other major innovation: the flexible narrative voice through which she traces her heroine's often anguished engagement with a predatory and unpredictable world. The praise for Burney's stylistic lucidity and clarity in 'perspicuous' is straightforward enough, but 'nervous' at this period can be used either in the now obsolete sense of a style 'vigorous, powerful, forcible' (*OED*), or with the emergent meanings associated with the nervous system and used within the language of sensibility to suggest particular sensitivity of temperament. Burney's sinuous third-person narrative importantly combines the two, guiding the reader through Cecilia's vigorous moral thought processes as she struggles to make sense of her experiences. Burney's heroine displays that ideal conjunction of reason with feeling which Mary Wollstonecraft would later celebrate as '*active* sensibility', and the novel establishes the inner life of its female protagonist as the focus of both interest and meaning.[33] The passage partially quoted above, in which Cecilia describes to herself the 'opulence, hospitality, and splendour' of London society, is typical:

> Yet, in her serious reflections, she could not but think herself strangely unfortunate that the guardian with whom alone it seemed proper for her to reside, should by parsimony, vulgarity, and meanness, render riches contemptible, prosperity unavailing, and œconomy odious ... in a city abounding with opulence, hospitality, and splendour, and of which the principal inhabitants, long eminent for their wealth and their probity, were now almost universally rising in elegance and liberality. (374)

This moves from directive third-person narration of Cecilia's thought processes to an unmediated representation of the enthusiastic terms she herself might use. In the classic mode of free indirect discourse, the heroine's scrupulous but surely still naïve evaluation is presented in her words, without authorial qualification or judgement, and it is the reader who must identify the point of view and supply any ironic distance. Such moments in *Cecilia* establish and define Burney's distinctive narrative technique, the third-person representation of a rational female consciousness which was to provide Austen with the blueprint for her more pervasive and sophisticated development of free indirect narration.

In her two later novels, *Camilla* and *The Wanderer*, Burney further refines this narrative method as her beleaguered heroines negotiate the gap between self and world, private consciousness and social persona. As in her earlier fiction, forms of violence, both physical and psychological, remain a constant threat. In *Camilla*, patriarchy's unreasonable demands bear down on the heroine in an insistence not this time on patrilinear inheritance, but on a code of propriety which requires self-repression and enforced inarticulacy. And in *The Wanderer*'s systematic examination of the limited opportunities for safe paid work, Burney is again concerned with the extreme difficulty for a woman of achieving, much less maintaining, independence. Like *Cecilia*, these are vast novels in which a huge cast of characters is, as Burney put it of *Camilla*, 'all *wove* into *one*, with a one *Heroine* shining conspicuous through the Group'.[34] In *Camilla*, the connecting thread is the marriage plot; in *The Wanderer*, the heroine's mysterious identity gives her the connective anonymity of an Everywoman.

Camilla is Burney's most unremittingly painful novel, an unbearable catalogue of constraint and inhibition. Its heroine is the victim of the men she loves, their conventionally protective role distorted into impossible or inappropriate expectations. Her uncle, Sir Hugh Tyrold, wants to keep her for himself; her suitor, Edgar Mandlebert (another Burney hero it's difficult to like), unduly influenced by his tutor, won't announce his affection until he is sure of hers; whilst her father presents her with a letter of advice on proper female 'discretion' which forbids the slightest betrayal of her feelings. Mr Tyrold's letter was taken straight by contemporaries, excerpted from the novel without Burney's consent and published separately in an anthology of conduct literature; Camilla does her best to follow its precepts, though she almost goes mad in the process; and, unlike *Cecilia*, the novel invites us to accept an unqualified happy ending. For these reasons, perhaps, *Camilla* has sometimes been misread as conformist, but Burney's narrative method invites a very different response. The effect of her mimetic representation of Camilla's mental anguish is to undermine rather than endorse her heroine's internalisation of male precepts which demand such a sacrifice of self. This process, and the novel's plot, reach their crisis in Camilla's much-cited, splendidly Gothic dream in which a disembodied voice of authority demands that she defend herself in writing, only to find that the iron pen provided 'made no mark' (875).

The Wanderer, too, is concerned with women's capacity for self-possession. Like all Burney's heroines, Ellis/Juliet enters the world essentially alone; even more starkly than the other heroines, she must secure her own financial and psychological survival in an environment inhospitable to a woman without name or family, a process which requires her to keep her inner self intact but hidden. At the end of the novel, the narrative voice sums up her experiences through comparison with those of a male fictional precursor:

> Here ... ended ... the DIFFICULTIES of the WANDERER; – a being who had been cast upon herself; a female Robinson Crusoe, as unaided and unprotected, though in the midst of the world, as that imaginary hero in his uninhabited island; and reduced either to sink, through inanition, to nonentity, or to be rescued from famine and death by such resources as she could find, independently, in herself.[35]

As in the Preface to *Evelina* some forty years earlier, Burney again aligns herself here, in what was to be her last novel, with the canonical male novelists of the eighteenth century. And as in the *Evelina* Preface, the acknowledgement is both a tribute and a challenge. Leaving aside for the moment her debts to Fielding's broad moral satire and Richardson's explorations of female subjectivity, Burney goes back to the novel's beginnings to announce herself as the inheritor of Defoe's paradigmatic myth of economic self-reliance. But in her latter-day realisation of that founding fictional narrative, the difference of gender reveals the known social and commercial world to be as alien as Crusoe's island.

Frances Burney's achievement as a novelist was the development of a narrative technique at once panoramic and intimate. Rooted in both satire and sensibility, her feminocentric novels establish a mode of psychological realism which minutely registers the often painful impact of social experience on the individual psyche. In her three longest, most characteristic novels, isolation tests her heroines to the limits of sanity, and female experience comes to stand as representation of and test case for the moral individual's negotiation with forms of social power. 'Self-possession', the narrator of *The Wanderer* tells us, 'is the highest attribute of fearless innocence' (815). The 'resources' which Ellis/Juliet in *The Wanderer* finds 'independently, in herself' signal that belief in an individualised core of identity, in a 'real self' separable, though never wholly separate from 'the world', which Burney's fiction helped define and which is so fundamental to the novel as it moved further into the nineteenth century.

NOTE ON EDITIONS

The best and most available modern editions of Burney's novels are the Oxford World's Classics reprints.

NOTES

1 *Monthly Review*, 67 (1782), 453; Jane Austen, *Northanger Abbey*, I, chapter 5; Anna Letitia Barbauld, 'Miss Burney', reprinted in Anna Letitia Barbauld, *Selected Poetry and Prose*, ed. William McCarthy and Elizabeth Kraft (Peterborough, ONT: Broadview Press, 2002), p. 443.

2 *Edinburgh Review*, 24 (1815), 336.

3 *Edinburgh Review*, 76 (1843), reprinted in Justine Crump (ed.), *A Known Scribbler: Frances Burney on Literary Life* (Peterborough, ONT: Broadview Press, 2002), pp. 374–5.

4 Ian Watt, *The Rise of the Novel* (1957; reprinted Harmondsworth: Penguin, 1972), p. 339.

5 Ibid., p. 340.

6 *Edinburgh Review*, 24 (1815), 337.

7 *Monthly Review*, 76 (1815), 412.

8 See Peter Garside, James Raven, and Rainer Schöwerling (gen. eds.), *The English Novel 1770–1829: A Bibliographical Survey of Prose Fiction Published in the British Isles*, 2 vols. (Oxford: Oxford University Press, 2000).

9 Frances Burney, *Evelina or the History of a Young Lady's Entrance into the World* (1778), ed. Edward A. Bloom, introduction and notes by Vivien Jones (Oxford: Oxford University Press, 2002), p. 9. Hereafter *E*.

10 *Critical Review*, 46 (1778), 202; *The Early Journals and Letters of Fanny Burney*, gen. ed. Lars Troide, 4 vols. to date (Oxford, Clarendon Press, 1988–), III, ed. Lars E. Troide and Stewart J. Cooke (1994), p. 6.

11 Garside, Raven, and Schöwerling, *The English Novel*, I, pp. 26–7, 34. Sixteen new novels were published in 1778; eighty in 1788.

12 *Monthly Review*, 67 (1782), 453, 456–7.

13 *Early Journals and Letters*, II, ed. Lars Troide (1990), p. 215.

14 For a full text of Burney's draft introduction, see Fanny Burney, *Cecilia, or Memoirs of an Heiress* (1782), ed. Peter Sabor and Margaret Anne Doody (Oxford and New York: Oxford University Press, 1988), pp. 943–5. Hereafter *Cecilia*.
15 *Diary and Letters of Madame d'Arblay*, edited by her niece [Charlotte Barrett], 7 vols. (London: Henry Colburn, 1842–6), II, p. 136.
16 Fanny Burney, *Camilla or A Picture of Youth* (1796), ed. Edward A. Bloom and Lillian D. Bloom (Oxford and New York: Oxford University Press, 1983), p. 7. Hereafter *Camilla*.
17 *The Journals and Letters of Fanny Burney (Madame d'Arblay)*, ed. Joyce Hemlow *et al.*, 12 vols. (Oxford: Clarendon Press, 1972–84), III (1973), p. 117.
18 *Critical Review*, 54 (1782), 414; *Monthly Review*, 67 (1782), 453, 457.
19 *Diary and Letters*, II, p. 195.
20 *Critical Review*, 54 (1782), 420.
21 Samuel Johnson, *The Rambler*, 4 (1750), in *The Yale Edition of the Works of Samuel Johnson*, ed. W. J. Bate and Albrecht B. Strauss (New Haven and London: Yale University Press, 1969), III, p. 22.
22 Ibid., p. 23.
23 *British Critic*, 8 (1796), 527; *Monthly Review*, 67 (1782), 453.
24 *Journals and Letters*, III, p. 186.
25 Barbauld, *Selected Poetry and Prose*, p. 449.
26 *Monthly Review*, 21 (1796), 161; *British Critic*, 8 (1796), 528.
27 *Monthly Review*, 76 (1815), 415; *Critical Review*, 5 (1814), 410.
28 *Critical Review*, 5 (1814) 406.
29 *Edinburgh Review*, 24 (1815), 337.
30 *Early Journals and Letters*, IV, ed. Betty Rizzo (2003), p. 293.
31 Austen famously described *Pride and Prejudice*, the title of which is taken from *Cecilia* (930), as 'rather too light & bright & sparkling', *Jane Austen's Letters*, 3rd edn, ed. Deirdre Le Faye (Oxford and New York: Clarendon Press, 1995), p. 203.
32 *Diary and Letters*, II, p. 128.
33 Mary Wollstonecraft, *The Wrongs of Woman: Or, Maria* (1798), *The Works of Mary Wollstonecraft*, ed. Janet Todd and Marilyn Butler, 7 vols. (London: Pickering and Chatto, 1989), I, p. 144.
34 *Journals and Letters*, III, p. 129.
35 Frances Burney, *The Wanderer; or, Female Difficulties* (1814), ed. Margaret Anne Doody, Robert L. Mack, and Peter Sabor (Oxford and New York: Oxford University Press, 1991), p. 872.

FURTHER READING

Doody, Margaret Anne, *Frances Burney: The Life in the Works*, Cambridge, Cambridge University Press, 1988

Epstein, Julia, *The Iron Pen: Frances Burney and the Politics of Women's Writing*, Madison, University of Wisconsin Press, 1989

Gallagher, Catherine, *Nobody's Story: The Vanishing Acts of Women Writers in the Marketplace, 1670–1820*, Oxford, Clarendon Press, 1994

Galperin, William H.,'Why Jane Austen Is Not Frances Burney: Probability, Possibility, and Romantic Counterhegemony', in *The Historical Jane Austen*, Philadelphia, University of Pennsylvania Press, 2003, pp. 82–105

Garside, Peter, James Raven, and Rainer Schöwerling (gen. eds.), *The English Novel 1770–1829: A Bibliographical Survey of Prose Fiction Published in the British Isles*, 2 vols., Oxford, Oxford University Press, 2000

Johnson, Claudia L., *Equivocal Beings: Politics, Gender, and Sentimentality in the 1790s: Wollstonecraft, Radcliffe, Burney, Austen*, Chicago and London, University of Chicago Press, 1995

Lynch, Deidre Shauna, 'Agoraphobia and Interiority in Frances Burney's Fiction', in *The Economy of Character: Novels, Market Culture, and the Business of Inner Meaning*, Chicago and London, University of Chicago Press, 1998, pp. 164–206

Newton, Judith Lowder, *Women, Power and Subversion: Social Strategies in British Fiction, 1778–1860*, Athens, GA, University of Georgia Press, 1981

Sabor, Peter (ed.), *The Cambridge Companion to Frances Burney*, Cambridge, Cambridge University Press, 2007

Schellenberg, Betty, 'From Propensity to Profession: Female Authorship and the Early Career of Frances Burney', *Eighteenth-Century Fiction*, 14 (2002), 345–70

Spencer, Jane, *The Rise of the Woman Novelist: From Aphra Behn to Jane Austen*, Oxford, Blackwell, 1986

Straub, Kristina, *Divided Fictions: Fanny Burney and Feminine Strategy*, Lexington, University Press of Kentucky, 1987

'Frances Burney and the Rise of the Woman Novelist', in John Richetti (ed.), *The Columbia History of the British Novel*, New York, Columbia University Press, 1994, pp. 199–219

Thaddeus, Janice Farrar, *Frances Burney: A Literary Life*, Basingstoke and London, Macmillan, 2000

6

JOCELYN HARRIS

Jane Austen

Two decades of intense experimentation and revision preceded the publication of Jane Austen's six major novels: *Sense and Sensibility* (1811), *Pride and Prejudice* (1813), *Mansfield Park* (1814), *Emma* (1815), *Northanger Abbey* (1818), and *Persuasion* (1818). Constantly playing off the tradition, she merges the dramatic interiority of Samuel Richardson with the authorial voice of Henry Fielding to expose characters' minds while prompting the judgement of readers. That flexible narrative voice would catch the attention of Henry James and Virginia Woolf, among others. Even in her last unfinished fragment, *Sanditon*, Austen was still evolving new techniques and subjects. But her affection for irony, satire, and parody derives just as clearly from Restoration and eighteenth-century drama. Thus Austen, poised between two centuries, writes novels that are as compact, witty, and incisive as plays.

Austen's relation to predecessors and contemporaries may be traced through the books she owned, says she has read, alludes to, or seems to echo. Even that may represent a mere fraction of what she knew, for as F. R. Leavis remarks, 'she read all there was to read, and took all that was useful to her – which wasn't only lessons'.[1] Like most authors, Austen made books out of other books as well as out of life. If readers are active rather than passive consumers of texts,[2] so too writers poach freely from other writers. Thus Austen's appropriations signify not lack of imagination, not plagiarism, not submission to 'influence', but sheer competitiveness. Her rewriting of fellow novelists particularly implies critique, for comparisons reveal her irresistible literary-critical impulse to improve upon them.

Although Austen was well acquainted with fiction, her knowledge of plays, poems, and other non-fictional works was just as extensive. A voracious and retentive reader, she devoured her way through volumes belonging to a book club or male relatives. Like Fanny Price in *Mansfield Park*, she was an eager 'renter, a chuser of books!' from circulating libraries.[3] Allusions to novels by Richardson, Fielding, Smollett, and Sterne, to Goldsmith, Mme de

Genlis, Rousseau, Frances Burney, Edgeworth, Charlotte Smith, Radcliffe, Robinson, More, Lennox, Lewis, Bage, Sarah Scott, and Walter Scott all surface in her novels and correspondence. But Austen absorbed many other genres including children's literature – nursery rhymes, Gay's *Fables* and the *Arabian Nights*. Her whole life long, she read, acted in, or attended performances of plays, pantomimes, melodramas, operas, musicals, and farces from Shakespeare to Fielding, Garrick, Otway, Sheridan, Bickerstaff, Centlivre, Dibdin, Moore, Goldsmith, Inchbald, Cowley, and the two George Colmans. The anarchic disjunctions of Fielding's farces especially inspired the juvenilia and spilled over into the novels.

Austen was familiar with philosophy, linguistics, and aesthetics from Locke to Gilpin, Burke, Smith, Hume, Repton, and Blair; she read poets from Chaucer to Spenser, Milton, Pope, Prior, Thomson, Gray, Cowper, Crabbe, Burns, Wordsworth, Coleridge, Southey, and Byron. The graphic art of Rowlandson was known to her, as were newspapers, periodicals from the *Spectator*, the *Rambler*, and the *Idler* to McKenzie's *Mirror*, Henry Austen's *Loiterer*, and the *Quarterly Review*; histories by Goldsmith, Robertson, and Henry; travel books by Johnson, Boswell, Smollett, Southey, Carr, and Macartney; and works on topics as diverse as characters and manners, the slave trade, the rights of woman, the French Revolution, sensibility, Christianity in India, and the military policy and institutions of the British empire.

Religious texts such as the Bible, the Book of Common Prayer, and Bunyan's *Pilgrim's Progress* formed as much part of her constitution as Shakespeare. She consulted navy lists, almanacs, works of heraldry and ancestry by Dugdale and Debrett, and sermons by Cooper, Secker, and Sherlock. The conduct books of More, Chapone, Chesterfield, Gisborne, Fordyce, Gregory, and Percival were probably known to her, as was the correspondence of de Staël, de Sévigné, Johnson, Baretti, and Anne Grant. She refers to anthologies assembled by Dodsley, Knox, and Jefferson, while biographies of Richardson, Johnson, Nash, Mary Robinson, and Nelson enter into her fiction.

The evidence lies in the novels, where Austen's interaction with her tradition seems often to spark invention. Translating precursors into other registers and contexts, she usually improves on her originals, although stumbles such as the plot resolution of *Persuasion* or the fleeting appearance of Richardson's *Clarissa* in *Sense and Sensibility* illuminate her creative process, as I shall explain. Resistance to other authors provides information just as striking about her methods and political beliefs.

Austen works through appropriation, elaboration, and improvement of other books. In the first category of her intertextual practice, she adapts without critique. For instance, if Emma Woodhouse remarks that a 'Hartfield edition of Shakespeare would have a long note' about the course of true love never running smooth (*E*, 80), her own history provides that long note, for Austen transposes ideas, characters, events, and significant vocabulary from *A Midsummer Night's Dream* into Emma's more modern time and place.

Austen plucks further ideas and anecdotes for *Emma* from Mary Wollstonecraft's feminist manifesto, *A Vindication of the Rights of Woman*. A veritable Wollstonecraft wannabe who longs to use understanding aright, Emma is resolutely uneducated, and cannot reason. Although she mocks Miss Bates for flying off, 'through half a sentence, to her mother's old petticoat' (*E*, 243), her own thought processes work in exactly the same dangerously associative way. Austen may be jesting when she applies the word 'vindicated' to the difference between men's and women's handwriting; when Emma thinks herself 'a better judge of such a point of female right and refinement' as Harriet marrying Robert Martin; or when a 'private dance, without sitting down to supper' was pronounced 'an infamous fraud upon the rights of men and women' (*E*, 321, 69, 273); but key words and concepts from the *Vindication* – 'understanding', 'fancy', 'mind', 'rational', 'reason', and 'education' – do recur significantly throughout the novel.

For the scene at Box Hill, Austen expands an anecdote from *Vindication* about a rich, idle woman insulting 'a worthy old gentlewoman, whom unexpected misfortunes had made dependent on her ostentatious bounty, and who, in better days, had claims on her gratitude': Emma, whom Miss Bates 'had seen grow up from a period when her notice was an honour', has 'in thoughtless spirits, and the pride of the moment' laughed at and humbled a poor woman 'sunk from the comforts she was born to', says Mr Knightley (*E*, 408).[4] Wollstonecraft attacked affectedly delicate women who 'neglect all the duties of life, yet recline with self-complacency on a sofa'. How she would have relished the imaginary complaints of Mrs Churchill, who though unable to 'leave the sopha for a week together', is impatient to take to the road to London (*E*, 331). The fact that Wollstonecraft's idle lady is the very same person who insults that worthy old gentlewoman, the progenitor of Miss Bates,[5] indicates that though some call Austen conservative, she draws readily on the radical *Vindication*.

Elsewhere, Austen turns to the landscape gardener Humphry Repton, whose remark about the ha-ha, that 'the *imaginary* freedom is dearly bought by the *actual* confinement, since nothing is so difficult to pass as a deep sunk fence', anticipates Maria Bertram's break for freedom past Sotherton's literal and symbolic restraints, in *Mansfield Park*.[6] Again in *Emma*, one can almost hear Austen laugh when Harriet Smith boasts of Mr Martin's 'eight cows, two of them Alderneys' (*E*, 26), for the breed was small, and Repton advised that introducing Alderneys into the landscape gave 'imaginary extent to the place, which is thus measured below a true standard; because if distance will make a large animal appear small, so the distance will be apparently extended by the smallness of the animal' (*Observations*, 6).

Austen appropriates Repton yet again for her account of Abbey-Mill farm, inhabited by Mr Knightley's tenant Robert Martin. Small detached farms, says Repton,

> adapted to useful and laborious life, unmixed with the splendours of opulence, but supporters of natural wealth, are indeed objects of interest in every point of view; they want not the adventitious aid of picturesque effect to attract peculiar notice; to a benevolent mind they are more than objects of beauty; they are blessings to society; nor is it incompatible with the pursuit of pleasure, sometimes to leave the boundaries of the park, and watch the exertions of laudable industry or visit the cottages 'Where cheerful tenants bless their yearly toil'. (*Observations*, 98)

Abbey-Mill offers likewise 'all its appendages of prosperity and beauty, its rich pastures, spreading flocks, orchard in blossom, and light column of smoke ascending'. Its situation, 'favourably placed and sheltered' half a mile from a bank 'of considerable abruptness and grandeur, well clothed with wood' (*E*, 391), echoes Repton's advice that the landowner should leave one or more houses in a dell, 'inhabited either as a keeper's house, a dairy, or a menagerie [building for animals], that the occasional smoke from the chimnies may animate the scene. The picturesque and pleasing effect of smoke ascending, when relieved by a dark hanging wood in the deep recess of a beautiful glen like this, is a circumstance by no means to be neglected' (*Observations*, 138). Abbey-Mill's cows, farm, view, and ascending smoke all suggest approval of Repton's nostalgic ethos. But whose? If Austen shares his nostalgia, she is conservative after all; if Emma endorses it, her attitude to Abbey-Mill's master and tenant has changed. Here, as usual, Austen complicates her source.

Repton's architectural ideas seem also to contribute to *Persuasion*. 'In magnificent town houses', he writes, 'we expect a suite of rooms, opening by folding doors, for the reception of those large parties for assemblies, when the proprietors are driven out of house and home, to make room for more visitors than their rooms can contain.' But that sort of state-room or drawing-room 'is now generally found a melancholy apartment, when entirely shut up, and only opened to give the visitors a formal cold reception'.[7] In their new home at Bath, Anne Elliot 'must sigh, and smile, and wonder too, as Elizabeth threw open the folding-doors, and walked with exultation from one drawing-room to the other, boasting of their space, at the possibility of that woman, who had been mistress of Kellynch Hall, finding extent to be proud of between two walls, perhaps thirty feet asunder'. As in Repton, a 'general chill' falls on the room, 'hushed into cold composure, determined silence, or insipid talk, to meet the heartless elegance of her father and sister'. Anne's snobbish sister Elizabeth has no intention of inviting the large parties that Repton deems suitable for rooms joined by folding doors, preferring 'a regular party – small, but most elegant'. Her excuse is 'Old fashioned notions – country hospitality – we do not profess to give dinners – few people in Bath do' (*P*, 149, 245, 238). In such ways, Austen turns Repton's incidental details into character and event.

In her second, more typical category, Austen plays the critic by improving on her predecessors – especially those who practised her own trade of novel-writing. Fearless in tackling even a favourite, she assimilated, inverted, and exaggerated Richardson's *Sir Charles Grandison* in the juvenilia. If, for instance, Sir Charles rejects a noble, beautiful, and wealthy Italian stalker armed with a poniard, Austen's Lucy, in spite of being 'possessed of Youth, Beauty, Wit and Merit', as she says herself, and 'the probable Heiress of my Aunts House and business', is sent an 'angry and peremptory refusal' by Charles Adams. She pursues him to his estate in Pammydiddle, only to be caught in a steel mantrap: 'Oh! cruel Charles to wound the hearts and legs of all the fair', exclaims the amiable but claret-loving Alice. As Lady Williams remarks, she has 'many rare and charming qualities, but Sobriety is not one of them' (*J*, 23–6).

Even in the mature novels, *Sense and Sensibility*, *Pride and Prejudice*, and *Mansfield Park*, Austen can still respond farcically to her predecessor. If Sir Charles asks, 'How many fatherless, brotherless, sonless families have mourned all their lives' on account of the horrors of duels; and grieves for the 'irreparable injury to the innocent family and dependents of the murdered',[8] Mrs Bennet cries out when Mr Wickham elopes with her daughter Lydia, 'And now here's Mr. Bennet gone away, and I know he will fight Wickham, wherever he meets him, and then he will be killed, and what is to become of us all? The Collinses will turn us out, before he is cold in his grave; and if you are not kind to us, brother, I do not know what we shall do.' But when her husband returns unharmed, she 'did not express so much satisfaction as her children expected, considering what her anxiety for his life had been before'. Who, she asks, 'is to fight Wickham, and make him marry her, if he comes away?' (*P&P*, 317, 328–9).

Austen just keeps on returning to Richardson. For instance, she runs not just one but four completely different variations on a scene following the marriage of Harriet Byron to Sir Charles, where the hero's congratulations to his 'dearest life' on her 'entrance into *your own* house' prompt the heroine to exclaim, 'Here I am! The declared mistress of this spacious house, and the happiest of human creatures!' (*Grandison*, part 3, 269). In *Sense and Sensibility*, it is deeply improper for Marianne Dashwood to visit Allenham alone with Willoughby, before they are engaged, before the property has passed to him upon its owner's death. In *Pride and Prejudice*, Elizabeth Bennet refuses Mr Darcy's proposal, views his magnificent home as a tourist, hears about his true character from the housekeeper, and realises that to be mistress of Pemberley might be something. In *Mansfield Park*, Maria boasts of Sotherton, her opulent future home, even though she loathes its owner, Mr Rushworth, to whom she is also engaged. In *Persuasion*, Anne turns down the chance to marry William Elliot, her father's heir, and return with him to Kellynch, the home she loves. Thus whereas Richardson's episode lacks consequence, Austen turns plot into character and character into plot.

As to her contemporaries, Austen's improvements on Maria Edgeworth provide striking examples of her competitiveness. For *Mansfield Park*, Austen calls on at least three of Edgeworth's novels, bearing out the seriousness of a joke made in a letter to her niece Anna on 28 September 1814, 'I have made up my mind to like no Novels really, but Miss Edgeworth's, Yours & my own.'[9] Although admiring of a popular writer, she diverges productively from her.

For example, Edgeworth's Lady Rackrent in *Castle Rackrent* seems to have launched Austen into her bravura creation of Mrs Norris in *Mansfield Park*. If Lady Rackrent, who is 'very charitable in her own way', had a charity school for poor children, 'where they were taught to read and write gratis, and where they were kept well to spinning gratis for my lady in return', Mrs Norris is no rich property owner, but a poor widow who ingeniously torments Fanny Price, the child adopted by her uncle, Sir Thomas Bertram. Claiming to be 'the last person in the world to withhold my mite', without the 'least intention of being at any expense whatever', she is 'thoroughly benevolent, and nobody knew better how to dictate liberality to others: but her love of money was equal to her love of directing, and she knew quite as well how to save her own as to spend that of her friends', says Austen's narrator. It proves 'impossible for her to aim at more than the credit of projecting and arranging so expensive a charity' as Fanny (*MP*, 6–9). Although the 'benevolence' of Mrs Norris is every bit as false as Lady Rackrent's, Austen's narrowing down of the focus from a school full of poor children to the suffering sensibility of one girl-child immediately arouses our sympathy.

If Lady Rackrent punishes a maid for being given a morsel of roast beef to keep body and soul together after she fainted three times on the last day of Lent, Mrs Norris is just as abusive to Fanny. Treating her as a servant, she induces headache by making her cut roses for three-quarters of an hour in the heat before sending her off on two more errands. Lady Rackrent promptly vanishes from Edgeworth's tale, but Mrs Norris's outrageous demand for Fanny to show gratitude resonates throughout *Mansfield Park*: 'I shall think her a very obstinate, ungrateful girl; if she does not do what her aunt and cousins wish her – very ungrateful indeed, considering who and what she is' (*MP*, 84–6, 172). Aunt Norris, the last and lowest in her own family, has only Fanny to pick on.

Austen develops further details from Edgeworth when Lady Rackrent, of the family of the Skinflints, is suspected of having Scottish blood, for she looks 'close to every thing'. The narrator says it is surprising 'how cheap my lady got things done, and how proud she was of it. Her table the same way, kept for next to nothing; duty fowls, and duty turkies, and duty geese, came as fast as we could eat 'em, for my lady kept a sharp look-out, and knew to a tub of butter every thing the tenants had, all round'. They never came 'without a present of something or other – nothing too much or too little for my lady – eggs, honey, butter, meal, fish, game, grouse, and herrings, fresh or salt, all went for something'.[10] Mrs Norris resembles Lady Rackrent in carrying off a beautiful little heath, a cream cheese, and four beautiful pheasant's eggs, before snapping up the theatre curtain because 'she happened to be particularly in want of green baize' (*MP*, 123, 228). But whereas the greed of Lady Rackrent has little effect on Edgeworth's novel, the obsessive sponging of Mrs Norris fatally distracts her from the physical and moral straying of her wards and nieces, the Bertram sisters. Thus Austen develops passing references from *Castle Rackrent* into the complex causes and effects of *Mansfield Park*. Her remark about *Fitz-Albini*, by Samuel Egerton Brydges, that 'There is very little story, and what there is told in a strange, unconnected way. There are many characters introduced, apparently merely to be delineated' (*Letters*, 22), could never be said of her.

For Maria's eventual fate, Austen darkens a scene from Edgeworth's *Vivian*, in which Lady Julia Lidhurst, rather than marry Vivian, chooses to retire and live with a relation, the ugly and prudish Miss Strictland, 'in a distant part of the country; where I shall no more be seen or heard of'. In Austen's far bleaker version, Maria leaves her husband, Mr Rushworth, for Henry Crawford. After the affair is over, she is banished to 'a retirement and reproach, which could allow no second spring of hope or character'. Even retirement with Miss Strictland must pale compared with being shut up with Mrs Norris in 'a remote and private' place, where, 'with little society, on one side no affection, on the other, no judgment, it may be reasonably supposed that their tempers became their mutual punishment'. As in *Vivian*, where Lord Glistonbury hopes that his daughter Julia will return 'tamed and docile' from her rustication, Sir Thomas hopes for penitence, but more bluntly refuses to sanction what he calls 'vice' (*MP*, 537–8).

Austen's irresponsible guardian, Mrs Norris, derives from Julia's guardian, Miss Bateman, of whom Lord Glistonbury says, 'all this could not have happened, if she had looked after her charge properly'. Calling Miss Strictland 'still less fit to guide a girl of Julia's genius and disposition', he even blames his wife for never managing Julia rightly when she was a child.[11] In Austen's more subtle analysis, Sir Thomas himself accepts responsibility for the 'grievous mismanagement'. Feeling 'anguish arising from the conviction of his own errors in the education of his daughters', he acknowledges the 'totally opposite treatment' between the 'excessive indulgence and flattery' of Aunt Norris and his own 'severity'. He himself has judged ill, for he has 'but increased the evil, by teaching them to repress their spirits in his presence, as to make their real disposition unknown to him, and sending them for all their indulgences to a person who had been able to attach them only by the blindness of her affection, and the excess of her praise'. Sir Thomas probes even more deeply into the situation when he fears that 'principle, active principle, had been wanting', that 'they had never been properly taught to govern their inclinations and tempers, by that sense of duty which can alone suffice' (*MP*, 535–6).

From Edgeworth's *Vivian*, too, Austen purloined a newspaper report of an elopement:

> Yesterday, the beautiful and fashionable Mrs W******, whose marriage we announced last year to the celebrated Mr W******, eloped from his house in St James's Street, in company with C****** V***** ... This catastrophe has caused the greatest *sensation* and astonishment in the circles of fashion ... What must increase the poignancy of his feelings [is] that the seducer was his intimate friend ... Mr W****** is, we hear, in pursuit of the fugitives. (*Vivian*, 186)

In *Mansfield Park*, Fanny reads a similar report of

> a matrimonial *fracas* in the family of Mr. R. of Wimpole Street; the beautiful Mrs. R. whose name had not long been enrolled in the lists of hymen, and who had promised to become so brilliant a leader in the fashionable world, having quitted her husband's roof in company with the well known and captivating Mr. C. the intimate friend and associate of Mr. R. and it was not known, even to the editor of the newspaper, whither they were gone.

Austen improves on Edgeworth's statement that 'the lady in question had always, till this fatal step, preserved the most unblemished reputation; and Mr and Mrs ****** were considered as models of conjugal felicity' (*Vivian*, 186), for Maria is 'prepared for matrimony by an hatred of home, restraint, and tranquillity; by the misery of disappointed affection, and contempt of the man she was to marry' (*MP*, 509, 236).[12]

From Edgeworth's *Patronage*, published just a few months before *Mansfield Park*, Austen may take elements for Henry Crawford. If the mother of Buckhurst Falconer in *Patronage* introduces him 'early to fashionable company, and to a life of dissipation and idleness', Crawford is 'thoughtless and selfish from prosperity and bad example', having been 'ruined by early independence' and the 'bad domestic example' of his uncle, the adulterous admiral (*MP*, 135, 540, 342). Having 'a high idea of the clerical character', Falconer knows himself to be unfit for the 'sacred profession' of clergyman his father chooses for him. His 'natural sensibility only hastened his perversion' when, endeavouring to 'distinguish himself as an eloquent preacher', but ashamed to tell of the 'better motives, by which he was partly actuated',

> he protested, that he preached only for fame and a deanery – His talents were such as soon accomplished half his wish, and ensured him celebrity – he obtained opportunities of preaching in a fashionable chapel in London, he was prodigiously followed – his theatrical manner, perhaps, increased the effect of his eloquence upon a certain class of his auditors; but the more sober and nice judging part of his congregation objected to this dramatic art and declamatory style, as tending to draw the attention from the doctrine to the preacher, and to obtain admiration from man, more than to do honor to God.[13]

This passage seems to prompt Austen's equally eloquent and theatrical Henry Crawford into his peroration about clergymen reading aloud: 'A thoroughly good sermon, thoroughly well delivered, is a capital gratification. I can never hear such a one without the greatest admiration and respect, and more than half a mind to take orders and preach myself.' Trying to find a way to Fanny's heart, he asserts that the 'eloquence of the pulpit ... is entitled to the highest praise and honour. The preacher who can touch and affect such a heterogenous mass of hearers ... is a man whom one could not (in his public capacity) honour enough. I should like to be such a man' (*MP*, 393–4).

But as Edgeworth warns, Crawford desires admiration for himself rather than honour for God. As he says, 'I never listened to a distinguished preacher in my life, without a sort of envy. But then, I must have a London audience. I could not preach, but to the educated; to those who were capable of estimating my composition.' He would preach 'perhaps, once or twice in the spring, after being anxiously expected for half a dozen Sundays together', but not for a constancy, or regular commitment. In Austen's more intricate rendition of Edgeworth, Crawford subsequently renews his suit to Fanny, without success (*MP*, 395–8).

Edgeworth finds it painful to 'recapitulate and follow the gradual deterioration of a disposition' such as Falconer's, 'to mark the ruin and degradation of a character, which, notwithstanding it's [*sic*] faults, had a degree of generosity and openness, with a sense of honor and quick feeling; which, early in life, promised well; and which, but for parental weakness and mistaken system, might have been matured into every thing good and great'. Instead, he becomes notorious as a 'man of talents' in private circles and at public dinners (*Patronage*, VII; 75–7). Austen writes just as regretfully about her 'man of talent', Henry Crawford, that if he could have been 'satisfied with the conquest of one amiable woman's affections' and deserved more, 'there can be no doubt that more would have been obtained'. As she says, 'Would he have persevered, and uprightly, Fanny must have been his reward.' And if Falconer suspects of the gentle Caroline Percy that 'such even as I am, she might readily be brought to love, honor, and obey me' (*Patronage*, VI; 36), Austen doubts whether the gentle Fanny 'could have escaped heart-whole from the courtship of such a man as Crawford ... had not her affection been engaged elsewhere' (*MP*, 378, 540, 270). But like Edgeworth's character 'French' Clay, whose principle it is 'to intrigue with every *married* woman who would listen to him' (*Patronage*, VI; 251), Crawford wrecks his chance with Fanny by eloping with the recently married Maria Rushworth. Thus Austen combines Edgeworth's Falconer and French Clay into the more complicated Crawford.

Julia and Edmund Bertram seem to enact other scenes first played by Falconer. In *Patronage*, his imitation of Colonel Hauton sets the table in a roar, when 'to his utter confusion, his patron, who he thought had left the room, returned from behind a screen'. As Edgeworth writes, 'Not Banquo's ghost could have struck more terror into the heart of the guilty. – Buckhurst grew pale as death, and sudden silence ensued.' He sat 'aghast'. Hauton consequently denies Falconer the clerical living he was counting on (*Patronage*, VII; 78–80). In a similar moment, Julia, 'with a face all aghast', exclaims, 'My father is come! He is in the hall at this moment', to the 'consternation' and 'absolute horror' of the party. Sir Thomas Bertram, as calm and composed as Hauton, speaks 'a language, a remonstrance, a reproof' that Edmund feels at his heart (*MP*, 202–5, 215–16). Once chastened, however, Edmund gains the living that Falconer lost, along with its income.

As the *Quarterly* reviewer noted sagely of *Patronage* in January 1814, 'the persons come in and out, exhibit themselves, and describe others – in an agreeable way enough, but without our well knowing why they came or why they went – without our much caring whether or not they ever appear again'. If it is true, as he argues, readers 'expect invention, combination, unity' from novels, Austen's attentiveness to cause, effect, and coherence in *Mansfield Park* explains its remarkable advance on *Patronage*.

Appropriation without assimilation, the third category of her intertextual method, can go horribly wrong, however. Most notably in the controversial resolution to *Persuasion*, scraps from a Shakespeare play, novels by Smollett and Richardson, and a memoir by Robinson lie insufficiently combined.

Just when Anne Elliot, uncertain of Captain Wentworth's fidelity, is beginning to look favourably on her father's heir William Elliot, her school friend Mrs Smith suddenly reveals his perfidy towards her dead husband. Othello's demand for proof of Desdemona's infidelity echoes in Mrs Smith's 'you ought to have proof … and you shall have proof'. When she declares that 'Mr. Elliot is a man without heart or conscience … He is totally beyond the reach of any sentiment of justice or compassion. Oh! he is black at heart, hollow and black!' she convinces Anne that 'This is full proof undoubtedly, proof of every thing you were saying.' Mrs Smith replies that she can give 'authentic oral testimony'. Her injunction to Anne to 'Hear the truth' sounds like Shakespeare's Emilia declaring she 'must needs report the truth' about 'the blacker devil' Othello.[14] Mrs Smith's comment, 'My expressions startle you. You must allow for an injured, angry woman' (*P*, 215–24), suggests that if Jane Austen had lived, she might have toned down her melodramatic representation of Mr Elliot.

The betrayal of generous Mr Smith by his 'most intimate friend' Mr Elliot resembles, rather, an inset tale in Smollett's *Humphry Clinker* about Mr Serle, who rescues Mr Paunceford from 'the lowest distress'. Once rich, Paunceford treats his friend with 'ungrateful neglect', just as the newly enriched Mr Elliot demonstrates 'hard-hearted indifference' to Mrs Smith. Her narrative is a 'dreadful picture of ingratitude', thinks Anne. Serle lodges in poverty in Stall Street, 'up two pair of stairs backwards, walks a-foot in a Bath-rug, eats for twelve shillings a-week, and drinks water as a preservative against the gout and gravel', rather as Mrs Smith lives 'in a very humble way' in a 'noisy parlour, and a dark bed-room behind', and treats her rheumatism at the warm bath. And if Serle is 'a perfect philosopher' who 'looks upon all superfluities with the most sovereign contempt',[15] Anne views her friend as a case of fortitude, resignation, and elasticity of mind, which counterbalanced almost every other want (*P*, 216, 227, 166–7).

When Mr Elliot says to Anne, 'I knew you by report long before you came to Bath. I had heard you described by those who knew you intimately … Your person, your disposition, accomplishments, manner – they were all described, they were all present to me', he echoes Richardson's treacherous Sir Hargrave Pollexfen in *Grandison*: 'And are at last my eyes bless'd with the sight of a young Lady so celebrated for her graces of person and mind? Much did I hear, when I was at the last Northampton races, of Miss Byron: But little did I expect to find report fall so short of what I see.' And if Mrs Smith describes Mr Elliot as a man 'without heart or conscience; a designing, wary, cold-blooded being, who ... would be guilty of any cruelty' and leads others into ruin (*P*, 203–4, 215), Sir Hargrave was 'cruel', a 'very dangerous and enterprising man ... malicious, ill-natured, and designing; and sticks at nothing to carry a point on which he has once set his heart'. He has 'ruined' three young creatures (*Grandison*, part 1, 43, 63).

Mrs Smith also recalls the beautiful and talented 'Perdita' – Mary Robinson, Romantic author, actress, and friend to Wollstonecraft, William Godwin, and Samuel Taylor Coleridge. Austen seems especially to invoke her relationship to 'Florizel', the Prince Regent, when Charles Musgrove cries out, 'Don't talk to me about heirs and representatives', adding, 'I am not one of those who neglect the reigning power to bow to the rising sun' (*P*, 243). Austen's hatred of the reigning king's heir and representative (*Letters*, 208), together with Robinson's reputation as a victim of the amorous regent, suggest a boldly satirical allusion.

Mary Robinson, who was represented as a warning against dangerous 'gaiety', led a life of 'wanton dissipation' that reduced her to 'penury and distress'. The *Morning Post*, reporting that her constitution and 'the use of her limbs are gone; death stares her in the face', crowed that to 'view the Perdita *now*, would be a lesson indeed!'[16] But her courage was much admired when

> *a violent rheumatism ... progressively deprived her of the use of her limbs* [author's italics]. Thus ... in the pride of youth and the bloom of beauty, was this lovely and unfortunate woman reduced to a state of more than infantine helplessness. Yet, even under so severe a calamity, the powers of her mind, and the elasticity of her spirits, triumphed over the weakness of her frame. This check ... led her to the more assiduous cultivation and development of her talents.[17]

Mrs Smith's involvement with a 'thoughtless, gay set' closely resembles Perdita's (*P*, 218). So does her subsequent decline, for impoverished by an extravagant husband and crippled by severe rheumatic fever, she alters from Anne's 'useful and good' schoolfellow, the 'fine-looking, well-grown Miss Hamilton, in all the glow of health and confidence of superiority, into a poor, infirm, helpless widow'. Austen adopts Robinson's term 'elasticity' for Mrs Smith, who like her cultivates her talents. Though in pain and among strangers, she can still 'converse and be cheerful' (*P*, 165–8). This cluster of unworked fragments illustrates Austen's process, her manner of building on other authors.

Even when she did have time to revise, appropriations can occasionally remain inert. In *Sense and Sensibility*, for instance, the inset tales of Eliza Brandon and her daughter Eliza Williams are twice-told, shrink-lit versions of Richardson's *Clarissa* (1748) – that repetition of the name 'Eliza' is unusually careless. The first Eliza's flight into a life of sin recalls Lovelace's abduction of Clarissa into a brothel, while Colonel Brandon's discovery of her in a spunging-house mirrors Mr Belford's visit to the dying and imprisoned Clarissa. As faded and sickly as she, Eliza also prepares to die.

Austen swerves away, however, from Richardson's doubly fatal ending. In *Clarissa*, Colonel Morden kills Lovelace in a duel, but when, in *Sense and Sensibility*, Colonel Brandon meets Marianne Dashwood's suitor Willoughby by appointment, he does not even wound him. Nor is Marianne ruined, although her resemblance to Clarissa and the first Eliza, together with her involvement like the second Eliza with Willoughby, make her look as though she has been. Marianne's illness copies that of Clarissa and the first Eliza so closely that the worst is feared (*S&S*, 354), and yet she lives.

Austen seems to critique Richardson when, instead of Clarissa driving on to her own death, Marianne regrets her desire for 'self-destruction'. But like his heroine, she is 'guilty of no misconduct' and need suffer 'no disgrace' – Clarissa was raped while drugged, and Marianne fell literally rather than sexually. Clarissa blamed herself for her approaching death, but Marianne's regret for her family's grief and her abhorrence of herself need only be imaginary (*S&S*, 238, 390–2). Like Clarissa, she entered into a prohibited correspondence with a man; unlike her, she is granted a second chance. Thus in spite of Austen's uncharacteristically slavish reliance on *Clarissa* for the two Elizas, she manages to wrench herself away.

In the fourth category of Austen's relation to her fictional tradition, inversion signals resistance. At the start of the nineteenth century, the English novel could go in two different directions: Austen's tightly written dramas or Scott's sprawling historical novels. Austen anticipated this rivalry when, on 4 February 1813, she threatened half-jokingly to stretch out the 'rather too light & bright & sparkling' *Pride and Prejudice* with a chapter of 'solemn specious nonsense' such as a 'critique on Walter Scott', and on 28 September 1814, just before he began his brilliant career as a novelist with *Waverley*, she complained that he had 'no business to write novels, especially good ones. – It is not fair. – He has Fame & Profit enough as a Poet, and not be taking the bread out of other people's mouths – I do not like him, & do not mean to like Waverley if I can help it – but fear I must' (*Letters*, 203, 277). It is of particular interest, therefore, to observe how she undermines Scott's deference to rank in *Persuasion*.

While writing her last novel, she read *Waverley*, *The Antiquary*, and probably *Guy Mannering* as well. In the first, Scott uncritically portrays Sir Everard Waverley admiring

> the tree of his genealogy, which, emblazoned with many an emblematic mark of honour and heroic achievement, hung upon the well-varnished wainscot of his hall. The nearest descendants of Sir Hildebrand Waverley … were, as this honoured register informed him, (and indeed as he himself well knew) the Waverleys of Highley Park, com. Hants.[18]

Austen's narcissistic, solipsistic baronet holds the satiric mirror up to Scott's:

> Sir Walter Elliot, of Kellynch-hall, in Somersetshire, was a man who, for his own amusement, never took up any book but the Baronetage; there he found occupation for an idle hour, and consolation in a distressed one … there any unwelcome sensations … changed naturally into pity and contempt. As he turned over the almost endless creations of the last century – and there, if every other leaf were powerless, he could read his own history with an interest which never failed – this was the page at which the favourite volume always opened:
>
> ELLIOT OF KELLYNCH-HALL. (*P*, 3)

Austen's 'foolish, spendthrift' Sir Walter also recalls Scott's Godfrey Bertram in *Guy Mannering*, drifting 'betwixt … misfortune, and imbecillity'. As the ruined father and daughter are expelled from 'the home that has sheltered us and ours for a thousand years', he dies of 'indignant anger', his heart broken 'in the effort to leave the mansion of his forefathers'. A 'torrent of sympathy' at once bursts out in the community, with the 'ancient descent and unblemished integrity of the family' being 'respectfully remembered'.[19] Sir Walter, by pointed contrast, drives away from his ancestral home 'in very good spirits', prepared with 'condescending bows for all the afflicted tenantry and cottagers who might have had a hint to shew themselves' (*P*, 270, 38). Thus, in *Persuasion*, Austen challenges the Tory assumptions of her famous contemporary.

Scott is renowned as a realist, but in the fifth and final category of her creative process, Austen shows that she too can splice an actual event into the literary tradition. For instance, she changes the topaz crosses brought home by her brother Charles into amber, a symbol of memory appropriate for the contemplative Fanny Price in *Mansfield Park*. As conspicuous as Belinda's sparkling cross in Pope's *Rape of the Lock*, Fanny's cross invites Edmund and Henry to link their lives with hers. Her choice of Edmund's plainer chain eventually foretells her fate.

Typically in her novels, then, Jane Austen expands, complicates, and integrates elements from a tradition chosen rather than imposed. Allusions may be openly parodic, tucked inside layers of accretion, or barely acknowledged in the speed of composition. Silent assimilation suggests kinship of ideas;

inversion amounts to critique. Once recognised, these references to texts and contexts work like metaphors, doubling the allusion up and rendering the passage as multiple and reverberating as poetry. Austen's imaginative act takes place between the original text and the new one as she enlarges, enhances, and remakes them both. Perhaps her sister, Cassandra, the ideal reader who read as she read and laughed as she laughed, made Austen into the confidently allusive writer she undoubtedly was.

Paradoxically, then, Austen's awareness of the tradition makes her original. Leavis was right to say half a century ago that 'Jane Austen, in her indebtedness to others, provides an exceptionally illuminating study of the nature of originality, and she exemplifies beautifully the relations of the "individual talent" to tradition.' Her relation to tradition is creative, he says, because she 'not only makes tradition for those coming after, but her achievement has for us a retroactive effect: as we look back beyond her we see in what goes before, and see because of her, potentialities and significances brought out in such a way that, for us, she creates the tradition we see leading down to her'. Her work, 'like the work of all great creative writers, gives a meaning to the past'.[20] But he was wrong to assume her tradition was only fictional, and wrong again to speak of indebtedness when her process is so markedly interactive and transformative.

Austen's creative practice seems in fact to anticipate Coleridge's theory of the imagination. Fancy he defines as 'a mode of Memory emancipated from the order of time and space', modified by 'that empirical phenomenon of the will, which we express by the word CHOICE', and receiving 'all its materials ready made from the law of association'. But what he calls the secondary imagination 'dissolves, diffuses, dissipates, in order to re-create; or where this process is rendered impossible, yet still at all events it struggles to idealize and to unify. It is essentially *vital*, even as all objects (*as* objects) are essentially fixed and dead.'[21]

Whenever Austen heaped up fragments from books or from life, she had only just begun. In the next stage of her creativity, her secondary imagination dissolved, diffused, and dissipated the world of matter in order to recreate reality. At the last, she unified and idealized it – transcended it, even – by weaving in allusions that resonate throughout her text. Those who love Jane Austen seek out biography to know her better, but her relationship with other authors offers an entrance to her mind.

NOTE ON EDITIONS

Until recently the standard edition has been the Novels of Jane Austen, ed. R. W. Chapman, 5 vols. (Oxford: Clarendon Press, 1923; 3rd edn, 1932–4;

reissued with changes and additions by Mary Lascelles, 1965–6). This is now being superseded by the Cambridge Edition of the Works of Jane Austen, ed. Janet Todd (Cambridge: Cambridge University Press, 2005–9).

NOTES

1 F. R. Leavis, *The Great Tradition: George Eliot, Henry James, Joseph Conrad* (London: Chatto & Windus, 1960), p. 5.
2 Michel de Certeau, *The Practice of Everyday Life*, trans. Steven Randall (Berkeley: University of California Press, 1984), p. 174.
3 *Mansfield Park*, p. 461. All references to Austen's novels are to the Cambridge Edition of the Works of Jane Austen. The following abbreviations are used: *Emma* (*E*), *Juvenilia* (*J*), *Mansfield Park* (*MP*), *Persuasion* (*P*), *Sense and Sensibility* (*S&S*) *Pride and Prejudice* (*P&P*).
4 Alison Sulloway, 'Emma Woodhouse and *A Vindication of the Rights of Woman*', *The Wordsworth Circle*, 7.4 (1976), 320–32.
5 Mary Wollstonecraft, *A Vindication of the Rights of Woman* (1792), ed. Miriam Brody (Harmondsworth: Penguin Books, 1985), p. 130.
6 Humphry Repton, *Observations on the Theory and Practice of Landscape Gardening* (London: T. Bensley and Son, 1803), p. 81. Hereafter *Observations*.
7 *Fragments on the Theory and Practice of Landscape Gardening* (London: T. Bensley and Son, 1816), pp. 54–5.
8 Samuel Richardson, *The History of Sir Charles Grandison* (1753–4), 3 parts, ed. Jocelyn Harris (London: Oxford University Press, 1972; reprinted 1986, 2001), part 1, p. 206. Hereafter *Grandison*.
9 *Jane Austen's Letters*, 3rd edn, ed. Deirdre Le Faye (Oxford: Oxford University Press, 1997), p. 278. Hereafter *Letters*.
10 Maria Edgeworth, *Castle Rackrent* and *Ennui* (1800), ed. Marilyn Butler (London: Penguin Books, 1992), pp. 68–9.
11 Maria Edgeworth, *Vivian* (1812), ed. Claire Connolly with Marilyn Butler, in *The Novels and Selected Works of Maria Edgeworth*, gen. eds. Marilyn Butler and Mitzi Myers, 12 vols. (London: Pickering and Chatto, 1999), IV, pp. 230–2.
12 Marilyn Butler calls links between *Vivian* and *Mansfield Park* 'readily identifiable borrowings from a notable recent novel' that would have been picked up by practised readers as 'witty allusions and compliments' to their literacy ('Jane Austen (1775–1817)', *Oxford Dictionary of National Biography* (Oxford: Oxford University Press, 2004; online edition accessed 22 October 2004: http://oxforddnb.com/article/904).
13 Maria Edgeworth, *Patronage* (1814), ed. Connor Carville and Marilyn Butler, in *The Novels and Selected Works* (London: Pickering and Chatto, 1999), VII, pp. 75–7.
14 William Shakespeare, *Othello*, ed. Michael Neill (Oxford: Oxford University Press, 2006), 5.2.128–31.
15 Tobias Smollett, *The Expedition of Humphry Clinker* (1771), ed. Thomas R. Preston and O. M. Brack, Jr (Athens, GA: University of Georgia Press, 1990), pp. 65–7.

16 Sarah Gristwood, *Perdita: Royal Mistress, Writer, Romantic* (London: Bantam Press, 2005), p. 219; Paula Byrne, *Perdita: The Literary, Theatrical, Scandalous Life of Mary Robinson* (New York: Random House, 2004), p. 232.

17 *Perdita: The Memoirs of Mary Robinson*, ed. M. J. Levy (London: Peter Owen, 1994), pp. 123–4.

18 Walter Scott, *Waverley; Or, 'Tis Sixty Years Hence* (1814), ed. Claire Lamont (Oxford: Clarendon Press, 1981), p. 8.

19 Walter Scott, *Guy Mannering* (1815), ed. P. D. Garside (Edinburgh: Edinburgh University Press, 1999), pp. 77–8.

20 Leavis, *Great Tradition*, p. 5.

21 Samuel Taylor Coleridge, *Biographia Literaria*, ed. James Engell and W. Jackson Bate, in *The Collected Works of Samuel Taylor Coleridge*, gen. ed. Kathleen Coburn (London: Routledge & Kegan Paul, 1983), VII, i, pp. 304–5.

FURTHER READING

Butler, Marilyn, *Jane Austen and the War of Ideas*, Oxford, Clarendon Press, 1975; reprinted 1976

Romantics, Rebels and Reactionaries: English Literature and Its Background 1760–1830, Oxford, Oxford University Press, 1981

Byrne, Paula, *Jane Austen and the Theatre*, London and New York, Hambledon Press, 2002

Deresiewicz, William, *Jane Austen and the Romantic Poets*, New York, Columbia University Press, 2004

Doody, Margaret Anne, 'Jane Austen's Reading', in *Jane Austen: Critical Assessments*, ed. Ian Littlewood, 4 vols., East Sussex, Helm Information, 1998, I, pp. 173–87

Duckworth, Alistair M., *The Improvement of the Estate: A Study of Jane Austen's Novels*, Baltimore, Johns Hopkins University Press, 1971; reprinted 1994

Gay, Penny, *Jane Austen and the Theatre*, Cambridge, Cambridge University Press, 2002

Gilson, David, 'Books Owned by Jane Austen', in *A Bibliography of Jane Austen*, Oxford, Clarendon Press, 1982, pp.431–46

Grundy, Isobel, 'Jane Austen and Literary Traditions', in Edward Copeland and Juliet McMaster (eds.), *The Cambridge Companion to Jane Austen*, Cambridge, Cambridge University Press, 1997, pp. 189–210

Harris, Jocelyn, *Jane Austen's Art of Memory*, Cambridge, Cambridge University Press, 1989; reprinted 2003

'Jane Austen, Jane Fairfax, and Jane Eyre', *Persuasions*, **29** (2007), 99–109

A Revolution Almost beyond Expression: Jane Austen's 'Persuasion', Newark, University of Delaware Press, 2007

Kirkham, Margaret, *Jane Austen: Feminism and Fiction*, Sussex, Harvester Press, 1983

Knox-Shaw, Peter, *Jane Austen and the Enlightenment*, Cambridge, Cambridge University Press, 2004

Lascelles, Mary, *Jane Austen and her Art*, Oxford, Oxford University Press, 1939; reprinted 1970

Moler, Kenneth L., *Jane Austen's Art of Allusion*, Lincoln, University of Nebraska Press, 1968

Pinion, F. B., 'The Influence of Certain Writers on Jane Austen', in *A Jane Austen Companion*, London, Macmillan, 1979, pp. 158–79

Stabler, Jane, 'Literary Influences', in *Jane Austen in Context*, ed. Janet Todd, Cambridge, Cambridge University Press, 2005, pp. 41–50

Sutherland, Kathryn, *Jane Austen's Textual Lives: From Aeschylus to Bollywood*, Oxford, Oxford University Press, 2005

Tuite, Clara, *Romantic Austen: Sexual Politics and the Literary Canon*, Cambridge, Cambridge University Press, 2002

7

ALISON LUMSDEN

Walter Scott

In *The Great Tradition*, F. R. Leavis famously dismisses the fiction of Walter Scott (1771–1832), arguing in a footnote that while he was 'a great and very intelligent man' he did not have 'the creative writer's interest in literature' and 'made no serious attempt to work out his own form and break away from the bad tradition of the eighteenth-century romance'. 'Out of Scott', he concludes, 'a bad tradition came.'[1] Leavis's dismissal of Scott, whose influence had been extraordinary, sets the tone for much of twentieth-century criticism.[2] It did not in itself destroy Scott's literary reputation, but it encapsulated a negative response that was typical of the modernist period.

Certainly, there is a sense in which Scott's long, usually three-volume, novels were antithetical to modernist aesthetics. Scott's primary interest is not with the inner life, and as such he was of little interest to the modernists, who shifted the locus of fiction from the exterior to the interior. Concomitantly, while writers such as Virginia Woolf concentrate on the precise details of psychological nuance and prose style, Scott is a master of what Franco Moretti has recently called the 'filler',[3] those acts of narration which exist between and beyond the 'essential' detail, and much of the interest of his fiction lies within the significances of such 'excess' material. Woolf herself, consequently, while recognising Scott's talent for what she wryly calls 'illumination' nevertheless sees his work as essentially limited, arguing that 'he has entirely ceased to influence others'.[4] Even within Scotland, writers working within the broad parameters of modernist concerns were dismissive of Scott, suggesting that his work was a failure not only in aesthetic terms, but that that failure was symptomatic of Scotland's failure as a nation in post-union Britain. Edwin Muir, for example, launched a bitter attack on Scott, arguing that the environment in which he lived marred Scott's work. As a consequence, he concludes, 'instead of a real framework he had to fall back on legend, and so his novels consist ... of flesh and blood and pasteboard'.[5]

By the middle of the twentieth century, then, Scott's literary credit was at a low ebb, and his work had largely disappeared from the canon of the English novel. However, Scott's fiction has undergone a significant reassessment in recent years. Perhaps not surprisingly much of this re-evaluation has taken place from within Scotland, where, if Scott's work was being critiqued, it was at least being read. Much of this re-evaluation has been generated by the appearance of the Edinburgh Edition of the Waverley Novels, a thirty-volume critical edition of all Scott's fictional output (see 'Note on Editions'). The Edinburgh Edition has not only made available works by Scott that were forgotten or little read, but by providing the reader with the historical, linguistic, contextual, and explanatory material necessary to fully understand the complexity of his fiction, it has provided a new framework in which criticism of Scott's work can take place. In addition its textual work (all novels have been re-edited from the evidence of manuscripts and proofs where these are available) has provided a modern readership with a version of Scott that challenges Woolf's version of him as creating 'carelessly',[6] suggesting that while he may not have the modernist concern with precision of language and punctuation, nevertheless he does take considerably more care with narrative craft than his reputation has allowed. This new version of Scott has gone hand in hand with a critical re-evaluation which has sought to reassess his work, particularly via its relationship to Scottish national identity, suggesting that it may reveal a more complex attitude to Scotland than that identified by Muir and his contemporaries. Recent work has also sought to re-evaluate his role in the development of the novel more generally.

Scott's relationship to the canon of the English novel is, then, vexed. Regarded in recent years as primarily a Scottish novelist and a problematic one at that, and dismissed by the modernists and Leavis, we must ask why Scott should be considered here, as a writer with a significant place in the discussion of English novelists? What is his relationship to the English novel, and why, having been dismissed so thoroughly in the early twentieth century, should his work now be undergoing a reassessment which positions it not only as significant in British literature, but indeed on the world stage?

An answer to some of these questions may be found if we consider how Scott viewed his own relationship to the novel in English. While Scott never formally theorises his ideas about the novel form, nevertheless some insight is given by his many reviews – of his contemporaries such as Jane Austen and Mary Shelley – and by a series of essays that he wrote as Prefaces to a collection called *Ballantyne's Novelist's Library*, which was published in 1821–5.[7] Under this format he wrote memoirs and commentaries on writers such as Samuel Richardson, Henry Fielding, Tobias Smollett, Laurence Sterne, Horace Walpole, Daniel Defoe, and Henry Mackenzie, to whom his own first novel, *Waverley*, is dedicated. Not only do these reviews and essays provide us with an insight into Scott's thoughts on these novelists, they also serve collectively as a survey of the British novel up until Scott's own time.

Moreover, what Scott actually has to say about these novelists is revealing, for it articulates what he saw as the main issues surrounding the novel in its early manifestations. For example, in his essay on Fielding he gives an outline of the qualities he sees as necessary in a good novel: 'Force of character, strength of expression, felicity of contrast and situation, a well-constructed plot, in which the development is at once natural and unexpected, and where the interest is kept uniformly alive, till summed up by the catastrophe – all these are requisites as essential to the labour of the novelist, as to that of the dramatist' (*PW*, III, 81). Contrary to Leavis's description of Scott as a mere writer of romance, repeatedly in these essays he praises the skill of the writer in painting what is 'true to life', and correspondingly he draws analogies between the writer and an artist drawing with a pencil. In his review of Jane Austen's novels, Scott commends what he sees as a new class of literature which has manifested itself in the nineteenth century, and of which he finds Austen to be an excellent exponent. In place of 'wild variety of incident' he praises 'the art of copying from nature as she really exists in the common walks of life, and presenting to the reader, instead of the splendid scenes of an imaginary world, a correct and striking representation of that which is daily taking place around him' (*PW*, XVIII, 210).

This discussion is also cast in terms of a variation on that recurring preoccupation of the eighteenth- and nineteenth-century British novel, the essentially Aristotelian distinction between the probable and the possible: 'a fiction is unnatural when there is some assignable reason against the events taking place as described', Scott comments in relation to Austen (*PW*, XVIII, 213–14). 'On the other hand, a fiction is still *improbable*, though not *unnatural*, when there is no reason to be assigned why things should not take place as represented, except that the *over-balance of chances is* against it' (*PW*, XVIII, 214). 'Now', he concludes 'though an author who understands human nature is not likely to introduce into his fictions any thing that is unnatural, he will often have much that is improbable' (*PW*, XVIII, 216). In this context, what is of merit in Austen's novels appears to be that she offers the perfect balance of plan and probability:

> Her fables appear to us to be ... nearly faultless; they do not consist ... of a string of unconnected events which have little or no bearing on one main plot, and are introduced evidently for the sole purpose of bringing in characters and conversations; but have all the compactness of plan and unity of action which is generally produced by a sacrifice of probability: yet they have little or nothing that is not probable. (*PW*, XVIII, 224)

Moreover, he assigns Austen's skill in achieving this in part at least to her narrative style and her manipulation of what we would now call point of view:

> The vivid distinctness of description, the minute fidelity of detail, and air of unstudied ease in the scenes represented, which are no less necessary than probability of incident, to carry the reader's imagination along with the story, and give fiction the perfect appearance of reality, she possesses in a high degree; and the object is accomplished without resorting to those deviations from the ordinary plan of narrative in the third person. (*PW*, XVIII, 225)

Her skill lies, he concludes, in achieving all of this while saying 'as little as possible in her own person' (*PW*, XVIII, 228).

Not surprisingly, this discussion of the probable and the possible is also evident in Scott's essay on Defoe. For Scott, Defoe is one of the most compelling of novelists. His skill, he suggests, lies in assuming '[t]he air of writing with all the plausibility of truth', so that 'All the usual scaffolding and machinery employed in composing fictitious history are carefully discarded.' The early incidents of the tale, for example, 'which in ordinary works of invention are usually thrown out as pegs to hang the conclusion upon' are here barely mentioned, and their details 'suffered to drop out of sight' (*PW*, IV, 274–5). So, too, the exactness and precision of the author adds to this plausibility effect, so that Robinson Crusoe is delineated 'as acting and thinking precisely as such a man must have thought and acted in such an extraordinary situation' (*PW*, IV, 275). Again, as with Austen, it is Defoe's writing style that is described as contributing to this overall effect, so that his tale is told with 'the indifference of an old bucanier [*sic*], and probably in the very way in which he may have heard them recited by the actors' (*PW*, IV, 276). This detailed commentary on the work of those novelists who have gone before him serves as a reminder that, however Scott may have been positioned by modern critics, he saw himself as operating within a tradition not of the Scottish novel – a tradition which in fact barely existed, Scotland being, as Francis Jeffrey pointed out 'a quarter of the island where materials and talents for novel-writing have been supposed to be equally wanting' (*CH*, 79) – but of British fiction.

Such reflections upon the details of the novelist's craft are also embedded within the Waverley Novels themselves. This is, of course, most overt in Scott's 'Prefaces', particularly those written in the 1820s, where the author uses those fictional narrators accrued as a result of his ostensible anonymity to offer a discussion of his own processes of creativity. Collectively, such reflections suggest that Scott was not a mere naïve writer of fictions who made no attempt to move on from his eighteenth-century predecessors, but a far more reflective practitioner of his art than Leavis's critique would imply. But if Scott is indeed a more complex exponent of the novel form than has been implied, and if he does, contrary to Leavis's claim, move beyond the parameters outlined by its eighteenth-century exponents, what exactly are Scott's achievements in terms of the development of the novel, and why is his work enjoying a new critical validity?

An answer may be found if we turn to Scott's first novel, *Waverley*, published anonymously in 1814. *Waverley* is often taken as a prototype for all of Scott's fiction, and while I would resist this attempt to contain his work within a recurring pattern it remains one of the most frequently read of his novels and may serve us here as an example of how Scott's work both engages with his fictional predecessors and moves beyond the parameters of the novel outlined by them. As Ina Ferris has recognised, an overt dialogue with Fielding is in fact opened near the start of the novel, when, as she puts it, 'Scott's narrator authorizes his text by declaring in a well-known passage that "the object of my tale is more a description of men than manners."' In *Joseph Andrews* Fielding had claimed that he described 'not Men, but Manners; not an Individual but a Species'.[8] Scott's formulation, Ferris notes, 'turns Fielding on his head, prefiguring the way in which Scott's nineteenth-century historical mode of fiction will overturn the hierarchy of men and manners affirmed by Fielding's eighteenth-century satiric fictions.[9]

This view of Scott's fiction as innovative was also one shared by his contemporaries. By the time he published *Waverley* Scott's reputation was already established as one of the most successful poets of his age with narrative poems such as *Marmion* (1808) and *The Lady of the Lake* (1810) enjoying unprecedented sales. Although *Waverley* was ostensibly published anonymously several readers recognised Scott's hand and applauded his move into fiction. Maria Edgeworth, for example, praised its 'new and bold delineations of character' (*CH*, 75), while Jane Austen wrote that 'Walter Scott has no business to write novels, especially good ones' (*CH*, 74). Perhaps most interesting of contemporary reviews is that by Francis Jeffrey, however, for it both assesses what Scott has apparently taken from eighteenth-century fiction and acknowledges the ways in which he has moved beyond it. For example, echoing Scott's own praise of his fictional predecessors Jeffrey praises *Waverley* for being 'true to nature', suggesting that 'the way in which [manners and customs] are here represented must satisfy every reader, we think, by an inward *tact* [original emphasis] and conviction, that the delineation has been made from actual experience and observation' (*CH*, 79, 81). However, Jeffrey also recognises that Scott does something more than this, in that he not only presents scenes from Scottish life, but does so in a way that delineates the forces which constitute historical process in operation. 'The object of the work before us' he writes, 'was evidently to present a faithful and animated picture of the manners and state of society that prevailed in this northern part of the island, in the earlier part of the last century':

> [A]nd the author has judiciously fixed upon the era of the Rebellion in 1745, not only as enriching his pages with the interest inseparably attached to the narration of such occurrences, but as affording a fair opportunity for bringing out all the contrasted principles and habits which distinguished the different classes of persons who then divided the country, and formed among them the basis of almost all that was peculiar in the national character. (*CH*, 80)

In recognising the significance of this aspect of Scott's novel Jeffrey to some extent pre-empts what was to be a major cornerstone of Scott's reassessment in the second half of the twentieth-century, namely Georg Lukács's view that what is of greatest interest in Scott's work is the fact that it deals with historical process. By placing his characters in moments of historical tension or crisis, Lukács argues, Scott 'finds in English history the consolation that the most violent vicissitudes of class struggle have always finally calmed down into a glorious "middle way"'.[10]

Lukács's thesis on Scott is still in many ways a convincing one, and it has recently been reiterated by Murray Pittock, who argues, similarly, that 'Scott writes of history as closure, as reconciliation, and as the civic settlement of ethnic differences.'[11] Such interpretations propose that Scott's plots are provided not merely to offer romance or 'wild variety of incident' as Scott puts it himself, but are, on the contrary, devised with the 'compactness of plan and unity of action' he praised in Austen, to the end of offering an analysis of the processes which had shaped modern Scotland and, indeed, modern Britain. Scott himself suggests as much in the much quoted 'Postscript, which should have been a Preface' to *Waverley*:

> There is no European nation which, within the course of half a century, or little more, has undergone so complete a change as this kingdom of Scotland ... The gradual influx of wealth, and extension of commerce, having since united to render the present people of Scotland a class of beings as different from their grandfathers, as the existing English are from those of Queen Elizabeth's time ... But the change, though steadily and rapidly progressive, has, nevertheless, been gradual; and, like those who drift down the stream of a deep and smooth river, we are not aware of the progress we have made until we fix our eye on the now-distant point from which we set out.[12]

And it is, indeed, easy to read *Waverley* in terms of an articulation of change. In this novel Scott brings his young English hero to Scotland at a Lukácsian moment of crisis – the 1745 Jacobite Rising – and through him, and the relationships he forms with both Lowland and Highland Scots, articulates the political and national tensions that converge at this moment in British history. As most readers will know, the novel's protagonist Waverley is seduced (needless to say via the attraction of a woman, Flora Mac-Ivor) into collaborating in the Jacobite Rising, fighting at the Battle of Prestonpans, and joining Charles Edward Stuart in his march into England. He then recognises the error of his ways, his friends negotiate a pardon for him, and the stability and future of the British state is expressed in his marriage to the more sober Lowland heroine Rose Bradwardine and his decision to retire into domestic security at his family seat of Waverley-Honour. By this process, the tensions involved in historical crisis are resolved in what Lukács calls the 'glorious middle way', and, as more negative critics have suggested, those elements of the plot that have accrued to Scottish identity via the association of the defeated Jacobite cause with Highland culture are consigned to the past.

However, as any reader of *Waverley* will recognise, and as more recent criticism has suggested, this synopsis can only be a gross parody of what actually occurs in *Waverley*, and indeed what happens between or in excess of these brief details of plot encourages us to read the novel in an altogether different and more complex way. While a reading of Scott in terms of an articulation of progress and change consistent with the Enlightenment ideas of stadial development which informed Scott's views of history is plausible, it is not entirely satisfactory; quite simply, it fails to take into account large sections of what occurs in *Waverley* and, indeed, the details by which this story of British harmony is mediated to the reader.

It is a mark of the acumen with which Francis Jeffrey read Scott's novel that this feature of the text is acknowledged even in his early review. Having quoted extensively from the novel, he acknowledges that he has, nevertheless, failed to capture much of what is expressed in it. 'Such is the outline of the story', he states, 'although it is broken and diversified with so many subordinate incidents, that what we have now given, will afford but a very inadequate idea even of the narrative part of this performance' (*CH*, 82). The 'subordinate incidents' which Jeffrey recognises form much of what is significant in *Waverley* and encourage more complex readings which cut across the narrative of progress and reconciliation, to some extent explaining the enduring appeal of this text to a modern readership well rehearsed in a postmodern aesthetics of disruption and reading against the grain. Franco Moretti observes that the effect of these 'fillers' – or the events that occur beyond the bare structures of the plot – is to 'enrich and nuance the progress of the story'.[13] But they also draw attention to what has been recognised in recent years as an ongoing feature in the development of Scott's fiction: a consummate interest in the relationship between the act of storytelling and the meaning of the story.

David Hewitt was one of the first critics to acknowledge this aspect of Scott's work. Writing primarily about Scott's habit of adding introductions and notes to his texts in the Magnum Opus edition of 1829–32, Hewitt recognises what is essentially a continuing fascination with the relationship between medium and message, suggesting that '[Scott] is never absolutely confident that truth can be captured in a particular form of words; it is as though he were constantly trying to work out the relationship of the literary artifact to what it conveys'.[14] Much recent criticism has recognised this aspect of Scott's work, suggesting that he is in fact a more self-reflexive writer than traditional criticism has implied, and that much of what drives his narrative style is an ongoing exploration of the potential and limitations of the novel form, particularly its capacity to articulate and communicate the past.

This becomes apparent if we revisit *Waverley*. While a Lukácsian reading can account for the bare bones of the story, it is what goes on in excess of this that is really of interest. While the main trajectory of the narrative may collude in a discourse of reconciliation with Scotland being subsumed into a peaceful British union, there are elements in the text that clearly operate to disrupt this reading.[15] For example, while the voices of Jacobite dissent are seemingly silenced at the end of the novel, this is disrupted by the power which is given to them in the main body of the narrative. As generations of readers of Scott have acknowledged, his descriptions of Scotland, and in particular the Highlands and Highlanders, have a powerful appeal for both his contemporary and modern readership; 'Through Scott the aura of romance finally settled upon Scotland' writes Andrew Hook: 'all those aspects of Scotland that had already acquired considerable romantic appeal – now appeared in a new and totally irresistible form'.[16] His claim is justified, for example, by the Highland tourist boom that was inspired by Scott's novels, and by the number of paintings that appeared in response to them. More importantly, however, while in the past some critics have seen this tendency in Scott as no more than the 'reduction of Scottish history to a set of stories',[17] postmodern critics have recognised that our understanding of the past can only ever be a set of discourses mediated through the eyes of a series of subjective observers. There can be, we now accept, no essentialist model of the past but, indeed, *only* a series of stories, and the significance of such stories, and what they mean for our understanding of the past, is part of what Scott is, in fact, exploring in his text.

This is apparent in the much-debated ending to *Waverley*. At the close of the narrative and in the wake of Culloden (a seminal event in the narrative of Scottish identity which Scott chooses to leave out of his tale of the '45), the novel's hero is married to the daughter of a Lowland Jacobite, Rose

Bradwardine. Her father having forfeited his estates as a result of his participation in the Rising, Waverley uses his newfound wealth as a result of his own father's death to buy the estate. He restores it to its original glory and presents it to Rose's father. As all readers of the novel will recall, however, 'There was one addition to this fine old apartment ... which drew tears into the Baron's eyes':

> It was a large and animated painting, representing Fergus Mac-Ivor and Waverley in their Highland dress, the scene a wild, rocky, and mountainous pass, down which the clan were descending in the back-ground. It was taken from a spirited sketch, drawn while they were in Edinburgh by a young man of high genius, and had been painted on a full length scale by an eminent London artist. Raeburn himself, (whose Highland chiefs do all but walk out of the canvas) could not have done more justice to the subject; and the ardent, fiery, and impetuous character of the unfortunate Chief of Glennaquoich was finely contrasted with the contemplative, fanciful, and enthusiastic expression of his happier friend. Beside this painting were hung the arms which Waverley had borne in the unfortunate civil war. (*W*, 361)

While some critics have seen this artifact at the heart of *Waverley*'s conclusion as a problematic consignment of the Highlands, Highlanders, and all that they have come to signify in the novel to the past and to the safe and contained realms of art, the painting can be read in a very different way.[18] Unless we are to believe that Scott felt art had no power at all (which seems unlikely given his constant analogies between novel-writing and graphic art), the painting, becoming a synecdoche for the novel itself, acts as a disruptive reminder of an uncomfortable event in Britain's recent past, and one which refuses to be silenced in spite of the seeming trajectory of the novel and British history. In this sense, therefore, the painting stands as yet another marker of what is in excess of the seeming containment of the story, since it spills out from the apparent fairyland that Waverley has created at Tully-Veolan, so that the reader cannot be allowed to conclude that everything is just as it was before.

The ending of *Waverley* is, then, problematic, and it sets the tone for what was to become a series of problematic endings in the Waverley novels. Repeatedly Scott's texts refuse to settle down into any straightforward closure but, on the contrary, erupt out of their apparent conclusions to suggest alternative possibilities. *The Tale of Old Mortality* (1816), for example, ends with the tragic death of one of its male protagonists, Lord Evandale, in the arms of his lover, only to have the more comic story of the marriage of this lover to the second male protagonist, Henry Morton, recounted as if at the insistence of his readership via the unlikely (and unauthoritative) source of a conversation with Miss Buskbody, a local Mantua-maker. As such two versions of the story of Scotland's past, and by implication her role within the British state, are allowed to coexist at the end of this text. Arguably Scott's greatest novel *The Heart of Mid-Lothian* (1818) also continues beyond its point of natural closure, where the heroine wins the pardon for her sister for which she has walked from Edinburgh to London. Scott added a whole additional volume to describe the events that take place after this moment of comic conclusion. The extra volume of *The Heart of Mid-Lothian* (it is one of only two novels that are four volumes in length rather than three) epitomises Scott's problematic relationship with conventional narrative closure, and, as so often in Scott's texts, the excess volume is used to problematise the story of national identity which the novel has offered and to disrupt the apparent discourse of reconciliation within which it has been set.

But if Scott disrupts conventional closure, he also problematises the openings of his texts. While he was to add further layers of introduction in the Magnum Opus edition, many of his novels are prefaced by introductory chapters even in their first-edition formats. Often these frames play upon the anonymous publication of the Waverley Novels, speculating on the role of authorship and authority, so that, as many critics have recognised, they offer a critique of the process of fiction writing itself. *The Tale of Old Mortality*, for example, is prefaced by an account of the figure of Old Mortality and his ongoing task of cleaning and repairing the graves of Scottish Covenanters so that their memorials remain readable. Scott's novel, like Old Mortality's cleaning of the graves, becomes a way of keeping the past alive and offering a commemoration of it. By such self-reflexive moments, the author thus comments upon his own narrative strategies.

It was, however, in the novels of the 1820s that Scott's most overtly self-reflexive Prefaces were to be written, specifically in the Introductory chapters of *Ivanhoe* (1820), *The Fortunes of Nigel* (1822), and *Peveril of the Peak* (1822), where Scott has his fictional narrators come together to discuss the practice of writing novels. At the point when he was writing these texts, Scott was at the height of his fictional career, 12,000 copies being the standard print run of his novels, well above the average for the period. It is, then, perhaps hardly surprising that he should have indulged himself in fictional game-playing in these Prefaces. However, there is also a serious point to them, and the 'Prefatory' and 'Introductory' chapters to these three texts, taken together, offer us an indication of the central problematics which vex Scott throughout his writing career.

There is insufficient space to deal with all of them here, but it is interesting to note that Scott's more vigorous period of Preface-writing coincides with a marked shift in subject-matter in the Waverley Novels. In spite of his original stated aim of writing fiction to '[preserve] some idea of the ancient manners' of Scotland (*W*, 363), it is clear that even by 1818 Scott was growing somewhat weary of Scottish subjects. In 1820, therefore, he dramatically relocated his subject-matter to England and, even more dramatically, beyond any kind of living and collective memory by setting it in the wake of the Norman conquests during the reign of Richard I. The novel that ensued, *Ivanhoe*, is arguably his great novel of English identity, and it secured his international reputation.

The Dedicatory Epistle to *Ivanhoe* is typical of the kind of self-reflexivity to be found in the 1820s, and in it Scott offers an unusually overt insight into the problems involved in writing historical novels. Supposedly written by the novel's author Laurence Templeton to the Rev. Dr Dryasdust, Scott's *alter ego* lays out the difficulties he sees in writing a novel of the English Middle Ages and, with a characteristic side-step, pre-empts criticism by acknowledging that 'the more grave antiquary will perhaps class [this publication] with the idle novels and romances of the day'.[19] Interestingly, Templeton's outline of the difficulties he foresees is framed in precisely the same terms as that debate between the probable and the possible that Scott is writing about elsewhere at this time in relation to the eighteenth-century English novel. One of the difficulties Templeton observes, for example, is that while a wilder and more ancient version of society is still remembered in Scotland, the author has to look much farther back into England's past to find a moment that shows the process of change that he is trying to articulate. The consequence, he suggests, is that the boundaries between the probable, the possible, and the impossible must be renegotiated; different standards to those which apply to tales of Scotland's past come into play. If one describes wild manners in Scotland to an English reader, he argues, he is inclined to believe them for 'he had either never seen those remote districts at all, or he had wandered through those desolate regions in the course of a summer-tour, eating bad dinners, sleeping on truckle beds, stalking from desolation to desolation, and fully prepared to believe the strangest things that could be told him of a people wild and extravagant enough to be attached to scenery so extraordinary' (*I*, 7). However, the boundaries of what will be accepted are altogether different when the novel is set in England:

> But the same worthy person, when placed in his own snug parlour, and surrounded by all the comforts of an Englishman's fire-side, is not half so much disposed to believe that his own ancestors led a very different life from himself; that the shattered tower, which now forms a vista from his window, once held a baron who would have hung him up at his own door without any form of trial; that the hinds, by whom his little pet-farm is managed, would have, a few centuries ago, been his slaves; and that the complete influence of feudal

> tyranny once extended over the neighbouring village, where the attorney is now a man of more importance than the lord of the manor. (*I*, 7–8)

As a result of this observation the fictional author of *Ivanhoe* outlines a set of rules by which to negotiate this tricky set of boundaries between probability and improbability in composition. While suggesting that his task is not insurmountable because 'opinions, habits of thinking, and actions' (*I*, 10) are constants of the human condition, he nevertheless sets out his own standards:

> The painter must introduce no ornament inconsistent with the climate or country of his landscape; he must not plant cypress trees upon Inch-Merrin, or Scottish firs among the ruins of Persepolis; and the author lies under a corresponding restraint. However far he may venture in a more full detail of passions and feelings, than is to be found in the ancient compositions which he imitates, he must introduce nothing inconsistent with the manners of the age; his knights, squires, grooms, and yeomen, may be more fully drawn than in the hard, dry delineations of an ancient illuminated manuscript, but the character and costume of the age must remain inviolate; they must be the same figures, drawn by a better pencil, or, to speak more modestly, executed in an age when the principles of art were better understood. His language must not be exclusively obsolete and unintelligible; but he should admit, if possible, no word or turn of phraseology betraying an origin directly modern. (*I*, 11)

However, in spite of this rather pompous statement by Laurence Templeton, the novel that Scott actually writes plays more complex games with the balance between probable and possible than this would imply. Indeed, the whole text seems to pivot on the intersection between what its author perceives as the balance between the probable, the possible, and the impossible, while simultaneously opening up spaces that invite the reader to consider possibilities beyond those circumscribed by the borders of period, history, and social convention. The tension that results in many ways encapsulates Scott's whole method of working throughout his novelistic career. While as a historical novelist he is unusually bound by the constraints of what is possible since he cannot change the course of history, he repeatedly also offers the reader that which is in excess of closure, conclusion, and the broad trajectories of historical process, opening up alternative, and often disruptive counter-narratives which offer a challenge to the very parameters of the possible by which his work appears to be delineated.

While the dynamics that operate within *Waverley* can be read in this way, it is also a process at work within *Ivanhoe*. As Templeton points out, the author of a work on medieval England is obliged to keep within such parameters of probability. For *Ivanhoe*, which deals with the codes of the Knights Templar, this involves operating within apparently strict boundaries and following the codes of chivalric values. Scott was perhaps better acquainted with these values than many, having written the *Encyclopaedia Britannica* entry on 'Chivalry' and, as the notes to the Edinburgh Edition of *Ivanhoe* indicate, having absorbed a great deal of relevant literature. However, it is clear that throughout this text Scott is repeatedly straining against the boundaries of what is probable within the period by offering us perspectives and attitudes that push beyond their twelfth-century parameters.

The best and most obvious example of this can be found in the scene where Wilfred of Ivanhoe lies wounded at Torquilstone while it is being attacked from without. Hearing the noise of battle outside, the wounded Ivanhoe, conforming to the probable sensibilities of his time and class, was 'glowing with impatience at his inactivity, and with ... ardent desire to mingle in the affray of which these sounds were the introduction' (*I*, 243). However, he cannot participate and instead must make do with a description of the battle by Rebecca the Jew who tends him in a medical capacity. But war is, as Ivanhoe tells her, '"no maiden's pastime"' (*I*, 243), and in fact Rebecca's description of what occurs serves as a critique of the chivalric (and warlike) values that seem to circumscribe the text. Ivanhoe attempts to explain to Rebecca '"how impossible it is for one trained to actions of chivalry, to remain passive as a priest, or a woman, when they are acting deeds of honour around him"'. But Rebecca, undermining this discourse, asks what remains to him as the prize of all the blood he has spilled. 'Glory', he responds, but again this is undercut by her answer:

> 'Glory?' continued Rebecca; 'alas, is the rusted mail which hangs as a hatchment over the champion's dim and mouldering tomb – is the defaced sculpture of the inscription which the ignorant monk can hardly read to the inquiring pilgrim – are these sufficient rewards for the sacrifice of every kindly affection, for a life spent miserably that ye make others miserable?' (*I*, 249)

While Ivanhoe may defend chivalry and tell Rebecca that she '"speakest ... of thou knowest not what"' (*I*, 249), Rebecca's words nevertheless, along with many aspects of the text, serve as a counterpoint to the discourse of chivalry which may appear on the surface to operate within this narrative.[20]

And as so often in Scott's texts this negotiation of the boundary between probable and possible is also inscribed within the ending. While *Ivanhoe* closes with its protagonist marrying the Saxon Rowena, thus, on the face of it, marking the reconciliation of Norman and Saxon factions within England, Rebecca, expelled as a Jew from this new England, haunts the end of the tale, recurring to the mind of Ivanhoe, and, of course, the reader, thus disrupting the apparent reconciliation at its conclusion. As Graham Tulloch puts it: 'Alongside the wedding of Ivanhoe and Rowena, the final chapter offers us another conclusion, not of reconciliation and harmony but of exclusion.'[21] Working within the parameters of the possible, Scott cannot have Ivanhoe marry Rebecca, but there are few readers of the novel who do not regret this; as such her presence in the text allows Scott to construct alternative possibilities that break out of the conventions he has set for himself.

If we recognise these aspects of Scott's work it is hardly surprising that his contemporaries should have regarded him not as a stale imitator of eighteenth-century fiction but as an innovator in the novel form, since it is clear that he takes the parameters of fiction set out by writers such as Defoe, Fielding, and Richardson and moves beyond them. Providing his readers with far more structured plots than those suggested by 'wild romance', he also renegotiates the boundaries of possible, probable, and impossible that he recognised as operating within his predecessors, extending them to allow dissonant voices to appear within his texts. As a consequence, disruptive discourses coexist within the seeming narratives of reconciliation that constitute the Waverley Novels, offering alternative versions of the past, nationhood, and even gender experience. What is perhaps more surprising, however, is that having been dismissed by the modernists, it is this innovative version of Scott that is being rediscovered today. Recent criticism has begun to look at Scott's position beyond Scottish literature, placing it in both a transatlantic and a European context. As Ian Duncan has put it recently, Scott's work casts a long and influential shadow, and it is one that falls not only on the novel in English but also on the development of the form in world literature.[22]

NOTE ON EDITIONS

The best edition of Scott's fiction is the Edinburgh Edition of the Waverley Novels (Edinburgh University Press, 1993–). Selected titles in this edition, including *Ivanhoe*, have been reprinted by Penguin in paperback. The best paperback edition of *Waverley* is Claire Lamont's Oxford World's Classics edition (1986).

NOTES

1 F. R. Leavis, *The Great Tradition: George Eliot, Henry James, Joseph Conrad* (London: Chatto & Windus, 1948), pp. 5–6.

2 John O. Hayden (ed.), *Scott: The Critical Heritage* (London: Routledge & Kegan Paul, 1970), cites commentaries from Austen, Stendhal, Balzac, Stevenson, and Twain, to name only a few of the many novelists who had read and absorbed Scott's work. Hereafter *CH*.

3 Franco Moretti, 'Serious Century', in *The Novel*, ed. Franco Moretti, 2 vols. (Princeton and Oxford: Princeton University Press, 2006), I, p. 367.

4 Virginia Woolf, 'Sir Walter Scott', in *Collected Essays* (London: Hogarth Press, 1966), I, p. 139. E. M. Forster also famously attacked Scott in *The Art of Fiction* (London: Edward Arnold, 1941).
5 Edwin Muir, *Scott and Scotland: The Predicament of the Scottish Writer* (London: George Routledge and Sons, 1936), p. 173.
6 Woolf, *Collected Essays*, p. 142.
7 These are republished in *The Prose Works of Sir Walter Scott, Bart.*, 28 vols. (Edinburgh: Robert Cadell, 1834–6). Hereafter *PW*.
8 Henry Fielding, *Joseph Andrews*, ed. Martin C. Battestin (Oxford: Clarendon Press, 1967), p. 189.
9 Ina Ferris, *The Achievement of Literary Authority: Gender, History and the Waverley Novels* (Ithaca and London: Cornell University Press, 1991), p. 96.
10 Georg Lukács, *The Historical Novel*, trans. Hannah Mitchell and Stanley Mitchell (London: Merlin Press, 1962), p. 32.
11 Murray Pittock, 'Introduction: Scott and the European Nationalities Question', in *The Reception of Scott in Europe*, ed. Murray Pittock, Athlone Critical Traditions (London and New York: Continuum, 2006), p. 2.
12 Walter Scott, *Waverley*, ed. P. D. Garside, Edinburgh Edition of the Waverley Novels (Edinburgh: Edinburgh University Press, 2007), p. 363. Hereafter *W*.
13 Moretti, 'Serious Century', p. 368.
14 David Hewitt, 'Walter Scott', in *The History of Scottish Literature*, vol. III, ed. Douglas Gifford (Aberdeen: Aberdeen University Press, 1988), p. 69.
15 Recent critical works by Caroline McCracken-Flesher and Julian Meldon D'Arcy have both offered convincing readings of Scott's work that serve to reposition the ways in which it deals with Scottish identity (see 'Further Reading').
16 Andrew Hook, 'Scotland and Romanticism: The International Scene', in *The History of Scottish Literature*, vol. II, ed. Andrew Hook (1987), p. 319.
17 Cairns Craig, 'The Body in the Kit-Bag: History and the Scottish Novel', *Cencrastus*, 1 (Autumn 1979), p. 20.
18 For a sceptical reading of the end of the novel see, for example, Claire Lamont's introduction to her edition of *Waverley* (Oxford: Oxford World's Classics, 1986), p. xiv, and for a more revisionist position Ian Duncan's essay '*Waverley*', in Moretti, *The Novel*, II, p. 175.
19 Walter Scott, *Ivanhoe*, ed. Graham Tulloch, Edinburgh Edition of the Waverley Novels (Edinburgh: Edinburgh University Press, 1998), p. 5. Hereafter *I*.
20 Graham Tulloch elaborates on this critique of chivalry in the Introduction to his edition of *Ivanhoe* (London: Penguin, 2000), p. xxii. Judith Wilt also comments on this passage in *Secret Leaves: The Novels of Walter Scott* (Chicago: University of Chicago Press, 1981), p. 41.
21 Tulloch, 'Introduction', p. xxv.
22 Ian Duncan, *Scott's Shadow: The Novel in Romantic Edinburgh* (Princeton: Princeton University Press, 2007).

FURTHER READING

D'Arcy, Julian Meldon, *Subversive Scott: The Waverley Novels and Scottish Nationalism*, Reykjavik, Iceland University Press, 2005

Duncan, Ian, *Scott's Shadow: The Novel in Romantic Edinburgh*, Princeton, Princeton University Press, 2007

Ferris, Ina, *The Achievement of Literary Authority: Gender, History and the Waverley Novels*, Ithaca and London, Cornell University Press, 1991

Gaston, Patricia S., *Prefacing the Waverley Prefaces: A Reading of Sir Walter Scott's Prefaces to the Waverley Novels*, New York, Peter Lang, 1991

Hayden, John O. (ed.), *Scott: The Critical Heritage*, London, Routledge & Kegan Paul, 1970

Hewitt, David, 'Walter Scott', in *The History of Scottish Literature*, vol. III, ed. Douglas Gifford, Aberdeen, Aberdeen University Press, 1988, pp. 65–85

Hook, Andrew, 'Scotland and Romanticism: The International Scene', in *The History of Scottish Literature*, vol. II, ed. Andrew Hook, Aberdeen, Aberdeen University Press, 1987, pp. 307–21

Jones, Catherine, *Literary Memory: Scott's Waverley Novels and the Psychology of Narrative*, Lewisburg, PA, Bucknell University Press, 2003

McCracken-Flesher, Caroline, *Possible Scotlands: Walter Scott and the Story of Tomorrow*, Oxford, Oxford University Press, 2005

McGann, Jerome, 'Walter Scott's Romantic Postmodernity', in *Scotland and the Borders of Romanticism*, ed. Leith Davis, Ian Duncan, and Janet Sorensen, Cambridge, Cambridge University Press, 2004, pp. 113–29

Muir, Edwin, *Scott and Scotland: The Predicament of the Scottish Writer*, London, George Routledge and Sons, 1936

Pittock, Murray (ed.), *The Reception of Scott in Europe*, Athlone Critical Traditions, London and New York, Continuum, 2006

8

ROBERT DOUGLAS-FAIRHURST

Charles Dickens

> They used to say I was an odd child, and I suppose I was. I am an odd man, perhaps. 'Gone Astray', *Household Words*, 13 August 1853

Going astray

Ever since John Forster published Dickens's autobiographical fragment in his *Life of Charles Dickens*, readers have known about the main events that marked Dickens's childhood and continued to trouble him as an adult: his father's arrest for bankruptcy and time in the Marshalsea prison; the period he spent working as a 'poor little drudge' in Warren's blacking warehouse; and his loneliness as he wandered the streets of London, slowly sinking into the dirt and misery of those other poor drudges living on the edges of recognition, never more than a few shillings away from his 'vagabond existence' hardening into a permanent way of life.

> The deep remembrance of the sense I had of being utterly neglected and hopeless; of the shame I felt in my position; of the misery it was to my young heart to believe that, day by day, what I had learned, and thought, and delighted in, and raised my fancy and emulation up by, was passing from me, never to be brought back any more; cannot be written.[1]

But it could be rewritten.

Throughout his career, the figure of an innocent child lost in the city is one that Dickens returns to like someone touching a bruise, at once drawing him back and driving him on. In 'Gone Astray', for example, an essay first published in *Household Words* in 1853, he explains how, as 'a very small boy indeed, both in years and stature, I got lost one day in the City of London',[2] and as the essay develops, what starts off as a sliver of autobiography quickly takes on the resonance of a founding myth. Although Dickens reports that he was taken to see the outside of St Giles's church in an attempt 'to quench my romantic fire, and bring me to a practical state' (*HW*, 156), once he has been lost by his guardian, or given him the slip, his adventures are described in a way that brings these rival modes of perception together into the characteristic double-act of his adult narrative style. Whether contemplating every merchant as 'a compound of Mr Fitz-Warren and Sinbad the Sailor' (*HW*, 160), or going to the theatre to watch a play in which the villain 'threw himself into the ocean from the summit of a curious rock, presenting something of the appearance of a pair of steps' (*HW*, 164), the transformative powers of the imagination repeatedly knock up against the urge to deflate and debunk. 'Up courts and down courts', Dickens recalls, 'in and out of yards and little squares – peeping into counting-house passages and running away – poorly feeding the echoes in the court of the South Sea House with my timid steps – roaming down into Austin Friars, and wondering how the Friars used to like it – ever staring at the British merchants, and never tired of the shops – I rambled on, all through the day' (*HW*, 160–1). The sentence too wanders and wonders, just as the essay as a whole repeatedly shifts gear between reportage, fairy-tale, and parable,[3] and in doing so it brilliantly dramatises the first stirrings of a young writer's mind as he encounters the world and establishes his place within it: syntax as a journey of self-discovery.

By the end of the essay, Dickens's narrative persona has given himself up to a watchman and been restored to his family, just as his real childhood self was eventually removed from the blacking warehouse and set on the path to success. However, his conclusion that 'I have gone astray since, many times, and farther afield' (*HW*, 165) refers to more than his adult obsession with pacing the same London streets, as if unsure whether he was trying to wind himself ever tighter in the coils of his past or pick up enough speed to escape its gravitational pull. It is also a knowing allusion to an idea that lies at the heart of his fiction: the child who is lost and found again, forever shadowed by the alternative stories of the waifs and strays who are lost for ever. From *Oliver Twist* (1837–9) to *David Copperfield* (1849–50) and beyond, the figure of the lost child reappears in ever more strange and haunting forms, as when Arthur Clennam, light-headed with want of sleep and food, worries that his mind is 'going astray' and is revived by the appearance of Little Dorrit ('"Your own poor child come back!"' (*LD*, 631)), or when the imprisoned Dr Manette, in *A Tale of Two Cities* (1859), tries to make sense of his daughter's sudden reappearance by touching her hair ('In the midst of the action he went astray, and, with another deep sigh, fell to work at his shoemaking'), and is only recalled to his senses by being taken in her arms and 'rocked … on her breast like a child' (*TTC*, 54).[4]

The foundling who earns his reward by discovering his origins is, of course, a stock literary figure, bringing together many of Dickens's formative influences as a novelist: Shakespeare's plays, Fielding's novels, popular melodramas, fairy-tales. But Dickens's use of the figure is not only a matter of plot; it is also a matter of style. Of all the buried selves and doubles that lurk in his fiction, the most important is the one that animates his own narrative voice: a childlike ability to be enchanted by the everyday, or what 'Gone Astray' describes as 'the marvellousness of everything' (*HW*, 160). Consequently, even when he is busily peopling his novels with images of his own potentially lost self – *Nicholas Nickleby*'s (1838–9) battered Smike, *Bleak House*'s (1852–3) ignorant Jo, the anonymous and absent lad in *The Old Curiosity Shop* (1840–1) who has been transported after being 'led astray' by wicked companions (*OCS*, 342) – his writing offers itself as a model of recovery, revealing a world that retained its capacity to surprise if seen through the right pair of eyes. As he noted when composing the latter stages of *The Old Curiosity Shop*, 'Keep the child in view'[5] – a local reminder to himself not to lose track of Little Nell in the dense weave of his plot which takes on the force of a more general piece of advice as his career develops. In its resistance to cliché, its openness to change, its overwhelming desire to love and be loved, his fiction sets out to keep the child in view and in hearing. Even when he is pointing out the dangers of treating the world as a living fairy-tale (David Copperfield's description of his 'fairy marriage' to sweet, silly Dora quietly acknowledges his error as well as the dazzle of his love when he notes that 'I am astray, and seem to see nothing' (*DC*, 614)), he is practising a childlike refusal to take anything for granted, least of all the genre or tone of his own voice.

A number of critics have wondered whether Dickens's childhood experiences can be held to account for a certain immaturity in his social and political thinking. Although he is often thought of as a social critic, argues George Orwell, 'He has no constructive suggestions, not even a clear grasp of the society he is attacking, only an emotional perception that something is wrong ... Whenever he departs from this emotional attitude he goes astray.'[6] For George Gissing, on the other hand, Dickens's greatness as a novelist resides precisely in the fact that he was unable to distinguish between what was true and what was rhetorically effective: 'Sadly as Dickens was led astray, now and then, by his melodramatic impulses, it is none the less one of his great qualities; in the best moments, it enables him to give tragic significance to the commonplace, and all through his finer work it helps to produce what one may call a romantic realism.'[7] Gissing's sympathy with Dickens is clear in that phrase 'romantic realism', which echoes Dickens's own preface to *Bleak House*, a short burst of self-justification which was also the closest he came to a literary manifesto: 'I have purposely dwelt upon the romantic side of familiar things' (*BH*, 6). However, Gissing's 'now and then' and 'best moments' also draw our attention to the most common critical complaint about Dickens, variations on which have dogged his reputation from the earliest reviews onwards, which is that while he is a genius of the sharp-eyed glimpse and the sharp-eared one-liner, he is less adept at weaving them together into a tight narrative pattern; that his style is too intimate with the stray figures it describes to capture the workings of society as a whole; that even if 'trifles make the sum of life', as David Copperfield claims (*DC*, 749), they do not necessarily add up to a satisfactory novel.

Dickens was far from alone among his contemporaries in wondering what form the novel should take or absorbing this question into the texture of his own writing. Looking at the England of 1851, Charles Kingsley also described it in a way that celebrated its diversity while worrying about its potential incoherence: '"See, I say, what a chaos of noble materials is here, – all confused, it is true, – polarised, jarring, and chaotic, – here bigotry, there self-will, superstition, sheer Atheism often, but only waiting for the one inspiring Spirit to organise, and unite, and consecrate this chaos into the noblest polity the world ever saw realised!"'[8] Like the London of 'Gone Astray', one notices here the self-extending syntax that seeks meaningful connections and patterns, but repeatedly threatens to break down, until the sentence gains a sense of momentum and direction as it reaches towards that final word 'realised'. In Dickens's novels, similarly, the growing complexity of the world manifests itself in bulging lists and narrative indirections, as his writing repeatedly threatens to collapse under its own weight of detail, even as he is sustaining a line of plot that promises to lead his readers out of the labyrinth. On the page, at least, the clutter of life can be resolved into a meaningful pattern, a redemption of contingency.

That is the theory, anyway. In practice, what many readers have found is that although Dickens sometimes toyed with the idea of the novelist as a benevolent 'Spirit' ruling his creation,[9] what drives his imagination is something far harder to organise into a settled 'polity': the unruly energies of his characters. Whereas the characters of other novelists can appear to exist principally to carry the events of their plot, Dickens's figures often seem larger than the novels attempting to contain them, drawing events into their orbit through sheer force of personality. Many of them seem less like human beings than emanations of their environment – *Oliver Twist*'s Fagin emerging from the poisonous atmosphere of the slums like a three-dimensional shadow, or *Our Mutual Friend*'s (1864–5) polished but superficial Veneerings presenting themselves as 'bran-new people in a bran-new house in a bran-new quarter of London' (*OMF*, 6) – as if giving grotesquely literal embodiment to that central Victorian worry that character is formed by circumstance. And yet, when engaged in dialogue or marshalled into the service of a plot, they can give the impression of being reluctant participants. However hard Dickens tries to turn *Martin Chuzzlewit* (1843–4) into a sustained warning against selfishness, the novel's presiding spirit remains the soliloquising Mrs Gamp. However long his reader spends in the company of *The Old Curiosity Shop*'s Little Nell, she cannot compete with the fire-drinking, dog-baiting, wife-beating energy of Quilp, her demonic double, who seems gleefully aware that so long as she is obliged to sustain the novel's main plot he is free to caper in the margins; *The Old Curiosity Shop* needs Quilp, but Quilp does not need *The Old Curiosity Shop*. Repeatedly, in Dickens's fiction, the details rebel against the whole; centre and periphery keep swapping places. Indeed, if one were to claim Dickens as the exponent of a single type of novel, it would be as a Gothic novelist; not in the sense of being interested in monsters and ghosts (though he is frequently drawn to both, as aspects of narrative style no less than as compelling kinds of subject-matter), but in the sense that Ruskin described the Gothic in *The Stones of Venice* (1851–3): a democratic aesthetic in which proportion gives way to proliferation, the ludicrous rubs up against the fearful, and the individual asserts itself within the assembled group.[10] Or, as Orwell pithily put it, when arguing that Dickens's parts are infinitely greater than his wholes, 'He is all fragments, all details – rotten architecture, but wonderful gargoyles.'[11]

Parts and wholes

As a number of more recent critics have pointed out, the charge that Dickens was brilliant but wayward applies far better to the early novels than the later ones. In moving away from the picaresque narratives of *The Pickwick Papers* (1836–7) or *Nicholas Nickleby*, Dickens's novels are constructed on increasingly ambitious plans, in which he attempts to keep the centrifugal energies of individual episodes in check through the centripetal force of a common theme. (In *The Pickwick Papers* the debtors' prison is a brief narrative interlude; in *Little Dorrit* it is the novel's inescapable centre.) The surviving rough notes for these later novels show how adept Dickens was becoming at creating complications for himself and then tidying them away, even if his writing remained haunted by the fear of how easily the novelist could turn into a figure like Jo in *Bleak House*, forever fighting against the waste piling up on the crossing he is trying to keep clean. A narrative voice that had started by moving onward now concentrated more on moving inward, burrowing into the characters whose lives are drawn together and drawn apart by the relentless rhythms of the city. 'London! – that great large place! – nobody – not even Mr. Bumble – could ever find him there!' is Oliver Twist's first thought when looking to escape into the anonymous bustle of the city's streets (*OT*, 54). What distinguishes Dickens's later novels, according to his more sympathetic critics, is his ability to turn this experience of London into a narrative form, by losing his readers in a tangle of close-up details and then revealing the threads of connection that link them all together. In a world that was becoming increasingly complex, and potentially illegible even to the most patient reader, Dickens's novels offered themselves as both a diagnosis and a form of therapy – a maze that resolves itself into a map.

There is some truth in this critical view, as there is in the claim that it was the pressures of serialisation that taught Dickens how to link the weekly or monthly parts of his novel together. Dickens's chosen mode of publication dovetailed neatly with some of his key preoccupations in these later novels, such as the stubborn persistence of the past – an idea that was written into the very form of serial novels such as *Little Dorrit* or *David Copperfield*, as each part asked its original readers to cast their minds back weeks or months in order to establish what needed to be remembered and what could safely be abandoned. In *Great Expectations* (1860–1), for example, Pip describes the 'dust-coloured' coat worn by Orlick: 'The watchman made more light of the matter than I did, and naturally; not having my reason for attaching weight to it' (*GE*, 300). One question confronting the reader, though, just as it confronts Pip, is how to tell which details can be made light of and which carry significant weight. When Jaggers tells his housekeeper to show off her wrist, she appeals to him 'with her eyes attentively and entreatingly fixed upon him' (*GE*, 196). More than twenty pages later, when Estella is icily refusing Pip's romantic overtures, he asks himself 'What *was* it that was borne in upon my mind when she stood still and looked attentively at me?' (*GE*, 217). One word – 'attentively' – is the trigger that would give him the answer he is seeking, that Jaggers's housekeeper is in fact Estella's mother, but it would take an unusually attentive reader to make the connection before he does. Similarly, when Wemmick fires his gun at sunset, Pip describes how it 'went off with a bang that shook the crazy little box of a cottage as if it must fall to pieces' (*GE*, 191). From one point of view, this is simply a realistic account of what happens if you use a cannon near a small wooden house, but from another point of view – the one which indicates Pip's consciousness of 'a vague something' nagging away at his thoughts – it also represents the shockwaves still reverberating from the guns firing to warn of Magwitch's escape and the 'small bundle of shivers' he encounters on the Kent marshes (*GE*, 1). As Pip will shortly discover with Magwitch's dramatic re-entry into his life, not everyone announces their arrival in the organised manner of Wemmick's DIY butler, with its 'ghostly tumbling open' of little wooden flaps inscribed 'John' or 'Miss Skiffins' (*GE*, 268); not everyone can be as snugly cut off from the outside world as the Aged P. And such lessons are to be learned by the reader alongside Pip, because at no stage are we given enough information to be able to distinguish with any certainty which details are key elements of plot and which merely the clutter of everyday description. Like so many of Dickens's narratives, *Great Expectations* brings together straightforwardness and stealth in a way that asks us to reflect on more than our reading of novels; it also asks us to reassess how we understand ourselves, each other, the world.

Not everyone was convinced by Dickens's attempts to subdue his great eccentrics to the demands of plot or symbolism. In 1858 Walter Bagehot complained that the novelist's 'irregular mind' manifested itself in 'incoherency of incident and aberration of character', and concluded that these two flaws were inextricably related:

> Interesting stories are founded on the intimate relations of men and women. These intimate relations are based not on their superficial traits, or common occupations, or most visible externalities, but on the inner life of heart and feeling. You simply divert attention from that secret life by enhancing the perceptible diversities of common human nature, and the strange anomalies into which it may be distorted.[12]

Put like that, Bagehot sounds as if he is criticising Dickens for not being George Eliot, just as many of his contemporaries (and Bagehot himself) compared his flashy populism unfavourably with the ironic restraint of Thackeray. Yet Bagehot's argument reads oddly when seen in relation to a novel like *Bleak House*, in which Dickens's double narrative turns the relations of parts and whole from a stylistic tic into a matter of serious psychological and sociological concern. What contributes to the development of an individual like Esther Summerson, and how happily are these elements reconciled in the same heart? On a larger scale, how successfully do the different parts of a society work together, and what do they add up to? Even in a city that seems to force private life onto its inhabitants, Dickens's novel shows how unavoidably we are connected through ties of blood, obligation, economic necessity, and a disease that refuses to know its place, like London's swirling fog or the rain which falls on the just and unjust alike.

How should the novelist tackle this world? Is it the novelist's task to depict things as they are, holding up a mirror to them in all their imperfection and incompleteness, or is it rather to persuade and inform his audience in such a way that the world can be made more like his fictionally ordered version of it? One of the oddest features of *Bleak House* is that it is a serialised novel which revolves around a parody of a serialised novel: the Chancery case, in which bundles of papers are brought together at regular intervals to try and reach the conclusion of a long-running story about inheritance. If this was deliberate on Dickens's part it showed a fair degree of courage, as it did to spend so much of the novel dwelling on the scenes of disintegration and collapse: 'broken sentences' (*BH*, 77), 'broken thoughts' (*BH*, 364), 'broken words' (*BH*, 777), a world where 'All is broken down' (*BH*, 790). Nor is this the only occasion on which he incorporated a commentary on his practice as a novelist into his fiction, like a set of critical footnotes absorbed into the main body of the text. Acts of writing are nervously dwelt on; words, like people, threaten to go astray;[13] there are even regular appearances by surrogate novelists, such as John Harmon, who busies himself rearranging Boffin's papers in *Our Mutual Friend*, or Mr Dick, whose unfinished 'Memorial' offers itself as a distorted reflection of the fragments of autobiography which Dickens was carefully working into *David Copperfield*. There is a wonderful moment in *Our Mutual Friend*, his last completed novel, as Silas Wegg opens the door to the shop of the taxidermist Mr Venus and notices that the stuffed and skeletal remains on display there 'show for an instant as if paralytically animated' (*OMF*, 77). Within the imaginative world of the novel, it is another clue that even what seems to be dead can come back to life in surprising ways; within the larger compass of Dickens's career, it is also a nervous reflection on what the novelist's work may amount to – opening the door to a shop in which nothing more than a few jiggling bodies are on show.

'Don't talk about it – do it!'[14] A favoured motto and theme, for Dickens. But was fiction a form of talking or a form of doing? One answer to this question of the relationship between words and the world can be found in Dickens's parallel career as an editor. By choosing to publish his serial novels in magazines such as *Household Words* (1850–9) and *All the Year Round* (1859–70), Dickens could place each episode alongside an assortment of other writings – from whimsical essays to hard-hitting investigative journalism – which implicitly asked his readers to consider what were the proper relations between fact and fiction, the individual and the group. If his novels dwelt on 'the romantic side of familiar things', they were also being braced and scrutinised by articles that revealed other ways of looking at these things: science, history, biography, fairy-tales, sociology, jokes. Another answer, which seems to have emerged from the intimacy of tone Dickens aimed at in these magazines, was to be found in the public readings of his work which occupied so much time and energy in his later years. How better to assure himself that his fiction had an effect on the world than by inviting his readers to cluster around him, like an extended family, and then observing their reactions? And what better story to choose than that fable of hospitality *A Christmas Carol* (1843)? In all, between 1853 and 1870, he gave no fewer than 127 performances of *A Christmas Carol*, by far his most popular full-length reading, drawing his readers together into a model society animated by sympathy and hope.

Of course neither the magazines nor the public readings were a democracy: it was Dickens who 'conducted' the other voices of *Household Words* and *All the Year Round*, rewriting his contributors' copy and using an editorial 'we' that was distinctly personal in tone; it was Dickens, again, who did all the voices in his readings, finally realising his childhood ambition of offering an entertainment like the 'monopolylogues' of the ventriloquist and quick-change artist Charles Mathews.[15] But both activities reflected the same conviction underpinning Dickens's fiction: that the writer can be an agent of change.

Escape-artists

One of Dickens's first publications was an edition of the clown Joseph Grimaldi's *Memoirs* (1838), which he hurriedly compiled from the notes left by Grimaldi and the wordy but incomplete version of an earlier editor. It was hackwork, but it paid well, and Grimaldi's life also offered a cautionary tale to a young man just starting out in the profession of entertaining the public; indeed, much of Dickens's version reads like a projected autobiography, with its account of Grimaldi's miserable childhood, his obsessive punctuality, his punishing work schedule ('Idleness wearied him more than labour'), and the exhaustion of his later years. One scene in particular seems to have struck a chord with Dickens, as he describes how the young Grimaldi was sent on a Sunday excursion to visit his grandfather dressed up in an embroidered green coat and breeches, a dazzling white satin waistcoat, silk stockings, shoes with shiny paste buckles, a cocked hat, a watch encrusted with fake diamonds, and 'a little cane in his hand, which he switched to and fro as our Clowns may do now'. Convinced that his son is 'a gentleman, and consequently perfectly able to take care of himself', Grimaldi's father sends him out into the streets, where he meets with hoots of derision until he comes across a beggar and slips a guinea (his only coin) into her hand, 'then away he walked again with a greater air than before.'[16] In the context of Grimaldi's life, the story is intended to show his need to learn the value of money that has been earned by 'industry and perseverance' (*Grimaldi*, 48) – a lesson he takes to heart in the thrift and sound business sense of his later career. By the time Dickens came to write *Great Expectations*, the story had mutated into a comic set piece within another admonitory fable about the need not to take on the 'air' of a gentleman until it has been earned, as Pip saunters down the street dressed in his new finery:

> I had not got as much further down the street as the post-office, when I again beheld Trabb's boy shooting round by a back way. This time, he was entirely changed. He wore the blue bag in the manner of my great-coat, and was

> strutting along the pavement towards me on the opposite side of the street, attended by a company of delighted young friends to whom he from time to time exclaimed, with a wave of his hand, 'Don't know yah!' Words cannot state the amount of aggravation and injury wreaked upon me by Trabb's boy, when, passing abreast of me, he pulled up his shirt-collar, twined his side-hair, stuck an arm akimbo, and smirked extravagantly by, wriggling his elbows and body, and drawling to his attendants, 'Don't know yah, don't know yah, pon my soul don't know yah!' (*GE*, 225)

The self-allusion is largely a private one – sales of Grimaldi's *Memoirs* were poor, and Dickens did not press his connection with the volume – but it slyly suggests Pip's real role in his story: not a hero who has been chosen to 'restore the desolate house, admit the sunshine into the dark rooms, set the clocks a going and the cold hearths a blazing, tear down the cobwebs, destroy the vermin – in short, do all the shining deeds of the young Knight of romance, and marry the Princess' (*GE*, 212), but a comic figure whose attempts to preserve his dignity in the face of laughter are precisely what make him vulnerable to further mockery. Like a pantomime clown, Pip enjoys the illusion of absolute freedom but must eventually subdue it to the demands of a certain kind of plot. His problem is that he hasn't yet recognised the nature of the story in which he finds himself: not quite a romance, and not quite a tragedy, but something uncomfortably close to a piece of refined slapstick.

Observers may have noted a touch of the clown in Dickens's own appearance at the time he was writing *Great Expectations* as, despite a painfully public separation from his wife and thin-lipped rumours of an affair with the young actress Ellen Ternan, he 'touched up his grizzling hair, dressed as gaily as ever, and continued to act like a young man'.[17] If there are echoes here of Grimaldi's behaviour after the death of his wife, 'summoned to the theatre to set the audience in a roar', like a modern Yorick, 'and chalking over the seams which mental agony had worn in his face' (*Grimaldi*, 112),[18] there are also hints of pantomime's more optimistic world, in which the ordinary rules of life were replaced by a sense of teeming possibility and romance, so that 'Everything is capable, with the greatest ease, of being changed into Anything, and "Nothing is, but thinking makes it so."'[19] Dickens's love of the pantomime was widely shared at the time. 'No words can express', one contemporary wrote, 'the animation, the gaiety, the boldness, the madness, the incoherence, the coarseness, the splendour, the whimsical poetry, the brutality of these Christmas pantomimes.'[20] Where Dickens differed was in his confidence that such variety could indeed be expressed in words. Every aspect of the pantomime that is praised here forms a key ingredient of his narrative style, together with some of the other features that made this theatrical form Dickens's first and lasting love: the way in which conventional character types – the lover, the villain, and so on – gained a vivid individuality in the hands of skilled performers; the tussle in the spectator's mind between enchantment and disenchantment, as this magical world teeters on the brink of collapse into cheap glitter and cardboard; and especially the controlled anarchy of the stage action, in which the clown's improvisation is always threatening to overwhelm the fragile mechanisms of plot.

There is a remarkable scene at the end of *Hard Times* (1854), Dickens's most sustained appeal to 'fancy', in which Gradgrind, the apostle of 'Fact, fact, fact', encounters the son who has decided to live out an ancient childhood fantasy by running away to join the circus. Sitting down forlornly on the clown's chair, Gradgrind observes the sulky youth dressed as a comic servant, 'In a preposterous coat, like a beadle's, with cuffs and flaps exaggerated to an unspeakable extent; in an immense waistcoat, knee-breeches, buckled shoes, and a mad cocked hat; with nothing fitting him, and everything of coarse material, moth-eaten and full of holes; with seams in his black face, where fear and heat had started through the greasy composition daubed all over it' (*HT*, 377) – a down-at-heels Grimaldi. Peter Ackroyd, animating the scene further than Dickens does, wonders if the spectacle of a boy covered in blacking could be a vision of the novelist himself: 'A young Dickens, in a nightmare of degradation, capering before his father? Or is it the young Dickens capering and gibbering before the older version of himself? Swallowed up, at last, by his past.'[21] But this doesn't go far enough, or at least doesn't take account of how far Dickens went to exorcise the ghosts of his past. Even if Dickens remained shadowed by the feelings of physical and moral taint that accompanied his time in the blacking warehouse, it is worth noting that young Tom Gradgrind escapes. If the scene stages a personal confrontation, it is principally one in which Dickens shows the pleasures of fancy confronting the demands of fact, greasepaint against grime. Even Tom's escape does not settle the matter: his final appearance comes in the form of a letter sent from 'many thousands of miles away', a fate that manages to suggest both that he has disappeared into an adventure story, an untold sequel to the novel, and that he had been exiled to the real world of Dickens's readers. A figure of the novelist he may be, but not as a clown or a comic servant. He is an escape-artist.

Throughout his career Dickens seems to have found a form of imaginative release by taking on certain restraints – the confines of plot, the potentially narrow tastes of his readers, the limitations on space imposed by serial publication – and then giving them the slip. Even his description in one letter of the imagination as a 'powerful Locomotive'[22] depicts it as another container of energy that could move forwards only if kept in check by orderly lines. His attitude towards his characters' ambitions, on the other hand, is sometimes more uncertain. As Garrett Stewart has shown,[23] many of the most sympathetic characters in Dickens's earlier fiction are escape-artists of the imagination: characters like the Marchioness in *The Old Curiosity Shop*, whose powers of fancy allow her to slip the leash of reality and disappear into an alternative world of her own creation, as she sits in her dank basement pretending that slices of old orange peel dipped in water are as good as wine ('If you make believe very much, it's quite nice' (*OCS*, 481)). Where Dickens's later characters go wrong is in mistaking this sort of dream for reality, as when Pip notices the drawers in Mr Pumblechook's shop and 'wondered when I peeped into one or two on the lower tiers, and saw the tied-up brown paper packets inside, whether the flower-seeds and bulbs ever wanted of a fine day to break out of those jails, and bloom' (*GE*, 48–9). The connection between seeds or bulbs and 'Pip' is a natural one, even if in his rush to escape the confines of village life Pip is forgetting that a seed must be rooted in the real world if it is to flourish. As Dickens noted in his memorandum book, loose talk about the 'virtue' of a seed ignores the fact that 'So there is in any grain of seed in a seedsman's shop – but you must put it in the ground before you can get any good of it.'[24] Anyone who is going to be involved in real life needs to start by keeping their feet on the ground. In this sense Pip's nearest fictional ancestor is probably *Barnaby Rudge*'s (1841) Simon Tappertit, who muses to himself about the 'ignoble existence' into which he has been born: 'A voice within me keeps on whispering Greatness. I shall burst out one of these days, and when I do, what power can keep me down?' (*BR*, 77). The answer comes shortly after he joins 'the very scum and refuse of London' who fan the flames of the Gordon riots, and ends up 'burnt and bruised, and with a gun-shot wound in his body; and his legs – his perfect legs, the pride and glory of his life, the comfort of his existence – crushed into shapeless ugliness' (*BR*, 574). Pip is not punished quite so brutally, but he too embodies Dickens's suspicion of how dangerous ambition can be if it is divorced from traditional virtues of self-determination and hard work. Admiring one's legs is not quite the same as using them to get on in life.

The need to keep moving is one that Dickens took seriously: he hated saying goodbye, brooded on the effects of different kinds of arrest and confinement, and according to George Sala, one of his favourite journalists, thought it necessary to spend the same number of hours walking every day as he did writing.[25] Yet even as he was gathering inspiration he was looking to master its source. 'As soon as I have fixed a place in my mind, I bolt',[26] he wrote in one letter, and the ambiguity of 'bolt' (to flee or to secure) is quietly telling. His novels are similarly divided, as the need for a conclusion attempts to subdue the narrative drive, even as the energy of the writing insists on keeping things on the move. It is an imaginative rhythm of contraction and expansion, a narrative heartbeat, which can be seen as early as *The Old Curiosity Shop*, in which the title promises one sort of 'curiosity', a static world of lovingly assembled clutter, even as the narrative is being kept going by a different sort of 'curiosity': the desire to know where Nell will end up. Repeatedly, promises of rest are held out for her – waxworks, melodramatic tableaux, graveyards – and then rejected, as the narrative refuses to settle down or find a single home-key. Not until Nell's deathbed scene does the narrative appear to slow to a halt, as Dickens drifts into the sort of blank verse that threatened to turn his most sentimental scenes into something as lifeless and static as the inscription on a gravestone: 'And still her former self lay there, unaltered in this change. Yes' (*OCS*, 538). But even this scene, with its self-affirming repetitions of 'She was dead', is not allowed to rest in peace; already punctured in advance by the Glorious Apollos' habit of reciting gobbets of mournful poetry at each other ('At the end of this quotation in dialogue, each gentleman struck an attitude, and immediately subsiding into prose walked into the office', *OCS*, 418), it is further deflated by the later response of Kit's children to the story of how she would laugh at their father, 'at which they would brush away their tears, and laugh themselves to think that she had done so, and be again quite merry' (*OCS*, 554). Unaltered in her change Nell may be, but the tone of her story is far harder to pin down.

'"The voice of Time"', according to the Phantom in *The Chimes* (1844), '"cries to man, Advance!"'[27] The momentum of Dickens's imagination often carried his characters far beyond his novels: in Thomas Hughes's *Tom Brown's Schooldays* (1857) a schoolboy is discovered 'reading and chuckling' over a comic episode in *The Pickwick Papers*, while in Elizabeth Gaskell's *Cranford* (1851) Captain Brown is so engrossed 'in the perusal of a number of "Pickwick", which he had just received' that he loses track of what he is doing and is run down by a train.[28] Add to this the vogue for Pickwick cigars, Pickwick hats, Pickwick coats, and the report of one tourist that he had found 'Pickwick' scrawled on an Egyptian pyramid, and it seems clear that from the start of his career Dickens was one of those rare novelists who is important to those who have read about him as well as those who have actually read him. But even within the limits of his fiction Dickens was skilled at leaving his audiences wanting more. *Bleak House* ends with Esther breaking off her account ('even supposing –') with a dash which offers itself as both a bridge and a barrier between the reader's world and the 'just suppose' world of fiction (*BH*, 914). *Little Dorrit* goes even further, turning the final paragraph into a passageway between the real world and its fictional counterpart (or supplement, or alternative) as Little Dorrit and Arthur Clennam slowly vanish from view:

> They went down into the roaring streets, inseparable and blessed; and as they passed along in sunshine and in shade, the noisy and eager, and the arrogant and the froward and the vain, fretted, and chafed, and made their usual uproar. (*LD*, 688)

Just as this description returns to the 'Babel' of sounds in the opening chapter (*LD*, 1), so in a beautiful modulation from 'they' to 'their' Dickens's syntax dramatises the couple returning to the anonymous throng from which they emerged at the start of the story. It is a span of thought which offers one of his most assured and subtle demonstrations of the art of the novel, in which figures are plucked from the crowd, meaningful structures are assembled from the chatter of everyday life, and events are given a narrative shape even as the writing is quietly acknowledging that such tidiness is a fiction of our own choosing.

The real world is far messier, far noisier, far more crowded, and it is Dickens's genius to create a version of it on the page that seems complete in itself while always suggesting there is more to be said. It is a fictional world in which the muffled sounds of London form a permanent soundtrack to events, like 'a distant ringing hum, as if the city were a vast glass, vibrating' (*BH*, 691). A world in which the novel, like Gothic architecture, celebrates the fact that 'Rigid perfection is impossible in anything living – it is never complete, always in part growing, in part decaying.'[29] A world in which Mr Datchery, in the last paragraph of *The Mystery of Edwin Drood* (1870), Dickens's incomplete final novel, 'opens his corner cupboard door; takes his bit of chalk from its shelf; adds one thick line to the score, extending from the top of the cupboard to the bottom; and then falls to with an appetite' (*MED*, 217).

NOTE ON EDITIONS

There is no single complete critical edition of Dickens's works. Oxford University Press's ongoing series of Clarendon editions provides the most authoritative texts for many of the novels, and these texts are reproduced along with comprehensive notes and introductions in the paperback Oxford World's Classics editions. Other recommended editions are those published by Penguin and Norton; both have good notes and introductions, and the latter also include a selection of critical extracts.

NOTES

1 John Forster, *The Life of Charles Dickens*, ed. J. W. T. Ley (London: C. Palmer, 1928), pp. 25–6.

2 *'Gone Astray' and Other Papers from Household Words, 1851–59*, ed. Michael Slater (London: Dent, 1998), p. 156. Hereafter *HW*.

3 The title of 'Gone Astray' alludes to a biblical passage that Dickens used as a touchstone throughout his career: 'And Jesus called a little child unto him, and set him in the midst of them, And said, Verily I say unto you, Except ye be converted and become as little children, ye shall not enter the kingdom of heaven ... How think ye? If a man have a hundred sheep, and one of them be gone astray, doth he not leave the ninety and nine, and goeth into the mountains, and seeketh that which is gone astray? ... Even so it is not the will of your Father which is in heaven, that one of these little ones should perish' (Matthew 18:2–14).

4 All page references to Dickens's fiction are taken from the editions published in the Oxford World's Classics series; see the Note on editions for more details. The following abbreviations are used: *Barnaby Rudge* (*BR*), *Bleak House* (*BH*), *David Copperfield* (*DC*), *Dombey and Son* (*DS*), *Great Expectations* (*GE*), *Hard Times* (*HT*), *Little Dorrit* (*LD*), *Martin Chuzzlewit* (MC), *The Mystery of Edwin Drood* (*MED*), *The Old Curiosity Shop* (*OCS*), *Oliver Twist* (*OT*), *Our Mutual Friend* (*OMF*), *A Tale of Two Cities* (*TTC*).

5 Dickens's number plans for the closing chapters are reprinted on p. 571 of the Oxford World's Classics edition of the novel, ed. Elizabeth M. Brennan (1998).

6 'Charles Dickens', *Critical Essays* (London: Secker & Warburg, 1946), pp. 56–7.

7 *The Immortal Dickens* (London: C. Palmer, 1925), p. 27.

8 *Yeast: A Problem* (1851) (London: Macmillan, 1888), p. 249.

9 In *Dombey and Son*, Dickens interrupts his narrative with an urgent warning about the blighting force of 'our wicked cities': 'Oh for a good spirit who would take the house-tops off, with a more potent and benignant hand than the lame demon in the tale, and show a Christian people what dark shapes issue from amidst their homes, to swell the retinue of the Destroying Angel as he moved forth among them' (*DS*, 685) – an appeal he was to answer himself four years later by writing *Bleak House*.

10 Peter Conrad discusses the connection between Gothic architecture and the Victorian novel in chapter 5 of *The Victorian Treasure-House* (London: Collins, 1973).

11 'Charles Dickens', *Critical Essays*, p. 52.

12 'Charles Dickens' (1858), reprinted in *Charles Dickens: A Critical Anthology*, ed. Stephen Wall (Harmondsworth: Penguin, 1970), p. 133.

13 In *Martin Chuzzlewit* one of the lodgers in Mrs Todgers's boarding-house is an old woman described as 'a perfect Tomb for messages and small parcels; and when dispatched to the Post Office with letters, had been frequently seen endeavouring to insinuate them into casual chinks in private doors, under the delusion that any door with a hole in it would answer the purpose' (*MC*, 438).

14 See Peter Ackroyd, *Dickens* (London: Sinclair-Stevenson, 1990), p. 533.

15 See Paul Schlicke, *Dickens and Popular Entertainment* (London: Unwin Hyman, 1985), pp. 234–41.

16 *Memoirs of Joseph Grimaldi* (1838), ed. Richard Findlater (London: MacGibbon and Kee, 1968), pp. 39–40. Hereafter *Grimaldi*.
17 Edgar Johnson, *Charles Dickens: His Tragedy and Triumph*, 2 vols. (London: V. Gollancz, 1953), II, p. 970.
18 In chapter 3 of *The Pickwick Papers* Dickens tells the story of a clown rising from his deathbed to entertain his audience.
19 'The Christmas Tree', *Household Words*, 21 December 1850, reprinted in *'A Christmas Carol' and Other Christmas Writings*, ed. Michael Slater (Harmondsworth: Penguin, 2003), p. 239.
20 Quoted by Ackroyd, *Dickens*, p. 37.
21 Ackroyd, *Dickens*, p. 711.
22 Letter to Sarah Hammond Palfrey (4 April 1868), *Letters*, XII, p. 91. References to *Letters* are to the Pilgrim Edition, gen. eds. Madeline House, Graham Storey, and Kathleen Tillotson, 12 vols. (Oxford: Clarendon Press, 1965–2002).
23 See his discussion in *Dickens and the Trials of Imagination* (Cambridge, MA: Harvard University Press, 1974).
24 *Charles Dickens' Book of Memoranda*, ed. Fred Kaplan (New York: New York Public Library, 1981), p. 4. Dickens's entry, which takes the form of a dialogue, goes on to compare the 'virtue' of a man: ' "You must set him in the earth, before you get any good out of him." '
25 'My Master in Letters', *Charles Dickens* (1870), reprinted in *Dickens: Interviews and Recollections*, ed. Philip Collins, 2 vols. (London: Macmillan,1981), II, p. 199.
26 Letter to John Forster (12 November 1844), *Letters*, IV, p. 217.
27 *'A Christmas Carol' and Other Christmas Books*, ed. Robert Douglas-Fairhurst (Oxford: Oxford World's Classics, 2006), p. 128.
28 I owe these examples to Andrew Sanders, *Dickens and the Spirit of the Age* (Oxford: Clarendon Press, 1999), p. 20.
29 Conrad, *The Victorian Treasure-House*, p. 161.

FURTHER READING

Ackroyd, P., *Dickens*, London, Sinclair-Stevenson, 1990
Bowen, J., *Other Dickens: Pickwick to Chuzzlewit*, Oxford, Oxford University Press, 2000
Butt, J. and K. Tillotson, *Dickens at Work*, London, Methuen, 1957
Carey, J., *The Violent Effigy: A Study of Dickens's Imagination*, London, Faber and Faber, 1973; 2nd edn, 1991
Chesterton, G.K., *Charles Dickens*, London, Methuen, 1906
Connor, S. (ed.), *Charles Dickens*, Longman Critical Readers, London, Longman, 1996
Hillis Miller, J., *Charles Dickens: The World of His Novels*, Cambridge, MA, Harvard University Press, 1958
House, H., *The Dickens World*, Oxford, Oxford University Press, 1941
Jordan, J.O. (ed.), *The Cambridge Companion to Dickens*, Cambridge, Cambridge University Press, 2001
Sanders, A., *Dickens and the Spirit of the Age*, Oxford, Clarendon Press, 2001
Schlicke, P., *Dickens and Popular Entertainment*, London, Unwin Hyman, 1985

Schlicke, P. (ed.), *The Oxford Reader's Companion to Dickens*, Oxford, Oxford University Press, 1999

Schwarzbach, F. S., *Dickens and the City*, London, Athlone Press, 1979

Slater, M., *An Intelligent Person's Guide to Dickens*, London, Duckworth, 1999

Stewart, G., *Dickens and the Trials of Imagination*, Cambridge, MA, Harvard University Press, 1974

Stone, H., *Dickens and the Invisible World: Fairy Tales, Fantasy, and Novel-Making*, London, Macmillan, 1980

Wall, S. (ed.), *Charles Dickens: A Critical Anthology*, Harmondsworth, Penguin, 1970

Wilson, E., 'Dickens: The Two Scrooges', in *The Wound and the Bow*, London, W. H. Allen & Co., 1941

9

NICHOLAS DAMES

William Makepeace Thackeray

Imagine, if you will, the following: a boy born to English parents, in Calcutta, during the waning years of the Napoleonic Wars. The boy's father dies four years later, and the boy is soon thereafter sent away from his mother – who had in the meantime resumed a prior attachment to an army captain – to distant England, where he will be schooled. (En route, the young boy catches sight of the exiled Bonaparte, tending the garden in his St Helena retreat.) His schooling is perfectly correct by the standards of his class and time, and perfectly nightmarish; he is initiated into the rituals of English social formation by the tyrannies, physical, moral, and sexual, of the pre-Victorian public school, and memories of these humiliations and the loneliness consequent upon them will follow the boy into adulthood and middle age. Youthful degradation leads to a prolonged period of diffident attempts to start a career and more serious cultural experimentation: an undistinguished period of time at Cambridge; travels to Paris, Weimar, and beyond, where the young man develops tastes for bohemian life; and a rapid dissipation of his patrimony thanks to gambling, unwise investments, and a bank failure. This once-genteel young man then turns to the London Grub Street of his day for a living, and begins to turn out spirited and witty sketches for newspapers and magazines. The list of his published pieces numbers in the hundreds, and the young man has married – unwisely, as it turns out, for his wife inexplicably and inexorably falls into a mental illness that results in her confinement in a series of asylums. Burdened with two daughters, tied to a shattered marriage, afflicted with guilt for his past failures and self-absorption, dubious of the social rewards he still feels compelled to win, the now no-longer-young writer works desperately at a bid for financial security: a serial novel that would satirically examine English society through the rise, and fall, of an unscrupulous female. The novel is a sudden and unforeseen success, and the writer proceeds to produce a corpus of fiction that is known for its savage cynicism, its sentimental tenderness, its improvisational looseness, its sharp acuity in picturing manners and morals, as well as its distinct unease. To the end of his life, this celebrated writer – now admitted into all the clubs, editorial offices, and drawing rooms that he had earlier envied and loathed in equal measure – never loses his signature tone of mockery, particularly self-mockery. His world is evidently one in which no one is exempt from the fate of having hollow desires despite knowing their hollowness.

Readers of W. M. Thackeray will immediately recognise this sketch of his life and career; they may also wonder why it is not better known. Aside from its bursts of melodrama, his career bears all the marks of what, in our own time, counts as worthy of interest. His experience of multiple cultures, particularly the culture of Anglo-Indian colonial governance and early nineteenth-century artistic bohemia; his recurrent concern with ambitious, rebellious, flawed, and emotionally flayed women, and the painful torsions that society asks of them; his intimate knowledge of the lies told by his social class, and the places where these lies are secretly admitted; his tendency to ironically deflate the moral precepts that he nonetheless repeats: these qualities would seem to ensure Thackeray the popular readership that so many of his fellow Victorian novelists still have. Yet such is not, in fact, the case. Aside from the towering example of *Vanity Fair* (1847–8), Thackeray is not usually read, and he has largely escaped the recent trend of film adaptations and rewritings that has kept other Victorian notables visible in contemporary mass culture.[1] The countless late nineteenth-century editions of Thackeray's collected works that sit on the shelves of used bookstores across the English-speaking world testify to a writer whose prestige, once immense, is now confined to one novel. Who, aside from specialist academics, now knows that his *History of Henry Esmond* (1852) was thought by the critic George Saintsbury in 1908 to be perhaps the greatest novel in existence?[2] Who would believe that that judgement was not then as eccentric as it now sounds?

The reason for this discrepancy is at least partly to be found in Thackeray's critics. Few major novelistic careers, in any era, have suffered from both admirers and detractors in the way that Thackeray's has. The usual praise offered in his own time stressed qualities unlikely to endear him to any subsequent age: Thackeray was all too often lauded as a 'gentleman', a 'moralist', a religious stoic, or a grave censor. Critics uncomfortable with Dickens's mass popularity used Thackeray, speciously and opportunistically, as an example of well-bred realism, thereby helping to ensure his neglect in times when gentlemanly breeding was no longer a sought-after quality in the aesthetic realm. Charlotte Brontë's decision to dedicate *Jane Eyre* (1847) to Thackeray, and her characteristically vivid description of him coming 'before the great ones of society much as the son of Imlah came before the throned kings of Judah and Israel', before whom he 'hurls the Greek fire of his sarcasm, and over whom he flashes the levin-brand of his denunciation', erases the irony and self-doubt that make Thackeray so potentially attractive to readers schooled in less scriptural modes.[3] At the same time, however, foreign readers of Thackeray detected moral hypocrisy. Hippolyte Taine, describing Thackeray for a French audience in his *Notes sur l'Angleterre* (1871), dismissed Thackeray's female characters as all 'more or less clergymen, more or less prudes'.[4]

Worse yet would come from critics who, by ridiculing the formal arrangements of Thackeray's novels, cleared space for their own *avant-gardiste* principles. Henry James famously used *The Newcomes* (1853–5) as his prime example of the 'large loose baggy monsters' of Victorian fiction, which, 'with their queer elements of the accidental and the arbitrary', would yield, as a result of the relentless march of aesthetic progress, to the tautly constructed forms of his own fiction.[5] James's charge stuck, not least because it turned the usual account of Thackeray on its head. After James, Thackeray went from being the gentleman moralist to being the clueless gentleman who may know good form but who cannot know good Form. What had earlier been understood as Thackeray's gentlemanly amateurism – oddly, given his long and fraught apprenticeship in journalism and sketch fiction – now seemed simply like bumbling amateurism. The post-war Great Tradition of F. R. Leavis, more Jamesian than James himself, had no space for multiplot, serial fictions like Thackeray's, with their authorial intrusions, plot digressions, panoramic scope, and sheer wordy elongation; reading Thackeray, Leavis claimed, is 'merely a matter of going on and on; nothing has been done by the close to justify the space taken – except, of course, that time has been killed (which seems to be all that even some academic critics demand of a novel)'.[6]

With such friends, and such enemies, even the most immediately appealing aspects of Thackeray's work faded from view. Only on the margins of the English-speaking world, it seems, far from the musty scents of his Victorian admirers and the disdain of his modernist detractors, could he be read with wonder and fervour. As for instance in Trinidad, in the early years of the twentieth century, where the young C. L. R. James found in *Vanity Fair* 'my Homer and my bible':

> Certainly of the lords and ladies and much of the world described, as a West Indian boy of eight, I hadn't the slightest idea. When I later told people how and when I had read the book some were skeptical and even derisive. It was not to me an ordinary book. It was a refuge into which I withdrew ... I laughed without satiety at Thackeray's constant jokes and sneers and gibes at the aristocracy and at people in high places. Thackeray, not Marx, bears the heaviest responsibility for me.[7]

Withdrawn from the suffocating atmosphere of his English reputation, Thackeray spoke to James of the codes of a class system James was just beginning to know: the restraint and self-discipline of English behaviour, mixed with a thorough knowledge of all the things restraint both gains and loses; the coruscating laughter at an aristocracy that will remain oblivious to it; the sense of a deep unrightness to things, poisoned by the inability to imagine them any other way. James's Thackeray, read in isolation from the history of his readers, can still be our Thackeray. Perhaps, at least, James's suggestion – that Thackeray trains us both to adapt to and recoil from a social world that might, *mutatis mutandis*, still be ours – is the right place to start.

Like many of his counterparts in Victorian fiction-writing, Thackeray's career began with an apprenticeship in the kind of periodical journalism available to quick and ambitious pens in the 1830s and 1840s: the 'sketch', the witty and spirited piece of cultural observation. The demands of the sketch form were many, including trend-spotting, maintaining a tone of mockery that stopped short of actual critique, and being able to entertain through the sheer pleasures of a discursive voice. Thackeray's initial solution to these demands was to develop a range of *alter ego* possibilities. Among the most popular of these early narrative voices was Charles James Yellowplush, a 'genteel' footman with a cockney accent and an unwittingly acute sense of the manners of his employers. At first, voices like Yellowplush's gave Thackeray the means to indulge his undoubted talents for parody and mimicry. If one cliché of novelistic careers is the need for the apprentice writer to 'find their voice', Thackeray begins instead by producing incisive parodies of cultural types and major novelistic styles already popular. His first novel, *Catherine* (1838), parodies the Newgate fiction of W. H. Ainsworth and Edward Bulwer-Lytton; a later sketch series, *Punch's Prize Novelists* (1847), took on an even wider range of targets, including Benjamin Disraeli, James Fenimore Cooper, and Charles Lever.

His gift for parody never deserted him, and in fact provided him with an education in the conventionality of *all* style – the way in which voices originate not from some authentic 'self', but from a social persona that is a matrix of numerous determining factors. The most important styles for Thackeray to have learned, however, were the styles of his servant-narrators, Yellowplush most prominently. From the start, that is, Thackeray refuses the godlike omniscience that would become such a dominant novelistic mode; instead he offers a narration from below-stairs. The servant and the writer are firmly linked in his imagination: like the writer, the servant exists to please, but is fully capable of enjoyment at our expense; like the servant, the writer is a socially marginal figure, one with unusual access but no security.

There are no transcendent or even particularly profound alibis for narration in Thackeray; his narrators are not gods, or sages, or mother or father, but footmen, clubmen, casual friends, gossipy servants, tradesmen. In part this servant-narration works effectively, particularly within the satirical genre of the sketch, to puncture social pretensions of various kinds; no man is a hero to his valet, of course, and Thackeray is quick to dispense with heroes of any kind.

More importantly, however, the servant offered Thackeray a key to an entire social ontology: snobbery. The very word 'snob', from the abbreviation *s.nob* for *sine nobilitate* ('without title'), had long been university slang for commoners, and that meaning persisted in the phrase 'nobs and snobs' throughout the nineteenth century. Thackeray, that is, begins with narrators who are 'snobs' in the way in which the term was understood in his youth. Yet by adopting the point of view of 'snobs' like Yellowplush, Thackeray revealed the entirely vulgar, and entirely human, desires of their kind – and began to insist, with greater clarity and force throughout the 1840s, that their desires are always also our desires. In so doing Thackeray turned 'snob' into snobbery proper: the great force of social cohesion, the thing that links all classes, all behaviours, that spans worlds. The term is for ever altered by Thackeray's intervention, from a vaguely feudal descriptor for a large, undifferentiated social class – those without titles – to a kind of desire that characterises the modern individual.

Few journalistic talents are as useful, or as important, as coining a new term for a social phenomenon that is apparent to everyone but not yet taxonomised; with the sketch series *The Snobs of England, by One of Themselves* (1846–7), serialised in *Punch* and later published as *The Book of Snobs*, Thackeray achieved one of these rare successes. The voice of these sketches in now the voice of the mature Thackerayan narrator: disillusioned, amused, and by no means able to exempt itself from the failures it deplores.

> There are only a few bland and not-in-the-least conceited philosophers, who can behold the state of society, viz., Toadyism organized: – base Man-and-Mammon worship, instituted by command of law: – Snobbishness, in a word, perpetuated, – and mark the phenomenon calmly. And of these calm moralists, is there one, I wonder, whose heart would not throb with pleasure if he could be seen walking arm-in-arm with a couple of dukes down Pall Mall? No; it is impossible, in our condition of society, not to be sometimes a Snob.[8]

Thus one of the early 'Snob' sketches proclaims, announcing the great theme of Thackeray's mature fiction. Snobbery, in Thackeray's world, is not a failing or a problem as much as the constitutive mark of any social activity. It is, in fact, the religion of his fictions: like religion, it operates through a complex mixture of hope (of a better future) and fear (of punishment or discovery); like religion, it underwrites both aspiration and abjection, both confidence and self-loathing. The self-alienation of snobbery, the way in which the snob is continually seeing the self through the eyes of others, is both a damaging self-estrangement and a strange form of clairvoyance, even a form of *ek-stasis* or 'ecstasy': seeing oneself from the outside, the way others see you. The snob is thus not a wholly lost or damned figure. The snob's sense of unfulfillable yearning and lack of self-satisfaction is a degraded version of more august things – Art, or Love, or Faith – and as such is not just a defect of character. Simply put, it is far too essential to the modern condition to be that.

This is not to say that snobbery, in its various guises, was invisible to other novelists of the time. Dickens's analysis of 'Podsnappery', from *Our Mutual Friend* (1864–5), is the culmination of a long line of condemnations of misplaced, venal, and *arriviste* social desires. But what is in Dickens a disease, curable and avoidable, is in Thackeray an ontology from which there is no escape. The subtitle of the original series, 'by One of Themselves', is not just an amusing squiggle; it is the key to Thackeray's sense of snobbery. Put another way, there is no 'outside' to snobbery for Thackeray, no place where one can opt out of its demands. As Thackeray well knew, claiming not to be a snob is in fact the surest sign that one is. It is not bounded by any particular social class or psychological disposition; it lent itself well to a sketch series, since its manifestations are theoretically infinite. (*The Snobs of England* aimed at a kind of comic encyclopaedism, from 'City Snobs' to 'University Snobs', 'Military Snobs', 'Literary Snobs', 'Dining Snobs', 'Irish Snobs', *et al.*) A later age might have called it an 'existential condition', such as, say, 'alienation' or 'ideology', just as an earlier age might have called it, like sin, the inescapable fact of our human fallenness. In the fallen world of Thackeray's fiction – a world that will, shortly after *The Snobs of England* finished its run, go under the name Vanity Fair – it is so fundamental that it will be impossible to determine the difference between snobbery and such things as love or faith or fidelity.

Snobbery is also, not coincidentally, a gift to the novelist. It is a religion of externals, and as such helps motivate the careful notation of details (dress, speech, possessions) that had become such a part of realist narration. It is also a religion of desire, and as such helps produce vivid, strongly mobile characters, characters whose self-dissatisfaction makes them willing to enter into narratives. With Becky Sharp, the central figure of *Vanity Fair*, Thackeray found the right novelistic corollary for his sense of snobbery's workings, and as a result he made his name as a novelist. Becky is an adventurer, an orphaned woman of talent who is determined to use her sharp eye for detail and sharp ear for the tones of class (both, of course, talents of Thackeray's own) in order to rise beyond the bohemian squalor of her upbringing. She therefore represents the active, restless side of snobbery, its ambition and narrative drive, rather than the inert judgementalism that is the hallmark of Dickens's snobs. In fact, Becky continually outrages the comfortably snobbish judgements of others – the reflections of various characters that she isn't, you know, quite the thing – which makes a reader's potential discomfort with Becky's scheming all the more complicated. On what ground can we stand in order to fairly judge Becky's transparently worldly desires? All too often the judgemental standpoint of *Vanity Fair*'s other characters is simply that they want the very same things Becky does. And if we are to reject Becky's desires simply on the basis of their restlessness, we have as our counterpoint the sluggish self-admiration of the Osborne family, whose slavish enjoyment of what they already possess makes Becky's cleverness all the more attractive by comparison – simply put, her company is more pleasant.

Becky's energy, that is, turns what could be a bleak portrayal of the ontology of snobbery into something frankly entertaining. Not that *Vanity Fair* lacks its moments of bleakness. Its characters all live out the psychological consequences of snobbery, particularly an essential loneliness. Whether it be Jos Sedley, in all the splendour of his dandyish evening dress, dining alone; Sir Pitt Crawley, dying of a stroke, abandoned by the nurse whose wages he had paid; or Amelia, waiting forlornly by her bedroom for her reluctant suitor to arrive, to be a character in Thackeray means to be caught constantly in the possession of a solitude without solace. In one of the novel's more desolate images, Thackeray imagines Jane Osborne, the spinster tyrannised by her clumsily snobbish father, trapped in a vulgar drawing-room waiting to receive the right kind of visitors, who never really arrive: 'The great glass over the mantelpiece, faced by the other great console-glass at the opposite end of the room, increased and multiplied between them the brown holland bag in which the chandelier hung; until you saw these brown holland bags fading away in endless perspectives, and this apartment of Miss Osborne's seemed the centre of a system of drawing-rooms.'[9] A system indeed: Miss Osborne's loneliness is far from extraordinary, but is instead part of a network of isolation stretching to every corner of Thackeray's fiction.

Vanity Fair, the quasi-autobiographical *Pendennis* (1848–50), and the sprawling family novel *The Newcomes* (1853–5) are Thackeray's most sustained and successful narratives of contemporary British life. While each starts in an earlier, pre-Victorian moment – as Thackeray saw it, the comparatively more robust and open society of Regency Britain – they inch into the near-present and offer a picture of a social universe locked into place.

Less interested than Dickens's sprawling multiplot novels of the 1850s in charting the connections between seemingly isolated worlds, *Vanity Fair* and *Pendennis* both depict an isolation that is far more complete and yet also far more irrelevant, since what grips all the individuals here is a 'system' experienced as personal frustration. Each novel is successively less comic than the previous one, as if the rambunctious Regency energy of Becky has successfully been contained by a system too invisible, and too all-encompassing, to be susceptible to her charms. Both *Pendennis* and *The Newcomes* have their own charms, but now those charms are limited to the rueful, detached voice that increasingly became Thackeray's signature. Never one to insist on the originality of his stories, Thackeray's real originality lay in the resigned, or bemusedly sophisticated, tone in which he insisted that there was really nothing new under the sun. The early love of Pendennis for a pretty, uneducated Irish actress? 'We are not going to describe his feelings, or give a dreary journal of his despair and passion. Have not other gentlemen been balked in love besides Mr. Pen? Yes, indeed: but few die of the malady.' Pen's initial circle of friends at 'Oxbridge' (a Thackerayan coinage)? 'Alas, the life of such boys does not bear telling altogether. I wish it did ... his neighbours are bad for the most part. Let us have the candour to own as much at least. Can you point out ten spotless men of your acquaintance? Mine is pretty large, but I can't find ten saints in the list.'[10]

This genially debunking voice, reminding us of the imperfections and constraints that we all live with, culminated in one of the more sour of *Pendennis*'s passages, and one of the more famous literary battles of the mid-Victorian period: the so-called 'Dignity of Literature' controversy that raged between Thackeray, Dickens, and their respective supporters. The controversy was initially spurred by a moment in which Pendennis experiences disappointment at the vulgar, common conversation of the literary men of London, with which the narrator wearily concurs:

> In fact, not one word about literature had been said during the whole course of the night: – and it may be whispered to those uninitiated people who are anxious to know the habits and make the acquaintance of men of letters, that there are no race of people who talk about books, or, perhaps, who read books, so little as literary men. (*P*, 440)

Pen is also taken in hand by the disillusioned, older George Warrington, a sometime writer himself, who proclaims: 'All poets are humbugs, all literary men are humbugs: directly a man begins to sell his feelings for money he's a humbug' (*P*, 520). (Warrington, it should be noted, has an estranged wife, much like Thackeray himself.) Sentiments like these were difficult for Dickens to accept passively, particularly as he was then engaged in efforts to found a guild or union for authors, and Dickens's friend John Forster – who seems to have been Dickens's proxy in most of the controversies of the 1850s – wrote a scathing critique of Thackeray, accusing him of the sin of snobbery, of currying favour with aristocracy by denigrating his own labour. Stung by an accusation that in earlier contexts he had been glad enough to accept as true, Thackeray swung back (in this as in other controversial matters, he was less cautious than Dickens) with an angry denunciation of the unseemliness of authors claiming for themselves some kind of 'dignity' – a screen, as Thackeray cynically read it, for asking for state support. Dickens responded by lampooning Thackeray in *Little Dorrit* (1855–7) in the figure of the feckless, lazy, self-hating, and snobbish artist Henry Gowan.

A minor enough skirmish, but it furnishes us with a clue to the complexity of Thackeray's fictional world. Within *Pendennis*, writers can talk only about money; and as Warrington insists, the fact that they market their feelings or memories makes them 'humbugs'. For Dickens's effort to produce a refuge from market forces – pensions, perhaps even state sinecures of some kind, for writers – Thackeray, however, has only scorn. The lesson: the market poisons, but there is no escape from it, and the act of believing in such an escape is at best wishful thinking, at worst a form of charlatanry. There is a willed stasis here, or what we might call a feeling of balked agency, that becomes the most important affective element of Thackeray's major fiction, and that increasingly drives his accounts of the social psychology of his time. What one hates (the market, the constraints of social life: the 'system' works in part because of its vagueness) cannot be changed – one is simply trapped by a set of forces that are too embedded, or too intractable, to be solved. Modern philosophy, after Peter Sloterdijk, has used the term 'cynical reason': a sensibility formed by a sensation of powerlessness, which is both highly adaptable to the unloved order of things and yet also made miserable by it.[11]

Thackeray's social novels, from *Vanity Fair* to *The Newcomes*, can be thought of as remarkably (and uncomfortably) incisive portrayals of the range of adaptive and maladaptive responses to the problem of cynical reason. Even his Prefaces bear the tinge of this problem. *Pendennis* starts with a complaint about the *de facto* censorship in Victorian fiction: 'Since the author of *Tom Jones* was buried, no writer of fiction among us has been permitted to depict to his utmost power a MAN. We must drape him, and give him a certain conventional simper' (*P*, lvi). The protest is bitter but ineffectual; knowing something is wrong is not, in Thackeray's world, tantamount to changing it, and his protest duly lodged, the novel proceeds to leave unmentioned those socially unmentionable parts of a young man's life. A residue of futile bitterness, which occasionally can sound like wise disillusionment, floats over the surface of these novels. Complaining about the limits of a form from within that form might sound metafictional to early twenty-first-century ears, but Thackeray is not interested in the subversiveness of metafiction; he is interested instead in the state of performing the roles we have to play all the while knowing their ridiculousness – that is to say, in the futility of self-knowledge. In a history of European consciousness, Thackeray stands beyond the cheerful and revolutionary reductivism of the eighteenth-century slogan *così fan tutte* and closer to the resigned jadedness of the nineteenth-century phrase 'that's the way of the world' – to say nothing of rather more profane late twentieth-century accounts of what 'happens'. Or, *vanitas vanitatum*, as the concluding page of *Vanity Fair* has it.

The power of Thackeray's portrayal of cynical reason is that within the tradition of the English novel, with its vaguely reformist hopes, expressions of balked agency are rare enough to be as explosive as revolutions. It is important that the most self-aware characters in his major novels, the characters most capable of seeing their place in the system and articulating their helplessness within it, their coerced participation, are women. Never the valorised women, the suitable wives, such as *Pendennis*'s Laura Bell, but the misfit women, such as Becky Sharp or *The Newcomes*'s Ethel Newcome. Ethel, the love of her cousin Clive, has been charged with finding a much wealthier and aristocratic mate; she is a pawn in the Newcome family's effort to raise itself. Her acute self-consciousness is raised to a kind of futile rebelliousness after a visit to an exhibition, when she notices green tickets marked 'Sold' attached to picture frames. She initially comments that 'we young ladies in the world, when we are exhibiting, ought to have little green tickets pinned on our backs, with 'Sold' written on them; it would prevent trouble and any future haggling, you know. Then at the end of the season the owner would come to carry us home.' When this acerbic commentary doesn't receive enough response, she decides to embody rather than simply speak:

> On that same evening, when the Newcome family assembled at dinner in Park Lane, Ethel appeared with a bright green ticket pinned in the front of her white muslin frock, and when asked what this queer fancy meant, she made Lady Kew a curtsey, looking her full in the face, and turning round to her father, said, 'I am a tableau-vivant, papa. I am Number 46 in the Exhibition of the Gallery of Painters in Water-colours.'[12]

The gesture is as futile as it is dramatic; the way in which Thackeray's least self-deceived characters express their helplessness is not by utopian dreaming but by *an angry acceptance of reality*. They protest by unusually dramatic surrenders.

Those characters more capable of self-deceit, or more comfortable with the world's alibis for things as they stand, go under the name 'gentlemen'. Even as Thackeray was characterised as such, and even as he has been read as a novelist dedicated to the ideal of gentlemanly behaviour, the truest 'gentlemen' in his novels suffer from their illusions. Rather than dramatise the insights of cynical reason in the manner of Ethel Newcome, they droop under the weight of an oppressive, even neurotic, boredom. *Vanity Fair*'s William Dobbin, a model of rectitude and faithfulness, is condemned to grow old waiting for his idealised image of Amelia Sedley to be finally shattered; in the meantime, he is described sleep-walking through years of army life. Clive Newcome is perhaps Thackeray's minor masterpiece in the portrayal of gentlemanly endurance; as marriage to his cousin Ethel becomes impossible, he fades from view, becomes prone to fits of mental abstraction, seems not all there. Pendennis, the narrator of *The Newcomes*, describes how Clive habitually 'bites his tawny mustachios, plunges his hands into his pockets and his soul into reverie': the posture of a character who has absented himself from his own plot (*N*, 827). His most characteristic facial expression, we are told, is a yawn. The gentleman's ultimate response to helplessness is therefore passive resistance at its most passive: refusing to pay attention. Boredom, melancholy, bitter irony, resignation, forms of suppressed panic: by the time of *The Newcomes* these affects increasingly dominate the supposedly 'comic' texture of Thackeray's novels. It is an odd testament to the liveability of cynical reason – the way in which it accustoms us to what might seem intolerable – that these painful affects were once, and can still be, read as genially humorous.

Thackeray's concentration on the lives of more or less ordinary individuals, the Clives, Ethels, and Pens of upper-middle-class British life, was focused not only through a social ontology but also through what could be called a historiography. In the process he altered the meaning of the 'historical novel' as it had come to him through Sir Walter Scott. Take, for instance, *Vanity Fair*'s announcement of the events of March 1815:

> 'Napoleon has landed at Cannes.' Such news might create a panic at Vienna, and cause Russia to drop his cards, and take Prussia into a corner, and Talleyrand and Metternich to wag their heads together, while Prince Hardenburg, and even the present Marquis of Londonderry, were puzzled; but how was this intelligence to affect a young lady in Russell Square, before whose door the watchman sang the hours when she was asleep; who, if she strolled in the square, was guarded there by the railings and the beadle: who, if she walked ever so short a distance to buy a ribbon in Southampton Row, was followed by black Sambo with an enormous cane: who was always cared for, dressed, put to bed, and watched over by ever so many guardian angels, with and without

> wages … Yes; Napoleon is flinging his last stake, and poor little Emmy Sedley's happiness forms, somehow, part of it.
>
> In the first place, her father's fortune was swept down with that fatal news. (*VF*, 211–12)

Despite its mock-uncertainty, the diffident 'somehow' that veils his logic, this passage demonstrates Thackeray's solution to the fundamental question of historical fiction since Scott: what kinds of experiences connect the individual to larger historical movements? How does that connection happen? Scott had offered bland, ambivalent heroes caught up in the middle of struggles, such as the series of eighteenth-century Scottish rebellions on behalf of the Stuart cause, that have sharp polarisations; his heroes negotiate the rift between the old (Jacobinism) and the new (Hanoverian rule), and as a result help to make that historical shift occur. Thackeray, however, seeks a historiography for a denser, more interconnected *world* history; not the intimacy of a civil war, but the far-flung consequences of trans-European conflict, connected to the individual by a series of mediating agencies, such as newspapers and finance capital. His solution is to offer the pole most seemingly far from history – the upper-middle-class young woman, sheltered and ignorant – and to expose it to a shock. There is no negotiation possible here, no decision to be made between, say, Scottish pride and English rule; it is only a question of surviving the sudden, catastrophic descent of History.

This is of course a deep problem for realism as well: how does one adapt a narrative technique that excels at intimacy, at the rather narrow radius of the human will, to historical processes much larger than any individual agency? *Vanity Fair*'s plot is spurred by the Hundred Days of 1815, but Thackeray is writing from the standpoint of the late 1840s, when mass history – the history of financial bubbles, transnational revolutionary movements, conscription – was increasingly recognisable. The logic of the Sedley family's sudden descent is a common one in the 1840s: a European political event spurs a financial crisis which destroys the investments of those who, like John Sedley, had bought heavily in French funds; the result is a young woman losing her home and her comfortable class position. The political theorist and geographer David Harvey has argued that the 'local', or the 'domestic', was no longer a self-sufficient frame of reference for fiction after the 1848 European revolutions, which made national boundaries as irrelevant as the railings of Russell Square.[13] Thackeray's fiction interprets history not as a crisis, as in the decisions of Scott's heroes, but as a *shock*.

Shock, of course, is not a mode of knowledge. As a result history in Thackeray is not entirely knowable. Great events, like Waterloo, are understandable only through their personal applications, such as the death of Amelia's fiancé, George Osborne, or through the lies and distortions through which they are filtered; Jos Sedley, who had fled Brussels out of fright, abandoning his sister, will later be known as 'Waterloo Sedley' thanks to his highly imaginative tales of his courage. History in Thackeray is not truth, it is instead an experience of something outside oneself, outside of the normal frames of life, which then gets rearticulated or re-experienced as a blurred, surreal glow. It is for this reason that Marxist literary critics, particularly Georg Lukács, condemned Thackeray's historical novels as a denial of the truth of historical processes, a reduction of the dialectics of history to the meaninglessness of individual perceptions.[14] The charge is both valid and irrelevant. Thackeray believes in no progress, no dialectics; his history is the record of catastrophes, much in the manner of Walter Benjamin's 'angel of history', who faces backwards and can see only the accumulation of wreckage and debris being hurled at its feet. Benjamin's description of 'progress' is appropriately Thackerayan: 'The angel would like to stay, awaken the dead, and make whole what has been smashed. But a storm is blowing from Paradise ... this storm is what we call progress.'[15]

The fruitless desire to make whole what has been smashed: another word for which would be 'nostalgia'. Where history is not experienced as a shock in Thackeray, it is experienced nostalgically, as a time defined by *what hasn't yet changed*. Frequently Thackeray's narrators will turn to the disappearance of the physical, quotidian details of childhood, particularly the demise of coaching; for future generations, *Vanity Fair* tells us, 'stage-coaches will have become romances – a team of four bays as fabulous as Bucephalus or Black Bess ... Alas! we shall never hear the horn sing at midnight, or see the pike-gates fly open any more' (*VF*, 87). This version of Thackerayan history is no small part of his nineteenth-century popularity; while Dickens more often mocked nostalgia as the make-believe of the privileged, Thackeray's talent tended towards indulging his fondness for the vanished past, particularly a vanished past that is a common, mass past, the past of technologies abandoned, buildings torn down, faces long since dead. Like photographs, Thackeray's descriptions memorialise even the present as the soon-to-be-disappeared; elegy seems encoded in his very way of seeing. With *The History of Henry Esmond*, Thackeray found the occasion to write a monument to this nostalgic historicity: a faux-memoir of the late seventeenth and early eighteenth century, it is suffused with longing for childhood memories. It was also published in an elaborately antique style, complete with an early eighteenth-century typeface and a dedication to a patron, all meant to create an artifact that signified not the resurrection of the past but its sheer, poignant inaccessibility. If Thackeray's description of historical shock has the capacity to frighten us, to make us realise how fragile our security is, his nostalgia offers us the comforts of a community: the impossibly large community of human desire for a vanished past. As such, he was perhaps the nineteenth century's finest nostalgist.

At the end of *Vanity Fair*, Thackeray refers to his characters as puppets, and tells his readers to put them back in their box; their game is over. As a commentary on Thackeray's conception of personality this is perfectly apt: we are lively when being manipulated, but dead, listless, limp when no one is around to manipulate us. But the naïve, or the entranced, reader might ask: do the puppets in the box continue to play when the lid has been shut on them? Listen carefully, for instance, to the moment when Becky, perhaps twenty years later, revisits Brussels and recalls the events of 1815, including George Osborne's attempt to seduce her:

> 'That poor Cupid!' she said; 'how dreadfully he was in love with me, and what a fool he was! I wonder whether little Emmy is alive. It was a good little creature: and that fat brother of hers. I have his funny fat picture still among my papers. They were kind simple people.' (*VF*, 821)

Given the unstated rules of realist representation, this moment is nothing less than shocking. The intimacy of British domestic realism depended upon a sense that we know all we need to know about central characters; even if we lack some details, we *know* them – we should know them better than a sibling, a lover, a parent. We should not, that is, have jealousy for some secret we can't grasp, some perspective of theirs we can't see. Yet here, Becky gives us something entirely different. Could she be misremembering? 'Kind and simple' is perhaps right for Amelia, but surely this is not quite right for Dobbin, who was her antagonist, or George, who may have been simple, but amply demonstrated his lack of kindness. Or could it be a belittlement? More unsettling still: is it possible that her recollection's lack of emotion and specificity show how the events of Brussels in 1815 – so central to the narrative of *Vanity Fair* – are to Becky just another incident in her life, and not even a particularly memorable one? Is it the case that Becky's experiences have been much larger, consequential, and complex than the part that involved the novel's characters – and us? In short, can we say that Becky's experience of herself is deeper and better informed than our experience of her?

Saying as much risks the naïveté, and terror, that informs a child's suspicion that when the lid is lifted, the puppets have just stopped playing among themselves. It also puts at risk the usual epistemological contract of realist fiction, in which we can understand what a character thinks, but in a way – and with a frame of reference – that they themselves could never understand. Thackeray seems to elevate the status of his characters; we know them as we know others in our lives, on the basis of sporadic intimacies, guesses, surmises; their reality surpasses our comprehension. But this extreme 'reality' comes at a cost – the cost of scepticism. What can we know of anyone else, even the fictional characters we think we know? In Thackeray the reader is not a god, nor even a parent; we have no privileged access. It is a remarkably diminished, if more palpably real, perspective; after all the vicissitudes of *Vanity Fair*, the lives lost or ruined, the men and women traduced, the loves faded, there is perhaps only that essentially solitary and detached comment to make: they were, after all, kind simple people.

NOTE ON EDITIONS

The best edition of Thackeray's complete works is still the seventeen-volume series prepared by George Saintsbury for Oxford University Press in 1908, commonly called the Oxford Thackeray. The current editions of Thackeray's major novels published as Oxford World's Classics are generally based on Saintsbury's texts, include copious annotations, and reproduce Thackeray's own images for the novels, such as *Vanity Fair*, that he originally illustrated.

NOTES

1 There have been, however, two notable exceptions: Stanley Kubrick's technically innovative 1974 film *Barry Lyndon*, based on Thackeray's 1844 picaresque novel, and Mira Nair's 2004 *Vanity Fair*, which reimagined the novel as an extended rumination on empire.
2 See George Saintsbury, introduction to *Henry Esmond*, Oxford Thackeray (Oxford: Oxford University Press, 1908), XII, p. x.
3 Charlotte Brontë, *Jane Eyre*, ed. Q. D. Leavis (Harmondsworth: Penguin, 1985), p. 36.
4 Hippolyte Taine, *Notes on England*, trans. Edward Hyams (Fair Lawn, NJ: Essential, 1958), p. 95.
5 Henry James, Preface to *The Tragic Muse*, in *The Art of the Novel: Critical Prefaces*, ed. R. P. Blackmur (New York: Scribners, 1947), p. 84.
6 F. R. Leavis, *The Great Tradition: George Eliot, Henry James, Joseph Conrad* (Garden City, NY: Doubleday, 1954), p. 21.
7 C. L. R. James, *Beyond a Boundary* (Durham, NC: Duke University Press, 1993), pp. 18, 39.
8 Thackeray, *The Book of Snobs*, ed. John Sutherland (New York: St Martin's Press, 1978), p. 35.
9 Thackeray, *Vanity Fair*, ed. John Sutherland (Oxford: Oxford University Press, 1983), p. 539. Hereafter *VF*.
10 Thackeray, *Pendennis*, ed. John Sutherland (Oxford: Oxford University Press, 1994), p. 152, 211. Hereafter *P*.
11 See Peter Sloterdijk's *Critique of Cynical Reason* (Minneapolis: University of Minnesota Press, 1987).

12 Thackeray, *The Newcomes*, ed. Andrew Sanders (Oxford: Oxford University Press, 1995), p. 362. Hereafter *N*.
13 See David Harvey, *The Condition of Postmodernity: An Enquiry into the Origins of Cultural Change* (Oxford: Blackwell, 1989).
14 See Georg Lukács's denunciation of Thackeray's historical fiction in his *The Historical Novel*, trans. Hannah Mitchell and Stanley Mitchell (Lincoln: University of Nebraska Press, 1983).
15 Walter Benjamin, 'Theses on the Philosophy of History', in *Illuminations*, trans. Harry Zohn (New York: Schocken, 1968), pp. 257–8.

FURTHER READING

Carlisle, Janice, *The Sense of an Audience: Dickens, Thackeray, and George Eliot at Mid-Century*, Athens, GA, University of Georgia Press, 1981
Dames, Nicholas, *Amnesiac Selves: Nostalgia, Forgetting, and British Fiction, 1810–1870*, New York, Oxford University Press, 2001
Gilmour, Robin, *The Idea of the Gentleman in the Victorian Novel*, London, Allen and Unwin, 1981
Harden, Edgar, *The Emergence of Thackeray's Serial Fiction*, Athens, GA, University of Georgia Press, 1979
Hardy, Barbara, *The Exposure of Luxury: Radical Themes in Thackeray's Fiction*, Pittsburgh, University of Pittsburgh Press, 1972
McMaster, Juliet, *Thackeray: The Major Novels*, Toronto, University of Toronto Press, 1971
Miller, Andrew, *Novels behind Glass: Commodity Culture and Victorian Narrative*, Cambridge, Cambridge University Press, 1995
Peters, Catherine, *Thackeray's Universe: Shifting Worlds of Imagination and Reality*, London, Faber and Faber, 1987
Ray, Gordon, *Thackeray: The Uses of Adversity, 1811–1846*, New York, McGraw-Hill, 1955
Thackeray: The Age of Wisdom, 1847–1863, New York, McGraw-Hill, 1958
Shillingsburg, Peter, *Pegasus in Harness: Victorian Publishing and W. M. Thackeray*, Charlottesville, University of Virginia Press, 1992
Sutherland, John, *Thackeray at Work*, London, Athlone, 1974
Taylor, D. J., *Thackeray*, London, Carroll and Graf, 1999
Tillotson, Geoffrey, and Donald Hawes (eds.), *Thackeray: The Critical Heritage*, London, Routledge & Kegan Paul, 1968

10

PATSY STONEMAN

Charlotte Brontë

'Master! How is he my master?'
Jane Eyre, 1847[1]

Every reader who remembers what it was like, as a child, to be hurt without reason and punished for crimes not committed, must warm to the first scene of *Jane Eyre*, where the young Jane breaks out 'like a mad cat' (*JE*, 12) against her bullying cousin, John Reed. Her protest, 'Unjust ! – unjust!' (*JE*, 15) claims common cause with categories of oppression well beyond her situation as an orphan and poor relation: 'Wicked and cruel boy!', she cries, 'You are like a murderer – you are like a slave-driver – you are like the Roman emperors!' (*JE*, 11). Her aunt's lady's maid, however, insists on a specific class and gender context, finding Jane's conduct 'shocking' because it fails in due deference to her 'young master' (*JE*, 12). Jane's reply, 'How is he my master?', opens up a dominant theme in Charlotte Brontë's work.

Jane Eyre's earliest readers were alarmed by this self-reliant heroine, who moves from childish 'mutiny' (*JE*, 12) to an adult claim to stand 'equal' with the man she loves, despite his apparent superiority in class and wealth (*JE*, 266). 'Every page burns with moral Jacobinism' wrote one reviewer: '"Unjust, unjust," is the burden of every reflection upon the things and powers that be',[2] while another found that 'the tone of the mind and thought which has overthrown authority ... abroad, and fostered Chartism and rebellion at home, is the same which has also written Jane Eyre'.[3] Nowadays, when *Jane Eyre* is read primarily as a love story, this response seems extreme. In 1847, however, when the novel appeared, the Chartist movement threatened civil anarchy in England. By January 1848 a version of *Jane Eyre* was on stage at London's Victoria Theatre, notorious for its insubordinate treatment of class issues.[4] By later in 1848, when these reviews were published, the whole of Europe was embroiled in 'the year of revolutions'.

Charlotte Brontë was not, however, an obstreperous member of the working class, or even an intellectual radical. Born in 1816, the third daughter of a West Yorkshire curate, Charlotte lived a life of personal endurance rather than public indignation. Her mother died when she was five, and at eight she suffered, with her two elder sisters, the harsh regime at Cowan Bridge School which she described as Lowood in *Jane Eyre*. Maria and Elizabeth died a year later. Then came a peaceful time at home with her brother, Branwell, and two younger sisters, Emily and Anne, looked after by a stern but caring aunt and encouraged by their father to read, write, draw, play music, and walk out on the moors. The Reverend Patrick Brontë was shown in early biographies as harsh and eccentric in his treatment of the children, but more recent research shows him as an active and benevolent parent, allowing his daughters an unusual latitude – they read, for instance, the scandalous Byron – and even teaching them Latin.

At fourteen, Charlotte went as a pupil to Roe Head School, a more liberal establishment where she later became a teacher. Then followed several rather wretched periods as governess in private families, but at twenty-five, she had never moved far from the small town of Haworth where she grew up. In this year, 1842, she gathered her courage and set out, with her sister Emily, to improve their languages at a school in Brussels. Here she encountered a remarkable teacher, M. Heger, and fell in love. Heger was, however, married, and after two years of increasing anguish she forced herself to go home, desperate for his letters, which, since he was a model of propriety, did not arrive. This, the most vivid experience of her life, furnished material for all her novels, and although at thirty-eight she married her father's curate, she died, in 1855, before she could take hold of this experience. There seems to be nothing in this life to account for revolutionary fervour. In class terms, indeed, she shared her father's oddly liberal conservatism, in which a deep sympathy with social deprivation, drawn from his poor Irish childhood, coexisted with a dread of mob action which led him to revere strong leaders.

The Marxist critic Terry Eagleton sees such contradictions as the key to the Brontë sisters' peculiar power. Living in an area and at a period of intense industrial friction, they were themselves placed 'at a painfully ambiguous point in the social structure', striving

> to maintain reasonably 'genteel' standards in a traditionally rough-and-ready environment. They were, moreover, socially insecure *women* ... And they were *educated* women, trapped in an almost intolerable deadlock between culture and economics – between imaginative aspiration and the cold truth of a society which could use them merely as 'higher' servants. They were *isolated* educated women, socially and geographically remote from a world with which they nevertheless maintained close intellectual touch, and so driven back on themselves in solitary emotional hungering.[5]

Charlotte's radicalism appears in her language for such 'hungering', which she found in the Romantic poets, in Sir Walter Scott, and George Sand, scorning the 'carefully fenced' world of Jane Austen, which scarcely acknowledges the 'stormy sisterhood' of 'the Passions'.[6] Her vehemence against class barriers is, however, ambiguous, and in *Jane Eyre*, like Dickens with his male protagonists in *Oliver Twist* (1837–9) and *David Copperfield* (1849–50), Charlotte protests rather that her heroine is misprised than that class divisions are iniquitous. This despised orphan is, like Cinderella, recognised by her Prince, but she hardly wishes to level class differences. Instead she is raised to her right level by discovering respectable relatives and inheriting a fortune. Even when acknowledged as equal in every way with the man she longs to marry, however, Jane prefers to address him as 'my master' (*JE*, 273), just as when she served in his household as governess to his young ward, and this apparently voluntary subjugation has earned her some scorn from modern feminists. The paradox of the conservative rebel is, however, worth unravelling, since the novel offers a sustained investigation of what constitutes 'mastery'.

Chapter 1 shows us that Jane is not prepared to submit to tyranny of class or gender, but it also shows her predisposed to revere those who can enlarge her mental world. This ten-year-old girl, confined within Gateshead Hall, already has access through her reading to Lapland and Siberia, to eighteenth-century love stories and to Roman tortures. At Lowood School, she is drawn to Helen Burns and to Miss Temple because of their liberal minds (*JE*, 53), and without them, finds Lowood oppressive (*JE*, 88). Installed at Thornfield Hall as governess to Adèle, she gazes at the horizon, longing 'for a power of vision which might overpass that limit' (*JE*, 114). Her first resource is imaginary; to turn her 'inward ear to a tale ... quickened with all of incident, life, fire, feeling, that I desired and had not in my actual existence' (*JE*, 114). Charlotte Brontë herself continued into adult life the fantastic imaginings which, as a child, she shared with her brother and sisters, and she was not alone in this habit. Florence Nightingale, before the Crimean War gave her a sphere of activity, confirmed that many 'daughters at home' lived a double life, in which a calm exterior hid the wildest daydreaming: 'It is', she writes, 'the want of interest in our life which produces it; by filling up that want of interest in our life we can alone remedy it.'[7] Heather Glen argues that Jane Eyre's daydreaming makes her 'a paradigmatic figure' in Victorian culture,[8] and indeed Jane protests on behalf of 'millions' who suffer a 'stiller doom' even than hers, and are 'in silent revolt against their lot' (*JE*, 114–15):

> Women are supposed to be very calm generally: but women feel just as men feel; they need exercise for their faculties, and a field for their efforts as much as their brothers do; they suffer from too rigid a constraint, too absolute a stagnation, precisely as men would suffer; and it is narrow-minded in their more privileged fellow-creatures to say that they ought to confine themselves to making puddings and knitting stockings, to playing on the piano and embroidering bags.
>
> (*JE*, 115)

When Mr Rochester takes up residence at Thornfield Hall, Jane is thus suffering 'the viewless fetters of an uniform and too still existence' (*JE*, 122). The presence of 'the master', however, means that 'Thornfield Hall was a changed place ... a rill from the outer world was flowing through it' (*JE*, 123–4). In their first long interview, Jane and Rochester explore the terms on which he is to be regarded as her master. She will not allow that age and experience confer 'the right to be a little masterful', since 'your claim to superiority depends on the use you have made of your time and experience'. Nor will her position as a 'paid subordinate' grant him automatic superiority, though he gains it, in her eyes, from having forgotten that part of their contract (*JE*, 140–1). As their relationship develops, she is charmed by his ability 'to open to a mind unacquainted with the world, glimpses of its scenes and ways' with an 'ease of manner' suited to 'my relation, rather than my master' (*JE*, 153). Finally goaded into declaring her feelings for Rochester, Jane cites her sense of

> communion with what is bright, and energetic and high. I have talked, face to face, with what I reverence; with what I delight in, – with an original, a vigorous, an expanded mind. I have known you, Mr Rochester; and it strikes me with terror and anguish to feel I absolutely must be torn from you for ever. I see the necessity of departure; and it is like looking on the necessity of death. (*JE*, 265)

This is the personal context in which Jane is able to cast off 'custom, conventionalities' and address Rochester 'just as if both had passed through the grave, and we stood at God's feet, equal, – as we are!' (*JE*, 266).

Gender differences are, however, more resistant than those of class. As prospective bridegroom, Rochester smiles a smile 'such as a sultan might, in a blissful and fond moment, bestow on a slave his gold and gems had enriched' (*JE*, 282). This is a kind of mastery which Jane will not tolerate:

> 'I'll not stand you an inch in the stead of a seraglio,' I said; 'so don't consider me an equivalent for one: if you have a fancy for anything in that line, away with you, sir, to the bazaars of Stamboul without delay; and lay out in extensive slave-purchases some of that spare cash you seem at a loss to spend satisfactorily here.'

She, meanwhile, will 'go out as a missionary to preach liberty to them that are enslaved' (*JE*, 282). Recognising that 'turtle-dove sensibility' would only 'foster ... his despotism', she uses 'the needle of repartee' to avoid the 'bathos of sentiment' (*JE*, 286–7).

There is still, however, an obstacle to their union. At the very altar, Jane discovers that Rochester is already married, to a madwoman, confined in the third storey, whose cries and night-time sorties have provided a mysterious background to their courtship. While the novel's first readers took the mad wife as a mere device of melodrama, feminist critics have pointed to parallels between Jane and her insane predecessor. It is in the third-storey corridor that Jane combats her sense of confinement with imaginative fantasies – while behind the wall, Bertha's unleashed mind is met with absolute physical constraint. Sandra Gilbert and Susan Gubar take 'the madwoman in the attic' as a significant feature of Victorian women's writing. Every sober heroine of the Jane Eyre type, they argue, is shadowed by a mad, bad double whose presence allows rage and sexual desire to be voiced, even though they are controlled by the novel's overt moral scheme.[9] More disturbing still, Jean Rhys's novel *Wide Sargasso Sea* (1966) shows how the naïve Antoinetta Mason became the mad Bertha by 'giv[ing] herself' too freely to Rochester.[10]

Jane, however, has Reason to master Feeling, and finds that after the failed marriage, when she is tempted to become Rochester's mistress, 'conscience, turned tyrant, held passion by the throat' (*JE*, 314). Jane's 'conscience' here provokes impatience in some modern readers. Even Charlotte Brontë's contemporary, George Eliot, who believed that 'all self-sacrifice is good', felt that 'one would like it to be in a somewhat nobler cause than that of a diabolical law which chains a man soul and body to a putrefying carcase'.[11] Jane's fear of giving way to the 'madness' of passion is reinforced when Rochester describes his past experience of 'kept women' as 'the next worst thing to buying a slave' (*JE*, 328), but when he urges his despair at losing her, she finds that

> my very Conscience and Reason turned traitors against me, and charged me with crime in resisting him. They spoke almost as loud as Feeling, and that clamoured wildly. 'Oh, comply! ... Who in the world cares for *you*? Or who will be injured by what you do?'
>
> Still indomitable was the reply – '*I* care for myself. The more solitary, the more friendless, the more unsustained I am, the more I will respect myself ... I will hold to the principles received by me when I was sane, and not mad – as I am now ... They have a worth – so I have always believed; and if I cannot believe it now, it is because I am insane – quite insane: with my veins running fire, and my heart beating faster than I can count its throbs. (*JE*, 334)

What Jane achieves here is self-possession, not as a mere social manner, but as a secure grounding in her own sense of self-worth. Although Rochester's 'fury was wrought to the highest', so that 'physically, I felt, at the moment, powerless as stubble exposed to the draught and glow of a furnace – mentally, I still possessed my soul'. He is forced to recognise that though 'frail', she is 'indomitable', since to assault her body would be to lose her spirit (*JE*, 335).

Jane leaves Rochester and takes up a humble post, 'free and honest', as a village schoolmistress. She yearns for his love, but not at the cost of being 'a slave in a fool's paradise' (*JE*, 378–9). Her rescuer, however, the young clergyman St John Rivers, offers an example of self-mastery which seems to her as dangerous as its opposite. He subdues his passion for the heiress, Rosalind Oliver, as 'ignoble; a mere fever of the flesh' (*JE*, 395), and as his pupil, Jane must also 'disown half my nature, stifle half my faculties' (*JE*, 420). As his wife, she would be 'forced to keep the fire of my nature continually low, to compel it to burn inwardly and never to utter a cry, though the imprisoned flame consumed vital after vital' (*JE*, 429). On the brink, nevertheless, of agreeing to this fate, she hears Rochester's voice – exactly how, we do not know – and is called back to a changed situation. Jane is now an heiress; St John and his sisters are her cousins; she has, therefore, a position in the world independent of Rochester. Rochester, on the other hand, is a free man but blind, scarred and crippled, and Thornfield Hall is a ruin. This redress of social and physical balance between the lovers seems harsh, but suggests Charlotte Brontë's distrust of marriage in an age when a woman was effectively vassal to her husband, who would legally own not only her possessions, but also her body and her children.[12] Jane can only trust Rochester not to invoke this mastery and in fact finds herself 'at perfect ease … in his presence I thoroughly lived; and he lived in mine' (*JE*, 460). His new dependence might, indeed, threaten self-pity, but for her 'needle of repartee': to his question, '"Am I hideous, Jane?"', she replies, '"Very, sir: you always were, you know"' (*JE*, 461).

Some modern readers are disappointed that such a fiery rebel should end satisfied with the life of a wife and mother, but the picture of companionate marriage given in the last chapter offered, for its Victorian readers, a way of loosening the 'viewless fetters' of women's lives without the penalties of being outlawed. We can be sure, for one thing, that Jane will enjoy physical love – Rochester's kisses and embraces are welcome, while to 'endure all the forms of love' while married to St John would have been 'a martyrdom' (*JE*, 426–7). When the married Jane writes, however, that 'I am my husband's life as fully as he is mine', this is only part of her meaning. 'We talk, I believe, all day long', she says (*JE*, 475), and we remember that her reason for loving him was her 'delight in … an original, a vigorous, an expanded mind' (*JE*, 265).

Jane Eyre was Charlotte Brontë's most successful novel,[13] but it was not her first effort at fiction. *The Professor* had already been offered to publishers with Anne Brontë's *Agnes Grey* and Emily's *Wuthering Heights*, but she was writing long before this. With her brother and sisters, she had invented a country called Angria, whose larger-than-life characters prompted all kinds of writing, from lyric poetry to political satire. At the age of twenty she could still be 'quite gone' into this world, so that in the schoolroom where she was a teacher, 'I ... saw the Duke of Zamorna leaning against that obelisk, with the ... African sky quivering and shaking with stars expanded above all'.[14] A year later, however, she bade farewell to Angria, turning 'to a cooler region where the dawn breaks grey and sober'.[15]

Soberness was the keyword for *The Professor*, and despite the success of *Jane Eyre*'s more sensational tone, Charlotte's next attempt at fiction returned to sober realism. On the first page of *Shirley* (1849), she asks, 'Do you anticipate sentiment, and poetry, and reverie? Do you expect passion, and stimulus, and melodrama? Calm your expectations; reduce them to a lowly standard. Something real, cool, and solid, lies before you; something unromantic as Monday morning.'[16] The very success of *Jane Eyre* woke in Charlotte Brontë a sense that she should broach more public issues, but she felt unequal to dealing with the current state of affairs in the industrial north. She had, however, a vivid knowledge of an earlier crisis which offered some parallels with the Chartist age. From stories told by her father, and by Miss Wooler, her teacher at Roe Head, she knew of violent scenes in the very area surrounding Roe Head School during the Luddite riots of 1811–12.[17] Augmented by research in the *Leeds Mercury*, these stories formed the context for *Shirley*.

'Who is to be master?' is the question implicit in these scenes of class warfare, but Charlotte Brontë's Victorian readers need not have feared insurrection at her hands: *Shirley* will not, like Frances Trollope's *Michael Armstrong, the Factory Boy* (1840), show the masters as 'child-torturers' or 'slave ... drivers' (*Sh*, 61). A brisk analysis of the local effects on trade, in these late years of the Napoleonic Wars, of the British 'Orders in Council', ensures that sympathy lies with her mill-owner hero, Robert Moore, rather than his desperate, machine-breaking workers (*Sh*, 30). Her middle-class male characters represent well-differentiated political positions, Mr Yorke taking the radical, anti-Establishment side; Mr Helstone the arch-conservative, Church-and-king line; and Robert Moore the pragmatic position of the entrepreneur, who wishes for peace almost at any price to revive his dying trade (*Sh*, 54–6, 37–8).

From among the workers, however, like Dickens in *Hard Times* (1854), she gives us extreme types – the drunken fanatic Moses Barraclough and the honest William Farren, driven by genuine desperation but 'not for pulling down mills and breaking machines', for his appeal is to authority – 'them that governs mun find a way to help us' (*Sh*, 137). Each of these figures is dealt with in individual terms – Barraclough jailed and Farren found work as a gardener – which leave the larger issues unresolved, settled only temporarily (as we know from history) by the repeal of the Orders in Council. Robert Moore appears to be converted from a hard master who regards working-class suffering as the price of progress (*Sh*, 138) to an interventionist prepared to build houses and schools, but these plans appear in the last pages as 'extravagant day-dreams', and the retrospective final paragraphs confirm only that they 'were, partially, at least, fulfilled' (*Sh*, 645).

The anti-romantic introduction to the novel points not only to its public themes but also to its effort to avoid the love-and-courtship plot. Most of the marriages in the novel are painful. Caroline Helstone's mother describes romance as 'the green tempting surface of the marsh' while marriage is 'the slough underneath' (*Sh*, 379); her father was a drunkard who mistreated wife and daughter (*Sh*, 102–3, 438); and for her uncle, marriage is 'a piece of pure folly' (*Sh*, 101, 217). Yet marriage at least provides a semblance of function for women. Uselessness afflicts not only dependent spinsters like Caroline, but even an heiress like Shirley Keeldar, who can still do very little without the agency of men (*Sh*, 270–4). Shirley and Caroline's position in society is symbolised by their physical stance during the riot at Moore's factory; they watch from a distance while Moore, Yorke, and Helstone fight off the attack, certain that they could do no good by 'a romantic rush ... into the mêlée' (*Sh*, 343, 345). Charlotte Brontë's pessimism here contrasts with Elizabeth Gaskell's hope, in words that seem deliberately to quote *Shirley*, that when *her* heroine throws herself 'into the mêlée, like a romantic fool', she nevertheless does 'some good' and 'a woman's work'.[18]

Caroline's first wish in *Shirley* is to do something useful, such as working in Robert's counting-house (*Sh*, 71, 77), while the description of Robert's sister, Hortense, who 'would give a day to the mending of two holes in a stocking' (*Sh*, 81), recalls Jane Eyre's protest against 'making puddings and embroidering bags'. Charlotte Brontë was closer to current affairs here than in her 'industrial' theme, since it was not long before the Langham Place Group, the Society for the Employment of Women, and *The English Woman's Journal* were to address the employment of women. Charlotte's focus, however, is not on practical crusading; it is on the inner damage done to individual women by 'solitary emotional hungering'.[19] Caroline's uncle will not allow her to work, and Robert Moore is too poor, and too preoccupied with business, to marry her. Bleakly she surveys her future: 'half a century of existence may lie before me. How am I to occupy it? What am I to do to fill the interval of time which spreads between me and the grave?' (*Sh*, 173).

The urgency of her plight is reflected in intense metaphors, and when she meets a mild rebuff from Robert, its pain is magnified by the conventions of feminine delicacy:

> A lover masculine so disappointed can speak and urge explanation; a lover feminine can say nothing ... You expected bread, and you have got a stone; break your teeth on it, and don't shriek because the nerves are martyrized ... You held out your hand for an egg, and fate put into it a scorpion. Show no consternation: close your fingers firmly upon the gift; let it sting through your palm. Never mind: in time, after your hand and arm have swelled and quivered long with torture, the squeezed scorpion will die, and you will have learned the great lesson how to endure without a sob. (*Sh*, 105)

Caroline knows that her disappointment is greater because 'women have so few things to think about' (*Sh*, 229), but she cannot be satisfied with the benevolent work thought appropriate for 'old maids': 'I perceive that certain sets of human beings are very apt to maintain that other sets should give up their lives to them and their service, and then requite them by praise: they call them devoted and virtuous. Is this enough? Is it to live?' (*Sh*, 174). Shirley's arrival mitigates her loneliness, but believing that Shirley will marry Robert, Caroline forms desperate plans to become a governess, only to have this escape closed by Mrs Pryor's warning: 'Better be a slave at once' (*Sh*, 241, 375–6). It is this absolute blankness of future which sends Caroline into a dangerous illness.

Like most Victorian novels, *Shirley* was published in three volumes, and most such works read seamlessly enough. The third volume of *Shirley*, however, shows a noticeable change of tone, and the reason is not hard to find. While Charlotte was writing her first, confident volume, before September 1848, she discussed it with Emily and Anne, as was their habit. By May 1849, her brother and both her sisters were dead. It is not clear exactly when volume II was written, but the third volume was written in the summer of 1849.[20] Little wonder that its first chapter is entitled 'The Valley of the Shadow of Death'. This volume is dominated by the need for love, and Caroline is saved from her illness by the devotion of Mrs Pryor, who proves to be her mother. As Shirley and Caroline move towards marital love with the Moore brothers, the tone of the language departs markedly from the realistic, often humorous narrative of volume I. Now we have purple passages, not only in the narrative voice (for example, *Sh*, 566, 568, 635), but within the dialogue. Robert Moore and Mr Yorke talk as if they were characters from Byron (*Sh*, 532–42), while Louis Moore quotes Shirley's embarrassingly high-flown schoolgirl essay, five pages long, verbatim (*Sh*, 485–90).

These deficiencies are a shame, since this final volume returns to Charlotte Brontë's characteristic theme of mastery between men and women. With Robert softened by illness, and released from financial hardship, his union with Caroline is only a matter of time, and the novel's focus shifts towards

Shirley and her love for Robert's brother, Louis, belatedly introduced at the end of volume II. Charlotte told Elizabeth Gaskell that Shirley was 'what Emily would have been, had she been placed in health and prosperity'.[21] As a child, Emily was lively, attractive, and precocious, and even in her more reserved adult life she was unconventional: like Shirley, she lay on the rug, and was devotedly fond of a fierce large dog.[22] We do not know, however, how Emily would have behaved in a courtship situation,[23] and it is, therefore, intriguing to see Charlotte's emphasis on Shirley's need to be mastered. Shirley cannot marry the otherwise eligible Sir Philip because he is '*not my master*' (*Sh*, 551, original emphasis). It is the pedagogic relationship which allows Louis the mastery which he lacks in social terms (*Sh*, 622–3), but its progress is interesting only in outline; it fails through lapsing, in George Eliot's words, 'from the picture to the diagram'.[24]

In *Villette* (1853), however, Charlotte Brontë offers her most sustained treatment of the master–pupil relationship, and this is intensified by the absence of positive female friendships. In *Jane Eyre*, Jane is supported by her relationships with Helen Burns, Miss Temple, and Mary and Diana Rivers. In *Shirley*, the friendship between Shirley and Caroline is almost as important as their relationships with men, although there is already a dismayed survey of other women's inadequate lives. *Villette* is almost schematic in its array of negative female existences. The young Paulina is a parody of feminine service to men; Miss Marchmont, like a benign version of Miss Havisham (in Dickens's *Great Expectations*) has spent thirty years in mourning for a dead lover;[25] Madame Beck's success depends on covert surveillance (*V*, 74); and Ginevra Fanshawe prefers catching a rich husband to Lucy's aim of 'earning a living' (*V*, 55–6). In an exhibition of paintings, Lucy sees other approved types of femininity: a sensual Cleopatra (*V*, 199), and four stages of 'La vie d'une femme', from prim maiden through pious bride and dispirited mother to grim widow. 'What women to live with!' Lucy comments, 'insincere, ill-humoured, bloodless, brainless nonentities' (*V*, 201–2).

Our heroine, meanwhile, though narrating her own story, is at pains to appear 'a mere looker-on at life' (*V*, 141). 'I, Lucy Snowe', she writes, 'plead guiltless of that curse, an overheated and discursive imagination' (*V*, 11), and in the face of Paulina's anguish, 'I, Lucy Snowe, was calm' (*V*, 22). She discovers, however, that the cold mantra of her name is no protection against the 'overheating' of desire. In *Jane Eyre*, St John Rivers, blond and coldly controlled, is contrasted with the dark and passionate Rochester. In *Villette* there is a comparable opposition between Lucy's cousin, the fair and sunny-tempered John Graham Bretton, and her teacher, M. Paul Emanuel, swarthy and emotional. It is tempting to see in this opposition the mythic rivalry of the rational Apollo and the sensualist Dionysus, but in Charlotte

Brontë's novels the dark 'Dionysian' attracts the heroine as much by his intellect as by his passion. Lucy finds that M. Paul's 'mind was indeed my library, and whenever it was opened to me, I entered bliss' (*V*, 381). Lucy herself, moreover, seems to combine these opposite qualities, as if Jane Eyre had swallowed the madwoman. There are always those who see her as 'quiet Lucy' (*V*, 333), 'inoffensive as a shadow' (*V*, 317), but M. Paul sees through her impassive surface: 'Other people in this house see you pass, and think that a colourless shadow has gone by. As for me', he tells her, he finds her savage, with her heart on fire and lightning darting from her eyes (*V*, 155, 318).

As the story progresses, its focus turns relentlessly inward to this volcanic charge of emotion which resists repression, and the power of the novel, which George Eliot found 'almost preternatural',[26] lies in this inward drama, where abstract qualities – Reason and Feeling – are personified in violent imagery. Lucy's solitude 'maintained in my soul the cravings of a most deadly famine' (*V*, 158), and against her better judgement (*V*, 228), she gives way to the 'strange, sweet insanity' of relying on Dr John's letters (*V*, 240). When these fail, she is thrown on the mercy of Reason, who, 'vindictive as a devil … turned me out by night, in mid-winter, on cold snow, flinging for sustenance the gnawed bone dogs had forsaken: sternly … she vowed her stores held nothing more for me – harshly denied my right to ask better things' (*V*, 229–30). With Reason in the ascendant, the sustained metaphor of famine gives way to that of burial: Lucy buries her letters in the garden of the school (*V*, 296), in a spot marked in legend as the tomb of a young nun, 'buried alive, for some crime against her vow' (*V*, 106). Months later, Lucy fears that she too has committed live burial: 'Sometimes I thought the tomb unquiet, and dreamed strangely of disturbed earth, and of hair, still golden and living, obtruded through coffin-chinks' (*V*, 362). In an inspired resurgence of a Gothic motif, she finds herself haunted by the figure of a nun, like a personification of Freud's perception that emotions too sternly repressed will return in uncanny shapes (*V*, 245, 297, 368).[27]

Lucy uses locks and keys – both real and metaphorical – to repress emotion, but for the feminist critic Kate Millett, 'escape is all over the book; *Villette* reads like one long meditation on a prison break'.[28] In the final chapters, when Lucy has admitted her love for her 'magnificent-minded' Paul (*V*, 488), she is goaded beyond endurance by being kept from him in the days before he leaves on a long sea-voyage. Now she does indeed break out of the confining school and, under a narcotic influence, enters the night-time park. In a scene of extraordinary vividness, she sees, in the lights and music of a national festival, a magical hallucination, 'a land of enchantment, a garden most gorgeous, a plain sprinkled with coloured meteors, a forest with sparks of purple and ruby and golden fire gemming the foliage; a region, not of trees and shadow, but of strangest architectural wealth – of altar and of temple, of pyramid, obelisk, and sphynx' (*V*, 453). This phantasmagoria, as Heather Glen demonstrates, is only an exaggerated version of Lucy's ordinary life, where society is a costly spectacle which dazzles, but does not include her.[29] It is only as she watches M. Paul with an apparent rival that 'something tore me so cruelly under my shawl, something so dug into my side, a vulture so strong in beak and talon, I must be alone to grapple with it' (*V*, 468).

The nun, the symbol of repressed emotion, now loses her power: 'thoroughly lashed up by a new scourge, I defied spectra ... I held her on high – the goblin! I shook her loose – the mystery! And down she fell – down all round me – down in shreds and fragments – and I trode upon her' (*V*, 470). The 'ghost' in this scene is nobody – nothing but an empty habit, discarded by Ginevra's lover, but the symbolism is apposite. Lucy's impassive behaviour has made her a 'nobody' (*V*, 308), just as Paulina's repressed anguish made the room she was in seem 'not inhabited, but haunted' (*V*, 12). Eugenia C. Delamotte argues that 'one of the dangers of living out the conventional life of a woman is that it will render one spectral, unreal, nobody. This association of proper and conventional womanhood with ghostliness makes Lucy's destruction of the nun an enraged assault on those ideals that render women "bloodless, brainless nonentities"'.[30]

Behind each of Charlotte Brontë's novels lies her hopeless love for M. Heger, and each of her heroes has one or more of his features – Mr Rochester is married, the Moore brothers are Belgian, William Crimsworth, in *The Professor*, is a teacher, and (since 'Villette' is a fictional version of Brussels) M. Paul is effectively a Belgian teacher. All are in some sense 'master' to the female protagonists. Like *Villette*, *The Professor* is set in a Brussels school modelled on the Pensionnat Heger.[31] Its focus, however, is different from the later novel, since Crimsworth, the teacher, is English. More important, he is the first-person narrator, and we see the female pupil, Frances Henri, through his eyes. In their eventual marriage, each of them retains their teaching profession and consequent income, even when Frances becomes a mother. *The Professor* is, therefore, a sanguine version of the love-theme, in which pupil and master attain a satisfactory mode of working and living as equals.

Villette, by contrast, emphasises the struggle for self-possession. Ginevra Fanshawe's question, 'Who *are* you, Miss Snowe?', is not to be answered in Ginevra's terms, in which only the rank of her relations would make her 'anybody' (*V*, 307–9). Nor does it depend on the social presence of a husband. Despite the unique intensity of Lucy's suffering, the novel's resolution is neither outright tragedy nor a happy union of souls. Instead we leave Lucy alone, but active, with engrossing work (*V*, 493). Her equilibrium is not, however, quite self-generated. Although M. Paul is not there at the end, and may never return, it is immensely important that he should have recognised Lucy's qualities and, as a result, have loved her. His letters, which confirm her importance in his eyes, are described as if to quell Caroline Helstone's tortures: M. Paul 'would give neither a stone, nor an excuse – neither a scorpion, nor a disappointment; his letters were real food that nourished, living water that refreshed' (*V*, 494). Self-possession, it seems, depends on one's sense of self-worth being reflected back from the eyes of another – especially a master.

The only power which is Lucy's own is the power of narration. Compared with Charlotte Brontë's earlier novels, Lucy's narrative in *Villette* shows an almost perverse pleasure in denying information: 'I must somehow have fallen over-board' (*V*, 35), she writes, metaphorically, of the disaster which throws her into the world without resources. When Lucy's English cousin John Graham Bretton reappears in Villette as 'Dr John', she conceals for a long time that she has guessed his identity (*V*, 96, 99, 174–5). The Lucy who narrates the story must know that the 'nun' who appears to Lucy at critical moments is Ginevra's lover in disguise; she must also know, but does not divulge, whether M. Paul is drowned at sea. These failures of candour could derive from the awkwardness of first-person narration, where a knowing hindsight could destroy the suspense of present scenes. Mary Jacobus, however, sees them as the narrative equivalent of repression – the 'buried letter' within the text which allows an ordinary life – *heimlich*, or homely – to appear *unheimlich*, or uncanny.[32]

It is, perhaps, Charlotte Brontë's particular gift that she is able to recount lives whose outward shapes are unremarkable and to invest them with the power to haunt us. If, in her hands, the 'action' of the novel turns inward, to the 'viewless fetters' of the dispossessed, her appeal to the 'millions' who are 'in silent revolt against their lot' (*JE*, 122, 115) means that what is 'solitary' also appears 'typical'.[33] She pleads, however, for recognition, not revolution. She is sure that 'undue humility makes tyranny' (*Sh*, 174), but to the question, 'How is he my master?' she replies in a paradox: 'By treating me as an equal.'

NOTE ON EDITIONS

For each novel, the Oxford Clarendon Edition provides the definitive text, and the Oxford World's Classics editions, which use the Clarendon text and notes, are the recommended paperback versions. The Penguin editions are also good, and the Norton editions have substantial editorial material including critical extracts.

NOTES

1 Charlotte Brontë, *Jane Eyre* (1847), ed. Margaret Smith, introduction by Sally Shuttleworth (Oxford: Oxford World's Classics, 2008), p. 12. Hereafter *JE*.
2 Anon., *Christian Remembrancer*, 15 (April 1848), 396–409. Jacobins were supporters of the French Revolution.
3 Elizabeth Rigby [Lady Eastlake], *Quarterly Review*, 84 (December 1848), 174.
4 John Courtney, *Jane Eyre or The Secrets of Thornfield Manor*, in Patsy Stoneman (ed.), *Jane Eyre on Stage, 1848–1898* (Aldershot and Burlington, VT: Ashgate Press, 2007).
5 Terry Eagleton, *Myths of Power: A Marxist Study of the Brontës* (1975), 3rd edn (Basingstoke: Palgrave Macmillan, 2005), p. 8.
6 Margaret Smith (ed.), *The Letters of Charlotte Brontë*, 3 vols. (Oxford: Oxford University Press, 1995, 2000, 2004), II, pp. 10, 383.
7 Florence Nightingale, *Cassandra* (1852), introduction by Myra Stark (New York: Feminist Press, 1979), p. 28.
8 Heather Glen, *Charlotte Brontë: The Imagination in History* (Oxford: Oxford University Press, 2002), p. 135.
9 Sandra Gilbert and Susan Gubar, *The Madwoman in the Attic: The Woman Writer and the Nineteenth-Century Literary Imagination* (New Haven: Yale University Press, 1979).
10 Jean Rhys, *Wide Sargasso Sea* (1966) (Harmondsworth: Penguin, 1983), p. 136.
11 Gordon S. Haight (ed.), *The George Eliot Letters*, 9 vols. (New Haven and London: Yale University Press, 1954–78), I, p. 268.
12 See Caroline Norton, *English Laws for Women* (London, 1854).
13 For *Jane Eyre*'s influence on later writers, see Patsy Stoneman, *Brontë Transformations: The Cultural Dissemination of 'Jane Eyre' and 'Wuthering Heights'* (Hemel Hempstead: Harvester Wheatsheaf/Prentice Hall, 1996).
14 Charlotte Brontë, 'Roe Head Journal', quoted in Christine Alexander, *The Early Writings of Charlotte Brontë* (Oxford: Basil Blackwell, 1983), p. 140.
15 Charlotte Brontë, 'I have now written a great many books', quoted in Alexander, *Early Writings*, p. 199.
16 Charlotte Brontë, *Shirley* (1849), ed. Margaret Smith and Herbert Rosengarten, introduction by Janet Gezari (Oxford: Oxford World's Classics, 2008), p. 5. Hereafter *Sh*.
17 E. C. Gaskell, *The Life of Charlotte Brontë* (1857), ed. Angus Easson (Oxford: Oxford World's Classics, 2001), pp. 86–9.
18 Elizabeth Gaskell, *North and South* (1854), ed. Angus Easson, introduction by Sally Shuttleworth (Oxford: Oxford World's Classics, 1998), pp. 190–1.
19 Eagleton, *Myths*, p. 8.
20 Margaret Smith, 'A Note on the Text', *Shirley*, p. xxvii.
21 Gaskell, *Life*, p. 315.
22 J. Barker, *The Brontës* (London: Phoenix, 1995; first published 1994), p. 134; Gaskell, *Life*, p. 214.
23 Sarah Fermi's *Emily's Journal* (Cambridge: Pegasus, 2006) offers a fictional account of a love relationship between Emily and a local boy which is consistent with known facts.

24 George Eliot, letter to Frederic Harrison, 15 August 1866, in *George Eliot: Selected Essays, Poems and Other Writings*, ed. A. S. Byatt and Nicholas Warren (Harmondsworth: Penguin, 1990), p. 248.
25 Charlotte Brontë, *Villette* (1853), ed. Margaret Smith, introduction by Tim Dolin (Oxford: Oxford World's Classics, 2008), p. 41. Hereafter *V*.
26 Haight, *George Eliot Letters*, II, p. 87.
27 Sigmund Freud, 'The Uncanny' (1919), *The Pelican Freud Library*, ed. Albert Dickson, vol. XIV, *Art and Literature* (London: Pelican Books, 1985), pp. 363–4.
28 Kate Millett, *Sexual Politics* (New York: Avon, 1969), p. 200.
29 Glen, *Charlotte Brontë*, chapter 7.
30 Eugenia C. Delamotte, *Perils of the Night: A Feminist Study of Nineteenth-Century Gothic* (Oxford: Oxford University Press, 1990), p. 278.
31 Charlotte Brontë, *The Professor* (1857), ed. Margaret Smith and Herbert Rosengarten, introduction by Margaret Smith (Oxford: Oxford World's Classics, 2008).
32 Mary Jacobus, 'The Buried Letter: Feminism and Romanticism in *Villette*', in *Women Writing and Writing about Women*, ed. Mary Jacobus (London: Croom Helm, 1979), pp. 42–60; Freud, 'The Uncanny', pp. 363–4.
33 Eagleton, *Myths*, pp. 8–9.

FURTHER READING

Barker, J., *The Brontës* (1994), London, Phoenix, 1995

Boumelha, P., *Charlotte Brontë*, Hemel Hempstead: Harvester Wheatsheaf, 1990

Eagleton, Terry, *Myths of Power: A Marxist Study of the Brontës*, Basingstoke, Macmillan, 1975; 3rd edn, Basingstoke, Palgrave Macmillan, 2005

Gaskell, E. C., *The Life of Charlotte Brontë* (1857), ed. Angus Easson, Oxford, Oxford World's Classics, 2001

Gilbert, S. and S. Gubar, *The Madwoman in the Attic: The Woman Writer and the Nineteenth-Century Literary Imagination*, New Haven, Yale University Press, 1979

Glen, H., *Charlotte Brontë: The Imagination in History*, Oxford, Oxford University Press, 2002

Glen, H. (ed.), *Jane Eyre*, New Casebooks, Basingstoke, Macmillan, 1997

Gordon, L., *Charlotte Brontë: A Passionate Life*, London, Vintage, 1994

Ingham, P., *The Brontës in Context*, Oxford, Oxford World's Classics, 2006

Michie, Elsie B. (ed.), *Charlotte Brontë's 'Jane Eyre': A Casebook*, Oxford, Oxford University Press, 2006

Nestor, P., (ed.), *Villette*, New Casebooks, Basingstoke, Macmillan, 1992

Shuttleworth, S., *Charlotte Brontë and Victorian Psychology*, Cambridge, Cambridge University Press, 1996

Smith, M. (ed.), *Selected Letters of Charlotte Brontë*, Oxford, Oxford University Press, 2007

Stoneman, Patsy, *Brontë Transformations: The Cultural Dissemination of 'Jane Eyre' and 'Wuthering Heights'*, Hemel Hempstead, Harvester Wheatsheaf/Prentice Hall, 1996

11

HEATHER GLEN

Emily Brontë

'*Wuthering Heights* stands alone as a monument of intensity owing nothing to tradition, nothing to the achievement of earlier writers. It was a thing apart, passionate, unforgettable, haunting in its grimness.' Thus the eleventh edition of *Encyclopaedia Britannica*, published in 1911. The sense that Emily Brontë's one surviving novel is quite unlike any other has been a persistent one. (She is the only writer in this volume with just one work of fiction to her name.) 'A kind of "sport"', F. R. Leavis famously called it.[1] 'In an age in which the realist novel seems both to come out of and to return to the ordinary life external to it, *Wuthering Heights* on the contrary represents something separate in itself, with its own geography, biology, and virtually untranslatable mythology', writes Philip Davis, in his volume on the Victorians for the *Oxford English Literary History* (2002).[2]

Even those closest to Emily Brontë seem to have shared this sense. In her Preface to the second, posthumous edition of the novel, Charlotte Brontë set out to defend it to a reading public that she feared would find it a 'rude and strange production' by giving some account of the author's life and also of 'the locality where the scenes of the story are laid'.[3] But in the end she offered less an explanation than a powerful contribution to the myth of Emily Brontë as an inscrutable genius whose extraordinary achievement was more baffling than intelligible. In the two final paragraphs of that Preface, reprinted in all subsequent editions, she developed an image that was to influence generations of readers, of *Wuthering Heights* as 'wrought ... from no model', 'colossal, dark, and frowning, half statue, half rock' (370–1) – more like a natural object than accomplished work of art.

Wuthering Heights was not, however, 'wrought ... from no model', nor in ignorance of literary tradition, as Charlotte Brontë well knew. The depiction in the novel of a 'remote and unreclaimed region' (368), 'alien and unfamiliar' (367) to polite metropolitan readers, was by 1847 less an innovation than a convention – one established and developed by the most successful novelist of the early nineteenth century. Sir Walter Scott was probably the only one of the novelists discussed in this volume (other than her own sister) whose works Emily Brontë had read. But she had read them with passion, and for years. In December 1827, as a child of nine, she had chosen Scott as her hero for the Brontë children's shared 'play' of 'Tales of the Islanders'. Her surviving Gondal writings, with their Scott-like scenery and characters, bear witness to the fact that his poetry, his history, and his novels continued to compel her throughout adolescence and beyond.[4] Many of the most distinctive features of the novel whose strangeness her sister tried to explain would not have been unfamiliar to readers familiar with Scott. Here, as in Scott's novels, there is a sustained attempt to represent regional dialect; here, as there, the central story is set within a framing narrative that foregrounds the limitations of the teller's point of view. If Nelly Dean, the housekeeper, recalls Scott's servant-narrators, Lockwood, the visiting stranger, coming from the city to a remote rural district and trying to make sense of its uncouth manners and customs, bears an even closer resemblance to the narrators of the Waverley Novels – polite young men with conventionally 'romantic' notions, who register the collision between a modern civilised culture and a ruder, more primitive one.

Yet *Wuthering Heights* has nothing of Scott's controlling geniality, with its pervasive implication of the ultimate triumph of civilised values. The point of the novel does not appear to lie in Lockwood's moral education; indeed, at the end it is doubtful whether he learns anything at all. Scott's picturesque landscapes are here replaced by a 'nature' that is neither prospect nor background but an intimate part of the action, violent, fruitful, animating, destroying, its importunate reality registered most immediately in the suffering, desiring, child-bearing, perishing bodies of three generations of characters. Lockwood's diary has a Latinate portentousness reminiscent of Scott's narrators: he describes himself as 'inspecting the penetralium' (3), and Catherine as 'wax[ing] lachrymose' (20). But it is largely displaced, after the first three chapters, by the directness and matter-of-factness of Nelly Dean's oral narrative, with its extensive reporting of others' spoken words. Here, in marked contrast to Scott's verbosity, his elaborate textual apparatus of introductions, appendices, dedications, there is the freshness and immediacy of a racy, economical prose. The sense is less of naïveté than of pondered, deliberate difference: as Mrs Humphry Ward was to put it, 'genius already matured and master of its tools'.[5]

'*Wuthering Heights* was hewn in a wild workshop', Charlotte Brontë wrote romantically (370); but the novel was actually written in a confined nineteenth-century household where its author worked in close proximity with two other aspiring novelists. She does not appear to have been indifferent to publication, nor unaware of the demands of the literary market-place. She was fiercely independent; she maintained reserves of privacy. But we know that she read and discussed *Wuthering Heights* with her sisters during the process of composition, and it is possible that she reshaped it, not in response to their criticisms ('to the influence of other intellects, [her mind] was not amenable', writes Charlotte (369)), but in order to facilitate ambitions that she shared with them. *Wuthering Heights* seems originally to have been conceived as a single-volume work, one of the '3 tales, each occupying a volume' that the sisters, as 'Currer, Ellis and Acton Bell', began to send out to publishers in July 1846.[6] When the tales by Ellis and Acton were accepted for publication by T. H. Newby in July1847, Charlotte's *The Professor* was either rejected or withdrawn. (*Jane Eyre*, her second novel, was in the event the first published, in October 1847.) Emily may then have expanded *Wuthering Heights* into a distinctively bifurcated two-volume work, so as to make up the 'three-decker' that was the most marketable form for fiction in the mid-nineteenth century.[7] For this novel that 'stands alone' in English literary history was not published alone. When it finally appeared in December 1847 its title-page announced it as '*WUTHERING HEIGHTS / A NOVEL, / BY /ELLIS BELL, / IN THREE VOLUMES*'. But the final volume consisted of Anne Brontë's *Agnes Grey*.

If Emily Brontë had read very few contemporary novelists, she was not unaware of new developments in English fiction, for they can be seen in the novel that appeared alongside hers. *Agnes Grey*'s tract-like sobriety, its confessional tracing of a singular life-trajectory, point back to one origin of the genre in spiritual autobiography. But this quietly original novel also points forwards to some of the greatest achievements of the evolving tradition of fictional realism in the nineteenth century. As a novel of education that raises unconventional questions about the treatment of the weak and dependent, including animals, it works to refine and enlarge its readers' moral sympathies. As the *Bildungsroman* of a marginalised, overlooked woman, it offers a subtly devastating critique of the 'cultivated' society it portrays. Its nuanced depiction of its narrator's turbulent interior life marks a significant stage in the nineteenth-century novel's increasingly complex representation of individual subjectivity.[8] In all these respects, however, it is quite different from *Wuthering Heights*.

Here, instead of a single controlling consciousness, there are sharply differing perspectives. *Wuthering Heights* ends not in closure, but in ambiguity. Instead of linear development there is an intricate time-scheme, pointing backwards as well as forwards, and an inter-generational plot, in which central characters die and are born. There is little attempt to consider moral issues. The main narrator is not a governess, but a nurse. Most surprisingly, perhaps (given the fact that critics have often discussed this novel in psychological terms), there is little here of *Agnes Grey*'s discursive elaboration of subjectivity. If the narrators and the characters occasionally speculate about motives, motives are not explored. Feelings are simple and direct – 'unbridled aversions' and 'headlong partialities', Charlotte Brontë called them (367). Passions are asserted, often by an appeal to elemental imagery, rather than analysed. What drives the protagonists is revealed in dialogue or observed from a distance: there is little of the analytic reflectiveness of free indirect speech, where the narrator enters into and comments on the mental state of the character. Instead of an ironic or morally complicating interweaving of differing points of view, there are vertiginous shifts between different existential realities.

Thus, in a pivotal scene, Nelly describes Catherine Earnshaw's unease as she prepares to accept Edgar Linton's proposal of marriage. Catherine's brother Hindley has just come home, drunk and violent, and almost killed his son Hareton by dropping him from the top of the stairs. Heathcliff, who has instinctively intercepted his fall, is now sitting morose and hidden behind the settle; and Nelly is lulling the child:

> I was rocking Hareton on my knee, and humming a song that began;
>
> 'It was far in the night, and the bairnies grat,
> The mither beneath the mools heard that,'
>
> when Miss Cathy, who had listened to the hubbub from her room, put her head in, and whispered,
>
> 'Are you alone, Nelly?'
>
> 'Yes, miss,' I replied.
>
> She entered and approached the hearth. I, supposing she was going to say something, looked up. The expression of her face seemed disturbed and anxious. Her lips were half asunder, as if she meant to speak; and she drew a breath, but it escaped in a sigh, instead of a sentence.
>
> I resumed my song; not having forgotten her recent behaviour.
>
> 'Where's Heathcliff?' she said, interrupting me. (76)

Nelly offers a vivid snapshot of a particular situation: the 'hubbub' just over, the child being rocked on the knee, a sharp but markedly external description of the signs of Catherine's feelings. It is a scene with complex antecedents and consequences. Heathcliff, the changeling in the Earnshaw household, is about to be driven away by what he sees as Catherine's betrayal; Hindley is maddened with grief at the death of his wife. The child whom Nelly is cradling is to marry Catherine's daughter, issue of the marriage whose prospect troubles her here. Yet relationships and emotions are dramatically rendered rather than analysed. The mode of presentation is quite different from that being refined and developed by those other novelists writing in Haworth Parsonage. But it is one that evinces a precise imaginative intelligence – and, I would argue, a sophisticated literary consciousness, signalled in its quotation from the song that Nelly hums.

For there is a striking literary parallel to what we see in scenes like this – terseness of narration, vividness of detail, the representation of complex situations through dialogue, passionate feeling sharply, externally observed – in the traditional ballads beginning to be collected and published in the latter half of the eighteenth century. Emily Brontë probably knew such ballads primarily through Scott's much-reprinted collection, *Minstrelsy of the Scottish Border* (1802–3). The ballad referred to here, called 'The Ghaist's Warning', appears, however, in an appendix to his poem *The Lady of the Lake* (1810). It tells of the cruelty of a stepmother to seven motherless children and of how their buried mother hears her children's piteous cries. She is permitted by God to return to them until cock-crow – not as a spirit, but as a decaying corpse whom her daughter does not recognise. She suckles her baby at her decomposing breast and terrifies the father and stepmother into treating the children more kindly. At the end, they are living in dread of her return. Sung here to a motherless child, whose father has just almost murdered him, this is hardly a soothing lullaby. But in its portrayal of familial cruelty, its matter-of-fact presentation of supernatural threat and revenge, its unsoftened confrontation of the facts of physical existence, its central focus on a passion that seems to transcend mortality, it points toward the world of *Wuthering Heights*.

If *Agnes Grey* is framed in a language of religious and Romantic sensibility, and if *Jane Eyre* evokes the more stirring Romanticism of 'incident, life, fire, feeling' to be found in the poems of Byron and in 'the bright pages of Marmion',[9] *Wuthering Heights* is quite different from either in its frequent allusions to ballads and ballad motifs. Ballad-echoes are most prominent in the novel's depiction of the love between Cathy and Heathcliff and their separation by death. Heathcliff's return from his three-year absence recalls the ballad of the demon lover who comes back from across the seas to find his betrothed has married another and takes her back with him to hell. For here, as in the ballads, the border between death and life is a charged and permeable space. '[W]e must pass by Gimmerton Kirk, to go that journey!' says the dying Catherine to Heathcliff. 'We've braved its ghosts often together, and dared each other to stand among the graves and ask them to come … I'll not lie there by myself; they may bury me twelve feet deep, and throw the church down over me, but I won't rest till you are with me … I never will!' (126). Like the revenants of such ballads as 'Clerk Saunders' and 'The Wife of Usher's Well' she returns, not a ghost, but corporeal – a wailing child with a 'little, ice-cold hand' (23). And the final paragraph of the novel evokes with a difference that commonplace of ballad endings, the sweetbriar and the rose entwining over the graves of two lovers, symbolising their union in death.[10]

The novel's evocation of what might be called the ballad mindset is evident not merely in tropes such as these but in its whole way of presenting and conceiving its world. Here, as in the ballads, the physical fact of the perishing body is central and untranscendable. Clerk Saunders's stark reply to the lover who pleads to lie at his side – 'My mouth it is full cold, Margaret, / It has the smell, now, of the ground'[11] – is recalled in Heathcliff's description of the opening of Catherine's grave. Here, as in the ballads, the feeling is less of Gothic melodrama than of a matter-of-fact materialism, of a piece with the novel's pervasive sense of the precariousness of bodily life. 'He had been active and healthy, yet his strength left him suddenly', recalls Nelly of Mr Earnshaw (39); 'You should have known better to choose such a rush of a lass', says the apothecary to Hindley, observing that 'the winter will probably finish' his wife (63). (Much of the novel, indeed, is a tale related beside a sickbed, where an invalid endures '[F]our weeks' torture, tossing and sickness' (90), after getting stuck in a snowdrift and 'benumbed' to the 'very heart' (30).) As in the ballads, action is unfolded without sentiment or moralising; difference registered less by subtle discrimination than by contrast and counterpoint. Here, as there, such contrasts appear not in schematic patterns, but with the vividness of the ordinary – Isabella's slatternly ways and burnt porridge; Nelly's pleasure in a tidy house.

The shape of this novel, spanning three generations in two volumes, is quite different from the tracing of a singular life-trajectory in *The Professor* and *Agnes Grey*. As in many traditional ballads, passions and consequences work themselves out not within a developing individual consciousness but through the histories of two families. There is a distinctive deployment of the most striking features of ballad narration: its abrupt time-shifts, its telescoped time-scale, its discontinuities. In *Wuthering Heights*, birth and death follow hard upon one another. Catherine's transition from child to wife, Heathcliff's from ploughboy to gentleman, are scarcely portrayed. Isabella's twelve years of marriage are marked by a break between chapters. Catherine, in her delirium, dreams that she is a child again: 'the whole last seven years of my life grew a blank!' (125). 'A gush of child's sensations flowed into my heart', says Nelly, describing where she played with Hindley 'twenty years before' (108). If the novels of the other Brontë sisters were beginning to explore the ways in which the selective processes of memory might constitute a continuing self, this registers the shock of collision between subjective and linear time.

For here, as in the ballad, the past is not left behind. The novel's narrative tempo is strikingly reminiscent of the ballad technique that scholars have called 'leaping and lingering'. As in the ballads, there are abrupt transitions, with little in the way of connecting narrative, counterpointed by a 'lingering' on critical or climactic scenes. As the novel is read, and reread, such scenes accrue resonances beyond their immediate narrative moment, interanimating one another to tantalising effect. Where in the traditional ballad, phrases, stanzas, and situations are repeated with slight variations, so here there is repetition with difference: Heathcliff's degradation and Hareton's brutalising; the first Catherine 'captured' at Thrushcross Grange, the second at Wuthering Heights. As with the likenesses to Catherine that Heathcliff sees everywhere, echoes such as these recur throughout the novel, at once suggesting and resisting meaningful patterning.

Last but not least, this novel recalls the ballads by the prominence of the figure of Nelly Dean – both the servant who acts as nurse to its succession of motherless children and the main narrator of its story of passion and revenge. Most of the telling takes place as she nurses Lockwood, reduced to a condition of childish dependence in the sickroom to which he is confined. As Scott indicated in his *Minstrelsy*, nurses and mothers played a major role in ballad transmission. (Nelly's songs disturb Joseph's Bible reading, she hums a ballad to Hareton, and tells that she taught 'old songs – my nursery lore' to the younger Catherine as a child (230).) But nurses and mothers also appeared within them, often as sinister figures: the 'cruel mother' who kills her child, the 'fause nourice'.[12] Just so, in *Wuthering Heights*, Nelly is not unambiguously nurturing, but sometimes obtuse, sometimes treacherous, sometimes spiteful, sometimes almost malevolent in her refusal to act. (As Mrs Humphry Ward complained, in her Introduction to the novel, 'she knowingly allows her charge Catherine, on the eve of her confinement, to fast in solitude and delirium'.)[13] Unlike the governess, who leads away from the body, towards civilisation and maturity, the nurse is a reminder of the terrors of embodiment and dependence, of the intensity of primal need. Like the ballads before her, Emily Brontë registers this, in the grisly song that Nelly hums to Hareton as a lullaby, the dark story she tells of violence within the family.

In *Wuthering Heights* that story is located in a world far more complex than that of the ballads and largely framed in discourses quite unknown to them. If Nelly appeals to superstition, she appeals also, and frequently, to the more rational moralising discourse of an emerging bourgeois individualism. The novel's imagery of growth and fruition and destruction and renewal, of the cycle of the seasons, of birth and death and heredity, draws on the languages both of Romantic poetry (especially Wordsworth and Shelley) and of the pre-Darwinian science that Emily Brontë seems to have known.[14] But its echoes of the ballad point perhaps most suggestively towards the nature of this novel's difference from those others being written beside it in Haworth Parsonage. If *Agnes Grey* and *The Professor* draw upon the traditions of confessional autobiography and of the self-help narrative to chart the difficulties of individual fulfilment within a particular society, *Wuthering Heights* seems more concerned with those more trans-historical realities of which the ballads speak: the primitive violence of human passions, the untranscendable facts of human embodiedness and mortality.

Yet what we see in this novel is very far from a naïve primitivism. As Charlotte Brontë indicated in her Preface, Emily Brontë knew the local oral traditions of the Haworth neighbourhood. But she knew the ballads also as a literary phenomenon. In *Minstrelsy of the Scottish Border*, she would have found them surrounded by three extensive introductions and detailed scholarly notes, their violence and horror set firmly within a distant historical past. She encountered 'The Ghaist's Warning' not as part of an oral tradition but as an antiquarian curiosity, in a learned appendix to an expensive volume produced for readers of taste. She could see very clearly that the primitive force and directness to which she responded was being framed and placed by the apparatus of scholarship, softened and sentimentalised for a polite reading public, displaced from its origins and brought within the confines of the world of books and print. And the novel that she produced for a similar reading public is concerned not merely with a ballad-world of primitive feeling but with how, within a particular, sharply imagined society, such feeling is entertained, distorted, accommodated, or repressed. She offers a sardonic view of that fashionable fascination with the primitive expressed in the ballad revival – the touristic interest in the harshness of 'uncivilized manners' evinced in Lockwood's choice of a country retreat, his curiosity about his uncouth landlord and his eager listening to Nelly's tale; the Romantic attraction toward them displayed in Isabella's disastrous passion for Heathcliff and Lockwood's fantasies about the younger Catherine. If she draws upon oral traditions, and places at her novel's centre a scene of oral storytelling, she is equally concerned with the significance of books and reading. From the scribblings in the 'musty' Testament (18) that trigger Lockwood's nightmare to the 'costly' illustrated volumes that bring the last pair of lovers together (315), books in this novel are powerful. Books are also futile. 'What in the name of all that feels', demands Catherine Linton of her husband, 'has he to do with *books*, when I am dying?' (122). Joseph's rantings from 't' Blessed Book' (308) on which he counts out his money are impotent to change the world of Wuthering Heights. If there is a sense of opening possibility in the novel's delicate portrayal of Hareton's learning to read, this is countered by the image, near the outset of Lockwood's narrative, of the books he piles against the window to keep the child-waif from coming in.

Antiquarian scholars (who often spoke of their own love of ballads in childhood) relegated the ballads to a now transcended past, mere quaint relics of the infancy of the race. But in *Wuthering Heights* the world of primitive feeling of which the ballads speak poses a radical, continuing challenge to the rational, morally progressive assumptions of modernity. The delicately bred Edgar has as little power to leave off his courtship of Catherine 'as a cat possesses the power to leave a mouse half killed, or a bird half eaten' (72); Isabella, trapped in her marriage to Heathcliff, eyes Hindley's pistol not with horror, but with 'covetousness' (140); the sobbing child at the window is insistent, implacable, still returning after 'twenty years' (24). Moreover, the novel's inter-generational plotting, its repetitions and its echoes, its patterning images of the changing seasons and the less predictable recurrences of heredity, work together to suggest that its concern is less with the vagaries of individual subjectivity than with a human condition all share. If nothing equals the intensity of that central and fractured love, likenesses, echoes, even parodies of it appear throughout the novel: in Lockwood's desire for and terror of romantic involvement; in Hindley's desperate grief for his young dead wife; in Isabella's mad passion and wild flight across the moors; in the startling appearance of the child Hindley, 'as fresh as reality', before the middle-aged Nelly, his early playmate; in Cathy and Hareton's fruitfully burgeoning love. And that informing imagery of a nature that is both destructive and regenerative, of which human beings are part, not merely in their working of the land, but because they have physical bodies that are born, that give birth, that die, likewise speaks not of a peculiar, individual experience, but of a predicament common to all.

The most powerful of human passions are those that seek to deny the facts of time and change, the limits of the body, human separateness: 'Nelly, I *am* Heathcliff'; 'If all else perished, and *he* remained, I should still continue to be' (82). But human beings are mortal – frail, dying inhabitants of an indifferent natural world. In setting this contradiction at the centre of her novel, Emily Brontë engages with the world of early nineteenth-century England in a wholly unconventional way. Implicitly she questions that ideology of progress which was transforming its landscapes and shaping its social arrangements; questions it not from the moralised perspective of a Dickens or a Mrs Gaskell, but from a powerfully realised awareness of the meanings of human creaturehood. And equally, in her stress not on a single individual but on birth and death and the replacement of one generation by the next, she questions that focus on self-making and self-fulfilment that was central to her culture's self-image and being given powerful imaginative expression by her sister novelists.

Charlotte Brontë's second novel is strikingly different from her first, in ways that bespeak the impact Emily's novel had on her. Whereas *The*

Professor told the story of a self-made man, this opens with the image of a rebellious, vulnerable child:

> A small breakfast-room adjoined the drawing-room. I slipped in there. It contained a bookcase: I soon possessed myself of a volume, taking care it should be one stored with pictures. I mounted into the window-seat: gathering up my feet, I sat cross-legged like a Turk and, having drawn the red moreen curtain nearly close, I was shrined in double retirement.
>
> Folds of scarlet drapery shut in my view to the right hand; to the left were the clear panes of glass, protecting, but not separating me from the drear November day. At intervals, while turning over the leaves of my book, I studied the aspect of that winter afternoon.[15]

There is much in this passage that recalls *Wuthering Heights*: the sharp domestic detail, the equally sharp sense of a natural world beyond, the fragility of that barrier between civilised comfort and cold. Yet it is startlingly unlike that earlier novel's image of a child at a window, near the beginning of Lockwood's narrative:

> The intense horror of nightmare came over me; I tried to draw back my arm, but the hand clung to it, and a most melancholy voice sobbed,
>
> 'Let me in – let me in!'
>
> 'Who are you?' I asked, struggling, meanwhile, to disengage myself.
>
> 'Catherine Linton', it replied, shiveringly (why did I think of *Linton*? I had read *Earnshaw* twenty times for Linton). 'I'm come home, I'd lost my way on the moor!'
>
> As it spoke, I discerned, obscurely, a child's face looking through the window – Terror made me cruel; and, finding it useless to attempt shaking the creature off, I pulled its wrist on to the broken pane, and rubbed it to and fro till the blood ran down and soaked the bed-clothes: still it wailed, 'Let me in!' and maintained its tenacious gripe, almost maddening me with fear.
>
> 'How can I?' I said at length. 'Let *me* go, if you want me to let you in!'
>
> The fingers relaxed, I snatched mine through the hole, hurriedly piled the books up in a pyramid against it, and stopped my ears to exclude the lamentable prayer. (23)

Shielded by glass, silently biding her time, the passionate, suffering yet coolly rational Jane Eyre is a distinctive, self-possessed individual, who is in the novel that follows to find her own place in the world. She is a heroine with a central place in one great tradition of the nineteenth-century novel – the paradigmatic narrative of individual development and socialisation which works by conscripting the reader into its confidence. It is, indeed, in this passage from *Jane Eyre*'s opening chapter that the reader's identification with its heroine is first subliminally established: Jane, like that reader, is turning the leaves of a book. But the child sobbing at the window, unable to get in, desperately, maddeningly clinging to Lockwood, the reader-surrogate, evokes a much older tradition of the ballad revenant. 'Obscurely' discerned, even her name uncertain ('I had read *Earnshaw* twenty times for Linton'), she haunts the novel that follows. Her image stays with the reader, undermining Catherine Earnshaw's lyrical assertion that 'Nelly, I *am* Heathcliff', confirming the separation that she seeks to insist is 'impracticable', eclipsing its depiction of her daughter's satisfied love. It is an image whose threat to those narratives of coherent selfhood and successful socialisation that were central to the culture of early Victorian England is registered in the terror with which Lockwood seeks to stave her off with a pyramid of books.

'Nothing like it has ever been written before; it is to be hoped, for the sake of good manners, nothing will be hereafter. Let it stand by itself, a coarse, original, powerful book ... It will live a short and brilliant life and then die and be forgotten', wrote one American reviewer of *Wuthering Heights*.[16] Yet more than many others in the English literary canon, this compelling, baffling novel has had a potent afterlife.[17] Perceived at once as strange and as somehow deeply familiar, it has been read and reread in different ways by generations of readers, appropriated for different critical emphases and methodologies. If it 'stands apart' from the emerging great tradition of Victorian social realism, it also implicitly questions it in ways that have proved impossible to forget. This is not the work of a genius beyond dialogue, but one that manifests a sophisticated sense of literary tradition and of narrative craftsmanship. Nowhere is this more evident than at its ending, where the sensible Nelly and the 'respectable character' Lockwood seek to lay the story to rest. For if, in this novel's resonant closing paragraphs there is a tantalising refusal of closure, as differing viewpoints are held suggestively in play, there seems also to be an ironic, prophetic figuring of its own continuing power to haunt and unsettle in the ballad echoes that here return, recharged with meaning – heath and harebells growing on graves and a countryside alive with the tales of the unquiet dead.

NOTE ON EDITIONS

The Oxford Clarendon Edition (1976), edited by Hilda Marsden and Ian Jack, is the authoritative edition. The Oxford World's Classics edition (1995) has the same authoritative text, with Ian Jack's notes and a new introduction by Patsy Stoneman, in cheap paperback form.

NOTES

1 F. R. Leavis, *The Great Tradition: George Eliot, Henry James, Joseph Conrad* (London: Chatto & Windus, 1948), p. 27.

2 Philip Davis, *The Victorians* (Oxford: Oxford University Press, 2002), p. 321.
3 'Editor's Preface', reprinted in the Oxford World's Classics edition of the novel, ed. Ian Jack, introduction by Patsy Stoneman (Oxford: Oxford World's Classics, 1995), p. 367. All page references in the text are to this edition.
4 Juliet Barker, *The Brontës* (London: Weidenfeld & Nicolson, 1994), p. 274.
5 Mrs Humphry Ward, 'Introduction' to *Wuthering Heights*, Haworth Edition of the Life and Works of Charlotte Brontë and Her Sisters (London: John Murray, 1900), V, p. xxiv.
6 Charlotte Brontë to Henry Colburn, 4 July 1846, in Margaret Smith (ed.), *The Letters of Charlotte Brontë*, vol. I, *1829–1847* (Oxford: Clarendon Press, 1995), p. 481.
7 See Edward Chitham, *The Birth of Wuthering Heights: Emily Brontë at Work* (Basingstoke: Macmillan, 1998).
8 On this aspect of the novel, see Jill L. Matus, *Unstable Bodies: Victorian Representations of Sexuality and Maternity* (Manchester: Manchester University Press, 1995), pp. 90–113.
9 *Jane Eyre*, ed. Margaret Smith, introduction by Sally Shuttleworth (Oxford: Oxford World's Classics, 2008), pp. 109, 371.
10 On ballad allusions and ballad and folklore motifs in *Wuthering Heights*, see Sheila Smith, '"At Once Strong and Eerie": The Supernatural in *Wuthering Heights* and Its Debt to the Traditional Ballad', *Review of English Studies*, 43 (1992), 498–517; Susan Stewart, 'The Ballad in *Wuthering Heights*', *Representations*, 86 (Spring 2004), 175–97.
11 Sir Walter Scott, *Minstrelsy of the Scottish Border*, 5th edn, 3 vols. (Edinburgh: A. Constable and Co., 1821), II, p. 410.
12 For a suggestive discussion of nurses, infanticide, and cruelty to children in Scottish balladry, see Ann Wierda Rowland, '"The fause nourice sang": Childhood, Child Murder, and the Formalism of the Scottish Ballad Revival', in *Scotland and the Borders of Romanticism*, ed. Leith Davis, Ian Duncan, and Janet Sorensen (Cambridge: Cambridge University Press, 2004), pp. 225–44.
13 Ward, 'Introduction', p. xxix.
14 See for example Jay Clayton, *Romantic Vision and the Novel* (Cambridge: Cambridge University Press, 1987), pp. 81–102; Stevie Davies, *Emily Brontë: Heretic* (London: Women's Press, 1994), pp. 53–5.
15 *Jane Eyre*, p. 7.
16 [George Washington Peck], *American Review*, 7 (June 1848), in Miriam Allott (ed.), *The Brontës: The Critical Heritage* (London: Routledge & Kegan Paul, 1974), p. 241.
17 For extensive discussion of this, see Patsy Stoneman, *Brontë Transformations: The Cultural Dissemination of 'Jane Eyre and 'Wuthering Heights'* (Hemel Hempstead: Harvester Wheatsheaf, 1996).

FURTHER READING

Allott, Miriam (ed.), *The Brontës: The Critical Heritage*, London, Routledge & Kegan Paul, 1974

Clayton, Jay, *Romantic Vision and the Novel*, Cambridge, Cambridge University Press, 1987

Davies, Stevie, *Emily Brontë: Heretic*, London, Women's Press, 1994
Emily Brontë, Writers and Their Work, Plymouth, Northcote House, 1998
Eagleton, Terry, *Myths of Power: A Marxist Study of the Brontës*, Basingstoke, Macmillan, 1975; 3rd edn, Basingstoke, Palgrave Macmillan, 2005
Gérin, Winifred, *Emily Brontë: A Biography*, Oxford, Oxford University Press, 1971
Hewish, John, *Emily Brontë: A Critical and Biographical Study*, London, Macmillan, 1969
Kermode, Frank, *The Classic*, London: Faber and Faber, 1975, pp. 115–41
Knoepflmacher, U. C., *Wuthering Heights*, Basingstoke, Macmillan, 1989
Leavis, Q. D., 'A Fresh Approach to *Wuthering Heights*', in *Collected Essays*, ed. G. Singh, 3 vols., Cambridge, Cambridge University Press, 1983–9, I, pp. 228–74
Miller, J. Hillis, *Fiction and Repetition: Seven English Novels*, Cambridge, MA, Harvard University Press, 1982
Smith, Anne (ed.), *The Art of Emily Brontë*, London, Vision Press, 1976
Stoneman, Patsy (ed.), *Emily Brontë: Wuthering Heights*, Duxford, Icon Readers' Guides, 2000

12

BRIGID LOWE

Elizabeth Gaskell

> every little, leetle, particular about yourself, and your concerns ... are most welcome to me ... down to the uninteresting in general basons of tapioca you have at lunch[1]

Henry James's description of the novelist simply as one 'upon whom nothing is lost'[2] suggests a complex ambition for the fiction of his century – the impulse not only to observe, but also to amass, record, preserve, recover, redeem. Such impulses – intensified, perhaps, by the experiences of loss accompanying accelerating social change – lie close to the heart of the nebulous mass of fictional conventions we call 'realism'. A shape begins to form in the mist if we read the fiction of Elizabeth Gaskell (1810–65) with an eye for such impulses. If the literary colossi of her generation seem in danger of overshadowing her on some fronts, her commitment to the capture, recording, and recovery of the texture of everyday human existence remains exemplary.

The fifth chapter of *Cranford* (1853), 'Old Letters', recalls how an elderly acquaintance, who took the failure of his bank 'with stoical mildness', nevertheless

> worried his family all through a long summer's day because one of them had torn ... out the written leaves of his now useless bank-book ... the corresponding pages at the other end came out as well, and this little unnecessary waste of paper ... chafed him more than all the loss of his money.[3]

Thus, a wistful chapter about loss begins with a comical exploration, registered in the very *stuff* of life, of an all too human urge to save and to spare in the face of inevitably changing times: 'Envelopes fretted his soul terribly when they first came in'; 'Even now ... I see him casting wistful glances at his daughters when they send a whole inside of a half-sheet of note paper, with the three lines of acceptance to an invitation, written on only one of the sides' (*C*, 41).

For her part, Gaskell always fills her page. Writing about her, Virginia Woolf expressed an 'irritation with the methods of mid-Victorian novelists ... they seem to have left out nothing that they knew how to say ... What we want to be there is the brain and the view of life; the autumnal woods, the history of the whale fishery ... omit entirely.' Her premises have been formative in later critical evaluations of Gaskell.[4] The latter was appreciated in her own time for precisely this diffused attention to the concrete, which was often considered feminine ('do be a woman', wrote Gaskell herself, 'and give me all possible detail'[5]). No slight was necessarily implicit in such a gendered evaluation – Dickens, too, was praised for such 'feminine' accomplishments.[6] But a certain strain in modernist aesthetics paved the way for sexist condescension towards Gaskell's realism, culminating in Lord David Cecil's damnation through faint praise.[7] Since then, rehabilitatory readings have downplayed Gaskell's investment in the details of life and emphasised instead her engagements with the grand themes of gender and class.

But Woolf was right that Gaskell's mode of fiction certainly would, if it could, leave nothing out – and our appreciation of her will leave out essentials if we accept the belittling of digressive detail. The narrator of *Cranford* feels with acquaintances 'grieved' by wasted butter scraps: 'Have you not seen the anxious look (almost mesmeric) which such persons fix on the article?' She shares the peculiar 'human weakness' for recouping apparently useless fragments: 'String is my foible. My pockets get full of little hanks of it, picked up and twisted together ... I am seriously annoyed if any one cuts the string of a parcel instead of patiently and faithfully undoing it fold by fold' (*C*, 41). So too Gaskell's mesmeric fictional gaze cherishes the skeins and rags of human existence and twists them into narrative. Hers is an imagination that cannot bear to see the knotted details of life cut through by abstraction: its patient thrift follows every little fold of a tangled reality. With a kindly Cranfordian frugality, it attends to 'fragments and small opportunities ... rose-leaves ... gathered ere they fell to make into a potpourri for someone who had no garden; the little bundles of lavender flowers sent to strew the drawers of some town-dweller ... Things that many would despise, and actions which it seemed scarcely worth while to perform, were all attended to in Cranford' (*C*, 15).

Cranford's formidable Miss Jenkyns shares Woolf's reservations about Victorian fiction and its trivia. Her Augustan style of letter-writing constrains itself to 'the brain and the view of life', making her young reader yearn for 'facts instead of reflections' (*C*, 47). Facts crop up at last in an account of a false alarm of French invasion, but the story told, Miss Jenkyns repudiates its interest: '"How trivial ... do all our apprehensions of the last evening appear ... to calm and enquiring minds!"' Miss Matty, though, resists the lofty dismissal: '"But, indeed ... they were not at all trivial or trifling at the time ... Many people talked of hiding themselves in the salt mines – and meat would have kept capitally down there, only perhaps we should have been thirsty"'(*C*, 48). The comedy of the remark only highlights its saving grace. Trivial recollection is preservative, like salt in the mine, of a whole history of human apprehension, contrivance, and chatter, rescuing it all, for a while, from the extinctionary sweep of time – whilst acknowledging still the inevitability of its loss. The details of the incident bring the past *alive* – we feel the imagination of thirst in our own throats.

Young Peter Jenkyns's teachers tried to keep such mundanities out of his letters, which consequently are generally 'of a highly mental description … but, now and then, the animal nature broke out in such a little sentence as this, evidently written in a trembling hurry … : "Mother dear, do send me a cake, and put plenty of citron in"' (*C*, 48–9). Gaskell makes us see the pale flecks of peel in the crumb and feel the craving in a lonely boy's tooth for something sweet and tangy, as well as the longing in his heart for the motherly love it substantiates.

Recurring in Gaskell's fiction is the suggestive image of a garden in which vegetables, herbs, and flowers mix. At Mr Holbrook's in *Cranford*, 'roses and currant-bushes touched each other … feathery asparagus formed a pretty background to the pinks and gilly-flowers' (*C*, 31), and in *Mary Barton* the farmhouse garden is 'crowded with a medley of old-fashioned herbs and flowers, planted … when the garden was the only druggist's shop … and allowed to grow in scrambling and wild luxuriance – roses, lavender, sage, balm (for tea), rosemary, pinks and wallflowers, onions and jessamine, in most republican and indiscriminate order'.[8] The 'scrambling and wild luxuriance' of detail in Gaskell's novels, seemingly 'allowed to grow' of itself without artistic control, is a brimming cornucopia of varied pleasures and virtues. 'Indiscriminate order' is not an oxymoron.

Sometimes the details add purely to the interest of the miscellaneous, the individual, and the unexpected, in the manner of the brooches worn by Cranford's ladies: 'some with dogs' eyes painted in them; some that were like small picture-frames with mausoleums and weeping-willows neatly executed in hair inside; some, again, with miniatures of ladies and gentlemen sweetly smiling out of a nest of stiff muslin'. Miss Pole wears seven: 'two were fixed negligently in her cap (one was a butterfly made of Scotch pebbles, which a vivid imagination might believe to be the real insect)' – a detail that is almost an ironic self-reflection on the jaunty artifice of excess in Gaskell's own (far from) 'negligent' realism (*C*, 74).

Sometimes the cherishing of small things is also ethically charged – it takes patience and faith, after all, to save up string. Whereas the weak and secretive Osborne in *Wives and Daughters* (1866) cannot remember at what time of year the roses of poetry bloom, *Cranford*'s man of integrity, Mr Holbrook, loves Tennyson for pointing out the colour of ash buds in March: '"they are jet-black, madam"'(*C*, 35). He considers it a 'shame' never to have observed as much for himself, but is dignified himself for having noticed, and held close to his heart for over forty years, the 'small' and 'mousey' Miss Matty.

This ethic of fine attentiveness is allied to the responsibilities of the scrupulous historian. *Cranford* makes passing allusion to Carlyle's review of Boswell's *Life of Johnson* (*C*, 61), in which he argues that Boswell's detailed account of daily life is more historically valuable than any formal history.[9] In like mode, Gaskell's fiction preserves a fascinating wealth of nineteenth-century particularities: the way in which ladies kept the flowers in their hair fresh; the exact social significance of particular foods and the times they are served; the logistics of land drainage, and so on. This attention to detail is most patient and faithful when, as in *Cranford* and *Wives and Daughters*, Gaskell writes about an age just beginning to fade from memory. Her concreteness staves off the imminence of loss.

Sometimes, too, Gaskell's detail does carry the deeper significance that Woolf demands. In health, the conjuror Signor Brunoni is a focus for the insular and xenophobic fears of the Cranford ladies; injured, he becomes a focus of their affection and generosity. Thus, the penny ball first encountered as a missile for checking for men in ambush under Miss Matty's bed is later covered 'with gay-coloured worsted in rainbow stripes' for Brunoni's child (*C*, 105), so becoming a symbol of the transformation of fear into love. But it is a playful symbol, tossed up underhand along with other particularities and caught up by the reader almost reflexively.

Cranford is the ideal vehicle for this miscellaneous aesthetic. Published in irregular instalments in *Household Words*, the early chapters were written before a full-length work was contemplated. *Pickwick Papers* features in the plot of the first number of *Cranford*, which, echoing Dickens's 'novel' in form,[10] is a series of vignettes, held loosely together by a simple plot and the individual streets, shops, and pieces of cat-chewed old lace from which a dense atmosphere emerges. As Gaskell's third novel, these vignettes draw on memories, anecdotes, and pieces of writing accumulated over the whole first half of her life, many rooted in her mother's Cheshire home-town, Knutsford, where Gaskell was raised by her maternal aunt. She was only two years old when her mother, of a well-connected Unitarian family, died, and afterwards she spent only limited time with the new family of her father, William Stevenson, erstwhile Unitarian minister and man of letters.

Cranford is conveyed through particularities because it is a feminine domain. The old letters humorously explore the tension between masculine abstraction and idealisation and feminine engagement with the matter of fact. One letter is labelled by Miss Matty's mother: 'Hebrew verses sent me by my honoured husband. I thowt to have had a letter about killing the pig, but must wait.' This practical young woman, bewildered by her future husband's idealising love-letters, 'could not quite understand what he meant by repeating the same thing over in so many different ways; but what she was quite clear about was a longing for a white "Paduasoy" –whatever that might be'. Again, lively littleness tells a story. As the mother's 'girlish vanity' is displaced by motherly love, 'the white "Paduasoy" figured again with almost as much vigour as before ... being made into a christening cloak for the baby' (*C*, 45, 43, 44).

Herein lie important clues to the conditions that made Gaskell such an exemplary realist of things. Of the twenty-seven writers discussed in this volume, only Gaskell and Burney were mothers – and Gaskell had the most complex and demanding domestic life of any of them. At twenty-two she married William Gaskell, a busy inner-city minister and committee-man, and bore seven children of whom four survived. Her letters and diary give a picture of a frenetic hands-on existence crammed full of teasets, caps, joints, drains: 'In this hour since breakfast I have had to decide on the following variety of important questions. Boiled beef – how long to boil? What perennials will do in Manchester smoke ... Length of skirt for a gown? Salary of a nursery governess ... ?' (*Letters*, 489). She also engaged in social relief-work. Bad times in Manchester saw Gaskell and her daughters on their feet all day until collapsing into bed. She travelled often and widely, the very energetic fullness and diversity of her practical life seeming to feed her writing. As well as six novels, she wrote numerous short stories, ranging from realistic sketches to ghost stories, as well as several novellas, the most highly regarded of which, *Cousin Phillis* (1864), capitalises on her strength in scene-painting. Her *Life of Charlotte Brontë* (1857) was immediately recognised as ground-breaking, in large part because of its meticulous grounding in diurnal details. She died at fifty-five, in the midst of frantically furnishing a house bought as a surprise for her husband and trying to finish *Wives and Daughters*. As John Carey observes, reading Jenny Uglow's account of this hectic life, 'you feel lost when the story suddenly stops'.[11]

Gaskell herself plays on the emotional dynamic between profuse, concrete, humdrum presence, and the poignancy of loss. The old letters embody 'a vivid and intense sense of the present time, which seemed so strong and full, as if it could never pass away, and as if the warm, living hearts that so expressed themselves could never die, and be as nothing to the sunny earth' (*C*, 42–3). Sensuous lyricism jostles with the comedy of the prosaic, as in the 'faint, pleasant smell of Tonquin beans' that wreathes the possessions of the late Mrs Jenkyns (*C*, 42). Comfortable and intimate concrete engagement runs straight through into lyrical grief, as in Miss Matty's recollection of the day Peter ran away: 'I was in the store-room helping my mother to make cowslip wine. I cannot abide the wine now, nor the scent of the flowers ... days after, I saw the poor, withered cowslip flowers thrown out to the leaf heap, to decay and die there' (*C*, 53).

This mastery of the tragic potentialities behind busy everyday life is what rendered Gaskell's first novel, *Mary Barton* (1848), 'the most moving response in literature to the industrial suffering of the 1840s'.[12] Readerly sympathy with loss comes most highly charged out of a vivid sense of presence, conjured here by the hypnotic power of the realism of things. Early reviewers recognised a new and powerful approach to the subject, and George Eliot saw a trail blazed: 'I was conscious, while the question of my power was still undecided for me, that my feeling towards Life and Art had some affinity with the feeling which had inspired *Cranford* and the earlier chapters of *Mary Barton*.'[13]

The success of Gaskell's effort to engage middle-class sympathy relies upon the deft balance she maintains between curiosity and emotional engagement, the strange and the familiar – a balance that is key to the attraction of all her novels. In introducing the humdrum Cranford, she emphasises the exotic: the description of a town 'in possession of the Amazons' prepares us for an investigation of the bizarre customs of a foreign place, even as the humour rests on the intimation that the savage practices of this provincial town will not be so shocking as to alienate our sympathies. The anthropologist-narrator explains local customs, taboos, and fetish objects: 'Do you know what a calash is? It is a covering worn over caps, not unlike the heads fastened on old-fashioned gigs; but sometimes it is not quite so large' (*C*, 65). But in *Mary Barton*, the opposite adjustment is needed. Here her reader really *could* be shocked out of sympathy by the details ahead, and such a response must be pre-empted by a recognition of the familiar amongst the strange. So the story begins not in Manchester amongst machinery, but on a holiday in the country – an ordinary enough bit of country, but, as the narrator assures the reader, 'you would not wonder, if you could see, or I properly describe, the charm of one particular stile, that it should be ... a crowded halting place'. There follows a delicately detailed description of landscape that, to the extent that the reader enjoys it, unites us in feeling with the working people. This is 'the April of the poets', and Gaskell stakes out the lives of her workers as fit subject for serious literature even as she emphasises the everyday subjective responses they share with genteel readers (*MB*, 1).

The reader seems to go home along with the Wilsons to the tea-party at the Bartons' – 'On the right of the door, as *you entered* ...'. This is an intimate occasion – 'blue-and-white check curtains ... were now drawn, to shut in the friends ... Two geraniums, unpruned and leafy ... formed a further defence from out-door pryers' – but the reader is one of those 'shut in', as Gaskell sets about transmuting us from curious 'pryer' into sympathetic friend (*MB*, 13, my italics).

On the other hand, determined to maintain the interest and authenticity of her picture of working-class life, Gaskell also emphasises unfamiliar things. A cupboard contains 'nondescript articles, for which one would have fancied their possessors could find no use – such as triangular pieces of glass to save carving knives and forks from dirtying table-cloths' – but the feelings they inspire are easy to sympathise with: 'it was evident Mrs. Barton was proud of her crockery and glass, for she left her cupboard door open' (*MB*, 13). Gaskell is at pains to let her reader visualise the room. But her images are by no means frozen: they invite us to move, in imagination, with the housewife around her cottage – 'on the opposite side to the door and window was the staircase, and two doors; one of which (the nearest to the fire) led into a sort of little back kitchen, where dirty work, such as washing up dishes, might be done, and whose shelves served as larder, and pantry, and storeroom, and all' (*MB*, 13). The economic fragility of this domestic comfort is only indirectly, though acutely, implied. Gaskell parenthetically remarks that the abundant furniture is a 'sure sign of good times among the mills' (*MB*, 13); Mrs Barton must borrow a cup if she is to invite a fourth guest, and that guest's address, simply stated as 'under 14, Barber Street', allows readers to make their own judgement about cellar-dwelling (*MB*, 14). Pity is not demanded; nevertheless, we register the lived reality of encroaching poverty.

Hospitable scenes like this, of which there are several in *Mary Barton*, are important throughout Gaskell's work. The accumulations of the novelist's attentively observant eye are laid out with an unstinting generosity before the reader's imagination, as though the solicitous host has much in common with the realist of things. Gaskell would not have thought this a patronising comparison: men as well as women act hospitably in this novel, and such tender care stands out against the dark background as truly heroic. The very scarcity of resource behind the welcome heightens its warmth. Alice spends her morning's wages on tea for three, and no description of qualities of mind could make us warm to her as much as watching her making an extra seat out of 'an old board arranged with some skill upon two old candle boxes set on end', and set 'her unlacquered ancient, third-hand tea-tray' 'with a black tea-pot, two cups with a red and white pattern, and one with the old friendly willow pattern, and saucers, not to match' (*MB*, 31). As a Unitarian, Gaskell believed in the shaping force of environment on character. These arduous hospitable preparations visibly shape the solidarity she admired in the working class.

However, the novel gets beyond any such generalised intuitions. Out of a particularised habitat grow strongly individualised characters. Extraordinary vitality imbues even minor figures such as Alice Wilson and Job Leigh. As a careful and systematic entomologist, Job not only gives the lie to the stereotype of the poor man as passive object of scientific inquiry, but is analogous to Gaskell herself in his attentiveness to tiny details, small lives, specific habitats. And as hedge doctor, Alice too aligns herself with the realist of common things: she collects 'all manner of hedge-row, ditch, and field plants, which we are accustomed to call valueless, but which have a powerful effect' (*MB*, 15).

As Jenny Uglow observes, Gaskell's thinking 'was not abstract or codified: she enacts and embodies rather than argues'.[14] Her impulse is at one with Thornton's vehemence in *North and South*: 'Indeed I have no theory; I hate theories.'[15] Nevertheless, not only *Mary Barton* but, to an even greater degree, her next novel, *Ruth* (1853), have been criticised for ideological incoherence. The title-character is an impoverished orphan seduced and then deserted by a rich man. Though her own innocent naïveté seems to rob her sexual lapse of all moral culpability, she spends the rest of her life in repentant acts of self-devotion to her child and her society and dies of a fever caught while nursing her unregenerate former lover. Readers have always felt uneasy with the exaction of this ultimate penalty from an essentially blameless heroine. However, if in theory *Ruth* is a flawed novel, it has the texture of a great one. George Eliot called 'its style ... a great refreshment ... from its finish and fullness ... how pretty and graphic are the touches of description! That little attic in the minister's house, for example, which, with its pure white dimity bed-curtains, its bright-green walls, and the rich brown of its stained floor, remind one of a snowdrop springing out of the soil.'[16]

In *Ruth*, Gaskell shows how effectively details of daily life conjure the intensity of subjective experience. Audrey Jaffe has complained about Ruth's lack of 'idiosyncratic identity'; her 'attention [is] always directed toward something other than herself'.[17] But what is true of Ruth's consciousness as Gaskell portrays it is true also of consciousness in general: to be conscious is to be conscious *of* something, and that something is usually outside ourselves. The novelist of detailed circumstance is at once the novelist of the intricacies of consciousness.

An early reviewer found 'the most obvious' peculiarity of *Ruth* to be the use, 'not more frequent than effective', of the pathetic fallacy (*CH*, 256). This was a suggestive observation, though Gaskell's scenic technique is both subtler and more varied than it implies. We first meet Ruth through her environment, as a description of a snowy night is focalised through her. The landscape, in turn, is a receptacle of memory for the orphan Ruth – it embodies her loss. '"At home I have many a time run up the lane all the way to the mill, just to see the icicles hang on the great wheel; and, when I was once out, I could hardly find in my heart to come in, even to mother ... even to mother".'[18]

These hanging icicles recall Coleridge's poem 'Frost at Midnight' (1798), and in Romantic vein, we sense the depth of Ruth's soul through the extent of the external greatness it comprehends – in moments when 'she knew not if she moved or stood still, for the grandeur of this beautiful earth absorbed all idea of separate and individual existence' (*R*, 65). We find the essential Ruth at the very times she all but loses herself:

> she forgot all doubt and awkwardness ... in her delight at the new, tender beauty of an early spring day ... Among the last year's brown ruins, heaped together by the wind in the hedgerows, she found the fresh, green, crinkled leaves and pale star-like flowers of the primroses. Here and there a golden celandine made brilliant the sides of the little brook ... the brown leafless woods in the foreground derived an almost metallic lustre from the golden mist and haze of sunset. (*R*, 40)

And at the juncture when all is lost – when she contemplates suicide – the agony of her numbness is registered exactly through the tiny things she continues to perceive: 'long afterwards – she remembered the exact motion of a bright green beetle busily meandering among the wild thyme near her, and she recalled the musical, balanced, wavering drop of a skylark into her nest, near the heather-bed where she lay' (*R*, 94).

The Brontës offer the nearest precedent in fiction for Gaskell's use of landscape and setting to project subjective depth. The novels of Gaskell and her friend Charlotte were often compared, and, indeed, Ruth's twisted Cinderella story powerfully recalls *Jane Eyre* (1847), and her absorption in the snow-scene outside the window is an echo of Jane reading Bewick's *History of British Birds* in the window-seat. But, as this example suggests, Brontë's invocation of landscape is more textually and symbolically mediated. Jane, after separating from Rochester, also lies on the ground observing the motions of the insects in the heather whilst hoping to die, but, unlike Ruth, her experience of the landscape is filtered through abstract allegorical reflections. In its refined naturalism, immediacy and psychological subtlety, Ruth's experience of landscape is more reminiscent of Wordsworth or Tennyson. It is a new, powerful importation to English fiction, which proved formative. Even more striking, for example, than the affinity between Gaskell's Ruth and Thomas Hardy's fallen, pure woman, Tess, is the marked similarity in the ways the two novelists fuse landscape and setting with subjectivity.

This new sense of the interpenetration of mind and world creates haunted places, where the consciousness of generations past hangs around places like an aura. *Ruth* begins with a description of the changes wrought by time on the 'assize-town in one of the eastern counties ... much distinguished by the

Tudor Sovereigns' (*R*, 1). Ruth's sensitive consciousness seems to conduct the sensibility of whole generations. The grand town houses have '(bend your ear lower, lest the shade of Marmaduke, first Baron Waverham, hear)' been converted into shops, but their 'body' is 'too solidly grand to submit to alteration'. Customers are occasionally surprised

> to find themselves at the foot of a grand carved oaken staircase, lighted by a window of stained glass, storied all over with armorial bearings. Up such a stair – past such a window (through which the moonlight fell on her with a glory of many colours) – Ruth Hilton passed wearily one January night.
>
> (*R*, 3)

In this novel, as in Hardy's fiction, it is as though the fractures of modernity can produce such isolation that individuals find their closest companionship in ghosts of the past. Ruth chooses the darkest part of the workroom, so that she may gaze at ancient panels, on which

> were thrown with the careless, triumphant hand of a master – the most lovely wreaths of flowers, profuse and luxuriant beyond description, and so real-looking, that you could almost fancy you smelt their fragrance, and heard the south wind go softly rustling in and out among the crimson roses – the branches of purple and white lilac – the floating golden-tressed laburnum boughs. Besides these, there were ... hollyhocks, fraxinella, monk's-hood, pansies, primroses; every flower which blooms profusely in charming old-fashioned country gardens ...
>
> Surely ... whoever the dead-and-gone artist might be, would have been gratified to know the pleasure his handiwork ... had power to give to the heavy heart of a young girl; for they conjured up visions of other sister-flowers that grew, and blossomed, and withered away in her early home. (*R*, 7)

The 'hand of the master', the smell of the flowers, the south breeze, though phantoms, seem more vivid and warm than the cold reality that surrounds her. The painting embodies the same instinct to resist loss, to capture the moment before the flowers wither, that guides the hand of Gaskell, realist of profuse and luxuriant description.

And so Gaskell, describing the view from the Welsh inn, herself takes the place of an artist leaving behind a sympathetic presence: 'I have seen ... sunny lights creeping down the purple mountain slope, and stealing over the green, soft meadows, till they reached the little garden, full of roses and lavender-bushes, lying close under the window. I have seen – but I shall see no more' (*R*, 63). 'Creeping', 'stealing', 'soft', 'close', 'no more': words redolent of change, loss, and the tenderness of recollection animate the setting of Ruth's tragedy. Among these same mountains, Gaskell's own baby son caught a fatal fever. Here, and for the rest of the novel, she leads her heroine through a sequence of thinly fictionalised places freighted with tender personal recollections of her own – a fact which both adds to the vividness of the descriptions and suggests an intense identification with her 'fallen' heroine. Though Gaskell sometimes seems to shrink from the prospect of her audience's disapproval of Ruth and her story, there is no sign of any shrinking from Ruth herself.

If Ruth's quivering responsiveness to what lies outside her creates the impression of subjectivity as a silver web suspended across the heather, we appreciate its delicacy all the more for the robustness of other characters. The powerful delineation of the complacent obtuseness and utilitarian self-righteousness of Mr Bradshaw and of the generous impetuosity of his daughter, Jemima, is closely echoed, and not bettered, by Dickens in *Hard Times* (1854). But best of all is noisy Sally, Charlotte Brontë's 'apple of gold' (*CH*, 201) – whose full-bodied existence is captured in her relation to things, and whose strong, hands-on approach to life is a perfect foil, and balance, to Ruth's hypersensitivity. The two are united – as well as subtly contrasted – through a shared appreciation of the connection between nature and memory: Sally 'gathered a piece of southern-wood, and stuffed it up her nose, by way of smelling it. "Whatten you call this in your country?" asked she. "Old Man," replied Ruth. "We call it here lad's-love. It and peppermint drops always reminds me of going to church in the country"' (*R*, 192).

As in *Cranford*, where the narrator has always 'vibrated' between Drumble (Manchester) and Cranford (*C*, 154), Ruth's movements between town and country reflect the vibrating tension between change and permanence, which Gaskell explores most systematically in *North and South* (1855). These binaries register in contrasting relations to the fabric of everyday life. Margaret Hale experiences the first fracture of her settled rural existence just as her father, in the walled garden of their family home, is taking his time over eating a pear, peeled 'in one long strip of silver-paper thinness' (*NS*, 30). It seems to Margaret that time is passing more quickly for her than for him. But even in Manchester, the Hales maintain a 'feminine' homeliness, lovingly described. To the stern mother of the capitalist Thornton, on the other hand, home comforts represent no more than extra dusting (*NS*, 78, 96). Like the house of Dickens's capitalist in *Dombey and Son* (1848), her son's is kept 'twenty times as fine; not one quarter as comfortable', the things in it alienated from everyday human contact by glass shades and dust-sheets (*NS*, 78, 112).

This novel brings out the tension between the realism of everyday life and narrative itself – the plotting inexorably leads Margaret, and the reader, away from homeliness, just as the lack of plot in *Cranford* allowed us to dwell on it. But here the balance between saving and loss is upset. Gaskell herself remarked that the novel might have been entitled 'death and variations' (*Letters*, 324), and the almost monotonous regularity of the deaths is numbing. Whilst the trauma of loss and change is powerfully expressed, greater distance is needed to give it shape. For that, Gaskell looked to history.

Set during the French Revolutionary wars, *Sylvia's Lovers* (1863), Gaskell's only strictly historical novel, follows Scott both in its choice of a period '*Sixty Years Since*' and of its central themes. Here, like the sailors, personal history is literally pressed into that of wars and nations. Scott's fiction is one well-examined manifestation of the connection between fictional realism and a preoccupation with historical change – between the urge to capture life as it is and the consciousness of time, change, and their annihilations. The motive of *Sylvia's Lovers* – with its epigraphs from Tennyson's *In Memoriam* – is to save the traces of individual lives from the wreck of time. For this novel, scrupulous as always in her historical research, Gaskell sought help in keeping her use of dialect vivid and accurate, and, as in her pictures of industrial poverty, the details of her account show an interest in difference and idiosyncrasy that is never voyeuristic, but permeated by her customary whole-hearted sympathy with the gamut of human life. When a peripatetic tailor calls, Sylvia fetches a bundle 'of small pieces of various coloured cloth, cut out of old coats and waistcoats, and similar garments, when the whole had become too much worn for use, yet when part had been good enough to be treasured by a thrifty housewife'.[19] Like such a housewife, Gaskell hoards the scraps of the fabric of existence to patch into symbols of mutability.

This acute sense of time, loss, the eternal and the transient, is also materialised in the novel's recurring image of waves, a trope echoing down from Dickens's *Dombey and Son*:

> Monkshaven is altered now into a rising bathing place. Yet, standing near the site of widow Dobson's house on a summer's night, at the ebb of a spring-tide, you may hear the waves come lapping up the shelving shore with the same ceaseless, ever-recurrent sound as that which Philip listened to in the pauses between life and death. (*SL*, 502)

As in *Ruth*, landscape unites subjective experiences through time. History is felt in the dynamic between the overwhelming intensity of consciousness and its watery inversion – absence and death. The vision is acutely self-reflexive: 'it appears curious to see how little our ancestors had the power of putting two things together ... Will our descendants have a wonder about us ... that we do not perceive ... that the logical consequence of particular opinions must be convictions which at present we hold in abhorrence?' (*SL*,

68). It is as though Gaskell anticipated that logic-chopping of precisely this kind would be applied to the inconsistencies of her own plots. She may have hoped too for the kind of compassion, sobered and made tender by a consciousness of the transience of all human perspectives, which she extends to her characters, even at their most prosaic, and which she invokes in us through the very littleness of the details:

> At this hour, all the actors in this story having played out their parts and gone to their rest, there is something touching in recording the futile efforts made by Philip to win from Sylvia the love he yearned for ... the grave, awkward, plain young man studying patterns and colours for a new waistcoat, with his head a little on one side. (*SL*, 133)

Tenderness towards the ugly, awkward, and imperfect was to be a vein explored further by George Eliot. Commenting on *Ruth*, Eliot had found fault with Gaskell's 'love of sharp contrasts ... She is not contented with the subdued colouring – the half tints of real life' (*CH*, 232). But Gaskell increasingly did adopt half-tints. Reviewing her last novel, *Wives and Daughters* (1865), the young Henry James remarked on 'the lightness of touch' which makes us forgetful of literary artifice, 'the admirable, inaudible, invisible exercise of creative power ... with which a new and arbitrary world is reared ... complete in every particular, from the divine blue of the summer sky to the June-bugs in the roses' (*CH*, 463).

The opening of that novel suggests the zoom of attention characteristic of realist novelist and child alike: 'In a country there was a shire, and in that shire there was a town, and in that town there was a house, and in that house there was a room, and in that room there was a bed, and in that bed there lay a little girl ... It was a June morning ... the room was full of sunny warmth and light.' The living warmth of the world of this novel is created through a profusion of 'solid' and 'heavy' stuff drenched in the vivacity of human habits and attitudes. Molly's bonnet is

> carefully covered over from any chance of dust, with a large cotton-handkerchief, of so heavy and serviceable a texture that, if the thing underneath it had been a flimsy fabric of gauze and lace and flowers, it would have been altogether 'scomfished' (... to quote from Betty's vocabulary). But the bonnet was made of solid straw, and its only trimming was a plain white ribbon put over the crown, and forming the strings. Still, there was a neat little quilling inside, every plait of which Molly knew; for had she not made it herself the evening before, with infinite pains?[20]

James marked the way 'the details ... so numerous and minute' contribute to the depth of the characters, and to our attachment to them. 'Molly Gibson [is] a product, to a certain extent, of clean frocks and French lessons'; the details educate the reader into 'a proper degree of interest in the heroine. He feels that he knows her the better and loves her the more for a certain acquaintance with the *minutiae* of her homely *bourgeois* life' (*CH*, 464–5). The morally grubby but socially fastidious Hyacinth spends some of her wedding money clearing her debts – 'a little sense of duty cropping out' – and the rest on clothes that will 'make a show' (*WD*, 144, 145): she is perfectly captured in her daintily mended underwear and in 'the dirty dog's-eared delightful novel from the Ashcombe circulating library, the leaves of which she turned over with a pair of scissors' (*WD*, 134). The choice of detail, rendered in prose tinged by the idiom of the character, makes for a revelation of personality that is searching, satiric, and yet – just because it takes such full account of the smallest circumstance – sympathetic.

The central characters of *Wives and Daughters* are embodiments of Gaskell's fictional ethic. Molly Gibson is a clear-eyed observer, whose marginal position renders her at once disinterested and poignantly engaged. She learns to go beyond preconceptions and literary clichés to engage with the complex details of reality. She makes her first intimate connection with Roger Hamley, another field biologist (modelled on Gaskell's relation Charles Darwin), when he finds and comforts her on his way back from dredging for pond specimens. He steps from the path to look at a rare plant: 'He was so great a lover of nature that, without any thought, but habitually, he always avoided treading unnecessarily on any plant; who knew what long-sought growth or insect might develop itself in what now appeared but insignificant?'(*WD*, 117).

Such attention is the stuff of love, and Gaskell lavishes it on her heroine. Molly's integrity and depth, like Ruth's, is registered through her closeness to her natural habitat. The crises of her development are vividly actualised in relation to changing seasons. They are minutely, though almost imperceptibly, embodied in the opening roses she smells, the damsons she goes to fetch, the crimsoning leaves she abstractedly admires – details on a par with Tennyson's March ash buds. On the day Roger leaves the country for years, Molly learns that he has proposed to her stepsister Cynthia. After their final interview, she 'caught the reflection of ... two faces in the glass; her own, red-eyed, pale, with lips dyed with blackberry juice, her curls tangled ... contrasted ... with Cynthia's brightness'. She notices the leaf full of blackberries she has brought home for Cynthia, 'the broad green leaf, so fresh and crisp when Molly had gathered it an hour or so ago, but now soft and flabby, and dying. Molly ... felt a strange kind of sympathetic pity for the poor inanimate leaf' (*WD*, 396). These details are themselves selected with unspeakable sympathy – we feel that Roger ought to love Molly the more for the blackberry stains.

Molly's great sorrow in the novel is the 'vanishing ... off the face of the earth' (*WD*, 392) of the sort of deeply appreciative attention that underlies such noticing. As her stepmother criticises the unfashionable curl of her hair,

> a recollection came before her like a picture ... a young mother washing and dressing her little girl; placing the half-naked darling on her knee, and twining the wet rings of dark hair fondly round her fingers, and then, in an ecstasy of fondness, kissing the little curly head. (*WD*, 471)

It is a representation that recalls another passage, from *Sylvia's Lovers*,

> in her after life, when no one cared much for her out-goings and in-comings, the ... figure of her mother, fronting the setting sun, but searching through its blinding rays for a sight of her child, rose up like a sudden-seen picture, the remembrance of which smote Sylvia ... with a sense of a lost blessing. (*SL*, 61)

These young women step outside themselves to glimpse their loss pictorially – and perhaps Gaskell does too. There is something of a mother's tender caress in the details she lavishes on the curls and cloaks, the out-goings and in-comings of her heroines – each one of them, in their hour of need, motherless, like herself. It is as though, tapping the overflow of her own motherly love, Gaskell seeks to assuage their loss, and her own.

NOTE ON EDITIONS

There have been two authoritative collected editions of Gaskell's fiction: the Knutsford Edition by A. W. Ward (8 vols., 1906) and Clement Shorter's edition for Oxford University Press (11 vols., 1906–19). Neither is in print. However, reliable annotated texts of the novels are available in Oxford World's Classics and Penguin Classics.

NOTES

1 Letter to Harriet Carr, 31 August and 1 September 1831, in *Further Letters of Mrs Gaskell*, ed. John Chapple and Alan Shelston (Manchester and New York: Manchester University Press, 2000), p. 6.

2 Henry James, 'The Art of Fiction' (1884), in *Henry James: Selected Literary Criticism*, ed. Morris Shapira (Harmondsworth: Penguin, 1968), p. 86.

3 Elizabeth Gaskell, *Cranford* (1853), ed. Elizabeth Porges Watson, introduction by Charlotte Mitchell (Oxford: Oxford World's Classics, 1998), p. 40. Hereafter *C*.

4 Virginia Woolf, review of Mrs Ellis Chadwick's *Mrs Gaskell: Haunts, Homes, and Stories*, *Times Literary Supplement* (29 September 1910).

5 *The Letters of Mrs Gaskell*, ed. J. A. V. Chapple and A. Pollard (Manchester: Manchester University Press, 1966), p. 540. Hereafter *Letters*.

6 For accounts of nineteenth-century attitudes towards this sort of realism see Naomi Schor, *Reading in Detail: Aesthetics and the Feminine* (New York: Methuen, 1987), and Ruth Bernard Yeazell, *Art of the Everyday: Dutch Painting and the Realist Novel* (Princeton and Oxford: Princeton University Press, 2008).
7 Lord David Cecil, *Early Victorian Novelists: Essays in Revaluation* (London: Constable, 1934).
8 Elizabeth Gaskell, *Mary Barton* (1848), ed. Shirley Foster (Oxford: Oxford World's Classics, 2008), p. 2. Hereafter *MB*.
9 Thomas Carlyle, review of James Boswell's *Life of Johnson*, *Frazer's Magazine*, 5 (May 1832), 379–413.
10 Hilary M. Schor makes a case for *Cranford* as 'a female version of Pickwick', in *Scheherazade in the Marketplace: Elizabeth Gaskell and the Victorian Novel* (Oxford: Oxford University Press, 1992).
11 John Carey, *Sunday Times* review of Jenny Uglow, *Elizabeth Gaskell: A Habit of Stories* (London: Faber and Faber, 1993), quoted on cover of paperback edition (1994).
12 Raymond Williams, *Culture and Society 1780–1950* (London: Pelican, 1961; first published 1958), p. 99.
13 *The George Eliot Letters*, ed. Gordon S. Haight, 9 vols. (New Haven and London: Yale University Press, 1954–78), III, p. 198.
14 Uglow, *A Habit of Stories*, p. 603.
15 Elizabeth Gaskell, *North and South* (1855), ed. Angus Easson (Oxford: Oxford World's Classics, 1998), p. 363. Hereafter *NS*.
16 Angus Easson (ed.), *Elizabeth Gaskell: The Critical Heritage* (London: Routledge, 1991), p. 232. Hereafter *CH*.
17 Audrey Jaffe, '*Cranford* and *Ruth*', in *The Cambridge Companion to Elizabeth Gaskell*, ed. Jill L. Matus (Cambridge: Cambridge University Press, 2007), pp. 46–58, 56.
18 Elizabeth Gaskell, *Ruth* (1853), ed. Alan Shelston (Oxford: Oxford World's Classics, 1985), p. 5. Hereafter *R*.
19 Elizabeth Gaskell, *Sylvia's Lovers* (1863), ed. Andrew Sanders (Oxford: Oxford World's Classics, 1982), p. 52. Hereafter *SL*.
20 Elizabeth Gaskell, *Wives and Daughters* (1865), ed. Angus Easson (Oxford: Oxford World's Classics, 2000), p. 1. Hereafter *WD*.

FURTHER READING

Easson, Angus, *Elizabeth Gaskell*, London, Routledge, 1980

Easson, Angus (ed.), *Elizabeth Gaskell: The Critical Heritage*, London, Routledge, 1991

Foster, Shirley, *Elizabeth Gaskell: A Literary Life*, Basingstoke, Palgrave Macmillan, 2002

Lansbury, Coral, *Elizabeth Gaskell: The Novel of Social Crisis*, New York, Barnes and Noble, 1975

Matus, Jill L. (ed.), *The Cambridge Companion to Elizabeth Gaskell*, Cambridge, Cambridge University Press, 2007

Schor, Hilary, *Scheherazade in the Marketplace: Elizabeth Gaskell and the Victorian Novel*, Oxford, Oxford University Press, 1992
Stoneman, Patsy, *Elizabeth Gaskell*, Brighton, Harvester Press, 1987
Uglow, Jenny, *Elizabeth Gaskell: A Habit of Stories*, London, Faber and Faber, 1993
Wright, Edgar, *Mrs. Gaskell: The Basis for Reassessment*, Oxford, Oxford University Press, 1965
Wright, Terence, *Elizabeth Gaskell: 'We are Not Angels': Realism, Gender, Values*, Basingstoke, Macmillan, 1995

13

DAVID SKILTON

Anthony Trollope

Of the great Victorian novelists, Anthony Trollope (1815–82) was the most prolific, and he was justly regarded as the foremost presenter of the lives of the professional and landed classes whose members provided the core of his readership. Many of his novels first appeared in parts or as serials in magazines, giving his fiction the currency which nowadays we can compare only to serial drama on television. One obituarist went so far as to write that his work 'will picture the society of our day with a fidelity with which society has never been pictured before in the history of the world'.[1]

Born in London in 1815, the fourth surviving child of a failing barrister with a difficult personality and grandiose expectations, the novelist spent a miserable childhood and youth. Because of his poverty he felt himself an outcast at Harrow and Winchester, where he was a scholastic failure. He felt further rejected when his mother abandoned him for four years at the age of twelve to go to America in a vain attempt to save the family's fortunes, leaving Anthony with his father, who was by now in a mental state verging on insanity. After his father's inevitable bankruptcy, Frances Trollope turned author in her early fifties, achieving fame and prosperity with *Domestic Manners of the Americans* (1832) and a flow of successful novels through the 1830s and 1840s. Through a family contact, Anthony was found a clerkship in the Post Office, and after a period in London he was posted to Ireland, where he became a reliable and energetic public servant. In 1844 he married Rose Heseltine, about whom we know little, except that she was an expert household manager, and her husband relied on her literary judgement throughout his life. Until retirement in 1867 he managed to combine full-time Post Office work, reorganising large parts of the postal service of Great Britain, Ireland and the West Indies, with a huge literary output, and with life in society and on the hunting field. He published his first novel in 1847, but had only just become well known on his return to London in 1859. He was immensely popular in the 1860s and made new efforts to retain his market position in the 1870s. He stood unsuccessfully for Parliament as a

Liberal candidate in 1868, believing membership of the House of Commons the highest honour to which a man could aspire. When he died in 1882 he had written nine volumes of stories and sketches, nine works of non-fiction and forty-seven novels, including two six-volume cycles, the Chronicles of Barsetshire and the Palliser Novels. He journeyed extensively in Europe, North America, Australia, New Zealand, and South Africa, incorporating his experiences in his fiction and travel books. He recounted his upbringing and his working life in a fascinating and moving autobiography, published posthumously in 1883. He is also renowned for introducing the pillar-box into Britain.

His most celebrated contributions to literature are extensive treatments of the life of the well-to-do in England, with Scotland and Wales featuring as they presented themselves to the eyes of a London-based but cosmopolitan Englishman. W. H. Auden considered that Trollope knew more about money than any other novelist, and it is true that he understands the socio-economics and the politics of everyday life among the prosperous classes and the processes of individual moral choice in a complex world. He dealt both humorously and seriously with the economic and emotional facts of life, and in his many love-stories, attraction to the opposite sex was not etherealised, but, within the strict limits of mid-Victorian self-censorship, desire was felt and expressed.

He was unusual in his generation in his admiration of Jane Austen and considered *Pride and Prejudice* the greatest novel in the language until Thackeray's *Esmond* appeared in 1852. Like Austen he dealt with the continuation of society through workable marriages. With a characteristic touch of Trollopian irony, in the last chapter of *Ayala's Angel* (1881) the narrator explains the conventional ending of the novel:

> If marriage be the proper ending for a novel, – the only ending, as this writer takes it to be, which is not discordant, – surely no tale was ever so properly ended, or with so full a concord, as this one. Infinite trouble has been taken not only in arranging these marriages but in joining like to like, – so that, if not happiness, at any rate sympathetic unhappiness, might be produced.[2]

This is a good example of Trollope both exploiting and playing with the conventions of Victorian fiction. He exploits his knowledge of the world gained in public life, and in particular of the mechanics of daily life, travel, commerce, communications, and administration. He was encouraged by the third novelist he most admired, Scott, to depict the interweaving of public events and private lives, but unlike Scott he did this in relation to the events of his own day. Unlike those of his contemporaries who set their fictions in the decades of their childhood and youth, he usually constructed fictional versions of the world as it was at the time he was writing. Thus, although his own miserable childhood and uncertain youth are clearly important, his fiction is never autobiographical in the sense that Dickens's is in *David Copperfield*.

Trollope concentrates on young adults and how they become mature adults. The issues surrounding the choice of a profession and of a marriage partner, and, more importantly, the choice of whether to pursue the profession and the marriage honestly or dishonestly, are central here, and that phrase, 'choice of a profession', must be taken to cover the administration of inherited estates, and, in the case of his women characters, the business side of managing a household and family: for Trollope was of his age in believing that a good marriage and child-rearing were the best occupations for a woman. Yet because he treats his women characters with the same seriousness as his men characters, giving them satisfyingly active mental lives and sense of self, he was and remains popular with intelligent woman readers, who have generally found him far superior in this respect to Dickens and Thackeray, though, of course, scarcely the equal of George Eliot. Susan Gay, a women's rights campaigner who knew Trollope, wrote, '[A]s regards imagination, he was unusually gifted ... and he would describe a woman's feelings in regard to a lover better than a woman herself.'[3] Most Victorian men insisted on a clear distinction between men's natures and women's, and men's mental lives and women's. Trollope did not. His women characters have a sense of identity as strongly developed as his men's, and although some when young regard their lovers as gods, and many later find fulfilment in domesticity and child-rearing, the best of his women have or crave exactly that 'position' on the map of human affairs which most Victorians attributed to educated men alone. Many, like Alice Vavasor in *Can You Forgive Her?* (1864), Lady Laura Standish in *Phineas Finn* (1876), or the Duchess of Omnium in *The Prime Minister* (1876), want a political role. Trollope is open-minded enough to make one sympathetic woman character, Madame Max Goesler in the Palliser Novels, a businesswoman and to allow her to propose to Phineas Finn without loss of authorial approval. Two of his most brilliant creations, Lady Mason in *Orley Farm* (1861–2) and Lizzie Eustace in *The Eustace Diamonds* (1873), are understood from the inside and do not become mere sensational criminal types, when in their different ways they take the law into their own hands – though the former is analysed sympathetically, while the latter is the creation of a comic genius. Such fictional women could certainly not be presented without as pronounced a social dimension to their characters as fictional men have in the period. It is not that Trollope was out of step with his age, but simply unusual among male novelists in giving imaginative form to such aspects of women's social and mental life. Yet his deliberate utterances on feminist issues were crass and uncomprehending, and his satires on feminists in *He Knew He Was Right* (1869) and *Is He Popenjoy?* (1878) are frankly embarrassing. It is difficult to reconcile these things with the fact that he knew some of the leading feminists of the day, some of whom he met through his friend George Eliot.

He was expert in the dynamics of human relationships, and, whether describing courtship, marriage, social life, business, or politics, he uses the strategies of interpersonal behaviour as a kind of higher-level language in which to present his fictional worlds. A reviewer suggested that Trollope was applying a systematic scientific knowledge of human social life – 'what we may call the *natural history* of every kind of man or woman he seeks to sketch'.[4] He never neglects the social construction of his characters' personalities, and treats the whole of human life in terms of individuals' sense of themselves interacting with those around them, and issuing in personal conduct and group dynamics. His contemporaries remarked on the dominance of an 'atmosphere of affairs' in all Trollope's fiction,[5] and this is true not just in the public and business lives he presents, but in the private lives as well. It is this that makes his fiction so unsentimental, whatever its subject, and makes his down-to-earth understanding of human motivation so uncynical, despite his comedy and his lack of idealism. His contemporaries agreed that he was pre-eminently 'a man of the world' in his fiction.

He was also unsurpassed in setting his fictional people in major British institutions: Parliament, the Civil Service, the Church of England, though, for the very Trollopian reason that he had no experience of them, not the Universities. Nor was he limited to Great Britain. Having worked in Ireland when young, he wrote five novels on Irish subjects, and is regarded as having made an important contribution to literature in Ireland. His treatment of Australian subjects, and even a story set in New Zealand, has enrolled him in the literary histories of those countries. He wrote frequently about America and American characters, and was on terms of friendship with many of the foremost American authors of his day, such as Bret Harte, Hawthorne, Russell Lowell, and Wendell Holmes. His mother and his one surviving brother were prominent members of the English expatriate community in Florence, and he followed the Risorgimento and Italian unification with close interest. When he travelled abroad, he wrote about it, setting scenes or complete stories and short novels in various parts of Europe and the Middle East and publishing books on *The West Indies and the Spanish Main*, *North America*, *Australia and New Zealand*, and *South Africa*.

However strong his single novels, he will always be best known as the author of two sequences of six novels each, the Chronicles of Barsetshire (1855–67), which develop an impressively ample picture of the social life of the clergy and the landed and other professional classes of the fictional county of Barsetshire, and the so-called Palliser Novels (1864–80), which centre on the lives and careers of Plantagenet Palliser (later Duke of Omnium) and his wife, Lady Glencora. His ability to produce what seems like a fully functioning society in addition to numerous individual characters is credited with influencing Tolstoy, while George Eliot is reported as saying that she was encouraged to write *Middlemarch* by his example. The Barsetshire Chronicles became popular reading during the Second World War, when they provided an escape into a world so much more secure than the reader's own. Nostalgia of this sort, though understandable, has probably distorted our appreciation of Trollope's fiction to a damaging extent. Although the cathedral city of Barchester is old-fashioned even when Trollope creates it, the stories he tells are of the modern and the metropolitan invading the country. Barchester is rapidly reached by train from London, but symbolically it is on a branch line, so that it is at once closely linked to the capital and a backwater. Trollope's contemporaries were adamant that this was not the world of Jane Austen, but the urgent, rapidly changing world of the age of railways. This point is important since there is disagreement about whether he is best read as a record of an attractive but long-vanished past or as a harbinger of the modern world in which we live. His corpus is so vast that evidence can readily be found for either position, and for a good many others besides. Yet the fact is that after the passing of over a century and a quarter, much of his fiction still looks as though it belongs to the modern world, or at least to a world closely linked to the world of today.

In part this is because of some obvious features which make the world it presents recognisable to us. Trollope's later characters travel on the London Underground, for example, and a firm of civil engineers in *The Claverings* (1867) is engaged in building London's Metropolitan line. Moreover Trollope's are among the first fictional characters to live lives controlled by rapid and efficient communications. Like their author, many of them are tireless train and steamship travellers in the British Isles and abroad, they exploit the penny post, and as soon as the telegraph is available, they use that too. While Dickens and Thackeray preferred to set their novels in the past, Trollope's seemed to their contemporary readers as up-to-the-minute as the latest topical cartoon in *Punch*. In *The Last Chronicle of Barset* he jokingly writes of a character's need to obtain an Austrian passport in order to travel to Venice, 'as was necessary in those bygone days of Venetia's thraldom' – that is to say a matter of months earlier than the date of publication, 1866.[6] Only those novelists who specialised in creating sensation by stories of crime and passion, made more sensational by their unexotic settings – writers like Wilkie Collins and Mary E. Braddon – had as close a relation as Trollope's with the world as it was when they were actually writing. As one critic remarked of the more lurid genre of fiction of some of Trollope's contemporaries, 'Proximity is ... one great element of sensation.'[7] It is equally one great element in the work of the leading proponent of what came to be called 'realistic' fiction – Anthony Trollope.

Novels such as *He Knew He Was Right* (1869) and *The Way We Live Now* (1875) contain details of London, presented with almost journalistic actuality, and every fictional journey within the metropolis has a distinct social and moral significance. *He Knew He Was Right* is strikingly centred on marital breakdown, a new and still relatively shocking subject when English novels more commonly sought to plot the various paths into and not out of marriage. The Divorce Court had been set up under Sir Creswell Creswell a decade before, but 'respectable' readers, used to reading about marital breakdown in the newspapers and in the works of Trollope's 'sensational' contemporaries, did not expect to encounter the subject in novels realistically depicting their own way of life. These recognisably modern qualities are reinforced by the feeling one has that for many of Trollope's characters – and for the narrators of his novels too, come to that – the world does not just consist of their own parish, county, or country, but includes half of Europe, North America, and Australia too. The need for today's reader of Trollope to adjust to a world without aeroplanes is less demanding than adapting to Jane Austen's novels, with their narrow geographical and social limits, restricted as they are to a few families in a few parishes.

Trollope built his knowledge of the world into his fiction, and, combined with a down-to-earth moral concern with personal conduct, it made him the darling author of the well-to-do and the proprietors of circulating libraries.[8] Yet the shadow of his childhood and youth hung over his vision of the world, making his understanding of misery acute and his appreciation of prosperity correspondingly lively. The shadow darkening Trollope's practical, middle-class view of the world is that the conditions which determined that someone 'belonged' to the landed and professional class, and was apparently secure in that class, might be illusory, to be negated in a trice by the ills he understood from his own past: bankruptcy, and obsession, anxiety, and outright insanity. In *The Last Chronicle of Barset* he examined the case of a man who remained a gentleman even when sorely afflicted with poverty, and how his afflictions turned his mind until he himself hardly knew whether he was sane or not. In *He Knew He Was Right* he takes the case of a man with a handsome income and drives him mad from jealousy, deploying intertextual references to *Othello* to brilliant effect. The nineteenth-century complex of thoughts and feelings in terms of which these two novels are to be read, and which framed the trauma of Trollope's youth, includes the heroism of the man who saves himself from potential ruin, as Trollope did most successfully. In justice, the *women* who worked to save themselves and their families, as Trollope's mother did when she turned writer in middle age, should have been just as feted, but they were not part of the major economic myths of the period. Most of Trollope's strong women are less active economically than they are in educating or controlling their wayward men. By all these means he dramatised the dangers, heroism, and cowardice of the precarious life of those who are as likely to be downwardly as upwardly mobile.

Debt and financial temptation are major themes. Mark Robarts, the vicar of *Framley Parsonage* (1861), a novel which Elizabeth Gaskell wished he 'would go on writing ... for ever',[9] nearly ruins his family by buying a pricey hunter and rashly signing a promissory note for an unscrupulous member of the county's 'fast' set, who uses his influence as a Member of Parliament to propose Robarts for inappropriate clerical advancement. This plot in the novel reveals several Trollopian techniques. Mark led astray is likened to Faust tempted by Mephistopheles, his fall being indirectly predicted by a well-known Latin quotation from the *Andria* of Terence, which provides the title to chapter one and tells the Victorian reader (at least the classically educated male reader) that although Mark's father was told 'all good things' about his son, that son, like Terence's protagonist, would soon run into difficulties. The narrator presents the social glamour, the hunting, and the lure of an enhanced clerical income as 'a naughty thing',[10] combining in this simple phrase the acknowledgement of sin in the sonorous language of the Book of Common Prayer – 'We have sinned, we have been naughty'[11] – with the language of the nursery, which reduces Mark to a child, who has to be guided and returned to good behaviour by Lady Lufton, the patroness of the parish, a neighbouring clergyman, and the support of his wife. By this means the attentive reader is kept in the world of the comedy of manners, while being given a glimpse of the mortal sin and ruin from which Robarts is saved.

This example of rashness and debt is one of dozens in Trollope, and facing up to or succumbing to debt are recurrent factors in the development of maturity in his male characters. The construction of masculinity involves various rites of passage before the character can happily move among his equals in his profession, his clubs, and the world of business and politics. In his posthumously published *Autobiography* Trollope explains:

> In my school days no small part of my misery came from the envy with which I regarded the popularity of popular boys ... And afterwards, when I was in London as a young man, I had but few friends. Among the clerks in the Post Office I held my own fairly after the first two or three years, but even then I regarded myself as something of a Pariah. My Irish life had been much better. I had had my wife and children, and had been sustained by a feeling of general

> respect. But even in Ireland I had in truth lived but little in society ... It was not till we had settled ourselves at Waltham that I really began to live much with others. The Garrick Club was the first assemblage of men at which I felt myself to be popular.[12]

He was then forty-six. These dramas of exclusion and belonging are the stuff of his fiction, found not only in his story patterns but in his narrator's relationship with his ideal reader, who is asked to recognise the way the world works, and a community of thinking and reading with the narrator, who quotes easily recognised phrases from the King James Bible, the Book of Common Prayer, Shakespeare, Milton, Burns, and other well-known sources, including Latin quotations which every schoolboy of Trollope's class will have learnt by heart. These act as handshakes of recognition between the reader, narrator, and characters that they are all in the same 'assemblage of men'.

There is in his treatment of all these issues a combination of seriousness and gentle levity. To be a hobbledehoy may be painful, yet the observation of social awkwardness may be humorous, whether seen in those around one, or, if one has passed through Trollope's maturing process, in one's former self. This does not exclude the possibility of real pain in memories, especially of bereavement – a more present reality in the nineteenth century than now. Trollope was one of seven children, and one of only three to reach adulthood. Beneath the surface of his comedy of manners lies an awareness of transience and potential insecurity. Looking back from the age of sixty at how his life and self-esteem were transformed when he moved to Ireland in his mid-twenties, he acknowledges

> how great is the agony of adversity, how crushing the despondency of degradation, how susceptible I am myself to the misery coming from contempt, – remembering also how quickly good things may go and evil things come ... There is unhappiness so great that the very fear of it is an alloy to happiness. I had then lost my father and sister and brother, – have since lost another sister and my mother; but I have never as yet lost a wife or a child.
>
> (*Autobiography*, p. 43)

We must remember that this seriousness is as much the basis of his mainly comic social vision as is his sense of humour, and that if in many of his novels things go right in the end, there are others in which things go distinctly wrong. Even in the happiness of a happy ending, there can be a feeling that things might have ended very differently.

It would nevertheless be wrong to identify religious argument in the fiction built on this perception. As a conforming member of the Church of England, Trollope wore his Christianity unobtrusively in social and professional life, as befitted a Victorian gentleman. The Barsetshire Chronicles, animated as they are with clerical characters, deal with the social life of the clergy and Church politics, and not with religious belief. In *The Bertrams* (1859) religious doubt is taken seriously. Daniel Thwaite, the tailor who marries an aristocrat in *Lady Anna* (1874), is a largely sympathetic free-thinker, and although the Moulders, 'low' characters in *Orley Farm*, are godless gluttons in the way they celebrate Christmas – 'swine from the sty of Epicurus' – they are nonetheless good examples of old-fashioned commercial integrity. But then, in Trollope, it is rare to find characters or situations which are not presented sympathetically at some stage. Lady Eustace is an outrageous liar and a cheat, but even her conduct is carefully explained, superficial and self-deceiving as she is. There is overwhelming sympathy for Lady Mason, who has forged a codicil to her late husband's will in order that her son shall inherit his estate. In *The Warden* (1855), Trollope apparently sets out to attack abuses in the management of Church charities, but in no time, his sympathy for all parties, the reformists and the incumbents, has overcome the satire, and the novelist is set on a course of portraying social issues and social mechanisms with an almost universal sympathy, examining individual cases of conscience – in his case, nearly always a secular conscience – as thoroughly as any seventeenth-century Protestant divine. As a result, various views of social and moral situations are present in each novel, and it is the rash critic who decides on the basis of selective quotation that Trollope 'thinks' or 'believes' this or that. It is rare to find characters who are roundly condemned, except in that attack on the modern world of company floatation and speculation, *The Way We Live Now*. Even the villainous Ferdinand Lopez in *The Prime Minister* (1876) is accorded a degree of sympathy, and it is not clear how far to accept the narrator's apparently light-hearted remark that Lopez's misfortune is that he does not know his grandfather. Trollope's narrator is not omniscient and all-wise, and his opinion is often one among many competing in a given novel, remarkably enough making the novels appear more intelligent than either their narrator or their author: the reader must be active in negotiating this rich mix of opinion. Trollope has been accused of outright anti-Semitism in *The Prime Minister*, but it is the reported attitudes of the generality of the characters of the novel, and not the authority of an omniscient narrator, which informs us that they assume that since they distrust Lopez, he must be Jewish. The novelist may be implicated, but in that case so may the reader too. After all, Trollope's angriest novel is entitled 'The Way *We* Live Now'. In most cases Trollope is too intelligent to let it be seen what prejudices he himself may have – though we must exclude publicly avowed feminism from the record of his fictional tolerance.

All this is to say, that although Trollope's fiction has often been regarded as unsophisticated, inattentive to point-of-view and other Jamesian concerns, and lacking in design, only hasty reading can support this view. Henry James deplored Trollope's frequent acknowledgement that the reader was reading a novel, finding these 'slaps at credulity' 'suicidal', though we can now recognise this feature as part of the tradition of fictional narrative throughout the ages, and in no way inferior to the pose of invisibility much vaunted by subsequent generations of novelists. After all, Trollope much preferred Fielding to Richardson, and may be acknowledging a debt to Sterne's self-aware approach to narrative when he tells us that the odious Mr Slope, the Bishop's Evangelical chaplain in *Barchester Towers*, is a descendant of the 'man midwife', Dr Slop, in *Tristram Shandy*. As for design or structure, we need to look at Trollope's very extensive reading of Elizabethan and Jacobean drama to understand how he utilised multiple plots in a dozen different ways to produce effects of contrast, comparison, and complication, as Peter K. Garrett has brilliantly explained.[13] These interrelated plots serve to produce the large social pictures which caused Tolstoy such delight. Each plot in one of these complex fictions may seem to suggest different views on the negotiation between moral principles and individual moral choices, so that the multiplot structure involves the reader in debating the issues, in a way which many find far less overt than the firm guidance of George Eliot's narrator in *Middlemarch*. In *Can You Forgive Her?* (1865) there are three plots which work in parallel. *The Last Chronicle* contains parallel plots which invite comparison of cases in this way, as well as a complex of other interlocking stories. In *Mr Scarborough's Family* (1883) there is a contrivance as complex as any Renaissance example to set up the *donnée* of the action, and an array of instances for readerly negotiation. Sometimes second plots are simply present to take the story beyond one single action and to provide events and characters to appeal to readers of all ages and inclinations, as when there is a love plot in *The Fixed Period* (1882), a futuristic story of compulsory euthanasia in an ex-colony, with 'regime change' (as we might now say) effected by a warship with a gun so powerful that it has never had to be used, and sent by the Ministry of Benevolence in Whitehall. In this novel, incidentally, the obsessed President, Mr Neverbend, is also an advocate of cremation, a cause which Trollope himself espoused.

Having excelled at social comedy in the early 1860s, he decided to contribute a new novel to the *Fortnightly Review*, a radical journal of which he was one of the founders, *The Belton Estate* (1866), written according to George Henry Lewes's theory of realism in *The Principles of Success in Literature*, also serialised in the *Fortnightly* in 1865. If we are tempted to characterise the Trollope of 1861 by the gentle world of *Framley Parsonage*, we are ignoring *Brown, Jones and Robinson* and 'Aaron Trow', published in the same year, the former about the promotion and advertising of a haberdashery business and the latter a brutal tale of a convict escaped from a British penal colony in Bermuda. Later Trollope added short novels set in other countries to his repertoire, including the anonymously published *Nina Balatka* (1867), set in Prague, and with a Jewish heroine, and *Linda Tressel* (1868), set in Vienna. He went on to write *The Golden Lion of Granpere* (1872), set in Lorraine, and his tale of the struggles of a sheep-farmer in Australia, *Harry Heathcote of Gangoil* (1874), researched (as we should say today) on a visit to his son, Fred, in New South Wales in 1871.

Trollope was deeply concerned throughout his life with the state of Ireland, and his first two novels, *The Macdermots of Ballycloran* (1847) and *The Kellys and the O'Kellys* (1848), were set there, the former centring on the murder of an excise officer and the latter framed by the state trials in Dublin in 1844. After a number of novels set in England, he returned to his beloved Ireland for *Castle Richmond* (1860), powerfully set in the Famine of 1845–7. The fourth Irish novel, *An Eye for an Eye* (1879), is a short tale of retribution for innocence betrayed, and the fifth, unfinished on Trollope's death, *The Landleaguers* (1883), concerns Protestant landowners beset by Irish nationalist violence and contains Trollope's only attempt at an important child character.

The other fiction of his early career includes *The Three Clerks* (1857), exploiting his knowledge of the Civil Service, and *The Bertrams* (1859), a novel using its author's travels in the Middle East and dealing more directly than any other of his books with religious doubt. He later confessed to knowing too little of Darwin to understand evolution, and it may be that after 1859 the terms in which religious doubt was framed were too little familiar to him, although he supported Colenso's attack on literal interpretation of the Bible. Alongside these novels, the Barchester Chronicles (not then envisaged as a series) began to appear. *The Warden* introduced the cathedral city of Barchester in 1855, and was followed by the brilliant *Barchester Towers* (1856), which understandably caused John Henry Newman to wake at night, laughing at memories of its scenes. The fictional settings expand over the county of Barsetshire in *Doctor Thorne* (1858), *Framley Parsonage*, and *The Last Chronicle of Barset* (1867), and beyond in *The Small House at Allington* (1864), which, because of its heroine, Lily Dale, has, with, *Doctor Thorne*, always been a favourite with a multitude of readers.

In *The Last Chronicle* an upright, poor, and scholarly clergyman is accused of stealing a cheque and becomes not only unsure of the facts of the case, but of his own sanity. Yet the most charged moment in the novel is arguably not the revelation of his innocence, but a gesture of inclusion in the acknowledgement by Archdeacon Grantly, his wealthy clerical superior, that '[w]e stand on the only perfect level on which such men can meet each other. We are both gentleman.' What makes the moment so very Trollopian is the narrator's comment that Grantly has been calculating: 'the archdeacon had hit his bird'.[14] The multiplot structure of the novel is complicated by the need to round off the five previous novels as well. Although *The Last Chronicle* is exactly what it says, and although the many story-lines are neatly tied up at the end, the impression of life continuing in an alternative world is maintained because that fictional life has been sustained through thousands of pages, published over a dozen years, making Trollope the greatest writer of the *roman fleuve* in English.

Trollope's publishing practice in the years of his greatest prosperity displays his utter professionalism. Some novels appeared in parts, after the pattern of many of Dickens's, but many more, starting with *Framley Parsonage*, Trollope's seventh novel and the fourth of the Barsetshire series, followed the then growing practice of serialisation in magazines, commencing in January 1860 with the first issue of one of the publishing successes of the age, Smith, Elder's *Cornhill Magazine*. Serialisation paid well, built up an author's popularity, and allowed a publisher two 'goes' at the market. *The Struggles of Brown, Jones and Robinson* followed in 1861–2, *The Small House at Allington* in 1862–4, and *The Claverings* in 1866–7, while *The Last Chronicle of Barset* was being issued in weekly parts by the same publisher in the same two years. So intensive was Trollope's output that in the period Chapman & Hall published his *Castle Richmond* (1860), *Orley Farm* (in parts, 1861–2), a travel book, *North America* (1862), *Rachel Ray* (1863), *Can You Forgive Her?* (in parts, 1864–5), *Miss Mackenzie* (1865), and *The Belton Estate* (in the *Fortnightly Review*, 1866). *Framley Parsonage*, *Orley Farm*, and *The Small House* carried distinguished wood-engraved illustrations by John Everett Millais, unequalled by any of Trollope's other illustrators. Trollope was also a regular writer for the *Pall Mall Gazette* (1865–8), and in 1867 he assumed the editorship of *St Paul's Magazine*, which was created as a vehicle for him, in an only partially successful attempt to emulate the successful periodicals Dickens founded and edited.

Can You Forgive Her? (1864) initiates the second six-novel sequence, developing characters who were marginal in the Barchester books from *Framley Parsonage* onwards, in particular Plantagenet Palliser, the heir of the immensely wealthy Whig magnate, the Duke of Omnium, whose enormous, ostentatious and uncomfortable country seat, Gatherum Castle, in Barsetshire, is almost a symbol of what the squirearchy of the county find wrong with the grandest of the aristocracy. A measure of the realistic spell Trollope casts is the fact that the reader soon forgets the comic names, and 'Omnium' and 'Gatherum' (from the cod-Latin phrase, 'omnium gatherum', or a miscellaneous gathering or hodgepodge) become like any other grand names. The arranged marriage of Palliser to the hugely rich heiress Lady Glencora M'Cluskie has an unpromising start, with Glencora almost eloping with a beautiful fortune-seeking ne'er-do-well, Burgo Fitzgerald. Lady Glen (as she is familiarly known) is passionate and impulsive, and Palliser is a 'cold fish'. In a complicated way which only Trollope or Austen could describe, the marriage works through five long novels, during which Plantagenet labours as Chancellor of the Exchequer, succeeds to the dukedom, and serves as a compromise Prime Minister. The sixth, *The Duke's Children* (1880), opens with one of Trollope's quiet and effective strokes, the sudden death of the Duchess:

> It was not only that his [the Duke's] heart was torn to pieces, but that he did not know how to look out into the world. It was as though a man should be suddenly called upon to live without hands or even arms. He was helpless, and knew himself to be helpless. Hitherto he had never specially acknowledged to himself that his wife was necessary to him as a component part of his life. Though he had loved her dearly, and had in all things consulted her welfare and happiness, he had at times been inclined to think that in the exuberance of her spirits she had been a trouble rather than a support to him. But now it was as though all outside appliances were taken away from him.[15]

It is difficult to think of another Victorian writer who could make such a passage ring true in relation to five preceding novels, and could find in this abandoned state and unapproachable man the germ of a new story in which to express profound changes which we now recognise as bringing in the twentieth-century world, including dynastic marriages between the British aristocracy and the American plutocracy.

The second and fourth of these novels, *Phineas Finn* (1869) and *Phineas Redux* (1874), follow the career of an Irish politician at Westminster and gave Trollope, as he says in *An Autobiography*, a 'method of declaring myself' politically, after his failure to enter the Commons as Liberal MP for Beverley in the general election of 1868. It is the Duke of Omnium, in *The Prime Minister* (1876), who comes closest to Trollope's description of himself as 'an advanced but still a conservative Liberal' (*Autobiography*, pp. 201 and 186), believing that inequalities in rank and wealth should be conscientiously but gradually reduced. (He reworks his painful electoral experiences in *Ralph the Heir* (1871).) He writes, 'By no amount of description or asseveration could I succeed in making any reader understand how much these characters with their belongings have been to me in my latter life, or how frequently I have used them for the expression of my political and social convictions' (*Autobiography*, p. 118). There were many other novels in the last dozen years, including *The American Senator* (1877) and *Is He Popenjoy?* (1878), each with its own unique features and critical champions.

His posthumously published *Autobiography* is a complex record of his early life and his writing career. It can best be understood as continuing his persistent theme of the choice of a career, in this case authorship, and of the honest or dishonest pursuit of it. Notoriously he includes a list of his literary earnings, amounting to some £70,000, which he regards 'as comfortable, but not splendid', and ends with the disavowal, 'It will not, I trust, be supposed by any reader that I have intended in this so-called autobiography to give a record of my inner life' (*Autobiography*, p. 232). Yet it is a work which if read carefully unlocks a good number of the questions of Trollope's life and opinions, with remarkably little direct writing of the self, as it is sometimes called today. In this it is just the extreme case of a work which must be quoted with care, from which it is rash to draw simple conclusions, but which leaves the reader with a haunting sensation that although much has been said, quite as much is left in the realm of suggestion, interpretation, and reinterpretation.

NOTE ON EDITIONS

The Penguin Classics and Oxford World's Classics editions of Trollope's novels are by and large the most useful and reliable and generally carry helpful explanatory notes. The Trollope Society/Pickering and Chatto uniform edition (1988–99) has texts checked against the part issue and serial versions of the novels and carries original illustrations but no notes. *An Autobiography*, which was published posthumously in 1883 with a seriously corrupted text, should be read in the Penguin or World's Classics editions.

NOTES

1 [Richard Holt Hutton], *Spectator*, 55 (9 December 1882), 1573–4.
2 *Ayala's Angel*, ed. Julian Thompson-Furnivall (Oxford: Oxford University Press, 1986), p. 624.
3 *Interviews and Recollections*, ed. R. C. Terry (Macmillan, 1987), pp. 61–2.
4 Anonymous review of *The Golden Lion of Granpere*, *Spectator*, 45 (18 May 1872), 630–1.
5 [Richard Holt Hutton], 'From Miss Austen to Mr. Trollope', *Spectator*, 55 (16 December 1882), 1609–11.
6 *The Last Chronicle of Barset*, ed. Stephen Gill (Oxford: Oxford University Press, 1980), p. 755.
7 [H. L. Mansel], 'Sensation Novels', *Quarterly Review*, 113 (April 1862), 488.
8 [E. S. Dallas], 'Anthony Trollope', *The Times* (23 May 1859), 12.
9 *The Letters of Mrs Gaskell*, ed. J. A. V. Chapple and A. Pollard (Manchester: Manchester University Press, 1966), p. 602.

10 *Framley Parsonage*, ed. P. D. Edwards (Oxford: Oxford University Press, 1980), p. 67.
11 'A Sermon on the Misery of All Mankind and of his Condemnation to Death by his own Sin', The Book of Common Prayer (1662).
12 *An Autobiography*, ed. David Skilton (Harmondsworth: Penguin, 1996), pp. 104–5. Further references are given in the text.
13 *The Victorian Multiplot Novel: Studies in Dialogical Form* (New Haven: Yale University Press, 1980).
14 *Last Chronicle*, p. 885.
15 *The Duke's Children*, ed. Hermione Lee (Oxford: Oxford University Press, 1983), pp. 2–3.

FURTHER READING

apRoberts, Ruth, *The Moral Art of Anthony Trollope*, London, Chatto & Windus, 1971

Garrett, Peter K., *The Victorian Multiplot Novel: Studies in Dialogical Form*, New Haven, Yale University Press, 1980

Hall, N. J., *Trollope: A Biography*, Oxford, Clarendon Press, 1991

Hall, N. J. (ed.), *The Letters of Anthony Trollope*, 2 vols., Stanford, Stanford University Press, 1983

Kincaid, James R., *The Novels of Anthony Trollope*, Oxford, Clarendon Press, 1977

Lansbury, Coral, *The Reasonable Man: Trollope's Legal Fiction*, Princeton, Princeton University Press, 1981

Marwick, Margaret, *New Men in Trollope's Novels: Rewriting the Victorian Male*, Aldershot, Ashgate, 2007

McMaster, Juliet, *Trollope's Palliser Novels: Theme and Pattern*, London, Macmillan, 1978

Morse, Deborah Denenholz, *Women in Trollope's Palliser Novels*, Ann Arbor, MI, UMI Research, 1987

Nardin, Jane, *He Knew She Was Right: The Independent Woman in the Novels of Anthony Trollope*, Carbondale, Southern Illinois University Press, 1989

Trollope and Victorian Moral Philosophy, Athens, OH, Ohio University Press, 1996

Sadleir, Michael, *Trollope: A Bibliography*, London, Constable, 1928

Skilton, David, *Anthony Trollope and His Contemporaries*, Harlow, Longman, 1972

Terry, Reginald C. (ed.), *Trollope: Interviews and Recollections*, Basingstoke, Macmillan, 1986

Turner, Mark, *Trollope and the Magazines: Gendered Issues in Mid-Victorian Britain*, Basingstoke, Macmillan, 2000

14

JILL L. MATUS

George Eliot

> My darling Marian!
>
> Forgive me for being so very affectionate but I am so intensely delighted at your success ... I can't tell you how I triumphed in the triumph you have made ... I saw the 1st review and read one long extract which instantly made me internally exclaim that is written by Marian Evans, there is her great big head and heart and her wise wide views ...Very few things have given me so much pleasure.
>
> 1st. That a woman should write a wise and *humourous* book which should take a place by Thackeray.
>
> 2nd. That you *that you* whom they spit at should do it![1]

So wrote Barbara Bodichon to her close friend Marian Evans after the pseudonymous publication of *Adam Bede* in 1859. Amid rumours of the novel's authorship, Marian Evans persisted in trying to keep her identity a secret. Nevertheless, Bodichon instantly recognised her as the author, divining even in an excerpt her friend's distinctive characteristics as a writer and thinker. I begin with this letter, and shall return to it on several occasions in the first part of this essay, as it helps us to understand the context in which George Eliot emerged as a writer and – especially in the phrase 'head and heart and ... wise wide views' – handily identifies future keynotes in George Eliot criticism and biography.

George Eliot (1819–80) was the pseudonym of Mary Anne Evans (also known at different stages of her life as Mary Ann, Marian, Pollian, M. E. Lewes, and, finally, Mrs J. W. Cross). Between 1859 and 1876 she published the several novels on which her reputation rests: *Adam Bede*, *The Mill on the Floss*, *Silas Marner*, *Romola*, *Felix Holt*, *Middlemarch*, and *Daniel Deronda*. She was in addition the author of shorter fiction (*Scenes of Clerical Life*, *Brother Jacob*, *The Lifted Veil*) and poems (*The Spanish Gypsy*, *The Legend of Jubal*), as well as essays and reviews. Throughout her career as a journalist and novelist, she supported herself and, for many years, the needy extended family of her common-law husband. In 1862, she negotiated what was then the highest sum ever paid to an English novelist – £10,000 – for her historical novel *Romola*, ironically the least successful of her works. Once shunned and excluded from polite Victorian society because of her irregular conjugal arrangement, she emerged as a cultural icon and sought-after celebrity in her later years. Queen Victoria (born on the same day as George Eliot) read her novels, commissioned paintings of their famous scenes, and expressed a desire to meet her. Excerpts were culled from her work and published in 1872 as *Wise, Witty and Tender Sayings in Prose and Verse Selected from the Works of George Eliot*. She became a Victorian sage.

As one of the feminist founders of *The English Women's Journal*, Barbara Bodichon was understandably delighted that a *woman* should write as good a novel as Thackeray. Her reference to him enables us to gauge the context of George Eliot's debut as a novelist. In 1859 Charles Dickens had already had a successful career of more than twenty years, the Brontë sisters were all dead, Elizabeth Gaskell had established a name for herself as a novelist and (most recently) biographer (of Charlotte Brontë), and William Makepeace Thackeray, who prided himself on being 'at the top of the tree' with Dickens, had produced his major work and would, within four years, be dead at the age of fifty-three. It was thus just the right time for the emergence of a new and powerful voice in English fiction.[2] Bodichon's description of her friend as 'you whom they spit at' refers to the social censure surrounding Marian Evans's marital status. She was unable to marry George Henry Lewes, the man with whom she lived, because he was already married, and, having condoned the adultery of his wife, was subsequently prevented from using it as grounds for divorce. Such was Victorian propriety that the social implications of this unsanctioned relationship were far-reaching. Marian Evans's self-consciously respectable family broke off all relations with her at the instigation of her stern and unyielding brother; even in metropolitan London she was excluded from polite society (though Lewes continued to receive dinner invitations) and looked upon as a home-wrecker or fallen woman. Although she wished to be known as Mrs Lewes and signed herself thus, dedicating her manuscripts to her 'beloved husband', few could overlook the fact that she was not legally married. 'I wish you *were* Mrs Lewes', wrote Gaskell regretfully.[3]

The pen name 'George Eliot' first appeared in January 1858, on the title-page of the book form of *Scenes of Clerical Life*, a collection of stories serialised anonymously in *Blackwood's Magazine* from December 1857. The mask of a pseudonym was presumably designed as a protection from gossip, since its author was already a woman who had attracted social opprobrium. Marian Evans wished her work to be taken seriously and 'judged quite apart from its authorship'.[4] But the adoption of a pseudonym speaks also to the nature and status of novel writing at the time and to George Eliot's own ambivalence about being a female author. It is often incorrectly supposed that a woman had to write under a *nom de plume* in order to find publication in the strongly patriarchal world of the nineteenth century. There were a great many women writing and publishing fiction at this time. Nevertheless, Bodichon's pride in the fact that 'a woman should write such a wise and humourous book' invokes a context in which much women's writing was relegated to the category of the frivolous and entertaining. In an essay entitled 'Silly Novels by Lady Novelists' (1856), George Eliot herself wrote scathingly of what she called the 'mind-and-millinery school'. She particularly singled out the 'lady novelist' who parades her learning, keeping a 'sort of mental pocket-mirror, and is continually looking in it at her own intellectuality'. For this reason, she concluded, 'the most mischievous form of feminine silliness is the literary form because it tends to confirm the popular prejudice against the more solid education of women'.[5]

Unlike the women writers she satirised, George Eliot was undisputedly the most profoundly intellectual of Victorian novelists, a view signalled by Bodichon's metonymic reference to her 'great big head'. As a largely self-educated generalist, Eliot demonstrated an unflagging capacity for absorbing and assessing complex ideas across the spectrum of nineteenth-century knowledge in an age of newly forming disciplines and burgeoning scientific enterprise. She read and spoke many languages, translated difficult historical and philosophical texts from German and Latin into English, conversed with the foremost scientists of the day in Europe, and lived an intellectual life quite astonishingly unprepared for by her conventional education and upbringing in Warwickshire. She thought carefully through questions of religious faith in an age of secularity and evolutionary theory, and although highly critical of prevailing social structures and attitudes, took a fairly conservative position on female suffrage and on radical political change and social revolution. Her stature in the field of English novelists rests in no small measure on the way her novels express the scope and complexity of her views about society, religion, gender, history, ethics, and morality. Though she did not embark on writing fiction until she was in her mid-thirties, it was the novel and not the philosophical treatise or essay that she chose as the medium for communicating her mature vision of life.

Charting George Eliot's intellectual growth, biographers have focused on her contact as a young woman with local liberal thinkers in Coventry, which drew her into an enlarged intellectual circle and exposed her to many exciting new developments: Charles Hennell's involvement in the 'Higher Criticism', which undertook to critique the Bible as a sacred text; George

Combe's ideas about phrenology and mesmerism; Sir Charles Lyell's work in geology and its implications for evolutionary thought; Thomas Carlyle's views on leadership.[6] Having left her native county for London when she was thirty-one, she worked for John Chapman, editor of the fading but once respected journal, the *Westminster Review*, nominally as his assistant but in reality the editor herself. It is difficult now to imagine how unusual, if not entirely unprecedented, must have been this move on the part of a young, unmarried woman from a respectable family to the big city and the hub of British intellectual life. There she continued to enlarge her acquaintance of influential writers and thinkers, meeting John Stuart Mill, Herbert Spencer, and, through him, the clever, versatile George Henry Lewes. In 1854 she and Lewes embarked on a trip to Germany as the first step in a life together that would endure for over twenty-five years until his death.

Having formed several unsatisfactory emotional attachments (Chapman and Spencer among them) before meeting Lewes, George Eliot has been characterised by biographers as emotionally dependent and even sexually susceptible, a designation that relies frequently on the contrast between her independent (masculine) head and her needy (feminine) heart. Not without a whiff of caricature, Virginia Woolf offers her up as an object for speculation, highlighting the incongruity of her predecessor's ambitious mind yet crippling emotional dependency:

> Thus we behold her, a memorable figure, inordinately praised and shrinking from her fame, despondent, reserved, shuddering back into the arms of love as if there alone were satisfaction and, it might be, justification, at the same time reaching out with a 'fastidious yet hungry ambition' for all that life could offer the free and inquiring mind and confronting her feminine aspirations with the real world of men.[7]

In accordance with Woolf's assessment, it is often remarked upon that this most wide-ranging and sagacious of novelists should be also, in her private circle, demandingly dependent and neurotically sensitive to criticism. We could, however, offer a counter-narrative foregrounding her emotional courage, since she was evidently prepared to chart her own life in defiance of social rules and norms, first in her relationship with the married Lewes, and then in her differently scandalous marriage after his death (and only months before her own) to John Cross, a family friend twenty years her junior.

In her letter, Bodichon refers to her friend's 'wise wide views'. Scholars have attributed the latter to George Eliot's increasingly broad range of reading and the formation of her mature attitudes to religion, epistemology, ethics, and morality, but they are also born of her own formative emotional experiences. In particular, Rosemarie Bodenheimer has pointed to the powerful but not always resolved psychological experiences that shape recurrent patterns in George Eliot's fiction.[8] An apt example lies in her changing views about religion. We know that her early education at neighbourhood schools was inflected by the religious mentorship of her teachers, first the Evangelical Maria Lewis and then the Franklin sisters, daughters of a minister. Mary Anne Evans's letters and compositions as an adolescent seem pious, ponderous, and judgemental. Along with her early religious convictions, she shed her own censoriousness, replacing it with a tolerance and liberal-mindedness that later enabled her to represent the diversity of religious views and communities in the world of her novels with sympathetic understanding, even if it was laced with gentle irony and satire. Although an agnostic, she drew in all her work on her Evangelical heritage. Her own 'Holy War', in which she asserted her revised convictions and opposed her father by refusing to attend church with him, resulted in a highly fraught family situation. The father, unbudging, threatened to disband their household at Rosehill on the outskirts of Coventry; the daughter continued her resistance but ultimately proposed the compromise of public conformity and private dissension.

The phases of their confrontation reveal a pattern often detected in the novels: strongly held convictions requiring renegotiation and, if necessary, modification in deference to moral commitments and emotional relationships. In the attempt to reconcile her independent religious views with her need for her father's love, she discovered the key notes of rebellion, self-sacrificial responsibility, and renunciation that would sound in the fates of fictional heroines like Maggie Tulliver in *The Mill on the Floss* and Dorothea Brooke in *Middlemarch*. Ties bind, in George Eliot's novels, and the affective bonds of the past are powerful influences. Moral crises are often about discovering the intransigence of others and taking the step to shoulder and accommodate those who cannot themselves change. Yet at the same time as the novels applaud an ethic of self-sacrifice and self-negation, they also register in elegiac terms the loss of personal welfare that duty and renunciation may entail. These views seem to arise as much from lived emotional experience as from intellectual and philosophical convictions about the collective need for compassion and sympathy in a world of cause and effect, where reliance on a providential deity is misguided and community becomes all the more important.

Individual experience and intellectual conviction, never truly separable, coalesce to make the power of affective bonds, and especially the moral power of sympathy, the cornerstone of her novelistic project and its aesthetics. Following Keats's pronouncement that 'axioms of philosophy are not axioms until they have been proved upon our pulses',[9] she writes:

> If Art does not enlarge men's sympathies, it does nothing morally. I have had heart-cutting experience that opinions are a poor cement between human souls; and the only effect I ardently long to produce by my writings is, that those who read them should be better able to *imagine* and to *feel* the pains and the joys of those who differ from themselves in everything but the broad fact of being struggling erring, human creatures.[10]

Like many of her contemporaries, however, she distrusted the raw feelings of social groups en masse and extolled the importance of education and informed opinion. One of the distinguishing enterprises of her fiction, which she called 'experiments in life', is the attempt to integrate or bring into alignment what we know with what we feel. As the narrator of *Middlemarch* remarks of Dorothea's painful passage to understand Casaubon's difference from the ideal husband she had anticipated:

> [I]t had been easier to her to imagine how she might devote herself to Mr Casaubon, and become wise and strong in his strength and wisdom than to conceive with that distinctness which is no longer reflection but feeling – an idea wrought back to the directness of sense, like the solidity of objects – that he had an equivalent centre of self, whence the lights and shadows must always fall with a certain difference.[11]

Distinguished from reflection or thought in this instance, feeling contributes to concrete as opposed to vague knowledge, as if it were (as indeed it is) informed by the direct evidence of the senses. It may seem odd to identify feeling, which is often opposed to fact, with distinctness, directness, and solidity. But what Eliot seems to argue is that feelings (emotions, sense impressions, perceptions) inform ideas through their connection to the world outside the self. Reflection, on the other hand, may prohibit one from being *in touch* with the real rather than imagined other. The passage conveys the idea both of Dorothea's growth as an acknowledgement of the alterity of others and of Mr Casaubon's obdurate otherness, a form of impediment that must nevertheless be reckoned with and furthermore deserves compassion.

From George Eliot's attempt to demonstrate the fusion of thought and feeling flow many of her key attributes as a novelist, not least the investment in emotion and especially sympathy as a way of shaping readerly attitudes. Her belief in the transformative power of affect arises from a particular conception of the psyche and its architecture – how the territory of inwardness is organised and shaped. D. H. Lawrence assessed the ground that George Eliot broke, often referred to as psychological realism, in the following way: 'You see, it was really George Eliot who started it all ... And how wild they all were with her for doing it. It was she who started putting all the action inside. Before, you know, with Fielding and the others, it had been outside.'[12] Lawrence's claim seems open to dispute on several levels. For one thing, a distinctive characteristic of the Victorian novel is its third-person narrator, artfully constructed with the privilege of seeming to know all and able to move in and out of the minds of its characters. And compared with novelists who precede her, George Eliot is clearly not alone in focusing on inner life and the problems of consciousness. There are, however, ways in which her conception of inside action is distinctive and may be said to have shifted the ground of the English novel. Although I have chosen to focus on the 'inside action' in this essay, I see this aspect of George Eliot's work as complementary to other well-known formulations of her distinctiveness in the tradition of the English novel: the moral seriousness of her fiction, which contributed to the elevation of the novel from a form of popular entertainment to a form of high culture; her realist manifesto, pitting truthful representations of ordinary life against sentimentalising or falsifying accounts; the poetic recreation of the English communal past, especially in the early novels; her critique of English nationalism and the cosmopolitanism of her later novels.

Drawing the reader's attention to the many activities that can take place inwardly in the space of a moment, the narrator of *Daniel Deronda* explains:

> For Macbeth's rhetoric about the impossibility of being many opposite things in the same moment, referred to the clumsy necessities of action and not to the subtler possibilities of feeling. We cannot speak a loyal word and be meanly silent, we cannot kill and not kill in the same moment; but a moment is room wide enough for the loyal and mean desire, for the outlash of a murderous thought and the sharp backward stroke of repentance.[13]

The distinction between the 'clumsy necessities of action' and 'the subtler possibilities of feeling' suggests that while feelings are not actions capable of external measurement, they are events. As the anguished Princess Halm-Eberstein puts it later in the same novel: 'events come on us like evil enchantments: and thoughts, feelings, apparitions in the darkness are events – are they not?' (*DD*, 540–1). Even if outwardly undetectable, and even if they occur without conscious awareness, interior events and their disturbing causal and determining power can constitute the stuff of narration. In her attention to the problems of consciousness – the ways in which people feel, dream, fantasise, and make decisions without realising the unconscious processes that inform them – George Eliot is a novelist of the psyche, but to say simply that is to neglect the important shift in the way she represents interior life.[14] The psyche, after all, is a concept with a history. George Eliot is arguably one who brings a particular conception of mind into the province of the novel and develops a language for describing it. If her emphasis on the inside action makes her a proto-modernist, it also links her to a very Victorian interest in the developing discipline of physiological psychology, and especially its concern with conscious and unconscious mental processes.

At the mid-nineteenth century, the concept of 'mind' was a subject of considerable debate and investigation, and psychology as a branch of study was in its infancy. In the early nineteenth century, psychology was the study of the soul; that is, everything spiritual as opposed to corporeal. Even by the 1850s, it was less a field, or a subject in its own right, than a flexible range of topics and issues, and it was porous to an extent that surprises readers in today's world of highly specialised disciplinary and professional distinction. In particular, the 'new psychology' sought to explore the embodiedness of mind and the mutual dependency of mind and brain. At the time George Eliot began writing fiction, there were several important contributions to this emerging field: Alexander Bain's *The Emotions and the Will* (1859), a companion volume to his earlier *The Senses and the Intellect* (1855); Herbert Spencer's monumental *Principles of Psychology* (1855); and George Henry Lewes's *The Physiology of Common Life* (1859).

Briefly put, Lewes brought the unconscious, the bodily, and the social into the conception of mind. He emphasised the interpenetration of neural and psychical processes and insisted that the mind is shaped and modified by social experience. In *The Physiology of Common Life* and *Problems of Life and Mind* (1874–9) Lewes set out and elaborated the view that 'Mind' is not equivalent to brain and does not designate intellectual operations only. It includes 'all Sensation, all Volition, and all Thought: it means the whole psychical Life; and this psychical Life has no one special centre, any more than the physical Life has one special centre'.[15] In this context it makes sense therefore to say that 'Consciousness forms but a small item in the total of psychical process.'[16] In large measure, George Eliot's fiction shares Lewes's views about the way sensation and feeling inform mental operations. What this means is that she understands 'mind' as a process inextricable from body and represents its movements (the inside action) in physical, often spatial terms. She shares too his interest in unconsciousness as an integral part of the psychical process. Given the conception of George Eliot as philosophical and analytical, an ordering, mastering intellect, it may seem odd to style her as the novelist of unconscious processes. But her unconscious is not a repository of anarchic impulses. It is not necessarily associated with chaos, irrationality, taboo, sexual desire, or madness, and, although it anticipates later Freudian models of the unconscious, it is markedly different from them.

Unconsciousness in George Eliot is figured as subtle web-work, the minute play of unattended motive and feeling. While such activity may go on unawares, it shapes and informs moments of decision and conscious thought. As the narrator quips in *Adam Bede*, 'Our mental business is carried on in much the same way as the business of the State: a great deal of hard work is done by agents who are *not acknowledged*. In a piece of machinery, too, I believe, there is often a small *unnoticeable* wheel which has a great deal to do with the motion of the large obvious ones ... The human soul is a complex thing' (emphasis added).[17] In *Middlemarch*, one of Lydgate's ambitions as a scientist is to 'pierce the obscurity of those *minute processes* which prepare human misery and joy, those *invisible thoroughfares* which are the first lurking-places of anguish, mania, and crime, that delicate poise and transition that determine the growth of happy or unhappy consciousness' (*M*, 154, emphasis added). 'Hidden' and 'invisible' also imply the work of the unconscious in consciousness, as in the narrator's description of Gwendolen in *Daniel Deronda*, where her fantasies are like 'dark rays doing their work *invisibly* in the broad light' of 'more acknowledged consciousness' (*DD*, 518, emphasis added). At times, the mandate of conveying the inner action confronts the novelist with a daunting infinitude of possibility: if the narrator of human actions were to do his work like the astronomer, he would 'have to thread the *hidden pathways of feeling and thought* which lead up to every moment of action, and to those moments of intense suffering which take the quality of action' (*DD*, 139, emphasis added).

The language of the web, which applies to the way external actions implicate everyone in the social network, applies also to internal events, which cause modifications and shifts in consciousness detectable only to the strongest lens. This is fiction that can reveal the 'naked skinless complication' of others' thoughts and emotions.[18] It is precisely because processes of unconscious thought are 'secret' and ordinarily difficult to detect that they require a knowing observer to explain them. So, for example, the narrator of *Adam Bede* explains that 'the secret of our emotions never lies in the bare object but in its subtle relations to our own past: no wonder the secret escapes the unsympathising observer, who might as well put on his spectacles to discern odours'.[19]

George Eliot remarked in a review of Charles Kingsley that the artist's task is to give us 'his higher sensibility as a medium, a delicate acoustic or optical instrument, bringing home to our coarser senses what would otherwise be unperceived by us'.[20] Drawing on new technologies of the nineteenth century, and particularly the imagery of the microscope and the manipulation of perspective that its powerful lenses allow, George Eliot's narrators open up for scrutiny what may otherwise be undetected. Auditory comparisons 'tune' the reader in to what is often unheard: '[t]here is much pain that is quite noiseless; and vibrations that make human agonies are often a mere whisper in the roar of hurrying existence'.[21] The fantastic premise of *The Lifted Veil* (1859), a Gothic tale and George Eliot's only first-person, fictive narration, is an acute sensitivity on the part of the narrator that amplifies the thoughts and feelings of others. The participation of Latimer's 'abnormal' consciousness in the minds of others is the din of an 'importunate, ill-played musical instrument' or the 'loud activity of an imprisoned insect'; it is 'a ringing in the ears not to be got rid of' or a 'preternaturally heightened sense of hearing' that makes 'audible to one a roar of sound where others find perfect stillness'.[22] Latimer can indeed hear the roar that lies on the other side of silence, as George Eliot would later famously formulate this audible insight in *Middlemarch*. And in her last work, a collection of essays entitled *Impressions of Theophrastus Such* (1879), she writes about the 'microphone which detects the cadence of the fly's foot on the ceiling, and may be expected presently to discriminate the noises of our various follies as they soliloquise or converse in our brains'.[23]

Such invocations of enhanced senses are more than apt analogies. They reveal an interior landscape that is physical and palpable could we but grasp it. Although the mind is never simply reducible to the physical constituents of the brain – what Lewes calls mere 'pulpy mass' – its workings are often expressed in terms of physical forces and laws of matter.[24] The transformations of thought, George Eliot demonstrates, have a chemistry of their own: 'No chemical process shows a more wonderful activity than the transforming influence of the thoughts we imagine to be going on in another' (*DD*, 362). Like the force of electricity, for example, whose physical nature could not be doubted by Victorian scientists though it remained perplexingly invisible to them, mental process is also physical. In line with growing scientific acceptance of the idea that nerve-force is closely akin to electricity, Eliot often likens powerful feelings and emotions to electric shocks, such as that experienced by Caterina in 'Mr Gilfil's Love Story': 'The vibration rushed through Caterina like an electric shock: it seemed as if at that instant a new soul were entering into her, with a deeper, more significant life.'[25] In *Middlemarch*, Dorothea on her honeymoon journey in Rome experiences the welter of sights and sounds as a jarring electric shock. And in the following example, Dorothea's electrifying effect on Will Ladislaw is closely observed and analysed by the narrator:

> When Mrs. Casaubon was announced he started up as from an electric shock, and felt a tingling at his finger-ends. Any one observing him would have seen a change in his complexion, in the adjustment of his facial muscles, in the vividness of his glance, which might have made them imagine that every molecule

> in his body had passed the message of a magic touch. And so it had. For effective magic is transcendent nature; and who shall *measure the subtlety of those touches which convey the quality of soul as well as body*, and make a man's passion for one woman differ from his passion for another as joy in the morning light over valley and river and white mountain-top differs from joy among Chinese lanterns and glass panels? Will, too, was made of very impressible stuff.
> (*M*, 363–4, emphasis added)[26]

Mid-century evolutionary and physiological psychology is often characterised in histories of emotion as *the* moment when emotions, which replaced terms like 'passions', 'sentiments', and 'affections', were reconceived as a physical rather than mental process. An 1855 review of Elizabeth Gaskell's work deplored novelists' concentration on the physical details of emotional change:

> [M]any novelists indulge [in] the description of minute changes in the *physical* expression in periods of deep feeling. This is, we are convinced, unartistic as well as false taste ... It would require a scientific man, intending to prepare 'plates' of the different emotions, to note these things. And the mind instinctively shrinks from the record of them. The grief and the love and the fear should absorb the attention, and not the resulting state of muscular action. It is uncomfortable, and always suggests the presence of an unparticipating spectator with a note-book.[27]

In the passage from *Middlemarch*, George Eliot pays attention to the emotion and the 'state of muscular action' with which it is associated. Her description of Will is evidence of the way emotion, internal feeling, is rendered bodily and physical, read through its corporeal manifestations. In this regard, George Eliot is very much in line with the way emotions themselves in physiological psychology were being conceptualised as a physical process. But in conjunction with the bodily changes Will experiences, we are encouraged to recognise the magical aspect of the transformation – even as Eliot details the physical process, she keeps alive a sense of the miraculous, marvellous, and inexplicable. And she preserves the language of soul. This is not, however, a remystification. If Will's emotional response is visceral it is also cognitive – the passage speaks of his evaluation and assessment of Dorothea's worth; his discrimination of her value among other women. To express the small but significant choices, preferences, and discriminations that reveal our cognitive schemes, George Eliot contrasts a preference for natural light and natural scenery with artful light and manufactured materials. The image of the lantern is an important one, allowing Eliot to draw on visual technologies to represent internal processes such as cognitive choice and involuntary memory. Finally, the statement about Will being made of impressible stuff – a good conductor of the emotional as electrical – is a light and slightly ironic touch, bringing us (and him) down to earth after the sublimity and seriousness of the previous remarks on body and soul.

Today, scholars and scientists of many different stripes continue to debate whether emotions are bodily or mental, cognitive or unintentional. Among those who have resisted these binary oppositions, Martha Nussbaum notes: 'Certainly we are not left with a choice between regarding emotions as ghostly spiritual energies and taking them to be obtuse, nonseeing bodily movements, such as a leap of the heart, or the boiling of the blood.'[28] Anticipating such critique, George Eliot represents emotion as a synthesis of physical and mental, bodily and cognitive. Her work demonstrates a kind of physiological aesthetics, a corporeal as much as an inward turn.

Although an interest in unconscious processes of the mind meant looking inward at the hidden and mysterious workings of memory, motive, emotion, and decision, this orientation was not in George Eliot a turning away from social representation – the acceptable domain of literary realism. Just as Lewes insisted that 'to understand the Human Mind we must study it under normal conditions, and these are social conditions',[29] so the two registers of the social and psychic seem ineluctably intertwined in George Eliot's work. 'Inner' and 'outer' may be conceptually opposed but the novels frequently assert their mutual dependency: 'there is no creature whose inward being is so strong that it is not greatly determined by what lies outside it' (*M*, 785).

In her essay 'The Natural History of German Life' (1856), George Eliot sounded an early criticism of Dickens's art as concerning itself exclusively with the 'external traits' of individuals (specifically 'idiom and manners') at the expense of 'psychological character – their conceptions of life, and their emotions'. Were he able to render this interior life, she argued, 'his books would be the greatest contribution Art has ever made to the awakening of social sympathies'.[30] In Lewes's 1872 essay on Dickens, he too lamented that '[i]t is this complexity of the organism which Dickens wholly fails to conceive; his characters have nothing fluctuating and incalculable in them'.[31] These remarks may miss an appreciation of the specifically Dickensian mode of conveying psychic life, but they usefully highlight a very different sense of how to narrate and represent psychic process. Even in comparison to Charlotte Brontë, a novelist often associated with the expression of inner life, George Eliot emerges as distinctive. The representation of interiority in Brontë depends particularly on a first-person voice that is frequently emotional, subjective, intense, intimate, and revelatory, whereas interiority in Eliot is mediated by a reflective and analytical narrator. Readers have responded variously to the demands of the narrator, some regarding her commentaries as the growing points of the novel, the provocative loci of ethical thinking and moral seriousness; others finding these so-called intrusions to be pedantic and ideologically suspect. Given the demands of trying to make narratable the most subtle and minute processes of emotion and thought, the narrator's remarks on 'Omniscience' in the following passage are pertinent to her own procedures:

> For Bulstrode shrank from a direct lie with an intensity disproportionate to the number of his more indirect misdeeds. But many of these misdeeds were like the subtle muscular movements which are not taken account of in the consciousness, though they bring about the end that we fix our mind on and desire. And it is only what we are vividly conscious of that we can vividly imagine to be seen by Omniscience. (*M*, 645–6)

While 'Omniscience' in Bulstrode's case refers to his conception of the all-seeing deity, the word reverberates in the context of the narrator's ability to make transparent the subtle movements of mind that lie outside consciousness. As far as narrative technique is concerned, it takes a special kind of authorial omniscience to detect and describe what, as we have seen, is represented as a virtually invisible process and goes on beyond the realm of consciousness; as the narrator inclusively suggests, 'we' may hold that what is not conscious cannot be seen by the all-seeing, but as readers, 'we' come to understand that what is not conscious may be a powerful determinant of action and as such is the novelist's province.

Bulstrode's silent thoughts are not directly rendered in the above quotation. Though George Eliot does occasionally make use of free indirect discourse, she is more likely to use a technique that narrative theorists have called psycho-narration, in which the character's thoughts are introduced by a verb of perception. The following passage deploys both free indirect discourse and psycho-narration: 'Then, he wished that he had begged Lydgate to come again that evening ... Should he send for Lydgate? If Raffles were really getting worse, and slowly dying, Bulstrode felt that he could go to bed and sleep in gratitude to Providence. But was he worse?' (*M*, 666).[32] The sentence including 'Bulstrode felt' is psycho-narration, but the two indirect questions are instances of narrated monologue, a narrative strategy allowing the author to fuse narratorial and figural presence. This technique superimposes two voices, hovering between what Dorrit Cohn describes as the 'immediacy of a quotation and the mediacy of narration'. She has suggested that narrated monologue gained ground in the realist novels of the nineteenth century roughly in proportion to the ascendancy of 'objective' over 'obtrusive' narrators, and that its use expanded greatly in the twentieth-century psychological novel, following the 'unprecedented importance given to the language of consciousness'.[33] I would argue, however, that George Eliot develops a language of consciousness that is both unprecedented and yet closely linked to the use of an obtrusive narrator. Unlike Flaubert, whose name is associated with *style indirect libre* and the use of an impersonal or 'objective' narrator, Eliot consistently makes use of narrators described (pejoratively, one might argue) as obtrusive or intrusive. The novels enlist the use of a commenting and analysing narrator in order to mediate consciousness and the unconscious processes that inform it. Without the narrator's commentary, the significance of those subtle movements of unconscious thought would be lost. The narrator's prompts to the reader to think himself or herself into the place of the other are as important as Bulstrode's questions to himself: 'Who can know how much of his most inward life is made up of the thoughts he believes other men to have about him, until that fabric of opinion is threatened with ruin?' (*M*, 647).

Bulstrode is a good example of what I am claiming about George Eliot's work because he is not a particularly introspective character, and introspective self-communing has been the focus for much theoretical analysis of how novels convey interiority. George Eliot's techniques of representing inarticulate and unselfconscious forms of interiority are thus worth further scrutiny, having been overlooked in the theoretical preference for highly self-conscious forms of 'inner speech'.[34]

Turning the spotlight on mental and emotional process at the most apparently trivial and undetectable level, George Eliot's fiction offers in abundance one of the particular pleasures of reading novels: access to the minds of imagined others. By configuring the psyche as physical rather than metaphysical, yet preserving rather than dispelling a sense of wonder at its subtle processes, she opens up new territory for the novel. Among the many distinctions of her work as a novelist is the significance it attaches at the individual, social, and formal levels to the question of knowing – uncertain and imperfect as that knowledge is – what goes on in our own minds and what we imagine to be taking place in the minds of other people. According to theorist Thomas Pavel, there are three grand shifts in the way human nature is represented by the novel: at the outset, immortal souls battle forces of good and evil in a contest whose stakes are damnation or salvation. Later sentimental fiction replaces souls with hearts and invests in romantic love. After that, the psyche takes the place of the heart as a system of 'unconscious drives, revealed in dreams not clear to the characters, though controlled by the author, who, like the analyst, understands the forms of energy and action'.[35] While that last formulation seems to describe a specifically post-Freudian movement, George Eliot, a Victorian, is surely in its vanguard.

NOTE ON EDITIONS

The best edition of George Eliot's works is the Cabinet Edition, published in 1878 by Blackwood. The Clarendon Edition of the Novels of George Eliot published by Oxford University Press is in the process of producing definitive editions. Thus far, *Scenes of Clerical Life*, *Adam Bede*, *The Mill on the Floss*, *Romola*, *Felix Holt, the Radical*, *Middlemarch*, and *Daniel Deronda* have been published.

NOTES

1 *The George Eliot Letters*, ed. Gordon S. Haight, 9 vols. (New Haven and London: Yale University Press, 1954–78), III, p. 56. Subsequent references will be cited as *GEL* with volume and page number.
2 See Rosemarie Bodenheimer's discussion of the 'outing of George Eliot' in *The Real Life of Mary Ann Evans: George Eliot, Her Letters and Fiction* (Ithaca: Cornell University Press, 1994), p. 137.
3 Gaskell to George Eliot, 10 November 1859, in *The Letters of Mrs Gaskell*, ed. J. A. V. Chapple and Arthur Pollard (Manchester: Manchester University Press, 1997), p. 592.
4 *GEL*, II, p. 505.
5 *Essays of George Eliot*, ed. Thomas Pinney (London: Routledge & Kegan Paul, 1963), p. 316.
6 See Jenny Uglow's account of this period in *George Eliot* (London: Virago, 1987), p. 29.
7 Virginia Woolf, 'George Eliot', in *The Common Reader I* (London: Hogarth Press, 1984), pp. 171–2.
8 My discussion in this and the following paragraph is indebted to Bodenheimer, *The Real Life*, pp. 58–84.
9 Keats to J. H Reynolds, 3 May 1818, in *Selected Letters of John Keats*, rev. edn, ed. Grant F. Scott (Cambridge, MA: Harvard University Press, 2002), pp. 122–3.
10 *GEL*, III, p. 111.
11 George Eliot, *Middlemarch* (1872), ed. David Carroll, introduction by Felicia Bonaparte (Oxford: Oxford World's Classics, 1998), p. 198. Hereafter *M*.
12 Jessie Chambers, *D. H. Lawrence: A Personal Record*, 2nd edn (London: Frank Cass and Co., 1965), p. 105.
13 George Eliot, *Daniel Deronda* (1876), ed. Graham Handley (Oxford: Oxford World's Classics, 1998), p. 33. Hereafter *DD*.
14 On George Eliot as a psychological novelist, see generally Michael Davis, *George Eliot and Nineteenth-Century Psychology: Exploring the Unmapped Country* (Aldershot: Ashgate, 2006).
15 George Henry Lewes, *The Physiology of Common Life* (New York: Appleton, 1859–60), II, p. 12.
16 George Henry Lewes, *Problems of Life and Mind*, second series, *The Physical Basis of Mind* (London: Trübner, 1877), p. 365.

17 George Eliot, *Adam Bede* (1859), ed. Valentine Cunningham (Oxford: Oxford World's Classics, 1998), p. 173.
18 George Eliot, *The Lifted Veil*, ed. Helen Small (Oxford: Oxford World's Classics, 1999), p. 15.
19 Eliot, *Adam Bede*, p. 199.
20 *Essays*, ed. Pinney, p. 126.
21 George Eliot, *Felix Holt, the Radical* (1866), ed. Linda Mugglestone (London: Penguin, 1995), p. 10.
22 Eliot, *The Lifted Veil*, pp. 13, 18, 18.
23 George Eliot, 'Shadows of a Coming Race', in *Impressions of Theophrastus Such*, ed. Nancy Henry (London: Pickering and Chatto, 1994), p. 138.
24 Lewes, *Problems of Life and Mind*; third series, *The Study of Psychology: Its Object, Scope, and Method* (London: Trübner 1879), p. 74.
25 George Eliot, 'Mr Gilfil's Love-Story', in *Scenes of Clerical Life*, ed. David Lodge (Harmondsworth: Penguin, 1973), p. 240.
26 See my extended discussion of this passage in 'Emergent Theories of Victorian Mind-Shock: From War and Railway Accident to Nerves, Electricity and Emotion', in *Neurology and Literature: 1860–1920*, ed. Anne Stiles (Basingstoke: Palgrave Macmillan, 2007), pp. 163–83.
27 'A Novel or Two', *National Review*, 2 (October 1855), 349–50.
28 Martha C. Nussbaum, *Upheavals of Thought: The Intelligence of Emotions* (Cambridge: Cambridge University Press, 2001), p. 25.
29 Lewes, *Problems of Life and Mind*, first series, 2 vols., *The Foundations of a Creed* (1874), I, pp. 127–8.
30 *Essays*, ed. Pinney, p. 271.
31 George Henry Lewes, 'Dickens in Relation to Criticism', *Fortnightly Review*, 17 (1872), 149.
32 On the terms 'psycho-narration' and 'narrated monologue' see Dorrit Cohn, 'Transparent Minds: Narrative Modes for Presenting Consciousness in Fiction', in *Theory of the Novel: A Historical Approach*, ed. Michael McKeon (Baltimore: Johns Hopkins University Press, 2000), pp. 493–514.
33 Cohn, 'Transparent Minds', p. 501.
34 Alan Palmer, *Fictional Minds* (Lincoln: University of Nebraska Press, 2004), p. 9.
35 Pavel's account is discussed by A. S. Byatt in 'Novel Thoughts: A Way Out of Narcissism?', *Times Literary Supplement*, 30 November 2007, p. 16.

FURTHER READING

Ashton, Rosemary, *George Eliot*, Oxford, Oxford University Press, 1983

Beer, Gillian, *Darwin's Plots: Evolutionary Narrative in Darwin, George Eliot and Nineteenth-Century Fiction*, London, Ark Paperbacks, 1985

Bodenheimer, Rosemarie, *The Real Life of Mary Ann Evans: George Eliot, Her Letters and Fiction*, Ithaca, Cornell University Press, 1994

Carroll, David, *George Eliot: The Critical Heritage*, London, Routledge & Kegan Paul, 1971

Haight, Gordon S. (ed.), *The George Eliot Letters*, 9 vols., New Haven and London, Yale University Press, 1954–78

Henry, Nancy, *George Eliot and the British Empire*, Cambridge, Cambridge University Press, 2002

Hertz, Neil, *George Eliot's Pulse*, Stanford, Stanford University Press, 2003

Levine, George (ed.), *The Cambridge Companion to George Eliot*, Cambridge, Cambridge University Press, 2001

Miller, Hillis, J., 'Optic and Semiotic in *Middlemarch*', in *The Worlds of Victorian Fiction*, ed. Jerome Buckley, Cambridge, MA, Harvard University Press, 1975, pp. 125–45

Pinney, Thomas (ed.), *Essays of George Eliot*, London, Routledge & Kegan Paul, 1963

Uglow, Jenny, *George Eliot*, London, Virago, 1987

15

PENNY BOUMELHA

Thomas Hardy

There is a Thomas Hardy (1840–1928) for almost any critical history of the English novel that you care to mention: Hardy the last Victorian or the proto-modernist, the rural idyllist or the social-problem novelist, bearer of the last vestiges of the folk-tale or pioneer of the feminist heroine and the working-class hero. Whether you are looking for a historical novel or a *Bildungsroman*, a tragedy or a social satire, there is at least one among Hardy's fourteen novels that can be pressed into service. At the beginning of his career in the early 1870s, when his first novels were published anonymously in accordance with a common convention of the time, reviewers were apt to compare him, whether in admiration or by way of reproof for a perceived excess of indebtedness, to George Eliot: this was particularly true of his first major success, *Far from the Madding Crowd* (1874). By the end of his time as a writer of fiction, his challenging last novels were seen by some of his contemporaries as fifth columnists within the solid ranks of English literature, subversively opening the way for the invasive forces of French naturalism, Scandinavian 'Ibscenity', or other foreign influences, most notably the case with *Jude the Obscure* (1895). Despite the often unsympathetic reviews that dogged his career, Hardy's reputation, both with the general reading public and with his successors, seems to have been less subject to vicissitudes than some. His work remains continuously in print in multiple editions, and novelists with as little in common as Marcel Proust and D. H. Lawrence, Virginia Woolf and John Fowles, have found much in him to praise and from which to learn.

And yet, despite the undoubted presence of a protean quality such as all this implies, a recognisable Hardyan voice nevertheless runs throughout his work. 'Voice', perhaps, does not quite capture what is most immediately recognisable about Hardy: there are, for example, relatively few quotable striking phrases in his fiction. He is above all a novelist of the long run. His most distinctive attributes lie in the shape and heft of his plotting, in the rhythms of its movement between the stasis of the great symbolic set-piece episodes and the impulsion of the plot, in the multiple perspectives and variable tones of his narration, in the shifts and swoops of a language that sometimes seems to take on a density and weight of its own. Perhaps paradoxically, the unmistakable singularity of the Hardy novel inheres in its multiple and many-voiced quality, in what, adapting a phrase of Hardy's own, might be called its 'multiplying eye'.

The 'multiplying eye' of Joseph Poorgrass, in *Far from the Madding Crowd*, is a comic and alcohol-induced affliction that, he says, 'always comes on when I have been in a public-house a little time' (*FMC*, 298).[1] In the case of Hardy himself, it is rather a habit of vision that leads him always to see his texts as plural: surrounding the events of his stories with variants, repetitions, and symmetries; reflecting his protagonists in doubles, cultural archetypes, and historic precursors; and setting them in a whispering gallery of echoes, quotations, and allusions. The strongly realised concrete particularities of his novels and the commanding central presences for which several of them are known are created within the framework of a notably wide range of perspectives, discourses, and modes of explanation. Late in his career as a novelist, in his Preface to *Jude the Obscure*, Hardy described his works, not as a uniform argument, but as an 'endeavour to give shape and coherence to a series of seemings, ... the question of their consistency or their discordance, of their permanence or their transitoriness, being regarded as not of the first moment' (*JO*, 27). It is in his willingness to embrace such multiplicity, to allow the discontinuities and the shadows to take their due place within the coherence of a single vision, that Hardy is at his most distinctive.

This quality derives in part from the fact that Hardy's novelist's eye is so firmly fixed on the histories and traditions of writing within which he sought to make a space for himself. From the outset of his writing career he immersed himself in the practice of literature as at once a history, an art, a trade, and a source of social capital. He was perfectly prepared, in literature as in his first career as an architect, to put himself through an apprenticeship. (He began training as an architect at the age of sixteen and worked for practices in Dorchester, London, and Weymouth until he was thirty-two.) It is perhaps a sign of class condescension towards this emerging author, famously lacking a university degree or a classical education, that others seem to have felt so free to offer him advice on improving himself. Nevertheless, these earlier years show him to have been eclectic and responsive in the identification of mentors and models. He was, for example, more than willing to learn from the novelist George Meredith, who in 1869, in his capacity as publisher's reader for Chapman & Hall, commented on the manuscript of Hardy's first attempt at a novel, 'The Poor Man and the Lady'. Meredith advised him to steer clear of the potential controversies of social criticism and satire and to head toward a more plot-based approach to the novel. Whether or not because of Meredith's counsel, this seems to have been a course to which Hardy adhered throughout his fictional practice, since the foregrounding – or the obtrusiveness, depending on the critic's point of view – of plot is one of the literary features most widely identified with him. Nor did this keep him out of deep waters of controversy, it must be said, and in the course of his career as a novelist he acceded with varying degrees of reluctance to all sorts of bowdlerisation of his plots in order to secure publication in the most lucrative conventional form, magazine serialisation followed by three-volume publication.

Another mentor was Leslie Stephen, who, as an editor and publisher, had a long and fraught relationship with Hardy. Stephen recommended a course of useful reading Hardy should undertake, focused on the French critic Charles Sainte-Beuve and on Matthew Arnold. Hardy's own Notebooks, as well as comments in the thinly disguised autobiography published in the name of his second wife,[2] show him to have undertaken a quite deliberate and notably wide-ranging study of models and examples of high literary style, a study that embraced *Times* leader articles as much as the essayist Addison or the novelists Sterne and Defoe. Never much given to reviewing or to public literary polemic, he nevertheless maintained a lively and at times opinionated dialogue with his writing contemporaries, through personal relationship, correspondence, or occasionally barbed commentary in diaries and notebooks. Although his published self-analyses were few, he was on occasion prepared to define his own characteristics as a writer by contrast, as when he compared the poet Browning to a man walking a narrow line, oblivious to the 'vertical cliff five hundred feet deep' alongside it, and defined himself in these terms: 'I know it is there, but walk the line just the same.'[3] So great was his engagement in the allegiances and rivalries of his literary milieu that, even on his deathbed, he composed a satirical mock-epitaph for his rival and antagonist George Moore.

As this continuing conversation with contemporaries suggests, Hardy was strongly aware of writers as a distinct group within society. Sometimes he viewed them on the literal or metaphorical model of the gentleman's club – he was, for example, pleased to be invited in 1879 to join the Rabelais Club dedicated to the pursuit and celebration of 'virility' in literature – and at other times he inclined more towards the model of the trade union or professional association, as in his enthusiastic response to the proposal to found an Incorporated Society of Authors, which he viewed as an opportunity to ensure that authors' rights were respected and prices kept up. Hardy's class background, as the son of a rural builder, meant that writing was to him from the first a professional career, not the gentlemanly hobby of a man with a private income, and he accordingly sought to be canny in the management of his publication rights and authorial earnings. The origin of his collected Wessex Edition of 1912–13, for which he wrote the famous General Preface as well as prefaces to individual works, lay in his admiration for the business acumen of Sir Walter Scott, as well as in the attempt to ensure that it was the novelist himself, and not some opportunist editor, who would profit from the processes of collection and contextualisation of the body of his work.

In other words, then, Hardy was not, as is still sometimes imagined, a barely lettered rustic who clumsily stumbled into occasional moments of greatness despite himself, but a professional writer with a strongly developed sense of his own place – at first as an aspiration, later as an achievement – within a continuing tradition of literature in English. The poet or novelist is, for Hardy, in part a participant in a conversation, in part an inheritor. All a writer can do, he is reported to have remarked to the poet Robert Graves in 1920, is to 'write on the old themes in the old styles' and hope in the process to achieve something that improves upon 'those who went before us'.[4]

This mixture of informed respect for what has gone before and assertive emulation in the present finds evident expression in the dense allusiveness that is woven into the texture of Hardy's writing. From the first, he uses quotations, epigraphs, and literary references to place his own writing firmly within the framework of what one of his writer-protagonists calls 'all that has been done in literature from Moses down to Scott' (*HE*, 311) – and, indeed, beyond, extending into the works of his own contemporaries. From the Bible to Swinburne, Socrates to Shelley, Shakespeare to Walt Whitman, the words of others ring through Hardy's novels. Some critics have interpreted this as a mark of intellectual insecurity, an autodidact's attempt to bolster his own artistic credentials by calling upon the dignity and power of his lofty predecessors. Yet the function of the pervasive allusions is more complex than that. For one thing, some of them are too obscurely phrased to be instantly recognisable by the majority of readers in any period: 'the ironical Tishbite' (*TD*, 101), for example, or 'as Hallam says of Juliet' (*DR*, 119). Their effect is less to awaken appreciative recognition of some particular echo in the mind of the reader than to draw attention to the fact that they *are* allusions. They clearly remind the audience, at least implicitly, that what they are reading is a work of fiction and that a history of literary conventions is at work, shaping and being shaped by the novel before them. So, when Hardy invokes 'dramas of a grandeur and unity truly Sophoclean' (*W*, 40) as the appropriate comparison for the tree-felling and cider-making, lapsed leases and hairpieces, of the world of Little Hintock, a claim is being made for the right of such a fictional world to the same kind and level of attention and engagement as the classical tragedy receives. There is in this an assertion, not just of the ambition of Hardy's own fictional project, but also of the cultural value of the novel itself, a form which in the course of the nineteenth century consolidated its position as the dominant literary genre in Britain.

The invocation of a framework of literary traditions need not always take quite so overt a form as direct allusion, of course. The sense of a dialogue between Hardy's fictional practices and those conventions of writing and histories of reading that shape and constrain the novel in the period is also palpable in his use of what might be called quoted plotting, the self-conscious evoking of tropes of plot that are taken up, explored, ironically reproduced, or challenged. Tess Durbeyfield's history as a 'ruined maid' at once calls up and hollows out the conventions of narrative expulsion or redemption through repentance that form the history of unmarried mothers in Victorian models like George Eliot's *Adam Bede* or Elizabeth Gaskell's *Ruth*. Ethelberta Chickerel's research trip, in *The Hand of Ethelberta*, to measure up and appraise the estate of a potential suitor gives a sardonically self-knowing twist to the marital careerism of the heroines of Jane Austen and her contemporaries. Scenes in which a woman writes down the truth of her own experience and feelings in a letter which then goes astray (as it does for Tess) or is suppressed by its writer (as in *The Hand of Ethelberta*) resonate with the lost, burned, and buried letters of such heroines as Charlotte Brontë's Lucy Snowe (in *Villette*) or George Meredith's Diana Warwick (in *Diana of the Crossways*). The night in the open which allows closeness to nature to bring Bathsheba Everdene or Tess Durbeyfield to a fresh perspective on their own social situation finds parallels in similar episodes everywhere from Brontë's *Jane Eyre* to Meredith's *The Ordeal of Richard Feverel*. The notably intractable obscurity that gives the story of Jude Fawley its title is, among other things, the vehicle of a savage onslaught on the meritocratic myth that underlies the characteristic denouements – inherited wealth or aspiration fulfilled – of the English *Bildungsroman*.

Such pervasive consciousness of intervening in an evolving history of writing – a history that cannot be ignored – is given a thematic exposition in the only two (in both cases, female) writer-protagonists of Hardy's novels, Elfride Swancourt in *A Pair of Blue Eyes* (1873) and Ethelberta Chickerel in *The Hand of Ethelberta* (1876). Viewed together, these heroines illuminate Hardy's acute sense of the writer's dilemma of emulation. Elfride, whose pseudo-medieval romance *The Court of King Arthur's Castle. A Romance of Lyonnesse* is written and published under a male pseudonym, is very much an amateur. Timid in her writing, petulant in her response to criticism, she wishes to be read on her own terms, as if she had no predecessors, and according to her own intentions: 'the young person who wrote the book did not adopt a masculine pseudonym in vanity or conceit ... and ... did not mean the story for such as he' (*PBE*, 165) is her objection when her book, like Hardy's own early novels, is unsympathetically reviewed as derivative. In a passage of dialogue that brings out very sharply the potentially disabling power of the cultural past, Elfride's stepmother attempts to console her over the reviewer's unflattering comparison: 'It proves that you were clever enough to make him think of Sir Walter Scott, which is a great deal.' Elfride is not for a moment placated: 'O yes', she retorts, 'though I cannot romance myself, I am able to remind him of those who can!' (*PBE*, 162).

As the plot of the novel unfolds, Elfride's tacit desire to set aside a cultural past that threatens to overwhelm her is placed in a relationship of complex symmetries to aspects of her two potential lovers. The first is Stephen Smith, whose social status as a self-made man depends upon maintaining an unsustainable level of secrecy about his class and educational background; and the second is Henry Knight, the reviewer of Elfride's romance, whose morbid aversion to the thought of any prior romantic or sexual history on her part is equally impracticable. Elfride achieves as a woman what she cannot as a writer, so charming her critic that he is utterly disarmed. In a significant irony of plotting, her ultimately revealed sexual secret – she has not only kissed Stephen but spent an innocent though compromising night in his company after a failed attempt to marry – destroys Knight's longing for romantic priority just as his accusations of derivativeness have undermined her own aspirations to cultural originality. He gives up on women in the same way that she abandons her writing.

If Elfride as a writer buckles under the weight of her predecessors, Ethelberta is made of sterner stuff. In a novel that in part constitutes a complex reflection on authorship, the young widow and servant's daughter Ethelberta sets out to earn a living as a professional. She achieves mingled notoriety and success by consciously exploiting the continuities and discontinuities between the conventions of fiction, the identity and experiences of the writer, and the expectations of an audience. Her first effort is a collection of poems, *Metres by E.*, the aim of which is said to be 'to justify the ways of girls to men' (*HE*, 46–7), and the Miltonic allusion immediately invokes an awe-inspiring instance of literary precursion. The success of the volume, it transpires, depends less upon the intrinsic quality of the verse than on the opportunity it provides for speculation and gossip about the morals of its avowedly female author. Whereas Elfride feels she is unfairly treated as a writer because her identity and life as a woman are not taken into account, Ethelberta's problem is the opposite. She attempts to draw a distinction between the author and the woman: 'It would be difficult to show that because I have written so-called gay and amatory verse, I feel amatory and gay', she tells her disapproving mother-in-law. But this argument gets her nowhere in the face of the conventional view that 'some, even virtuous, ladies' become 'improper ... when they get into print' (*HE*, 96–7).

Ethelberta's next venture is as a storyteller, in person rather than on the page. In this role, she draws on the example of Defoe for tales of adventure and exoticism that the embodied nature of her telling nevertheless once again encourages her audience to take for the story of her own life: 'For Heaven's sake, Ethelberta ... where did you meet with such a terrible experience as that?' interjects one excited listener (*HE*, 111). But the moment when Ethelberta *does* set out to recount her own life-story leaves her audience consternated rather than excited – 'this was not at all the kind of story that they had expected' – and the storyteller herself reduced to silence: 'her voice trembled, she moved her lips but uttered nothing' (*HE*, 296). Just as the honest letter she begins to write to the man she thinks she loves is abandoned and an ironically conventional one substituted, so Ethelberta can only find a voice, can only be heard, when she tells her audience what they are expecting to hear.

Ethelberta seems, like Elfride before her, to abandon writing in favour of the pursuit of marriage; and yet, with her socially glorious but emotionally void marriage achieved, she is reported at the end of the novel to have reverted to her Miltonic beginnings by embarking upon the composition of an epic poem. Where Elfride's attempts to write show her overwhelmed by the burden of the literary past and the audience expectations it has formed, Ethelberta is a survivor, able to turn the models afforded by her predecessors to her advantage, but only at the cost of a self-alienation that exposes her to the fanciful or censorious scrutiny of her audience while enforcing the suppression of her own feelings and experiences.

These writing protagonists make palpable Hardy's vivid awareness of literary history as a perpetual present which is at once the enabling condition of his imagination and the threat to its fulfilment. The female writers of Hardy's novels find their counterparts in a series of usually male scholar-protagonists, reading men who seek in the distilled wisdom of their predecessors some key or code by which to understand and interpret their own experience. Henry Knight has made his name and his living as a reviewer and essayist on general topics including the nature of women, and his personal tragedy results in part from the lack of connection between such accumulated wisdom and any personal experience: 'And do you mean to say', asks his cousin Mrs Swancourt of one opinion-piece about women, 'that you wrote that upon the strength of another man's remark, without having tested it by practice?' He confirms that this is indeed the case, going on to add that 'having written it, I would defend it anywhere' (*PBE*, 303). Clym Yeobright in *The Return of the Native* (1878) is another such scholar-protagonist who painfully experiences a disseverment between his intellectual principles of conduct and the demands of his actual situation. Convinced by his exposure to contemporary French social thought that 'the want of most men was knowledge of a sort that brings wisdom rather than affluence' (*RN*, 190), he fails to notice that his fellow heath-dwellers, scrabbling for a living in difficult conditions, are not the right audience for a message that he is doomed to preach even though it will not be heard: 'To argue upon the possibility of culture before luxury to the bucolic world may be to argue truly, but it is an attempt to disturb a sequence to which humanity has long been accustomed' (*RN*, 191).

At such moments, Hardy sets out to demonstrate the futility of adopting received wisdom as a guide to living, prising petrified categories of morality and knowledge apart from the material realities of social life. Ethelberta's admonition to her sister – 'But don't you go believing in sayings, Picotee: they are all made by men, for their own advantages. Women who use public proverbs as a guide through events are those who have not ingenuity enough to make private ones as each event occurs' (*HE*, 153) – is echoed elsewhere, as in the narrator's ironically phrased comment on Tess, that:

> If before going to the d'Urbervilles' she had rigorously moved under the guidance of sundry gnomic texts and phrases known to her and to the world in general, no doubt she would never have been imposed on. But it had not been in Tess's power – nor is it in anybody's power – to feel the whole truth of golden opinions while it is possible to profit by them. (*TD*, 126)

But Hardy's most thorough, and most devastating, exposure of the gap between the tired and partial wisdom of public proverbs and the unformulated nature of raw experience is to be found in the very evident narrative strategy of discordant contrasts in *Jude the Obscure* (1895). Here, character after character struggles to align their personal experience with the maxims, models, or principles by which they variously seek to live. Sue Bridehead, once married, cannot associate her sense of herself as an individual with the 'Mrs Richard Phillotson' that now constitutes her social identity (*JO*, 223); the schoolmaster Phillotson is torn by the sense that his 'instinct' as a man and his 'doctrines' and 'principles' lead in different directions (*JO*, 246); and Jude's enforced journey out of the orderly harmony of his early 'neat stock of fixed opinions' into 'a chaos of principles' lies at the core of the novel's critique of the English *Bildungsroman* (*JO*, 336–7). Each of these characters carries with them through the novel a habit of quotation that clearly becomes less and less closely related to the experiences they undergo. Sue, at the height of her conviction that through rationality and the power of her will alone she can transform her society to match her expectations, gives this graphic expression by producing her own literally cut-and-paste version of the New Testament. But as she is confronted more and more brutally by the limits of her capacity to impose her will upon the world, she is forced to abandon this attempt to make her textual authorities suit her own purposes and instead moves progressively toward silence, so that the reader's two last sightings of her are of her blocking her ears so that she cannot hear Jude and clenching her teeth so that she expresses nothing to the first husband she has remarried, Phillotson. If Sue learns that she cannot rewrite the texts of social ideology to support her own experience, Jude, on the other hand, becomes bitterly alienated from the scriptural and literary history that had at first appeared to offer him a means of personal fulfilment and social mobility as well as a way of understanding his experience through the medium of the received wisdom of authorities. His quotations are increasingly sardonically counterpointed with the situations and relationships in which he finds himself, from his drunken recitation of the Nicene Creed in a pub to the culminating scene of his death, accompanied as it is by the desolating words of Job ('Let the day perish wherein I was born, and the night in which it was said, There is a man child conceived') interspersed with cheers from the celebrating crowd on the river bank (*JO*, 408).

In this way, Hardy's reader- and author-protagonists alike are carefully positioned at the point of intersection of past exemplum and present uniqueness. The sense of this continuous and challenging interplay is not peculiar to the domain of writing, however. Indeed, Hardy's work, both as a novelist and as a poet, is saturated with consciousness of belatedness. Just as his greatest poetry is often thought to lie in the poems of love for a wife already dead, so 'Too Late Beloved', an early title for the manuscript that was to become *Tess of the d'Urbervilles* (1891), could almost stand as the epigraph to his fiction. His imagination is possessed by missed opportunities, failed encounters, returns too long postponed, and all the exquisite agonies of bad timing. The most common shape of his plots takes the form of a struggle by one or more of his characters to leave definitively behind them a past that refuses to stay buried: a sexual secret, a broken promise, a rash act with irrevocable consequences.

So the graveyards and funerals that feature so prominently in Hardy's writing do not only convey a characteristically Victorian preoccupation with mortality, but also figuratively remind us that the past is at best an unquiet sleeper. Burial in its most literal form is on occasion potently evoked, as in the sleep-walking Angel Clare's attempt to carry to her grave the chaste and virginal Tess now dead to him following her wedding-night confession (*TD*, chapter 37). But it is only one of a congeries of metaphors Hardy draws on to suggest at once the urgency and the impossibility of rupturing temporal continuity to start afresh. There is also, for example, Sergeant Troy's ill-fated planting of flowers on Fanny Robin's grave, so soon washed away by the torrents of water that issue from the mocking gargoyles (*FMC*, chapters 45 and 46), or the uncanny effigy of Michael Henchard, wearing his discarded clothes, which he finds 'floating as if dead in Ten Hatches Hole' (*MC*, 300).

It is not only natives that return in Thomas Hardy's novels, in which it seems that nothing can lie long concealed. Tess Durbeyfield's increasingly desperate attempts to prove that 'the recuperative power which pervaded organic nature' is 'not denied to maidenhood alone' (*TD*, 127); Michael Henchard's strenuous efforts to fashion a new and sober life over which the earlier drunken sale of his wife casts no shadow; Jude Fawley's nomadic striving to move on to a new start from each of the scenes of rejection that structure his life: all are thwarted by an apparent law of eternal recurrence that allows the power of the past to reclaim the fresh beginnings of the present. Sometimes – as in the muted satisfactions of the ending of *Far from the Madding Crowd*, for instance – the reassertion of past commitments over more newly formed and more tentative allegiances appears relatively benign, but characteristically, such reclamations lead toward tragedy.

Set against the evocation of a past that constantly threatens to overshadow the present are the attempts of the characters to inscribe the uniqueness of their own lives within the continuous loop of human narrative. Henry Knight's longing for priority – to be the first to have loved Elfride, first to have kissed her, and so on – may be absurd in its extremism and poignant in its disproportionate effects on the lives of both characters, but it is nevertheless of a piece with the sensibility of other Hardyan protagonists. It is reflected, for example, in Hardy's first published novel, *Desperate Remedies* (1871), where the young Cytherea Graye is abused by her employer Miss Aldclyffe once she discloses that she has already been kissed once or even twice before: 'I – an old fool – have been sipping at your mouth as if it were honey, because I fancied no wasting lover knew the spot. But a minute ago and you seemed to me like a fresh spring meadow – now you seem a dusty highway' (*DR*, 110). Miss Aldclyffe is a rare – even a unique – example in Hardy of a female character gripped by the need to be first in the sexual sense. Actual or presumed virginity commonly does double duty in Hardy's fiction: as an oppressive social ideology that unduly circumscribes moral virtue in women to no more than simple chastity, but also as a powerful image of the imaginary nature of personal chronological priority. Several of Hardy's men are shown in the process of being progressively, and painfully, disabused of this fantasy.

If male virginity does not have the same significance for his heroines, there is nevertheless a corresponding movement in the novels in relation to women. The difference between the two recurrent plots marks a particular understanding of a division between the spheres of experience of the sexes that persists almost throughout Hardy's work. For his women, the desire for priority and its inevitable disappointment are played out in their experience of formal or informal education, often at the hands of their male lovers, and bring forth in heroine after heroine similarly melancholy reflections on their own lack of uniqueness. 'O, other people have thought the same thing, have they?' ponders Elfride. 'That's always the case with my originalities – they are original to nobody but myself' (*PBE*, 295). Similarly, Tess Durbeyfield doubts the value of 'learning that I am one of a long row only – finding out that there is set down in some old book somebody just like me, and to know that I shall only act her part', going on to surmise that 'the best is not to remember that your nature and your past doings have been just like thousands' and thousands', and that your coming life and doings 'll be like thousands' and thousands'' (*TD*, 153–4). These female protagonists learn in the sphere of the intellect what their male counterparts must learn in the domain of sexuality: that the longing to be first and unique can never be fulfilled.

Hardy is primarily thought of as the novelist of a delimited region, his fictional Wessex. But if he is generally content with restricted and localised space, that highly specific setting serves to anchor an intense awareness of temporality, so that any given location places the drama of the protagonists within the perpetual present of living history. Landscapes and urban settings alike can function as embodied histories, staging confrontation between a particular character and an encompassing personal or historical past: Jude wandering among the phantom worthies on the streets of Christminster, Tess and her homeless family amid the ancestral graves of Kingsbere churchyard, and Michael Henchard's meeting with his long-abandoned wife in the Roman amphitheatre with its history of ill-fated 'appointments of a furtive kind' (*MC*, 98).

A flamboyantly symbolic episode in *A Pair of Blue Eyes* graphically represents the way in which Hardy configures the axes of temporality and spatiality in order to place the localised experience of one character in the context of its inevitably multiple precursors. Set mostly in the small community of Endelstow, the novel nevertheless frames the lives of its protagonists within a set of concentric histories that range from the vast sweep of pre-human existence to local community narratives. When Henry Knight slips on the edge of the Cliff without a Name and holds on grimly, waiting for the ingenious Elfride to rescue him, he comes face to face with embedded fossils telling of 'the world in its infancy' and time closes up 'like a fan' before his eyes (*PBE*, 222), allowing him imaginative access to the aeons of geological time and the world of the prehistoric. In the next chapter, the passage of time is domesticated as Stephen Smith listens in on the conversations of the local inhabitants about such matters as a clock that has stopped, the cyclical regrowth of weeds, and a family history of pig-killing; and shortly afterwards, the scene of Lady Luxellian's burial adds to these perspectives a further layer of history, those dying generations whose coffins can be seen lying in their 'order of interment' in the family vault (*PBE*, 255). Such foreshortening of chronological perspective is one among a number of narrative strategies by which the unique particularity of the moment and the long view of history are combined, with neither allowed to predominate.

These strategies include those moments in which the engrossing, even moving, story of an individual becomes flattened by the pragmatic tones of a local storyteller into the repetition of some (often comic) type, as when Tess Durbeyfield is obliged to listen to the dairy-workers' tale of the wronged maid and her fleeing lover, Jack Dollop, hiding in the milk churn. A counterpart to this technique can be found in those episodes in which the voice of a narrator distances the characters – perhaps sympathetically, perhaps ironically – by assimilating them momentarily into historical, mythological, or cultural prototypes. In the following passage, for example, Eustacia Vye's momentary fright at the threat of gossip is coolly contextualised in a historical setting which at once generalises its significance and lessens its emotional impact:

> The reddleman's hint that rumour might show her to disadvantage had no permanent terror for Eustacia. She was as unconcerned at that contingency as a goddess at a lack of linen. This did not originate in inherent shamelessness, but in her living too far from the world to feel the impact of public opinion. Zenobia in the desert could hardly have cared what was said about her at Rome. (*RN*, 116)

Then again there are those repeated intimations of family histories apparently re-enacting themselves through the medium of the present, as in the spectral coach and mailed ancestors of *Tess of the d'Urbervilles* or the marital curse that seems to hang over the Fawleys. Individuals and their stories may be multiplied and mirrored within a text in other ways too, through repetition, contrast, or substitution: the three Avices who in turn engage the affections of Jocelyn Pierston in the strikingly non-naturalistic romance at the centre of *The Well-Beloved* (1897); or Jude and Sue aghast at what is implied by finding themselves waiting alongside their pregnant, drunken, or pock-marked fellow clients at the registry office; or Picotee Chickerel fulfilling in the actualities of the plot the reconciliation with her sister Ethelberta's discarded suitor that has been misleadingly foreshadowed throughout as a possible denouement for the heroine herself.

The simultaneous presence of such multiple possible narratives within the framework of a single story highlights an oscillation between resignation to what appears fated by historical precedent or social maxim and rebellious resistance to it. This dialectic is in a sense the mechanism of social change for Hardy. Tess's defiance of official Christian ritual in devising her own version of a midnight baptism for her dying infant is as much part of the novel's meaning as her passive compliance with the force of the law at Stonehenge. The hesitation between compliance and resistance, resignation and flight, is often most clearly visible in the case of Hardy's heroines, and at times it is structured into the narrative in a willed ambivalence that is drawn insistently to the attention of his readers. So, there hangs over the events of Tess Durbeyfield's life-determining night in the Chase an equivocation – was she raped or seduced? – that parallels the similarly critical episode of Eustacia Vye's drowning in *The Return of the Native*, a death that cannot unambiguously be declared to be suicide or attempted flight from the Heath, accident or final assertion of choice. The uncertainty about such crucial elements of the plot may well have been in part an attempt – not entirely successful, of course – to head off the more extreme potential responses of censorious Victorian reviewers. More importantly, however, it also directs us towards something that lies close to the heart of Hardy's narrative technique: a refusal to allow his readers to slip comfortably into the mode either of affective identification with his characters and their histories or of settled judgement upon them.

Many readers and critics have been troubled by the presence in the novels of multiple, even contradictory, emotional and ethical perspectives deployed through the medium of a single narrative voice. This has been most extensively discussed (probably because most insistently noticeable) in relation to *Tess*, where a range of irreconcilable commentaries upon the heroine's sexual history is displayed, from noting the 'pity of it' that her 'beautiful feminine tissue' should be marked by 'such a coarse pattern' (*TD*, 101–2) to the summary defence of her experience as 'simply a liberal education' (*TD*, 127). Alongside this flurry of direct commentaries in the narrative voice, and alongside the opinions expressed in direct speech by various characters, runs another set of moral perspectives and social ideologies conveyed through allusion. Tess appears beset by community judgements on her post-virginal life, which are incorporated into the novel through quotation (as in the pious

Clare family's biblical understanding of the virtuous woman whose price is far above rubies) or on occasion given starkly material form through graffiti and emblazoned texts, such as the sign-writer's equally biblical reminder 'THY, DAMNATION, SLUMBERETH, NOT' that confronts her on her travels (*TD*, 108). Each new explanation and commentary appears to be offered with the same degree of rhetorical confidence and without reference to neighbouring contradictions. Such discontinuity of perspective has sometimes been viewed as evidence of authorial carelessness or as a mark of the episodic nature of serial publication and the forgiving lapses of the reader's concentration that it permits. Yet the tendency to write in this way, even if at its most evident in *Tess*, is so consistent in Hardy's technique that inadvertence hardly seems sufficient explanation.

Instead, such equivocations can be read as the counterpart at the level of voice of a tension already noted in relation to narrative structures, between that aspect of the character and story that is repetition and their status as new-minted and unique. The manipulation of narrative distance is a notable feature of Hardy's writing, where the dynamic between sympathetic engagement with the characters and detached commentary upon them is often strongly visualised. The novels are full of sudden and surprising shifts of perspective that take the reader abruptly from an intimate evocation of human particularity – the precise shade of Elfride Swancourt's squirrel-coloured ringlets, or of the 'Prout's or Vandyke brown' that could render Grace Melbury's eyebrows (*W*, 69) – to a mode of observation so dispassionately remote that it seems almost heartless. Such moments either assimilate particularity to a historical type – Clym Yeobright's face, we read, is 'the typical countenance of the future' (*RN*, 185) – or even remove it altogether from the sphere of the human, as when Ethelberta watches the dwindling figure of her departing lover, 'the black spot diminishing to the size of a fly as he receded along the dusty road' (*HE*, 248).

Emotional distance fluctuates just as evidently. Sudden flashes of inwardness with a character seem to suggest the momentary presence of an embodied first-person narrator: 'our Eustacia – for at times she was not altogether unlovable' (*RN*, 94). Yet at the same time, Hardy's narration is littered with distancing generalisations on the basis of a type, a class, a sex: 'Woman's ruling passion – to fascinate and influence those more powerful than she' (*PBE*, 202); 'It was, to some degree, Northern insight matched against Southron doggedness – the dirk against the cudgel' (*MC*, 137); or 'The beautiful youth usually verges ... perilously on the incipient coxcomb' (*TT*, 311). However tempting it may be to take such maxims as expressions of an authorial world-view, they form only one element in a complex movement of retreat and advance in the evocation of character and address to the reader. The very awkwardness of such disconcerting shifts in the narrative mode serves to interrogate the relationship between the precepts and 'public proverbs' (to recall Ethelberta's phrase) that represent interpretative frameworks drawn from consciousness of human repetition and the sudden spurts of sympathetic engagement that accompany the poignant recognition of specificity.

This, then, is the textual manifestation of Thomas Hardy's 'multiplying eye'. The play of narratorial distance, between close focus on the unique nature of the moment for the individual and the long view of cultural history, is perhaps the most characteristic element of Hardy's writing. It crystallises his sense of the individual human life as the meeting-point of a set of intersecting histories: the slow processes of evolution, family traits, social traditions, material inheritances of privilege and dispossession, community histories, legends and precepts, all come together in the complex and vivid particularity of the moment. Like one of those visual puns in which silhouetted shape and background predominate alternately as we look at them, Hardy's characters and their lives shade imperceptibly from singularity to archetype, from incident to legend, and back again. Every life in Hardy is inhabited by the ghosts of earlier selves and cultural forerunners, just as every setting in his novels is a haunted site and every text resounds with the background clamour of earlier voices.

NOTE ON EDITIONS

There are many scholarly and popular editions of individual novels by Hardy. Most are based upon the Wessex Edition of the fiction and poetry, published by Macmillan in twenty-four volumes in 1912–13 and incorporating Hardy's final revisions as well as a General Preface to the novels, written specifically to accompany this collected edition. The only widely available complete edition of Hardy's fiction to incorporate these revisions is the New Wessex Edition, reset from the original Wessex Edition, and published by Macmillan in fourteen volumes under the general editorship of P. N. Furbank in 1975–6. It is to this edition that reference is made throughout this chapter. There are Penguin Classics editions of all the novels, under the general editorship of Patricia Ingham, based with one exception on the first volume edition of each; they have been well edited and often include very good introductions. Oxford World's Classics editions (and in some cases an associated Clarendon edition) have been published, with Simon Gatrell as the general editor. Where available, these are excellent in editorial practice and critical introductions, but unfortunately the series does not include all of Hardy's novels.

NOTES

1 All references to Hardy's novels are to the New Wessex Edition, gen. ed. P. N. Furbank (London: Macmillan, 1975–6). The following abbreviations are used: *Desperate Remedies* (*DR*), *Far from the Madding Crowd* (*FMC*), *The Hand of Ethelberta* (*HE*), *Jude the Obscure* (*JO*), *The Mayor of Casterbridge* (*MC*), *A Pair of Blue Eyes* (*PBE*), *The Return of the Native* (*RN*), *Tess of the D'Urbervilles* (*TD*), *Two on a Tower* (*TT*), *The Woodlanders* (*W*).

2 The two volumes of biographical material first published after Hardy's death by his second wife, Florence Emily Hardy (1928, 1930), have now been re-edited by Michael Millgate and published as Hardy's own work under the title, *The Life and Work of Thomas Hardy* (London: Macmillan, 1984). For Notebooks, see *The Literary Notebooks of Thomas Hardy*, ed. Lennart A. Björk, 2 vols. (London: Macmillan, 1985), and *The Personal Notebooks of Thomas Hardy*, ed. Richard H. Taylor (London: Macmillan, 1978).

3 Michael Millgate, *Thomas Hardy: A Biography* (London: Oxford University Press, 1982), p. 409.

4 Millgate, *Hardy*, p. 534.

FURTHER READING

Bayley, John, *An Essay on Hardy*, Cambridge, Cambridge University Press, 1978

Boumelha, Penny, *Thomas Hardy and Women: Sexual Ideology and Narrative Form*, Brighton, Harvester, 1982

Fisher, Joe, *The Hidden Hardy*, Basingstoke, Macmillan, 1992

Garson, Marjorie, *Hardy's Fables of Integrity: Woman, Body, Text*, Oxford, Clarendon Press, 1991

Goode, John, *Thomas Hardy: The Offensive Truth*, Oxford, Basil Blackwell, 1988

Higonnet, Margaret R. (ed.), *The Sense of Sex: Feminist Perspectives on Hardy*, Urbana, University of Illinois Press, 1993

Ingham, Patricia, *Thomas Hardy*, Authors in Context, Oxford, Oxford University Press, 2003

Irwin, Michael, *Reading Hardy's Landscapes*, Basingstoke, Macmillan, 1999

Kramer, Dale (ed.), *The Cambridge Companion to Thomas Hardy*, Cambridge, Cambridge University Press, 1999

Mallett, Phillip (ed.), *Palgrave Advances in Thomas Hardy Studies*, London, Macmillan, 2004

Miller, J. Hillis, *Thomas Hardy: Distance and Desire*, Cambridge, MA, Harvard University Press, 1970

Millgate, Michael, *Thomas Hardy: A Biography*, London, Oxford University Press, 1982

Page, Norman, *The Oxford Reader's Companion to Hardy*, Oxford, Oxford University Press, 2000

Pite, Ralph, *Hardy's Geography: Wessex and the Regional Novel*, Basingstoke, Palgrave, 2002

Tomalin, Claire, *Thomas Hardy: The Time-Torn Man*, London, Viking, 2006

Widdowson, Peter, *Hardy in History: A Study in Literary Sociology*, London, Routledge, 1989

Wright, T. R., *Hardy and His Readers*, London, Palgrave Macmillan, 2003

16

ADRIAN POOLE

Robert Louis Stevenson

In a volume entitled, at once defiantly and wistfully, *I Can Remember Robert Louis Stevenson*, Flora Masson recalls a dinner party at the Stevensons' family home in Edinburgh, sometime in the 1870s. The twenty-something Louis, as he was known to family and friends, was enthusing about Balzac, his style and vocabulary. This set off a heated debate between father and son about language.

> Mr Stevenson upheld the orthodox doctrine of a 'well of English undefiled', which of course made Louis Stevenson rattle off with extraordinary ingenuity whole sentences composed of words of foreign origin taken into our language from all parts of the world – words of the East, of classical Europe, of the West Indies, and modern American slang … It was a real feat in the handling of language, and I can see to this day his look of pale triumph.[1]

Mr Stevenson was prosperous, pious, an eminent lighthouse engineer. He had hoped his only child would follow the family profession or become a lawyer, but young Louis recoiled from respectability. He was sickly, volatile, mutinous, hungry for play, performance, sensation. After his early death in 1894, his friend Henry James declared 'the filial relation quite classically troubled'.[2]

In this duel over language the son roams the globe. Like his own immediate literary father, Walter Scott, Stevenson drew to fine effect on the variations between Scots and English, in *Kidnapped* (1886) and the unfinished *Weir of Hermiston* (1896), as well as in shorter tales such as 'Thrawn Janet' and 'The Merry Men' (both 1881).[3] But by the time he came to maturity – if he ever did so, for there are detractors who dispute it – the world was rapidly changing. When *Jekyll and Hyde* turned him into a superstar in 1886, the printed word was being flashed to the ends of the earth at increasing speed. Too popular for most of his immediate British successors, Stevenson has recently come to seem, alongside James and Conrad and Wilde, a pivotal figure for English literary culture on the brink of its development into 'modernism'.[4]

'A real feat in the handling of language': Stevenson is one of the great improvisers, an acrobat with words and stories, a Scots Scheherazade, rattling on and off without end. For inspiration he looked everywhere. France was a good place to start, still distinctly risqué for Victorian Britain: he admired Balzac and Baudelaire, Hugo and Dumas, and further back, Montaigne and Molière. In a prophetic early essay on 'Victor Hugo's Romances' (1874) he reflects on modern 'romance' and sketches a lineage for himself as the heir to Scott, Dumas, and Hawthorne (XXVII, 1–23).[5] He liked the idea of the *flâneur*, the strolling and dawdling observer, and created an anglo-scot version *en plein air* for the travel books that made an early mark, *An Inland Voyage* (1878) and *Travels with a Donkey* (1879). His admiration for the French would be reciprocated by Mallarmé, Proust, and Gide.

Of his English antecedents Stevenson was drawn to Defoe and Sterne and, closer in time, to Thackeray and Meredith. But he looked beyond English literary culture to Dostoevsky ('Henry James could not finish it [*Crime and Punishment*]: all I can say, it nearly finished me'),[6] to Poe and Hawthorne and Twain. What is more, he rejected the distinctions between high and popular culture on which most of his educated contemporaries were trying to take their stand. He was not exempt from anxieties about this, but he threw himself into writing that did not sharply discriminate between its readers, between making art and making money.

Look – and listen – to the ring of the coins at the end of *Treasure Island* (1883): 'English, French, Spanish, Portuguese, Georges, and Louises, doubloons and double guineas and moidores and sequins ... nearly every variety of money in the world' (II, 215). Stevenson welcomed the polyglot, the multiracial, the hybrid.[7] His works anticipate the gleeful exploitation of generic convention in the best kinds of popular cinema. This is no less true of *New Arabian Nights* (1882), *Prince Otto* (1885), *The Dynamiter* (1885), *The Wrong Box* (1889), and *The Wrecker* (1892), than of his more enduring successes.

Stevenson's writing has global and perhaps imperial ambitions. He took a traditional interest in the European heritage near to hand, but he travelled in body and spirit to the New World and beyond, heading so far west that it turned into east. In *The Wrecker*, on which his stepson Lloyd Osbourne collaborated, the protagonist Loudon Dodd describes himself as 'a waterside prowler, a lingerer on wharves, a frequenter of shy neighbourhoods, a scraper of acquaintance with eccentric characters' (XII, 115). In San Francisco he compares himself to a Roman legionary looking north towards the mountains of the Picts:

> For all the interval of time and space, I, when I looked from the cliff-house on the broad Pacific, was that man's heir and analogue: each of us standing on the

> verge of the Roman Empire (or, as we now call it, Western civilisation), each of us gazing onward into zones unromanised. (XII, 118)

It is a clue to Stevenson's dealings with 'imperial romance' that he should latch on to such a figure on the verge of first contact. By the time Stevenson settled in Samoa in 1890, the 'zone' could no longer be seen as simply 'unromanised'. On the contrary, the Romans' successors (British, French, German) were eagerly jockeying for position, and Stevenson was in the thick of real living history.

Flora Masson remembers with particular vividness young Louis's 'look of pale triumph'. The pallor connotes both fear and anger. Stevenson was obsessed with courage and cowardice, with the fears that can never be wholly dispensed with, disposed of, especially as these afflict 'manhood'. To read Stevenson is to be absorbed in reading male faces and bodies, the signs by which men, boys, and beasts distinguish themselves from each other. Quite where women and girls fit in is a mystery, but this may be part of the fun; they can certainly look too and listen, like young Miss Masson.

John Jay Chapman thought Stevenson's art was a sham. In 1898 the American concluded that Stevenson was just an extraordinary mimic: 'The instinct at the bottom of all mimicry is self-concealment.' Stevenson had hidden himself well but when we did reach deep inside, all we would find was 'a pale boy'.[8] Mimicry advertises itself, as its more sinister sibling, plagiarism, does not. (In the 1880s Oscar Wilde provoked not dissimilar anxieties.) Mimicry can be a more complex activity than Chapman allows, as recent critical thinking about colonial and post-colonial writing has helped to suggest. Stevenson resists the terms of Chapman's accusation, that mimicry represents failure, inadequacy, a reluctance to find your own selfhood and voice. The well of English undefiled is a myth; so too perhaps is the singular self to be true to. Stevenson was ahead of his time in making Jekyll write of 'the perennial war among my members' and hazard the guess 'that man will be ultimately known for a mere polity of multifarious, incongruous and independent denizens' (II, 58). Chapman's complaint suggests that Stevenson's appeal – even or especially when it provokes exasperation – is based on a certain precariousness, if not downright antagonism, between a Jekyll and Hyde, or the two brothers Durie (in *The Master of Ballantrae*), or the Justice-Clerk and his son Archie (in *Weir of Hermiston*).

With more kindly intent Henry James observed in 1887 that setting aside *Prince Otto* and *Jekyll and Hyde*, everything Stevenson had written so far was 'a direct apology for boyhood'.[9] *Treasure Island* certainly fits this bill, though it is very much more than the 'children's classic' it is often supposed to be. Its first young readers were not half as enthusiastic as the grown-ups. J. M. Coetzee indicates why when he remembers, in the third person, how he could not work out whether Long John Silver was good or bad: 'He wishes Squire Trelawney would kill Long John instead of letting him go: he is sure he will return one day with his cutthroat mutineers to take his revenge, just as he returns in his dreams.'[10] *Swiss Family Robinson* was much more comforting: a strong father, no bad brothers or murderous pirates.

Treasure Island is an exceptional case of the one and the many. Imperceptibly senior to his younger boy-self, the first-person narrator, Jim Hawkins, is confronted by a multitude of grown-ups, the loyal party of surrogate fathers, Squire Trelawney, Dr Livesey, Captain Smollett, and the mutineers led by the bewildering Long John Silver. The story does contain nightmares of violence, but these are enveloped by a good dream about the boy who gains his manhood not by slaying fathers but by saving them. Jim risks life and limb to save the good trio, and they are grateful, though the most severe, the Captain, never relaxes his objection that Jim is 'too much the born favourite' (II, 214).

Long John is a different matter, the first of the mesmeric outlaws who raise Stevenson's best fiction to the level of myth or legend. Silver can be mistaken for another father-figure but he is more an irregular double, a more violent, calculating, and shameless version of Jim's youthful recklessness. Jim and Silver are both ingenious tricksters, and Jim learns a lot from watching the older man closely, mostly about techniques for survival, but also, more mysteriously, about loyalty, treachery, and justice. To what ends? In its own brilliant way this is a *Bildungsroman*, a story about the development of a youth into adulthood, but Stevenson avoids drawing conclusions and allows events to 'speak for themselves' in a way that anticipates his modernist successors, Hemingway for example. He leaves Jim with Captain Flint's 'Pieces of eight! pieces of eight!' still ringing in his ears, as if the island and its memories will keep him (and us) for ever entrapped and entranced.

Like all the best dreams, this one is packed full of detail, like the list of things in Billy Bones's sea-chest, from the suit of very good unworn clothes to some curious West Indian shells. Billy Bones is just one of the huge cast who lurch into focus and out again: Black Dog, Blind Pew, Ben Gunn the idiot maroon, Israel Hands whom Jim shoots dead, and a host of others accorded fleeting but vivid attention. Tom Redruth, for instance, the Squire's gamekeeper, 'sullen, old, serviceable servant', who dies uncomplainingly at the stockade: 'After a while of silence, he said he thought somebody might read a prayer. "It's the custom, sir", he said apologetically' (II, 112–13); or Abraham Gray, who bravely deserts the mutineers to join the loyalists; or Dick Johnson, a lad who has gone to the bad as Jim himself might have done: 'He had been well brought up, had Dick, before he came to sea and fell among bad companions' (205). Dick is one of the three pirates marooned at the end, who kneel and raise their hands in supplication to the departing ship.

There is more than one way of grouping the four fictions written and published between 1881 and 1889 by which Stevenson is best known: *Treasure Island*, *Kidnapped*, *Jekyll and Hyde*, and *The Master of Ballantrae*. All sport an unforgettable 'outlaw': Long John Silver, Alan Breck, Edward Hyde, and James Durie. These figures cast a magical spell, fascinating to the point of obsession the more conventional males, the boys who would be men and the men who would be boys, from whose perspective the story is told. And yet they are finely distinct. Mr Hyde and James Durie are much the most menacing, while Alan Breck is the sunniest, or least deeply troubling, a fiery, reckless but innocent Jacobite rebel, tinged with incipient pathos.

Kidnapped (1886) started life as a serial in the same magazine (*Young Folks*) as *Treasure Island*. Its protagonist David Balfour is an older boy, indeed a classic adolescent on the brink of manhood. As headlong youthful narrators David and Jim are as different as possible from the main ones of *Jekyll and Hyde* and *The Master*: the lawyer Utterson and the steward Mackellar, dry, buttoned-up, celibate professionals, whose tales are very much darker throughout, not least in their endings.

At one point David's path is crossed by a boatload of lamenting Scots emigrants bound for the New World. The real wounds and trauma of history ensure that there is no such benign enveloping dream as there was in *Treasure Island*. There is no question of saving a father. Wicked Uncle Ebenezer is squatting on David's paternal property, and nearly sends the lad to his death up a broken-off staircase, before having him kidnapped by Captain Hoseason and consigned to oblivion as a slave in the Carolinas. To escape and find his way back to the showdown with this usurping uncle David must deal with the Captain and his piratical men on the brig, one of whom kills in a drunken fit the young cabin boy Ransome (an *alter ego* for David as Dick had been for Jim Hawkins). The good dream of which David is the beneficiary involves a brave big brother, Alan Breck, with whose help he vanquishes his captors and crawls his way across Scotland, grazing the historical events surrounding the murder of the English king's factor, Colin Campbell or 'Red Fox', and risking his life in the process. David is brave and resourceful but less impulsive than Jim Hawkins, less lucky and more prone to despair, most notably when he is wrecked on the island of Earraid. His nightmares are deeper and more protracted than Jim's, especially in the long 'flight across the heather', where he wants to lie down and die. As Jim was saved by Long John, so David is saved by Alan Breck, but this is a deeper, more fraternal bond – a benign inverse to the murderous rivalry between the two Duries, or indeed between Jekyll and Hyde. As in

Scott, there is a political significance to the union of reckless Highlander and canny Lowlander, King James's man and King George's, and a pathos in our knowledge that it cannot last. There is also pathos to our knowledge that the boy's racing pulses will slow down when he claims his property and turns into a man. So at least the conventional story goes – the one that would have appealed to Stevenson's parents. *Kidnapped* was published in 1886, the year before his father died.

The novel ends inconclusively, like so many of Stevenson's fictions, longer and shorter.

> 'Well, well,' said the lawyer, when I had quite done, 'this is a great epic, a great Odyssey of yours. You must tell it, sir, in a sound Latinity when your scholarship is riper; or in English if you please, though for my part I prefer the stronger tongue.' (VI, 203)

Stevenson likes to invoke traditional models, like the ballad of the beggar returning to his birthright that David recalls in the penultimate chapter, 'I Come into My Kingdom'. There is a fine climactic scene in which Alan confronts Uncle Ebenezer with the force of 'the law' behind him (Mr Rankeillor and his clerk Torrance). Yet the novel ends with the wicked kinsman still in possession: 'It stood there, bare and great and smokeless, like a place not lived in.' David can see the peak of his uncle's nightcap in one of the top windows 'bobbing up and down and back and forward, like the head of a rabbit from a burrow' (222). Arrived in the big city yet still thinking of the Alan he has left behind, David confesses to 'a cold gnawing in my inside like a remorse for something wrong' (223). He is still adrift, at sea one might say, or yearning to be back there and out there, not settled safely inside.

The dreams of boyhood in *Treasure Island* and *Kidnapped* can be seen as good training for what has been called 'imperial romance', a genre typified by Rider Haggard's *King Solomon's Mines* (1885), Rudyard Kipling's *Kim* (1901), and the collected works of another Scot, John Buchan (1875–1940).[11] Stevenson's later fiction engages critically with the 'romance' of imperial experience, not only in the South Sea tales, but also in the proto-colonial contexts sketched in *The Master of Ballantrae*. But in any case Stevenson was too restless and experimental an artist to settle into a single style, form, or genre. And if anything were wanted as a sharp contrast to the expansive and breezy topographies of *Treasure Island* and *Kidnapped* it is the claustrophobic metropolitan fable of *Jekyll and Hyde* (1886).

Or to give it its accurate first title, *Strange Case of Dr Jekyll and Mr Hyde*. The lack of the definite article makes it sound like the cry of the news-vendors in the tale itself. Several of the episode headings – should we call them 'chapters'? – follow suit: 'Story of the Door', 'Incident of the Letter',

'Remarkable Incident of Dr Lanyon'. Nor are these sections numbered, thus denying a sense of order and progress. (This is also true of *The Master* and *The Ebb-Tide*.) It creates the impression that these narratives are a collection of 'incidents', like news items, little fragments of story from various sources, loosely bundled together. Here the third-person narration is focalised by the lawyer Mr Utterson, who conducts us to the first-person stories, the confessions of the two eminent doctors, Lanyon and Jekyll.

Is *Jekyll and Hyde* a 'novel' at all? Does it matter? Penguin Classics confidently calls it, along with 'The Beach of Falesá' and 'The Ebb-Tide', a 'short story'.[12] But Stevenson is testing such generic distinctions, just as in other respects he questions the categories by which we try to distinguish this from that, ethically, ethnically, Jekyll from Hyde, Durie from Durie, light from dark and white from black. Stevenson liked dynamite. He explodes the whole idea of fictional form and revels in the number of things you can call a story, a tale, a yarn, a romance, a 'panorama',[13] a fable. He worked for over twenty years on a collection of *Fables* published after his death – they include one of his most chilling pieces, 'The House of Eld' (V, 86–91). He was impatient with long novels and especially with 'realism' (a temporary aberration, not the French at their best); he deplored 'the insane pursuit of completion' ('A Note on Realism' (1883), XXVIII, 74). He felt surrounded, he said, by 'an art that is like mahogany and horse-hair furniture, solid, true, serious, and as dead as Caesar' (*L*, IV, 276). Looking back on 'My First Book' a few months before he died, he reflected: 'It is the length that kills ... I remember I used to look, in those days, upon every three-volume novel with a sort of veneration, as a feat – not possibly of literature – but at least of physical and moral endurance and the courage of Ajax' (II, xxix). It was absurd to expect 'art' to compete with 'life', Stevenson argued, politely dissenting from Henry James's 'The Art of Fiction' (1884). Art requires omission, selection, 'geometry'. James listened, and they became friends.[14]

Two volumes of Stevenson's tales boast their lineage from a favourite model: *New Arabian Nights* (2 vols., 1882) and *More New Arabian Nights* (1885), on which his wife Fanny collaborated. This latter is better known by its subtitle *The Dynamiter*. It is not the only tale that anticipates Joseph Conrad, in this case *The Secret Agent* (an association that caused the later writer discomfort).[15] One of Stevenson's first reviewers, Edward Purcell, shrewdly praised it:

> Mr Stevenson flushes a regular three-volume covey of incident, pursues it for a while ... and then gaily tosses it aside .... The 'Dynamiter' contains a whole library of possible novels. Its charm lies in this wanton profusion of a spendthrift whose resources seem inexhaustible.[16]

A whole library of possible novels: this would appeal to one of Stevenson's later admirers, the great Argentinian writer, Jorge Luis Borges.

'Make him [the reader] *think* the evil, make him think it for himself', recommended Henry James, of his own horror-story, 'The Turn of the Screw' (1898).[17] Stevenson's is an art of economy, ellipsis, of questions not asked, and *Jekyll and Hyde* is its apogee. What is Mr Richard Enfield up to, the well-known man about town, walking home at three o'clock in the morning from 'some place at the end of the world' (V, 3)? Why exactly are he and his kinsman, Mr Utterson, so devoted to each other? What is Sir Danvers Carew doing out in the middle of the night accosting young men? Just what are the 'irregularities' committed by the ultra-respectable Dr Henry Jekyll, M.D., D.C.L., LL.D., F.R.S., &c.? As for Mr Hyde, he is a figure for the unspeakable, something his name tells us is – impossibly – a hidden surface, at once concealed and unmissably visible, like the hide of an animal. And there is indeed a strong sense of regression in Hyde, something 'troglodytic', 'ape-like', atavistic, inextirpably creaturely, the obverse of the blithe child, the innocent primitive.

Amongst everything else, a prime model for the mutual dependency of Jekyll and Hyde is indeed that of father and son: 'Jekyll had more than a father's interest; Hyde had more than a son's indifference' (66). So writes the man who gives birth, as it were, to the Hyde in himself. Creator and creature: Stevenson's is a version of Dr Frankenstein and his monster for a post-Darwinian age. Mr Hyde is not just Dr Jekyll's personal production. He is the work of the 'patriarchy' that dominates the tale:[18] Mr Utterson the lawyer and Dr Lanyon, abetted by the man about town Richard Enfield, supported by Poole the butler and Guest the head clerk, not forgetting Inspector Newcomen of Scotland Yard. This is a community of childless men, who do not know joy or families or children – save for Jekyll and the distorted, deformed, malignant other he hides in himself and brings forth.

It is an indication of Stevenson's working methods and rhythms that he started *Kidnapped* and abandoned it in spring 1885, then picked it up again in January 1886 after completing *Jekyll and Hyde*. Even then, he had unfinished business with David Balfour and returned to the sequel known as *Catriona* (or *David Balfour* or, together, *The Adventures of David Balfour* – Stevenson's titles are often shifty, provisional). By the time it was published in 1893, Stevenson had long escaped to America and on into the Pacific, where he settled in Samoa and built his 'great house' at Vailima.

But for all the labour that went into it *Catriona* is not one of Stevenson's most vital creations,[19] and a truer successor to *Kidnapped* can be found in *The Master of Ballantrae* (1889). It continues the fable about Scottish identity begun in *Kidnapped*, focused in the amicable precarious bond between wild Highlander and circumspect Lowlander, precisely dated and confined to the year 1751. *The Master* draws on a more protracted phase of Scottish history, the long aftermath to the catastrophe of 1745. The ancient House of Durrisdeer is torn apart by the rivalry between two brothers, James (the Master) and Henry Durie, who have taken different sides in the Jacobite war. They have not, however, been moved to do so from any principle or belief; the family has just hedged its bets and tossed a coin. The Master wins and joins the rebels and so loses everything, at least officially, including his title. The Master is charismatic, unprincipled, ruthless, Satanic, 'all I know of the Devil', said Stevenson (*L*, VI, 86–7), while his younger brother Henry is conscientious, honourable, and sexless. This is another version of the relations between 'inlaw' and 'outlaw' that we met in Jim Hawkins and Long John Silver, or more pertinently David Balfour and Alan Breck, save that the two Duries are as consumed by fratricidal enmity as David and Alan were bound together by love, of some sort. Now there is real sex and money at stake: an heiress, kinswoman Alison, on whom the future of the House depends for its heirs and its solvency. There is no tottered House of Shaws to be repossessed; the House of Durrisdeer will be bled dry and ruined, hollowed out from inside, without prospect of redemption, political, economic, emotional, sexual.

The novel is subtitled 'A Winter's Tale'. Stevenson invokes the allure of traditional narratives, including comforting ones about the young challenging and superseding the old, coming through their rites of passage, a seasonal myth of death and renewal. So does Shakespeare, not least in *The Winter's Tale*, one of Stevenson's favourites. In *Weir of Hermiston* young Archie is associated with Perdita's anxious glance at youth's frailty ('a malady most incident to only sons', XVI, 21).[20] The tenderness Stevenson shows towards childhood and youth draws on his lack of much faith in the future. In *The Master* the hope of rejuvenation is cruelly deceptive: there will be no spring after winter. The brothers die together, thousands of miles from their ancestral home, in the frozen North American wilderness. Henry Durie succeeds to the title of Lord Durrisdeer and fathers a son and a daughter, but we know they will die childless and heirless. We know this from the main narrator, the steward Ephraim Mackellar.

Mackellar is a remarkable creation, as fine in his way as the loyal butler who narrates Kazuo Ishiguro's *The Remains of the Day* (1989). Mackellar is more consciously artful, indeed he is a 'master of arts' from the University to rival the arts of the Master. Yet over and above Mackellar's head the novel advertises its literariness. The setting is borrowed from Scott's *Redgauntlet*, and inspiration for the Master drawn from Captain Marryat's *The Phantom Ship*. There are contributions from Stevenson's previous writing, including some pirates (themselves derived from *The General History of Pirates* (1724), possibly by Defoe), and a cameo appearance by Alan Breck. There are references to grand narrative models such as Virgil's *Aeneid*, the epic of migration and empire. Old Lord Durrisdeer and his son James are great readers, and so perhaps is Mackellar. There are other high cultural references, to Shakespeare, Milton, Lovelace, and others. But there are also popular lyrics and ballads, Scots and Irish, traditional ones such as 'Shule Aroon' and the ballad of the 'Twa Corbies', or in the case of 'Wandering Willie' a version by Stevenson himself (better than Burns, he boasted).

The novel takes a sharp interest in questions of authenticity and masquerade. If not a whole library of possible novels, it provides a spectrum of possible models and angles, a vertiginous sense of fractured perspectives. None more so than on the voyage across the Atlantic when the Master and Mackellar become most intimate. One reads Richardson's *Clarissa*, the other the Bible. The Master tells a menacing tale that sounds like Poe or Hawthorne, and Mackellar reacts by trying to kill him. He tries to break the hold the Master has over him, a spell cast not just by the tale but the way he has told it, swaying up and down to the rhythm of the ship, and sitting back now in a graceful posture, 'fítting the swíng of the shíp with an éxquisite bálance' (X, 171) – an exquisite dactylic pentameter. No wonder Mackellar is seduced, and reduced to violence. He too, like his master Henry Durie, tries to rival the Master, and fails. Mackellar writes; the Master speaks, sings, performs. Here we touch one of Stevenson's great subjects: the intricate relations between the written word and the voice (spoken, sung, whispered, or 'soothed', to use a good Scots word). On the one hand there is the glamour of presence and utterance – unstable, ephemeral, magical. On the other is the enduring but orphaned power of the written word, its mastery and control – the only means, it seems, by which the Duries will endure. Hence the significance of the double gravestones at the end, ordered and inscribed by Mackellar, with their enigmatic confession that he has served two masters, only one of them 'A MASTER OF THE ARTS AND GRACES' (X, 233)

Stevenson's sudden death left several writing projects incomplete, most notably the fragment that has come to be known as *Weir of Hermiston*. Admirers have hailed it as the consummation of Stevenson's artistry, and the confrontation between the ferocious Justice-Clerk, Lord Hermiston, and his mutinous son, Archie Weir, looks set to be the climactic staging of the troubled filial relation. It is tantalising, magnificent as far as it goes, certainly in its portrayal of the father, 'this adamantine Adam', as his son thinks of him, and the rendition of his virulent Scots: 'No son of mine shall be speldering in the glaur with any dirty raibble' (XVI, 10); 'Ye daft auld wife! ... A bonny figure I would be, palmering about in bauchles!' (13); 'Na, there's no room for splairgers under the fower quarters of John Calvin' (34). It is harder to be confident about the handling of young Archie's dealings with women, the childless but emotionally vibrant Kirstie, a surrogate mother, and the young namesake about to supplant her.

If *Weir* promised to be the culmination of a traditional nineteenth-century tale of fathers and sons, then Stevenson's Pacific writings push into new territory, both in their matter and style. He had always been attracted to boundaries and margins, but *The Wrecker* suggests the new form they were taking in the wharves and beaches, the flotsam and jetsam, human and otherwise, of what we now think of as the Pacific rim. He was particularly drawn to the 'beachcomber', that distant dissolute down-at-heels kinsman of the leisured urban *flâneur*. Or of the poet, Loudon Dodd notes, as he contemplates the yarn-spinners in the South Sea Club at the back of a San Francisco bar: 'All had indeed some touch of the poetic, for the beach-comber, when not a mere ruffian, is the poor relation of the artist' (XII, 123). Though *The Wrecker* is far less well-finished a work than the short masterpieces of these years, 'The Beach of Falesá' (1892) and *The Ebb-Tide* (1894), Stevenson's account of its ambitions points to a new kind of work: 'The tone of the age, its movement, the mingling of races and classes in the dollar hunt, the fiery and not quite romantic struggle for existence with its changing trades and scenery' (XII, 405).

In *The Ebb-Tide* the not quite romantic struggle for existence has sunk to a new low. The title ironically inverts the lines recalled by its epigraph: 'There is a tide in the affairs of men.' (Shakespeare's Brutus goes on – 'Which, taken at the flood, leads on to fortune.')[21] One of a trio of outcasts who have washed up on a Pacific beach, Robert Herrick is down and out en route to oblivion. At the end of his tether, he has taken up with a disgraced American sea-captain and a sparky, shameless Cockney clerk. In the first part, entitled 'The Trio', they get hold of a ship full of champagne which they aim to sell off at life-saving profit. But drink and incompetence lead them to an island in the middle of nowhere, run by the formidable figure who makes good the novel's subtitle, 'A Trio & Quartette' [*sic*]. Quite the match for Lord Hermiston, Attwater is an invincible patriarch in whom Stevenson combines the commercial and theological motives dominating Western interests in the Pacific. Attwater's dealings in pearls and the Bible are backed by a gun. He is authority and certitude incarnate, as almighty as Herrick is feckless. No hope of slaying this father. Attwater ends in triumph, having easily cowed the trio who challenge him, though the tale concludes on the equivocal prospect of release, for Herrick at least.

Herrick's mind is stuffed with scraps of literary and musical high culture, all of which are as useless as the 'meaningless gibberish' of the music-hall song the Cockney remembers: 'Hikey, pikey, crikey, fikey, chillinga-wallaba dory' (XIV, 83). The tattered Virgil Herrick carries round with him is only good for forging a bond with Attwater, who names his beautiful island after a line from the *Aeneid*, 'nemorosa Zacynthos' (87).[22] They are Oxbridge men. But this is all too romantic, this romanising of the Pacific, in which Herrick finds himself complicit. He needs a new language, or idiom, as does his author. Stevenson cursed and swore with the pains he took over *The Ebb-Tide*, its 'forced, violent, alembicated style' (*L*, VIII, 70); he had found a new, old mentor in Flaubert. Yet when it was done he was pleased with the result, 'as I see I *can* work in that constipated, mosaic manner, which is what I have to do now with *Weir of Hermiston*' (*L*, VIII, 250). The intricate texture of its unobtrusive rhythms is as satisfying as the visual 'mosaic' had seemed, in the making, laborious:

> The captain drummed with his thick hands on the board in front of him; he looked steadily in Herrick's face, and Herrick as steadily looked upon the table and the pattering fingers; there was a gentle oscillation of the anchored ship, and a big patch of sunlight travelled to and fro between the one and the other. (83)

'There have been – I think – for men of letters few deaths more romantically right', Henry James daringly wrote to Stevenson's widow, in December 1894 (*HJ & RLS*, 249). (One needs to read the whole letter.) Of the other figures in this volume only the Brontës have inspired such a romantic interest in the writer's life and a comparable curiosity about what was still to come. Given his mistrust of endings and aversion to completeness, let alone his physical frailty, it is astonishing that Stevenson produced as much as he did. His writing has certainly travelled. It says a good deal about the nature of his genius that he has been admired by masters of twentieth-century fiction well beyond the traditions of the English novel, including Borges, Nabokov, and the young Italo Calvino, whose first novel draws on *Treasure Island* and whose second rewrites *Jekyll and Hyde*.[23]

NOTE ON EDITIONS

Even before his death in 1894 Stevenson's works were being collected by his friend Sidney Colvin and published in the Edinburgh Edition, 28 vols. (1894–8), the basis for subsequent collected editions, including the Tusitala Edition, 35 vols. (1923–4). A new complete edition is currently under way, to be published by Edinburgh University Press under the general editorship of Stephen Arata, Richard Dury, and Penny Fielding. The most popular novels and tales are widely available in paperback editions by Penguin, Oxford World's Classics, and others.

NOTES

1 Rosaline Masson (ed.), *I Can Remember Robert Louis Stevenson* (Edinburgh and London: W. R. Chambers Ltd, 1922), p. 128.
2 Janet Adam Smith (ed.), *Henry James and Robert Louis Stevenson: A Record of Friendship and Criticism* (London: Rupert Hart-Davis, 1948), p. 255. Hereafter *HJ & RLS*.
3 For a useful modern collection see *Stevenson's Scottish Stories and Essays*, ed. Kenneth Gelder (Edinburgh: Edinburgh University Press, 1989).
4 See in particular Alan Sandison, *Robert Louis Stevenson and the Appearance of Modernism* (Basingstoke: Macmillan, 1996).
5 All references to Stevenson's writings are to the Tusitala Edition, 35 vols. (London: Heinemann, 1923–4), by volume and page number. Dates given here for tales and novels are those of first publication in volume form; many of Stevenson's writings were first issued serially in periodical magazines (see Roger Swearingen, *The Prose Writings of Robert Louis Stevenson: A Guide* (London and Basingstoke: Macmillan, 1980)).
6 *The Letters of Robert Louis Stevenson*, ed. B. A. Booth and E. Mehew, 8 vols. (New Haven and London: Yale University Press, 1994–5), V, pp. 220–1. Hereafter *L*.
7 See Cairns Craig, 'Scotland and Hybridity', in Gerard Carruthers, David Goldie, and Alastair Renfrew (eds.), *Beyond Scotland: New Contexts for Twentieth-Century Scottish Literature* (Amsterdam: Rodopi, 2004), pp. 229–53.
8 Paul Maixner (ed.), *Robert Louis Stevenson: The Critical Heritage* (London: Routledge & Kegan Paul, 1981), pp. 488–94. Hereafter *CH*.
9 *HJ & RLS*, p. 131.
10 *Boyhood: Scenes from Provincial Life* (London: Secker & Warburg, 1997), p. 46.
11 See for example Wendy R. Katz, *Rider Haggard and the Fiction of Empire: A Critical Study of British Imperial Fiction* (Cambridge: Cambridge University Press, 1987), and Susan Jones, 'Into the Twentieth Century: Imperial Romance from Haggard to Buchan', in Corinne Saunders (ed.), *A Companion to Romance* (Oxford: Blackwell, 2004), pp. 406–23.
12 *Dr Jekyll and Mr Hyde, and Other Stories*, ed. Jenni Calder (Harmondsworth: Penguin Books, 1979).
13 He described *The Wrecker* to its dedicatee, W. H. Low, as 'less a romance than a panorama' (XII, 404).
14 James's 'The Art of Fiction' and Stevenson's 'A Humble Remonstrance' are reprinted in *HJ & RLS* and elsewhere. For a useful collection of Stevenson's essays on writing, see Glenda Norquay (ed.), *R. L. Stevenson on Fiction: An Anthology of Literary and Critical Essays* (Edinburgh: Edinburgh University Press, 1999).
15 See Sandison, *Stevenson and Modernism*, pp. 117–41.
16 *CH*, p. 196.
17 Preface to 'The Turn of the Screw', in *Literary Criticism: French Writers, Other European Writers and the Prefaces to the New York Edition*, ed. Leon Edel with the assistance of Mark Wilson (Cambridge: Cambridge University Press, 1984), p. 1188.

18 See William Veeder's 'Children of the Night: Stevenson and Patriarchy', in William Veeder and Gordon Hirsch (eds.), *Dr Jekyll and Mr Hyde after One Hundred Years* (Chicago and London: University of Chicago Press, 1988), pp. 107–60.

19 Barry Menikoff makes the case for reading the two novels as a serious study of Scottish history in *Narrating Scotland: The Imagination of Robert Louis Stevenson* (Columbia, SC: University of South Carolina Press, 2005).

20 Perdita is meditating on the 'flowers o'th' spring', including 'pale primroses, / That die unmarried ere they can behold / Bright Phoebus in his strength – a malady – / Most incident to maids' (*The Winter's Tale*, ed. Stephen Orgel (Oxford: Oxford University Press, 1996), 4.4.122–5).

21 *Julius Caesar*, ed. Arthur Humphreys (Oxford: Oxford University Press, 1984), 4.2.268–9.

22 Virgil, *Aeneid*, II, 270.

23 *Il sentiero dei nidi di ragno* (1947, *The Path to the Spiders' Nests*), and *Il visconte dimezzato* (1952, *The Cloven Viscount*). See Ann Lawson Lucas, 'The Pirate Chief in Salgari, Stevenson, and Calvino', in Richard Ambrosini and Richard Dury (eds.), *Robert Louis Stevenson: Writer of Boundaries* (Madison and London: University of Wisconsin Press, 2006), pp. 344–7.

FURTHER READING

Ambrosini, Richard, and Richard Dury (eds.), *Robert Louis Stevenson: Writer of Boundaries*, Madison and London, University of Wisconsin Press, 2006

Calder, Jenni (ed.), *Stevenson and Victorian Scotland*, Edinburgh, Edinburgh University Press, 1981

Colley, Ann C., *Robert Louis Stevenson and the Colonial Imagination*, Aldershot, Ashgate, 2004

Harman, Claire, *Myself and the Other Fellow: A Life of Robert Louis Stevenson*, New York and London, HarperCollins, 2005

Jones, William B., Jr (ed.), *Robert Louis Stevenson Reconsidered: New Critical Perspectives*, Jefferson, NC and London, McFarland, 2003

Maixner, Paul (ed.), *Robert Louis Stevenson: The Critical Heritage*, London, Routledge & Kegan Paul, 1981

McLynn, Frank, *Robert Louis Stevenson: A Biography*, London, Pimlico, 1993

Menikoff, Barry, *Robert Louis Stevenson and 'The Beach of Falesá': A Study in Victorian Publishing*, Stanford, Stanford University Press, 1984

Reid, Julia, *Robert Louis Stevenson, Science and the Fin de Siècle*, Basingstoke, Palgrave Macmillan, 2006

Sandison, Alan, *Robert Louis Stevenson and the Appearance of Modernism*, Basingstoke, Macmillan, 1996

Smith, Vanessa, *Literary Culture and the Pacific*, Cambridge, Cambridge University Press, 1998

Swearingen, Roger, *The Prose Writings of Robert Louis Stevenson: A Guide*, London and Basingstoke, Macmillan, 1980

Veeder, William, and Gordon Hirsch (eds.), *Dr Jekyll and Mr Hyde after One Hundred Years*, Chicago and London, University of Chicago Press, 1988

17

MICHIEL HEYNS

Henry James

Henry James (1843–1916) was, like Joseph Conrad, an English novelist by choice and naturalisation rather than by birth. Born in New York, he settled in England in December 1876 and became a British citizen in 1915, shortly before his death. But if James seemed to turn his back on his native America, he never ceased to keep an analytical eye on it. From his first acknowledged novel, *Roderick Hudson* (1875) – an earlier novel, *Watch and Ward*, was disowned[1] – to his last completed novel, *The Golden Bowl* (1904), James sustained a complex dialogue between America and Europe, renegotiating repeatedly a relation capable of apparently infinite variation.

Perhaps no major novelist is more prone to reinterpretation than Henry James: his works are constantly being mined for meanings buried or assumed to be buried under their apparently placid surfaces. This may be because the relatively overt moral purpose as manifested variously in, for instance, the novels of Austen, Gaskell, Dickens, Eliot, and Hardy, shades off, in James, into something less determinate, more negotiable. Combining uniquely the influence of his compatriot Nathaniel Hawthorne and the tradition of English realism with the example of such French writers as Balzac, Flaubert, and Maupassant, James can now be seen as an early modernist in his experimentation with his chosen form, favouring a partial perspective rather than omniscience as narrative medium, and generating implications and suggestions rather than packaged meanings.

Modern criticism tends to assume the right to supplement authorial reticence with its own speculations and extrapolations. In the case of James, in particular, many 'new readings' have undertaken to reveal unspoken tensions and anxieties in the fiction, producing interpretations that would find little warrant in any statement of James's own as to his intentions – and it is worth noting that in the exhaustive Prefaces that he wrote for the revised New York Edition of the Novels and Tales (1907–9), James was unusually explicit in this regard.

But if much of what is taken for meaning in new readings of James may not have, indeed *could* not have, presented itself in just this form and just this language to James, such readings, without necessarily invalidating older ones, do supplement them, fill in the outlines, shift the emphasis, and reinforce our sense of why James is still worth reading. In what follows I advance my own readings, taking tacit account of an evolving critical tradition; but readers would be well advised to follow up some of the studies listed under 'Further Reading' for alternative takes on these richly controversial texts.

One reason for the proliferation of readings of James may be that he eschewed, temperamentally and intellectually, the repose of final certainty. His fiction is characteristically driven by the bewilderment of his central characters, as he recognised in his Preface to *The Princess Casamassima*: 'It seems probable that if we were never bewildered there would never be a story to tell about us' (V, ix).[2] Of course, the relative ignorance and ensuing enlightenment of the protagonist does not differ essentially from the classic trajectory of the realist plot: from Elizabeth Bennet having to revise her opinion of Mr Darcy in Austen's *Pride and Prejudice* to Kurtz muttering 'The horror! The horror!' in Conrad's 'Heart of Darkness', there is some continuity of pattern, of ignorance or blindness followed by elucidation. What distinguishes James from most of his predecessors is the more tentative, partial, even elusive nature of such enlightenment as his characters achieve. Some insight they are generally vouchsafed, as part of what James called, in the Preface to *The Ambassadors*, 'the process of vision' (XXI, vi). Such insight, however, rarely brings about the closure that tradition has accustomed us to expect; hence the famously and to some readers frustratingly indeterminate nature of so many of James's endings.

The early novels (1875–1881)

The best introduction to James remains his first acknowledged novel, *Roderick Hudson* (1875). The young artist, torn between dedication to his craft and infatuation with the beautiful Christina Light, initiates James's lifelong weighing up of the rival claims of art and life. The artist, as exceptional creature, may claim exemption from the strictures of conventional morality; and yet, in order to create, he needs stability, application, and abstemiousness, and may have to forgo the pleasures of sensual and social living. Against Roderick, the irresistible but irresponsible artist, is set Sam Singleton, 'the little noiseless worker' (I, 109), humbly admiring of Roderick (who hardly notices him). Singleton, by 'patient industry' develops his meagre talent into something 'incontestable' (I, 108); Roderick squanders his lavish talents in an infatuation with Christina. Inspiration wanes as passion waxes, and Roderick dies, romantically but pointlessly, in an Alpine storm.

Read like this, *Roderick Hudson* is a tragically abbreviated *Künstlerroman*, tracing not so much the development of an artist as his decline. But James complicates the matter both technically and thematically by telling Roderick's story largely through the observer-participant Rowland Mallet, his would-be benefactor. The use of Mallet as controlling consciousness inaugurated James's cherished though not inveterate reliance on a limited point of view, whereby the 'action' of the novel is not to be distinguished from the telling of it, in a perfect fusion of technique with theme: the means of representing the story is itself of the essence of the drama.

Roderick Hudson also takes James's first American to Europe. In his beguilement and eventual defeat, his infatuation and disillusionment, Roderick is the harbinger of a procession of Americans discovering, like the young James himself, the beauties of the Old World, there to be charmed and baffled in about equal measure (those who are too wadded with complacency to be charmed, like Sarah Pocock in *The Ambassadors*, are also immune to bafflement).

Roderick Hudson prefigures later novels also in its central relationship, that between Rowland Mallet and Roderick. Current critical trends discern something more than disinterested patronage in Rowland's concern for Roderick – not, necessarily, overt sexual desire, but an erotic charge animating this relationship as no other in the novel. Roderick Hudson's infatuation with Christina drives the plot; but the more poignant love story is Mallet's equally unrequited enthralment to Roderick.[3] As he waits by the body of his dead friend, Mallet recognises that for two years he has lived vicariously through and for Roderick: 'Now that it was all over Rowland understood how up to the brim, for two years, his personal world had been filled. It looked to him at present as void and blank and sinister as a theatre bankrupt and closed' (I. 526).

In James there are ever those who live life and those who observe it; and if his art yearns to imply that the observer may live as intensely as those others, it never quite escapes the sense that a life vicariously lived must rely upon the performance of somebody else more gifted in the art of living, as poor Mallet's image of the bankrupt theatre implies. This, too, is a theme on which James was to write numerous variations, to culminate in *The Ambassadors* and *The Wings of the Dove*.

In *The American* (1877), James's first novel to be set in Paris, the 'international' aspect moves closer to the thematic centre of the novel; indeed, Old World deviousness drives the plot as it impels Christopher Newman to seek revenge for the iniquities of the aristocratic de Bellegardes. Like

Roderick Hudson, *The American* prefigures some of James's mature concerns, but whereas *Roderick* is interesting in its own right, *The American* is notable mainly for what it anticipates in later and better novels. Christopher Newman is an odd choice of hero, being signally lacking in that 'finer grain' that James elsewhere sees as a precondition of his interest. (*The Finer Grain* (1910) was the title of James's last volume of tales.) Newman is successful, driven, direct, and supremely confident of the power of his money. In this he is a precursor of Caspar Goodwood, that dogged suitor of Isabel Archer's, and of Adam Verver, the enigmatic plutocrat in *The Golden Bowl*. In his determined pursuit of Claire de Cintré, if not in his wealth, Newman also anticipates that other square-jawed American, Basil Ransom of *The Bostonians*; but where the comparatively uninteresting Ransom is set against the complex, intriguing Olive Chancellor, Newman has only the highly conventional de Bellegardes to contend with – and a heroine whom James himself came to pronounce, in his Preface, 'a light plank' (II, xxii).

If in *The American* intercontinental misunderstanding produces high melodrama, in *The Europeans*, the superb little novel that followed in 1878, it generates sharp but gentle comedy. Instead of discord and mistrust, here there is an enriching interchange, even in the midst of mutual incomprehension. Felix, the irrepressible Bohemian, revels as much in Gertrude Wentworth's earnestness as she delights in his gaiety; and the Europeans are almost as shocked by the freedom of association given to American youth as the Americans are by the irregularity of the Baroness's marital situation and the flightiness of her brother. If old Mr Wentworth is as perplexed as he is dismayed by the foreign ways of his visitors, the worldly-wise Robert Acton and his pert sister Lizzie, as well as Clifford, the puppyish young Wentworth scion, take the European invasion very much in their free New England stride.

The ending, with Felix and Gertrude, Mr Brand and Charlotte, Clifford and Lizzie all 'charmingly' paired off in the kind of multiple marriage that comedy delights in, is exceedingly rare in James. More in keeping with his characteristic tenor is the unresolved relationship between the Baroness and Robert Acton. It is never quite clear whether Acton rejects Eugenia or vice versa: unspoken meanings are exchanged, with crucial but unacknowledged effect. Attracted to Eugenia and yet perturbed by her want of rectitude, Acton hesitates; and Eugenia, also attracted to him and yet insulted by his distrust, withdraws, asking herself 'Was she to have gained nothing?'[4] It is a question Madame Merle is to ask herself at the end of *The Portrait of a Lady*, and to mark that is to note also that, though Eugenia's machinations are as nothing to Madame Merle's, nevertheless, in her James touches on darker matters than in the rest of this scintillating tale.

James did not include *The Europeans* in the New York Edition, perhaps judging it too slight a thing. *Washington Square* (1880) was also given the cold shoulder by late James, but it is an exquisite little tale, adroitly combining the gently comical with the poignant. James may have judged his central character, Catherine Sloper, too dim to hold the reader's interest: he maintained, in his Preface to *The Princess Casamassima*, that 'We care, our curiosity and our sympathy care, comparatively little for what happens to the stupid, the coarse and the blind' (V, vii–viii). Whereas it would be harsh to call poor Catherine coarse and blind, she is not intellectually gifted. Her father, indeed, sees her as stupid; and whereas Dr Sloper is in his way more coarse and blind than Catherine, he does have a sharp intellect, which he exercises at his daughter's expense: 'You would have surprised him', the narrator tells us, 'if you had told him so, but it is a literal fact that he almost never addressed his daughter save in the ironical form.'[5] Catherine, with her unfortunately sumptuous taste in dress and her sweet trustfulness in the face of manifest duplicity, is an easy target for irony. But beneath the upholstered front beats a sentient heart; if it at first leads Catherine horribly astray, it eventually enables her to recognise the pain her father inflicts on her as a form of contempt, and 'something that there was of dignity in Catherine resented it'.[6]

If, as I have noted, many of James's protagonists are perplexed in the face of the contending claims of existence, they are often surrounded (not always helpfully) by remarkably clear-sighted, goal-directed pragmatists: Basil Ransom in *The Bostonians*, Paul Muniment in *The Princess Casamassima*, Mrs Gereth in *The Spoils of Poynton*, Kate Croy in *The Wings of the Dove*, Adam Verver in *The Golden Bowl*. Dr Sloper belongs with these: acute, articulate, analytical, and utterly assured of his own rightness. He possesses, like many of these, an admirable 'lucidity' (James's word for this hard clarity of insight), lacking only a certain humanity that would subordinate his judgement to his heart.

Dr Sloper is, of course, right in believing Morris Townsend to be a fortune-hunter; but he is wrong about Catherine. She has a simple dignity that outbraves her father's contempt, her Aunt Penniman's heartlessly prurient machinations, and Townsend's callous opportunism. In a tale in which nobody achieves what he or she wanted, Catherine finally attains the clarity of mind to make two choices: she refuses to give her father the assurance that she will not marry Townsend, and she refuses Townsend when he reappears. In neither case is Catherine's decision registered as a triumph; but in both cases the dignity is all on her side.

If *The Portrait of a Lady* (1881) harbours, in Madame Merle, one of the most ruthlessly clear-sighted of James's characters, it also contains, in Isabel

Archer, one of the most beguiled. Isabel's misfortune, indeed, is that she fancies herself enlightened and independent, whereas in truth she is for the first half of the novel manipulated, albeit in some instances with the best of intentions, by those she has chosen to trust: Mrs Touchett, in bringing her to Europe; Ralph Touchett, in asking his father to leave her a fortune; and Madame Merle in recommending her to Gilbert Osmond.

But mainly Isabel is misled by her own notions. She turns down the offers of marriage of Caspar Goodwood and Lord Warburton because she fears they will deprive her of her freedom, only to marry Gilbert Osmond, who values her mainly as a decorative adjunct to publish to the world his superiority. But though Isabel is less free than she assumes, she accepts responsibility for her choice and its consequences: 'One ought to choose something very deliberately, and be faithful to that', she says to Osmond in the early days of their courtship (III, 381); and if there is a ghastly dramatic irony here at the expense of her naïve presumption, it is also her distinction, or perversity, to remain faithful to her youthful notions even when they prove to be based on error and deception.

Through Isabel James explores the connection between the aesthetic and the moral that informs much of his fiction. 'Don't you remember my telling you that one ought to make one's life a work of art?' Osmond asks Isabel during their courtship. 'You looked rather shocked at first; but then I told you that it was exactly what you seemed to me to be trying to do with your own' (IV, 15).

Osmond may well be right, but the novel develops a distinction between his notion of life as a work of art and Isabel's. The two notions have something in common, hence Osmond's appeal for Isabel: both strive to give their lives a pleasing appearance. But to Osmond this is purely a matter of making an impression on the world, as Ralph Touchett comes to see: 'under the guise of caring only for intrinsic values Osmond lived exclusively for the world' (IV, 144). Isabel, on the other hand, cares that the appearance should reflect a reality: 'Her life should always be in harmony with the most pleasing impression she should produce; she would be what she appeared, and she would appear what she was' (III, 69).

This aspiration regulates Isabel's conduct to the end of the novel, but it is worth asking whether she succeeds in it. Her concept of morality is a matter of harmony and appearance as much as of content, with no very clear distinction between the two. In this lies her weakness in dealing with Osmond: he can appeal to her in the name of values she to an extent shares. When she tells him that she wants to go to Ralph's deathbed, he counters with an appeal couched in terms he knows she will find cogent: 'Because I think we should accept the consequences of our actions, and what I value most in life is the honour of a thing!' Isabel is, as Osmond calculated, paralysed by his words, for 'they represented something transcendent and absolute, like the sign of the cross or the flag of one's country' (IV, 356).

Isabel's return to Osmond at the end of the novel needs to be seen in the light of her youthful 'unquenchable desire to think well of herself' (III, 68). For if she were to leave Osmond, she would be guilty in her own eyes of having repudiated 'the most serious act – the single sacred act – of her life' (IV, 246). For Isabel, consistency is a value in itself: having chosen freely, as she thinks, she has to abide by that choice, even as embodied in an obnoxious husband. The 'traditionary sanctities and decencies' (IV, 245) of marriage transcend the merely incidental fact of an individual's unhappiness within a particular marriage. It is not a doctrine that appeals to an age and culture in which divorce is a common remedy for a common mistake; but it is difficult to imagine Isabel doing anything other. If to us her decisions seem riddled with contradictions, that is because, in trying to live her life as a work of art, she is attempting the impossible: it is James's constant implication that art and life are driven by different dynamics and ruled by different values. In art, the appearance is the reality; in life the two do not necessarily coincide. Nobly consistent or perversely obdurate, Isabel is a victim as much of her own high-mindedness as of the machinations of Madame Merle and Gilbert Osmond.

The middle years (1886–1890)

Another masterpiece slighted by the late James was *The Bostonians* (1886).[7] Something of a rarity in the Jamesian *œuvre* in being exclusively set in America, it is, with *The Princess Casamassima*, James's most political novel. But the tug-of-war between Olive Chancellor and Basil Ransom for the appealing, passive Verena Tarrrant is more than a political difference: it is a fierce sexual rivalry. It is also, as regards Verena, part of a complex of abusive relationships: 'rescued' (in actual fact *bought*) from her exploitative parents and the squalid ambition of the newspaperman Matthias Pardon by the high-minded Olive Chancellor, Verena becomes the willing but progressively disenchanted acolyte–protégée–possession of her 'benefactor', until she is once again 'rescued' by the militantly chauvinist Basil Ransom. Whereas Ransom is more clear-sighted about his own motives than Olive, they both find sanction for their possessiveness in their political principles. Basil indeed feels no need of a sanction: the heterosexual imperative need not clothe itself in ideological garb.

Verena is the least realised of the major characters; but that is part of her significance, that she is a blank page upon which various people try to sign their names, and to whom she represents such different things: Olive, Ransom, her parents, Matthias Pardon, the New York socialite Mrs Burrage and her son, the great public. It is a theme that James explored in *The Portrait* and was to return to in *The Tragic Muse* and *The Wings of the Dove*: what one person *represents* to somebody else as opposed to what, if anything, that person might be taken to *be* in herself.

The distinction of *The Bostonians* lies in its mordant analysis of the springs of political action, and in its wonderful portrait of Olive Chancellor: self-deluded as only a thoroughly humourless idealist can be, tortured as only a very conscientious person can be, her tenderness as implacable as her hatred, in her defeat she is yet more heroic that Ransom in his triumph. He is a romance hero claiming the girl; she is a tragic heroine embracing at last the opportunity to sacrifice herself to a cause.

A somewhat similar juxtaposition of public and private marks James's next novel, *The Princess Casamassima* (also published in 1886). James thought more highly of it than of its predecessor, a judgement that by and large posterity has not shared. However brilliantly James imagined the impoverished world of the London slums and the murky underworld of anarchist plotting, it is difficult to give it the same credence as to his rendering of a milieu more familiar to him.

Paris features significantly in *The Princess* and it appears even more prominently in James's next novel, *The Tragic Muse* (1890), as the site of a conception of art that James found lacking in England. Indeed, this novel about the artist's life, or about the conflict between art and life, suffers from being too obviously 'about' something. This could be because at this stage of his career James was seriously contemplating writing for the stage, and in this novel gives himself scope to expatiate on the subject of the theatre (he was not to publish another full-length novel till 1897).

The story is lively, the dialogue almost un-Jamesian in its directness, the minor characters vivid and often amusing – in particular Gabriel Nash, who floats in and out of the story, an aesthete with apparently no other identity or profession. But with the exception of the extraordinary Miriam Rooth, the central characters, distinguishable mainly by their places in the 'debate', do not seem to interest James as individual consciousnesses. If we care less than James does about the rival claims of life and art, the novel loses much of its point – and struggles to justify its inordinate length.[8]

Later James (1896–1901)

After the failure of his play *Guy Domville* in London in 1895, James abandoned the long-cherished ideal of writing for the theatre, and applied something of the techniques of playwriting to his novels; indeed, he adapted a project for a play into a novel, *The Other House* (1896), which in its convoluted plotting and implausible denouement goes some way towards explaining why James had so little success on stage.[9] The three 'London' novels that followed, *The Spoils of Poynton* (1897), *What Maisie Knew* (1897), and *The Awkward Age* (1899) (interspersed with the very successful tale 'The Turn of the Screw' in 1898), all concern themselves much more plausibly with the upper-middle-class society that James by now knew intimately – and from which he distanced himself by moving in 1897 to Lamb House, Rye. Witty and acerbic, these novels evince a growing disenchantment (though also an abiding fascination) with drawing-room society, which James was finally, in *The Wings of the Dove*, to anatomise most devastatingly. Often seen as a social conservative because of his veneration for the forms of social intercourse, James was yet not beguiled by the polished surfaces he rendered so well: underlying them, he finds rapacity, exploitation, and betrayal.

In *The Spoils of Poynton*, admittedly, drawing-rooms are mainly settings for furniture. Mrs Gereth cares for 'things' more than for human beings: the 'Spoils' of the title are in fact the beautiful objects she and her late husband spent a lifetime collecting. If, in this, she harks back to Gilbert Osmond and anticipates Adam Verver, she is distinguished from the sterility of the former and the acquisitiveness of the latter by the fact that she is animated not by 'the crude love of possession' but by 'the need to be faithful to a trust and loyal to an idea' (X, 46).

Fleda Vetch, her protégée or perhaps her captive (Mrs Gereth also recalls Olive Chancellor and other coercive 'benefactors'), cherishes, like the Jamesian heroine she is, what to a more pragmatic age seems a perversely high standard. She is in love with Owen, Mrs Gereth's sweetly dim son, and more than suspects that he may be regretting his engagement to the awful Mona Brigstock. He tells her that Mona 'won't have' him if the spoils, which Mrs Gereth has clandestinely removed from Poynton, are not returned: Fleda can thus, simply by making this known to Mrs Gereth, prevent their return, leaving Owen free to marry Fleda, and Mrs Gereth in possession of both Poynton and the spoils. But Fleda will not benefit by playing a double role, and cannot lend herself to a scheme that would bring her a compromised happiness.

Her high moral tone, however, involves some self-blinding: she does not want Owen on morally dubious grounds, but she does want Owen. What she in fact wants is a clear conscience *and* the man, and when she seems likely to lose the man, she abandons the moral high ground, but too late to gain the man. A terrible consistency is enforced when Poynton burns to the ground just before Fleda can retrieve from it the one token of Owen's affection that he has offered her, leaving her only 'the raw bitterness of a hope that she might never again in life have to give up so much at such short notice' (X, 265). The drawing-room comedy modulates, as often in James, into a bleak vision of loss and devastation.

What Maisie Knew, also published in 1897, is partly a comedy of bad manners, the atrocious Beale and Ada Farange vying to outdo each other in selfishness and self-indulgence. As the offspring of such a union, Maisie should have been doomed to delinquency or worse; but for James the challenge was to show how 'not less than a chance of misery and of a degraded state, the chance of happiness and of an improved state might be here involved for the child' (XI, vi).

As the title signals, the novel is centred on the question of knowledge, always in James a potent theme. The question of what Maisie knows interests James as a way of exploring the nature of knowledge when stripped of the linguistic categories we have devised as guides to understanding. Maisie is surrounded by adults lying, cheating, committing adultery; but because she does not possess these categories of conduct, what her governess Mrs Wix calls 'a moral sense', she interprets actions in terms of their human consequences – usually but not exclusively their effect on her. James does not sentimentalise childhood – Maisie is willing, if need be, to sacrifice Mrs Wix in order to retain Sir Claude, the lover of her father's ex-wife – but he does convey through Maisie a saving imperviousness to the intrigue and manipulation surrounding her. As funny as it is devastating, *What Maisie Knew* is an unlikely success: the mature James undertaking to interpret for us the mind of a young girl.

In *The Awkward Age* London is more than a location: it is a centre of value and negotiation, more specifically of upper-middle-class society, in whose drawing-rooms the action almost exclusively takes place. The elderly visitor from Suffolk, Mr Longdon, is implicitly and at times explicitly used to comment on London's difference not only from remote Suffolk, but from the London of his youth.

If we are never sure, in *What Maisie Knew*, what Maisie does know, here the assumption is that Nanda, though not wholly 'downstairs', knows everything; and yet, in the concern for appearances that serves here as a code of conduct, her mother feels inhibited by her company, for which reason, along with several others, she wants to marry her off. Mrs Brook's associates pride themselves on their 'talk', in which freedom of reference to matters sexual is taken for granted – though Vanderbank proves too fastidious to marry a young woman contaminated by the circle he frequents.

Again the brittle comedy, here carried largely by dialogue, gradually darkens; and by the end of the novel, the circle of Buckingham Crescent is 'smashed' by the relentless working out of its own premises, for all that it is Mrs Brook who, according to Vanderbank, 'pulled us down ... as Samson pulled down the temple' (IX, 439). Working others for all they are worth, obsessed with sex and money, the denizens of this world can sustain not even the camaraderie of a band of predators. The Countess succeeds in marrying little Aggie to Mitchy, whose ugliness is more than offset by his wealth; and thus Mrs Brook does not succeed in marrying him to Nanda. Mrs Brook does manage to get Mr Longdon to look after Nanda for life, but she loses Van; as do Nanda and Mr Longdon. Nanda retreats into nun-like seclusion in Suffolk, while Mrs Brook settles down in her drawing-room, for life, as it were, exchanging listless platitudes with her vacant husband ('he suggested a stippled drawing by an inferior master' (IX, 66)) and her 'utterly disgusting' son (IX, 43).

The kind of over-heated speculation that *The Awkward Age* invites (who is doing what with/to/for whom?) attains a fictional apotheosis in *The Sacred Fount* (1901), its anonymous first-person narrator avidly enquiring into the private lives of his fellow guests at a country house.[10] James was surprised that anybody took it as anything other than a joke; in its infinitely deferred signification it may figure as a parody of the kind of elusiveness that non-Jamesians find so uncongenial.

The major phase (1901–1904)

The Ambassadors, the first of James's three great last novels (it was published in 1903, after *The Wings of the Dove*, but written earlier, in 1901) revisits many of James's most urgent themes. Once again we have an American invasion of Europe, in this instance in an attempt to rescue a native son from the toils of evil old Paris. The novel is indeed almost schematically structured upon the sustained contrast between Woollett, a New England manufacturing town, and Paris, traditionally the centre of high living and low morals. Here, as in all three of the last novels, cities are not just settings, but sites of symbolic value. In *The Ambassadors* Paris figures as the place that it is wonderful to be young in, the place to experience life. In this, it is emphatically unlike the pious and prosperous Woollett, the seat of the pious and prosperous Mrs Newsome.

Lambert Strether, somewhat bemusedly engaged to be married to Mrs Newsome, and the first of the eponymous ambassadors, is one of James's most appealing heroes: impressionable, diffident, scrupulous, wry. In spite of the expert guidance of his more experienced compatriot, Maria Gostrey, he is also one of the most bewildered of heroes, in suffering a double disillusionment: first in coming to realise that Woollett could be wrong about the effects of Paris on Chad Newsome, Mrs Newsome's wayward son; and then, more painfully, that, nevertheless, Chad has not been as miraculously transformed by his association with the charming Madame de Vionnet as Strether has wanted to believe.

Strether's famous injunction to Little Bilham, one of Chad's associates: 'Live all you can. It's a mistake not to' (XXI, 217), offers itself readily as the novel's statement of theme. But the novel calculates, as Strether cannot at this stage, the price of living all one can. For Chad, who has beautifully mastered the art of living, is one of those charming young Jamesian men who contrive to live at the expense of others – if not, in his case, financially, then emotionally. Strether is moved to conclude ruefully that Madame de Vionnet's influence can, after all, only be finite: 'She had made him better, she had made him best, she had made him anything one would; but it came to our friend with supreme queerness that he was none the less only Chad' (XXII, 284). And Chad, being Chad, is more than likely to leave Marie de Vionnet for the prosaic seductions, or at any rate rewards, of Woollett.

By novel's end Strether has alienated his old friend Waymarsh, been lambasted by Mrs Newsome's daughter, the militantly upright Sarah Pocock, and by implication been disowned by Mrs Newsome. He has also belatedly come to recognise the true nature of Chad and Marie de Vionnet's relationship. In return he has gained nothing, which seems to be the way he wants it: 'Not out of the whole affair, to have got anything for myself' (XXII, 326) is how he explains his refusal of Maria Gostrey's 'offer of exquisite service, of lightened care, for the rest of his days' (XXII, 325–6) – her offer, in short, of marriage. The reason he gives for declining her offer is Jamesian enough not greatly to surprise us – it is a rare Jamesian hero or heroine who is rewarded for his or her scruples – but, to judge by the critical literature, almost nobody believes him, even if Maria does; and critical speculation has readily occupied what Eric Haralson calls 'the narrative space created by Strether's evasion of conventional heteromasculine standards'.[11] Given the glamour of Chad, the likeability of Little Bilham, the charisma of the artist Gloriani, that space is vividly enough populated to create for Strether a richer emotional life than he thinks of himself as having.

If *The Ambassadors* is deeply personal in its lament for the life unlived, *The Wings of the Dove* (1902) is a profound study of a social and commercial mechanism, and its cost in human terms. As *The Ambassadors* represents James's most heartfelt exploration of the ambiguous beauty of Paris, *The Wings of the Dove* is his most searching analysis of the great marketplace that is London.

The novel's interrelated stories, those of the dying Milly Theale and of the lovers Kate Croy and Merton Densher, converge in London and are negotiated in London terms. Milly may represent 'in respect to the mass of money so piled on the girl's back, a set of New York possibilities' (XIX, 106); but New York possibilities fade into fable as they confront London, the real, the hard present, as personified most of all by Maud Lowder, 'Britannia of the Market Place' (XIX, 30): as Kate sees, 'Mrs. Lowder *was* London, *was* life – the roar of the siege and the thick of the fray' (XIX, 32).

Mrs Lowder equals London equals life: that equation dominates the novel, as the impecunious Kate and Merton and the fabulously rich Milly all strive somehow to lay claim to life in its various senses. For Densher that means Kate; for Kate it means having Densher's love as well as 'squaring' Aunt Maud; for Milly it means merely surviving: 'It was perhaps superficially more striking that one could live if one would; but it was more appealing, insinuating, irresistible in short, that one would live if one could' (XIX, 254).

Kate has, as Merton knows, a 'pure talent for life' (XX, 176), and various people try to appropriate this talent: she realises early on that 'she was in her way a tangible value' (XIX, 9) – to her father, her sister, her aunt, and, in a different sense, to Merton and to Milly. The plot of *The Wings* is driven by Kate's determination to cash in her value without sacrificing anything, to make Densher's 'long looks ... most completely her possession ... as if she might work them in with other and alien things, privately cherish them and yet, as regards the rigour of it, pay no price' (XIX, 61). But in Aunt Maud's world, into the spirit of which Kate now enters, everything has a price; as Lord Mark explains to Milly, 'Nobody here, you know, does anything for nothing' (XIX, 160); or, as Kate explicates the matter: 'the working and the worked were, as one might explain, the parties to every relation ... The worker in one connexion was the worked in another' (XIX, 178–9).

Caught up in this relentless market mechanism, Densher, torn between his love and desire for Kate and his moral qualms, is drawn into the plot to inherit Milly's wealth; but if the lovers are united in their purpose, they are ultimately driven apart by their complicity. Merton's own corruption is marked not so much in his lending himself to Kate's plot as in his 'working' Kate, in accordance with Lord Mark's principle, to sleep with him in return for his co-operation: 'If you decline to understand me I wholly decline to understand you. I'll do nothing' (XX, 230–1).

Milly, for all her wealth, is not robust enough to negotiate 'the roar of the siege and the thick of the fray'. In the novel's symbolic geography, Venice represents a retreat from the fray into a timeless world, part of Milly's identification with such life as a work of art may be said to have. Her identification with the Bronzino portrait at Matcham that she is told she so uncannily resembles now becomes complete: her life here is, in Susan Stringham's term, 'a Veronese picture' (XX, 206). But life pursues her even here, in the coerced figure of Merton Densher and the devious presence of Lord Mark, and she is destroyed by it.

In structure Milly's story is a reprise of the tale of the innocent American falling prey to the Old World, and we gather from the Preface that that was how James had planned it. But 'one's plan, alas, is one thing and one's result another' (XIX, xiii), and in the event much of the balance of interest is shifted to the relationship between the conniving couple. If one woman's plotting to marry off the man she loves to another woman recalls the intrigue of *The Portrait*, here the plotters themselves are given centre stage and a good deal of imaginative sympathy. Their accord, contest of strength, and eventual estrangement form a kind of drawing-room *Macbeth*, with Kate, utterly clear-eyed as to her own motives and desires, playing Lady Macbeth to Densher's Macbeth – with this difference, that she never repents or relents: 'I'm just where I was', she tells Densher as Milly lies dying, 'and you must give me some better reason than you do, my dear, for *your* not being' (XX, 348). Densher, on the other hand, never achieves Macbeth's singleness of purpose: his 'horror, almost, of her lucidity' (XX, 350) is a baffled moral revulsion. The last achievement of Kate's lucidity is to pronounce the novel's tragic closing line: 'We shall never be again as we were!' (XX, 405).

Adam Verver, in *The Golden Bowl* (1904), is the last of James's American 'innocents' abroad, and in his deceptively mild fashion he avenges the beguilement of all those others. He has not only bought a magnificent European prince with working parts for his daughter, he is buying up as much of Europe as he can ship back to American City. If, on the one hand, his Jamesian lineage can be traced back to Christopher Newman, a different line runs through Mrs Gereth and Gilbert Osmond, the collectors. Like them, he applies the same value to human beings as to objects of art: 'the instinct, the particular sharpened appetite of the collector, had fairly served as a basis for his acceptance of the Prince's suit' (XXIII, 140).

The impoverished Italian Prince Amerigo acquiesces more than willingly to his acquisition; he has little national or, apparently, personal pride; as the packed opening sentence of the novel has it: 'The Prince had always liked his London, when it had come to him; he was one of the Modern Romans who find by the Thames a more convincing image of the truth of the ancient state than any they have left by the Tiber' (XXIII, 3). But the Prince's pleasant historical reflections are out of date: in the world of *The Golden Bowl*, the city to which tribute is paid is not London, but American City, and its conquering hero is an American, Adam Verver. The Prince thinks he will share in the power of the man who has bought him, 'the power of the rich peoples' (XXIII, 18), but he is to discover that he constitutes a possession, not a partner.

The Ververs, father and daughter, have been the subject of critical debate for decades. Earlier readings tended to take the Ververs at their own valuation, Adam presiding beneficently over the restitution to his beloved daughter Maggie of what is hers by right: the love of her husband, temporarily led astray by the wiles of the scheming Charlotte Stant. But more recent, more suspicious critical methods have found darker strains in the father–daughter relationship and a more insidious power in Adam's practice of benevolence. On this reading, the Prince and Charlotte figure not so much as the erring spouses (though they are that as well, with whatever provocation) as the signs and victims of 'a rare power of purchase' (XXIV, 360), objects bought in for Adam's aesthetic satisfaction and for Maggie to play with.

The elusiveness of *The Golden Bowl* derives partly from what James called, with monumental understatement, 'a certain indirect and oblique view of my presented action' (XXIII, v). As in earlier novels, but more bewilderingly, James here entrusts his tale to the perspective of his characters, with little narrative intervention, leaving the reader at the mercy of the self-deceptions and rationalisations of characters intent upon casting the most amiable light upon their own actions. Maggie wants to believe in the benevolence of her father's power, which is also the source of her power over the Prince; Adam wants to believe that in marrying Charlotte he has relieved Maggie of the suspicion that in marrying the Prince she has abandoned her father; Charlotte and the Prince want to believe that in resuming their affair they are serving the interests of their spouses; and Fanny Assingham, who originally introduced the Prince and Charlotte, wants to believe that 'there were beautiful intentions all round' – 'Otherwise ... I should have been a wretch' (XXIII, 392).

In the complex linguistic play of the novel, apparently simple terms ('good', 'evil', 'right', 'wrong', and especially 'beautiful') are insistently invoked, changing their meaning according to whoever is using them and in what context.[12] Given the floating of the novel's moral terminology, power is also a matter of controlling language; and here, ultimately, all meaning is referred back to Adam Verver, the omnipotent creator of this world and the fixer of its meanings. He is to this novel what Mrs Lowder is to *The Wings of the Dove*, and the source of his power is the same: money. But his power, like his wealth, is immeasurably greater than hers: if she is Britannia of the Market Place, he is 'one of the powers, the representative of a force – quite as an infant king is the representative of a dynasty' (XXIII, 324).

Adam's power is exercised so subtly that those subject to it believe themselves to be free to indulge their desires, whereas in fact they are indulging an illusion sponsored by him; when they exceed the limits of their silken halters, he pulls them up. His apparently benevolent inscrutability blinds them to the conditions of their own servitude, but James allows the reader the odd glimpse into Verver's 'lucidity' – as when deciding that his marrying Charlotte is just the thing to reassure Maggie: 'When … he had simply settled this service to his daughter well before him as the proper direction of his young friend's leisure, the cool darkness had again closed round him, but his moral lucidity was constituted' (XXIII, 208).

Adam's lucidity does not safeguard him from error – Charlotte proves less tractable to his idea of 'the proper direction of [her] leisure' than anticipated – but he has the means and the power to re-establish the equilibrium of his little world. How much Adam knows is never revealed, but somehow the vexed affairs of the two families are rearranged: since his provision for Charlotte's leisure has failed so spectacularly, he ships her back to America so that everyone can sustain the beautiful fiction of their beautiful lives, and Maggie can have the Prince to herself.

The novel's sardonic conclusion finds the Prince and Charlotte arranged for inspection by their owners in Maggie's drawing-room:

> The fusion of their presence with the decorative elements, their contribution to the triumph of selection, was complete and admirable; though to a lingering view, a view more penetrating than the occasion really demanded, they also might have figured as concrete attestations of a rare power of purchase. There was much indeed in the tone in which Adam Verver spoke again, and who shall say where his thought stopped? '*Le compte y est.* You've got some good things.' (XXIV, 360)

Reified as 'good things', the erstwhile lovers embark on the rest of their lives as tributes to Mr Verver's 'rare power of purchase'. Maggie can now, secure in her possession, surrender to the Prince's sexual power – or assert her claim to him. The novel ends on an embrace, that time-honoured closing clinch; but in this novel most embraces seal a deception, and this is no exception. As the Prince 'encloses' Maggie, he pledges himself to blindness to all but her: '"See"? I see nothing but *you*.' And Maggie, too, blinds herself to the full implication of his words: 'And the truth of it had with this force after a moment so strangely lighted his eyes that as for pity and dread of them she buried her own in his breast' (XXIV, 369). Pity and dread, of course, are the tragic emotions; and *The Golden Bowl*, for all its coerced 'happy' ending, and for all the comedy of 'beautiful intentions all round', is as much a tragedy of wasted passion as *The Wings of the Dove*. Like Kate and Densher at the end of their novel, the Prince and Maggie are driven by 'the need to bury in the dark blindness of each other's arms the knowledge of each other that they couldn't undo' (XXIV, 393).

Given the lucidity of James's own insights, one hesitates to ascribe to him the bewilderment he visits upon his characters; but much contemporary criticism is in fact premised upon an assumption of some limit to James's understanding of his own creations: somewhere beyond the bafflement of his characters, the modern critic finds James's own perplexity. But he was never helpless in the face of his perplexity: firmly convinced of the significance of his art, labouring tirelessly at refining it and reflecting on it, he transmuted his bewilderment into a body of work unsurpassed in the English novel for craftsmanship, range, and depth, continuing to intrigue, amuse, and provoke his readers.

NOTE ON EDITIONS

Henry James revised most of his novels and some of his tales for a definitive edition, what came to be called the New York Edition, published by Scribner's, New York, from 1907 to 1909 (reprinted by Augustus M. Kelley, Fairfield, NJ, 1976). Most modern reprints have reproduced this edition. The unrevised versions are currently being reprinted by the Library of America. Readers looking for more readily accessible texts of all the major novels will find them in Oxford World's Classics or Penguin editions. A complete new scholarly edition of the novels and tales is in preparation, to be published by Cambridge University Press.

NOTES

1 Henry James, *Watch and Ward* (1871), in *Henry James: Novels: 1871–1880* (New York: Library of America, 1983).
2 Unless noted otherwise, references in the text to James's novels, including the Prefaces, are to the volume and page numbers of the New York Edition published by Scribner's (New York, 1907–9), reprinted by Augustus M. Kelley (Fairfield, NJ, 1976).
3 For a discussion of this and related matters in *Roderick Hudson* and later novels, see Eric Haralson, *Henry James and Queer Modernity* (Cambridge: Cambridge University Press, 2003), and the more emphatically argued *Henry James and Sexuality* by Hugh Stevens (Cambridge: Cambridge University Press, 1998).
4 Henry James, *The Europeans* (1878), in *Henry James: Novels 1871–1880*, p. 1017.
5 Henry James, *Washington Square* (1880), in *Henry James: Novels 1881–1886* (New York: Library of America, 1985), p. 22.
6 *Ibid.*, p. 127.
7 Henry James, *The Bostonians* (1886) in *Henry James: Novels 1881–1886*.
8 For a more appreciative discussion of *The Tragic Muse* as 'a greatly entertaining and interesting confrontation of issues and situations that mattered profoundly to James: art, the theatre, sex, power, and the various uses of "representation"', see

Peter Brooks, *Henry James Goes to Paris* (Princeton, Princeton University Press, 2007), p. 80.

9 Henry James, *The Other House* (1896), in *Henry James: Novels 1896–1899* (New York: Library of America, 1996).

10 Henry James, *The Sacred Fount* (1901), in *Henry James: Novels 1901–1902* (New York: Library of America, 2006).

11 Haralson, *Henry James and Queer Modernity*, p. 104.

12 I discuss this and related matters in *Expulsion and the Nineteenth-Century Novel* (Oxford: Oxford University Press, 1994), chapter 5.

FURTHER READING

I am grateful to Rebekah Scott and Adrian Poole for their help in compiling this list.

Brooks, Peter, *Henry James Goes to Paris*, Princeton, Princeton University Press, 2007

Buelens, Gert (ed.), *Enacting History in Henry James: Narrative, Power, and Ethics*, Cambridge, Cambridge University Press, 1997

Coulson, Victoria, *Henry James: Women and Realism*, Cambridge, Cambridge University Press, 2007

Edel, Leon, *Henry James*, 5 vols., London, Rupert Hart-Davis, 1953–72

Freedman, Jonathan (ed.), *The Cambridge Companion to Henry James*, Cambridge, Cambridge University Press, 1998

Gordon, Lyndall, *A Private Life of Henry James: Two Women and His Art*, London, Chatto & Windus, 1998

Hadley, Tessa, *Henry James and the Imagination of Pleasure*, Cambridge, Cambridge University Press, 2002

Haralson, Eric, *Henry James and Queer Modernity*, Cambridge, Cambridge University Press, 2003

Heyns, Michiel, *Expulsion and the Nineteenth-Century Novel: The Scapegoat in English Realist Fiction*, Oxford, Oxford University Press, 1994

Horne, Philip, *Henry James and Revision*, Oxford, Oxford University Press, 1990

Horne, Philip (ed.), *Henry James: A Life in Letters*, New York, Viking Penguin, 1999

McWhirter, David, *Desire and Love in Henry James: A Study of the Late Novels*, Cambridge, Cambridge University Press, 1989

Poole, Adrian, *Henry James*, Harvester New Readings, Hemel Hampstead, Harvester Wheatsheaf, 1991

Rawlings, Peter (ed.), *Palgrave Advances in Henry James Studies*, Basingstoke, Palgrave Macmillan, 2007

Rowe, John Carlos, *The Other Henry James*, Durham, NC, and London, Duke University Press, 1998

Sedgwick, Eve Kosofsky, *Epistemology of the Closet*, Berkeley, University of California Press, 1990

Seltzer, Mark, *Henry James and the Art of Power*, Ithaca and London, Cornell University Press, 1984

Stevens, Hugh, *Henry James and Sexuality*, Cambridge, Cambridge University Press, 1998

18

ROBERT HAMPSON

Joseph Conrad

Joseph Conrad, the pen-name adopted by Józef Konrad Korzeniowski (1857–1924), earned his early reputation as a writer of colonial fiction. His first two novels, *Almayer's Folly* (1895) and *An Outcast of the Islands* (1896), were set in Southeast Asia, and reviewers saw him as annexing a new territory for British fiction. They compared his work, for example, with Louis Becke's (1855–1913) stories of the South Pacific.[1] He was also, perhaps inevitably, termed 'the Kipling of the Malay Archipelago'.[2] And yet, as a colonial story, *Almayer's Folly* is highly disconcerting. It is very different from the imperialist and masculinist fiction produced by the writers of W. E. Henley's circle (such as Stevenson and Kipling). Andrea White has written illuminatingly about Conrad and adventure fiction, showing how Conrad worked from within the genre of adventure fiction, but, at the same time, 'wrote a fiction at odds with the traditional assumptions of the genre'. As White notes, adventure fiction 'traditionally celebrated an unqualified kind of heroism' and provided 'the energizing myth of English imperialism'.[3] By comparison, Kaspar Almayer is a singularly unheroic hero.

In the opening chapter of *Almayer's Folly*, he thinks back to the start of his career in Macassar and remembers his first impressions of the adventurous Captain Lingard, but his admiration is not for the adventures Lingard has had ('his loves, and ... his desperate fights with the Sulu pirates').[4] Lingard has become a 'hero' to him because of 'his smart business transactions' and 'enormous profits'. Like Stevenson's *Treasure Island* (1883) and Rider Haggard's *King Solomon's Mines* (1885), *Almayer's Folly* has a plot involving a search for treasure. Almayer dreams of becoming wealthy and leaving the up-river trading station where he has spent twenty-five years of his life. *Almayer's Folly* makes explicit a latent element of adventure fiction. Despite their foregrounding of tests of courage, the treasure plot means that adventure novels are often as materialistic as Almayer. At the end of *Treasure Island*, the pirates' hoard is divided up between Jim, the doctor and the squire, and the reader is assured that 'All of us had an ample share of the treasure.'[5] Similarly, at the end of *King Solomon's Mines*, Quatermain, Good, and Curtis's younger brother Neville have to be careful not to flood the market with the diamonds they have brought back from Africa. The major differences are that Almayer is explicitly motivated by the search for wealth and that Almayer is a failure. Not only does he not find the gold, but it is apparent from the start that his whole life is a failure: his business in Sambir has failed; he has lost his patron; and he is trapped up a Borneo river with a wife he despises. This is a very different image of the European in the tropics from the masterful white men of colonial adventure fiction.

Another unconventional feature of Conrad's first novel is the prominence of women. *Treasure Island* was intended, from the start, as 'a story for boys', and the only female character is Jim's mother, whom he leaves at the start.[6] Haggard's narrator proudly asserts that there is 'not a *petticoat* in the whole history'.[7] By contrast, Mrs Almayer's plotting drives the first half of the narrative, while her daughter Nina effectively takes over the central position in the second. The story of Almayer's failure and decline is counterpointed by the story of Nina's discovery of a new identity. She had been brought up by Almayer to think of herself as a 'white woman', but this identity doesn't survive her move to Singapore to be educated. In the end she finds her new identity by aligning herself with her Malay heritage. Thus, not only is Almayer a failure, but his daughter finds a solution to the problems caused by her mixed descent by choosing her mother's Malay traditions rather than her father's European ones.

In his 'Author's Note' to *Almayer's Folly*, Conrad addressed himself to Alice Meynell's criticism of what he describes as 'that literature which preys on strange people and prowls in far-off countries' (*AF*, vii). Where Meynell had criticised this literature as 'decivilised', Conrad insists on the common humanity shared by people 'no matter where they live, in houses or in huts, in the streets under a fog, or in the forests behind the dark line of dismal mangroves' (*AF*, viii). Conrad was conscious of the category of colonial fiction to which his own first novel would be assigned; at the same time, he was strongly influenced by another tradition. Conrad's own conception of the novel was derived from his reading of nineteenth-century French fiction: the works of Alphonse Daudet, Anatole France, Guy de Maupassant, and Gustave Flaubert were all intimately known to him. With his emphasis on technique and style Flaubert, in particular, provided Conrad with a concept of the novel very different from the dominant literary modes of Dickens, George Eliot, or Thackeray. In *A Personal Remembrance*, the memoir written by Ford Madox Ford after Conrad's death, Ford recalls how they 'talked about Flaubert and Maupassant', how they both had 'immense passages of *Madame Bovary*, *La Nuit*, *Ce Cochon de Morin*' by heart, and how they would drive around the Kent countryside searching for *le mot juste* to render details of the passing landscape.[8] (Conrad and Ford, along with Henry James and James Joyce, can be seen to constitute the Flaubertian tradition in the English novel.) The period of collaboration and intense friendship between Conrad and Ford from 1898 to 1909 was certainly an important moment in the development of literary modernism. During this period, they hammered out their own conception of the modernist novel, but its impact went further. From 1908 onwards, Ford also became closely involved with Ezra Pound, and, from these early conversations with Ford, Pound developed the aesthetic ideas which flowered as imagism. The Flaubertian concept of the novel which fed into the discussions of Conrad and Ford thus provided the basis for what Pound called 'the prose tradition in poetry'.[9]

Sea fiction: *The Nigger of the 'Narcissus'*

Conrad's career at sea provided him with experiences which he was to draw on throughout his writing life, and his professional connection with the sea was one of the ways in which his work was marketed. However, what this narrative leaves out is Conrad's literary background. His father, Apollo Korzeniowski, was a poet, dramatist, and translator. From an early age Conrad was in contact with English and French literature. In addition, Apollo also gave Conrad a grounding in Polish Romantic literature: Mickiewicz, Słowacki, and Krasiński, in particular. Subsequently, during his years at sea, Conrad was a voracious reader. When he started to write, therefore, he was well read in three literatures (English, French, and Polish) and drew on the resources of all three.

Conrad's first sea-story was *The Nigger of the 'Narcissus'* (1897). This recounts a homeward-bound voyage from Bombay to London and was based on Conrad's own 1884 voyage as second mate in the *Narcissus*. However, the story is far from being a sailor's reminiscence of a voyage. Early reviews were puzzled by its lack of plot: 'The story is simply an account of an ordinary voyage made by an ordinary sailing ship', wrote Arthur Quiller-Couch (or 'Q', as he was known). They were also puzzled by its lack of women: 'There is no love-making – no word of it. The *Narcissus* carried no woman on board', Q continued.[10] The anonymous reviewer for the *Daily Mail* similarly complained that 'The tale is no tale, but merely an account of the uneventful voyage of the *Narcissus*', and 'the only female in the book is the ship herself'.[11] A modern reader might think there are plenty of events in the story – the insubordination and near-mutiny of the crew, the illness and death of the West Indian sailor James Wait, not to mention the ship going over on her side in a storm off the Cape of Good Hope. What the early criticism points to is a conception of the appropriate plotting for a sea-story, which Conrad's text doesn't supply. Q's review in the *Daily Chronicle* indicates, by comparison, what such a plot should include: 'There is no pirate in it, no wreck, no desert island, no treasure trove.' Writers of popular sea fiction were also expected to find ways of smuggling women into the narrative to provide some romance – some love-interest for the reader.

Conrad's sea story is, at first glance at least, an impressionistic account of a voyage. The opening chapter presents the roll-call on board the *Narcissus* with careful attention to precise visual and aural phenomena, describing, through concrete detail, a ship readying itself for departure. From the start, however, the description also plays with the contrast of black and white, darkness and light, that are present in the novel's title. The muster itself involves a similar play: each man is briefly individuated, summoned into the light by his name, and then, almost immediately, returns into darkness. It is precise realistic detail, but, at the same time, it seems to imply both the submerging of individuals in the collective identity of the crew, which is the ideological position from which actions are judged in the course of the narrative, and also the wisdom enunciated later in the chapter: 'a generation of men goes – and is forgotten, and it does not matter!' *(NN*, 25). Conrad has already developed the technique of creating an aura of meaning around his concretely realised realistic details

He has also given considerable thought to the structure of the narrative. As Peter McDonald has noted, the narrative as a whole is constructed according to easily recognisable patterns: the opening departure is answered by the final arrival, the initial roll-call by the final paying-off of the crew, the storm scene by the scene of becalming.[12] In addition, as McDonald shows, it is 'constructed as a series of ethically and politically charged moments, the relations between which are often neither causal nor explicit' (37). This novella doesn't simply invite us to read for the plot, but to be aware also how the construction of the narrative is an important part of the literary work's meaning. The linear movement of plot is replaced by the spatial relations of structure.

Another major difference between *The Nigger of the 'Narcissus'* and a sailor's reminiscence of a voyage is the novella's depth of psychological exploration. To begin with, there is the development of Wait. Wait is dying of TB, but he handles his fear of dying by pretending to be pretending to be dying. This is why he is pleased that Donkin treats him as a malingerer, since this reassures him that he is not actually ill but only pretending to be ill. In the second part of the novella, when he is undeniably dying, Wait handles his fear of death by the simpler process of denial: simply asserting that he is fit to work, when he manifestly isn't.

However, Conrad is not just interested in Wait: he is concerned with the group psychology of the crew and in Wait's impact upon that. Wait is the centre of 'the ship's collective psychology' (as Conrad observed in 'To My Readers in America', written for the Doubleday Sundial Edition, 1920). Conrad uses him to explore the mechanisms people employ to avoid awareness of their own mortality and the errors into which this self-deception leads them. Throughout the narrative, Wait plays on the crew's unacknowledged fear of death. In the first half, he takes control over the crew by asserting his illness. They both believe in his illness and suspect that he is malingering to avoid work – and Wait encourages this suspicion. He controls them not through their belief but through their doubt – and through the resulting ambiguity of their response: 'we oscillated between the desire of virtue and the fear of ridicule; we wished to save ourselves from the pain of remorse, but did not want to be made the contemptible dupes of our sentiment' (*NN*, 41). In the second half of the narrative, it is again because of their own fear of death that the crew will want to believe that Wait is not really dying. Because they cannot face the fact of their own mortality, and cannot acknowledge their own fear of death, they are vulnerable to being controlled through these unacknowledged fears.

Modernist fiction and popular fiction: *Lord Jim*

As we have seen, Conrad's work created generic problems for early reviewers and critics. In the case of his first novel, he is working within the genre of imperial adventure fiction, but writes a fiction at odds with the traditional assumptions of that genre. In the case of *The Nigger of the 'Narcissus'*, contemporary reviewers recognised the power of the work, but could not reconcile it to their sense of the popular genre of sea fiction. Some of the ways in which it departs from or exceeds that genre have been addressed in the previous section. What has not been mentioned yet is the well-known Preface which Conrad published with the novella. The very fact of a Preface again moves the work out of the realm of popular fiction into that of serious literature. Famously, in this Preface, Conrad asserts his vision of his task: 'by the power of the written word, to make you hear, to make you feel – it is, before all, to make you *see*!' (*NN*, x). These words are often quoted as Conrad's literary manifesto. There has been considerable discussion about the ambiguity of the word 'see', which seems to mean both truth to the visible world and the attempt to penetrate appearances to a deeper truth. There has also been some discussion of the word 'make' – a coercive attempt to make us see in a particular way. But not enough attention has been paid to the context in which this task is asserted, the position that it opposes, namely that 'wisdom', orientated towards 'immediate profit', which seeks edification, consolation, or amusement. None of these, Conrad asserts, is the aim of art. At the same time, the Preface is careful not to follow the aesthetic doctrines of the separation of art from life. Conrad is concerned with the 'truth' of experience, with finding ways of rendering that 'truth' for his readers, but also, as Giles Foden has suggested, the ethical concerns of the work are embedded in and emerge from its 'essential organisation'.[13]

Since the 1950s, when Conrad's current reputation began to be established – alongside and contemporaneous with academic attention to 'modernist' literature – the primary works on which that reputation has been built have been *Lord Jim* (1900), 'Heart of Darkness' (1902), and Conrad's important political novels, *Nostromo* (1904), *The Secret Agent* (1907), and *Under Western Eyes* (1911). In *Lord Jim*, Conrad self-consciously confronts the models of popular fiction. Jim's 'vocation for the sea' declares itself after 'a course of light holiday literature', and his career thereafter is explicitly plotted against the generic conventions and expectations of such 'light literature' (*LJ*, 5, 6). He misses taking part in a real adventure, caused by the collision between a coaster 'running in for shelter' and 'a schooner at anchor' (*LJ*, 7), because he is day-dreaming, living 'beforehand ... in his mind the sea-life of light literature' (*LJ*, 6). What that sea-life consists of is mapped out for us: 'He saw himself saving people from sinking ships, cutting away masts in a hurricane, swimming through a surf with a line ... He confronted savages on tropical shores, quelled mutinies on the high seas, and in a small boat upon the ocean kept up the hearts of despairing men – always an example of devotion to duty, and as unflinching as a hero in a book' (*LJ*, 6). Conrad runs through a series of motifs from popular sea fiction, but what he then provides in the novel is a counter-version of such fiction. Jim famously does not 'save people from sinking ships' – he jumps overboard to save himself. Jim, 'in a small boat upon the ocean', does not 'keep up the hearts of despairing men'. He spends the night awake and alert, ready to defend himself from his companions in the 'small boat' into which he has jumped. In other words, Conrad engineers his own collision between 'the sea-life of light literature' and the reality of sea-life – at least as represented in his fiction. Marlow at one point comments: 'In no other kind of life is the illusion more wide of reality – in no other is the beginning *all* illusion – the disenchantment more swift' (*LJ*, 129). Conrad shows this to be the case with Jim. At the start of chapter 2, the narrator comments: 'After two years of training [Jim] went to sea and entering the regions so well known to his imagination, found them strangely barren of adventure' (*LJ*, 10). Instead of the romantic world he imagined, 'the fanciful realm of recklessly heroic aspirations' (*LJ*, 83), he encounters 'the prosaic severity of the daily task that gives bread' (*LJ*, 10). Jim's response is to retreat further into his world of dreams with the disastrous results that then follow in the *Patna*.

The first part of the novel deals with the *Patna*, the enquiry, and its aftermath. Once the judgement has been made by the official inquiry, Marlow then conducts his own unofficial investigation into Jim's case. Interestingly, this part of the novel draws on another popular genre which was then being developed, the detective story. Marlow interviews, in succession, his series of 'witnesses': the French Lieutenant, Chester, Stein. As with *The Nigger of the 'Narcissus'*, this sequence of interviews produces a series of 'ethically charged moments', which are complexly interrelated with each other and with other moments in the novel. In effect, the sequence of interviews enacts a dialectic which ends by moving Jim out of the world of the sea and sea fiction into another world. The French Lieutenant, who brought in the *Patna* after Jim and the other European officers had abandoned her, at first seems to offer hope for Jim. His assertion that 'One is always afraid' (*LJ*, 146) seems to offer the possibility of a 'lenient' or indulgent view of Jim, but he quickly makes it clear that Marlow has misunderstood him ('What life may be worth ... when the honour is gone' (*LJ*, 148)). Chester's cynical attitude towards Jim represents the opposed position: having asserted of Jim that 'he's no good' (*LJ*, 166), he wants to offer him a job guarding coolies on an island of guano. Stein provides a way out, and he does it by moving Jim out of the sphere of the code of the sea (by which Jim has failed) into the inland world of Patusan. In the second part of the novel, Jim is allowed to achieve success in a world where he can play another kind of hero: the hero of adventure romance. Indeed, Jim welcomes the offer precisely as an opportunity to enter a different fictional world. He describes Stein's story of the exchange of rings with Doramin as 'like something you read of in books' (*LJ*, 233–4). Later on, in Patusan, he describes Doramin and his wife as 'like people in a book' (*LJ*, 260). However, in this particular book, the world of Patusan is described with ethnographic accuracy. If Jim continues to live in the world of romance, a world governed by the codes and values of adventure-romance fiction, Conrad's novel (as we would by now expect) does not reproduce the motifs of adventure romance. In other words, in both parts of the novel Jim lives according to the codes of a popular genre which the novel itself does not follow in its representation of the world. Jim wants to be the hero of a popular sea-fiction story, but the novel's own mode of representation is quite different. Subsequently Jim wants to be the hero of an adventure-romance story – and again the novel's ethnographic mode of representation refuses to conform to that dream.[14]

I mentioned above how the interviews conducted by Marlow are complexly interrelated with other moments in the novel. For example, during the interview with the French Lieutenant, after he asserts that 'the fear ... is always there', Marlow observes that 'He touched his breast near a brass button, on the very spot where Jim had given a thump to his own when protesting that there was nothing the matter with his heart' (*LJ*, 146). This gesture brings together two moments: the genuinely heroic French Lieutenant, admitting the fear he felt, despite which he stayed on board the *Patna* while it was being towed, even though it could have sunk at any moment, and Jim, whose assertion of his lack of fear is what might be expected from a hero in a book, but is disabling in the face of emergencies. The unacknowledged fear of death is as treacherous for Jim as it was for the crew of the *Narcissus*. Jim derives his heroic model ('as unflinching as a hero in a book') from his 'course of light holiday literature' (*LJ*, 6). At his death, he achieves this ideal and Conrad consciously echoes the earlier passage: Jim, we are told, 'sent right and left at all those faces a proud and unflinching glance' (*LJ*, 416). Or, at least, that is what was reported by the bystanders. With this final uncertainty, Conrad leaves open the judgement on Jim's case.

Marlow's inquiry is complex, explorative, and, ultimately, inconclusive. We are left (or made) to draw our own conclusions from the prolonged play of Marlow's curiosity and intelligence over Jim's character and psychology. One of the complications is that it is Marlow's inquiry. Why has Marlow involved himself in Jim's case? What are his personal investments in possible outcomes? We know, in part, that Marlow is involved for professional reasons: he is a ship's captain, and, as he notes at one point, he would have trusted his ship to Jim – on the strength of his appearance – and it would have been a mistake. To some extent then, Marlow's professional judgement is at stake. Another of the complications is Jim's disappearance into Patusan: as a result Marlow has to construct his conclusion from various sources of information – Gentleman Brown, Tamb' Itam – with varying degrees of reliability. Marlow's narrative attempts to explain another person and concludes with more questions rather than answers.

Modernist fiction: 'Heart of Darkness'

'Heart of Darkness' has become the paradigmatic 'modernist' novel. Its modernist elements are its indeterminacies, its epistemological uncertainties, its spatial form, its mythic logic. The reader is warned early on what to expect – or, rather, what not to expect – from the story. One of Marlow's audience observes: 'we knew we were fated, before the ebb began to run, to hear about one of Marlow's inconclusive experiences' (*HD*, 51). We have also been told that Marlow's stories are not like the tales of other sailors, 'the whole meaning of which lies within the shell of a cracked nut'. In Marlow's case, 'the meaning of an episode was not inside like a kernel but outside, enveloping the tale' (*HD*, 48). As with *Lord Jim*, much of the work is taken up with Marlow's narration – with his attempt to understand, and make sense of, his experience. And, as with *Lord Jim*, the reader is given the task of interpreting Marlow's interpretation, knowing all the time that what we are being told is only an interpretation. As Edward Said has remarked, Conrad's fiction characteristically presents us with embodied statements, related to a specific individual in a specific situation, and we have to take into account both the individual and the situation in evaluating the statement.[15]

In his Author's Note to 'Heart of Darkness', Conrad describes the story as 'experience pushed a little (and only a very little) beyond the actual facts of the case' (*HD*, xxxv). Certainly, as Conrad's *Congo Diary* makes clear, Marlow's experiences in 'Heart of Darkness' follow fairly closely the route that the author himself took from the interview in Brussels (through a female relative's influence) to Kinshasa.[16] There are various omissions: Boma, for example, was far more populous than 'Heart of Darkness' suggests – with a hotel, tramway, and government buildings. There are also various changes – the *Florida* was wrecked, but it was then salvaged and brought back to Kinshasa. Conrad was not, like Marlow, delayed there for three months and involved in salvage work. There was also, of course, no Kurtz. There was a Klein – an agent of the company who boarded the steamer, the *Roi de Belge*, at Stanley Falls and died of dysentery on the voyage down-stream. There were also numerous agents of the Company who were involved in atrocities against the local people. Rom, Hodister, a whole gallery of Belgian agents have been suggested as models for Kurtz.

What Conrad's account of 'Heart of Darkness' leaves out is the extraordinary qualities of the writing: the complex and multi-layered engagement with experience that the novel embodies and the structural complexities of the narrative. Conrad's misleading description of his work is the beginning of a game played with the reader. Near the start, there is the following, generally unremarked passage:

> 'I don't want to bother you much with what happened to me personally,' [Marlow] began, showing in this remark the weakness of many tellers of tales who seem so often unaware of what their audience would best like to hear.
>
> (*HD*, 51)

This shows, again, a Conrad who is aware of his audience, aware of their expectations, and aware also that he has no wish to satisfy them. The audience might want to hear about Marlow's personal experiences, and the reader might want to know about Conrad's personal experience, but testimony or confession is not the same as a work of literary art.

Modernism was concerned with the expression of complexity of experience through complexity of form. In this context, one of the priorities for modernist writers was compression. Hence, for example, Pound's interest in Chinese ideograms, and his development, in the *Cantos*, of what he called the ideogrammatic method: producing a montage, collage, or constellation of informations around a particular node. In the case of 'Heart of Darkness', that drive to compression found expression in two forms: the use of the tale within a tale, and the use of what T. S. Eliot, in writing of Joyce's *Ulysses*, was later to call 'the mythical method'.[17]

To take the tale within a tale first. As in *Lord Jim*, Conrad uses Marlow as narrator, telling his story in a particular context to a particular audience. The device is at least as old as Scheherazade and the *Arabian Nights*, but Conrad's immediate source was probably H. G. Wells's recent novel, *The Time Machine* (1895), where the Time Traveller recounts his experiences to a suburban audience at his home in Richmond. His fantastic voyages are set within the frame of contemporary London, and the implications of the inset tales (in terms of class divisions or human appetites, for example) are allowed to flow back into the present moment of narration and raise questions about the apparently safe and comfortable world of the audience. 'Heart of Darkness' works in exactly the same way. The setting on the Thames, where the narration takes place, anchors the tale's telling in familiar surroundings, but the implications of the tale are allowed to reflect back upon the world of London. Conrad's narrative in *The Nigger of the 'Narcissus'* works by asking the reader to make connections between ethically and politically charged moments in the text: the device of the tale within a tale is another spatialisation of literary form.

Eliot's example of the 'mythical method' is Joyce's use of the *Odyssey* as the underlying framework for *Ulysses*. Apart from the title, Joyce makes no mention of the *Odyssey* in the novel, but it provides him with his structure – each chapter of the novel corresponding to an episode from the classical epic. The *Odyssey* provides, as it were, the basic grammar, which Joyce then complicates by overlaying other mythic frames, including, for example, Shakespeare's *Hamlet*. Where these overlapping frames contradict each other, interpretative spaces open up within the text for the reader. Conrad similarly augments the details of his own journey up and down the Congo with a range of other journeys. First, there are the other narratives of exploration with which he was familiar. McClintock's quest for Sir John Franklin in Arctic waters and Henry Stanley's quest for Emin Pasha in Africa are only two of the intertexts on which Conrad drew in his development of the narrative he created around the dying agent Klein. His narrative is also disrupted and over-written by a variety of literary and mythical journeys, and it is here that Conrad can be seen to adumbrate the mythic method of *Ulysses*. His narrative can be read as a quest; as an inverted version of a pilgrim's progress; as an inverted version of Jatakas, Buddhist stories of enlightenment. Marlow's journey up-river draws on the literary tradition of the *katabasis*, of descent into the underworld, that features in Homer, Virgil, Dante, and the Christian myth of the Harrowing of Hell; while Kurtz's experience suggests a version of the Faustian pact, a story of damnation familiar from Christopher Marlowe's play, Goethe's great work, and numerous operas. Again, Conrad was following *The Time Machine* here, which also features the protagonist's descent into an underworld, with echoes of the *katabasis* and Harrowing of Hell. As a result of all these mythic overlays, Marlow's physical journey from London to the Congo becomes a moral and political journey in which he confronts the workings of colonialism, but also a psychological journey, undertaken by Marlow, his audience, and the reader, in which we descend into ourselves to confront our basic drives and impulses, our needs and our weaknesses.

The device of the tale within a tale also touches on the structural complexities of the narrative and its multi-layered engagement with experience. First of all, it has to be emphasised that Marlow is not Conrad; nothing in this work is said by Conrad in his own voice. The narrative begins with a beautiful, extended description of the sun setting over the Thames estuary that leads into an eloquent celebration of British imperial history. A casual remark made by Marlow later ('you say Knights?', *HD*, 49) reveals retrospectively that all of this has been a speech made by one of the group on board the *Nellie*. In other words, the passage shifts its status from written address to the reader to the reported address of one character to others. And this shift of status is accompanied by a shift – and loss – of authority. This is not an omniscient narrator, perhaps carrying the authority of the writer, but just another voice, another perspective. The speech is embodied and situated in exactly the way that Said noted. The unnamed narrator has a nautical past, like Marlow and Conrad, but his patriotic rhetoric is not theirs. Indeed, his speech subverts itself as it proceeds. His reference to Sir John Franklin subtends a dark story of exploration, disaster, and possible cannibalism among Europeans. His final references to 'Hunters of gold or pursuers of fame ... bearing the sword and often the torch' (*HD*, 47) is also carefully poised. How noble are the motives behind exploration? British imperialism might often bear the torch, but it always (by implication) bears the sword – 'the might within the land'. Also, this image of the torch is later revalued by Kurtz's sinister painting of a blind figure carrying a torch – as it were, perhaps, invading a country with no understanding of its culture and politics – while the sword reappears up-dated as the 'thunder and lightning' (*HD*, 128), the sophisticated firepower, with which Kurtz 'came to' his African followers. What we are seeing here is what Cedric Watts calls the 'tentacular' nature of this text: the 'qualifications, modifications, ifs and buts, discriminations' that emerge when we reflect retrospectively on the work – or as we read and reread it.[18]

The novella begins with an unnamed narrator, but the narration is then taken up by Marlow. This figure had already appeared, in *Blackwood's Magazine*, in Conrad's story 'Youth' (1898), and he was to appear again in *Lord Jim* and *Chance* (1913–14), in each case as the main narrator. Marlow enters our consciousness with the arresting and wonderfully gnomic utterance: 'And this also ... has been one of the dark places of the earth' (*HD*, 48). We are then given Marlow's narrative – his attempt to explain and understand his experiences. But we also have to remember that he knows in advance how this story ends, and this extra awareness gives him an advantage over his audience (and his readers) that can be used by Conrad to mislead us. This is apparent in the prompt which starts the account of his experiences in Africa. His reflections on the Romans in Britain lead to more abstract reflections on imperialism, expressing first of all a condemnation of imperialist conquest of territory ('the taking it away from those who have a different complexion or slightly flatter noses than ourselves') and then an apparent revaluation of that condemnation ('What redeems it is the idea only' (*HD*, 50–1)). As often in the narration that follows, the reader is caught up in the flux and reflux of Marlow's thoughts, but here there is a particular reader-trap. Because we don't know the story that follows, we assume it will reveal to us that redeeming 'idea'. But Marlow knows, as he fails to complete his sentence, that his story is not about a redeeming idea, but about setting something up to be worshipped and offering sacrifices to it.

Similarly, later, when he asserts that 'I hate, detest, and can't bear a lie' (*HD*, 82), we tend to take this as a sign of his trustworthiness. It is, then, slightly disturbing when he, more than once, allows others to believe what is not strictly true. For example, he allows the brick-maker to believe that he and Kurtz represent 'the new gang – the gang of virtue' (*HD*, 79), when there is no 'new gang' outside the brick-maker's paranoid interpretation of the coincidence that Marlow and Kurtz have been 'recommended' by the same people. King Leopold's plans for the Belgian Congo had no place for a 'gang of virtue'.[19] And yet the brick-maker's mistaken interpretation of the texts he has read – the Company's correspondence – has been kept alive by generations of critics and readers. Furthermore, if this 'white lie' is disturbing, a form of lying by omission, what are we to make of Marlow's final, active lie to Kurtz's Intended, when he returns to Brussels? One of the striking features of his narration is the constant play of interpretative effort over the events of his narration.

As the story proceeds, it becomes more and more directed towards Kurtz. The Company's chief accountant first mentions Kurtz, 'a first-class agent ... a very remarkable person' (*HD*, 69). Subsequently, Marlow becomes associated with Kurtz as part of the 'gang of virtue'. Marlow feels alienated from the atmosphere of greed and plotting at the Central Station: against this, Kurtz stands out as a believer in the 'civilising mission': 'an emissary of pity, and science, and progress' (*HD*, 79). As Marlow feels more and more alienated from those around him, he becomes increasingly attached to the idea of Kurtz. Kurtz alone seems to have some 'moral ideas'. What is more, Kurtz is 'a gifted creature', and his pre-eminent gift is 'his ability to talk, his words – the gift of expression' (*HD*, 113). What Kurtz holds out for Marlow is not only the chance to see 'whether this man, who had come out equipped with moral ideas of some sort, would climb to the top after all, and how he would set about his work when there' (*HD*, 88), but also the chance of someone whose gift for words will enable Marlow to make sense of his experiences. One of the disappointments of the novella – a deliberate and structural disappointment – is that Kurtz doesn't tell his story. The only utterance we are given is the famous (and ambiguous) 'The horror, the horror'. This stands in for the story that is not told.

I suggested earlier that one of the narrative patterns that Conrad uses in 'Heart of Darkness' is that of the quest. We can see here how Marlow searches for Kurtz, but also how, when he finds him, the result is disappointing for him and difficult for us to interpret. We can contrast this with the much more straightforward quests of *Treasure Island* or *King Solomon's Mines*. At the end of these works, the various quests have been successfully completed – treasure has been found, identities established, brothers reunited – and everyone returns home satisfied. 'Heart of Darkness' is more like *To the Lighthouse*. Virginia Woolf's novel ends with the arrival at the lighthouse and the completion of Lily Briscoe's painting, but the reader is left to put this together and puzzle over the significance of that arrival. In the same way, in 'Heart of Darkness', the end of the quest does not flood the text with meaning, but rather leaves the reader with more questions to consider.

Political novels

Between 1904 and 1911, Conrad produced his three great political novels: *Nostromo*, *The Secret Agent*, and *Under Western Eyes*. Since his unfinished second novel, *The Sisters*, Conrad's ambition had been to write a novel of the cities and to be part of the European tradition of the novel. With these works, Conrad achieved that ambition.

Through his collaboration with Ford Madox Ford on *Romance* (1903), he had learned how to use research (rather than personal experience) as the basis for fiction. *Romance* was a story of English smugglers, Cuban pirates, and Jamaican planters based on materials Ford had found in the British Library. Straight after *Romance*, Conrad began work on *Nostromo*. Through the creation of a fictional (or, rather, a composite) South American country, Conrad engages with the new North American imperialism that had announced itself through the Spanish–American War. Under the treaty of December 1898 that concluded the war, America acquired (among other things) Cuba and the Philippines: this clearly marked the decline of Spain and the emergence of the USA as an imperial power. Subsequent North American support for the secession of Panama from Colombia (which allowed the New Panama Canal Company to build the canal which the government of Colombia had rejected) also had an impact on the novel's representation of the functioning of the new imperialism and the operation of 'material interests' (what we might call 'market forces') in the third world. These 'material interests' (*N*, xix) are embodied in the novel by the Gould silver mine.

Nostromo, indeed, is the great British political novel, on the grounds of both its literary and political sophistication. It is not only a technical *tour de force* in its handling of time-shifts, multiple viewpoints, and symbolic action. It is also one of the few novels in English that adequately registers the dynamics of a society; one of the earliest English novels to engage with the rhetoric and practices of American imperialism that came to dominate the twentieth century; and one of the few English novels that deals, with any sophistication, with the world of multi-national corporate enterprise that we all inhabit. At the same time, through its complex narrative presentation of the fictional history of Costaguana, it also engages with the problematic nature of history and of historiography.

Central to the novel are two figures, Charles Gould, the owner of the silver mine, and Gian' Battista Fidanza (known as 'Nostromo'), an Italian sailor 'in exile from the sea', who has come ashore and become the Capataz de Cargadores, the leader of the dock-workers. In his Author's Note, Conrad links these two individuals together as 'both captured by the silver of the San Tomé mine' (*N*, xix). Gould inherits the mine from his father and determines to make it a success in order to bring peace and order to Costaguana. The novel traces the outcomes of this project, based on his faith in 'material interests', and shows its impact on the country, its politics, and its people – and, not least, the impact on the character of Charles Gould and his marriage. Nostromo's enslaving by the silver comes about through his willingness to serve those in power in order to make a name for himself. Around this central armature, Conrad builds up his picture of Costaguana and its relations to a larger world, national and international, of politics and finance. As Arnold Kettle observed, the narrative technique that Conrad developed in *Nostromo* was designed to show life in modern society with its various political and social processes acting at conscious, semi-conscious, and unconscious levels.[20] The temporal dislocations prevent readers from losing themselves in the pleasures of narrative sequence and force them to engage with how the past becomes the present; how the present becomes the future; how individuals (and societies) are shaped by past experience. The novel's interest is in the process of historical change and the process of becoming, but the novel is also concerned with how these processes are conceptualised and represented by individuals to themselves and by different classes and groups in society.

The Secret Agent was apparently inspired by a conversation with Ford about anarchists. It takes as its subject the alleged anarchist attempt to bomb the Greenwich Observatory, but Conrad's narrative follows the anarchist interpretation of the incident as the work of an *agent provocateur*. In contrast to the complex construction of *Nostromo*, this is, indeed, as the subtitle claims, a 'simple tale'. Conrad deploys a sustained ironic narration, and there is only one major narrative trick: the time-jump from Verloc's assignment by the foreign embassy to carry out a bomb attack on the Observatory to the anxious discussion of the outcome of the attempted bombing among the anarchists. After that, the narrative follows the working out of the process of detection through a single day in the restricted space of central London. However, there is nothing simple about the novel's social vision. If the novel shows its anarchists as (with one exception) a group of ineffectual fakes, it shows a police force motivated by private alliances and considerations, a society organised to protect those who have from those who have not, and the underside of international politics with its spies and secret agents, its 'terrorist' scares created to bring about oppressive domestic legislation.

The Secret Agent is a novel of anarchists, *agents provocateurs*, police-spies, secret agents for foreign powers, but at its centre is a domestic tragedy. The novel charts the destruction of the Verloc family: the death of Stevie as the direct outcome of the self-sacrificing plans of his mother and sister designed expressly to protect him; the misalignment at the heart of the Verloc marriage whereby Verloc had mistakenly believed he was loved for himself; and the madness and suicide of Winnie. The remorseless destruction of this family is part of a deeply pessimistic vision of the atomisation of society, with each individual pursuing their own separate schemes, and the apprehension of a larger chaos, in which human plans go awry and nothing can be relied upon.

In *Under Western Eyes*, Conrad again engages with the underside of politics. Where *The Secret Agent* brought the lower-middle-class domestic world of H. G. Wells's social comedies (or Arnold Bennett's later *Riceyman Steps*, 1923) into the interplay of anarchists, international 'terrorism', and the policing of terrorism, *Under Western Eyes* brings Dostoevsky's *Crime and Punishment* into the shadowy, looking-glass world of spies and double agents made familiar later by the fictions of Graham Greene and John Le Carré.[21] *Under Western Eyes* takes place in tsarist Russia in the dying days of the Romanov autocracy. Conrad's protagonist, Razumov, the illegitimate son of Prince K–, becomes entangled in the aftermath of the assassination of a Minister of State. Razumov, who has focused his life on winning the silver medal for the prize essay as a step towards an academic career, finds that his behaviour has been misinterpreted by his fellow students as revolutionary sympathy, when Haldin, the surviving assassin, takes refuge in his room. Razumov is now forced to take sides between autocracy and revolution, but soon discovers that, under the oppressive conditions of tsarist autocracy, he can never clear his name from suspicion. At the same time, his betrayal of Haldin to the authorities preys on him in the same way as Raskolnikov's murder of the two women operates on his unconscious, forcing him compulsively into disguised confessions of guilt.

In the first part of *Under Western Eyes* Conrad's narrator, an English 'teacher of languages' in Geneva, recounts Razumov's life as a student in St Petersburg up to the time of the assassination and the betrayal of Haldin. This account is based on 'documentary evidence', Razumov's journal (*UWE*, 3). However, the narrator does not present us directly with the journal, but rather with his own interpretation and novelisation of it. Parts II and III describe Razumov's life among the Russian political exiles in Geneva; here the narrator supplements his use of Razumov's journal with his own experience of these circles and his own impressions of Razumov. Part IV takes us back to the moment at which Part I ended and reveals the process by which Razumov came to be in Geneva. This new information enforces a radical revisioning of Razumov and his motives. At the same time, the narration throughout is coloured by the narrator's claimed inability to understand Russians, his antipathy to Razumov, and Razumov's antipathy to him. As with *Crime and Punishment*, the narrative is driven towards the protagonist's confession. Razumov's partial confession at the end of Part I to General T– is completed, at the end of the novel, by full confessions, written and spoken to Miss Haldin and the revolutionaries respectively. However, this sense of narrative closure – Razumov's confessions finally bring his sense of himself in line with the identity others ascribe to him – is problematised by the method of narration. The narrator's repeated reflections on his task and Razumov's identity as a writer (of essays, reports, journals) make this a novel very self-conscious about writing. Also, as Frank Kermode has pointed out, the insistent imagery of souls, ghosts, and phantoms or the attention to eyes, ears, writing, and hearing that permeates the narrative produce a hermeneutic excess that escapes the closure of interpretation.[22]

Conclusion

Conrad continued to write until his death in 1924. Although one of these novels, *Chance* (1913), was his first popular success, and another, *Victory* (1915), was included by F. R. Leavis in his 'great tradition', Conrad's late novels have suffered from critical neglect and undervaluation until comparatively recently. The paradigm of 'achievement and decline' that was established by Conrad critics in the 1950s has remained dominant despite repeated attacks on it. Gary Geddes, for example, convincingly demonstrated that the paradigm misread late Conrad because it privileged 'fictional modes and techniques that were no longer of paramount importance to Conrad'.[23] Certainly, in his later fiction, Conrad maintained his interest in developing new modes and techniques in a continuing experimentation with the novel form.[24] The interest in women, gender, and sexuality (in novels like *Chance*, *Victory*, *The Arrow of Gold* (1919), and *The Rescue* (1920)) and the exploration of ageing in *The Rover* (1923) and *Suspense* (1925) also show Conrad opening new territories. In the last phase of his writing career, despite the recurrent anxieties and problems with his health, Conrad continued to develop as a novelist and continued to produce work that repays attention.

NOTE ON EDITIONS

There is no single complete critical edition of Conrad's works available: Cambridge University Press has such an edition in hand and has so far published *Almayer's Folly*, *The Secret Agent*, and *Notes on Life and Letters*. It is current scholarly practice to refer to the Dent Uniform Edition (J. M. Dent, 1923–4). This was reprinted as the Dent Collected Edition (1946–55). The Oxford World's Classics editions of Conrad's novels are published with useful introductions and notes and have the same pagination as the Dent Uniform and Collected editions. There are Norton Critical editions of some of Conrad's key texts which additionally include a selection of critical essays.

NOTES

1 Louis Becke, *By Reef and Palm* (London: T. Fisher Unwin, 1894), *The Ebbing of the Tide* (London: T. Fisher Unwin, 1896), *The Mutineer* (London: T. Fisher Unwin, 1898).

2 Unsigned review, *Spectator* (19 October 1895), 530.

3 Andrea White, *Joseph Conrad and the Adventure Tradition* (Cambridge: Cambridge University Press, 1993), pp. 5 and 7.

4 *Almayer's Folly* (London: J. M. Dent, 1923), p. 7; hereafter cited as *AF*. Other abbreviations used are as follows: 'Heart of Darkness' (*HD*), *Lord Jim* (*LJ*), *The Nigger of the 'Narcissus'* (*NN*), *Nostromo* (*N*), *Under Western Eyes* (*UWE*). All references to Conrad's work are to the Dent Uniform Edition, 1923–4.

5 Robert Louis Stevenson, *Treasure Island*, Tusitala Edition (London: Heinemann, 1923), p. 219.

6 Stevenson, *Treasure Island*, p. xxvi.

7 H. Rider Haggard, *King Solomon's Mines* (London: Penguin, 2008), p. 10. Despite this, he does give prominent roles to two women, Gagool and Foulata, neither of whom, of course, wears a petticoat.

8 Ford Madox Ford, *Joseph Conrad: A Personal Remembrance* (London: Duckworth, 1924), pp. 35, 36.

9 See Robert Hampson, '"Experiments in Modernity": Ford and Pound', in Andrew Gibson (ed.), *Pound in Multiple Perspective* (Basingstoke: Macmillan, 1993), pp. 93–125.

10 *Daily Chronicle* (22 December 1897), in Norman Sherry (ed.), *Conrad: The Critical Heritage* (London: Routledge & Kegan Paul, 1973), p. 89. Hereafter *CH*.

11 *Daily Mail* (22 December 1897), in *CH*, p. 83.

12 Peter McDonald, 'Men of Letters and Children of the Sea: Conrad and the Henley Circle', *The Conradian*, 21.1 (Spring 1996), 15–56.

13 Giles Foden, 'The Moral Agent', *Guardian Review* (1 December 2007), 4.

14 For a fuller discussion of this point, see Robert Hampson, *Cross-Cultural Encounters in Conrad's Malay Fiction* (Basingstoke: Palgrave, 2000), chapter 6.

15 Edward Said, *The World, the Text and the Critic* (London: Vintage, 1991), pp. 94–5.

16 The most accurate transcription of *The Congo Diary* is my own. First published with my edition of 'Heart of Darkness' (Penguin, 1995), it was reprinted for a new edition (Penguin, 2007).

17 T. S. Eliot, '*Ulysses*, Order, and Myth', in *Selected Prose of T. S. Eliot*, ed. Frank Kermode (London: Faber, 1975), p. 178.

18 Cedric Watts, *Conrad's 'Heart of Darkness': A Critical and Contextual Discussion* (Milan: Mursia International, 1977), pp. 2, xx.

19 See Adam Hochschild, *King Leopold's Ghost* (London: Pan Books, 2002) for an account of Leopold's policies and practices in the Congo.

20 Arnold Kettle, *An Introduction to the English Novel* (London: Hutchinson, 1951), II, p. 66.

21 For a detailed discussion of the connections between Conrad and Dostoevsky, see Keith Carabine, *The Life and the Art: A Study of Conrad's 'Under Western Eyes'* (Amsterdam: Rodopi, 1996).

22 Frank Kermode, 'Secrets and Narrative Sequence', in *Essays on Fiction, 1971–82* (London: Routledge & Kegan Paul, 1983), pp. 133–53.
23 Gary Geddes, *Conrad's Later Novels* (Montreal: McGill-Queen's University Press, 1980), p. 1.
24 For a fuller account, see my essay 'The Late Novels', in J. H. Stape (ed.), *The Cambridge Companion to Joseph Conrad* (Cambridge: Cambridge University Press, 1996), pp. 140–59.

FURTHER READING

Dryden, Linda, *Joseph Conrad and the Imperial Romance*, Basingstoke, Macmillan, 2000
Gibson, Andrew, and Robert Hampson (eds.), *Conrad and Theory*, Amsterdam, Rodopi, 1993
GoGwilt, Christopher, *The Invention of the West: Joseph Conrad and the Double-Mapping of Europe and Empire*, Stanford, Stanford University Press, 1995
Hampson, Robert, *Joseph Conrad: Betrayal and Identity*, Basingstoke, Macmillan, 1992
Henricksen, Bruce, *Nomadic Voices: Conrad and the Subject of Narrative*, Urbana, University of Illinois Press, 1992
Jones, Susan, *Conrad and Women*, Oxford, Oxford University Press, 1999
Kaplan, Carola M., Peter Lancelot Mallios, and Andrea White (eds.), *Conrad in the Twenty-First Century: Contemporary Approaches and Perspectives*, New York, Routledge, 2005
Knowles, Owen, and Gene Moore (eds.), *The Oxford Reader's Companion to Conrad*, Oxford, Oxford University Press, 2000
Najder, Zdzislaw, *Joseph Conrad: A Chronicle*, Cambridge, Cambridge University Press, 1983
Roberts, Andrew Michael, *Conrad and Masculinity*, Basingstoke, Macmillan, 2000
Stape, J. H. (ed.), *The Cambridge Companion to Joseph Conrad*, Cambridge, Cambridge University Press, 1996
Watt, Ian, *Conrad in the Nineteenth Century*, London, Chatto & Windus, 1980
White, Andrea, *Joseph Conrad and the Adventure Tradition*, Cambridge, Cambridge University Press, 1993

19

MICHAEL BELL

D. H. Lawrence

David Herbert Lawrence (1885–1930) was, and remains, a highly controversial outsider, never quite assimilable to successive orthodoxies. Born with weak lungs and the lifelong expectation of an early death, and having internalised in childhood the conflicting pressures of his parents, he had what some psychologists call a 'skinless' sensitivity. While this made him on occasion a 'difficult' person socially and domestically, it also contributed to his unique characteristic as man and writer: the intensity of his existence in the passing moment. For this reason, he represents a strong conception of the novel, which, although it commands widespread theoretical assent, can be controversial in practice. His own practice is illuminating in its very unevenness and occasional extremity, for these arise from his being always something more than a novelist. In his own words, he was 'a passionately religious man', which does not mean the adherent of a sect but having a fundamental conviction about the human relation to the cosmos.[1] In this respect, the meditation on Being in a philosopher such as Martin Heidegger provides a significant analogue. At the same time, the novel was his crucial arena for testing his shifting insights into human and non-human existence, and the sequence of his novels therefore provides the best structure through which to understand the shape of his *œuvre*. Accordingly, what follows is a survey of his novelistic career and personal life leading to reflections on the nature and significance of his writing.

In retrospect, his first three novels show Lawrence feeling his way and, in his own words on *Sons and Lovers*, shedding his sicknesses (*Letters*, II, 90). *The White Peacock* (1911) is consciously modelled on George Eliot in its story of two couples in a provincial English setting. When Lettie Beardsall marries the socially desirable Leslie rather than the lower-class, more physical, but also less developed and articulate suitor, George Saxton, the outcome is frustration and stagnation for the principal characters. Meanwhile the tone of the book is caught in its narration by Lettie's sensitive, but rather ineffectual, brother, Cyril, nicknamed Sybil, as well as a Thomas Hardy-like,

Schopenhauerian emphasis on the indifferent 'cruelty' of the natural world in which George is more at home. The emotional impasse of the book reflected Lawrence's own. Although his parents were not so far apart in objective social terms, they enacted a mutually exacerbating conflict between a culturally and socially aspirant mother and a recalcitrantly working-class father. This early experience underlies the gender bias focused in the parenthetical story from which the novel derived its eventual title. The local gamekeeper, Annable, nurses a resentment after his affair with a lady referred to as the 'white peacock'. He attributes her rejection of him to a specifically female idealism, the flip side of the initial attraction. It would take Lawrence some years to fight free of his over-identification with his mother and his rejection of his father, and throughout his career he was liable to misogynist outbursts arising from his underlying female identification and his reactive need for masculine assertion. This first novel has the vividness of Lawrence's sensibility but with a world-weariness and sentimentality he would quickly come to reject. He would have one day to kill off the Cyril in himself.

Lawrence trained as a schoolteacher at Nottingham College and had his first post from 1908 at Croydon, in suburban South London. *The Trespasser* (1912) reworks a manuscript by his schoolteacher friend, Helen Corke, who had suffered the suicide of her older, married lover when she broke off the affair. In Corke's own story, published as *Neutral Ground* (1933), the heroine comes to recognise her own lesbian nature whereas in Lawrence's version it is once again the woman whose emotional idealism resists the physical demands of love and drives the man to despair. But instead of the emphasis on a Schopenhauerian natural world, much of the action of this novel takes place in the Isle of Wight, where the lovers go for an idyllic short holiday. The musician lover is called Siegmund as part of an elaborate creation of a Wagnerian world both beautiful and febrile, desirable and destructive. Lawrence is now concerned with the cultural forms that create worlds and is beginning to unmask the dangers of romantic love as such. Even as it lays blame on the woman within the relationship, the novel probes the cultural premises of the relationship itself.

If Lawrence had died in 1912 he might be remembered as a talented 'Edwardian' novelist, and he unfairly dismissed his first two novels as 'a florid prose poem and a decorated idyll running to seed in realism' (*Letters*, I, 184). But he was right to recognise a significant new ambition in his next novel, *Sons and Lovers* (1913). He had been working on 'Paul Morel' for some time and consulting as always with his friend Jessie Chambers, in whose family at the Haggs Farm, a short walk from his home in Eastwood, Lawrence had been almost an adoptive extra brother. He resigned his teaching post in 1912 owing to pneumonia and was in a very low and uncertain state psychologically. He had broken off his long and ambiguous relationship with Jessie and was briefly engaged to another local friend, Louie Burrows. Planning to go to Germany, he visited for advice his former professor of languages, Ernest Weekley, whom he admired, and was immediately struck by Weekley's wife Frieda, née von Richthofen. She was likewise attracted to the young man some five years her junior, and, partly influenced by the Austrian psychologist Otto Gross, she believed in the benefit of sexual love beyond the confines of monogamy. But Lawrence wanted a permanent commitment to which she eventually agreed despite a very painful divorce from Weekley and separation from her children during their youth. The story of Paul Morel, closely based on Lawrence's relationship with Jessie, now had Frieda as its creative sounding-board, and, as an account of the blocked relationship, it is unfair in attributing to Jessie a sexual inhibition more crucially present in the young Lawrence himself. But it is a novel, and, as the change of title indicates, it seeks to illuminate a more general theme of the son's need to free himself emotionally from the mother. The generalising of the theme may reflect Lawrence's acquaintance, through Frieda, with Freudian thought although he strongly resisted 'Oedipal' readings of the novel. His writings on Freud, *Psychoanalysis and the Unconscious* (1921) and *Fantasia of the Unconscious* (1922), indicate his resistance, endorsed by many subsequent thinkers, to the normative premises of Freudian thought.

The novel is a remarkable achievement and a deserved classic of adolescent development. Its observation of working-class family life is as compelling as it is sometimes painful. It is true that it does not entirely escape a *parti pris* whereby identification with Paul as the Lawrence-figure distorts both the central relationship and the presentation of the parents. But for Lawrence the novel emphatically had achieved '*form*' (*Letters*, I, 476), and if his special capacity as a novelist was to give his narrative an independent dramatic life that could speak beyond, and even against, the author's conscious purpose, then this dramatic even-handedness can be seen in memorable sections of *Sons and Lovers*, such as the description of Walter Morel repairing boots, making fuses, and telling stories about the underground world of the mine.[2] Not surprisingly, its overall success remains a matter of readerly disagreement, and the case is further complicated by the radical emendations, largely cuts, effected by Lawrence's early mentor, the civil servant Edward Garnett. In order to make the work publishable, Garnett cut what he saw as repetitious material, whereas Lawrence was developing, somewhat intuitively, what was to become his characteristic method of incremental development through repetition with variation. Garnett removed, for example, moments of intellectual discussion with Miriam (the Jessie-figure) which gave a different substance to the character and the relationship. Moreover, although the constant adoption of Paul's viewpoint, both morally and technically, threatens the impersonality of the work, it is appropriate to the subjective intensity of the experience at stake, and it shows Lawrence's own process of discovery beginning to work through that of his major character. One such discovery is the self-transcendence, or impersonality, that Paul experiences making love with his married lover, Clara Dawes. Although that relationship does not last, it anticipates the crucial intuition of *The Rainbow* (1915) and the central problematic of *Women in Love* (1920), the two novels which embody Lawrence's mature world-view.

In 1913 Lawrence began work on a novel which was years later to become *The Lost Girl* (1920), a serio-comic implosion of the moral world and the novel form of Arnold Bennett, but he put it aside for what he initially thought of as a 'pot-boiler' which rapidly developed into an 'earnest and painful work' (*Letters*, I, 536). This was the story of a young woman who was to become, after many different drafts, Ursula Brangwen, and in the process Lawrence recognised that the two resulting novels were his most summative and profound achievement as a novelist. Having more or less willingly accepted Garnett's advice on *Sons and Lovers*, he adopted a newly authoritative tone in reproving Garnett's incomprehension of the new work in progress (*Letters*, II, 182–3).

Lawrence's romantic diagnosis of modernity, fed by reflection on the anthropology of his day, saw the processes of mental development and enlightenment as occurring at the expense of psychic wholeness in relation to the self, the community, and the cosmos. Following the century of Darwin, however, he found that, in order to tell his modern story, the substance of *Women in Love*, he needed to precede it with a family prehistory of evolutionary scope which he achieved in *The Rainbow* by a narrative art of philosophical subtlety that is rarely recognised even today.[3] Whether his romantic world-view was ultimately true is not the point, even if such a matter could be decided; what counts is the internal complexity, coherence, and power of its instantiation as a way of mapping human experience. By incorporating the story of Ursula's grandparents and parents, Lawrence rehearses, in a compacted multi-layered form, the three evolutionary phases of human development which can be seen in various nineteenth- and early twentieth-century conceptions such as positivism. In the course of the book the characters' sensibility, and way of relating to the world, shift from mythic monism, through religious dualism, to scientific modernity. The book, that is to say, has a double myth of origins: the Genesis myth signalled in the title, and reinforced by the biblical allusions throughout, is polarised with an evolutionary account signalled in the opening reference to the family home as Marsh Farm. These are not essentially to be understood as historical statements about the world, as in the earlier nineteenth-century confrontation of science with biblical literalism, but as two permanent, contrary motives of the human psyche: the desire to be rooted in a spot and the desire to explore beyond the given horizon. So in each generation there are characters who develop their individuality without losing their existential confidence and those who become hollow, often in association with leaving the home environment.

The philosophically ambitious scope of the narrative is effective because it is implicit, and because the evolutionary process is not presented 'sideways on' in the inconceivably large time-scale that would require but as a felt impact of the past within the present. The multi-layered psyche of the Brangwens meant that, in contrast to other modernists, Lawrence did not just enact the dissolution of the 'old stable ego' (*Letters*, II, 183) but absorbed it into something larger and potentially more positive. This sense of the ego's relation to something other than itself underlies the 'impersonality' of the characters' emotional lives especially at moments of profound feeling or crisis as when Lydia Brangwen looks at Tom after the birth of their first child with an 'impersonal' look.[4] Above all, the underlying analysis remains implicit, a function of the narrative language, which constantly assimilates the emotional lives of the characters to its larger rhythm. A supra-personal dimension permeates the narrative medium as in the insistent, rhythmic intensity in the opening description of the farm life. This is sometimes attributed to a heavy-handed authorial celebration of a sentimental Edenic ruralism, but it is rather a subliminal indication of the emotional claustrophobia from which most of the characters wish to escape. We participate half-consciously in this double pressure rather than know it externally as descriptive fact. So too, a relation of continuity between man and environment in the early part of the book gradually modulates into a symbolic relation depending on a new duality. The early Brangwens 'harnessed their horses at the wagon, and, with hand on the bridle-rings, drew the heaving of the horses after their will' (*R*, 10); a joint activity felt in the effortful alliteration but whose intensity requires no further explanation. In the third generation, by contrast, Ursula's mysterious experience with a group of horses (*R*, 450–5) calls out for interpretation. She is no longer in continuity with her world, yet neither has it become merely inert matter to be instrumentally manipulated. The horses have become symbolic, and 'symbolism' has for Lawrence a resonant indeterminacy. Symbols for him are not conscious attributions of meaning but 'organic units of consciousness' connecting us to older modes of being.[5] Just as modernity is only a tiny late moment in the great process of human development, so in Lawrence's account of the human story the dark vision of modernity is overwhelmed by the onward-looking optimism invested in Ursula and her hopeful vision of the rainbow with which the book ends. In 1909 Lawrence had encountered the writings of Friedrich Nietzsche, who anticipated or influenced many of the modernist generation. The early Nietzsche was deeply influenced by Arthur Schopenhauer's pessimistic philosophy of the Will, by which human beings are merely the unwitting instruments of natural process, a view expressed in the grim naturalism of Thomas Hardy. Nietzsche kept much of the framework of Schopenhauer's conception while reversing its implication. For Nietzsche, the most admirable human type is the figure whose personal life can be a conscious endorsement of this impersonal process. Hence tragedy, for him, was affirmative, just as for Lawrence, objecting to the pessimism he saw in Arnold Bennett, it should be 'a great kick at misery'.[6] The difficult double logic here is that Nietzsche affirmed the individual but not as mere ego, a category whose modernist dissolution he also anticipated. This was to be a central theme of *Women in Love*, but before Lawrence could continue Ursula's story in the contemporary generation, contemporary history was catastrophically to intervene.

With the publication of *The Rainbow*, Lawrence should have been comfortably established as a writer, both critically and financially, but its publication after the outbreak of the war was a compound disaster with immeasurable consequences. *The Rainbow* was banned on grounds of obscenity, so that his financial prospects were dashed. He was bitterly opposed to the war and, with his German wife, he attracted official attention such that they were required to leave their cheap cottage in Zennor, Cornwall, yet were forbidden to leave the country. Hence, like Thomas Mann's *The Magic Mountain* (1924), *Women in Love* was conceived before, but gestated during, the war, so that the impact of the war became a significant aspect of the novel's substance and tone. Although it makes no direct reference, he said that the 'bitterness' of the war is to be felt throughout, intensifying his diagnosis of modernity.[7]

In *Women in Love* the 'Lawrencean' couple, Rupert Birkin and Ursula Brangwen, are contrasted with her artist sister Gudrun and the industrialist Gerald Crich. The 'moral' truth at the centre of the novel is that those who have lost their capacity simply to be, and to acknowledge the unknowability of the other, are driven to dominate and possess. But this clash of egos is not a moral truth in the mode of George Eliot so much as a process, both psychological and metaphysical, which works itself out impersonally over the course of the novel. Perhaps for that reason, the contrast between the couples is analytic rather than simply evaluative: Gudrun and Gerald have admirable qualities while Birkin in particular can be tiresome and ineffective even as he articulates the novel's central concerns. Birkin is acutely aware of the power and possessiveness of love relations at all times and of the sublimative illusion in romantic love. He refuses to use the word 'love' at all except as he is forced to by Ursula, who is intuitively close to his recognition but initially shocked and suspicious at his refusal of conventional romantic expression. Birkin seeks an 'impersonal' commitment: an equivalent of the relationship of Ursula's grandparents, which is no longer possible, at least in the same way, for the modern couple. The relationship in *The Rainbow* is imaged as an arch: a stable, rooted form which depends on the separation of its two ends. It is also an image invoked by the narrative voice bypassing the self-consciousness of the characters. By contrast, Birkin images relationship as two stars held in mutual equilibrium by a gravitational pull yet free of the ground on all sides. But more significantly, perhaps, the image is Birkin's own and it becomes, in the 'Mino' chapter, a focus of disagreement between the couple despite her emotional readiness (*WL*, 145–54). For the crucial difference in the modern couple is that their form of joint life is no longer simply inherited like the earlier Brangwen marriages but has become self-conscious. It exists at the level of the personal ego.

The typically damaging self-consciousness of these modern characters, especially those most out of touch with themselves and their world, is depicted in a number of complex symbolic scenes, many involving water, as their less conscious condition is projected on to the world around them. An unconscious process of creating a murderous world out of the repressed self is worked out from the early 'Diver' episode, through the turning-point of 'Water Party', and culminates in the icy peaks in which Gerald is finally frozen into the environment his repression has unwittingly created. These episodes, which combine to make this novel one of the major works of modern literature, are largely revelatory and diagnostic, however, and difficulty arises as Lawrence seeks to articulate a positive fulfilment. There is no ready equivalent in *Women in Love* for the language of impersonality that underwrites such moments in *The Rainbow*; only the strident rhetoric of the 'Excurse' chapter, at once too direct and yet obfuscatory.

Women in Love is both the apogee of Lawrence's novelistic *œuvre* and the fulcrum on which it turns. Within its radical diagnosis of modernity there is an exploratory, creative process of feeling for a new form of life; what Lawrence called the 'struggle for verbal consciousness' (*WL*, 486), which has been well analysed by Michael Ragussis as the contradictory pressures put on key words such as 'individuality'.[8] 'Individuality' means both the achievement of Lawrencean wholeness and its opposite, the empty modern ego. But even as Birkin focalises this process he dramatises the predicament of the author as a radical outsider. The banning of *The Rainbow* was not just an external disaster; it represented a gulf of understanding between Lawrence and his social world in a way that affects the possibility of the novel form as such. Wittgenstein has said: 'It is what human beings *say* that is true and false; and they agree in the *language* they use. That is not agreement in opinions but in form of life.'[9] Lawrence's case suggests a further possibility: that human beings may have to share the same language while living different forms of life. The traditional form of the novel assumes a measure of cultural consensus, and from this point on Lawrence's longer narratives became frankly personal explorations using the traditional powers of the novelist to test experience dramatically, but shot through with an awareness of his distance from the likely common reader. In this respect he makes an illuminating contrast with other modernists, such as Joyce, who deliberately changed the novel form; Lawrence attempted to keep faith with the traditional form but found it imploding from within. It may be significant that his classic essays on the novel as the supreme form of sensitivity to life in its complex and shifting wholeness date from the mid-1920s.[10] As elsewhere in his *œuvre*, he describes most eloquently a possibility that is already lost.

Lawrence's next published novel, *Aaron's Rod* (1922), begins with the hero, a flautist, walking out of his domestic and social worlds with the most minimal explanation either to his wife or to the reader. He wanders through post-war Europe guardedly seeking a new mode of life for himself and fearing always his own loss of integrity, partly symbolised by the fragility of his flute. His cautious relationship with the Lawrencean character, Rawdon Lilly, is a hint that the male-to-male relationship, which was already significant in the previous fiction, was to become a major focus of the *œuvre*, and also a premonition of the overtly prophetic characters of Lawrence's fiction in the Twenties. *Kangaroo* (1923) draws closely on the Lawrences' visit to Australia for several months in 1922. The central figure, Somers, is a writer, with a marriage and wartime experience similar to Lawrence's. In post-war Australia, Somers observes the political choice between socialism and a proto-fascist movement of male bonding led by a charismatic leader, Ben Cooley, known as Kangaroo. Somers is a journalist rather than a novelist, and the novel is a consciously fragmentary *bricolage* turning over the new experiences with a sceptical curiosity. He eventually rejects Cooley before leaving the country altogether, and, although there is no mention of the aborigine peoples, Somers's responsiveness to the non-human presence of the Australian outback anticipates his next major relocation: to the Indian country of the American Southwest.

Lawrence had been invited by the wealthy and wilful Mabel Dodge Luhan to come to New Mexico, where she had settled on the edge of the Taos pueblo with her third husband, the native American Tony Luhan. Lawrence was suspicious of the exotic sentimentalism behind white interest in native American life, but once he arrived he began gradually to see beyond this immediate inauthenticity. The native peoples had an archaic relation to the cosmos which gave vital clues to what he thought was missing in modernity. At least they had until recently, for the Indian way of life was itself largely extirpated not just by external dispossession but by the more subtle and inward impact of modernity. Moreover, Lawrence insisted on the separateness of the two forms of life, so that he knew he could never join the Indians, although they nonetheless confirmed his intuitions about the radical failure of his own civilisation. Lawrence wrote impressive essays on the Indians but his next major attempt at a novel came with his trip to Mexico in 1923.

The decade of brutal internecine warfare known as the Mexican Revolution was just about over as the Lawrences arrived, and there were idealistic attempts to form a new political order and to recover indigenous, pre-Columbian culture. José Vasconcelos, Minister of Education, commissioned indigenist murals by Diego Ribera for the ministry building in Mexico City, while the anthropologist Manuel Gamio investigated the ancient Aztec world. This brief moment of hopeful openness before the Cristero Wars and the institutionalising of the revolutionary party fired Lawrence's imagination to write what he for some time believed was his most important book. Like many other observers, he saw the indigenous peoples of the region as doubly bereft: in their deepest psychological formation they had never really accepted Christianity, yet they had lost their former relation to a religious cosmos. He therefore imagined the possibility that a Mexican anthropologist, Ramón Carrasco, might revive essential qualities of the old religious life form to replace Christianity. Ramón wishes the movement to be religious and explicitly separate from the political order although he has to work in parallel with the President, Montes, and more problematically again, with the military leader, General Cipriano, who becomes part of the movement.

The Plumed Serpent is full of memorable scenes and descriptions partly approaching the mode of Lawrence's travel writings, a genre which he made peculiarly rich. Yet the work has been almost universally seen as a failure overall for a variety of reasons. The most fundamental is that the sensibility underwriting the religious revival is by definition pre-conceptual: it is experienced through symbols, gods, and rituals but cannot be put into the form of ideas. But in order to communicate its meaning in a modern novel Lawrence expounds and paraphrases in ways that negate the intended effect. In many ways the sensibility of the revival is comparable to that attributed subliminally to the early Brangwens in *The Rainbow*, but once it becomes a conscious project it is radically falsified. The story is focalised, at a high level of self-consciousness, through Kate Leslie, the forty-year-old widow of an Irish political activist, who is both attracted and repelled by the movement. She too is looking for something deeper than politics, while Ramón and

Cipriano would like her to join them as an avatar of the Goddess Malintze, and thus as a symbolic reversal of the Mexican myth of Malinche. Malinche, the interpreter and concubine of Hernan Cortés, was a mythic figure in the Mexican imagination: the Mexicans, as 'sons of Malinche', carry an ancient humiliation. The native Virgin of Guadalupe, an object of popular pilgrimage, was a Christian answer to this figure, but the marriage of the white woman, Kate Leslie, to Cipriano is an even more complete reversal of the old myth. Once again, such a mixture of the everyday and personal with the mythic remains impossibly abstract, although placed next to the work of a Mexican writer like Carlos Fuentes, such as *A Change of Skin* (1967), the project is less weird than when seen from a purely European viewpoint.

Through the first half of *The Plumed Serpent* Kate Leslie is principally the Lawrence-figure, sceptically sympathetic to the revival, but in the last half she becomes the Frieda-figure over whom Cipriano wishes to exert a male authority; or more precisely he wishes her to recognise an impersonal 'phallic' power. Once again, in other words, one can see here an underlying commitment to the intuitive emotional impersonality of the early Brangwens being falsified by becoming a conscious programme, at which point it is hopelessly contaminated by Lawrence's own reactive male assertion. The degree of internal scepticism represented by Kate remains a crucial question for reading the novel. Is it, as Bertrand Russell thought, a naïve fantasy in which Lawrence imagines a fascistic exercise of political power by a thinly disguised Lawrence-figure? Or is it a thought-experiment in which Lawrence subjects this idea, and the authority of his own world-view, to testing in a realistically imagined arena and against a sceptical female consciousness? And the question is intensified rather than resolved by the fact that his earlier version, now published as *Quetzalcoatl* (1995),[11] is a more discreet and sceptical treatment of the theme. The final version, with the ritual killing of Ramón's would-be assassins, seems to push the theme to a deliberate extremity. But however we read its possible intentions, the falsifying self-consciousness of the narrative makes it an unwitting parody of the Lawrencean world-view expressed elsewhere, and within two years Lawrence himself had rejected the 'leadership' notion at its core (*Letters*, VI, 321). He was by now engaged in his last novel, which represents a radical change in direction.

Lawrence caught malaria in Mexico in 1925, was barely allowed back into the US, and was seriously ill for his remaining five years. He returned to Europe, including Italy, where he became interested in writing a popular book on the Etruscan tombs. *Etruscan Places* (1932), only published after his death, presented a different image of the primitive self from the sanguinary toughness of the Aztecs, who were after all, even if this was not the aspect that interested Lawrence directly, a military and imperial power. Now living in a fascist Italy consciously modelled on ancient Rome, Lawrence prized the ancient civilisation of the Etruscans which the Romans had destroyed. He affirmed the easy-going physicality, the love of the passing moment of existence, that he saw in the art of their tombs. Although the tombs are carved out of rock under the ground, they are painted internally as if they were tent-like structures in the open air. And the tombs were placed like a second city opposite the city of the living. The Etruscan art suggested an ease of transient bodily existence expressed in 'touch', and it was this that Lawrence sought to recover in *Lady Chatterley's Lover*.

Lawrence wrote this novel three times. The earlier versions are better thought of as different novels on a similar theme and have now been published separately.[12] Parkin, the original of Mellors, the gamekeeper, is initially a union official, and the novel focuses on the social divide between the central couple. The third and final version is more of a romance between two characters who are already déclassé, Mellors himself being in a state of suspicious withdrawal from social and sexual contact. Lawrence edged the political dimension out of the novel to concentrate on the quality of personal relationship and bodily being. Connie Chatterley's young husband, Clifford, returns from the war impotent and in a wheelchair. The event is unfortunate and unfair, though symbolic of a 'tragic' generation. What matters are the responses which this disaster provokes: Clifford denies the importance of the body while Constance suffers not so much from his impotence *per se* as from the attitudes it intensifies and brings to the surface in him. At the centre of the novel is the series of sexual encounters in which Mellors overcomes his reserve and Connie discovers the power of sexual passion in a relationship of physical tenderness. But because of his concern with cultural attitudes, Lawrence depicted not only the progressive stages of intimacy and trust in the sexual relations between Connie and Mellors; he sought also to decontaminate the common language for sexual activity and bodily parts. Indeed, he was concerned with how we talk about such topics at all, and the theme of 'chatter', signalled in the title, is as significant as that of sexuality. *Lady Chatterley's Lover* is not one of Lawrence's most ambitious novels, stylistically and thematically. It has a more palpable moral design on the reader, and its notoriety has significantly distorted its reception with inappropriate expectations. Nonetheless, it is humorous, brave, defiant, and wistful: a conscious last word from the dying novelist.

Lawrence and the novel

Along with his unique practice, Lawrence represented a classic conception of the novel which he developed through wide and critical reading. English novelists have always assimilated wider influences, especially from other European writers, but Lawrence is remarkable for combining a peculiarly English sensibility with a global outlook and an intensely international formation.

In the first instance, of course, he learned from his native tradition. He was steeped in George Eliot, and the intensive mixture of appreciation and critique in his reading of Thomas Hardy clearly underwrote the creative gestation of *The Rainbow* and *Women in Love*.[13] Even as he rejected the moralism of Eliot, and saw in Hardy hints of the dissolution of 'the old stable ego' on which it depended, his critique was adaptive rather than rejecting. Where some other modernists turned too precipitately against the Romantic inheritance, the young Lawrence, as Ford Madox Ford noted, had a deep knowledge of it.[14] It ultimately underlies his growing appreciation of the non-human, whether within the human itself, or in the natural worlds of Australia and the American Southwest.

He also absorbed French literature and appreciated, for example, the power of life and truth-telling in Balzac (*Letters*, I, 91–2). He was, however, resistant to the literary ideal of Flaubert and to the Joycean/Poundian modernism which it influenced. Introducing his own translation of the Sicilian novelist Giovanni Verga, he spoke eloquently of Verga's artistic impersonality and how it was occasionally corrupted by self-conscious Flaubertian techniques of narrative detachment.[15] Lawrence's own artistic impersonality would have been equally damaged by such technique partly because emotional impersonality was an important question within his writing. An academic criticism schooled in a different kind of modernism has frequently failed to see Lawrence's artistry because it works so much, as it were, from inside the character. A narrative posture of ironic detachment would kill the sense of open-ended, exploratory struggle conducted within the momentary horizon of the individual. Only in the longer view do the limits of the characters' horizons become evident, and that is often through a process of recognition for which the earlier state was a necessary condition. Lawrence's 'technique', if one must call it that, is not of objectivity but of a shifting subjectivity. He would, I think, have resisted the later academic privileging of technique as a means of understanding and control. Highly self-aware as a writer, he exercised an essential technique only as an epiphenomenal aspect of his command of the emotional material. To appreciate this more fully, one may turn to his assimilation of Russian and American fiction.

Lawrence eagerly read and commented on nineteenth-century Russian fiction, which he saw as the most advanced in Europe for engaging the condition of modernity. His friend Koteliansky kept up with Russian literature, and the teens of the century saw a European vogue of Dostoevsky, on whom another friend, John Middleton Murry, wrote a book, while Edward Garnett's wife, Constance, was his major translator. The peculiar conditions of Russian cultural history meant that the novel, a generally secular form in Europe at large, was posing primordial questions in religious terms yet in modes of extreme, modern self-consciousness. But in the end, Lawrence came to feel, this self-consciousness was locked within itself, unable to break out into a new life form. Unbeknown to Lawrence, Mikhail Bakhtin was writing in the 1920s his thesis on Dostoevsky, which was to influence Western academic thinking on the novel in the 1980s.[16] Bakhtin reversed the 'doctrinal' reading of Dostoevsky, which was common at the time, arguing that, as a novelist, he subjected all doctrine, even his own most passionately held convictions, to a radical dramatic testing. From this thought Bakhtin was to develop a conception of the novel as a unique means of exploratory self-investigation in modern culture. Although Lawrence subscribed to the doctrinal reading of Dostoevsky, and attacked him fiercely, he seems creatively to have shared the Bakhtinian intuition. Even more doctrinally convinced and passionate than Dostoevsky, he had so much the greater need for it. Whereas the generational sweep and impersonality of *The Rainbow* are Tolstoyan, *Women in Love* is highly Dostoevskeyan in the destructive self-consciousness and extreme behaviour of its characters. Lawrence's great essays on the novel, and his incidental remarks in *Lady Chatterley's Lover*, are contemporary with Bakhtin's thinking. He defines the 'morality' of the novel as lying 'in the trembling instability of the balance' such that the cardinal sin of the novelist is to put a 'thumb in the scale'.[17] But there is an issue of self-consciousness here that is lost on some of Bakhtin's later disciples. It may be a different thing to *create* a novel on Bakhtinian principles if what drives it is an impassioned conviction. The Bakhtinian recognition may follow the creative event it would have killed in prospect, and in that respect it is once again suggestive that Lawrence's essays *follow* his major creative achievement in the novel. Lawrence's sense of creation as a genuine and radical struggle between conflicting forces is further illuminated by his reading of American fiction.

Trapped in Britain during the war, Lawrence read American literature with a view to earning some money afterwards from a lecture tour. Although the tour never happened, America had given him a better reception than his own country, and he was eventually to perform the opposite trajectory to Henry James. Where James settled in England for its dense social milieu, Lawrence eventually acquired a ranch in the New Mexican desert which he appreciated for its non-human environment and for the native Americans, who had a living relationship with it. Nonetheless, white America, which he saw as the most advanced form of modernity, was an important part of the story.

The essays that make up *Studies in Classic American Literature* (1923), originally entitled *The Symbolic Meaning*, are one of the foundational interpretations of the national tradition. At a time when it was still seen largely as children's or adventure literature, Lawrence saw in it the genuine breakthrough he had missed in the Russians. American literature for him enacted a great psychic adventure: he saw the importance of the male-to-male, interracial relation, and traced in a succession of American writers a struggle between their conscious moral purpose and their repressed responsiveness to the New World. This is significantly different from the Bakhtinian notion of an artistic arena for conflicting opinions: it is rather a matter of honesty versus a colluding repression. It also indicates the importance of achieving impersonality within the process, as it were, rather than by a general technique of modernist detachment. Hence the importance in this text of the one critical adage that Lawrence has bequeathed to posterity: 'Never trust the artist. Trust the tale.'[18]

At the same time, it takes one to know one, and Lawrence has remained controversial because of the continuing struggle of art and doctrine in his own fiction. Perhaps for this reason none of his novels, unlike much of his short fiction, is a completely satisfactory artistic achievement. The novels are always in some degree the workshop as well as the product. For this reason, too, it is actually very difficult, though deceptively easy, to write him down ideologically, which is why the ideological turn in literary studies during the late twentieth century led to a dramatic drop in his academic reputation, although not in his common readership around the world. Indeed, the unboundedness of his creative process has an equivalent at the level of response: he constantly challenges the reader to participate in radical revaluations.

That helps to explain why he has been an object of anger and contumely from many feminists while retaining the respect of highly intelligent women readers not lacking in political consciousness. Most notably, Carol Siegel's fine study, *Lawrence among the Women* (1992), after observing that some early reviewers assumed he was female, places him in a tradition of women writers. A number of his books, including a further Australian novel, *The Boy in the Bush* (1924), were written with women collaborators (this, with Mary Louisa Skinner), and female identification is a strong feature of his *œuvre* throughout. There is more at stake here than the patriarchal ventriloquising of which he has been accused and is sometimes guilty. His excellent play *The Daughter-in-Law* (1912) is one of those works in which the women are the strong characters, as the daughter-in-law, Minnie, seeks to break the emotional hold of her mother-in-law, Mrs Gascoyne, over her husband, Luther. The dialogue and action are emotionally vehement with bitter things said but in a spirit of emotional struggle whereby all parties can come to recognise the necessary unfairness. Mrs Gascoyne identifies this mode of utterance as specifically female when she says scornfully to her son: 'Th'art a fool, our Luther, if ter tae's a woman at her word. Well, tha deserves what ta gets.'[19] In truth, this is Lawrence's own normal mode, the homely, folk version of the Bakhtinian principle, by which absolutes are constantly relativised by time and circumstance. Or as he put it elsewhere: 'My yea! of today is strangely different from my yea! of yesterday.'[20] If you take Lawrence at his word you deserve what you get, or what you fail to get, although that is what many academic readers continue to do. In this sense, although Lawrence has been consciously excluded for his masculinist assertions, he has been more truly and unconsciously unheard as a woman.

What is really at stake here, then, is a conception of literature itself. Literature for Lawrence expresses the vividness and wholeness with which he responded to all experience, sensory and intellectual, internal and external. He used the expression 'the fourth dimension', most likely taken over from P. D. Ouspensky's *Tertium Organum* (1922), to indicate that this is not merely an individual emotional intensity but an insight into the nature of being.[21] The phrase refers not to a further dimension, like time, within a perspectival logic, but to a felt intensity of the being of the world such as one can imagine van Gogh and Rilke to have felt. Although Lawrence went to live in the New World, the momentary present was for him the true and always inaccessible *terra incognita*. Philosophically speaking, he may be located as a modern thinker between, or as a combination of, Friedrich Nietzsche and Martin Heidegger, both of whom pushed the boundaries of philosophical discourse towards literary utterance. The iconoclastic revaluing, and the assertion of individual wholeness, in the foreground of his fiction are subtended by an awareness of the sheer mystery of being, always present and always unattainable. He was a great writer not because he always enjoyed such fullness of being in himself, but because of the difficulty, intensity, and insight of his pursuit, and his uncanny capacity to capture it, over and again, in language.

NOTE ON EDITIONS

The standard edition is the Cambridge Edition of the Works of D. H. Lawrence, ed. M. H. Black, James T. Boulton, Lindeth Vasey, and John Worthen (Cambridge: Cambridge University Press, 1979–). The Complete Novels are available in an eleven-volume set.

NOTES

1 *The Letters of D. H. Lawrence*, 8 vols. (Cambridge: Cambridge University Press, 1979–93), II, p. 165. Hereafter, *Letters*.
2 *Sons and Lovers*, ed. Carl and Helen Baron (Cambridge: Cambridge University Press, 1992), pp. 88–9.
3 I discuss this at length in Michael Bell, *D. H. Lawrence: Language and Being* (Cambridge: Cambridge University Press, 1992), pp. 51–96.
4 *The Rainbow*, ed. Mark Kinkead-Weekes (Cambridge: Cambridge University Press, 1989) p. 77. Hereafter *R*.
5 *Apocalypse and the Writings on Revelation*, ed. Mara Kalnins (Cambridge: Cambridge University Press, 1980), p. 48.
6 *Letters*, I, p. 459.
7 *Women in Love*, ed. David Farmer, Lindeth Vasey, and John Worthen (Cambridge: Cambridge University Press, 1987), p. 485. Hereafter *WL*.
8 See Michael Ragussis, *The Subterfuge of Art: Language and the Romantic Tradition* (Baltimore: Johns Hopkins University Press, 1978), pp. 172–225.
9 Ludwig Wittgenstein, *Philosophical Investigations*, trans. G. E. M. Anscombe (Oxford: Blackwell, 1958), p. 88e.
10 These essays are to be found in *Study of Thomas Hardy and Other Essays*, ed. Bruce Steele (Cambridge: Cambridge University Press, 1985).
11 *Quetzalcoatl*, introduction by Louis L. Martz (New York: New Directions, 1998).
12 *The First and Second Lady Chatterley Novels*, ed. Dieter Mehl and Christa Jansohn (Cambridge: Cambridge University Press, 1999).
13 See *Study of Thomas Hardy*.
14 See John Worthen, *D. H. Lawrence: The Early Years 1885–1912* (Cambridge: Cambridge University Press, 1991), p. 122.
15 'Preface to *Cavalleria Rusticana*', in *Introductions and Reviews*, ed. N. H. Reeve and John Worthen (Cambridge: Cambridge University Press, 2005), pp. 170–1.
16 *Problems of Dostoevsky's Poetics*, ed. and trans. Caryl Emerson, introduction by Wayne C. Booth (Manchester: Manchester University Press, 1984).
17 *Study of Thomas Hardy*, p. 172.
18 *Studies in Classic American Literature*, ed. Ezra Greenspan, Lindeth Vasey, and John Worthen (Cambridge: Cambridge University Press, 2003), p. 14.
19 *The Plays*, ed. Hans-Wilhelm Schwarze and John Worthen (Cambridge: Cambridge University Press, 1999), p. 345.
20 *Study of Thomas Hardy*, p. 196.
21 Lawrence uses the phrase especially in the title essay of *Reflections on the Death of Porcupine*, ed. Michael Herbert (Cambridge: Cambridge University Press, 1988), pp. 349–76.

FURTHER READING

Bell, Michael, *D. H. Lawrence: Language and Being*, Cambridge, Cambridge University Press, 1992
Clarke, Colin, *River of Dissolution: D. H. Lawrence and English Romanticism*, London, Routledge & Kegan Paul, 1969

Leavis, F. R., *D. H. Lawrence, Novelist*, London, Chatto & Windus, 1955
Moynahan, Julian, *The Deed of Life: The Novels and Tales of D. H. Lawrence*, Princeton, Princeton University Press, 1963
Ragussis, Michael, *The Subterfuge of Art: Language and the Romantic Tradition*, Baltimore, Johns Hopkins University Press, 1978
Siegel, Carol, *Lawrence among the Women: Wavering Boundaries in Women's Literary Traditions*, Charlottesville and London, University of Virginia Press, 1992
Spilka, Mark, *The Love Ethic of D. H. Lawrence*, Bloomington, Indiana University Press, 1955
Swigg, Richard, *Lawrence, Hardy and American Literature*, London, Oxford University Press, 1972
Worthen, John, *D. H. Lawrence: The Life of an Outsider*, New York, Counterpoint, 2005

20

MAUD ELLMANN

James Joyce

On Sunday 11 March 2001 a huge crowd gathered to watch the first arrival into Dublin harbour of a new car ferry, reputedly the largest in the world. It was not the ferry's size that mattered to the crowd, however, but its name – the *Ulysses*. At the ferry's naming ceremony ten days later, the then Taoiseach of Ireland, Bertie Aherne, announced, 'Of course, it took a Dubliner – James Joyce – to see that Ulysses was not in fact Greek, but was in fact Irish!!'[1]

The ferry *Ulysses* met with a much warmer reception in Dublin than the novel. In 1920 Joyce wrote that a great movement against the publication of *Ulysses* was being prepared by puritans, English imperialists, Irish republicans, and Catholics: 'What an alliance! Good grief, I deserve the Nobel Peace Prize!'[2] Four instalments of *Ulysses*, serially published in *The Little Review*, were seized by the United States Post Office between 1919 and 1920, and the *Review*'s editors, Margaret Anderson and Jane Heap, were fined and fingerprinted for their crime. In 1922, five hundred copies of the Egoist Press edition of *Ulysses* were seized by Post Office authorities in New York, and a further consignment of 499 copies was destroyed by British Customs at Folkestone. Banned in Britain, Australia, Canada, and the United States, *Ulysses* escaped official censorship in Ireland because it had been published abroad, but only under-the-counter copies were available until the early 1970s.[3] In 1967 Joseph Strick's film version was banned outright by the Irish censors, and it was not until 2001 that the movie was released in Ireland, when it was granted a '15' certificate – a measure of the distance travelled in thirty years by what Brian Moore once called 'a nation of masturbators under priestly instruction'.[4]

Having been exiled from Ireland for the best part of a century, *Ulysses* has now come home to Dublin with a vengeance, quashing its detractors much as the homecoming Odysseus routed the suitors. *Ulysses* and its author have been noisily repatriated, to the lucrative benefit of Dublin's tourist industry. The Martello Tower where Stephen Dedalus bickers with Buck Mulligan in the first episode of *Ulysses* has been turned into a Joyce museum; the front door of the Blooms' house at 7 Eccles Street is now enshrined in the James Joyce Centre, which also offers guided tours of 'Joyce's Dublin'. In Dublin fashion, Joycean monuments have been greeted with irreverent rhymes: a statue of the author in Earl Street, unveiled in 1990, was promptly renamed 'the prick with the stick', while a fountain depicting Anna Livia Plurabelle, the personified River Liffey in *Finnegans Wake*, earned the nickname 'the floozy in the jacuzzi', just as the statue of Oscar Wilde in Stephen's Green is now known as 'the quare in the square'. Dublin itself is becoming a museum, refashioned in the image of Joyce's works, which reinvented the Irish capital for the world.

In honour of the first centenary of Bloomsday, 16 June 1904, the day on which the action of *Ulysses* takes place, the Irish government helped to sponsor six months of celebration culminating in 'Bloom's breakfast', when 10,000 people sat down in O'Connell Street to indulge in fried kidneys washed down with Guinness. Bloomsday is now celebrated all over the world, or as Joyce might put it, 'yanked to glory most half this planet from Frisco Beach to Vladivostok', competing with St Patrick's Day as a national holiday.[5] 'The Joyce of cooking' – to borrow the title of Alison Armstrong's Joycean cookbook – has also spread to Joyce's European haunts.[6] In Zurich, where Joyce wrote much of *Ulysses*, the James Joyce pub offers Bloom's breakfast – fried kidneys (improved with a continental dash of cognac) – and Bloom's lunch – a Gorgonzola sandwich – served by tuxedoed waiters at prices beyond Bloom's wildest dreams.[7]

In the academic world, the fortunes of *Ulysses* have risen steadily throughout the century, the novel having proved remarkably adaptable to critical fashion. While the New Critics focused on recurrent patterns and motifs, feminists have stressed the subversion of gender roles, Freudians the psychopathology of everyday life, and Lacanians the crisis of the paternal function. As for deconstruction, Derrida confessed to the uncanny feeling that his insights had been remembered in advance by Joyce's 'hypermnesia'.[8] More recently, Marxists, historicists, post-colonial and cultural critics, reacting against what they perceive as the aestheticisation of Joyce's writing, have insisted on restoring it to time and place, probing its agonistic relations to consumerism, popular culture, British imperialism, and Irish nationalism.[9] The sheer variety of these approaches confirms Cheryl Herr's view that critical responses to *Ulysses* recapitulate the wanderings of its Homeric namesake.[10] This critical variety also echoes the multiplicity of Joyce's voices, ranging from the 'scrupulous meanness' (*SL*, 83) of *Dubliners* to the forked-tongued ironies of *A Portrait of the Artist*, the polyphonic styles of *Ulysses*, and the multilingual puns of *Finnegans Wake*.

One of the paradoxes of the 'Joyce industry' is that *Ulysses* is much more feted than read, whereas *Finnegans Wake* is scarcely read at all. Classes on *Ulysses*, oversubscribed by eager students, shrink to manageable numbers after the first foray into 'Proteus', the forbidding third chapter, and only the most intrepid venture into *Finnegans Wake*. Intimidated by the lexical challenges of Joyce's prose, readers are also daunted by its encyclopaedic aspirations. Both *Ulysses* and *Finnegans Wake* aspire to incorporate the whole of human knowledge; these are books that strive to gobble up the world, with all its languages, legends, and literatures, and even to absorb the sounds of wind and water, animals and plants: 'to allow water to speak like water, birds to chirp in the words of birds, to liberate all sounds from their servile, contemptible role and to attach them to the feelers of expressions which grope for definitions of the undefined'.[11] In view of this linguistic gluttony, it is appropriate that the best-known passages in Joyce's work are scenes of eating. If few readers have digested *Finnegans Wake*, a much wider audience has relished the memorable Christmas dinners of 'The Dead' and *A Portrait of the Artist as a Young Man*. Even more celebrated is the love-scene that concludes *Ulysses*, where Molly's famous 'yeses' assent to food as well as to her future husband, specifically to the seedcake that the kissing lovers exchange between their mouths. 'Yum' is Bloom's response to the same memory.

Henry Fielding famously observed that Homer's *Odyssey* is a great 'eating Poem' and that Odysseus enjoys 'the best Stomach of all the Heroes'.[12] Joyce is equally concerned with the stomachs of his heroes, although their digestion is much less robust than Odysseus's. Leopold Bloom's quest for lunch is constantly at risk of being shipwrecked on the rocks of nausea, and Stephen Dedalus abjures food altogether, imbibing only liquid refreshment on 16 June 1904. Yet *Ulysses* itself is shamelessly omnivorous, gorging on the Western literary tradition, seasoned with liberal helpings of popular culture. In *Finnegans Wake*, this *grande bouffe* goes on eternally; a wake is a funeral feast in which the spirit of the dead is reincorporated into the community.

Joyce's meals provide an illuminating vantage-point for gauging his transformations of the novel. Joyce, of course, is scarcely the only European novelist with an 'eatupus complex'.[13] Jane Austen's *Emma* (1815), for example, tests its heroine's morals through a series of meals, from the suppers at Hartfield, where Emma handsomely supplies the guests while her father begs them to restrict themselves to gruel, to the disastrous picnic on Box Hill, where eating out-of-doors opens the floodgates to incivility.[14] Dickens's *Great Expectations* (1860–1) exposes the discrepancy between table manners and morals; Pip picks up the London way of handling a knife and fork as promptly as he forgets the lessons of love. Beginning with a stolen pork pie and climaxing in a putrefying wedding-cake, food and consumption – as well as the failure to consume – mark all the 'partings welded together' of Dickens's narrative.[15]

If the feast is the hallmark of the epic – Odysseus's return to Ithaca is delayed by a series of banquets – the family dinner is the staple of the bourgeois novel, where the diurnal rotation of meals helps to create what Roland Barthes describes as 'the reality effect'.[16] Gertrude Stein, in her memoir of the Nazi occupation of Paris, *Wars I Have Seen* (1945), remarks that it is 'a queer life one leads in a modern war, every day so much can happen and every day is just the same and is mostly food, food and in spite of all that is happening every day is food'.[17] By presenting human life as 'mostly food', the realist novelist asserts the value of the everyday, defending the importance of the unremarkable routines of life. In *Ulysses* Stephen Dedalus says, 'I fear those big words ... which make us so unhappy' (*U*, 2:26.264). Joyce, writing *Ulysses* during the First World War, uses food to counter those big words, stationing his hero Bloom in the kitchen rather than the battlefield.

Marcel's memorious *madeleine* in Proust's *À la recherche du temps perdu*, Mrs Ramsay's *boeuf-en-daube* in Woolf's *To the Lighthouse*, the wedding-banquet in Flaubert's *Madame Bovary*: these also testify to the centrality of meals in the European novel. For the novelist, meals serve as a device to gather the characters together, revealing both their personal foibles and collective traits. Conflicts between classes, genders, and generations play themselves out over the dinner table. The Christmas dinner in 'The Dead', for instance, offers a microcosmic view of middle-class society in Dublin, staging the divisions between men and women, employers and servants, Catholics and Protestants, nationalists and unionists, scroungers and creditors, intellectuals and philistines, Westerners and Easterners, the sober and the drunk – Freddy Malins, who turns up 'screwed', exemplifies the rampant alcoholism that menaces the flimsy fabric of respectability.[18] At the centre of the story lies the struggle of the living and the dead: Gabriel Conroy belatedly discovers that his wife Gretta is still in love with the memory of Michael Furey, her childhood sweetheart from the West of Ireland. Gretta believes that Furey died of love for her, and Gabriel, feeling incapable of such a passion, realises that he is deader than the furious ghost. His deadness reflects the stagnancy of Dublin, which Joyce described as a 'centre of paralysis', 'hiberniating after seven oak ages' – the seven centuries of Irish subjugation (*SL*, 83; *FW*, 316.15–16).

Furthermore the struggle between the living and the dead is re-enacted at the dinner table, where animals are sacrificed to feed the living and to reaffirm their social bonds: 'A fat brown goose lay at one end of the table and at the other end, on a bed of creased paper strewn with sprigs of parsley, lay a great ham, stripped of its outer skin and peppered over with crust crumbs, a neat paper frill round its shin and beside this was a round of spiced beef' (*D*, 197). With these appetising details, Joyce distinguishes himself from those novelists criticised by Virginia Woolf for telling us what people say, but neglecting what they eat at dinner parties. 'A good dinner', Woolf insists, 'is of great importance to good talk.'[19] Yet a good dinner also depends on violence. Animals are slaughtered to produce meat, vegetables are torn up, peeled, and chopped, most of what we eat is scorched or scalded by fire, while chewing completes the destruction that killing and cooking began.[20] One of the chief roles of etiquette, according to Margaret Visser, is to 'keep a lid on the violence' entailed in eating.[21]

In the Catholic Communion, worshippers unite together through the shared consumption of bread and wine, the staple food and drink of the Mediterranean, which are transubstantiated into the body and blood of Christ. In this ritual, you are what you eat; as Saint Augustine's God explains, 'I am the food of full-grown men. Grow and you shall feed on me. But you shall not change me into your own substance, as you do with the food of your body. Instead you shall be changed into me.'[22] Joyce, who repudiated the Catholicism of his youth, begins *Ulysses* by mocking the Communion service. Here Buck Mulligan assumes the role of priest, replacing the chalice with his shaving bowl:

> Stately, plump Buck Mulligan came from the stairhead, bearing a bowl of lather on which a mirror and a razor lay crossed. A yellow dressinggown, ungirdled, was sustained gently behind him by the mild morning air. He held the bowl aloft and intoned:
> – *Introibo ad altare Dei.*
>
> (*U*, 1:3.1–5)

It is probable that lather, mirror, and razor stand for sentimentality, narcissism, and sadism, which Joyce regarded as the three-sided emotional seduction of Catholicism. 'For this, O dearly beloved, is the genuine Christine: body and soul and blood and ouns', Mulligan continues, here supplanting Christ with a sexier 'Christine' to be sacrificed in this make-believe black mass (*U*, 1:3.21–2). The theme of Communion resurfaces in 'Lotus-Eaters', the fifth chapter of *Ulysses*, when Bloom the free-thinking Jew drops into a church to marvel at the superstitions of his Catholic neighbours: 'Rum idea: eating bits of a corpse. Why the cannibals cotton to it' (*U*, 5:66.352). Like Marx, Bloom views religion as the opiate of the people, the lotus-flower that drugs them into apathy: 'Good idea the Latin. Stupefy them first' (*U*, 5:66.350–1).

Despite these lampoons of Catholicism, T. S. Eliot shrewdly diagnoses Joyce as a blasphemer rather than a heretic, who 'profoundly believes in that which he profanes'.[23] By opening *Ulysses* with a Communion service, however travestied, Joyce frames his novel in a Catholic world, where iconoclasm serves as a backhanded form of fidelity. Food is one of the most amusing ways that Joyce proves himself a blasphemer, since he rarely writes about eating without an ironic allusion to the sacrament. His meals play up the cannibalistic element of the Communion feast, so that the diner is always liable to become a dish. 'Eat or be eaten. Kill! Kill!' Bloom thinks as he escapes the macho carnivores in Burton's restaurant (*U*, 8.139.703).

In the Christmas dinner of *A Portrait of the Artist*, the scene is set for a Communion feast, the pater familias distributing turkey and gravy much as the priest dispenses bread and wine, but the communal spirit is shattered by an outburst of cannibalism. No sooner does Simon Dedalus begin to carve the turkey than the adults begin to carve up one another. A furious row breaks out about the late Charles Stewart Parnell, the great campaigner for Irish home rule, whose political career was destroyed by the public exposure of his ten-year affair with a married woman, Katherine O'Shea. Although Parnell married Mrs O'Shea in 1891, and died in her arms a few months later, the Catholic hierarchy united in condemnation of Parnell, and many nationalists blamed the Church for driving their 'chief' to an early grave.[24] Joyce, however, explains nothing of this background, but places the reader in a similar position to the child, Stephen Dedalus, who witnesses the adults' battle without grasping its full implications. Stephen's nationalist father, flanked by Mr Casey, rails against the clergy, Mrs Riordan (known as Dante) defends the priests, while Stephen's mother begs them to stop talking politics.

> Mrs Dedalus laid down her knife and fork, saying:
> – For pity's sake and for pity sake let us have no political discussion on this day of all days in the year. (*PAYM*, 30)

An early champion of Ibsen's drama of social criticism, Joyce sets the stage for this showdown with an Ibsenite attention to detail.[25] Possibly in homage to Ibsen's Christmas play *A Doll's House* (1879), in which a stove burns near the footlights, Joyce positions his characters around an open fire: 'A great fire, banked high and red, flamed in the grate and under the ivytwined branches of the chandelier the Christmas table was spread' (*PAYM*, 25–6). This sentence aspires to the condition of a stage direction, bringing narrative as close as possible to drama. But in a premonition of the stage directions in the 'Circe' episode of *Ulysses*, which acquire an uncanny life of their own, this scene-setting sentence bristles with symbolic innuendo. The fire, ostensibly a sign of festive cheer, forming the centre of the family circle, also evokes a funeral pyre where the 'dead King', together with the aspirations of the

Catholic middle class, burns to ashes (*PAYM*, 39). Similarly, the 'ivytwined' chandelier accrues a funerary resonance from its association with Parnell, whose death on 6 October 1891 is still commemorated by Ivy Day, so named because Parnell's mourners in Glasnevin Cemetery, awaiting the cortège delayed by the enormous crowds in Dublin's streets, plucked ivy to wear in their lapels. Meanwhile the Christmas colours green and red, enshrined in the fire and the ivy, recall the green- and maroon-backed brushes, mentioned in the opening pages of the novel, which Dante identifies with Parnell and his betrayer, Michael Davitt (*PAYM*, 3–4).

This technique of imbricating naturalistic detail with symbolic resonance is scarcely unique to Joyce; the leitmotif of red-and-green, for instance, can be compared to the file in *Great Expectations*, which resurfaces throughout the narrative like the return of the repressed, harking back to Pip's fateful encounter with the convict in the marshes. In the *Portrait*, the colours red and green – the 'red in the grate and the green ivy and red holly' – unite the political and the religious themes, implicating Parnell's downfall in the sacrifice of Christ (*PAYM*, 28). Both sacrificial victims are suggested by 'the plump turkey, which had lain, trussed and skewered, on the kitchen table' (*PAYM*, 28). There is a sense in which the diners partaking of the turkey are sharing the flesh and blood of the 'dead King', an epithet applicable to either the political or the religious martyr.

It is hard to read this scene without being reminded of the Christmas dinner in *Great Expectations*, which is also recounted from a child's point of view. In Dickens's dinner, it is Pip who is trussed and skewered by the conversation at the Christmas board. 'Squeezed in at an acute angle of the tablecloth, with the table in my chest, and the Pumblechookian elbow in my eye', Pip is accused of ingratitude to the sister who brought him up 'by hand' and condemned as 'naterally wicious'. The little boy is thus devoured by the diners' talk much as the pork is devoured by their teeth: 'What is detestable in a pig, is more detestable in a boy', Mr Wopsle scolds.[26] These porky barbs reach a climax when Mrs Joe discovers the theft of the pork pie, and Pip is rescued from a further roasting by the sudden arrival of the police.

The kindly Joe attempts to parry these assaults by ladling bucketfuls of gravy onto Pip's plate, a detail echoed in Joyce's Christmas dinner when Simon Dedalus tries to deflect the argument about Parnell by heaping food and sauce on Stephen's plate. A moment later, however, Simon fans the flames of Dante's pious wrath by offering the 'pope's nose' to any takers, a pun in which the turkey, formerly suggestive of Parnell, is transformed into this leader's most exalted persecutor. In the ensuing stony silence, Simon devours the pope's nose himself (*PAYM*, 31–2). From this point onwards, Simon gives up his half-hearted attempts to quell the argument, and the violence latent in the Christmas feast, no longer disguised by table manners, erupts into a verbal spitting match.

Pip differs from Stephen in the obvious sense that Dickens deploys first-person narrative, whereas Joyce uses the third person. But Joyce's free indirect discourse is often coloured by Stephen's juvenile idiom, which enhances the illusion that Stephen is living rather than revisiting his childhood. For this reason Stephen lacks Pip's ironic hindsight or Jane Eyre's retrospective indignation at the injustice and hypocrisy of adults. Like Henry James in *What Maisie Knew* (1897), Joyce exploits the child's vision to defamiliarise the adult world, thus creating the dramatic irony whereby the reader intuits more than the child understands – although Joyce's readers, distanced by a century (and possibly a hemisphere) from Parnell's downfall, may be as mystified as Stephen by the adults' argument. Yet Maisie's immature diction makes little impact on James's labyrinthine syntax, whereas Joyce adapts his style to the child's lisping speech. As Stephen grows from childhood to youth, Joyce's style alters in accordance with the seismic changes in his hero's consciousness. The notorious discontinuities of style in the *Portrait* reflect the epistemological breaks experienced in growing up: 'Molecules all change. I am other I now', as an older Stephen puts it in *Ulysses* (*U*, 9:156.4).

What is startling about the Christmas scene is that Stephen's consciousness is temporarily effaced by the verbal carnage of the dinner table. In formal terms, this ill-fated feast marks an abrupt change of narrative stance.[27] Up to this point, the narrator has adopted Stephen's point of view, showing how the frail, myopic schoolboy gropes his way around his puzzling world by testing the sonic and semantic possibilities of language: 'Suck was a queer word' (*PAYM*, 8). When the Christmas scene begins, Stephen is characteristically musing on the double meaning of the word 'turkey': 'Why did Mr Barrett in Clongowes call his pandybat a turkey?' (*PAYM*, 28). The answer to this question, unguessed by Stephen, is that the pandybat, a leather strap used to strike the hands of fractious schoolboys, makes the victim's skin turn red like turkey-flesh. This explanation reinforces the association between food and violence, between the carving of the 'turkey' and the persecution of the sons of God and men. But Stephen is no longer meditating double meanings by the time that Mr Casey mentions 'champagne', meaning explosives, and it is left to the reader to decode the term; the same is true of 'the birthday present for Queen Victoria' to which Mr Casey attributes his crippled fingers (*PAYM*, 26–7). As the Parnell argument intensifies, and jibes ricochet across the table, Stephen's inner voice is silenced by the crossfire. Thus the child is cut out of the narrative much as he is cut out of the argument, and this elision of the personal perspective by the rival claims of Church and nationalism epitomises the Irish colonial predicament.

Historically Parnell's downfall coincided with the bankruptcy of Joyce's father, which sent the Joyce family tumbling down the social ladder. For this reason, the Christmas dinner is the last time the Dedalus family joins together for a hearty meal. Similarly, *Dubliners* presents a world of dearth alleviated only by a Christmas feast. The lavish Christmas dinner of 'The Dead', combined with the opulence of Joyce's elegiac style, marks a radical departure from the 'scrupulous meanness' of the other stories, in terms of both the menu and the prose. Yet even in 'The Dead', as the title implies, the omnipresence of the dead transforms the food into a form of 'moriture', to borrow a coinage from the *Wake* (*FW*, 167.24). The ghost of Michael Furey, like the ghost of Parnell in the *Portrait*, slips into the meat, the music, and the merry-making.

If the *Odyssey* is a great eating poem, *Dubliners* is a lean and hungry book, whose ill-fed characters and pared-down prose reflect the starving culture of a country devastated by the Great Hunger. In 'Two Gallants', Lenehan exclaims three times that Corley's exploitation of young women 'takes the biscuit' – 'the solitary, unique, and, if I may so call it, *recherché* biscuit!' (*D*, 44) – and biscuits are indeed '*recherché*' in the sense that they are hard to get in Dublin, though not as hard as more substantial fare. Joyce's Dublin is awash with alcohol, but the food on offer is rarely more substantial than a biscuit, and sometimes even biscuits are declined. In 'The Sisters' cream-crackers are rejected by the boy narrator, who fears that chewing them will break the funereal hush; in 'An Encounter', musty biscuits lie bleaching in the grocers' windows; in 'A Painful Case', a tray of arrowroot biscuits, washed down with lager, is all that Mr Duffy eats for lunch. Having rebuffed the caresses of Mrs Sinico, his loving friend, Duffy learns too late that he is 'outcast from life's feast', a condition prefigured by his dry and unsustaining biscuits (*D*, 113).

In 'Grace' Mr Kernan, who has fallen downstairs outside a pub and bitten off a corner of his tongue, gags on his own mucus. The only nourishment he tastes is cold black tea, which he promptly spits into the grate, as if his injured tongue were lapping backwards, thrusting the tea out instead of in. Later in the story, Mr Cunningham regales Kernan's bedside party with an old joke in which a sergeant flicks cabbage off a spoon onto the soldiers' plates across the room, crying: '*65, catch your cabbage!*' (*D*, 160). This unappetising ritual could be seen as a perversion of the Communion feast, in which the congregation 'takes the biscuit' from the priest; indeed the Irish male diet of booze and biscuits is grimly reminiscent of the wine and wafers of the sacrament.

In 'Two Gallants', there is a suggestion of cannibalism when Lenehan insists that he is not going to 'eat' Corley's 'tart'. Instead it is Corley who devours the girl's earnings, while Lenehan indulges in a plate of peas, a puny vegetable that puns on 'pee'. Apart from the Christmas dinner in 'The Dead', the only substantial meal in *Dubliners* is the Samhain feast celebrated in 'Clay', but this dinner is marred for Maria by the loss of her hard-earned plumcake in the tram. The game of blind man's buff, in which Maria is tricked into handling 'a soft wet substance' with her fingers, substitutes an excremental lump of clay for the gift of food (*D*, 101). With the exception of 'The Dead', food in *Dubliners* is lost, scanty, bleaching, flavourless, inedible, or unavailable; in the most unnerving cases food is 'abject', in Julia Kristeva's usage of the term, meaning that the body is infiltrated by its own refuse, invaded by its own peas and clay, or flooded by its own spit and mucus.[28]

After the slim pickings of *Dubliners* and the *Portrait*, it is a pleasure to join Bloom for breakfast in the 'Calypso' episode of *Ulysses*.

> Mr Leopold Bloom ate with relish the inner organs of beasts and fowls. He liked thick giblet soup, nutty gizzards, a stuffed roast heart, liver slices fried with crustcrumbs, fried hencods' roes. Most of all he liked grilled mutton kidneys which gave to his palate a fine tang of faintly scented urine.
>
> (*U*, 4:45.1–5)

In contrast to his hero, Joyce detested offal, but he invites the reader to munch the consonants that designate Bloom's favourite dishes.[29] Whatever we think of kidneys scented with urine, Bloom's dietary gusto earns him a place in the pantheon of greedy comic heroes, notably Cervantes's Sancho Panza, whose surname means stomach. Valery Larbaud enthused that Joyce was 'as great as Rabelais', and that Bloom was 'an immortal like Falstaff'.[30] Yet Joyce's hero differs from Shakespeare's fat knight in that Bloom's meals, which are far from lavish, are consumed in poignant solitude, even though his wife is lolling upstairs during breakfast, and distant acquaintances surround him during lunch.

It is Bloom's lunch – a Gorgonzola sandwich and a glass of burgundy – that I propose to chew over. Bloom eats this modest snack in Davy Byrne's 'moral pub' after beating a speedy exit from Burton's Restaurant, which is packed with Lestrygonian flesh-eaters (*U*, 8:140.732). Bloom has also spurned the vegetarian theosophists, George Russell and his sidekick Lizzie Twigg. Instead the wandering hero tries to steer between these alimentary antitheses, avoiding both Scylla and Charybdis, both the constipating rock of meat and the diarrhoeic whirlpool of 'weggebobbles', which 'keep you on the run all day' (*U*, 8:136.535–7). Bloom solves the lunch dilemma by choosing wine, bread, and cheese, all produced by rotting or fermentation combined with human ingenuity. 'Mity cheese', which 'digests all but itself', makes a satisfying compromise between the carnivore and the herbivore, since cheese is animal in origin but manufactured without bloodshed (*U*, 8:141.755).[31] While bread and wine conform to the Communion menu, cheese is Bloom's addition to the Catholic recipe. But cheese is mammary in origin, and thereby violates the patriarchal purity of the Communion service, in which the male priest appropriates the role of the maternal breast, feeding the communicants the 'substance' of the son, as opposed to the mere 'matter' of the mother's milk.

In Bloom's case, the wine is transubstantiated into the voluptuous body of his wife, rather than the tortured body of the son of God. Like Marcel's *madeleine*, Bloom's beaker full of the warm south conjures up a vision of his 'sweetsour' past:

> Stuck on the pane two flies buzzed, stuck.
>
> Glowing wine on his palate lingered swallowed. Crushing in the winepress grapes of Burgundy. Sun's heat it is. Seems to a secret touch telling me memory. Touched his sense moistened remembered. Hidden under wild ferns on Howth below us bay sleeping: sky ... Ravished over her I lay, full lips full open, kissed her mouth. Yum. Softly she gave me in my mouth the seedcake warm and chewed. Mawkish pulp her mouth had mumbled sweetsour of her spittle. Joy: I ate it: joy. Young life, her lips that gave me pouting. Soft warm sticky gumjelly lips. Flowers her eyes were, take me, willing eyes. Pebbles fell. She lay still. A goat. No-one. High on Ben Howth rhododendrons a nannygoat walking surefooted, dropping currants. Screened under ferns she laughed warmfolded. Wildly I lay on her, kissed her: eyes, her lips, her stretched neck beating, woman's breasts full in her blouse of nun's veiling, fat nipples upright. Hot I tongued her. She kissed me. I was kissed. All yielding she tossed my hair. Kissed, she kissed me.
>
> Me. And me now.
>
> Stuck, the flies buzzed. (*U*, 8:144.896–918)

This tableau, in which Bloom and Molly exchange seedcake and kisses on Howth Head, is also recollected by Molly at the end of *Ulysses*, where her interior monologue concludes with her apocalyptic 'Yes'. In the passage above, Bloom says 'yum' to Molly's 'yes', food and kisses having coalesced in his ecstatic confusion of the senses: 'Joy: I ate it: joy.' In accepting the seedcake 'mumbled sweetsour of her spittle', Bloom is also devouring Molly in an amorous form of cannibalism: 'Hot I tongued her.' The term 'mumble' conflates eating with kissing and speaking; according to the *OED*, to mumble is to eat without making much use of the teeth, 'to turn over and over in the mouth'; 'to fondle eagerly with the lips, as if devouring'; 'to speak indistinctly'; 'to maul; to mix up in confusion'; or 'to cook to a soft pulp'. All these meanings 'mumble' in Joyce's usage of the word. Also mumbled in

Bloom's memory is the other end of the digestive process, represented by the nannygoat 'dropping currants'. Under the spell of Bloom's alimentary Midas touch, even goat-turds are transformed into food – 'currants'.

In formal terms, Bloom's stream-of-consciousness differs from the free indirect discourse of the *Portrait* in that the scene is wholly engorged into his mind. 'Take me', say Molly's eyes, and Bloom responds by taking everything in. In the *Portrait*, where Stephen still believes in God, his author still believes in grammar, retaining conventional sentence-structure up until the end, when the novel closes with the fragmentary notes of Stephen's diary. Bloom's monologue, by contrast, chops up syntax into bite-size portions; his thinking is staccato where Molly's is legato. In recollecting the love-scene on Howth Head, Bloom constructs a pointillist word-painting, composed of little dabs and splashes of sensation. Ezra Pound, glossing his pointillist poem 'In a Station of the Metro', explains that 'in a poem of this sort one is trying to record the precise instant when a thing outward and objective transforms itself, or darts into a thing inward and subjective'.[32] Joyce captures such a moment when Bloom sips his wine, and it is appropriate to the digestive motif of the episode that the outward becomes inward with a swallow. After the sentence, 'Glowing wine on his palate lingered swallowed', the external narrator disappears and we are plunged into Bloom's subjectivity, as it lurches between me then and me now.

Bloom's prandial ruminations are framed on either side by the repellent image of the flies copulating on the window-pane, but it is hard to ascertain whether these insects are noticed by the hero or the narrator. 'Stuck on the pane', the flies mark the threshold between the present and the past, the outside and the inside of Bloom's pain, yet cannot be assigned to either. Both their buzzing and their liminality recall Emily Dickinson's poem, 'I heard a fly buzz when I died', where the fly provides a distraction from the deathbed but also functions as a kind of shaman, buzzing between the living and the dead. Bloom broods on the tragic difference between the 'me' who Molly kissed and the 'me' who contemplates the flies: 'Me. And me now. Stuck, the flies buzzed.' The word 'stuck' evokes the lovers Molly and Boylan ('Stuck together! Covered with kisses!' whoops the barmaid who spies on them in 'Circe' (*U*, 15:462.3800–1)), but also alludes to Bloom and Molly, 'stuck' with one another after desire has flown. Moreover Bloom is 'stuck' like a broken record on his joyful memories, unable to bring his 'hiberniating' marriage bring back to life.

Arguably the most distractible character in modern literature, Bloom is distracted from his food by the memory of love, distracted from his memory by buzzing flies, and even distracted by a defecating goat from the most passionate encounter of his life. When Molly's thoughts return to the same moment, she is equally distracted by the other 'he's' that crowd into her memory. It is telling that neither Bloom nor Molly is wholly 'in the moment', for their mutual distraction in this love-scene presages their estrangement to come. While Bloom's memory is full of food, however, Molly's recollection of the same event is full of flowers.

> the day I got him to propose to me yes first I gave him the bit of seedcake out of my mouth and it was leapyear like now yes 16 years ago my God after that long kiss I near lost my breath yes he said I was a flower of the mountain yes ... and I knew I could always get round him and I gave him all the pleasure I could leading him on till he asked me to say yes ... and Gibraltar as a girl where I was a Flower of the mountain yes when I put the rose in my hair like the Andalusian girls used or shall I wear a red yes and how he kissed me under the Moorish wall and I thought well as well him as another and then I asked him with my eyes to ask again yes and then he asked me would I yes to say yes my mountain flower and first I put my arms around him yes and drew him down to me so he could feel my breasts all perfume yes and his heart was going like mad and yes I said yes I will Yes. (*U*, 18:643–4.1573–609)

Like Molly, Bloom remembers 'the rhododendrons on Howth Head' and the flowers of that were Molly's eyes: 'Flowers her eyes were, take me, willing eyes.' But his oral and alimentary sensations overwhelm the ocular dimension of the scene: 'Soft warm sticky gumjelly lips.' Glued to these lips, Bloom has no inkling that Molly is 'leading him on'. Yet her own manipulations are belied by her breathless orgasmic surrender to her memories. 'And I thought as well him as another' may seem a lukewarm acceptance of a husband, especially since this 'him' is ill-distinguished from another 'he' who kissed her under the Moorish wall. If her words seem cynical, however, they could also represent a poignant resignation to the fate of love; the world is full of others, and there is always something arbitrary in the choice of one, however we romanticise this great subtraction. What is more, the rush of flowers that concludes her monologue punningly alludes to Bloom, adding a floral affirmation to her yeses.

The term 'mumbled', with its connotations of mixing, speaking, kissing, and eating, looks forward to *Finnegans Wake*, where food, sex, and language are constantly commingling in Joyce's puns. A relatively accessible example may be found in the seventh chapter of the *Wake*, in which the writer Shem the Penman is lambasted by his jealous brother Shaun the Postman. The battle of these 'doubleparalleled twixtytwins' (*FW*, 286, footnote 4) takes many forms within the *Wake*, where the brothers metamorphose into Justius and Mercius, Dolph and Kev, Burrus (butter) and Caseous (cheese), and many other wrangling duos. In chapter 7, Shaun deplores his brother's eating habits:

> Shem was a sham and a low sham and his lowness creeped out first via foodstuffs. So low was he that he preferred Gibsen's teatime salmon tinned, as inexpensive as pleasing, to the plumpest roeheavy lax or the friskiest parr or smolt troutlet that ever was gaffed between Leixlip and Island Bridge ... None of your inchthick blueblooded Balaclava fried-at-belief-stakes or juice-jelly legs of the Grex's molten mutton or greasilygristly grunters' goupons or slice upon slab of luscious goosebosom with lump after load of plumpudding stuffing all aswim in a swamp of bogoakgravy for that greekenhearted yude. Rosbif of Old Zealand! he could not attouch it. See what happens when your somatophage merman takes his fancy to our virgitarian swan? He even ran away with hunself and became a farsoonerite, saying he would far sooner muddle through the hash of lentils in Europe than meddle with Irrland's split little pea. (*FW*, 170.25–171.6)

This passage, which recalls the toothsome list of offal in the 'Calypso' episode of *Ulysses*, turns out to be an epic catalogue of Shem's refusals. Evidently Shem is no Irish nationalist when it comes to food, for he prefers tinned salmon to the freshest caught in Ireland. Unlike Joyce's favourite heretic, Giordano Bruno, Shem is not prepared to fry at the stake for his beliefs; nor does he participate in bloodshed, whether on the table or the battlefield of Irish nationalism. By declining a smorgasbord of meats ('stakes', 'mutton', 'grunters', 'goosebosom'), Shem recalls the broken-hearted Jew of Joyce's Greek-inspired novel *Ulysses*, where Bloom shuns the meat-eaters of Burton's Restaurant. At this point Shaun interrupts his diatribe to put the question: see what happens when a flesh-eating merman couples with a virgin, vegetarian swan? It was this grotesque annunciation that engendered Shem, the prodigal son, who eloped to the Continent and became a farsoonerite, saying he would far sooner muddle through the wars of Europe than meddle with the squabbles of partitioned Ireland. Like the biblical Esau, Shem is willing to sell his Irish birthright for a European 'mess of pottage', which means a 'hash of lentils'.

'Rosbif', the French term for the English, derives from the English national dish, just as 'frogs', the English term for the French, derives from the French predilection for frogs' legs. But 'roastbeef of old England' is now exported from a British colony, New Zealand. The 'old' *Zee*land is an island in the Netherlands, from which the Vikings set forth to conquer Ireland, entering the River Liffey in the ninth century when they founded the cities of Dublin (the site of Island Bridge) and Leixlip, which means Salmon Leap. Joyce rarely misses a chance to undermine the myth of Celtic purity by showing that the Irish are a mumbled, hybrid, merman race. Hence Shem's father, the somatophage merman, has a Viking ancestry, while his mother, the virgitarian swan, is identified with the River Liffey, the channel through which the

Vikings deflowered Ireland. At the same time the virgitarian swan evokes Shakespeare, the swan of Avon, as well as Virgil, the poet of the *Aeneid*. Shem's fancy for Shakespeare and Virgil means that he would far sooner muddle through Europe's polyglot hash than meddle with the Irish language. The 'split little pea', in addition to its alimentary significance, refers to the 'p/k split' in Celtic languages, whereby Irish is distinguished by its alteration of 'p's into 'k's. In *Finnegans Wake*, Joyce is constantly splitting and reuniting 'p's and 'k's, as well as minding his p's and q's, 'those mirror twins in print', where 'q' is the Celtic predecessor of the Irish k-sound.[33]

If Shem refuses both Irish fresh fish and the blue-blooded beef of British imperialism, what does he consent to eat? This 'stinksome inkenstink' consumes the leftovers of others (*FW*, 183.6). A filthy eater and a filthy writer, Shem lives in a 'mess', in the double sense of meal and muddle:

> The warped flooring of the lair and soundconducting walls thereof, to say nothing of the uprights and imposts, were persianly literatured with burst loveletters, telltale stories, stickyback snaps, doubtful eggshells, bouchers, flints, borers, puffers, amygdaloid almonds, rindless raisins ...
>
> (*FW*, 183.8–13)

and the catalogue continues for another page. Joyce uses the portmanteau 'rindless raisins' to pre-empt those critics who find neither rhyme nor reason in the *Wake*, while he also 'makes a meal' of such derision. The *Wake* is a world of word-eat-word where language is reduced to the primeval (or post-eval) chaos of its elements; a 'flamend floody flatuous world' where monstrous hybrids tear each other in the slime of 'solubles' (*FW*, 23.10.299, footnote 3).

But there is method in this punster's madness. Most of Joyce's portmanteaux combine ideas of food with sex, letters, litter, and 'litteringture' (*FW*, 570.18). In the passage about Shem's lair quoted above, 'burst loveletters' puns on 'French letters', meaning burst condoms, an accident liable to produce a 'litter' of progeny. 'Messes of mottage' mixes the French term for 'word' (mot) into a 'mess of pottage', referring again to the 'hash of lentils' for which Esau sold his birthright; throughout the *Wake*, the story of Jacob and Esau haunts the fraternal rivalry of Shem and Shaun. Another scrumptious portmanteau is 'quashed quotatoes' (*FW*, 183.22), which mashes quotations with potatoes. The word 'quotatoes' represents an Irish mispronunciation of 'potatoes' – the blighted national dish – based on the p/q split. As penman and punman, Shem's role is to gobble up these quashed quotatoes into the gigantic maw of *Finnegans Wake*. He devours other people's words in order to excrete them into writing, producing 'from his unheavenly body a no uncertain quantity of obscene matter not protected by copriright' – an allusion to Joyce's tribulations with the censors and pirates of his former works (*FW*, 185.29–30).

This brief foray into *Finnegans Wake* provides only a foretaste of its pleasures and frustrations. But the same might be said of the lengthiest excursions, since any analysis of Joyce's 'hash of sounds' is necessarily interminable.[34] Joyce explained: 'I'd like a language which is above all languages, a language to which all will do service. I cannot express myself in English without enclosing myself in a tradition.'[35] Instead, Joyce strives to enclose every tradition in his own neologisms, incorporating all the 'verbage' of the world into Joyce Inc. In a charming story called *The Cat and the Devil* written for his grandson Stephen, Joyce appends the following postscript: 'The devil mostly speaks a language of his own called Bellsybabble which he makes up as he goes along but when he is very angry he can speak quite bad French very well though some who have heard him say he has a strong Dublin accent.'[36] The *Wake*'s Bellsybabbling belly incorporates more than seventy-seven languages, each strongly inflected with a Dublin accent. In the vast digestive system of the *Wake*, words are broken down in order to be re-enfleshed in Joyce's ink, engendering what is probably the greediest 'eating poem' in the history of literature. Although *Ulysses* also gorges on the writings of the past, incorporating every style of English prose, *Finnegans Wake* refuses even to restrict its diet to English, consuming both the lowest and the highest foodstuffs of oral and literary culture.

Joyce's voracious epic has proved indigestible to many readers, and even its most passionate defenders agree that a little goes a long way. For the *Wake* yields its flavours best when it is sniffed or sipped or nibbled, not when it is swallowed whole. Had Joyce survived the perforated stomach ulcer that caused his premature death in 1941, there is some speculation that he might have given up his verbal bulimia for anorexia, and returned to the scrupulous meanness of his early style. Yet both these styles – to paraphrase Blake – are roads of excess that lead to the palace of wisdom. Fat or thin, rapacious or abstemious, Joyce's four greatest works provide no end of food for thought.

NOTE ON EDITIONS

There is no standard edition of Joyce's works, nor any prospect of producing an authoritative text of *Ulysses*. The first edition of Joyce's masterpiece, published in 1922 in Paris by Shakespeare and Company, carries the following caveat from its publisher, Sylvia Beach: 'The publisher asks the reader's indulgence for typographical errors unavoidable in the exceptional circumstances.' Despite later corrections by the author and his editors, these errors have never been eradicated; indeed later editions have added more corruptions than they have expunged. In 1984 Hans Walter Gabler published what was described as the 'corrected edition' of *Ulysses*, but his decision to base the text on Joyce's incomplete manuscripts, rather than the first edition of the novel, caused a critical furore. Recent editors (Declan Kiberd for Penguin, Jeri Johnson for Oxford World's Classics) have reverted to earlier versions of the work: both contain excellent introductions, notes, and other explanatory material. Such problems do not arise with *Finnegans Wake* since the pagination has never been altered since the first edition (Faber and Faber, 1939); the page and line references provided here therefore conform to all editions of the work. For *Dubliners* and *A Portrait of the Artist as a Young Man*, the Penguin Classics editions are recommended.

NOTES

1 Speech by the Taoiseach, Mr Bertie Ahern TD, 21 March 2001, www.irishferries.com/ulysses/taoiseach_speech.shtml.
2 Joyce, *Selected Letters*, ed. Richard Ellmann (New York: Viking, 1975), p. 270: my translation. Hereafter *SL*.
3 See Paul Vanderham, *James Joyce and Censorship: The Trials of 'Ulysses'* (New York: New York University Press, 1998).
4 See Tania Sillem, 'It's 'Innocent Stuff Now'', *Guardian*, 3 February 2001, http://film.guardian.co.uk/features/featurepages/0,,432616,00.html.
5 James Joyce, *Ulysses* (1922), ed. Hans Walter Gabler (London: Bodley Head, 1986), chapter 14, p. 349, ll. 1584–5. Hereafter cited as *U*, followed by chapter, page, and line numbers.
6 Alison Armstrong, *The Joyce of Cooking: Food and Drink from Joyce's Dublin* (Barrytown, NY: Station Hill Press, 1986).
7 Armstrong, *Joyce of Cooking*, p. 49.
8 Jacques Derrida, 'Two Words for Joyce', trans. Geoff Bennington, in *Post-Structuralist Joyce: Essays from the French*, ed. Derek Attridge and Daniel Ferrer (Cambridge: Cambridge University Press, 1984), p. 147.
9 For a well-informed, engaging history of Joycean criticism, see Joseph Brooker, *Joyce's Critics: Transitions in Reading and Culture* (Madison: University of Wisconsin Press, 2004).
10 Cheryl Herr, 'Art and Life, Nature and Culture, *Ulysses*', in Derek Attridge (ed.), *James Joyce's 'Ulysses': A Casebook* (Oxford: Oxford University Press, 2004), p. 55.
11 Joyce, speaking to the Polish writer Jan Parandowski, quoted by Petr Skrabanek, 'Night Joyce of a Thousand Tiers', *Hypermedia Joyce Studies*, 4.1 (2003), www.geocities.com/hypermedia_joyce/skrabanek2.html.
12 Henry Fielding, *The History of Tom Jones, A Foundling*, ed. Thomas Keymer and Alice Wakely (London: Penguin, 2005), p. 446.
13 *Finnegans Wake* (1939), 3rd edn (London: Faber and Faber, 1964), p. 128, l. 36. Hereafter cited as *FW* followed by page and line numbers.

14 See Maggie Lane, *Jane Austen and Food* (London: Hambledon Press, 1995), especially chapter 8, pp. 153–68.
15 Charles Dickens, *Great Expectations*, ed. Margaret Cardwell (Oxford: Oxford University Press, 1994), p. 222.
16 Roland Barthes, 'The Reality Effect', in *The Rustle of Language*, trans. Richard Howard (New York: Hill and Wang, 1986), pp. 141–8.
17 Gertrude Stein, *Wars I Have Seen* (New York: Random House, 1945), p. 12.
18 James Joyce, *Dubliners* (1914), ed. Terence Brown (London: Penguin, 1993), p. 176. Hereafter *D*.
19 Virginia Woolf, *A Room of One's Own* (1929), ed. Susan Gubar (New York: Harcourt, 2005), pp. 10, 18.
20 See Margaret Visser, *The Rituals of Dinner: The Origins, Evolution, Eccentricities, and Meaning of Table Manners* (New York: Grove Weidenfeld, 1991), pp. 3–4.
21 Visser, *Rituals*, p. 4. See also Maggie Kilgour, *From Communion to Cannibalism: An Anatomy of Metaphors of Incorporation* (Princeton: Princeton University Press, 1990), pp. 16–17.
22 St Augustine, *Confessions*, quoted in Kilgour, *From Communion to Cannibalism*, p. 15.
23 T. S. Eliot, *After Strange Gods* (London: Faber, 1934), p. 52.
24 Mr Casey calls Parnell 'the chief' in Joyce, *A Portrait of the Artist as a Young Man* (1916), ed. Seamus Deane (London: Penguin, 1992), p. 35. Hereafter *PAYM*.
25 Joyce, *On Ibsen*, ed. Dennis Phillips (Los Angeles: Green Integer, 1999), contains four of Joyce's essays on Ibsen. In 1915, Joyce argued eloquently for Ibsen's superiority to Shakespeare; see Richard Ellmann, *James Joyce* (1959; rev. edn Oxford: Oxford University Press, 1982), p. 398; hereafter *JJ*.
26 Dickens, *Great Expectations*, pp. 25–6.
27 See Hans Walter Gabler, 'The Christmas Dinner Scene, Parnell's Death, and the Genesis of *A Portrait of the Artist as a Young Man*', *James Joyce Quarterly*, 13.1 (1975), 27.
28 Julia Kristeva, *Powers of Horror: An Essay on Abjection*, trans. Leon Roudiez (New York: Columbia, 1982), p. 56.
29 Brenda Maddox, *Nora: A Biography of Nora Joyce* (London: Hamish Hamilton, 1988), p. 105.
30 Robert H. Deming (ed.), *James Joyce: The Critical Heritage* (London: Routledge & Kegan Paul, 1970), I, p. 185.
31 See Richard Ellmann, *Ulysses on the Liffey* (Oxford: Oxford University Press, 1975), pp. 74–81.
32 Ezra Pound, *Selected Prose*, ed. William Cookson (New York: New Directions, 1975), p. 89.
33 Brendan O'Hehir, *A Gaelic Lexicon for 'Finnegans Wake' and Glossary for Joyce's Other Works* (Berkeley: University of California Press, 1967), quoted in *FinnegansWiki*, www.finneganswebb.com/wiki/index.php/P/K_split. As Derek Attridge points out in *How to Read Joyce* (London: Granta, 2007), the Internet seems to have been invented to help us read *Finnegans Wake* (p. 87).
34 Apropos of *Finnegans Wake*, Joyce claimed: 'With this hash of sounds I am building the great myth of everyday life' (quoted by Skrabanek, 'Night Joyce of a Thousand Tiers').

35 Quoted by Stefan Zweig in *The World of Yesterday: An Autobiography* (New York: Viking Press, 1943), p. 275.

36 This story was published as *The Cat and the Devil* by Dodd, Mead and Company (New York, 1964) and Faber and Faber (London, 1965), but the text cited here is Joyce's letter to Stephen Joyce (10 August 1936): *SL*, p. 384.

FURTHER READING

Attridge, Derek (ed.), *James Joyce's 'Ulysses': A Casebook*, Oxford, Oxford University Press, 2004

Bishop, John, *Joyce's Book of the Dark, Finnegans Wake*, Madison, Wisconsin University Press, 1993

Budgen, Frank, *James Joyce and the Making of 'Ulysses'*, London, Oxford University Press, 1972

Deming, Robert H. (ed.), *James Joyce: The Critical Heritage*, London, Routledge & Kegan Paul, 1970

Devlin, Kimberly J., and Marilyn Reizbaum (eds.), *Ulysses: En-Gendered Perspectives: Eighteen New Essays on the Episodes*, Columbia, University of South Carolina Press, 1999

Ellmann, Richard, *James Joyce* (1959), rev. edn, Oxford, Oxford University Press, 1982

Froula, Christine, *Modernism's Body: Sex, Culture, and Joyce*, New York, Columbia University Press, 1996

Gibson, Andrew, *Joyce's Revenge*, Oxford, Oxford University Press, 2002

Gifford, Don, *Ulysses Annotated: Notes for Joyce's Ulysses*, Berkeley, University of California Press, 1998

Kenner, Hugh, *Joyce's Voices*, Berkeley, University of California Press, 1978

Kitcher, Philip, *Joyce's Kaleidoscope: An Invitation to Finnegans Wake*, New York, Oxford University Press, 2007

Mahaffey, Vicki, *Reauthorizing Joyce*, Gainesville, University Press of Florida, 1995

Mullin, Katherine, *James Joyce, Sexuality and Social Purity*, Cambridge, Cambridge University Press, 2003

Nolan, Emer, *Joyce and Nationalism*, London, Routledge, 1996

Rabaté, Jean-Michel, *James Joyce, Authorized Reader*, Baltimore, Johns Hopkins University Press, 1991

Wolleger, Mark A., *Joyce's 'A Portrait of the Artist as a Young Man': A Casebook*, Oxford, Oxford University Press, 2003

21

SANTANU DAS

E. M. Forster

If we were to have all the English novelists 'seated together in a room, a circular room, a sort of British Museum reading-room – all writing their novels simultaneously', where would we place our author? One could picture him sitting between his favourite novelist Jane Austen and D. H. Lawrence, who might nettle him but whom he regarded as the 'only prophetic novelist writing today'.[1] Aspects of both are present in the novels of Edward Morgan Forster (1879–1970). From Austen, he inherits the realist comedy of manners and mode of delicate irony with which he probes under the surface of middle-class English life. But his social satire is regularly invaded by Lawrentian impulses. A passionate kiss in a field of violets connects a boy and a girl from disparate classes; a Cambridge-educated gentleman runs away with a friend's gamekeeper. 'No one seizes more deftly the shades and shadows of social comedy', writes Woolf of her friend 'Morgan', 'but the neat surface is always being thrown into disarray by an outburst of lyric poetry.'[2] Beneath the wit and the wisdom that mark Forster's writing, and giving his novels their poignant undertow, are deep, unfulfilled longings: for a life of the senses rather than of thoughts, for an English greenwood, for some spiritual home, and, above all, for the male 'Friend' who 'never comes yet is not entirely disproved'.[3]

Belonging 'to the fag end of Victorian liberalism',[4] Forster was an observant participant in a culture into which literary émigrés such as Henry James and T. S. Eliot were seeking to gain entry: a pre-war England marked by conversation, conventions, personal relations, style, suavity, money, manners, irony, texture. This milieu was epitomised by turn-of-the-century Cambridge, where he spent four wonderful years (1897–1901). Here, he came under the indirect influence of G. E. Moore, whose philosophy of 'the pleasures of human intercourse'[5] informed the Cambridge Apostles, an exclusive society to which Forster was elected in 1901, and which influenced his cult of 'personal relations'. But culture brings along its discontents. Muddles abound. And one can hear the whirr of the motor car. In this Edwardian world, poised between tradition and modernity, Forster wrote all his novels, except his last one: *Where Angels Fear to Tread* (1905), *The Longest Journey* (1907), *A Room with a View* (1908), *Howards End* (1910), and *Maurice*, largely written in 1913–14 but published after his death in 1971. An inheritance of £8,000 from his great-aunt Marianne Thornton enabled him to have an independent writing career. In 1924, he published *A Passage to India* to great acclaim. He then continued a busy and public literary life, writing reviews, essays, memoirs, short stories – but no longer fiction. Perhaps his homosexuality prevented him from writing another novel; perhaps eros, once satisfied, took away the creative spark; perhaps the red rust Helen sees in *Howards End* had irretrievably tarred his beloved countryside; perhaps his pen just ran dry. We can never know.

In the history of English fiction, we cannot place Forster either with the realist, fob-chained Edwardians such as Bennett and Galsworthy, or the iconoclastic, clock-smashing moderns such as Joyce and Woolf. Forster mentioned Austen, Marcel Proust, and Samuel Butler as the three major influences on his writing. Though periodic attempts are made to claim him as 'modernist' and though his novels register the shock of modernity – motor cars, urbanisation, colonialism – he retains an angular relation to modernism: the countryside remains more attractive than the city and even in *A Passage to India*, his most innovative work, he does not break up the fictional clock. His complexity lies not in radical experimentation but in something almost more fundamental, more psychological, more transcendental: like Lucy Honeychurch, we are made to 'cross' some boundary.[6] There is always something that eludes, unsettles, lingers. His power lies in realising the wider currents of history and morality as intimate vibrations within the soul, in exploring the soul enmeshed in the minutiae of the social world but shaken by strange fits of passion, and in suffusing that passion with an inexpressible sense of loss. He shows us the supreme power of love, which is never far from yearning, as in Godbole's song 'Come, come, come' to Krishna (*PTI*, 96). When he returned to India in 1921, Woolf worried that 'he will become a mystic, sit by the roadside and forget Europe'.[7] This mystical strain in his writings – as in Margaret Schlegel's intimations of some 'eternal adventure'[8] in King's Cross – has been traced back to Romanticism. Its intrusion into the socio-comic novel results in a 'double vision' of worldliness and spirituality that disturbed Woolf and has provoked critics ever since. Yet this unresolved tension, this longing for something afar makes the realist also an idealist: it fills his protagonists with a strange restlessness and propels them from their solid, secure worlds into 'adventures' in which we no longer know where the exhilaration ends and the anguish begins.

Few novelists capture as finely as Forster the delicacies of human feeling, or articulate with such eerie precision the relationship between sexual desire and emotional longing. 'Far more mysterious than the call of sex to sex', notes Margaret, 'is the tenderness that we throw into that call' (*HE*, 205). This wistfulness can be read as the complex expression of homosexual alienation, but perhaps draws more actively from his experiences of unrequited love, as for his Indian friend Syed Ross Masood: 'I wish very much he had felt, if only once, what I felt for him.'[9] Restraint, rather than consummation, seems to give his pre-war novels their erotic pulse. It was only during his war service with the Red Cross in Alexandria in 1916 that he had his first complete sexual experience, and a year later he began his first relationship, with the Egyptian tram-conductor Mohammed-el-Adl. Consider the following extract from a letter Forster wrote him over seven years after his death, now in the King's College archives:

> The last instants we sat together, in the train at Cairo, you nudged me twice with your right elbow, out of love. But when we got out of the train to say farewell on the platform, and I asked you to remove your specs, because I found you more beautiful without them, you refused irritably. I want to record that refusal as well as the nudge. Also, when the train moved out, you did not watch for the last of me, but turned away with an Egyptian acquaintance.[10]

The same combination of acute observation and heartbreaking pathos marks some of his finest fictional moments, as in the conclusion of *Where Angels Fear to Tread*, when Philip Herriton says farewell to Italy and 'thank you' to Caroline Abbott and closes the window of the train carriage.[11]

Forster's fullest critical engagement with fiction is in *Aspects of the Novel* (1927), which began life as the Cambridge Clark lectures. The categories of 'fantasy and prophecy' and 'pattern and rhythm' join the ingredients of nineteenth-century fiction – 'story', 'people', 'plot' – as he provides subtle insights into fictional form. But the focus is firmly on the human:

> The intensely, stiflingly human quality of the novel is not to be avoided; the novel is sogged with humanity; there is no escaping the uplift or the downpour, nor can they be kept out of criticism. We may hate humanity, but if it is exorcised or even purified the novel wilts, little is left but a bunch of words. (*AN*, 39)

One realises his distance from the intellectual gymnastics of Joyce or the endless refinements of James. He did not like *Ulysses* (1922) and he fretted about Jamesian style: 'Most of human life has to disappear before he can do us a novel.' To him, in contrast, 'human beings have their great chance in the novel'. The intimate, the contingent, the impure in human life are of such value that they can lead fictional form astray: the novel pays homage to the unruliness of life rather than to the rules of art. What is important is 'the power of the writer to bounce the reader into accepting what he says' (*AN*, 142, 149, 82). There are then for Forster, as Frank Kermode notes, 'no limits to what you could do in a novel so long as you got away with it'.[12] For the ultimate 're-examiner' of fiction is 'the human heart' (*AN*, 38).

The reputation of Forster the liberal sage can overshadow the emotional quirks and perverse impulses of the man and the novelist. The prophet of 'personal relations' also wrote: 'I want to love a strong, young man of the lower classes and be loved by him and even hurt by him.'[13] In *The Longest Journey*, the sensitive Rickie is attracted not just to the brutish saviour-hero Stephen but, more masochistically, to the handsome school bully Gerald. Stephen Spender described Forster as 'one of the most comforting of modern writers, and at the same time one of the most uncomfortable'.[14] He can be mischievous too. In *A Passage to India*, the 'strong, young' Aziz asks Fielding: 'Let me put in your stud. I see ... the shirt back's hole is rather small and to rip it wider a pity' (*PTI*, 83). Forster has become young in recent years. There has been a swell of interest, particularly from queer and post-colonial perspectives, though he was always wary of theories and did not find criticism useful. Fresh biographical and literary research has, however, illuminated a writer at once mystical, mischievous, philosophic, playful, familiar, and disturbing; one who loved life in all its unruliness and caprice; and valued pleasure. He was thrilled when, once in Long Island, he was told that his lecture would take place on a basketball court; it was the same spirit of fun that made him turn from Christ to Krishna, 'that vulgar blue-faced boy ... [who] ... does admit pleasure and fun and jokes and their connection with love'.[15] The pleasure-loving god refuses to come and fills the world with yearning.

Why are Forster's early novels, inspired by his first trip to Italy – *Where Angels Fear to Tread* (1905) and *A Room with a View* (1908) – still widely read and admired? Sparkling irony, comedy, satire, wit, characterisation are obvious answers but do not wholly define our reading experience; Edwardian middle-class life lifts off the pages with a soufflé-like weightlessness, and the novels outlast their Merchant–Ivory adaptations. When Lilia, Caroline, and Philip all succumb to the charms of the sensual Italian Gino, when Lucy receives her first kiss by the violet-clad meadows, or when Mr Beebe and Freddy and George plunge naked into the pond, the exuberant style makes us 'lend them our dreams' (*AN*, 63). We enter a world of romance and rapture; we become light-headed and youthful; we are carried away by the young, ready-to-fall-in-love writer who believes in love's magic. Our novelist lends Lucy his dreams and consummates his yearnings: Forster fell down twice in Italy, first spraining his ankle, then breaking his arm, and was looked after by his mother; Lucy also falls down twice, each time into the arms of George Emerson. Breaking through the satire on middle-class English life is a fierce affirmation of the life of the body and the spirit. The novels also alert us to life's 'muddles'. Mrs Moore in *A Passage to India* prefers mysteries to muddles. To Forster, both have value, related to the education of the 'undeveloped' English heart, as he famously observed, and to ways of knowing.[16] 'Mr Beebe', asks Lucy, 'Old Mr Emerson – is he nice or not nice? I do so want to know' (*ARVW*, 57).

The fizz and brio of these Italian novels also come from Forster's celebrated irony. It can puncture social snobbery with the observational skill, ethics, and lightness of Austen, as in Charlotte Bartlett's encounter with 'ill-bred' tourists:

> Miss Bartlett, in reply, opened her mouth as little as possible, and said: 'Thank you very much indeed ...'
>
> 'My father,' he said, 'is in his bath, so you cannot thank him personally'...
>
> Miss Bartlett was unequal to the bath. (*ARWV*, 25, 32)

Or it can gesture towards Edwardian camp, combining the wit of Lytton Strachey with delicate self-mockery. Watch Cecil Vyse having his first taste of heterosexual romance:

> As he touched her, his gold pince-nez became dislodged and was flattened between them. (*ARWV*, 127)

Or it can combine situational comedy and sexual knowledge in unsettling ways, as Gino strolls into the drawing-room and into the heart of Caroline Abbott:

> He padded upstairs, and looked in at the open door of the reception-room without seeing her. Her heart leapt and her throat was dry when he turned away and passed, still singing, into the room opposite. It is alarming not to be seen.
>
> He had left the door of this room open, and she could see into it, right across the landing. It was in a shocking mess. Food, bedclothes, patent-leather boots, dirty plates and knives, lay strewn over a large table and on the floor. But it was the mess that comes of life, not of desolation.
>
> ...
>
> His back was turned and he was lighting a cigar. (*WAFT*, 115–16)

Austen would have alerted us to the impropriety of the encounter, Eliot to its moral consequences. Forster simply has fun as the 'open door' lets more of life itself – in all its risk, messiness, and disorder – into English domestic fiction. Italy here stands partly for the life of the instinct, partly for life's impurity, and partly for the great unknown: all that 'Sawston' suppresses.

Voyeurism is staged as comedy, but the shift to the present tense ('It is alarming') hints at more. It is the voyeurism of an author who is distanced from a central preoccupation of society and realist fiction: heterosexual love. The narrative thrill at the furtive encounter points beyond Caroline's hysteria to the novel's object of desire: Gino. Homoerotic longing, prevented from articulating itself directly, gets converted through plot reversals into physical combat between Gino and Philip, the Forsterian aesthete. The eroticised violence of this fight looks forward to his short stories such as 'The Other Boat' and, beyond it, to the sadomasochistic world of Lawrence's 'The Prussian Officer' (1914). Even in his first novel, Forster views English comedy through a cross-cultural lens while the compulsory heterosexuality of bourgeois fiction encounters transgressive eros.

On the other hand, *A Room with a View* with its marriage plot and comic cast resembles Austen. But it is also her vision turned upside-down as her disciple repudiates sense and sensibility for muddles and mysteries. Between Austen and Forster falls the shadow of Beethoven, and Lucy, like her creator, is a talented pianist. Music floods the text, functioning both as imaginative expansion and as escape from suburbia. Forster also pays homage to George Eliot, as Lucy, like Dorothea in *Middlemarch*, is placed in situations that lie outside the Baedeker. But he subtly puts his formal signature, or what he calls 'rhythm'. It can be a 'little phrase' that recurs, as in Proust's *À la recherche du temps perdu*, like 'an echo, a memory': 'not to be there all the time like a pattern, but by its lovely waxing and waning to fill us with surprise and freshness and hope' (*AN*, 147, 148). As the Italian gets stabbed and Lucy faints, George Emerson appears, looking 'across something', and recalls us to the first chapter when he smiled 'across something' (*ARWV*, 62, 27). In the 'Old Lucy' draft begun as early as 1901–2 – which was supplanted by the 'New Lucy Novel' in 1903 and finally became *A Room with a View* in 1907 – the word marches ahead of Lucy or the murder: Arthur 'began to cross/was crossing' to the Uffizi arcade.[17] In the final version, Lucy, 'as well as the dying man, had crossed some spiritual boundary' (*ARWV*, 64). For Lucy and George, it was not just that a man had died: 'something tremendous has happened' and, a few paragraphs later, 'something had happened to the living' (*ARWV*, 64, 66). The rhythm accretes intensities of meaning, threatening the realism of the scene. Forster here moves beyond the immediate demands of story or plot to hint at the 'obscure recesses of our being', or what he calls the 'lower personality', which is a 'very queer affair' but without which 'there is no literature'.[18] According to the novelist Zadie Smith, 'his was a study of the emotional, erratic and unreasonable in human life': it is not Austen's world of prudence but Keats's notion of being in 'uncertainties, mysteries and doubts' that characterises Lucy's 'being in the world'.[19] The child of poetry, Lucy is later borne away on the 'viewless wings' of 'Phaethon' to receive her first kiss: social comedy melts into mythic romance and the plot 'drifts' to follow the intricacies of the heart.

In *Aspects*, Forster distinguishes between 'the life in time' and 'the life by values' (*AN*, 42). 'Value' erupts amidst chronological time in *A Room* – first, when Lucy crosses the piazza and later when Freddy, George, and Mr Beebe splash each other joyfully – as Forster abandons realism for fantasy. The jouissance of the bathing scene, gesturing towards Walt Whitman and Edward Carpenter – prophets of (homo)sexual liberation – makes us regard the concluding marriage plot with deep ambivalence. After all, the kiss has already been parodied in Miss Lavish's novel. Moreover, why does Mr Beebe, who for 'profound reasons' is 'chilly' towards the opposite sex, turn 'inhuman' when Lucy confesses her love for George (*ARWV*, 53–4)? This ambivalent ending throws a cloud over Forster's sunniest novel, and we realise its emotional value when we read his personal works.

Like Lawrence's ill-health and Woolf's mental instability, Forster's 'effeminancy'[20] – as he misspells or coins the word – gives his life its poignant rhythm. Woolf, meeting him for the first time, described him 'as a woman, a clever woman'; his first attempt at fiction, 'Nottingham Lace', was concerned with the transformation of a feminised boy into a manly one.[21] In 1916, he writes to Carpenter: 'This physical loneliness has gone on for too many months ... Awful to live with an unsatisfied craving, now and then smothering it, but never killing it or even wanting to.'[22] Erotic and emotional loneliness informs the mystical yearning that floods *A Passage to India*: 'Less explicit than the call to Krishna, it voiced our loneliness nevertheless, our isolation, our need for the Friend who never comes yet is not entirely disproved' (*PTI*, 119). In the pre-war novels, 'effeminancy', loneliness, and eros result in the idealisation of non-intellectual, unselfconscious, athletic bodies: Gino, George, Stephen, Alec. This fantasy is written into the conception of his two most personal novels: *The Longest Journey*, inspired by his encounter with a lame shepherd at Figsbury Rings, and *Maurice*, which was 'conceived' when Edward Carpenter's working-class lover George Merrill 'touched my backside – gently and just above the buttocks'.[23] Read together, they provide singular insights into his psychic life: the former is a tortured working out of some of his innermost conflicts which, in the latter, are transformed into a radical, if escapist, vision of same-sex love. They are formally not his most accomplished novels but perhaps his most moving.

The Longest Journey is like a long cry of pain that tears apart the conventions of fiction. Like the foot of the protagonist Rickie Elliot, the text itself is deformed: it is messy, melodramatic, crammed with symbolism but intensely powerful. Of all his creations, Rickie – frail, feminised, and an aspiring writer – most closely resembles his creator. The book lurches from realism to polemic to fantasy under the pressures of memory and wish-fulfilment: Forster's miserable years at Tonbridge School, the romance of Cambridge, and the intense craving for that perfect 'friend'. It was the novel Forster was 'most glad' to have written, the 'only one of my books that has come upon me without my knowledge' (*LJ*, lxvi). There is much that is disturbing, even emotionally ugly, in this novel: Rickie's combination of self-denigration and masochism, Ansell's misogyny, or the financial machinations of Agnes. People die sudden deaths in Forster's novels: Lilia Herriton and her child in *Where Angels Fear*, the Italian in *A Room*, Leonard Bast in *Howards End*. But in *The Longest Journey*, young men – who cannot be touched and loved by other men – are killed with an air of improbability that jeopardises the realism: 'Gerald died that afternoon'; 'Robert had been drowned'; 'the train went over his [Rickie's] knees' (*LJ*, 51, 238, 282). On the other hand, as Rickie's married life festers, Stephen, half-brother, half-Pan, appears. Fantasy floods the text like a 'bar of light' (*AN*, 102). Rickie and Stephen ride across the mystical Cadbury Rings, leaving the marriage-plot of nineteenth-century fiction far behind.

Is Forster a realist or a symbolist? How important is his homosexuality in reading his heterosexual plots, and what is its relation to fantasy? *The Longest Journey* shows intimate connections between these questions. While discussing Butler's *Erewhon*, Forster notes that he likes the 'idea of fantasy, of muddling up the actual and the impossible'[24] and in *Aspects*, he remarks that 'fantasy asks us to pay something extra' (*AN*, 104). *The Longest Journey* asks us for 'that extra' through its lyric intensity: '"Come with me as a man," said Stephen, already out in the mist' (*LJ*, 257). Self-mutilation and wish-fulfilment are combined as the train runs over Rickie's leg while he saves Stephen: out of Rickie's disfigured body rises the powerful Stephen, the spiritual and erotic centre of the book. *The Longest Journey* is not only a shedding of sickness like Lawrence's *Sons and Lovers* (1913), to which it has been compared. A searing portrayal of alienation is overlaid by a fantasy of male intimacy and organic wholeness that skewers novelistic form but remains haunting. In 1964, when Forster revisited the Figsbury Rings, he remarked:

> I shall lie in Stephen's arms instead of his child. How I wish that book hadn't faults! But they do not destroy it, and the gleam, the greatness, the grass remain. I don't want any other coffin. (quoted in *LJ*, lxii)

A similar longing underwrites *Maurice* as he releases two masculine lovers into the 'greenwood' of fiction (*M*, 220). *Maurice* is the first homosexual *Bildungsroman* by a canonical author in the history of English fiction, articulating the cries and whispers of Howard Sturgis's *Tim: A Story of Eton* (1891) or A. E. Housman's *A Shropshire Lad* (1896). It was published posthumously in 1971 to mixed responses. While the happy ending led some to hail it as the first 'gay liberation masterpiece' – which it is not, as the gloomy terminal note shows – most critics echo the reservations of Lytton Strachey: 'The Maurice–Alec affair didn't strike me as so successful.'[25] The sudden union and escape of the middle-class Maurice and working-class Alec are unconvincing and politically naïve but it is also the most poignant demonstration of the Forsterian fantasy: it is a vision of 'manly love' rooted in old Albion, a vision that reconciles homosexuality, manliness, class differences, and his beloved English countryside.

Forster longed for a relationship of the kind enjoyed by Carpenter. Maurice's Cambridge friendship with Clive echoes J. A. Symonds's notion of same-sex desire, underpinned by classical learning, while his love of Scudder the gamekeeper reflects Carpenter's ideal of comradely love rooted in nature. Yet, this concluding fantasy of 'manly love' leaves out the feminised 'Forsterian intellectual'.[26] Mourning for lost youth and the lost friend breaks through the 'happy' ending as Clive is 'left to correct proofs':

> Out of some eternal Cambridge his friend began beckoning to him, clothed in the sun, and shaking out the scents and sounds of the May Term. (*M*, 218)

Not a word can be removed from the sentence without ruining its music or the fusion of nostalgia and synaesthesia, which have a Proustian glow. If we try to understand Forster only through his more successful novels, we risk overlooking the potent forces of conflict and fantasy that drive his writing and losing out on some of his most beautiful and heartfelt prose. If other writers extend the boundaries of fiction by breaking the rules of art, Forster does so by breaking the rules of life.

The first three novels and *Maurice*, in their different ways, affirm the poetry of the earth, a life of instinct and emotion. In *Howards End* (1910) and *A Passage to India* (1924) the scope expands to a social vision. The virtues of tolerance, goodwill, and personal affection are now tested against the complexities of Edwardian England and colonial India. 'Modern fiction', notes Woolf, has 'no plot, no comedy, no tragedy, no love interest or catastrophe in the accepted style.'[27] What happens to early twentieth-century fiction that registers the shock of the modern – suburbia, fragmentation, post-war gloom, race – but cannot wholly let go of nineteenth-century realism?

Howards End, in Lionel Trilling's classic phrase, shows Forster's 'war with the liberal imagination'[28] – and his deep commitment to it. To connect the 'inner life' of the cultured Schlegel sisters with the Wilcoxes' world of 'telegrams and anger' (*HE*, 255, 23) as well with the depressed lives of the Basts, Forster devises the most ramshackly of plots: an improbable marriage, an improbable death, and an even more improbable birth. Yet the *Daily News* described *Howards End* as 'the most significant novel of the year';[29] it remains endlessly fascinating. Why? Between the plot summary and our reading comes the 'atmosphere' of the book. We sink, like Helen among the cushions of the motor car, into a world of dinner parties, Beethoven's Fifth Symphony, a broken umbrella, Votes for Women, Anglo-German relations. Like Aunt Juley on the same motor, we sit up in alarm when the novel takes symbolic routes, as when the bookcase descends on Leonard Bast. Yet, this violent yoking allows Forster not only to investigate the Edwardian socio-moral world with intricate subtlety but also to examine liberalism itself against historical reality and change. When Margaret observes 'More and more do I refuse to draw my income and sneer at those who guarantee it' (*HE*, 148), Forster points to a central dilemma: the lifestyle of the liberal intelligentsia is guaranteed by the capitalist forces they propose to despise. *Howards End* echoes anxieties voiced by C. F. G. Masterman in *The Condition of England* (1909), but it continues to provoke us by asking questions no less urgent today: how can one lead a decent and responsible life in an unequal society? Can capitalism be tempered with mercy? How democratic is 'culture'?[30]

Forster did not believe in a prescribed craft of fiction, but he held that a work of art 'answers to its own laws, supports itself, internally coheres'.[31] Woolf found this unity missing in *Howards End*: 'Elaboration, skill, wisdom, penetration, beauty – they are all there, but they lack fusion; they lack cohesion.'[32] This lack is partly the result of the work being too scrupulous a testimony to the historical complexity of the period. The novel's mode of nineteenth-century realism, inherited from a liberal-humanist tradition, can no longer sustain the belief in progress as liberalism itself crumbles: paradoxically, Forster's vision of a pre-modern England must be conveyed through modernist symbolism.[33] Realism and symbolism clash as fictional form registers the tension between a deep yearning and the impossibility to 'see life steadily and see it whole'. Leonard Bast is a critique of Arnold's dream of 'sweetness and light', but as Margaret walks through the Hertfordshire countryside, the Arnoldian rhythm returns: 'in these English farms, if anywhere, one might see life steadily and see it whole' (*HE*, 229). Howards End, based on Forster's childhood home Rooksnest, suddenly becomes the symbol of England. But realism intrudes. Helen points to the 'red rust' on the meadows and warns Margaret, 'London's creeping':

> 'And London is only part of something else, I'm afraid. Life's going to be melted down, all over the world.' (*HE*, 290)

The world embodied in Howards End quivers before the 'real' nation of industrial modernity. Against such 'melting', the Schlegels and the house with its wych-elm make their last precarious stand. The symbolic mode returns, like the affirmative second fugue after the lament at the end of the final movement in Beethoven's Piano Sonata no. 31 in A flat major, op. 110. Like his favourite composer, Forster reinstates his vision: the power of the novel lies in the tension between the affirmation of a pastoral England and a deep awareness of its fragility.

In 'A Note on the Way' (1934), Forster observes 'Arnold's "bad days" are halcyon when compared with our own.'[34] He would have felt similarly about the world of *Howards End* when viewed from a post-war perspective. *A Passage to India* was begun after his first trip to India in October 1912 but completed after his nine-month-long visit in 1921 as private secretary to the Maharajah of Dewas State Senior. Meanwhile, the Amritsar massacre of 1919, particularly after India's contribution to the First World War, had irreversibly altered colonial relations. Forster began the novel 'as a little bridge of sympathy between East and West, but this conception has had to go'. He bleakly remarks: 'I think that most Indians, like most English people, are shits.'[35] *A Passage to India* is his most acclaimed and ambitious novel, redefining the contours of twentieth-century fiction. It is nowadays read as the ur-text of post-colonial literature, both 'inheriting and interrogating the discourses of the Raj'.[36] Forster, however, wanted the work to be 'something wider than politics', to be 'philosophic and poetic', indicated in his borrowing of its title from Walt Whitman's 1871 poem.[37] What is remarkable is the imaginative intensity with which he inhabits British, Muslim, and Hindu India and fuses it with a sense of the numinous on one hand and erotic longing on the other. Consider the celebrated ending as Aziz and Fielding ride together:

> '[I]f it's fifty or five hundred years we shall get rid of you, yes, we shall drive every blasted Englishman into the sea, and then' – he rode against him furiously – 'and then,' he [Aziz] concluded, half-kissing him, 'you and I shall be friends.'
>
> 'Why can't we be friends now?' said the other, holding him affectionately. 'It's what I want. It's what you want.'
>
> But the horses didn't want it – they swerved apart; the earth didn't want it, sending up rocks through which riders must pass single-file; the temples, the tank, the jail, the palace, the birds, the carrion, the Guest House ... they didn't want it, they said in their hundred voices, 'No, not yet,' and the sky said, 'No, not there.'
>
> (*PTI*, 316)

The East and West are here brought tantalisingly close.[38] So are the novel's several worlds – the physical, the metaphysical, the political, and the personal – touching each other with breathtaking fluency.

The above scene of parting, retrospectively considered, marks Forster's own farewell to fiction; it is a fitting finale. Politics, poetry and passion are fused and confused in Aziz's rhythmic spurring between 'if' and 'shall' as he furiously rides up to Fielding, while the phrase 'and then' – syntactically distanced, repeated, forlorn – teases narrative closure with historical possibility, negation with promise. The half-kiss gives the encounter an erotic frisson and looks back, beyond the duo's half-articulate intensities behind the half-shut door over the collar-stud, to the flames in the cave which 'touch one another, kiss and expire' (*PTI*, 139). One realises by contrast the limpness of the handshake in David Lean's film version. Colonial and erotic ambivalence are evoked through the movements of a single sentence. If the novel's avoidance of Indian politics is periodically deplored, its subtlety also often goes unnoticed. Colonial history is recorded not through 'events', such as the ship in Joseph Conrad's 'Heart of Darkness' (1902) firing its guns into the jungle, or through engagement with political activities, as in Rabindranath Tagore's *The Home and the World* (1915), but through unspoken vibrations of doubt, desire, or meaning in the heart of Mohammed Aziz. 'He was inaccurate because he was sensitive' (*PTI*, 168): hungry for intimacy with his liberal English 'friend', he lies about the collar-stud; embarrassment parades as gruffness when Fielding visits him during his illness; invested with a 'moment's brief authority' during the Marabar expedition, he grows wings; misled by Hamidullah, he repudiates Fielding. He is not just an 'oriental' or the 'colonial other': he is a warmly human, and complex portrayal of the 'damaged psyche' produced by colonialism.[39]

Like Woolf and Joyce, Forster finally abandons the nineteenth-century plot in *A Passage to India*, but the genre does not change as radically as it does with *Ulysses* (1922) or *Mrs Dalloway* (1925). Rather than plunging us into the mind's 'myriad impressions'[40] that explode conventional form, Forster devises an intricate system of symbols and rhythm, like the motif of the 'wasp' or the much-noted use of the word 'extraordinary', which internally 'stitch' the narrative. The plot refuses to solve the central mystery: what happened to Adela in the caves? Above all, we have the nullifying 'bou-oum, or ou-boum' (*PTI*, 159) which cancels all meaning and value and sends Mrs Moore to her grave. Nature is threatening and eerily alive, a world where Marabar thrusts its fists and fingers into the sky and Kawa Dol mirrors its darkness to infinity. These descriptions have a symbolic intensity comparable to Lawrence, but it is the vision of the Edenic Brangwen farm reversed: the caves are the anti-sublime, they rob 'infinity and eternity of their vastness' (*PTI*, 161). Against this, we have Godbole's mystical 'Come, come, come' and finally the rapturous birth of Krishna, which is based on Forster's own experience of the Hindu Gokul Ashtami festival and recounted in *The Hill of Devi* (1953).

Just when we think that the birth of Krishna has countered the negativity of the caves, just when Aziz and Fielding reach a moment of perilous intimacy, the symbolic bursts upon the human with singular drama. Horses swerve apart, echoes multiply, Marabar itself seems to loom up with its fists and fingers between the friends. The 'hundred voices' of the earth and sky recall the 'hundred Krishnas' and 'the hundred mouths' of India (*PTI*, 96, 149), while the final 'no' has the cumulative force of the hundred negatives that strew the text. Yet the cosmic refusal paradoxically fills with cosmic yearning the monosyllabic lyricism of 'It's what I want. It's what you want.' The moment is at once transcendental and poignant: it gathers up the passion of Philip for Gino, of Rickie for Stephen, of the author for the book's dedicatee, Masood, as Forster distils all the strength and all the sweetness of personal relations and eros into a foreclosed possibility of colonial friendship. In contrast to the 'yes – oh dear yes' of the greenwood of *Maurice*, we have the no, not yet, no, not there, of reality, as it were. What we are left with, however, is yearning coupled with rapture, the rapture of language, the exhilaration of 'song' (*AN*, 126) from a writer whom Benjamin Britten called 'our most musical novelist'.[41]

In Penguin paperback alone, *A Passage to India* has sold over a million copies, a figure unmatched by much modernist fiction. The immense popularity of Forster is often forgotten, underrated, or even mistaken. In a climate when modernist criticism tends to equate formal innovation and complexity with literary greatness, the power and subtlety of his art make us question such assumptions. Is radical experimentation the main criterion of literary value? What are the languages in criticism to address emotions such as love and longing and pleasure, which define our understanding of Forster and our experience of reading more generally and can go beyond concepts such as 'narrative' or 'modernism'? The novelist David Mitchell has recently observed, 'It might take a lifetime to learn to write like Forster, whereas it might only take a couple of years to learn to be experimental.'[42] The humanism and chattiness of *Aspects* may be the result of his shrewd understanding that 'the final test of a novel will be our affection for it, as it is the test of our friends, and of anything else which we cannot define' (*AN*, 38). This affection Forster inspires not only in academic critics but also writers and countless 'common readers': like Stephen's arms, he could not have longed for a happier grave.

NOTE ON EDITIONS

The most scholarly edition is the Abinger Edition of E. M. Forster, published by Edward Arnold from 1972 and by André Deutsch from 1996.

The Penguin paperback editions usually use the Abinger text and are excellent: they provide lively introductions and notes.

NOTES

1 E. M. Forster, *Aspects of the Novel*, ed. Frank Kermode (Harmondsworth: Penguin, 2005), pp. 27, 130. Hereafter *AN*.
2 Virginia Woolf, 'The Novels of E. M. Forster', in *The Essays of Virginia Woolf*, ed. Andrew McNeillie (London: Hogarth, 1994), IV, p. 494.
3 E. M. Forster, *A Passage to India*, ed. Oliver Stallybrass (Harmondsworth: Penguin, 1989), p. 119. Hereafter *PTI*.
4 E. M. Forster, 'The Challenge of Our Time', in *Two Cheers for Democracy* (Harmondsworth: Penguin, 1970), p. 65.
5 G. E. Moore, *Principia Ethica* (Cambridge: Cambridge University Press, 1903), p. 188.
6 E. M. Forster, *A Room with a View*, ed. Oliver Stallybrass (Harmondsworth: Penguin, 2000), p. 64. Hereafter *ARWV*.
7 Quoted in P. N. Furbank's biography, *E. M. Forster: A Life* (London: Secker & Warburg, 1978), II, p. 67.
8 E. M. Forster, *Howards End*, ed. Oliver Stallybrass, introduction by David Lodge (Harmondsworth: Penguin, 2000), p. 11. Hereafter *HE*.
9 Entry for 31 December 1914, 'Locked Journal', EMF/12/8, Papers of E. M. Forster, King's College Archive Centre, Cambridge, p. 41. I gratefully acknowledge the Society of Authors as agent for the Provost and Scholars of King's College, Cambridge for allowing me to use this extract, and the following one from his unpublished 'Memoir'.
10 'Memoir', EMF/11/10/1, Papers of E. M. Forster, King's College Archive Centre, Cambridge.
11 E. M. Forster, *Where Angels Fear to Tread*, ed. Oliver Stallybrass (Harmondsworth: Penguin, 1976), p. 160. Hereafter *WAFT*.
12 Frank Kermode, 'Fiction and E. M. Forster', *London Review of Books*, 10 May 2007, p. 15.
13 Francis King, *E. M. Forster* (London: Thames & Hudson, 1978), p. 80.
14 Stephen Spender, *World within World: The Autobiography of Stephen Spender* (London: Hamish Hamilton, 1951), p. 167.
15 E. M. Forster, *The Prince's Tale and Other Uncollected Writings*, ed. P. N. Furbank (London: André Deutsch, 1998), p. 317.
16 E. M. Forster, 'Notes on the English Character', in *Abinger Harvest* (London: Edward Arnold, 1965), p. 13.
17 E. M. Forster, 'Old Lucy', in *The Lucy Novels*, ed. Oliver Stallybrass (London: Edward Arnold, 1977), p. 35. See Kermode, 'Fiction and E. M. Forster', p. 20.
18 E. M. Forster, 'Anonymity: An Inquiry', in *Two Cheers*, p. 91.
19 Zadie Smith, 'Love, Actually', *Guardian Review*, 1 November 2003, http://books.guardian.co.uk/review/story/0,12084,1074217,00.html.
20 E. M. Forster, 'A Plot 17/7/04', quoted in introduction to *The Longest Journey*, ed. Elizabeth Heine (Harmondsworth: Penguin, 1989), p. xlviii. Hereafter *LJ*.

Interestingly, the *OED* dates the first use of 'nancy' to mean 'an effeminate man or boy; a homosexual' to 1904.

21 Virginia Woolf, *The Diary of Virginia Woolf*, ed. Anne Olivier Bell (London: Hogarth, 1977), I, p. 263.
22 Quoted in Furbank, *Forster*, II, p. 35.
23 E. M. Forster, 'Terminal Note', in *Maurice*, ed. P. N. Furbank (Harmondsworth: Penguin, 2000), p. 219. Hereafter *M*.
24 Forster, 'A Book That Influenced Me', *Two Cheers*, p. 226.
25 Michael Holroyd, *Lytton Strachey* (London: Chatto & Windus, 1994), p. 726.
26 John Fletcher, 'Forster's Self-erasure', in *Sexual Sameness: Textual Differences in Lesbian and Gay Writing*, ed. Joseph Bristow (London: Routledge, 1992), p. 65.
27 Virginia Woolf, 'Modern Fiction', in *The Common Reader*, ed. Andrew McNeillie (London: Hogarth, 1984), p. 150.
28 Lionel Trilling, *E. M. Forster* (London: Hogarth Press, 1944), p. 14.
29 *Daily News*, 7 November 1910.
30 David Lodge asks some of these questions in his excellent introduction (*HE*, p. xx).
31 Forster, 'Anonymity: An Enquiry', *Two Cheers*, p. 89.
32 Woolf, 'The Novels', p. 498.
33 See Michael Levenson, 'Liberalism and Symbolism in *Howards End*', in *Modernism and the Fate of Individuality* (Cambridge: Cambridge University Press, 1991), pp. 78–101.
34 Forster, 'A Note on the Way', in *Abinger Harvest*, p. 87.
35 Quoted in Furbank, *Forster*, II, p. 106.
36 Benita Parry, 'The Politics of Representation', in *E. M. Forster*, ed. Jeremy Tambling, New Casebooks (Basingstoke: Palgrave, 1995), p. 134.
37 Forster, 'Three Countries', quoted in introduction to *PTI*, p. 25.
38 Edward Said, *Orientalism* (New York: Pantheon Books, 1978), p. 224.
39 For an explanation of the 'damaged' colonial psyche, see. Ashis Nandy, *The Intimate Enemy: Loss and Recovery of the Self under Colonialism* (Delhi: Oxford University Press, 1983).
40 Woolf, 'Modern Fiction', p. 160.
41 Benjamin Britten, 'Some Notes on Forster and Music', in *Aspects of E. M. Forster*, ed. Oliver Stallybrass (London: Edward Arnold, 1969), p. 81.
42 David Mitchell, 'Interview', *Serendipity*, www.magicalrealism.co.uk/issue1/interview.php.

FURTHER READING

Beer, John, *The Achievement of E. M. Forster*, London, Chatto & Windus, 1962
Bradshaw, David (ed.), *The Cambridge Companion to E. M. Forster*, Cambridge, Cambridge University Press, 2007
Beauman, Nicola, *Morgan: A Biography of E. M. Forster*, London, Hodder and Stoughton, 1993
Colmer, John, *E. M. Forster: The Personal Voice*, London, Routledge, 1975
Kermode, Frank, 'Fiction and E. M. Forster', *London Review of Books*, 10 May 2007, pp. 15–24
Furbank, P. N., *E. M. Forster: A Life*, 2 vols., London, Secker & Warburg, 1977–8

Martin, Robert K., and George Piggford (eds.), *Queer Forster*, Chicago, Chicago University Press, 1997

Smith, Zadie, 'Love, Actually', *Guardian Review*, 1 November 2003, http://books.guardian.co.uk/review/story/0,12084,1074217,00.html.

Tambling, Jeremy (ed.), *E. M. Forster: Contemporary Critical Essays*, London, Palgrave, 1995

Trilling, Lionel, *E. M. Forster*, London, Hogarth Press, 1944

Woolf, Virginia, 'The Novels of E.M. Forster', in *The Essays of Virginia Woolf*, ed. Andrew McNeillie, London, Hogarth, 1994, IV, pp.491–502

22

MARIA DIBATTISTA

Virginia Woolf

Even before she was enshrined among the most important women writers of the twentieth century, Virginia Woolf fretted that such might be her fate. 'One does *not* want', she insisted in a diary entry from 1921, 'an established reputation, such as I think I was getting, as one of our leading female novelists.'[1] Be that as it may, that is the reputation she possessed then and still enjoys, although on different and ever shifting grounds, today. At the time she voiced this worry, her reputation was based on two novels, the adventurous but ultimately abortive female *Bildungsroman*, *The Voyage Out* (1915), the more conventional, but socially shrewder *Night and Day* (1919), and a volume of experimental short fiction, *Kew Gardens* (1919). The revolutionary modernist works – *Mrs Dalloway* (1925), *To the Lighthouse* (1927), *Orlando* (1928), *The Waves* (1931), *The Years* (1937), and *Between the Acts* (1941) – were yet to be written. Nor could their innovative forms have been predicted of the writer whose protests against the 'masculinist' conception and domination of life were more ideological than artistic. *The Voyage Out* and *Night and Day* were eloquent in denouncing the hypocrisies and inequities that buttressed patriarchy, but their feminism was not yet allied to a revolutionary programme for the novel. Her apprentice works did little to confute the assumption widely held then – and arguably still prevalent today – that women novelists, whether conservative or radical in their conception of society and women's role and destiny within it, are unlikely to join in the more aggressive assaults on tradition spearheaded by the combative male modernists of the day.

Such assumptions seemed warranted in the case of the refined woman writer who enjoyed, as her contemporary Winifred Holtby enumerated them, the 'advantages of being Virginia Stephen'. Woolf acknowledged the more obvious ones when, in her partial memoir, 'A Sketch of the Past' (1939), she addresses the question of 'Who was I then?':

> Adeline Virginia Stephen, the second daughter of Leslie and Julia Prinsep Stephen, born on 25th January 1882, descended from a great many people,

> some famous, others obscure; born into a large connection, born not of rich parents, but of well-to-do parents, born into a very communicative, literate, letter writing, visiting, articulate, late nineteenth century world.[2]

The dominant figure and intellectual influence in this large and literate connection was her father, Leslie Stephen, author of such philosophical works as *The History of English Thought in the Eighteenth Century* (1876 and 1881) and *The Science of Ethics* (1882) and, most notably, editor of that monumental work, *The Dictionary of National Biography*, an alphabetic labour mock-heroically recalled in the agony of Mr Ramsay, the patriarch of *To the Lighthouse*, straining to advance his thought from his stalled position at the letter 'Q' on to 'R', where further enlightenment awaits. To her father Woolf owed an upbringing in which Henry James, George Meredith, Oliver Wendell Holmes, and Thomas Hardy were not just household names, but family friends who supplied her 'very early with a vision of greatness and great men' (*MB*, 136).

Yet being ensconced within a literate, articulate, sociable circle of eminences before you have any independent standing within it can be as dismaying to an aspiring writer as being excluded from it. Woolf insinuates as much in *Night and Day*, remarking of her heroine, Katherine Hilbery, also born into a distinguished literary family, that 'the quality of [her] birth oozed into her consciousness from a dozen different sources as soon as she was able to perceive anything'.[3] 'Ooze' suggests an ambivalence never fully resolved in Woolf's relation to family, privilege, and social importance, as if something vaguely toxic seeped through the polished veneer of a family that was, Woolf later remarked, 'a complete model of Victorian society' (*MB*, 127).

More but quite different advantages accrued after her legendary move to Bloomsbury in 1904, where, as a young woman 'full of experiments and reforms', she became part of that small concentrated world in which there was nothing that one could not say, 'nothing that one could not do' ('Old Bloomsbury', *MB*, 163, 174). To many latter-day, outside observers, among them Elizabeth Hardwick, the arrangements of Bloomsbury, 'shored up by stout logs of self-regard', appear 'insular in the extreme'.[4] Yet it was in this apparently cloistered world that Virginia Stephen was exposed to a wider and less self-regarding, even humbling acquaintance with a world unsettled by social inequities, economic unrest, and the wrongs systematically inflicted by the machinery of empire. The agitation for intellectual and political change was not just reflected but provoked and advanced by the Hogarth Press that Virginia and her husband Leonard Woolf founded in 1917. Besides Woolf's own fiction and polemical tracts like *A Room of One's Own* (1929) and *Three Guineas* (1938), the Hogarth list came to include T. S. Eliot's *The Waste Land*, short fiction by Katherine Mansfield and E. M. Forster, Gertrude Stein's *Composition as Explanation*, political and social tracts by Leonard Woolf, including *Imperialism and Civilization*, John Maynard Keynes's *The End of Laissez-Faire*, anti-imperialist works like C. L. R. James's *The Case for West-Indian Self Government* and Lord Olivier's *The Myth of Governor Eyre*, Roger Fry's *Art and Commerce*, as well as translations of Freud's *The Future of an Illusion* and *Civilization and Its Discontents*.

Although raised in the traditions and domestic rituals of the late Victorian and Edwardian household and so accustomed to a life 'ordered with great simplicity and regularity' ('Reminiscences', *MB*, 28), Woolf, as both writer and publisher, was more at home and more herself in the epicentre of Georgian modernity, in which established institutions, conventional ideas, and traditional artistic methods were under scrutiny and, more often than not, under attack. Still, as Winifred Holtby recalled in her 'critical memoir' of Woolf, to identify yourself as a rebel Georgian – as Woolf famously did in her generational quarrel with Arnold Bennett and the Edwardian 'materialists' – meant something different for a woman from what it meant for a man:

> ... a woman who was a Georgian was not to be left in peace to her claim of immunity. If the Georgians had deposed the Reason, they had discovered the Nerves. They had discovered sensibility and intuitions, and memories, and the subconscious mind, and sex. Particularly they had discovered sex ... At the very moment when an artist might have climbed out of the traditional limitations of domestic obligation by claiming to be a human being, she was thrust back into them by the authority of the psychologist. ... All the doubts and repudiations of those who reacted against the Edwardian tradition were hers, combined with all the tumult of the conflict surging round ... the Pankhursts [suffragettes]. The full weight of the Freudian revelation fell upon her head. She was told to write like a human being, to write like a woman, to write like a political propagandist, and not to write at all.[5]

In the clamour and tumult of the Georgian rebellion, it apparently hardly mattered to a woman whether she was Inside or Outside the centres where power and ideas were wielded and exchanged. What seemed to matter more was that you were a woman, beset by conflicting demands to write as a modern – in revolt against outworn and oppressive conventions – and as a woman – a creature of intuitions, sensibility, and, as the Freudian 'revelation' ungallantly dumped on scores of female heads proclaimed, a trembling, tightly coiled sexual character.

Woolf not only defied but surmounted such daunting obstacles, hurdling over them with the unexpected ejaculation that announces her fearless leap into modernity: 'What a lark! What a plunge!'[6] Joyce's *Ulysses*, a book very much on Woolf's mind as she was writing *Mrs Dalloway*, strolls into modernity in the wake of the 'Stately plump' showman, Buck Mulligan, celebrant of the jocoserious and faultless mimic of the verbal pomp that augurs the magnificent literary performance to come. Although of a different temperament, education, class, and literary idiom, Woolf also enters modernity in high spirits, plunging, as if in free fall, into 'life, London, this moment in June', not quite sure where she will land, but seemingly unafraid – or serenely unaware – of any hazards ahead.

This unladylike impulse not only propels Woolf's heroine and narrative downward and onward, but backward and inward as well. All sense of narrative direction seems to be confounded as Mrs Dalloway, pausing on the threshold of her plunge, immediately recalls a similar rush of feeling when she had 'burst open the French windows and plunged at Bourton into the open air': 'How fresh, how calm, stiller than this of course, the air was in the early morning; like the flap of a wave, the kiss of a wave; chill and sharp and yet (for a girl of eighteen as she then was) solemn, feeling as she did, standing there at the open window, that something awful was about to happen.' More than windows are burst open in the rapidly shifting course of this recollection. Woolf is determined to ventilate the well-appointed but shuttered world of the conventional novel, opening it up to the brisk movements of the mind as it responds to the stimuli assailing it (sometimes pleasurably, sometimes painfully) from without and to the memories, thoughts and emotions erupting from within. In the subtle folds and turns of this sentence, Woolf blazes a new trail for prose narrative, one whose tortuous, often contorted but ultimately fluid syntax takes us deep into the mind and backwards into time without losing its foothold in the present.

Marcel Proust, a writer she read and admired, had made similar revolutionary inroads into the domain of Past Time, resurrecting the indwelling and eternal reality that slumbered there through the unpredictable but sovereign powers of involuntary memory. In the course of writing *Mrs Dalloway*, Woolf exulted in a novelistic discovery of similar importance to the modern understanding of time, memory, and the creative consciousness: 'I dig out beautiful caves behind my characters ... the idea is that the caves shall connect, & each comes to daylight at the present moment' (*Diary*, II, 263). She resorted once more to the geological image of underground, labyrinthine worlds in naming this discovery her 'tunnelling process, by which I tell the past by instalments, as I have need of it' (*Diary*, II, 272). The emotional effect of Woolf's narrative excavations, however, was more disquieting than the rapture experienced in the Proustian recovery of lost time. She had unearthed the past by instalments, rather than, like

Proust, as monumentally complete social and emotional universes. In *Mrs Dalloway*, the past is broken up even as it is returned and restored to the present, so that what might initially be greeted and enjoyed as a moment of exhilaration ultimately subsides into a mood of retrospective anticipation, in which one recalls what it was like to be anxious about a future yet to unfold and already behind one.

Such moments that suspend us on the brink of a catastrophe that may or may not come to pass in a time that is at once behind and before us are what Woolf supplies to satisfy the narrative demand that something of consequence happen. What *are* the consequential moments or events in our lives is precisely what the moderns set out to question and redefine. Like Joyce, Lawrence, and the Forster of *A Passage to India*, Woolf abandoned the intricate and melodramatic plotting that gave the Victorian novel its moral compass as well as its emotional excitement. Her achievement as a novelist, like theirs, was to return the idea of the momentous – in the life of a person or of a nation – to the singular if nondescript 'moment in June' from which it emerged. This is the revolution she explained and promoted in 'Modern Fiction' (1925), an essay in which she urged us to 'Look within' and 'examine for a moment an ordinary mind on an ordinary day', noting especially how it 'receives a myriad impressions – trivial, fantastic, evanescent or engraved with the sharpness of steel'. Should we do so, we might observe that 'as they fall, as they shape themselves into the life of Monday or Tuesday, the accent falls differently from of old; the moment of importance came not here but there'.[7] Woolf's reassuring emphasis on the ordinariness of the moment, the mind, and the day that concern her as a novelist makes her argument seem less unsettling than it proves to be: for in describing how our impressions, whether they barely ruffle or cut deep into the tissue of the mind, have acquired a new importance in modern life, she is laying the groundwork for a tectonic shift in the foundations of the novel. The word 'accent', which traces the 'fall' of our impressions over the course of our days, becomes the stress point where this shift linguistically and conceptually occurs. As a musical, metrical, or orthographical term, an accent indicates where stress *should* be; Woolf calls on these associations to indicate a shift in the way we 'pronounce' value. In the newly accented life represented in modern fiction, the momentous is no longer limited to great love-affairs, the doings of great men, or the enterprise of powerful nations, but can unexpectedly arrive in the midst of the apparently ordinary 'life of Monday or Tuesday' in which most of us live out our lives.

It was perhaps inevitable, as Woolf herself would later argue in *A Room of One's Own*, that women's sense of what was or was not momentous and important in the ongoing life of Monday and Tuesday would differ, in ways both large and small, from that of men.[8] Her temperament as much as her social position might have kept her from actual contact with the coarser, more raucous, and debauched life the gritty naturalists – all men – had explored, but they also gave her a vantage-point from which to view and appreciate another form of existence that the novel had generally overlooked or dismissed – the 'lives of the obscure' as she identified them. These were the unhistoric lives George Eliot also represented (but tended, unlike Woolf, to idealise), lives of those 'who lived faithfully a hidden life', ministering to the 'growing good of the world', but who now 'rest in unvisited tombs'.[9] In contrast, the obscurity attributed to Jude Fawley, Hardy's last novelistic hero, is dense and clotted with the black irony of his hope and ambition to rise – that great plot of the Victorian novel. Woolf's interest in obscurity, like George Eliot's, is not in the greatness it eclipses, but in the common oblivion that overtakes unremarkable and therefore unrecorded lives.

More than a feeling for a common, unobserved humanity, however, drives Woolf to focus on the unheralded moment rather than on the epic and emotionally transformative – or shattering – event. The philosopher in her had an equally intense interest in divining the 'real' nature of time, a problem she took up somewhat in the spirit, if not with the rigour of Henri Bergson, who had distinguished between the real time of Duration (*la durée réelle*) and the time mechanically partitioned and ticked off by the hands of a clock. Woolf reached similar conclusions, positing that our consciousness of time alternates between moments of non-being, which take up most of our waking life and are spent in largely unconscious activities; and moments of being, when the mind is aroused, aware of its pleasures, and alert to its pains. In such moments of being, Woolf believed, the mind attains its most active visionary state, seeing beyond its own individual existence into the greater and ultimate truth of things. These convictions reflected and served her own imaginative disposition to seek reality in places most other novelists (with the grand exception of Proust) had not thought to look – within those interstices of time where, so she believed, being and pattern and order are sequestered.

These moments of being, as Woolf memorably described them in 'A Sketch of the Past', are not encountered or recollected in tranquillity, but experienced as 'sudden shocks ... embedded in many more moments of non-being':

> I feel that I have had a blow; but it is not, as I thought as a child, simply a blow from an enemy hidden behind the cotton wool of daily life; it is or will become a revelation of some order; it is a token of some real thing behind appearances; and I make it real by putting it into words. It is only by putting it into words that I make it whole ... From this I reach what I might call a philosophy; at

> any rate it is a constant idea of mine; that behind the cotton wool is hidden a pattern; that we – I mean all human beings – are connected with this; that the whole world is a work of art; that we are parts of the work of art. *Hamlet* or a Beethoven quartet is the truth about this vast mass that we call the world. But there is no Shakespeare, there is no Beethoven; certainly and emphatically there is no God; we are the words; we are the music; we are the thing itself. And I see this when I have a shock. ('Sketch of the Past', *MB*, 71–2)

What Woolf 'sees' may be revealed by a shock, but is not determined or obliterated by it. She does not present us with a blank or distorted image of the phenomenal world seen through the lens of the stunned and traumatised eye. She reports, rather, a genuine vision of the order and unity of things, a vision that delivers a sudden blow to the somnolent, unobservant spirit, rousing it from the habits and routines that muffle it in the nondescript cotton wool of everyday life. This vision provides the motive and subject for a new kind of narrative. Without this narrative, reality, she implies, might cease to exist, since there is no Shakespeare, no Beethoven, and no God but only the pattern that we ourselves, at any given 'moment of being', compose.

Woolf's 'constant idea' accounts for the symbolism that, beginning with those leaden circles of Time dissolving in the air of *Mrs Dalloway* and triumphing in the totemic lighthouse that gives her next novel its name and trajectory, more and more had come to overtake the material facts and objects with which her fiction is, in fact, richly furnished. In 'Modern Fiction' and the more contentious 'Mr Bennett and Mrs Brown' (1924), Woolf dismissed Arnold Bennett and John Galsworthy and H. G. Wells as blinkered 'materialists' who had failed to notice that life had moved on or beyond or beneath its physical surfaces. But this was the controversialist in Woolf asserting herself; the novelist in her had an equal but different respect for the significance of material objects, the humbler the better. *Jacob's Room* (1922) concludes, rather abruptly, with a distraught and grieving mother displacing her sorrow onto a pair of suddenly useless shoes. This poignant tableau would not be out of place in any of Bennett's Five Town novels or in the remoter corners of Galsworthy's *The Forsyte Saga*. Where Woolf departs from realist representations is in investing certain objects with talismanic power, like the skull that adorns the children's nursery in *Jacob's Room* and *To the Lighthouse*; the knives, one real, one fantasised, with which Peter Walsh, Clarissa's former suitor in *Mrs Dalloway*, and James Ramsay, the aggrieved son of *To the Lighthouse*, assert and defend their menaced manhood; the cross Mrs Swithin caresses throughout *Between the Acts* to symbolise the unity she hopes to ritually coax into being. The writer who begins an essay with 'Nothing is more remarkable in reading the life of Crabbe than his passion for weeds'[10] cannot be faulted for failing to appreciate our powerful, often passionate attraction to objects, however fossilised, murderous, sacrosanct, or aggressively proliferating they may be.

But unlike the Edwardian realists, Woolf took the Romantics' part in the quarrel with 'real standard things',[11] even as she made fun of herself for doing so in the droll experimental story, 'The Mark on the Wall' (1917), in which the mark that suggests so many shapes, stories, and philosophical reflections to the narrator is finally identified as your standard, garden-variety snail. Her objection to the Edwardian and, in fact, all novelistic 'materialists', was not that they described the external features of people and things, but that they described them as if they had only one meaning or reality to convey. She declares with and through her heroine, Mrs Dalloway, that she 'would not say of anyone in the world now that they were this or were that' (*MrsD*, 8). Mrs Dalloway's general reluctance to define people and things is elevated into a philosophical principle in *To the Lighthouse*, a novel that comically but earnestly wrestles with the question of subject, object, and the nature of reality. There is no finer demonstration of Woolf's desire to radicalise our sense of reality than in James Ramsay's new-found and quite modern understanding of how many things a lighthouse might be: 'The Lighthouse was then a silvery, misty-looking tower with a yellow eye, that opened suddenly, and softly in the evening. Now – .' That dash arrests James on the brink of a mythic, that is a momentous, vision in which both his mother's silvery tower and his father's lighthouse – 'the tower, stark and straight' – are accepted as real and true, 'for nothing was simply one thing'.[12]

This is a view of objects that the novelist may share with the painter, and indeed Woolf's technique was enormously influenced by the writings of Roger Fry, whose biographer she was to become, and the example of the Post-Impressionists he championed. Woolf's fiction abounds in such painterly, half-fantasised objects that may alternately submit to or resist, confirm or dispute, the mind's symbolising, vatic power. Their very existence points to a third order of being that may only be experienced, perhaps, in the realm of modern narrative, where it was first systematically described. These are states of consciousness in which the mind, even on the most ordinary day, vacillates between – and in some mysterious way partakes of – being and non-being. These are the moments of vision when ordinary objects seem both symbolically resonant of the order of the world and at the same time, like that snail making its mark on the wall, possessed of an irreducible materiality devoid of any discrete identity, meaning, or purpose.

These moments of vision possess more than philosophical importance for what they can disclose about the nature of time and the reality of things both in themselves and as elements in a larger design. They fulfil an important structural role in stabilising her narrative. Without them, her narratives would come perilously close to slipping off into nonsense or, worse, into empty space. What abysses seem to be invoked and avoided by the dashes that halt her narratives in mid-sentence! Woolf's idiosyncratic punctuation contributes to the syntactical suspense her elaborately distended sentences create, but the dash, a danger signal of the precipice just beyond the horizon of intelligible thought, or the ellipsis, which eases the mind gently into blankness, are not forceful enough in themselves to ward off or withstand the most wayward impulses of a mind working at full speed. Woolf recognised this peril and so worked diligently to channel into symbolic grooves the imaginative fluency that would allow her nameless narrators to go in and out of the minds of her characters and to follow a wandering thought or stray fantasy wherever it might illogically but irresistibly lead them.

The vagrancy as well as fluency of these narrative motions capture what Woolf herself identified as the 'most marked characteristic' of modern experience – 'the strange way in which things that have no apparent connection are associated' in the mind: 'Beauty is part ugliness; amusement part disgust; pleasure part pain. Emotions which used to enter the mind whole are now broken up on the threshold.'[13] In this respect Bennett, one of the 'materialists' Woolf indicted, with less justice than the evidence supported, for ignoring the inner workings of the mind and spirit, understood something about her fiction that more sympathetic readers had missed. Although Bennett had conceded the originality and 'cleverness' of the 'new school' of novelists 'of which Mrs Woolf is the leader', he complained that he could not finish *Mrs Dalloway*, being unable to 'discover what it was really about, what was its direction, and what Mrs Woolf intended to demonstrate by it'.[14] Showing professional as well as personal displeasure with the upstart Georgians, he protested that the 'new practitioners have simply returned to the facile go-as-you-please methods of the eighteenth century, ignoring the important discoveries and innovations of Balzac and later novelists' (*CH*, 192). Bennett, understandably peeved at Woolf's often tactless criticism of his own novelistic manners, dismisses Woolf's modernist methods as if they were facile rather than inordinately difficult. Yet he rightly places Woolf in the tradition of eighteenth-century novelists, primarily Sterne (whom Bennett did not mention but most likely had in mind), the author of the quintessentially 'go-as-you-please' novel, *Tristram Shandy*. Woolf's vivacious and beloved friend Vita Sackville-West may have been the muse of *Orlando*, that lark in which Woolf defies time, leaps from age to age, style to style, and most notoriously from sex to sex, but *Tristram Shandy* was its progenitor.

Less spectacularly, but of more consequence for the development of her art, Sterne's whimsy and comic bravura embolden Woolf to follow her own imaginative inclinations in *Jacob's Room*, the apprentice novel in which she so carefully prepared for her plunge into modernity. Take the following digression, in which the narrator, with an insouciance inherited from Sterne, diverts our attention to a character who does not have the remotest relation to the novel's principal characters or to whatever plot the novel purports to have:

> 'Holborn straight ahead of you,' says the policeman. Ah, but where are you going if instead of brushing past the old man with the white beard, the silver medal, and the cheap violin, you let him go on with his story, which ends with an invitation to step somewhere, to his room, presumably, off Queen's Square, and there he shows you a collection of birds' eggs and a letter from the Prince of Wales's secretary, and this (skipping the intermediate stages) brings you one winter's day to the Essex coast, where the little boat makes off to the ship, and the ship sails and you behold on the skyline the Azores; and the flamingoes rise; and there you sit on the verge of the marsh drinking rum-punch, an outcast from civilization, for you have committed a crime, are infected with yellow fever as likely as not, and – fill in the sketch as you like.[15]

This near-hallucinatory instance of Woolf's 'go-as-you please method' would seem without point or purpose had it not a semi-ethical tag attached to it: 'As frequent as street corners in Holborn are these chasms in the continuity of our ways. Yet we keep straight on.' Chasms, nicely alliterative with the continuity it disrupts, sounds the modernist note of rupture portentously enough. But the sudden gravity seems forced, a way of giving respectability to the genuinely subversive, patently irresponsible suggestion that we depart from the straight and presumably narrow path and actually *enjoy*, as Clarissa will in the novel to come, the prospect of an invigorating leap into the chasms that interrupt the continuity of our ways. Rather than cower before these chasms, we should pause before them, heed the stranger who crosses our path, and listen to the story he carries within him – a preposterous sort of story whose ending we may even need to invent ourselves! A 'go-as-you-please' digression, silly and truncated, yes, but one in which we can glimpse not only the modern, but postmodern novel in which all the protocols regulating the relationship between fiction and reality, author and reader are flouted with abandon.

Woolf's imaginative exercise here has, then, the value of all experiments that, however inconclusive, even negligible their individual results might be, teach us something about the nature of the materials we are working with – in this case, the novel's unique ability to render the mind's association of ideas, no matter how erratic or fantastical or obscene. Such experiments also reveal surprising but real affinities between one writer and another. Here Woolf playfully travels out of her way to join up with Conrad, for surely that outcast of the island infected with fever is not to be found anywhere on the globe except on some Conradian atoll. T. S. Eliot, with his customary if sometimes supercilious acuity, saw beyond the superficial differences between the teller of sea tales and the lady novelist from Bloomsbury to glean the profound kinship between them:

> Of all the contemporary authors Mrs Woolf is the one who reminds me most of Joseph Conrad. For if you remove from Conrad's books the Strong Man, the lonely man warring against the forces of nature of the jungle – and this lonely European of Conrad's stories is a residual survival of the moral purpose, of the 'deeper psychology' of Shakespeare and Racine – then you will have the equivalent of the novels of Virginia Woolf. If the loss of the strong man is not a great loss, then Mrs Woolf should be praised for having accomplished at Kew and on the English beaches what Conrad has accomplished in the Tropics and the South Seas. (*CH*, 192)

We might reverse as well as borrow Eliot's terms of praise and propose that if you replace the figure of the Strong Man with the figure of the Determined Woman, then you may not feel the loss of the Strong Man as keenly, if at all. You will find in Woolf's London and on her English islands and in her country houses the same residual moral purpose and the same 'deeper psychology' of Shakespeare and Racine, but also of the Russians, especially Chekhov, Tolstoy, and Dostoevsky, who were as great an influence on her.

The Determined Woman has, in fact, many avatars in Woolf's fiction. We glimpse her in the determination of Clarissa Dalloway to buy the flowers herself and to hold her party, despite all the self-doubts and criticism that assail her throughout the day. We wonder at her in Mrs Ramsay's determination to make 'Life stand still here' (*TL*, 165); we honour her when she finally rises up within Lily Briscoe, drawing a line down the centre of her painting, overcoming and thereby confuting the doubts that women can't write, women can't paint. We have our last look at her in the unaccommodating figure of Miss La Trobe, the Determined Artist who has shed all the feminine graces her predecessors had flashed with greater or lesser effect and taken on the uningratiating role of Old Bossy, furiously set on staging her pageant despite insufficient money and materials, the wandering attention of her audience, the spectre of war, and her own fear of failure, the failure of illusion, which, as any artist knows, 'is death, death, death'.[16]

Like the Strong Man, the Determined Woman is not afraid to confront the finality of death in whatever form it presents itself – the death of illusion, the death of a loved one, the madness and despair of a suicide. In fact only *Night and Day* and *Orlando*, a fantasy whose hero-heroine defies the laws of both gender and mortality, do not make Death the dominant fact and power to which their form must submit. But the novels' formal compliance with the universal mandate of Death never collapses into servility. The 'Time Passes' section of *To the Lighthouse* dutifully reports the fatalities of war and timely as well as untimely deaths (an overworked mother's sudden death; the death of a young woman in childbirth), yet confines these emotionally staggering events to the cramped space of a parenthesis. Such a rhetorical gesture weakly defends the humanly significant fact from the obliterating darkness historically and metaphysically surrounding it, but it also frees the novelist from her obligations to be always *personally* concerned with Death as Annihilation. It frees her to turn her attention to the more impersonal aspect of Death as a dynamic force in the perpetual making and unmaking of the world, what Bernard in *The Waves* affirms as 'the eternal renewal, the incessant rise and fall and fall and rise again'.[17] Determination – that moral alliance between effort and endurance – finds here its worthy enterprise. Bernard's last words, 'unvanquished and unyielding', are a challenge to Death, the enemy. The novel's final words impassively record, whether as a concluding irony or in muted benediction, that the waves broke against the shore.

Something else besides Bernard's defiant cry seems to be dashed by those incoming waves; their tidal onslaught seems to exhaust Woolf's own patience with heroic myths of Death. She took heart from the example of Cervantes, seemingly so indifferent to the cruelty rampant in the characters and world of *Don Quixote*, and Shakespeare, who, she reminds us, 'dismissed Falstaff callously enough': 'The great writers', she marvelled, 'have this large way with them, nature's way; in which we who are further from nature call cruel, since we suffer more from the effects of cruelty, or at any rate judge our suffering of greater importance, than they did.'[18] Woolf's plunge into modernity, into the ongoing life of Monday and Tuesday where Death inevitably makes its way, was facilitated by her determination to get, in her words, 'closer to nature' and so surmount any particular attachments to the characters, things, and moments that imaginatively engaged and often bewitched her. She understood that for a writer of her temperament, immersion and over-identification with her subject was a danger attending every sympathetic description or poetic flight – or plunge – that took her deep into the heart of Being.

For, as Woolf knew and dramatised quite well, she could as easily lose as find herself in such deep identifications. Septimus's fatal plunge in *Mrs Dalloway*, Rhoda's euphoric madness in *The Waves*, Lady Ermyntrude, who drowned herself and whose legend haunts *Between the Acts*, are figures of the madness and fatal melancholy that shadowed Woolf's excursions into the innermost recesses of the mind. Her natural defence against the waves of despondency that periodically overwhelmed both her characters and her narrators was 'a natural delight in humour and comedy' instinctive to English fiction from Sterne to Meredith.[19] One of her first efforts at novelistic portraiture attempts to capture this uplifting spirit as it irradiates Rachel Vinrace's face: 'She was amused, and yet she was respectful; if such a thing could be, the upper part of her face seemed to laugh, and the lower part to check its laughter.'[20] Rachel's face becomes a sort of mask, a mask put on, we might say, not just by Rachel, but by the narrative itself. It is the mask that both radiates laughter, even joy, and limits their power. E. M. Forster was the first critic of the novel to register the salutary force of its comedy, remarking that humour 'does not counteract her tragedy and at the close enhances it' (*CH*, 54).

Woolf's restorative sense of comedy was not, however, let loose, as it was in the works of her contemporaries, to sport freely with the vernacular. She might play with colloquialisms and the demotic idioms of modernity, but not with the tireless ingenuity of Joyce, or the 'cocksure' iconoclasm of Lawrence, or the mischievous humour of Gertrude Stein. For an artist who thought so imaginatively about words, she never troubled herself unduly to capture the sound of her own times. She was just as dismissive of novels that paraded 'the last flings of topical slang ... the last toss of colloquial jargon' as she was of those which reported 'what skirt is being worn in Bond street'.[21] The language of her fiction remains by and large an English spoken by everyone and no one in particular, the language of the mind conversing with itself. This language becomes more poetic and interpersonal as she moves from Septimus's rhapsodic prophesies in *Mrs Dalloway*, through the ensemble soliloquising of *The Waves*, to the stylistic parodies, refurbished clichés, broken nursery rhymes, and lyrical declamations of *Between the Acts*.

As her language became more poetic and generalised, it also became more representative. In her late works, she sought to create a style enlivened by 'real little incongruous living humour' in which '"I" was to be rejected and We substituted' (*Diary*, V, 135). Woolf's conception of the artist as the anonymous voice of collective humanity is a late one, developed in reaction to the rhetoric of fascism, the politics of mass movements, the spectacle of mass rallies, and the 'virtual' communities created by the gramophone and radio. In Mrs Dalloway's troubled vision of 'people feeling the impossibility of reaching the centre which, mystically, evaded them' (*MrsD*, 202), Woolf had prefigured a politics of the decentred. In her final works she returns to this possibility, but with an intensified feeling for the difficulty of forging the Unity in Dispersity envisioned in *Between the Acts*.

This difficulty is first encountered in *The Years*. Woolf initially conceived this work as an essay-novel in which novelistic incertitude and ideological conviction might interact without diminishing each other's force or integrity. It devotes its last instalment, 'Present Day', to imagining 'another life, a different life'. In the restless musings of North Pargiter, the family outsider who does not believe in signing manifestos or joining societies, Woolf suggests another way to realise the dream of a new life that such collective action, however compromised, hopes to secure: 'Not halls and reverberating megaphones; not marching in step after leaders, in herds, groups, societies caparisoned. No; to begin inwardly, and let the devil take the outer form.'[22] Woolf's revolutionary fiction and her feminist, anti-totalitarian politics ultimately unite in this injunction 'to begin inwardly', perhaps the injunction all novels deliver to their readers. 'Look within', she had exhorted us in 'Modern Fiction', to find out what life is; now, years later, she again urges us to look within, this time to discover what life *might* be. Eleanor Pargiter, who, like Woolf, was born into a late nineteenth-century world and fears for the future of the 'present day', shows us what we might glimpse if we do:

> There must be another life, she thought, sinking back into her chair, exasperated. Not in dreams; but here and now, in this room, with living people. She felt as if she were standing on the edge of a precipice with her hair blown back; she was about to grasp something that just evaded her. There must be another life, here and now, she repeated. This is too short, too broken. We know nothing, even about ourselves. We are just beginning, she thought, to understand, here and there.

We return one last time to the image of a Determined Woman on the edge of a precipice, about to grasp something that just evades her, only this time the fate of humankind and not of any single individual seems to hang in the balance. And yet how little Woolf chooses to take with her to meet the challenges ahead. So successful was the modernist revolution in changing our ideas about fiction that we now tend to forget or take for granted how *complete* was her refusal of the novelistic tools and conventions she had inherited: 'no plot, no comedy, no tragedy, no love interest or catastrophe in the accepted style, and perhaps not a single button sewn on as the Bond Street tailors in slavish imitation of the fashion of the hour'.[23] The effort 'to break every mould and find a fresh form of being, that is of expression, for everything I feel & think', required, she admits in her diary, 'constant effort, anxiety and risk' (*Diary*, IV, 233). She was regularly visited, like Lily Briscoe, by moments of panic: 'Was there no safety? No learning by heart the ways of the world? No guide, no shelter, but all was miracle, and leaping from the pinnacle of a tower into the air?' (*TL*, 183). No, Woolf's novels tell us, there is no safety, no learning by heart the ways of the world, no guide, no shelter. Looking back on Woolf's imaginative daring, we might feel our own moment of retrospective anticipation at the marvel of this Determined Woman Novelist taking her momentous leaps into the brisk and empty air.

NOTE ON EDITIONS

The most complete scholarly editions of Woolf's novels are Blackwell's Shakespeare Head Press and the Cambridge University Press editions of her works. The common reader may enjoy any of the excellent paperback editions published by Penguin, Oxford World's Classics and Harcourt. All offer helpful introductions and notes.

NOTES

1 *The Diary of Virginia Woolf*, ed. Anne Olivier Bell and Andrew McNeillie, 5 vols. (London: Hogarth Press, 1978), II, p. 107. Hereafter *Diary*.
2 Virginia Woolf, 'Sketch of the Past', in *Moments of Being*, ed. Jeanne Schulkind (New York and London: Harcourt Brace Jovanovich, 1976), p. 65. Hereafter *MB*.
3 Virginia Woolf, *Night and Day* (Oxford: Oxford University Press, 1992), p. 32.
4 Elizabeth Hardwick, *Seduction and Betrayal* (New York: Random House, 1975), p. 135.
5 Winifred Holtby, *Virginia Woolf: A Critical Memoir* (Chicago: Academy Press, 1978), pp. 9, 30.
6 Virginia Woolf, *Mrs Dalloway* (New York: Penguin, 1991), p. 3. Hereafter *MrsD*.
7 Virginia Woolf, 'Modern Fiction', in *The Common Reader*, ed. Andrew McNeillie (San Diego and New York: Harcourt Brace; London: Hogarth Press, 1984), p. 150.
8 Virginia Woolf, *A Room of One's Own* (San Diego and New York: Harcourt Brace, 1981), pp. 73–4.
9 George Eliot, *Middlemarch* (Oxford: Oxford University Press, 1997), p. 822.
10 Virginia Woolf, 'Crabbe', in *Captain's Death Bed* (New York: Harcourt Brace, 1950), p. 28.
11 Virginia Woolf, 'The Mark on the Wall', in *The Complete Shorter Fiction of Virginia Woolf*, ed. Susan Dick (San Diego and New York: Harcourt, 1989), p. 86.
12 Virginia Woolf, *To the Lighthouse* (New York: Harcourt, 2005), p. 189. Hereafter *TL*.
13 Virginia Woolf, 'The Narrow Bridge of Art', in *Granite and Rainbow* (New York: Harcourt Brace, 1958), p. 16.
14 Arnold Bennett, 'Another Criticism of the New School', in *Virginia Woolf: The Critical Heritage*, ed. Robin Majumdar and Allen McLaurin (London: Routledge, 1997), p. 192. Hereafter *CH*.
15 Virginia Woolf, *Jacob's Room* (London: Penguin, 1992), p. 82.
16 Virginia Woolf, *Between the Acts* (New York: Harcourt Brace Jovanovich, 1969), p. 180.

17 Virginia Woolf, *The Waves* (San Diego and New York: Harcourt Brace Jovanovich, 1959), p. 297.
18 'Reading', in *Captain's Death Bed*, p. 179.
19 'Modern Fiction', p. 150.
20 Virginia Woolf, *The Voyage Out* (Oxford: Oxford University Press, 1992), p. 25.
21 'Life and the Novelist', *Granite and Rainbow*, p. 46.
22 Virginia Woolf, *The Years* (New York: Harcourt Brace, 1965), p. 410. Hereafter *Y*.
23 'Modern Fiction', p. 150.

FURTHER READING

Abel, Elizabeth, *Virginia Woolf and the Fictions of Psychoanalysis*, Chicago, University of Chicago Press, 1989

Beer, Gillian, *Virginia Woolf: The Common Ground*, Ann Arbor, University of Michigan Press, 1996

Bowlby, Rachel, *Virginia Woolf: Feminist Destinations*, Oxford, Basil Blackwell, 1988

Briggs, Julia, *Virginia Woolf: An Inner Life*, San Diego, Harcourt, 2005

DiBattista, Maria, *Imagining Virginia Woolf: An Experiment in Critical Biography*, Princeton, Princeton University Press, 2008

Froula, Christine, *Virginia Woolf and the Bloomsbury Avant-Garde: War, Civilization, Modernity*, New York, Columbia University Press, 2005

Lee, Hermione, *Virginia Woolf*, New York, Knopf, 1996

McLaurin, Allen, *Virginia Woolf: The Echoes Enslaved*, Cambridge, Cambridge University Press, 1973

Marcus, Jane, *Virginia Woolf and the Languages of Patriarchy*, Bloomington, University of Indiana Press, 1987

Roe, Sue, and Susan Sellers (eds.), *The Cambridge Companion to Virginia Woolf*, Cambridge, Cambridge University Press, 2000

Zwerdling, Alex, *Virginia Woolf and the Real World*, Berkeley, University of California Press, 1986

23

VICTORIA COULSON

Elizabeth Bowen

Elizabeth Bowen was born to Anglo-Irish parents in Dublin in 1899. She was the only child of a middle-class Protestant Unionist family, part of the Ascendancy class that monopolised political power in Ireland until the civil war resulted in partition and home rule (1920) and in the Irish settlement (1922). As a young child, Bowen experienced the privileged exclusivity of her class: her family spent winters in Dublin, where her father had a law practice, and summers at Bowen's Court, the 'Big House' on their land in County Cork. When Bowen was five, the protective intimacy of her family was disrupted by her father's mental breakdown; his subsequent illness was so severe that family separation was considered necessary, and his wife departed with their daughter to the south coast of England for a five-year period. In 1912, Bowen's father was sufficiently recovered to allow the family to reunite at Bowen's Court, but within the year Bowen's mother was to die from cancer. After her mother's death, Bowen's upbringing was organised by her aunts; she attended boarding schools in Hertfordshire and Kent and spent summers with her father at Bowen's Court. In 1923 she married Alan Cameron, who worked in education and later for the BBC; their marriage lasted until his death in 1952, and coexisted peacefully with her numerous love-affairs with men and women. Throughout the 1920s and 30s, Bowen divided her life between countries, returning regularly from the literary circles of Oxford and London to Bowen's Court, which she inherited when she was thirty-one. Her travels between Britain and Ireland continued during the Second World War as she wrote secret reports for the British Ministry of Information on the socio-political situation in Ireland. After the war she lectured in the US and wrote for American magazines but found it increasingly difficult to afford Bowen's Court and eventually sold it in 1960. She spent her last years in Hythe, Kent, and died in 1973.

Bowen began writing in her early twenties and completed ten novels and almost eighty short stories. Her non-fictional work includes a family chronicle and a memoir of her Dublin childhood (*Bowen's Court* and *Seven*

Winters (both 1942)), critical essays, travel writing, and journalism. Her ten novels represent her major work: though I have chosen to focus on the five published between 1931 and 1949, her other novels are equally rich and – in the case of her three late novels – wonderfully strange. *A World of Love* (1955), *The Little Girls* (1964), and *Eva Trout, or Changing Scenes* (1969) stage destabilising encounters between the perplexing and at times exhilarating demands of the post-war world and a seam of mourning that runs deeply through Bowen's fiction. A vivid apprehension of loss can be felt, too, at the heart of the early novel *The Last September* (1929) with its analysis of the end of Ascendancy rule in Ireland.

Bowen is a great psychological novelist; like the literary ancestor whom her work most frequently invokes, Henry James, Bowen's focus on the texture of human relationships and the emotional structures of the self is both forensic and poetic. And like James, Bowen's attention to intersubjective experience is always political, alert to the vicissitudes of power that shape even the most recondite intimacies. Bowen analyses emotional life as an arena of competing demands, desires, and necessities that reproduces the matrix of family, class, and culture which created it. Correspondingly, Bowen's two novels to address national and international politics directly, *The Last September* and *The Heat of the Day* (1949), develop a psychological analysis of war as a manifestation of internal conflict, in the form of civil war or treachery from within the state.

Bowen's work vibrates to a tradition in nineteenth-century fiction that insists on the political nature of family relationships and on the psychological roots of public life; significant texts in this tradition include Austen's *Mansfield Park*, Charlotte Brontë's *Jane Eyre*, George Eliot's *Daniel Deronda*, and James's *The Princess Casamassima*. Such novels locate the determinants of adult subjectivity in the experiences of early childhood, and are especially interested in the formative effects of parental behaviour and identity on the lives of their heroes or heroines. Life in the family is presented as a small-scale version of national and international political realities: *Mansfield Park* identifies a structural kinship between a father's authority over his family and a colonial landowner's mastery of his plantations; *Jane Eyre* implies a similar parallel between British colonial possession and Rochester's repudiation and imprisonment of his Creole wife. In this model of repression and resistance, the family is an authoritarian structure that generates revolutionary energies: James's Hyacinth Robinson, son of a working-class woman and a male aristocrat, discovers a violent political energy within the intolerable contradictions of his own identity, while Eliot roots Deronda's visionary political aspirations in his Jewish maternal parentage. These fictions belong to an influential tradition of nineteenth-century psychological thought which would achieve its most extensive elaboration in the case histories and cultural criticism of Freud. For Freud, there could be no understanding of any adult's public or private behaviour, or of the most intimate feelings and experiences, or of the organising structures of an entire culture, without reference to the explanatory power of the child's development in relation to his or her parents and their authority within the family.

But Freud's work did not merely codify a powerful nineteenth-century view of the self: his work broke new ground by proposing that the force of the relationship between parents and children be understood primarily in terms of desire. According to Freud, what children most want, and what they must not be allowed to imagine that they can have, is their mother's exclusive love, and it is against the energy of this desire that the authoritarian structures of the family and of society at large – what Freud calls *repression* – must contend. Bowen's work needs to be understood in relation to this intellectual context because her fiction represents one of the first, and certainly one of the most serious, engagements with Freudian theory in the English novel's post-nineteenth-century history. Thus, while the affinities between Bowen's work and that of Austen, Brontë, and James are compelling, we would lose an important sense of Bowen's psychological modernity if we were to overlook her profound commitment to a distinctively Freudian view of childhood loss and adult identity. This essay will trace two parallel, chronological trajectories through Bowen's fiction: from childhood, through adolescence, to adulthood; and from fictions that first repress and then explore the outrages of the abandoned child, to a novel that analyses the familial roots of political mastery to suggest that although it seems an unthinkable challenge we may need to learn how to live without parents.

Childhood: *Friends & Relations* (1931), *To the North* (1932), *The House in Paris* (1935)

Complex family structures form a richly rebarbative context in Bowen's fictions, yet Bowen's imagination circles most compellingly around the figure of the orphan, the unparented or under-parented child, as if insisting on the internal flaws and vulnerabilities of these otherwise intransigent networks of kinship, love, and obligation. In Bowen's early novels, separation from parents can afflict even the youngest children, and it tends to be sudden and absolute; this model of trauma lives on as the pattern by which adults recognise the shocks and losses of their own lives. As *To the North* (1932) accelerates towards its violent finish, Mark Linklater tells his lover, Emmeline Summers, that despite his sexual infidelities she must not end their love-affair. 'If you take this away, I go right to pieces, Emmeline.' Appalled,

Emmeline asks, 'Have I done you harm?', to which Mark replies: 'No one is dropped, you know, without being damaged.'[1]

Friends & Relations (1931) explores the constellations of love, intimacy and desire that pivot in traumatised formation around the novel's scandalous prehistory: Elfrida's affair and desertion of her husband and five-year-old son Edward. Decades later, Elfrida recalls Edward's last Christmas before she abandoned him:

> Considine [Elfrida's lover] had sent [Edward] a small stuffed bear that stood by the tree, upright, with brown paper over its head. It was a stuffed real bear, not jointed, not a teddy-bear; Edward, who had wished for a teddy-bear, pulled at its limbs in silence. 'It's a real bear, Edward.' 'I know it was once.' It was a dead bear now and appalled him. Prey to this or some other obscure disappointment he soon afterwards wept and asked to be taken to bed early. (*F&R*, 39)

Considine has stolen Edward's safety, leaving in its place isolation and a premature apprehension of adult sexuality as an urgent and implacable compulsion. Wishing for a teddy-bear, Edward had hoped for something to hold on to, a comforting object that makes parental absence bearable through the paradoxical logic of substitution. Instead he is offered a diminutive fetish whose showy claim to life is perversely underwritten by the organic reality of its deliberate killing. As an envoy from Considine to his lover's five-year-old son, the small dead bear is a communication too brutally truthful to function as a bribe: it only reiterates the reality of Edward's loss, condensing Considine's traumatic presence with a voodoo-like image of Edward himself, who, '[s]olitary in velvet ... attempt[s] to group himself at the foot of the tree' (39). In velvet, like fur, Edward is another young animal blindfolded and positioned as if for execution.

The bear also confirms the psychic mortality shadowing Edward's mother. Shortly afterwards, Elfrida exiles herself to Paris, leaving Edward to live with unmarried aunts; when he asks if his mother is dead, they answer: 'Practically' (24). Unconsoled by toys, Edward waits for adulthood and the permitted restitution of comfort in sexual relationships; decades later, Edward tells his wife about his childhood 'in the dark, with his head close to hers and his arms round her. Had he spoken of this before? He said, till now he had not ever let himself think or feel. Once she comforted him so much that he wept. They had designed, wordlessly, that he must re-live his childhood' (25). In Bowen's understated but thoroughgoing Freudian tragedy Edward will indeed relive his childhood: he condemns himself a second time to separation from a woman he loves – Janet – by choosing to marry her sister instead. In the next generation, Edward's niece Hermione seems determined to avoid the catastrophe of separation from Janet, her own mother: having no truck with even the most conciliatory substitutes, Hermione causes a public scene by sacrificing teddy-bears on the balcony of a London house. '[A]lways too much with her mother, too tensely present', Hermione suffers from bad dreams and difficulty going to sleep (78). Taken back to bed by her mother – who encourages her to 'Curl up tight and think about your dormouse' – Hermione says to Janet, 'Oh, go on holding me tight, don't go; I wish we were the same person!' (109–10).

These bears and dormice must separate Bowen's children from their mothers without contributing to the effect of being dropped, offering comfort without becoming implicated in the pain of desertion, providing consolation for real life without seeming either to endorse or to compete with it. Theirs is an elusive ontological status not to be confused with reality. Henrietta, one of two under-parented children in *The House in Paris* (1935), carries with her Charles, 'a plush toy monkey with limp limbs', whom she has had since she was born: Henrietta's mother has died, but Charles does not have to be imagined as living (*HP*, 17). 'I like to think he enjoys things', Henrietta explains (18); but she is genuinely surprised by the apparent misapprehension that he might be a real animal:

> 'You travel, I hear, with a monkey?' [Henrietta is asked.]
> 'Yes, called Charles. I left him down in the salon.'
> 'Will he wreck the salon?'
> 'Oh no, he's not *alive*.' (48)

Yet these creatures should not be dead either. Edward's children discover the stuffed bear 'all moth-eaten now' (*F&R*, 85): as the real fur succumbs to organic processes of mortality, the object's decay echoes its first death. Contrastingly, Charles remains in excellent condition after eleven years of collaborative life, and the threat to his material form – that his ears may come off when he is picked up by them – emphasises his manufacture as a toy. Only an object abstracted from the vicissitudes of mortality can survive the pain of maternal absence, and by so doing Bowen's soft toys meditate on complex relationships between loss, imaginative life, and the capacity for love. The house in Paris is a way-station in two children's transitions through orphanhood: the motherless Henrietta is travelling towards her grandmother, while nine-year-old Leopold is returning from foster-parents to the mother he has never known. 'Look –' Leopold asks Henrietta, 'now your mother's dead so you can't possibly see her, do you still mean to love her, or is that no good now? When you want to love her, what do you do, remember her? But if you couldn't remember her, but heard you could see her, would you enjoy loving her more, or less?' (*HP*, 31). In Bowen's fiction, Leopold's questions are as pertinent as they are absurd, clarifying the enigmatic core of absence that both enables and destabilises love. If love requires a remembering of what is lost, the teddy-bear's job is to protect memory with sufficient forgetfulness to render it bearable through the long years of childhood until a mother can be found again in marriage. Paradoxically, Edward cannot navigate towards a woman he loves, or love a woman whom he has found, because his bear failed to distract him from his mother Elfrida: his traumatised loyalty to the real thing makes any other real thing impossible. Unable to accept the diversions of childhood, the grown-up Edward is correspondingly unable to recognise whom he loves: his wedding-day displays 'the fatal climax of his hesitations, a misdirected lover's' (*F&R*, 77–8).

There is a profound tenderness for the pain of orphan experience in Bowen's early novels, but it is a tenderness lodged within the objects that children are equipped with for distracting themselves, and each novel bears these objects much as Henrietta carries Charles: instead of the raw wound of Henrietta's bereavement we encounter the eminently presentable plush monkey. Bowen identifies the presence and location of the pain, but rather than *articulate* the sadness of, for example, the orphaned adolescent Pauline in *To the North*, the novel describes the pet of a house in which Pauline is a weekend guest. 'An apologetic white dog coasted round the chair-backs; he belonged to the house and desolated by too many departures dared form no more attachments, looking at newcomers with a disenchanted eye: a nervy luckless little white dog that yearned for a sweet routine' (*TTN*, 155). The suggestive but studiedly disavowable connection between Pauline and this desolated pet is representative of more general relationships between pain and literary performance in Bowen's early fiction. Bowen's writing incorporates powerful diversionary structures to create internal distance from the losses that can be named but not directly felt; these novels quiver with an orphan sensibility that nobody, including the orphans, wants to take charge of. Pauline belongs to nobody in particular: she 'circulat[es] among relations', 'coast[ing] round' without ever being offered a seat at the table (35, 155); in like fashion, Bowen's early novels host but do not domesticate their internally dislocated emblems of pain.

Attending to these desolated symbols is thus a project that can only be ambivalently received by Bowen's early novels. For all the poetic plangency of the little white dog, to insist on Pauline's sadness risks an earnestness at odds with the ravishingly merciless wit that characterises exactly these same fictions. Compelled by an adolescent self-consciousness to ever more ham-fisted performances of girlish whimsicality, Pauline is a sorry trial for her uncle Julian, who consequently avoids her.

> Then she [Pauline] heard Julian's key in the flat door. He perceived for a moment her pensive figure among the cushions, and, as she sprang up to

> embrace him and kiss him just short of the ear, could not be thankful enough this was not his wife.
>
> 'All alone?' he said heartily.
>
> 'Ever so happy,' said Pauline.
>
> The remark was unanswerable. (42)

Pauline is not 'ever so happy' alone, but, 'controlled ... by a committee of relatives' (35) and living in a boarding-school, she has been plentifully equipped with pet notions about herself, notions that seem to fit her experience but which simultaneously divert her from it. 'Pauline thought to herself what a good thing it was that she was a dreamy child, full of interests, who liked playing the gramophone' (40): housed but unloved, Pauline evidently could not manage without the teddy-bear-like companionship of these familiar ideas, yet it is exactly this strain of hapless internal falsity that makes her unbearable to Julian, deliciously amusing to Bowen's reader, and another minor and deniable figure for the relations between pain and style in Bowen's early writing.

Adolescence: *The Death of the Heart* (1938)

Bowen's primary figure for thinking about the persistent yet provisional mechanisms of repression is the adolescent schoolgirl. Adolescence in Bowen's fiction is a time of widespread, normalised expulsion from the family home, as the tragic orphan is joined in large numbers by girls whose parents have delegated their care to the professionals – governesses, tutors, and the matrons and teaching staff of day- and boarding-schools. Bowen is fascinated by these substitute child-rearers and the places and techniques that they use to perform the labour that the real mothers of these fictions puzzlingly characterise as 'motherly' or 'home-like'. Here we again encounter the magical status of the teddy-bear: governesses, boarding-schools, pets, sports, and hobbies are the teddy-bears of adolescence, objects, activities, and environments whose task is to make parental loss bearable through a mixture of distraction, suspension, and consolation.

Bowen's adolescent girls thus inhabit an ostensibly frugal interregnum whose emotional austerity is secured by the proximity of forbidden ideas. Precisely because the Plasticine animals, window-sill botany, and afternoon teas crowding the schoolgirl's life seek to satisfy her licensed appetites, they cannot help but allude to her unacceptable hunger for the family intimacies of childhood or the sexual relationships that may later reiterate these earliest bonds. Nature studies and the keeping of pets, in particular, bear complex information about the management of such taboo desires. At Pauline's school, the girls' activities manifest a rigorous overriding of live appetites: their gardens are 'planted like rows of neat little graves' and 'someone had a cement rabbit' (*TTN*, 77); simultaneously, however, these obstacles to intimacy cannot help but intimate what they seek to obscure. During a discussion of 'impure curiosity' at her confirmation class, Pauline 'had been offered, and had accepted, a very delicate book and still could not think of anything without blushing ... So that now flowers made her blush, rabbits made her blush excessively; she could no longer eat an egg. Only minerals seemed to bear contemplation' (41).

Bowen uses adolescence to think about the ways in which desire may be unbearable. Adult composure cherishes cement rabbits over live creatures, finding support against destabilising gushes of feeling in the brittle integrities of mineral forms. The lapidary quality of Bowen's early novels may itself be understood as a way of securing a poised and highly self-controlled prose style against the losses and shocks of separation, desertion, and death. Bowen's mid-period novel *The Death of the Heart* (1938) meditates on the costs of such a passage from childhood experience to adult identity: but here Bowen's writing relaxes its commitment to composure, exploring the possibilities of a much more direct communion with an adolescent girl's hunger for what she has lost.

The novel begins with an image of mineral integrities too fragile to bear further contemplation: 'That morning's ice, no more than a brittle film, had cracked and was now floating in segments' (*DH*, 7). Anna is walking in a snowy Regent's Park with her friend St Quentin, telling him about her distress at the contents of Portia's diary. Portia is sixteen, an orphan, and has come to stay with her half-brother Thomas and his wife Anna. Anna explains to St Quentin why, when she had gone into Portia's room on an errand, she came to find Portia's diary:

> 'All I did ... when I had hung her dress up, was to take one look round ... Well, one thing I had thought she'd like was a little escritoire thing ... It has drawers that lock and quite a big flap to write on. The flap locks too: I hoped that would make her see that I quite meant her to have a life of her own ... But she seems to have lost the keys – nothing was locked ... She had crammed it, but really, stuffed it, as though it were a bin ... The flap would not shut – papers gushed out all round it and even stuck through the hinge. Which made me shake with anger – I really can't tell you why.' (9)

Anna has equipped Portia's room with the furniture for an adult's self-concealment: the gushing desk and absent keys demonstrate Portia's failure to adopt this mode of identity. Far from resenting her half-sister-in-law as another woman in the house (as Anna says of Portia, 'she and I are hardly the same sex' (312)), Anna finds Portia intolerable because she has not yet acquired the privacies that internalise privation. Portia cannot be borne by

Anna – whose own mother died when she was a child and who has suffered two miscarriages – because Portia bears too much evident pain and longing with her. 'Anna … asked herself why she liked Portia so little. The idea of her never leaves me quiet, and by coming into this room she drives me on to the ice. Everything she does to me is unconscious: if it were conscious it would not hurt. She makes me feel like a tap that won't turn on. She crowds me into an unreal position' (245).

Like an unsuccessful teddy-bear, Portia carries too much meaning with too little forgetfulness, bearing back to Anna the experiences of loss against which Anna has had to construct her frozen integrity. Through this opposed pair of female characters, Bowen suggests that the threat posed by children to adults is that of a powerful desublimation, an undoing of repression; a contagious reminder of unconscious forces. 'As I read [Portia's diary]', Anna reports, 'I thought, either this girl or I are mad' (10); neither is mad, but the rigidity of the split on which adult identity depends makes less traumatic forms of engagement impossible. Adult identity, Bowen implies, is the form we find for forgetting our childhood experiences – to quote St Quentin, 'if one didn't let oneself swallow some few lies, I don't know how one would ever carry the past' (249): but in Bowen's unsparing analysis, repression remembers itself through the very forms of its erasure. The objects that we use for forgetting will also carry the meanings that we have tried to lose.

In contrast, the novel's narrative form is careful not to reproduce the split between Portia's experience and Anna's: parts of the text take the form of Portia's diary, while indirect free-style narration moves fluidly between different characters' perspectives, at times simply voicing their internal monologues. There is an overt emotionalism in Bowen's writing here that seems connected to a powerful sense of outrage on Portia's behalf. Bowen grieves the loss of mothers and understands Anna's intolerance of Portia as a symptom of the adult woman's fragile treaty with her own motherless childhood; rather than seeking relief in an aggressive partisanship, the novel works to remember the connections between adolescent and adult femininity.

Portia and her mother had lived for years in hotels in Switzerland, in a relationship of déclassé intimacy: 'Untaught, they had walked arm-in-arm along city pavements, and at nights had pulled their beds closer together or slept in the same bed – overcoming, as far as might be, the separation of birth' (56). Portia's memory of her mother is visible in the collection of Swiss carved wooden bears that she installs on the mantelpiece of the room assigned her in London. The bears disturb Anna, who asks the housekeeper if they make dusting difficult; the housekeeper, Matchett – from whose motherly attention Portia is distanced by class – defends the bears as 'Miss Portia's hobbies' (25). However, they are rigid figures, and Portia petrifies them further by coating them in varnish; she spills the varnish on to the bedside rug that Anna had put in Portia's room. In her diary, Portia notes that she wishes the rug would come back from being cleaned, and when it does: 'My white rug has come back, it is fluffier than it was, it is fluffy like the underneath of a cat. I hope I shall not upset something on it again' (114).

Cats are everywhere in *The Death of the Heart*, and the flexibility of their symbolic and psychological import is notable. Despite their proximity to Anna and Thomas – who doodles cats on his blotting-paper – cats problematise but do not disallow the longings embodied in Portia's bears. The numerous appearances of kitten imagery invoke the loss of connection between mothers and daughters, but these are moments not of repression so much as of thoughtful sadness. When Portia finds a childhood portrait of Anna holding a black kitten, the image opens up in her an empathetic passage for the first time: 'She had not been kind to Anna; she had never been kind ... That kitten, for instance – had it died? Anna never spoke of it ... Did Anna also, sometimes', Portia wonders, 'not know what to do next? ... Inside everyone, is there an anxious person who stands to hesitate in an empty room?' (141). As if connecting dream life with waking thought, cats mediate between conscious and unconscious zones, bearing communications between adults and adolescents.

Like teddy-bears, these cats model the work of translation that Bowen identifies as the structure of adult sexuality. To survive in the world without her mother's love, Portia has no choice but to swap bears for cats, to exchange a form of identity that other adults cannot tolerate for one that they can accommodate. This is an angry novel, but Bowen's tragic vision recognises that the outrages of loss are nobody's fault. The novel is emphatic that love is a longing for what has been lost – 'when you love someone all your saved-up wishes start coming out' (115): but Bowen is clear that Anna could not replace Portia's mother – the best she can do is put a soft lining in her alien new room. At the novel's end Portia takes refuge from her relations' house with an acquaintance of the family, Major Brutt, who lives at the Karachi Hotel, but it is evident from the architecture that there is in fact no adult alternative to the kind of relationship that Anna and Thomas exemplify; there can be no restoration of the child's intimacy with her mother. 'The Karachi Hotel consists of two Kensington houses, of great height, of a style at once portentous and brittle, knocked into one – or, rather, not knocked, the structure might hardly stand it, but connected by arches at key points' (285). Thus this novel which at the level of form opens itself to a melting of icy integrities ends with the thought that adult relationships may at best be able to bear connections between separate and brittle structures.

Adulthood: *The Heat of the Day* (1949)

The Heat of the Day is a troubling meditation on the causal relationships between familial and political systems. In this wartime story, there is obvious danger in bombs dropping nightly out of the sky, but by daylight a more insidious risk can be inferred: 'Parks suddenly closed because of time-bombs – drifts of leaves in the empty deck chairs, birds afloat on the dazzlingly silent lakes – presented, between the railings which still girt them, mirages of repose' (*HD*, 91). If daytime is a repression of night, adult identity may be merely a repression of childhood, a mirage of repose concealing latent violence. In this novel, Bowen reviews her previous compassion for children's thwarted desire with a newly sceptical eye, suggesting that it motivates political violence of many kinds. In marked contrast to *The Death of the Heart*, which empathises with adolescent deprivation, *The Heat of the Day* critiques the adult child's hunger for mastery that drives submission to various forms of authoritarian rule. The railed-in place nurtures the time-bomb that will eventually devastate it.

In the central plot, Harrison, a counter-spy, informs Stella that her lover Robert has been passing information to the enemy; if Stella will agree to a sexual relationship with Harrison he will protect Robert from exposure. Eventually Robert confesses his fascist allegiances to Stella and then, to escape arrest, flees on to a roof from where he either jumps or falls to his death. Other narrative strands include the inheritance by Stella's son, Roderick, of an Irish estate, and the daily lives of Louie and Connie, young working-class women in London. The novel uses its historical setting to allegorise the relations of conflict and collaboration that organise its characters' intimate interactions; and it uses its characters' most private experiences to illuminate the psychological dynamics of the Second World War. In particular, Bowen uses three grown-up children – Robert, Roderick, and Louie – to analyse conflicting political systems in terms of their familial structure, articulating through her characters an erotic pathology of war.

Louie's wartime Britain, Roderick's neutral Ireland, and Robert's projected fascist state each address what appears to be an internal crisis in patriarchal authority. Louie's parents, for example, have been killed in an air-raid and her husband, Tom, is away fighting; in an attempt to reproduce her husband's governing place in her life, Louie roams London seeking out casual sexual encounters. She seems unable to live without a master, and this is embodied by the figure of a lost dog which (as Louie will do moments later) approaches a restaurant table occupied by Stella and Harrison.

> Patiently knocking itself against a leg of their table, the dog had distracted Stella's attention: it pushed its muzzle up at her, pleading to be allowed to be

> under obligation to *someone* – there was something umbilical about its trailing leash. Harrison reaching round, pushed at the dog with his foot: a masochistic quiver ran down its spine but it stood firm, having now lodged its head upon Stella's knee. (234)

Louie's canine avatar contrasts significantly with the little white dog that carried Pauline's disavowed pain in *To the North*. Whereas Bowen's earlier fiction bore its loss as internally distanced symbols, *The Heat of the Day* engages directly with a longing for direct communication between orphans and parents: this dog seeks out new bonds, and Louie will claim ownership of it. But the directness with which, in this later novel, Bowen confronts the child's longing for parents is accompanied by a disconcertingly infantile quality in many of the novel's adult characters. Despite the adult status of Louie and other grown-up children in this novel, there is an absolute quality to their needs that makes them seem much closer to babyhood than the real children of Bowen's earlier fiction – the five-year-old Edward, for example, who had hoped for a teddy-bear for Christmas. Louie seems less a child than an infant: the lost dog trails its umbilical leash as if it were a newborn baby. And if a need is absolute, it cannot be borne except as a form of servitude: the umbilical leash identifies hunger with slavery, as if the earliest bond of all is also an experience of bondage. Thus Louie, who appears to represent a problem of female promiscuity that demands firm masculine control, opens up a much deeper anxiety about an uncontrollable dependence on mothers.

As if a child's intense hunger for its mother cannot be tolerated except through a rigorous repression, Louie and the other adult children of this novel seek not substitute mothers but men who will protect them from remembering the mothers that they cannot bear to need. Through images such as the 'umbilical leash', Bowen communicates to her readers an understanding of Louie's longing for a mother that is too powerful to be acknowledged by Louie herself. During her husband Tom's absence, Louie's friend Connie provides domestic companionship for her and even occupies Tom's side of the bed, but as if Louie cannot bring herself to engage fully with Connie's presence she continues to seek out promiscuous sexual encounters with men and eventually becomes pregnant. As Connie puts it, in an unfinished letter to Tom, 'She has been quite a curious girl in the way she has been missing and fretting for you, always straying about like a dog with no one' (327). Through Louie, Bowen suggests that an adult's desire to be mastered by men paradoxically demonstrates the child's unbearable dependence on its mother. As love-objects, the women of this novel can be no more than ineffectual, precisely because their forgotten power is absolute.

Roderick is the under-parented grown-up child that the novel uses to think about the political culture of rural Ireland. He grew up without a father, believing incorrectly that his parents' divorce resulted from sexual misbehaviour on his mother's part. From his father's family he inherits Mount Morris, an estate in Ireland. Nettie, the wife of the previous owner, Cousin Frankie, had taken permanent refuge in a mental asylum, and the only remaining servants are the 'ageless, wifeless Donovan' (165) and his two virtually silent daughters, Mary and Hannah, who embody a politically regressive fantasy of female peasant virginity. 'Having not a thought that was not her own, [Hannah] had not any thought; she was a young girl already upon her unmenaced way to Heaven' (179). Through Roderick and Mount Morris, Bowen stages a nostalgic yearning for a feudal mastery unmenaced by a mother's sexual waywardness or a wife's hysterical withdrawal. Correspondingly, the canine population appears well to heel, emblematised by the dog-collar noted by Stella in Cousin Frankie's library. The collar belonged, perhaps, to Cousin Frankie's big old dog; Donovan undertakes to find one of this dog's puppy descendants for Roderick.

But if, as Louie's umbilical leash suggests, a craving for men forgetfully memorialises a dependence on women, the symbols of masculine control may carry silent reminders of maternal power. If fathers are a repression of mothers, dogs may be a repression of cats. Instructions drawn up by Cousin Frankie for all imaginable emergencies – notes about fire extinguishers, telegrams, and beggars – include two suggestive messages: '*Live Mice* caught in traps, to be drowned *Not* dropped into kitchen fire' and '*Hysteria, Puppies*, in case of ... [*sic*]' (164). If mice are being caught in traps, Cousin Frankie must be confident that cats can be excluded and substituted for. Hysteria in puppies, however, suggests that feline qualities cannot be eradicated from the house. Hysteria is an illness associated with problems of authority; it suggests a disguised resistance to patriarchal control and carries an implication of feminisation. It recalls Cousin Nettie's retreat to a mental asylum. Insufficiently submissive puppies are behaving like kittens, and more like women than men. Cousin Frankie appears to have produced instructions for responding to resurgences of feline and female power, but the text seems unable to imagine what a response might be: Bowen's ellipsis intervenes, leaving unanswered the problem that Roderick will have to address.

This question resounds throughout Bowen's fiction: How are we to bear our need for our mothers? For Louie, remembering is intolerable, and for Roderick, forgetting cannot work. The problem attains pathological intensity in the bourgeois matriarchy of Holme Dene, Robert's family home and the arena of psychic operations of Muttikins, a mother who seems like a monstrous joke at the expense of the unhappy orphans who circulate homelessly through Bowen's earlier fictions. Ruled by Muttikins, Holme Dene, with its perverse and terrifying architecture of 'swastika-arms of passage leading to nothing' (258), is a miniature totalitarian state whose inhabitants act as agents and victims of a remorseless internal surveillance. This might seem far from Bowen's earlier, desolated landscape of orphanhood with its teddy-bear consolations: but Muttikins, too – whose grotesque diminutive pet-name retains its primacy for her adult children – is a kind of pet object, who renders her children's dependence tolerable by making what is loved unbearable. Muttikins is a thrillingly toxic figure, a juicy invitation to hatred who demonstrates that matrophobia is a special form of repression. Her identity thus manifests an unstable duality that can neither be reconciled with itself nor done away with: she wields enormous psychological power, yet her pet-name suggests that she is the littlest puppy; she is definitively British and yet her pet-name incorporates the German *Mutti*, 'mummy'. Like a perverse teddy-bear, Muttikins commemorates longing in the form of loathing. Muttikins's dominance as a monster carries the forgotten memory of her children's absolute need.

Robert and his sister Ernestine have turned Mrs Kelway into Muttikins because their father offered no protection from their mother's power. Robert despises his father for having 'let himself be buckled into his marriage like Ernie's labrador used to let itself be buckled into its collar' (119). What kind of a creature, then, is Robert, the traitor? Ernestine suggests that he might know his way around in the dark like a cat, but Robert's suicidal jump, or fall, from the roof disproves that theory. (Ernestine herself is compared to a ferret, a hunting creature more specialised than the novel's populous slave race of dogs but no less in hock to authority.) Robert's political betrayal certainly seems to represent a rebellion against the canine subservience required by Muttikins; but when he voices his fascist credo to Stella, his rejection of his mother's power resolves back into a fanatical submissiveness.

> 'Look at your free people – mice let loose in the middle of the Sahara. It's insupportable – what is it but a vacuum? Tell a man he's free and what does that do to him but send him trying to dive back into the womb? ... We must have something to envisage, and we must act, and there must be law. We must have law – if necessary let it break us: to have been broken is to have been something.' (268–9)

Like Louie and Roderick, Robert tries to master his need for his mother by submitting to a law that could outdo her. Yet by casting himself as a mouse, Robert imagines submission to, and destruction by, a *feminine* embodiment of power: cats. Of course, mice are perfectly safe in the middle of the Sahara, an environment empty of predators. But bred in the police state of Holme Dene, Robert does not want to be 'free': more craven even than the novel's dogs, Robert is a mouse who plots for feline omnipotence. As the adult child whose mother-loathing is most intense, Robert demonstrates Bowen's laws of repression by pushing most eagerly back towards the swastika-shaped womb that bore him. Hatred, Bowen intimates, forgetfully preserves desire, and treachery may be a continuation of loving by other means.

Bowen's contribution to the English novel lies in the elegance, rigour, and mordant wit with which she explores the inexorable hungers that subtend the self and the social world at large. For Bowen, as for a generation of novelists who shaped the early years of modernism, Freudian thought provided an intellectual matrix for the fiction of the new century; writers such as Bowen, Rosamond Lehmann, Djuna Barnes, Virginia Woolf, and Katherine Mansfield sought to engage directly with those unconscious energies that the nineteenth-century novel had kept more firmly in check. The Victorian novel had imagined repressed desire as a force that could be harnessed to drive the engine of plot, but which had to be kept well tamped down to prevent explosions. In contrast, modernist practitioners of the novel sought to engage with what Freud had characterised as the ubiquity as well as the volatility of tabooed energies. Through the course of her writing life Bowen experimented with a range of perspectives on children's powerful orientation towards parental, and especially maternal, love; many of her earlier novels communicate in richly comic terms a bitterly painful vision of destiny as recursive, a hopeless adult re-enactment of the losses of childhood.

In *The Heat of the Day*, however, Bowen interrogates the political consequences of adults acting in the service of their most infantile hungers, and the result is a rigorously anti-patriotic novel. Here, Bowen suggests that loyalty and betrayal are equally infantile and ethically indistinguishable postures in relation to authority. Bowen challenges us to recognise our desire for parental control and encourages us to consider how we might live without demanding it from the state. When we see Stella for the last time, she is seeing out an air-raid in a rented upper-floor flat, alone except for a cat. The cat belongs to her absent neighbour, and it barely co-operates with Stella's project of comforting it: it hides under furniture from which it cannot be coaxed out; eventually it emerges warily. The neighbour's cat is like a teddy-bear for Stella, and it models a self-protective autonomy and a wariness of authority that offer a real alternative to the violence that Bowen's characters face from within and from without.

Bowen's fiction engages deeply with Freud's tragic vision of the self, yet in the immediate aftermath of the Second World War her work holds out the possibility of something less absolute: a version of adult identity that is not defined by a covert war between the grown-ups that we need to believe ourselves to be and the forgotten children that we cannot help but remain.

NOTE ON EDITIONS

Bowen's first novel, *The Hotel* (1927), *Friends & Relations* (1931), *Bowen's Court*, and *Seven Winters* (1942) are out of print at the time of writing. The following are currently available from Vintage Press (London): *The Death of the Heart* (1998), *Eva Trout, or Changing Scenes* (1999), *The Heat of the Day* (1998), *The Last September* (2000); and the following from Anchor Press (New York): *The House in Paris* (2002), *The Little Girls* (2004), *To the North* (2006), *A World of Love* (2003).

NOTE

1 *To the North* (New York: Anchor, 2006), p. 241. All references to Bowen's novels are to the editions indicated in the 'Note on Editions', with abbreviations as follows: *The Death of the Heart* (*DH*), *Friends & Relations* (*F&R*), *The Heat of the Day* (*HD*), *The House in Paris* (*HP*), *To the North* (*TTN*).

FURTHER READING

Bence-Jones, Mark, *Twilight of the Ascendancy*, London, Constable, 1987

Bennett, Andrew, and Nicholas Royle, *Elizabeth Bowen and the Dissolution of the Novel*, Houndmills, Macmillan, 1995

Bloom, Harold (ed.), *Elizabeth Bowen*, New York, Chelsea House, 1987

Corcoran, Neil, *Elizabeth Bowen: The Enforced Return*, Oxford, Clarendon, 2004

Craig, Patricia, *Elizabeth Bowen*, Harmondsworth, Penguin, 1986

Ellmann, Maud, *Elizabeth Bowen: The Shadow across the Page*, Edinburgh, Edinburgh University Press, 2003

Hoogland, Renee C., *Elizabeth Bowen: A Reputation in Writing*, New York and London, New York University Press, 1994

Jordan, Heather Bryant, *How Will the Heart Endure: Elizabeth Bowen and the Landscape of War*, Ann Arbor, University of Michigan Press, 1992

Lee, Hermione, *Elizabeth Bowen*, London, Vintage, 1999

24

BHARAT TANDON

Henry Green

[F]iction, or indeed any book, if good, is not lying, it is a world, a life of its own. Marginal, perhaps, but the marginal, or oblique, has great value.

Henry Green, *The Times*, 1961[1]

'I can't seem able to express myself but there you are.'

Raunce, in *Loving*, 1945[2]

'What is wrong with this picture?' It is a question with which generations of late twentieth-century British children became familiar, as they scanned treated photographs in magazines, trying to place the trim missing from a policeman's uniform, or locate an invisible football; it is also a question pertinent to Henry Green, English modernism's most evasive and idiosyncratic talent. (He was born Henry Vincent Yorke in 1905 and died in 1973.) Reading one of his elliptical yet precisely pitched novels, we might well find ourselves becoming gradually aware that something more, less, or other than straightforward 'representation' is going on. In its most overt form, this displacement of attention involves literally leaving things out – notably the articles which go missing from Green's work in the late 1920s, such as the unpublished 'Saturday' ('Noise came from streets but only murmuring. Sun shone on flowers' (*S*, 53)) and his second novel, *Living*:

> As Mr Dupret and Bridges walked through the shops Mr Tarver followed them. This man was chief designer in Birmingham factory. He was very clever man at his work. (*LLPG*, 211)

But such formal experiments are only the most easily visible (or invisible) features of a fictional *œuvre* which makes a creative virtue of wrong-footing its readers, even as it depicts the numerous ways in which its characters accidentally or deliberately wrong-foot each other. Seen as a whole, Green's writing comes to look like a long series of tough yet affectionate questions about how novels are written, read, and written about.

When an artistic schoolboy at Eton, Henry Yorke experimented with the baroque, unwieldy *nom de plume* of 'Henry Michaelis', but by the time he came to fictionalise and rework that period in his first novel, *Blindness* (1926), he had settled on the unassuming, yet more resonant 'Henry Green'. Whilst it could be described as Green's most 'conventional' novel, one can already perceive the first stirrings of the qualities which animate the later and more avowedly strange works. Meandering in directions and manners which can be neither predicted nor definitively attributed, Green's sentences explore the ground between perceptions and their limitations; for instance, in his most celebrated novel, *Loving*, Raunce, the new butler, is sneaking into his deceased predecessor's room to purloin his secret account-books, leaving his subordinate Albert on guard:

> He slipped inside like an eel into its drainpipe. He closed the door so that Bert could not see. Within all was immeasurable stillness with the mass of daffodils on the bed. He stood face averted then hurried smooth and at his quietest to the roll-top desk. He held his breath. He had the top left-hand drawer open. He breathed again. And then Bert whistled.
>
> Raunce snatched at those red and black notebooks. He had them. He put them away in a hip pocket. They fitted. 'Close that drawer,' he said aloud. He did this. He fairly scrambled out again. He shut the door after, leaving all immeasurably still within. (*LLPG*, 24)

Green's prose gives with one hand what it takes away with the other: rather than offering the authority of so-called 'omniscient' narration, this sequence combines privileged insight with deliberate withholding. We can follow Raunce visually into the room in ways that Bert can't, with the magical mobility through walls and doors possessed by movie cameras, yet Green keeps us at arm's length from any intimate psychological inwardness with the focal character, confining himself to external, sensory details ('He breathed again ... He had them. He put them away in a hip pocket'), with just that idiomatic flicker of what might be Raunce's own valuation and phrasing ('fairly scrambled out again'). Alfred Hitchcock created the innovative distortion effect in *Vertigo* by tracking the camera back and zooming in simultaneously;[3] and while Green is justly celebrated for his sense for particulars, for what A. Kingsley Weatherhead calls 'those tiny, anecdotal incidents, which appear to be true since they are too strange for fiction',[4] his writing, too, often appears to be tracking back from those particulars even as he closes in on them, with the result that it makes complex and sometimes conflicting demands upon our sight-lines and sympathies.

Laurence Sterne's *Tristram Shandy* reflects: 'our minds shine not through the body, but are wrapt up here in a dark covering of uncrystallized flesh and blood; so that, if we would come to the specifick characters of them, we must go some other way to work';[5] Green's best-known remark on the nature of his own art tries to grapple with the same kind of problem. In *Pack My Bag* (1940), the mid-life autobiography prompted by the fear of impending death in wartime, he justifies his own evasiveness over naming his contemporaries, in ways that are illuminatingly applicable to his fiction:

> Names distract, nicknames are too easy and if leaving both out as it often does makes a book look blind then that to my mind is no disadvantage. Prose is not to be read aloud but to oneself at night, and it is not as quick as poetry but rather a gathering web of insinuations which go further than names however shared can ever go. Prose should be a long intimacy between strangers with no direct appeal to what both may have known. It should slowly appeal to feelings unexpressed, it should in the end draw tears out of the stone, and feelings are not bounded by the associations common to place names or to persons with whom the reader is unexpectedly familiar.[6]

'[A] long intimacy between strangers': particularly from *Living* onwards, Green makes much of the invitation, or challenge, for the reader to 'go some other way to work'. Indeed, that 'long intimacy' often begins with the narrative equivalent of a stranger's handshake: we know the nebulous complex of conventions for which it stands, we know that it means something, but we can't initially be certain exactly what that something is in this instance. This is partly attributable to Green's parsimony with exposition: if he does not always plunge a reader directly *in medias res*, his scene-setting is often perfunctory. Take, for example, the openings of *Living*, *Loving*, and *Caught*:

> Bridesley, Birmingham.
>
> Two o'clock. Thousands came back from dinner along streets.
>
> 'What we want is go, push,' said works manager to son of Mr Dupret. 'What I say to them is – let's get on with it, let's get the stuff out.'
>
> Thousands came back to factories they worked in from their dinners.
>
> (*LLPG*, 207)

> Once upon a day an old butler called Eldon lay dying in his room attended by the head housemaid, Miss Agatha Burch. From time to time the other servants separately or in chorus gave expression to proper sentiments and then went on with what they had been doing.
>
> (*LLPG*, 18)

> When war broke out in September we were told to expect air raids. Christopher, who was five, had been visiting his grandparents in the country. His father, a widower, decided that he must stay down there with his aunt, and not come back to London until the war was over.[7]

In each of these openings, Green offers a distinctive means of 'placing' a reader in relation to the characters and events. *Living*'s terse, telegraphic opening resembles a theatrical scene direction, or, more pointedly, a cinematic shot (Green was a devotee of the cinema from his Oxford days until he became a recluse in later life); *Loving* establishes its connections (however skewed) with older models of romance, by glancing parodically at the stock formulae of fairy-tales, as 'Once upon a day' anticipates the novel's final sentence ('Over in England they were married and lived happily ever after'

(*LLPG*, 204)); and *Caught* provides a succinct outline of Richard Roe's family relationships as his wartime fire service begins. In each instance, though, Green provides further evidence for the idea that no narrative can begin from a point of absolute rest and satisfaction, since each opening leaves a reader creatively unfulfilled, wanting to know more, in its own way. Whether leaving us at a loss to a pronoun's referent ('them' in *Living*, 'we' in *Caught*), or detaching itself, as *Loving* does, from the very traditions of storytelling to which it alludes, Green's writing alerts us to the fact that it cannot and will not tell us everything, and that, in this 'long intimacy between strangers', we are going to have to 'go some other way to work', as we piece out Green's hints, silences, and obliquities with our own imaginations. To 'place' a reader at the opening of a work is often also, on another level, to *displace* them, to energise them to find out more; in this light, Green's openings can be read as a microcosm of his method, as they navigate the boundaries between how things operate outside the imaginative world of fiction, and how they operate on his side of the looking-glass. Like so many of the best works of innovative art, his novels serve as primers for their own interpretation.

It is this idea of fiction as an ongoing process of distanced acclimatisation to which Green refers repeatedly in his pair of radio talks from 1950, 'A Novelist to His Readers'. Complaining that 'novelists have taken to explaining what they think is going on in their dialogue' (*S*, 138), he offers a smart send-up of narratorial intrusiveness, then comments:

> Writing in this sort of way the novelist speaks directly to his readers. The kind of action which dialogue is, is held up while the writer, who has no business with the story he is writing, intrudes like a Greek chorus to underline his meaning. It is as if husband and wife were alone in the living room, and a voice came out of a corner of the ceiling to tell them what both were like, or what the other felt. And do we know, in life, what other people are really like? I very much doubt it. We certainly do not know what other people are thinking and feeling. How then can the novelist be so sure? (*S*, 139)

One does not have to concur completely with the thought that Green voiced in 1955, that 'we are, all and each one of us, always and always alone' (*S*, 193), to recognise the stylistic virtue of what the novelist's conviction led him to: like Tristram Shandy before them, Green's narrators, characters, and readers have to make do without privileged access to other consciousnesses. Indeed, while Henry Yorke may have been a son of economic privilege, the art of Henry Green is, more variously, an art of 'making-do-without', whether those lacks be emotional or material, as when Richard Roe in *Caught* 'clutched at her arm, which was not there' (*C*, 31).

What are characters and readers to do in the absence of these forms of privileged access? This is the problem to which the writing of Green's most creative period – from *Party Going* in 1939 to *Concluding* in 1948 – repeatedly and inventively addresses itself. Antic comedies of misprision, loss, and coping, the novels of the 1940s deal with living-without in numerous ways. At the most basic level, characters have to deal with any number of temporary and permanent absences. Much of *Party Going*'s plot depends on the off-stage presence of 'Embassy Richard'; in *Caught*, Roe has lost his wife, while Pye's sister is in an institution; and in *Back*, Charley Summers, having already lost his beloved Rose, returns from the war minus one of his legs:

> And, as he was forever asking himself things he could seldom answer, and which, amassing in his mind, left a great weight of detail undecided, the next question he put was, what he could say if a woman came while he searched, if she were to observe that he was lame who was of an age to have lost a leg, in fact what should he do if seen by a village gossip, who might even recognize him, but who, in any case, would have her sense of scandal whetted, so he felt, by a young man with a wooden leg that did not fit, searching for a tomb.[8]

This effect is furthered by the ways in which Green's narrative subtly picks away at, and throws out of joint, some of the engrained habits of idiomatic phrasing: a linguistic 'eccentric' in the root sense of the term, Green rarely lets his readers rest easy with received phrases, anticipating the frustration which he expressed directly in 1950, when he claimed that Good English was 'a style preserved in the school-room and which has not changed in a hundred years, although the language currently spoken every day alters quicker than women's fashions ... In "good English" the brain is dulled by clichés'.[9] But, as befits a novelist with such an accurate ear for the minutiae of vernacular speech, including the surreally figurative language overheard on the floor of the Yorke family's Birmingham factory ('His eyes started out of his head like little dog's testicles' (*PMB*, 156)), he acknowledges that one cannot wholly avoid them; instead, he delicately repitches and deranges them, so that we hear their precise force anew. The very opening of *Pack My Bag* provides a signal instance, as Green recounts the beginning of his (or Henry Yorke's) own tale; it merits quotation at length, since its effects are, as Green's so often are, cumulative and sequential:

> I was born a mouthbreather with a silver spoon in 1905, three years after one war and nine before another, too late for both. But not too late for the war which seems to be coming upon us now and that is a reason to put down what comes to mind before one is killed, and surely it would be asking much to pretend one had a chance to live.
>
> That is my excuse, that we who may not have time to write anything else must do what we now can. If we have no time to chew another book over we must turn to what comes first to mind and that must be how one changed from boy to man, how one lived, things and people and one's attitude. All of

> these otherwise would be used in novels, material is better in that form or in any other that is not directly personal, but we I feel no longer have the time. We should be taking stock.
>
> Most things boil down to people, or at least most houses to those who live in them, so Forthampton boils down to Poole, who did not live in but was gardener about the place for years. (*PMB*, 1)

It is a *tour de force* of a beginning, both in its inventiveness and its ability simultaneously to locate and dislocate its readers' purchase on the story to come. 'I was born a mouthbreather with a silver spoon' brilliantly reawakens and literalises the old complaint about a rich person's being 'born with a silver spoon in their mouth', especially since it is no longer clear exactly what 'with' denotes in this new context; however, some of Green's other idiomatic juxtapositions are more unsettling, the nasty proximity of 'put down' to 'killed', and of 'stock' to 'boil down', casting an extra flicker of mortality across Green's already gloomy thoughts in the advent of the Second World War. In fiction, much depends on the means by which writers situate their readers in space and time, and Green has a particular facility with one of the most crucial, the preposition. His 1941 'Apologia' for C. M. Doughty's *Travels in Arabia Deserta* (1888) – an acknowledged influence on his own style – echoes some of the thoughts on prose from *Pack My Bag*. 'Doughty puts words together', he argues, 'which, entering by our ears if they are read out loud, or slipping in by our eyes if they are scanned in print, express their meaning in our bones' (*S*, 93). Doughty's baroque, idiosyncratic English, syntactically inflected with biblical and Arabic influences, marks out its sensory priorities by deviating, both subtly and overtly, from the habitual orientations of the 'good English' sentence, as when he describes a scene of punishment:

> The writhing worm and no man, after the first cries drawn from him, now in a long anguish groaned hideously; I thought, within a while he must be beaten in pieces and is already a broken man for his life after.[10]

By delaying the active verb 'groaned hideously', Doughty puts that much more emphasis on the circumstances of the groaning, circumstances which move prepositionally from the externally measurable ('after the first cries') to the internally subjective ('in a long anguish'), in ways that would not be perceptible in quite the same way had the author stuck to a more conventional English structure. And while Green's idiosyncrasies are only rarely as sustained as Doughty's, he shares with the nineteenth-century traveller a determination to let his sentences cleave to what is most noteworthy in what they describe, as they live out their processes of perception.

In this light, Green's skill with prepositions is of great value: prepositions can 'place' their referents both literally and figuratively, as the above example from Doughty shows; indeed, they often hover between literal and figurative senses and can therefore offer a creative resource to writers who explore the interplays of bodily and psychological existence. Christopher Ricks argues, with reference to Wordsworth, that '[i]f as a poet you are concerned above all with relations and relationships, you are bound to give special importance to those words which express relationships: prepositions and conjunctions'.[11] Similarly, Jane Austen's inventive play with idiomatic prepositional phrases such as 'beyond me' betrays her focus on the blurred conjunctions between the spatial and psychological in the world of her novels.

These effects attest to some of the challenges put to language (especially narrative language) by the brute facts of the simultaneous dimensions which people are constrained to inhabit: German even has to come up with two different nouns for it, with *Existenz* denoting the sheer, abstract fact of being and *Dasein* the multi-dimensional complex that is situated existence, the errant maze whose dimensions fiction always heroically fails to measure completely. We do not live just 'in space and time': rather, we have to occupy at once any number of contiguous versions of each, which can work in any number of different spaces and time-scales – with the result that prepositions like 'in' are pressed into service to cover what is in fact a palimpsest of locations. One practical consequence of this awkward circumstance is that, as Green's fiction demonstrates, some of the most essential parts of our characters remain occluded, whilst others, often the most embarrassing, are all too visible or audible despite our best efforts. In Plato's *Symposium*, Aristophanes provides one of Western culture's founding metaphors for desire, when he claims that its pangs spring from the ancient sunderings of souls into two, but this is not the only plausible account. Indeed, reading novelists such as Sterne and Green, one might offer a different originary myth for human misunderstanding: that at some point in the distant past, we were not so much split in two as turned inside out, hence the continual problems of physical and mental location. Green's facing up to these problems in his prose bears comparison with the twentieth century's greatest novelist of mind–body problems, Samuel Beckett – another writer whose prepositions embody much that is essential to him. For example, Moran's enforced banter with Father Ambrose in *Molloy* derives its slapstick power from the way in which comic timing can temporarily turn the metaphorical into the literal:

> He informed me that Mrs Clement, the chemist's wife and herself a highly qualified chemist, had fallen, in her laboratory, from the top of a ladder, and broken the neck –. The neck! I cried. Of her femur, he said, can't you let me finish.[12]

But in late, stripped-down works such as *Worstward Ho*, relational words run out of things to relate, becoming themselves the primary matter and condition of 'Thenceless thitherless there': 'Know better now. Unknow better now. Know only no out of. No knowing how know only no out of. Into only.'[13]

Time and again in Green's novels of the 1940s, the wavering, uncertain locations provided by his prose answer to a state of affairs, almost a psychological politics, which Michael North has identified with this particular generation of twentieth-century writers, one preoccupied with 'the fluid boundary between public materials and the most intimate parts of the self ... Green's novels are based on the belief that the self is not a truth to be expressed but an expression itself, a fiction'.[14] That 'fluid boundary' is one which surrounds and perplexes both Green's characters and his readers, and relational words can register the occlusions and sudden exposures that make up so many of the novels' actions and inactions. Early on in *Caught*, Richard Roe, back at his family home in the country, finds himself '[s]eparated by privet from the aspect of those lawns and borders familiar to him' (*C*, 4). This turns out to be only the prelude to any number of major and minor separations, all distant relations of the irrevocable separation of death which hangs like a pall over the novel. Although Green excels at depicting group experience – see, for instance, the evocations of the factory and the cinema in *Living* or the nightclub in *Doting* – he is as alert to the apartness as to the togetherness, as when Richard and his workmate Hilly finally go out on a dinner date:

> They had not been out eating together at night before. So that they had never until this moment shared the spectacle, dreary, commonplace and sad, of dim lit faces leaning two by two towards each other beside pink-shaded table lamps, solid, rosy, not so young couples endlessly talking, talking within their little coral pools, in half whispers, waited on by those hopeless, splay-footed, black-coated waiters. (*C*, 99)

A description bled so dry of mutuality that it questions the very idea of 'sharing', this passage not only reworks more sadly *Living*'s sight of 'every head in this theatre tumbled without hats against another, leaning everywhere' (*LLPG*, 217), but places its characters in several incompatible locations at once, 'leaning two by two *towards* each other *beside* pink-shaded table lamps', '*within* their little coral pools, *in* half whispers' (my italics). The couples appear almost as mechanically reproducible as the tables and lamps – an impression enhanced by the way in which 'solid, rosy' could seemingly apply to either the table lamps or the 'not so young couples', or indeed to both, which may be Green's point. Critics have justly praised Green for the depth with which he imagines the lives and psychologies of working-class characters (or simply those beyond the narrative consideration of a novelist like his friend and contemporary Evelyn Waugh), as he exposes the 'tremendous fictional depth just where life is thought most shallow'.[15] However, this cuts both ways: as psychologically rich as these selves are, Green's fiction, as *Caught* demonstrates, is also pointedly attentive to how vulnerable they can be.

Faced with these barriers and pitfalls, Green's characters can only attempt to talk their way around the hazards, however doomed that attempt may eventually be. Recognising the spaces between each other, in which understanding and misunderstanding both occur, they fill those spaces as best they can, with the elliptical semi-sequiturs which are so typical of the major novels. Green is a virtuoso of obliquity: indeed, 'oblique' is one of his favourite adjectives for describing his own style, and Jeremy Treglown's excellent biography *Romancing* registers its sympathy with its subject by being comparably fond of the word.[16] Spiralling off into the furthest corners of the novels' narratives, characters play out in their talk Green's conviction that '[w]e certainly do not know what other people are thinking and feeling'. The twentieth-century philosopher of language Paul Grice argued that spoken communication was governed by what he termed the 'Cooperative Principle' which he summarised simply thus: 'Make your conversational contribution such as is required, at the stage at which it occurs, by the accepted purpose or direction of the talk exchange.'[17] While his central idea is a salutary one, Green's characters appear not to have read that particular script. Rather, the characteristic mode of his fictional dialogue is one of misinterpretation or downright incomprehension, leavened by moments of incomplete understanding, or of transcendental redundancy. Mr Bridges in *Living* sets the tone when he mishears 'defeatist' as 'Diabetes?' (*LLPG*, 327), and from then on, Green delights in spinning bits of plot-business out of misapprehensions, like a stage *farceur* partially transfigured into a poet of the wanderingly melancholic. The influence of stage comedy is most evident in *Loving*, where the servants, temporarily in charge of the house at Kinalty, suspect an insurance assessor of being something far more serious on the basis of his company's unfortunate acronym: 'Why spell me out those letters. Irish Regina Assurance. I.R.A. boy. So 'e was one of their scouts, must a' been' (*LLPG*, 143). But Green can also play out this motif in altogether sadder ways: Charley Summers in *Back*, obsessed with his dead lover Rose, seems fated accidentally to hear versions of her name in others' conversations, as the narrative compounds his condition of disordered mourning:

> When Charley got back to his room Mrs Frazier spoke of rising prices. 'Why,' she said, 'they rose, they've rose …' and the words, because he had not paid attention, the words pierced right through. (*B*, 32)

Conversely, the condition of perpetual indirectness can also produce some extraordinary flourishes: for example, Jane Weatherby's muddled meanderings in *Nothing* show Green to be as much an inheritor of Austen's Miss Bates and Dickens's Flora Finching as he is a contemporary of Joyce, Woolf, and Anthony Powell:

> 'It's too wicked the wicked tongues there are,' she cried in great indignation and at once. 'I only hope my dear you won't ever have some such terrible experience you can look back on in your life and be sure that all your poor ills date right from it. Oh I went to my lawyer but he said let sleeping dogs lie, don't stir up mud, better not throw glass stones. I don't know if I did right, yet oh they should have been punished!'[18]

Green's practice is, as he argues in his non-fictional writing, to leave his characters to their own devices and their own words, and delegate to his readers the responsibility of reckoning their significance (or otherwise). In this, he stands in marked contrast to the schoolmaster whose ways he describes – perhaps for that reason – with damning economy in *Pack My Bag*: 'In his presence we were small mirrors changing in colour to the hues of his moods' (*PMB*, 16). His is an art, not of coercion, but of swerves and distractions, his characters appearing all the more three-dimensional in their partial opacity. It is a testament to Green's methods that a reader would have trouble defining clearly what any of his characters 'represent'; rather, his fiction constitutes an experiment in what can happen when characters are let off the leash, excused the burden of signification. And this applies not only to his characters, but to the larger architectonics of the novels themselves: it is an aspect of Green's art for which some readers will forgive him, while it will always keep others at arm's length, that, as James Wood finely summarises it, 'he is too generous towards drift and half-thought'.[19] Most of the novels possess, not so much plots, as what appear initially as loosely concatenated sequences of episodes, episodes which are only revealed much later to be the mutually supporting parts of a large and delicate structure. Some of the novels play out their dissent from plotting conventions with comic directness – notably *Party Going*, whose stranded characters are always 'going' but never gone, and *Concluding*, whose missing-persons mystery remains unresolved at the end of the day, with the final focus moving instead to the protagonist Mr Rock ('On the whole he was well satisfied with his day. He fell asleep at once in the yellow woollen nightshirt').[20] But even the less overt works make much of the bathetic possibilities of narrative. The final line of *Doting*, which ended up being Green's last published line of fiction, could be read as a summary of this: 'The next day they all went on very much the same.'[21]

In a 1959 interview with Alan Ross, Green returned to some of the questions he had raised in his two radio talks from the beginning of the decade:

A. R.: Are your novels, would you say, non-representational alternatives to real life, or at a different level extensions of it?

H. G.: Oh I think they must be extensions every time, even *Doting* and *Nothing*.[22]

While Green does not dispute the description of his work as 'non-representational', he does, tellingly, defend the novels' link back to 'real life', even if that link is not a directly representational or mimetic one; and in doing so, he pinpoints one of his signal contributions to British modernist fiction. In contrasting the aesthetics of modernism with those of Romanticism, Gabriel Josipovici makes a valuable distinction: 'It might be thought', he remarks, 'that such an art, an art of total potentiality, of laws rather than subject-matter, would result in a dry abstraction ... What is important is that such an art need be neither solemn nor cold. On the contrary, there has never been an art more joyous, or one that brings joy back to our response to older art, than that of Stravinsky, Picasso and Eliot.'[23] To this list, one could also add Green – for in posing so many variations on the question 'what is wrong with this picture?', he creates an art which is indeed non-representational, but manages, in its non-mimetic indirections, to engage its readers all the more creatively and emotionally with the world it isn't miming – how true it is that 'the marginal, the oblique, has great value'. For example, the 1940s works, through their stylisation, offer fresher perspectives on the impact of war than a more strictly naturalistic treatment might have provided, whether registering the impact of violence on the very vocabulary of description in *Pack My Bag* ('the light of imminent death, that rather ghastly colour in the sky of mustard yellows with the sirens wailing their call of now you may have to die' (*PMB*, 134), exploring the mental and sexual claustrophobia of wartime London in *Caught*, or fashioning a mournful tone-poem out of post-traumatic stress in *Back*. In each case, a crucial aspect of the fiction's effect involves a reader's active experience of disorientation, and their subsequent readjustments of perspective. This may be one reason why *Nothing* (1950) and *Doting* (1952), despite their more rigid adherence to Green's ethic of showing rather than telling, read like less accomplished works. The last two novels eschew description and narration almost completely in favour of dialogue, but in so doing they also deny themselves that performative shift between perspectives on which so much of Green's art depends: it is there, by the most oblique processes of refamiliarisation, that the fiction does its work and 'draws tears out of the stone'.

'Living one's own life', Green wrote, 'can be a great muddle, but the great writers do not make it plain, they palliate, and put the whole in a sort of proportion' (*S*, 281–2). Green is arguably twentieth-century British fiction's finest chronicler of that 'great muddle', and his writing puts the whole into proportion by availing itself consummately of the resources of disproportion; he may even be speaking too modestly of his achievement, since to be freshly energised to the commonplace by fiction is so much more than a palliative. Repeatedly in the novels, his game, befuddled characters resort to variations on the conversational phrase 'there you are'. In *Caught*, for instance, the inane fireman Piper observes to Richard Roe: 'So then I looks you up and it is you. So there you are then' (*C*, 32); and in *Back*, Green composes a moment of finely pitched comic awkwardness for Charley's first encounter with his late lover's husband:

> 'It's my leg,' Charley explained. He drawled rather when he spoke.
> 'Yes well there you are,' James said.
> 'There it is,' Charley agreed. (*B*, 8)

'There you are': like umming and ahing, or talking about the weather, it is one of those characteristic markers of English speech, at once semantically almost redundant and conversationally indispensable, which are 'marginal, perhaps,' but 'have great value'. When Lambert Strether ends Henry James's *The Ambassadors* with 'Then there we are!',[24] a reader is invited to take the phrase as a marker of Strether's shift to a clearer habit of perception; in Green, it works more as a stoical shrug of resignation, simply denoting the condition of being there, in the muddle. 'There you are': there we all are, in that world which Green imagines – a world in which there is no *mot juste*, but there are, magnificently, the *mots*.

NOTE ON EDITIONS

There is, unfortunately, no uniform edition of Green's novels currently in print. The 1990s Collins/Harvill reprints of the novels, with introductions by Jeremy Treglown, are, however, readily available from second-hand sources. Currently in print in the UK are *Pack My Bag* and the omnibus edition of *Loving*, *Living*, and *Party Going*, both published by Vintage. For American readers, Dalkey Archive Press also publishes paperback reprints of *Blindness*, *Back*, *Concluding*, *Nothing*, and *Doting*.

NOTES

1 Henry Green, 'Unloving' (1960), in *Surviving: The Uncollected Writings of Henry Green*, ed. Matthew Yorke, introduction by John Updike (London: Chatto & Windus, 1992), p. 281. Hereafter *S*.

2 Henry Green, *Loving, Living, Party Going*, introduction by John Updike (London: Picador, 1978), p. 149. Hereafter *LLPG*.

3 François Truffaut, *Hitchcock* (London: Martin Secker & Warburg, 1968; rev. edn, London: Paladin, 1986), pp. 372–4.

4 A. Kingsley Weatherhead, *A Reading of Henry Green* (Seattle: University of Washington Press, 1961), p. 154.

5 Laurence Sterne, *The Life and Opinions of Tristram Shandy: Text*, ed. M. New and J. New, The University Press of Florida Works of Laurence Sterne, vols. I–II (Gainesville: University Press of Florida, 1978), I, p. 83.

6 Henry Green, *Pack My Bag: A Self-Portrait*, introduction by Alan Ross (London: Vintage, 2000), pp. 55–6. Hereafter *PMB*.

7 Henry Green, *Caught*, introduction by Jeremy Treglown (London: Harvill, 1991), p. 1. Hereafter *C*.

8 Henry Green, *Back*, introduction by Jeremy Treglown (London: Harvill, 1998), p. 5. Hereafter *B*.

9 Henry Green, 'The English Novel of the Future', *Contact*, 1.2 (July–August 1950), p. 23.

10 Charles M. Doughty, *Travels in Arabia Deserta*, introduction by T. E. Lawrence, 2 vols. (London: Jonathan Cape, 1936), I, p. 53.

11 Christopher Ricks, *The Force of Poetry* (Oxford: Oxford University Press, 1984), p. 120.

12 Samuel Beckett, *The Beckett Trilogy: Molloy, Malone Dies, The Unnamable* (London: Picador, 1979), p. 93.

13 Samuel Beckett, *Nohow On: Company, Ill Seen Ill Said, Worstward Ho* (London: John Calder, 1989), p. 104.

14 Michael North, *Henry Green and the Writing of His Generation* (Charlottesville: University Press of Virginia, 1984), p. 12.

15 *Ibid.*, p. 216.

16 'Green's is an intuitive, oblique, often wayward kind of art'; 'As with much in his life, its effects on him were powerful but oblique'; 'Here, as elsewhere, his fiction is an oblique form of self-portrait'. Jeremy Treglown, *Romancing: The Life and Work of Henry Green* (London: Faber and Faber, 2000), pp. 3, 17, 191.

17 Paul Grice, 'Logic and Conversation' (1967), in *Studies in the Way of Words* (Cambridge, MA and London: Harvard University Press, 1989), p. 26.

18 Henry Green, *Nothing*, introduction by Jeremy Treglown (London: Harvill, 1992), p. 46.

19 James Wood, *The Irresponsible Self: On Laughter and the Novel* (London: Jonathan Cape, 2004), p. 300.

20 Henry Green, *Concluding*, introduction by Jeremy Treglown (London: Harvill, 1997), p. 213.

21 Henry Green, *Doting*, introduction by Jeremy Treglown (London: Harvill, 1998), p. 226.

22 Alan Ross, 'Green, with Envy', *The London Magazine*, 6.4 (April 1959), p. 23.

23 Gabriel Josipovici, *The World and the Book* (London: Macmillan, 1971; 2nd edn, 1979), p. 199.

24 Henry James, *The Ambassadors*, ed. Adrian Poole (London: Penguin, 2008), p. 470.

FURTHER READING

Holmesland, O., *A Critical Introduction to Henry Green's Novels: The Living Vision*, Basingstoke, Macmillan, 1986

Josipovici, G., *The World and the Book: A Study of Modern Fiction*, London, Macmillan, 1971; 2nd edn, 1979

Kermode, F., *The Genesis of Secrecy: On the Interpretation of Narrative*, Cambridge, MA, Harvard University Press, 1979

Melchiori, G., *The Tightrope Walkers: Studies of Mannerism in Modern English Literature*, London, Routledge & Kegan Paul, 1956

Mengham, R., *The Idiom of the Time: The Writings of Henry Green*, Cambridge, Cambridge University Press, 1982

North, M., *Henry Green and the Writing of His Generation*, Charlottesville, University Press of Virginia, 1984

Ryf, R.S., *Henry Green*, New York and London, Columbia University Press, 1967

Stokes, E., *The Novels of Henry Green*, London, Hogarth Press, 1959

Treglown, J., *Romancing: The Life and Work of Henry Green*, London, Faber and Faber, 2000

Weatherhead, A.K., *A Reading of Henry Green*, Seattle, University of Washington Press, 1961

Wood, J., *The Irresponsible Self: On Laughter and the Novel*, London, Jonathan Cape, 2004

25

ANTHONY LANE

Evelyn Waugh

The novels of Evelyn Waugh (1903–66) occupy an unstable place in the canon. On the one hand, they have been disdained for the narrowness of their social range and the coldness, even the cruelty, of their moral temper. On the other hand, even Waugh's detractors find it hard not to appreciate the prose in which his stories are couched, and which marks him out – in its exactitude, in the curtness of its controlled irony, and in a fanatical pursuit of the *mot juste* – as what might be termed the last of the Augustans, while rarely retreating into the archaic or subsiding into pastiche. His published letters and journals find him creating, as though by reflex, and as much for his own enjoyment as for that of others, unceasing miniature narratives of comic ferocity; they suggest an author sharpening his knives for the preparation of a feast.

Waugh himself, aware of the accusations ranged against him, sought to confound his critics, in the spirit of mischief which underlay most of his public pronouncements, by owning up to the majority of the charges and yielding to others that had not even been levelled. The disingenuity was nicely calculated: 'I regard writing not as an investigation of character, but as an exercise in the use of language, and with this I am obsessed', he said in an interview of 1963. 'I have no technical psychological interest. It is drama, speech, and events that interest me.'[1] The fact that his fiction dealt with but a fraction of British society – a failing, if it is a failing, that haunts many of the authors considered in the present volume – he never denied, maintaining that it would be presumptuous to venture into territories with which he was unacquainted. Against that, it could be pointed out that in the 1930s he became an indefatigable traveller, and that to record your progress through the Amazonian jungle, whilst never evincing the slightest wish to explore, say, the industrial cities of the North of England, is itself the index of a particular social prejudice.

More fraught is the stand that Waugh came to take against the modernist innovations of his period. 'Experiment? God forbid!' he remarked in the same interview, claiming of Joyce that 'He started off writing very well, then you can watch him going mad with vanity.'[2] Waugh's own progress, however, did not entirely square with this bluster. He must have read T. S. Eliot's 'Sweeney Agonistes', for example, in the *Criterion*, where it appeared in 1927, because in 1930, two years before it became available in book form, he commended the experimental advances of its second half, 'Fragment of an Agon', in a review of Henry Green's *Living*. Lines such as these from the poem –

> *DUSTY:* Yes I know you've a touch with the cards
> What comes next?
> *DORIS:* What comes next. It's the six.
> *DUSTY:* 'A quarrel. An estrangement. Separation of friends.'
> *DORIS:* Here's the two of spades.
> *DUSTY:* The *two of spades!*[3]

– received a sharp echo in the opening pages of Waugh's *Vile Bodies*, which came out in the same year as the review:

> 'Hullo, Mr Henderson. What's that spade?'
> 'That's the ace, that is.'
> 'I can see it's the ace. What I mean you didn't ought to have trumped that last trick not if you had a spade.'
> 'What d'you mean, didn't ought to have trumped it? Trumps led.'
> 'No, they did *not*. Arthur led a spade.'
> 'He led a trump, didn't you, Arthur?'
> 'Arthur led a spade.'[4]

Most readers of Waugh remember Anthony Blanche, the corrupting (if perceptive) exotic of *Brideshead Revisited*, standing on a balcony and reciting *The Waste Land* through a megaphone,[5] and the scene duly takes its place in a languorous comedy of privilege, but the tribute paid to Eliot by *Vile Bodies* – and paid continually, right up to the schizophrenic exchanges in Waugh's late and disquieting novella, *The Ordeal of Gilbert Pinfold* (1957) – is subtler and more adventurous. As this essay hopes to show, Waugh's political and religious conservatism was cross-hatched, in ways that he did not always choose to acknowledge, with a fearful interest in the anarchic and the fragmentary, and in the forms that they assume on the page.

Waugh was born in 1903, the second son of Arthur Waugh, a noted – and notably unprovocative – man of letters. ('That category, like the maiden aunt's, is now almost extinct', wrote Evelyn in his 1964 autobiography, *A Little Learning*.)[6] He was educated at Lancing College, where he devoted far less time to writing than to draughtsmanship, which he took to be his destined *métier*. This preference for the graphic arts continued at Oxford, where Waugh arrived as an undergraduate at the beginning of 1922. He had been awarded a history scholarship to Hertford College; he would leave in 1924 with a Third, a term early, and without completing his degree. (The sense of pleasure being cut short, which pervades the university scenes of both *Decline and Fall* and *Brideshead*, was thus born of a literal curtailment.) The period of his attendance at Oxford has become, since the publication of *Brideshead* in 1945, a rich, not to say cloying, source of suggestion. Waugh's biographers plunge the reader into a cluster of dramatis personae, including John Betjeman, Harold Acton, Brian Howard, Cyril Connolly, Christopher Hollis, and Robert Byron. All were acquaintances of Waugh's, and all were to achieve either fleeting notoriety or a more lasting distinction. The nostalgic impulses that propelled much of *Brideshead* thus played directly and corrosively into the British fixation on the idea of a gilded set.

Waugh himself was ungilded. An embarrassed, and frequently embarrassing, scion of the professional middle classes, he spent much of his university career either drunk or broke, and the reason that his early novels rise with such withering ease above the cacophony of 'names' and 'japes', is that he revelled in the follies of the upper ranks while positioning himself on the fringes of the proceedings and regarding them from an oblique angle. Socially, sexually, and morally, Waugh was under the influence, but the prose that emerged from his observations was cold sober:

> There is tradition behind the Bollinger; it numbers reigning kings among its past members. At the last dinner, three years ago, a fox had been brought in in a cage and stoned to death with champagne bottles. What an evening that had been! This was the first meeting since then, and from all over Europe old members had rallied for the occasion. For two days they had been pouring into Oxford: epileptic royalty from their villas of exile; uncouth peers from crumbling country seats; smooth young men of uncertain tastes from embassies and legations; illiterate lairds from wet granite hovels in the Highlands; ambitious young barristers and Conservative candidates torn from the London season and the indelicate advances of debutantes; all that was sonorous of name and title was there for the beano.[7]

That is the second paragraph of Waugh's first novel, *Decline and Fall*, published in 1928. What is remarkable is that, in its scornful and elaborate amusement, it could hail from any period of his writing career. Waugh, in short, already sounds like Waugh. You could argue that the exclamation mark, which nudges the exhilaration towards *style indirect libre* (it could be the fond remembrance of a former Bollinger rake), is recognisably youthful in its high spirits; but so much else about the paragraph establishes patterns that Waugh would never break. There is the long sentence, marked out with colon and semi-colons, marshalling order from its account of a populous chaos. There is the judicious nod towards 'tradition', which starts with royalty and is then dissected into its component absurdities. To expose the venalities of individual aristocrats, by way of indicting the entire stratum from which they hail, is among the most tested methods of radical complaint, yet that is not the spirit in which Waugh's litany unrolls. His choice of adjectives is biting and precise, as though inscribed with an engraver's tool, yet, even as the evidence accrues ('epileptic', 'uncouth', 'illiterate', and the delicately scandalous 'indelicate'), there is remarkably little sense of attack, and the carousing Wodehousian slang of the last word – a light resting-place for such a heavily-packed paragraph – is happy to hint that there is far more to relish, in these unworthies, than there is to lambast. Waugh will both beat them and join them; or, at any rate, express the dim hope that he could.

Decline and Fall is a depleted *Bildungsroman*, detailing the adventures of Paul Pennyfeather, the joke being that anyone less equipped for adventure it would be hard to conceive. Thackeray subtitled *Vanity Fair* 'A Novel without a Hero', not just because, among its array of male characters, none stood out with any prominence, but also, by implication, because few conducted themselves in a sustained heroic manner. It is that sense of deflation which Waugh inherited, and, from the moment when Pennyfeather's trousers are removed by a rowdy throng, in the quad of an Oxford college, we embark upon a string of leading men, threading all the way to Guy Crouchback in the *Sword of Honour* trilogy (1965), who will be defined less by the thrust of their activity than by the nicety of their humiliation. A Waugh hero does not make his mark upon the world; he waits, not with any masochistic thrill but in a near-trance of resignation, to see what damage the world will choose to inflict upon him.

Pennyfeather is sent down from Oxford for indecent exposure. One could argue that, for the unwilling Waugh hero, any exposure to the wider environment, beyond the stone walls of his spiritual home, is doomed to indecency – emotional and professional, as well as sartorial. (The most elegant variation on this theme comes in *Scoop*, where Mr Salter and William Boot, the town mouse and the country mouse, trade places; the suburban-dwelling Salter is as wretchedly stranded in Boot Magna, with its chatter of horses and heraldry, as William is in the din of the metropolis.) Pennyfeather is hired as a master at a private school in Wales, and the set pieces that ensue, such as the school sports, display a comic athleticism that Waugh would never surpass. Some of the supporting cast – Dr Fagan, Grimes, and Prendergast, all of them fellow teachers – impose themselves on our perception with an immediacy denied to the central figure. This is one reason, incidentally, why most adaptations of Waugh, on stage or screen, fall flat: there is a blank at the heart of them that no actor can fill. We know that Captain Grimes, for instance, has a red moustache and a wooden leg, and within a dozen pages we have been led through his previous history, whereas Pennyfeather is barely supplied with any physical description until the closing pages of the book, at the precise point when – after marrying a pupil's mother, going to jail for a crime that he was unaware of having committed, and being declared legally dead – he returns to his old college in disguise, with a moustache of his own. He has failed at one life, and must try another.

There is a passage of reflection, halfway through this first novel, and mirrored nowhere else in Waugh's fiction, when he steps back from the narrative (not unlike Thackeray, in his opening declaration as 'Manager of the Performance'), and admits that 'the whole of this book is really an account of the mysterious disappearance of Paul Pennyfeather', who was destined to become a respectable citizen of solid opinions, but who was diverted and 'disembodied' by the plot that befell him: 'Paul Pennyfeather would never have made a hero, and the only interest about him arises from the unusual series of events of which his shadow was witness' (*D&F*, 122–3). For a novel of such robust and cheerful reputation, this strikes a fragile note. In the ranks of questing young men, the 'shadow' in question owes less to the Pip of *Great Expectations*, say, than to the Frédéric Moreau of Flaubert's *L'Éducation sentimentale*, who was swept up and along in his times and, as T. S. Eliot observed, 'constructed partly by negative definition'.[8] This dissolving of the self is hard to spot in Waugh's fiction; it tends to be confounded by the pains that he took to construct his own outward persona, especially in later years, into a pugnacious presence. But *The Ordeal of Gilbert Pinfold*, grounded in an episode of his own mental dissolution on board ship, demonstrates what was always there: an acute awareness not just of all that menaced one's sanity but of the ease with which a person could vanish inside the modern throng.

Vile Bodies (1929) was responsible for hardening and fixing those qualities which posterity has assigned to the work of the younger Waugh: a metallic lustre, a narrative briskness that verged on the peremptory, and a froideur designed to cool anything that smacked of emotional warmth. The book was a success, not least among those whom it purported to satirise; its modish, invented vocabulary ('shame-making', 'sad-making', 'bogus', 'divine'), itself became *à la mode*, and that sense of Waugh as an observer of a localised scene, with his finger on a quickening social pulse, led some to prescribe a limit to the book's effects. 'If you don't read it now you'll be too late', predicted Richard Aldington in a review.[9] If the novel has confounded such cautions, it is because it refuses to parade its credentials as a period piece. When the hero, Adam, is chastised by his paramour, Nina Blount, for being dull – 'Do be amusing, Adam. I can't bear you when you're not amusing' (*VB*, 90) – the etiolated phrasing answers not to the passing fancies of the Bright Young People, as transcribed by Michael Arlen in *The Green Hat* (1924), but to something permanent in our capacity for boredom.

The epigraph to *Vile Bodies* comes from Lewis Carroll's *Through the Looking-Glass*, and, as though to fulfil that forewarning, the subsequent plot is deliberately stripped of the logical momentum that drove *Decline and Fall*. In its stead is a tessellation of incidents, fitted together to provide a tonal clash; one long parenthesis unrolls the events to which the young lovers have been invited ('Masked parties, Savage parties, Victorian parties, Greek parties ... ' (*VB*, 123)), and the entire book wears the air of a social gathering on the brink of collapse, with guests of incompatible backgrounds forced into harsh proximity and the characters distilled to an essence of conversation. Chapter 11 is scored for voices only, with Adam and Nina on the telephone, and the reader eavesdropping as if on crossed wires:

> 'You haven't got any money?'
> 'No.'
> 'We aren't going to be married today?'
> 'No.'
> 'I see.'
> 'Well?'
> 'I said, I see.'
> 'Is that all?' (*VB*, 183)

This back-and-forth – a form of stichomythia, updated and whittled down – marks one of the distinctive verbal beats in Waugh, yet it was not wholly of his devising. It sprang from a lesser figure:

> 'Love isn't logical, Gerald.'
> 'Alas!'
> 'Oh, Gerald!'
> 'What has your friend a year?'
> 'How should I know, dearie?'
> 'It's important to know.'
> 'It's better to be poor – I've often heard mum say – than to have a soft seat in hell.'
> 'An Italian is often very easily enamoured.'[10]

The passage comes from *Inclinations*, Ronald Firbank's novel of 1916. Waugh acknowledged Firbank as a tutelary spirit, hailing him in an article of 1929 as 'the first quite modern writer to solve for himself, quite unobtrusively and probably more or less unconsciously, the aesthetic problem of representation in fiction', and noting that 'his compositions are built up, intricately and with a balanced alternation of the wildest extravagance and the most austere economy, with conversational nuances'.[11] What will surprise Waugh's readers, in particular those who know only his later dismissals of anything that savoured of the *avant-garde*, is, first, his grappling with what we now recognise as one of the prime conundrums of modernism, and, secondly, how closely his account of 'extravagance' and 'economy' fits his own narrative tactic in *Vile Bodies* – far more so than it does the manner of Firbank, whose lines, quoted above, are not so much dramatised as stagey, grabbing at plush epigrams instead of holding fast to character. It is Waugh, rather than his mentor, who sounds 'unobtrusive'.

The most assiduous of his biographers, Martin Stannard, has established that the writing of *Vile Bodies* was broken off half-way through.[12] The cause of the interruption was the breakdown of Waugh's marriage. He had married Evelyn Heygate – they were known among friends as 'He-Evelyn' and 'She-Evelyn' – in June 1928. Little over a year later, on 9 July 1929, his wife informed him in a letter that she had fallen in love with somebody else. Waugh was away in the country at work on the novel, which he abandoned at once and did not resume until September. 'I am relying on a sort of cumulative futility for any effect it may have', he wrote in a letter of that month.[13] He embarked not just on a new direction in the plot, and on what Stannard calls 'a conscious desire to give the novel a consistently "darker" tone',[14] but also on a reshading of all that had come before.

There is no denying Stannard's chronological argument, nor the fact that *Vile Bodies* is nudged to the brink of collapse; on the other hand, Waugh could be seen as well prepared for such a rupture, with *Decline and Fall* and his earlier apprentice work being already committed to a view of human relations as both burdensome and transient. As early as 1923, in a story entitled 'Antony, Who Sought Things Lost', Waugh had described a man inhabiting a prison cell with his fiancée, who cuckolds him by sleeping with their pockmarked jailer.[15] The fear of betrayal, in other words, predated its actual onslaught. A biographical reading of the novels would, with some justice, emphasise the failure of the marriage as the wellspring of all the other disenchantments in his subsequent work. It could equally be claimed, however, that Waugh's writing was instinctively drawn to disruption (consider not only the plots but the jagged paragraphing of *Vile Bodies* or *Black Mischief*, which suggests an impatience with unbroken rhythms and moods), and that his marital distress was but one of many templates that would serve that literary need. 'He liked things to go wrong', in the words of one commentator,[16] and that headlong comic preference remains more pertinent than his private shame.

Waugh soon separated from his wife, though the divorce was not finalised until 1935. In 1930 he was received into the Roman Catholic Church. In the ensuing years he travelled widely, and the novels that emerged – *Black Mischief* (1932), *A Handful of Dust* (1934), and *Scoop* (1938) – can be read as an informal trilogy of restlessness. Many readers have been struck, if not repelled, by the heartlessness of their plotting and mood; most of the characters are funny, few are likeable, and the author himself was rarely disposed to offer them a saving charity. The first concerns a cad, Basil Seal, who makes himself useful, or otherwise, in the attempts of a young African emperor to launch his country into the modern age; the second sees an ineffectual English squire who leaves his wife, in the wake of her adulterous affair, and, having submitted to the grim legal rigmarole that attends a divorce, journeys to a fever-ridden exile in South America; in the third, the timorous Boot, mistaken for an eminent novelist of the same surname, is dispatched abroad (again, to Africa) to cover a complicated war. This he does at first woefully and then with a triumphant, if inadvertent, flourish, the success of which smothers him with British embarrassment. His reports are filed by telegram, a medium that allowed Waugh to compress his taste for surreal juxtaposition into its most concentrated form: 'LOVELY SPRING WEATHER BUBONIC PLAGUE RAGING'.[17]

There was an authentic precedent for such silliness. 'NURSE UNUPBLOWN' was one message sent by Waugh himself and cited in his travel book, *Waugh in Abyssinia* (1936),[18] which was based on his reports for the *Daily Mail* on the Italian invasion of that country; it stands in much the same relation to *Scoop* as *Ninety-Two Days* (1934) does to the latter stages of *A Handful of Dust*, and as *Remote People* (1931) – Waugh's earlier account of Abyssinia, with its description of the coronation of Haile Selassie – to *Black Mischief*. In each case the travel book is, though unblinking in its curiosity, necessarily shapeless: a sketch for the compressed finesse of what came after. 'Nothing is more insulting to a novelist than to assume that he is incapable of anything except the mere transcription of what he observes', Waugh had written in 1930. 'One has for one's raw material every single thing one has ever seen or heard or felt, and one has to go over that vast, smouldering rubbish-heap of experience, half stifled by the fumes and dust, scraping and delving until one finds a few discarded valuables.'[19] The sentiment here is hardly unusual; the image is peculiar to Waugh, in its melding of determination and disgust.

Unlike Robert Byron, Peter Fleming, and other travel-writers of his generation, who were enthused and educated by their experiences, Waugh, by his own admission, went abroad with a set of prejudices and came back with them intact, and his characters, too, seem no wiser for their wanderings. The lure of elsewhere, throughout the novels, is balanced with the horrors of home. Everywhere on earth, things go wrong; amelioration, whether by government decree or personal effort, is hard to come by and transient in its effects; urban civilisation is no less rabid and raw than the supposedly primitive conditions under which less developed cultures are said to toil. There is no point in concealing Waugh's lapses into what we now read as blatant racism; *Black Mischief* is the worst offender, with its lazy, cinematic flashes of 'Tireless hands drumming out the rhythm; glistening backs heaving and shivering in the shadows.'[20] Yet what truly excites his mockery is the emperor's scheme to mimic, both in morals and machinery, the advances of a Western society that Waugh increasingly took to be unfit for emulation. Boot writes, after all, for the *Daily Beast*. Its rival is the *Brute*. The cushioned existence of Lord Copper, proprietor of the *Beast*, is and will remain 'full to surfeit of things which no sane man seriously coveted' (*Scoop*, 220).

This dissatisfaction was brought to full bloom by *Brideshead Revisited*, which came out in 1945. It was not Waugh's first novel of the Second World War; 1942 had seen the publication of *Put Out More Flags*, his acidic tale of the Phoney War, with Basil Seal – none the worse for having unwittingly eaten his own girlfriend at the close of *Black Mischief* – forging an illicit profit from the discomforts of others. There is little combat in the novel, and none at all in *Brideshead*, which was explicitly written as a response to the privations of wartime life. The result has an overflowing, unrationed quality, as the author admitted in a later Preface: 'the book is infused with a kind of gluttony, for food and wine, for the splendours of the recent past, and for rhetorical and ornamental language, which now with a full stomach I find distasteful' (Preface to *BR*, 7). It was also a great commercial success, a novelty for Waugh, who was gratified and appalled in equal measure, confident that his new readers had misread his intentions. To him its theme had been 'the operation of divine grace on a group of diverse but closely connected characters' (*BR*, 7), whereas what had snared the attention of his fans, and indeed his detractors, was its memory of Oxford in the Twenties, 'irrecoverable as Lyonnesse' (*BR*, 23), and its portrait of an old Catholic family rich in land, possessions, servants, and internal strife. The book 'lost me such esteem as I once enjoyed among my contemporaries' (*BR*, 7), and the debate over its merits – whether its snobbery outglares its beauty and its comedy, or whether the three are inextricable – has never ceased.

What tends to be passed over, in discussions of *Brideshead*, is its divergence from a rule that Waugh, in his completed novels, never otherwise broke, before or after: it is written in the first person. (The novel that it most closely resembles, in its refraction of a dazzling but finally disappointing figure through the eyes of a duller narrator, as in its prevailing wistfulness, is *The Great Gatsby*; but Waugh did not read Fitzgerald's book until after the war (*LL*, 181).) Gone are the harsh, snapping paragraphs of the early books and the drastic reversals of fortune that beset Waugh's heroes of the Thirties. Frustration still intrudes, but it is handled with regret, and the clauses tend to unfurl in leisurely rumination, as though in tribute to 'the mind sequestered and self-regarding' (*BR*, 77) that is lauded as one of the primary attributes of youth. *Brideshead* trades one loftiness for another, the aesthetically formal for the wearily social: where Waugh, as narrator, inspected his earlier characters from on high, wielding a dry malice, Charles dwells among them, reporting on their affairs, and yet, by meeting Sebastian Flyte and thus becoming an honorary member – or, at any rate, a temporary mascot – of the British aristocracy, he is still furnished with a vantage-point from which to observe, at an ironist's comfortable distance, the habits of the quotidian world.

The effects of that hauteur were soon subjected to critical debate. Conor Cruise O'Brien, writing under the pseudonym of Donat O'Donnell, argued in 1946 that *Brideshead* 'breathes from beginning to end a loving patience with mortal sin among the aristocracy and an unchristian petulance towards the minor foibles of the middle class' (*CH*, 258). In Waugh's eyes, this charge impugned 'the good faith of my conversion to Catholicism' (*CH*, 270), and he was equally stung when it was repeated and expanded by Frank Kermode in an article of 1960 (*CH*, 279–87). Both commentators had noted the novel's untrammelled repulsion at the figure of Hooper, Charles's wartime platoon-commander, whose brief but vivid appearances act as bookends to the main action, and who represents all that his creator saw as dull, grasping, and spiritually inert. After centuries of pious and graceful flowering, in oases such as *Brideshead*, 'came the age of Hooper' (*BR*, 331) – a sudden frost, as the novel's final page insists. Waugh claimed that 'the Common Man' was 'an abstraction invented by bores for bores',[21] but with Hooper – and then with Trimmer, his even cockier successor in *Sword of Honour* – he gave the abstraction fierce concrete form, leaving some readers to ask: if, as a Catholic writer, Waugh believed that all were possessed of an immortal soul, what does it mean for the Trimmers and the Hoopers, and the aspiring class from which they hail, to be drawn as virtually soulless? Why are they not permitted to feel, as Sebastian, his sister Julia, and his errant father, Lord Marchmain, so obviously do, the 'twitch upon the thread' that will draw them back to the centrality of the Faith?[22]

This 'conflict between style and morality', which Terry Eagleton identified in his study of *Brideshead*,[23] and which, in his view, assigned spiritual seriousness only to those who have lived with – and, if possible, finally dispensed with – a flourish of ineffable glamour, makes no more than fitful appearances in the later works of Waugh. These can be divided into the abrupt, forthright novellas and short stories, such as *Scott-King's Modern Europe* (1947), *The Loved One* (1948), *Helena* (1950), and *The Ordeal of Gilbert Pinfold*, and into the more extensive reach of the *Sword of Honour* trilogy, which began with the publication of *Men at Arms* in 1952, continued with *Officers and Gentlemen* three years later, and came to a close with *Unconditional Surrender* in 1961. The three instalments touch at many points on the author's own wartime experiences, which saw him joining the Royal Marines and then the Commandos. He saw action against the Vichy French at Dakar and in the battle for Crete before taking part in a military mission to Yugoslavia. Waugh was known on the one hand for his imperturbable physical bravery and, on the other, for being, in the words of one Commanding Officer, 'so unpopular as to be unemployable'.[24]

In 1965 Waugh combined the three parts of the trilogy into what he called a recension. The changes he imposed were profuse and often far from superficial, with implications for the organising structure of the books; even on the very last page, for instance, the hero, newly remarried, is described in one version as the father of twins and in another as childless.[25] On this hangs the whole question of the house of Crouchback: will Guy's heirs be truly his, or will they descend from the illegitimate child that his former wife, now deceased, conceived with her lover – the despised Trimmer, no less – and that Guy, in a gesture both noble and demeaning, has raised as his own? Will they be old Catholic blood, in short, or the Modern Age made flesh? Even the reader unbothered by such a distinction will realise the weight that it bears within the moral environment of the books, and the case for a scholarly edition of Waugh's complete works (not least *Brideshead*, which underwent many important transformations in 1960) is overwhelming.

Read as a whole, the trilogy – the summit of Waugh's achievement – comes across as both crowded and lonely: crowded, as one would expect of any fiction that lays forth the experiences of a combatant during the Second World War; and lonely, because the soldier in question feels himself from the start to be excluded from that throng. Guy's otherness has many causes. He is older than most of his fellow recruits, and, indeed, soon acquires the adhesive nickname of 'Uncle'. He is, like the majority of Waugh's heroes, from Tony Last onward, a Roman Catholic. Above all, as though pursuing the course of solitude charted by Charles Ryder (who described himself to Hooper as 'homeless, childless, middle-aged, loveless' (*BR*, 330)), Guy is a man adrift – 'destitute, possessed of nothing save a few dry grains of faith' (*SoH*, 24). The note of desiccation is struck again when he meets his former wife, Virginia, whose brightness of manner is a rebuke to his inanition: 'as she drifted into ever ampler felicity, Guy shrank the further into his own dry, empty place' (*SoH*, 71).

At the outset of the novels, nonetheless, we find him clinging, with some alacrity and even joy, to the moral cause of the war: something to die for is a reason to live. 'The enemy at last was plain in view' (*SoH*, 4). He returns from his exile's home in Italy to fight, and the early chapters of *Men at Arms* see him delighting in his new regiment, the Halberdiers, whose customs and companionship stir an affectionate memory of school: 'he loved the whole corps deeply and tenderly' (*SoH*, 42). That full-hearted, almost fulsome phrasing is highly unusual in Waugh, and the experienced reader will already catch, buried within it, an ominous hint that such love will be disappointed, and that the hero must be riding for a fall. And so it proves. Guy's age proves to be more of a liability than a cause for veneration. His country is 'led blundering into dishonour' (*SoH*, 440). He is scandalised by the embrace of Stalin's Russia as an ally of the Christian West. And, above all, when men go into action, what awaits them is not glory but shame and foul-up: first in a commando raid on the coast of France – it was aiming at a nearby island, but missed – for which the cowardly Trimmer is decorated; then in the battle for Crete, with its ignominious scurry to the departing ships; and finally in Yugoslavia, where even the smallest gesture of charity on Guy's part – an attempt to find safe haven for a number of displaced Jews – is compromised and stifled in the prevailing mêlée.

That 'one frustrated act of mercy' (*SoH*, 656) had been recounted before, in a short story entitled 'Compassion' (1949).[26] Like much of late Waugh, *Sword of Honour* is littered with a wealth of self-borrowings. Names alone loop back to the early work: Margot Beste-Chetwynde, who seduced Paul Pennyfeather in *Decline and Fall*, and who earned either cameo roles or alluring mentions in *Vile Bodies*, *A Handful of Dust*, *Scoop*, *Put Out More Flags*, and *Brideshead Revisited*, is rediscovered in 'Basil Seal Rides Again' (1962), living in a London hotel and addicted to television, 'her old taut face livid in the reflection'.[27] As for the lovely Julia Stitch, whose social accomplishments had been hymned in *Scoop*, she seems undiminished seventeen years later, in *Officers and Gentlemen*, at once businesslike and unfathomable:

> As he drove away she waved the envelope; then turned indoors and dropped it into a waste-paper basket. Her eyes were one immense sea, full of flying galleys. (*SoH*, 444)

That strange last sentence takes its place in a long litany of classical images that reverberate through Waugh. Not only was he unusual among his contemporaries in an unabashed fondness for Latinate diction ('it was his example which fortified me to that desperate expedient' (*LL*, 219)); he would also, timing his moment carefully, elevate his descriptive diction into the mock-epic. This rise lent a brief mythical status to the lowliest and most risible of beings ('Had he not moved unseen when the darkness covered the waters?' we are asked of Grimes in *Decline and Fall* (199)), not so much poking fun as proffering a verbal magnificence that life, in its graceless let-downs, could never supply. When the Earl of Balcairn, a newly sacked gossip columnist in *Vile Bodies*, puts his head in an oven and turns on the gas, his passing is linked to that of his noble forefathers, one of whom 'had been picked white by fishes as the tides rolled him among the tree-tops of a submarine forest' (*VB*, 107). Like those men, Mrs Stitch is honoured with a glimpse of the aquatic (those same eyes are elsewhere described as 'portable and compendious oceans' (*SoH*, 330), a quotation from the seventeenth-century poet Crashaw),[28] but something has changed. The laughter has leaked away, and, if there is laceration here, it is not in Waugh's lampooning of unfortunates but in Mrs Stitch herself – in her own insouciant gesture, which *Sword of Honour* construes as the mark of a terrible indifference. In the envelope that she throws away is the identity tag that Guy has taken, in duty and piety, from the body of a British soldier that he came across in Crete. He has asked her to forward it to the authorities, so that the family of the deceased can be notified, but this brilliant, well-connected woman feels nothing for an unknown soldier. Her mind is elsewhere, all at sea.

Waugh's greatness, at such moments, is that of a writer who has seen fit (or found good cause) to transform a comic ruthlessness into a modulated despair. The war, as he perceived it, piled one treachery upon another ('courage and a just cause were quite irrelevant to the issue' (*SoH*, 123)), and thus confirmed, in the wider political field, what he had always suspected of private emotional transactions. The surprise is that work of such shrunken expectations should strike the ear as anything but dispiriting. For Waugh himself, the hopelessness of the given world was nothing to be surprised by, or – in prose, at least – to complain about. It was a necessary concomitant of a belief in a better world to come, and his task was to make sport of our abandoned predicament. 'In my future books there will be two things to make them unpopular', he wrote in the aftermath of *Brideshead*. 'A preoccupation with style and the attempt to represent man more fully, which, to me, means only one thing, man in his relation to God.'[29] In planning for unpopularity he was unsuccessful; all his novels remain in print. But the two parts of that plan were in fact as one: his was a style calibrated to register the precise degree of foolishness with which every man and woman clung to the false gods, as Waugh understood them, of earthly life. In this light, his conservatism was not an uneasy mismatch for his comic stringency but its essential source, furnishing him with ceaseless examples of the disorder and deceit in which he rejoiced; 'the anarchic elements in society are so strong that it is a whole-time task to keep the peace', he wrote in 1939.

'Once the prisons of the mind have been opened, the orgy is on.'[30] His prose existed to prove a point, and, in his mature work, he blended the effulgences of *Brideshead* with the parsimonious, puncturing farce of his first novels to arrive at an urbanity that was responsive to error and yearning alike. The ageing author who had initially dreamed of being a draughtsman still saw himself as a maker of verbal objects, and his late books find kinship with those who, whether in sacrilege or sanctity, are possessed of practical gifts: with the lost souls who practise the ghastly minutiae of the Californian mortuary in *The Loved One*, or the mother of the Emperor Constantine, in *Helena*, whose quest to find the True Cross climaxes in a brisk rummaging through cellars blocked with rubble. Saddest of all is the impractical Guy Crouchback, struggling to meet the time-scuffed demands of the rifle range, the parade-ground and the officers' mess. Trying and failing, he is described as 'Philoctetes set apart from his fellows by an old festering wound; Philoctetes without his bow' (*SoH*, 410). Waugh's own wounds can only be guessed at, by his biographers; he preferred to identify, explore, and sometimes laugh at the unhealable wounds around him. Unlike Guy, however, he never mislaid his bow, and the novels are there to prove it.

NOTE ON EDITIONS

The Penguin edition of Waugh's fiction is most readily and cheaply available to the general reader. The Everyman series, each with an introductory essay and short bibliography, is also recommended. Neither option, however, confronts the many textual issues that arise in the study of Waugh; the original *Brideshead Revisited* of 1945, for example, as opposed to the revised version of 1960, is currently unavailable in any form.

NOTES

1 Alfred Kazin, introduction to *Writers at Work: The Paris Review Interviews*, third series (London: Secker & Warburg, 1967), p. 110.
2 Ibid., pp. 110–11.
3 T. S. Eliot, *Collected Poems and Plays* (London: Faber and Faber, 1969), p. 117.
4 *Vile Bodies* (Harmondsworth: Penguin, 1938), p. 18. Hereafter *VB*.
5 *Brideshead Revisited* (rev. edn 1960; Harmondsworth: Penguin, 1962), p. 34. Hereafter *BR*.
6 *A Little Learning* (Harmondsworth: Penguin, 1983), p. 72. Hereafter *LL*.
7 *Decline and Fall* (Harmondsworth: Penguin, 1937), p. 9. Hereafter *D&F*.
8 T. S. Eliot, 'Ben Jonson', in *Selected Essays*, 3rd edn (London: Faber and Faber, 1951), p. 152.
9 *Evelyn Waugh: The Critical Heritage*, ed. Martin Stannard (London and New York: Routledge, 1984), p. 104. Hereafter *CH*.

10 *The Complete Firbank* (London: Duckworth, 1961), p. 283.
11 'Ronald Firbank', in *The Essays, Articles and Reviews of Evelyn Waugh*, ed. Donat Gallagher (London: Methuen, 1983), pp. 57–8.
12 Martin Stannard, *Evelyn Waugh: The Early Years 1903–1939* (London: Dent, 1986), chapter 6 passim.
13 To Henry Yorke, in *The Letters of Evelyn Waugh*, ed. Mark Amory (London: Weidenfeld & Nicolson, 1980), p. 39.
14 Stannard, *Evelyn Waugh: The Early Years*, p. 206.
15 Reprinted in *The Complete Short Stories and Selected Drawings*, ed. Ann Pasternak Slater (London: Everyman, 1998), pp. 565–9.
16 Shirley Hazzard, 'Greene and Waugh on Their Own Terms', in *Writing among the Ruins: Graham Greene and Evelyn Waugh* (Austin, TX: Harry Ransom Humanities Research Center, 2004), p. 10.
17 *Scoop* (Harmondsworth: Penguin, 1943), p. 146.
18 Reprinted in *Waugh Abroad: Collected Travel Writing* (London: Everyman, 2003), p. 654.
19 'People Who Want to Sue Me', in *Essays, Articles and Reviews*, p. 73.
20 *Black Mischief* (Harmondsworth: Penguin, 1965), p. 230.
21 'Fan-Fare', in *Essays, Articles and Reviews*, p. 302.
22 The phrase is used first by Cordelia Flyte in conversation with Charles Ryder and then as the title of Book Three. It comes originally from 'The Queer Feet', a story by G. K. Chesterton, reprinted in *The Complete Father Brown* (London: Penguin 1981), p. 50.
23 Terry Eagleton, *Exiles and Émigrés: Studies in Modern Literature* (London: Chatto & Windus 1970), chapter 2, 'Evelyn Waugh and the Upper-Class Novel', p. 68.
24 *The Diaries of Evelyn Waugh*, ed. Michael Davie (London: Weidenfeld & Nicolson, 1976), p. 532. Waugh reports this comment by Colonel Robert Laycock.
25 'Now they've two boys of their own', in the original version of *Unconditional Surrender* (1961), reprinted in *The Sword of Honour Trilogy* (London: Everyman, 1994), p. 710. Compare: 'Pity they haven't any children of their own', in the recension of 1965, reprinted in *Sword of Honour* (London: Penguin, 1999), p. 663. Hereafter *SoH*; citations are from the Penguin edition.
26 Reprinted in *Complete Short Stories*, pp. 419–40.
27 Ibid., p. 495.
28 'Sainte Mary Magdalene, or The Weeper', *Crashaw's Poetical Works*, ed. J. C. Martin (Oxford, 1957), p. 312.
29 'Fan-Fare', in *Essays, Articles and Reviews*, p. 302.
30 'Robbery under Law', in *Waugh Abroad*, pp. 730, 917.

FURTHER READING

Amory, Mark (ed.), *The Letters of Evelyn Waugh*, London, Weidenfeld & Nicolson, 1980

Davie, Michael (ed.), *The Diaries of Evelyn Waugh*, London, Weidenfeld & Nicolson, 1976

Gallagher, Donat (ed.), *The Essays, Articles and Reviews of Evelyn Waugh*, London, Methuen, 1983

Hastings, Selina, *Evelyn Waugh: A Biography*, London, Sinclair-Stevenson, 1994
Heath, Jeffrey, *The Picturesque Prison: Evelyn Waugh and His Writing*, London, Weidenfeld & Nicolson, 1982
Myers, William, *Evelyn Waugh and the Problem of Evil*, London, Faber and Faber, 1991
Stannard, Martin, *Evelyn Waugh: The Early Years 1903–1939*, London, Dent, 1986
Evelyn Waugh: No Abiding City 1939–1966, London, Dent, 1992
Stannard, Martin (ed.), *Evelyn Waugh: The Critical Heritage*, London and New York, Routledge, 1984
Stopp, Frederick J., *Evelyn Waugh: Portrait of an Artist*, Chapman & Hall, London, 1958
Sykes, Christopher, *Evelyn Waugh: A Biography* (1975), rev. edn, Harmondsworth, Penguin, 1977
Walia, Shelley, *Evelyn Waugh, Witness to Decline: A Study in Ideas and History*, New Delhi, Sterling, 1998
Waugh, Alec, *My Brother Evelyn and Other Profiles*, London, Cassell, 1967

26

DOROTHEA BARRETT

Graham Greene

Introduction

Born in the same generation as Borges, Beckett, and Barthes, Graham Greene (1904–91) studiously avoided postmodernism: not for him, the myth-making, the magic, the bizarre hilarity of a world gone crazed after the death of God. Although his career spanned the period that, in England, ran from the height of modernism in the 1920s to that of postmodernism in the 1980s, his major novels display little of the self-consciousness characteristic of these literary movements, and their only implausible events are the result of his Catholicism (though even these are always capable of a natural explanation). Occasionally a character speaks to God, and God replies. How are we to construe that? The odd unobtrusive miracle takes place – or does it? Apart from these brief flashes of the supernatural, Greene is relentless in portraying the world as absurd, grotesque, and deeply disappointing. His first novel, *The Man Within*, appeared in 1929, two years after Virginia Woolf's *To the Lighthouse*. It contains passages that could be described as stream of consciousness, but Greene soon abandoned this modernist technique for a tougher, more muscular stance that he shared with George Orwell: enough of this effete introspection – let's portray the real world in all its horror and squalor.

He wrote twenty-six novels[1] (including two that were never published and those he called 'entertainments') plus short stories, poetry, plays, screenplays, biographies, autobiographies, children's books, travel writing, journalism, essays, and film criticism. At least thirty-eight films and seventeen television adaptations have been made of his fictions so far. With an author as prolific as this, it is even more necessary than usual to indicate a select few works to recommend as his best. My choice would be as follows: *Brighton Rock* (1938), *The Power and the Glory* (1940), *The Heart of the Matter* (1948), *The End of the Affair* (1951), *The Quiet American* (1955), *The Comedians* (1966), *The Honorary Consul* (1973), and his fine short story

'The Destructors' (1954). These are complex works that focus on major religious, political, and ethical themes, and they will be the main subjects of this discussion, but the selection excludes another important aspect of his fiction: the comedies. Perhaps the best introduction to Greene would be *Our Man in Havana* (1958), *Travels with my Aunt* (1969), and *Monsignor Quixote* (1982). Here some of the same themes are treated with whimsical humour and a touch of magic.

By the 1950s, Greene was generally acknowledged as one of the finest writers of his generation, and that opinion was voiced again and again over the years. V. S. Pritchett claimed that Greene was the first English novelist since Henry James to represent evil in the world. In her introduction to the centenary edition of *The Quiet American*, the novelist Zadie Smith had this to say about his moral sensibility:

> No twentieth-century writer had a subtler mind for human comparison. Where lesser novelists deploy broad strokes to separate good guy from bad, Greene was the master of the multiple distinction; the thin lines that separate evil from cruelty from unkindness from malevolent stupidity. His people exist within a meticulously calibrated moral system. They fail by degrees. And so there is no real way to be good in Greene, there are simply a million ways to be more or less bad. (*QA*, v)

In each of these assessments, the writer tries to isolate what is special about Graham Greene, and that will be my focus here too: the essay will glance at Greene's life then discuss various aspects of his works – his style; his treatments of religion, sexuality, and politics – in the hope of arriving at conclusions about his place in the literary canon.

Life

Henry Graham Greene was born in Berkhamsted – a small town about one hour north of London by train – in 1904. The Greene family was large and prosperous. One ancestor – Benjamin Greene III – founded the Greene King brewery in Bury St Edmunds in the early nineteenth century and owned sugar plantations in the West Indies. Graham's parents were cousins, and his mother was a cousin of Robert Louis Stevenson.

Graham attended Berkhamsted School, where his father was headmaster. There Graham had his first painful experiences with divided loyalties, betrayal, and persecution. He overheard other boys ridiculing his father and knew that in order to be accepted he would have to laugh with them. One of the boys bullied him, and another, whom Graham had considered his friend, turned out to be in league with the bully. This situation – a banal enough example of the everyday brutality of school life – provided a basic pattern for his fiction. As

Greene's biographer Norman Sherry has observed, *The Power and the Glory* is based on this template: the whisky priest is the persecuted hero, the lieutenant the persecutor, and the mestizo[2] the Judas-figure. The hunted protagonist, alone in a frightening and treacherous world, became Greene's specialty. The persecution is often political – the Tontons Macoute in *The Comedians*, the Paraguayan police in *The Honorary Consul* – but Greene had learned the nature of torture and gratuitous evil not in exotic Third-World situations of political tyranny but as a bullied schoolboy in an English boarding-school.

In 1920, when his depressive tendencies became obvious, his parents sent him to live with a psychiatrist. Greene kept a dream diary and underwent therapy sessions every day. This early experience with psychotherapy (early in both his own life and the history of psychoanalysis) would serve him well later as a novelist: it taught him the value of dreams and the subconscious. Greene sometimes uses the dreams of his protagonists to reveal what they are repressing. He also relied on sleep and the subconscious as part of his writing method: every morning, he wrote five hundred words, and every night before he went to sleep he read over what he had written so that the subconscious could work on it overnight.

At Oxford he was more interested in drinking and pranks than in studying. At one point he joined the Communist Party as a joke. But he was already deeply committed to literature: as editor of the literary magazine *Oxford Outlook*, he accepted works from Louis Golding, Edith Sitwell, Louis MacNeice, W. H. Auden, C. Day-Lewis, Rex Warner, and Emlyn Williams. His first book – a volume of poetry entitled *Babbling April* – appeared in 1925. Despite this apparently full life, he was always plagued by boredom. He claimed that at Oxford he had played Russian roulette, simply to alleviate the sense of stultifying boredom that oppressed him.

After university, under the influence of his love for Vivien Dayrell-Browning, he began to work hard and eventually got a job as a sub-editor at *The Times*. In this period, he was romantic and politically conservative. He was a strike-breaker at *The Times* during the General Strike of 1926. His letters to Vivien, who married him after a great deal of hesitation in 1927, reveal an enthusiastic, foolish, traditional young man, deeply in love with a rather remote young woman. In order to persuade her to marry him, Greene offered her a celibate marriage in which they would live together but have no sexual relations. His conversion to Catholicism in 1926 was in part another attempt to win Vivien, but it also went deeper than that. In a letter to her of 5 November 1925, he wrote:

> I admit the idea came to me, because of you. I do all the same feel I want to be Catholic now, even a little apart from you. One does want fearfully hard,

> something fine & hard & certain, however uncomfortable, to catch hold of in the general flux.[3]

In the years that followed, Greene's personality and beliefs evolved. Marriage, the discovery of his vocation as a writer, and disastrous political events transformed him from a traditional and conservative romantic into the iconoclastic, radical, cynical mind we recognise behind the major novels. For example, as a boy, he had loved to read the adventure stories of John Buchan, but years later, in *Ways of Escape* (1980), he had this to say about Buchan's view of Britain and the empire:

> Patriotism had lost its appeal, even for a schoolboy, at Passchendaele, and the Empire brought first to mind the Beaverbrook Crusader, while it was difficult, during the years of the Depression, to believe in the high purposes of the City of London or of the British Constitution. The hunger-marchers seemed more real than the politicians. It was no longer a Buchan world.[4]

The influence of adventure and detective stories stayed with him: Robert Louis Stevenson, H. Rider Haggard, and G. K. Chesterton left their traces in Greene's imagination. But there are also palpable influences of a darker and more modern kind: Henry James, Joseph Conrad, T. S. Eliot, and Ford Madox Ford.

With this new persona came the restlessness, the itch to travel as a way of escape but also as the satisfaction of his voracious desire to see the world – all of it, in all its aspects, no matter how ugly or difficult. He was very good at getting newspapers, publishing houses, and intelligence services to pay for his travels. He crossed Liberia and Mexico in the 1930s; he worked for British intelligence in Sierra Leone during the Second World War; he travelled, sometimes in difficult and dangerous conditions, in Estonia, Israel, Vietnam, Argentina, Cuba, Kenya, the Belgian Congo, Haiti, Panama, Paraguay, Chile, Nicaragua – the list goes on. He was attracted to trouble spots, to war, poverty, and persecution, and these became the raw materials for his fiction.

His incessant travels might also have been a way to escape from his family: he and Vivien now had two children, and Greene found the domesticity stifling. The boredom he dreaded had set in once more, and he was determined to resist it. He had affairs and went to brothels. His first important affair was with Dorothy Glover, with whom he spent much of his time during the war in London, while Vivien and the children were safely out of the way in Oxford. He then fell in love with Catherine Walston, a married woman and mother of five, who was the original for Sarah in *The End of the Affair*. His affair with Catherine Walston lasted many years, and for several of those he was still seeing Dorothy Glover. Finally, in the 1960s, he formed a new and lasting relationship with another married woman: he left (though never divorced) his wife and settled in Antibes, where he spent the last thirty years of his life with Yvonne Cloetta.

His travels, then, were both physical and psychological: he spent his professional life roaming the world and his personal life moving from one love to another, often playing a double game of betrayal and deception that mirrored the still cloudy complications of his espionage activities. Betrayal, marginality, crossing borders – these were to him the central weapons in the battle against boredom and the forging of his consciousness as a writer. From the provincial, middle-class, Home-Counties boy, Greene had become a citizen of the world and, in doing so, had produced a truly global body of work.

Style

In 1948, the novelist Evelyn Waugh had this to say about Greene's style:

> [T]he style of writing is grim. It is not a specific literary style at all. The words are functional, devoid of sensuous attraction, of ancestry and of independent life. Literary stylists regard language as intrinsically precious and its proper use as a worthy and pleasant task. A polyglot could read Mr. Greene, lay him aside, retain a sharp memory of all he said and yet, I think, entirely forget what tongue he was using. The words are simply mathematical signs for his thought.[5]

It is true that Greene is no stylist in the ordinary sense of the term; we remember him for his content. Although he was a rigorous rewriter, honing his prose to a point of absolute precision and economy, his focus was more decidedly on content rather than form. His prose, like Hemingway's, shows the influence and discipline of his experience in journalism, but, unlike Hemingway, he does not encourage the reader to pay as much attention to the sound as to the sense of his words. His own estimation of his style, in an interview with the novelist Anthony Burgess, is not very different from Waugh's:

> I started off with the desire to use language experimentally. Then I saw that the right way was the way of simplicity. Straight sentences, no involutions, no ambiguities. Not much description, description isn't my line. Get on with the story. Present the outside world economically and exactly.[6]

The choice of simplicity has a political dimension: he seems determined to avoid the ivory-tower aspect of literary greatness. His novels are complex in their ideas and imagery, but he makes them accessible to the ordinary reader. For example, in *The Heart of the Matter*, Scobie receives a telegram from his wife, Louise, who has been in South Africa for some time. During the interval, Scobie has become involved in an affair with Helen. Louise's telegram reads: '*Have written am on my way home have been a fool stop love*' (*HM*, 173). In a telegram, the word 'stop' simply indicates punctuation, but on the symbolic level Scobie must indeed 'stop love', now that Louise is coming home. This is the sort of thing that critics make a living decoding, but Greene precludes that by repeating the phrase a few pages later, so that even the untutored reader gets the double meaning. It may be irritating for the literary critic, whose services are thus rendered superfluous, but for the ordinary reader it is liberating.

People quoting Greene tend to choose the moral pronouncements, the pearls of wisdom, such as the line in *Brighton Rock* about the 'appalling … strangeness of the mercy of God' (*BR*, 268) or the great simile in *The Quiet American*: 'innocence is like a dumb leper who has lost his bell, wandering the world, meaning no harm' (*QA*, 29). However, Greene's incisiveness is also evident in simple powerful observations. This is from the scene in *The End of the Affair* in which Henry and Bendrix go to a pub: 'A little hilarious man darted in and called out, "Wot cher, everybody," and nobody answered' (*EA*, 6). In a single sentence, Greene evokes not only the loneliness and disappointment of an individual life but also the lack of social cohesion in the twentieth century that was first explored by T. S. Eliot in *The Waste Land*. Had a similarly hilarious little man walked into a tavern in a nineteenth-century novel – the Rainbow in George Eliot's *Silas Marner*, for example – he might have been ridiculed as the village idiot (social cohesion is not always a positive thing), but this is no nineteenth-century village: it is London after the Second World War, and nobody cares whether the little hilarious man is an idiot or not.

Religion

For the first decade after his conversion to Catholicism in 1926, Greene did not write about Catholics, because he felt he knew too little. His best novels focus on the Catholicism of their central characters; at the same time, politics becomes increasingly central. He was always irritated by being seen as a Catholic writer:

> Many times since *Brighton Rock* I have been forced to declare myself not a Catholic writer but a writer who happens to be a Catholic … Nevertheless it is true to say that by 1937 the time was ripe for me to use Catholic characters. It takes longer to familiarize oneself with a region of the mind than with a country, but the ideas of my Catholic characters, even their Catholic ideas, were not necessarily mine.[7]

As often in *Ways of Escape*, one feels the gentleman doth protest too much. There is no doubt that Greene is fascinated by Manicheanism and Jansenism.[8] Pinkie in *Brighton Rock* believes firmly in hell but not necessarily in heaven. Brown in *The Comedians* declares himself a Manichean. The Catholic ideas that predominate in Greene's fiction are generally heretical ones: that people are incapable of keeping God's commandments without special grace from Him; that the presence of evil in the world proves that God cannot be both omnipotent and benevolent.

At the end of *Brighton Rock*, Rose goes to a priest and confesses that she wishes she had committed suicide with her husband, Pinkie. The priest replies as follows:

> There was a man, a Frenchman ... who had the same idea as you. He was a good man, a holy man, and he lived in sin all through his life, because he couldn't bear the idea that any soul could suffer damnation ... This man decided that if any soul was going to be damned, he would be damned too. He never took the sacraments, he never married his wife in church ... some people think he was – well, a saint. I think he died in what we are told is mortal sin ... You can't conceive, my child, nor can I or anyone the ... appalling ... strangeness of the mercy of God. (*BR*, 268)

The Frenchman is the writer Charles Péguy (1873–1914). Greene's epigraph to *The Heart of the Matter* is from Péguy: 'The sinner is at the very heart of Christianity ... No one is more competent than the sinner to understand Christianity – no one except the saint.'[9] In *The Lawless Roads* and *Brighton Rock*, Greene modifies Wordsworth's happy Pelagian phrase to his own sinister formulation: 'Hell lay around him in his infancy.' In *The Power and the Glory* and *Monsignor Quixote* (which were written over forty years apart), Judas is seen as a heroic figure, a saint in the Ethiopian Church.

Orwell, in a review of *The Heart of the Matter*, famously attacked Greene's concept of 'the sanctified sinner':

> He appears to share the idea, which has been floating around ever since Baudelaire, that there is something rather *distingué* in being damned; Hell is a sort of high-class nightclub, entry to which is reserved for Catholics only.[10]

But it is important not to detach the Catholic ideas from their contexts: Greene interweaves them with politics and the theme of betrayal. The connection between religion and politics in Greene's work has been remarked by many commentators. For Greene, Catholicism at its best is revolutionary, opposing tyranny and oppression in defence of the poor and powerless. He often expressed his admiration for the 'liberation theology' of South America and frequently criticised the Vatican for its conservatism.

Late in his career, Greene makes the connection between Catholicism and Communism playfully explicit in *Monsignor Quixote*. The Quixote-figure is a Catholic priest in bad odour with his bishop; the Sancho-figure is the Communist mayor of El Toboso, who has just lost his seat in an election. This is from a conversation between the two:

> Someone had painted a hammer and sickle crudely in red upon the crumbling stone.
>
> 'I would have preferred a cross,' Father Quixote said, 'to eat under.'
>
> 'What does it matter? The taste of the cheese will not be affected by cross or hammer. Besides, is there much difference between the two? They are both protests against injustice.' (*MQ*, 38)

In his controversial lecture, 'The Virtue of Disloyalty', delivered in Hamburg in 1969, Greene brings together three of his major themes – Catholicism, Communism, and betrayal – under the canopy of defining the writer's vocation:

> The writer is driven by his own vocation to be a protestant in a Catholic society, a catholic in a Protestant one, to see the virtues of the capitalist in a Communist society, of the communist in a Capitalist state ... Loyalty confines you to accepted opinions: loyalty forbids you to comprehend sympathetically your dissident fellows; but disloyalty encourages you to roam through any human mind; it gives the novelist an extra dimension of understanding.[11]

Catholic novelist and critic David Lodge has argued that Greene's Catholicism – far from being a drawback, ghettoising him as a 'Catholic author' and alienating non-Catholic readers from his works – enriches his fiction immensely by giving it a vivid sense of humanity's yearning for good in a world full of evil.

Minds and bodies

Greene achieves something that is very rare in literature but common enough in the visual arts: the representation of the mind's relation to the body. As a Catholic, Greene presumably believes in the soul, and he represents these souls as trapped in repulsive bodies from which they are utterly alienated. Even non-Catholic readers can identify with this, because, regardless of our personal beliefs, most of us have been formed by cultures rooted in religions that encourage a sense of alienation from the body.

For example, sex in his works is a rather unsavoury business, usually linked to betrayal and/or disgust. Most of the sexual relationships he describes are adulterous, and the dominant emotion is jealousy. Brown in *The Comedians* is in this respect not unlike Bendrix in *The End of the Affair*. Sexual advances in *Stamboul Train* are furtive and predatory. Pinkie (*Brighton Rock*) finds the prospect of sex frightening and repulsive. Scobie's affair with Helen (*The Heart of the Matter*) is characterised more by pity, sadness, and guilt than by desire. At the centre of Fowler's love-affair with Phuong (*The Quiet American*) is not sex but the ritual of preparing opium pipes. This grim view of sexuality is perhaps epitomised in his short story 'May We Borrow Your Husband?' (1967), in which a couple of homosexual men seduce a bridegroom on his honeymoon, while the middle-aged male narrator, observing from another table in the same hotel dining-room, debates whether to make advances to the stunned and despairing young bride.[12] Squalor was Greene's *métier*, and the twentieth century gave him plenty of scope to develop it.

Loving relationships between men in Greene's fiction are much more convincing than those between men and women: Bendrix's ménage with Henry at the end of the novel; Scobie's affection for Ali; Fowler and Pyle; Querry and Deo Gratias in *A Burnt-Out Case*. In *Ways of Escape*, Greene is silent about his affairs with women, claiming that he is protecting their copyright, but he describes deep friendships with men with a kind of wistful romanticism.

Greene's most convincing and three-dimensional female characters are the waifs – Coral in *Stamboul Train*, Rose in *Brighton Rock*. They are small and slim, strangely reminiscent of Dostoevsky's women – souls with faces but no real bodies. Perhaps his most dynamic and fully realised female character is Aunt Augusta in *Travels with My Aunt* – a flamboyant, red-haired, spirited, adventurous, bawdy, and intensely vital old lady, an aged twentieth-century Moll Flanders.

But the love objects of Greene's male protagonists rarely 'come alive'. Bendrix insists on describing Sarah in specific physical detail, but in fact we do not see her; she never 'comes alive' in the way Bendrix, Henry, and Parkis do. The female beloveds of Greene's fiction may have orgasms, but we get no sense of how their bodies look or feel or what it is like to inhabit them. Only the repulsive women have bodies: the drunken lesbian journalist Mabel Warren in *Stamboul Train*; Ida Arnold in *Brighton Rock* ('her big breasts bore their carnality frankly down the Old Steyne' (*BR*, 84)).

Male characters, by contrast, have bodies we can see, feel, and smell. We understand what it is like to inhabit the bodies of Wilson in *The Heart of the Matter*, with his bald pink knees, and Mr Smith in *The Comedians*, with his large innocent hairy ears. In *The Quiet American*, the one truly loving relationship is between Fowler and Pyle. The lovely young Vietnamese woman Phuong represents Vietnam, but Pyle is a complex, convincing, three-dimensional character, and, despite or perhaps because of his atrocious innocence, Fowler loves him.

One part of the particularity of Greene's vision is his sense of how our bodies betray us. Few other writers have attempted it, and most of them were writing about extreme conditions. It is there in the great novels of torture – George Orwell's *1984*, Arthur Koestler's *Darkness at Noon*, and J. M. Coetzee's *Waiting for the Barbarians* – and in fiction about old people, like Muriel Spark's *Memento Mori* and T. C. Boyle's short story 'Rust'. Milan Kundera and Pat Barker have done it more recently, but Greene was the first novelist fully to explore the alienation of the mind from the body it inhabits, even when that body is young, healthy, and not in pain.

Politics, espionage, and empire

In his essay 'Henry James: The Private Universe' (1936), Greene writes, 'It is always the friend, the intimate who betrays.'[13] He is referring to James's fictional worlds, but the statement is as true of his own, and this is one of the few links between Greene and his postmodernist contemporaries. His fascination with and sympathy for the Judas-figure has led to much speculation about whether Greene was a double agent. We know he worked for British Intelligence during the war under Kim Philby, who later defected to Moscow. In *Stamboul Train* (1932), Mr Savory gives his unsavoury definition of the novelist: '"'E's a spy!"' (51). If it were not so early, this could be construed as Greene's private joke about his own espionage activities,[14] but by his own account the Depression, the hunger marches, and the rise of Nazism precipitated the central change in his political views:

> I think of those years between 1933 and 1937 as the middle years for my generation, clouded by the Depression in England ... and by the rise of Hitler. It was impossible in those days not to be committed, and it is hard to recall the details of one private life as the enormous battlefield was prepared around us.[15]

Despite the tone of commitment here and elsewhere in his writings, Greene's political choices were not always explicit or consistent. The conflict between his political and religious allegiances divided him over the issue of the Spanish Civil War – a Catholic Republican could support neither one side nor the other. When in June 1937 a booklet entitled *Authors Take Sides* appeared, in which leading left-wing authors of the day declared their support for the Republican government of Spain and their opposition to fascism, Greene's name was conspicuous in its absence from the list, as Anthony Powell noticed in his review of the booklet.

A certain left-wing distrust of Greene as a political ally has pervaded commentary on his life and work. Post-colonial critics like Martin Green and

Elleke Boehmer tend to see Greene as endorsing colonial perspectives even as he tries to criticise imperialism.[16] Jon Thompson, by contrast, sees him as working in 'the critical or ironic tradition' beginning with Conrad's *The Secret Agent* and continuing in Somerset Maugham, Greene, Ambler, and Le Carré.[17]

Greene may be accused of representing British imperialism in a rosy light in the benign and fair-minded character of Scobie, but in the end Scobie's condescending pity for everyone – the women who love him, the Africans under his jurisdiction – is seen as dangerous and wrong. And surely *The Quiet American* is one of the best anti-imperialist novels of the twentieth century, vivid in its representation of the political complexities and the major actors' inability to understand them, startling in its historical foresight.

The critic Paul O'Prey argues that Fowler (*The Quiet American*), Brown (*The Comedians*), and Plarr (*The Honorary Consul*) all begin by cultivating a detached position of non-involvement but are forced by events to become involved.[18] In an article of 1967, Anthony Burgess links Greene's political engagement to his religious heterodoxy: 'The Jansenist in him is led to the places where the squalor of sin is exposed in its rawest forms.'[19] In his discussion of politics in Greene's novels, Burgess focuses on Dr Magiot's letter at the end of *The Comedians* as Greene's most explicit discussion up to that time of the connection between religion and politics – or, more specifically, Communism and Catholicism. Dr Magiot, the quiet, heroic, Haitian dissident, writes to Brown, the narrator. Magiot's letter is given great weight by appearing very near the end of the novel and when Magiot himself is dead:

> I have grown to dislike the word 'Marxist'. It is used so often to describe only a particular economic plan. I believe of course in that economic plan – in certain cases and in certain times, here in Haiti, in Cuba, in Vietnam, in India. But Communism, my friend, is more than Marxism, just as Catholicism ... is more than the Roman Curia. There is a *mystique* as well as a *politique*. We are humanists, you and I ... Catholics and Communists have committed great crimes, but at least they have not stood aside, like established society, and been indifferent. I would rather have blood on my hands than water like Pilate. (C, 290–1)

Catholic writers from Dante to Greene have shared the contempt for indifference expressed here, but it seems excessive and dangerous when we consider that the indifferent are usually harmless. Wars are waged, people are blown up or beheaded, entire populations are exterminated by the passionate, the committed. Dr Magiot's letter is a fine piece of rhetoric. Its power lies partly in the language (Greene may be no stylist, but his prose nevertheless has great impact) and partly in the characterisation of Magiot. He is symbolic of an original Haiti, unspoiled by the Duvalier regime, much as Phuong is symbolic of an original Vietnam, unspoiled by imperialism (before the scatologically named Fowler and Pyle get to her). Readers who sympathise with the population he represents are likely to be moved by this passage in a way that is more common in political writing and speeches than in fiction: moved to a sense that something must be done. This is a striking contrast between Greene and many of the postmodernists; Borges, Grass, and Kundera all warn us against joining up, taking sides, getting in a uniform, or chanting with a crowd; Greene on the other hand repeatedly leads us on a journey from blameless indifference to bloodstained commitment.

His protagonists are, for the most part, lonely men living in foreign, usually Third-World countries, and as such they are the literary descendants of unromantic representations of agents of imperialism like the Boy in Kipling's 'Thrown Away', Kayerts and Carlier in Conrad's 'An Outpost of Progress', and Alban in Somerset Maugham's 'The Door of Opportunity'. The difference is that Greene's protagonists are usually wandering the world after the European empires have collapsed. He explores the aftermath of imperialism in meticulous detail with great insight, and in this his fictions have a contemporary relevance and historical dimension that are unequalled.

Greene's fiction addresses twentieth-century global history as no other fiction writer has. This is clear in politically motivated reactions to it: the Duvalier government in Haiti issued a pamphlet denouncing Greene after the publication of *The Comedians*; the release of the 2001 film of *The Quiet American* was delayed for a year because its subject – an American involved in terrorist activity – was considered too politically sensitive. It is often said that dictators went pale at the sight of Greene setting up his typewriter in their capitals. Some commentators have suggested that his focus on contemporary politics reduces his fiction from literature to mere journalism, a point of view Greene gently ridicules by putting it in the mouth of his character Dr Saavedra in *The Honorary Consul*. Saavedra is a novelist who believes that political fiction must have a historical setting in order to attain universality; his own novels are romantic, false, and steeped in a sentimental reverence for *machismo*.

Even when the subject matter is not explicitly political, Greene's fictions vibrate with subliminal political meaning. In his brilliant short story 'The Destructors', a gang of boys systematically destroys the beautiful house of their old neighbour. The destruction is perceived, by the leader of the gang, as a work of art: it has to achieve perfection; it has nothing to do with financial gain; it is characterised by the perverse idealism we see again and again in the great destructions of the twentieth century.

Conclusions

Novelist and critic Allan Massie, writing in 1990, saw *The Honorary Consul* and *The Human Factor* as among Greene's best works, because in them pity is represented as 'the emotion which makes life tolerable',[20] whereas in earlier Greene novels it is seen as corrupting. Pity may be a fine moral quality, but simply promoting it in one's fiction does not win one a place in the literary canon. As Oscar Wilde said in his Preface to *The Picture of Dorian Gray*, 'The moral life of man forms part of the subject-matter of the artist, but the morality of art consists in the perfect use of an imperfect medium.'[21]

Greene is important not because of the ethical content of his fiction, but because he is one of the best and most accomplished writers of the mid-twentieth century. He made groundbreaking contributions in the three main areas that have been discussed here: he was the first novelist in English since Henry James to portray evil in the world, the first fully to explore the alienation of the mind from the body it inhabits, and he addressed twentieth-century global history as no other fiction writer has.

One of the reasons why he could do this was that he had deliberately placed himself on the periphery – becoming a Catholic in a Protestant culture, avoiding the ivory-tower aspects of literary fame, spending much of his time in the world outside the narrow enclave of middle-class Western privilege into which he was born. He always considered himself a marginal man, writing from the borders. In *A Sort of Life*, he quotes a passage from Robert Browning's poem 'Bishop Blougram's Apology', saying he would choose it as the epigraph for his collected novels, and the passage is perhaps the best last word on Graham Greene:

> Our interest's on the dangerous edge of things
> The honest thief, the tender murderer,
> The superstitious atheist, demi-rep
> That loves and saves her soul in new French books –
> We watch while these in equilibrium keep
> The giddy line midway.[22]

NOTE ON EDITIONS

All Greene's novels have been recently reissued in the Vintage Classics Centenary Edition, except the following, which have not yet appeared: *It's a*

Battlefield (1934), *Loser Takes All* (1955), and *The Captain and the Enemy* (1988); also two early novels, *The Name of Action* (1930) and *Rumour at Nightfall* (1931), which Greene later suppressed.

NOTES

I would like to thank Tom Bourke, Lisa Cesarani, John Cox, Peter Kennealy, Father Joseph Kolb, Nigel Leask, and Adrian Poole for their help with this essay.

1 References to Greene's works are to the texts reprinted in the Vintage Classics Centenary Edition (2001–). The following abbreviations are used: *Brighton Rock* (*BR*), *The Comedians* (*C*), *The End of the Affair* (*EA*), *The Heart of the Matter* (*HM*), *Monsignor Quixote* (*MQ*), *The Quiet American* (*QA*).

2 A 'mestizo' is a person of mixed blood.

3 Norman Sherry, *The Life of Graham Greene*, vol. I, *1904–1939* (London: Jonathan Cape, 1989), p. 256.

4 Graham Greene, *Ways of Escape* (London: Vintage, 1999), p. 69.

5 Evelyn Waugh, 'Felix Culpa?', in *Graham Greene: A Collection of Critical Essays*, ed. Samuel Hynes (Englewood Cliffs, NJ: Prentice-Hall, 1973), p. 97.

6 Anthony Burgess, 'Monsieur Greene of Antibes', in *But Do Blondes Prefer Gentlemen? Homage to Qwert Yuiop and Other Writings* (New York: McGraw-Hill, 1986), p. 21.

7 *Ways of Escape*, pp. 74–5.

8 Manicheanism, which was widespread in the third and fourth centuries, was based on belief in a primeval conflict between light and darkness, good and evil, and that the two sides were equally powerful. Jansenism was a seventeenth-century heresy based on the idea that man has no free will: he either has God's grace and so can obey His commandment, or he has not, in which case he is bound to sin.

9 The translation is mine.

10 George Orwell, 'The Sanctified Sinner', in Hynes (ed.), *Graham Greene*, p. 107.

11 Graham Greene, 'The Virtue of Disloyalty', in *The Portable Graham Greene*, ed. Philip Stratford (Harmondsworth: Penguin, 1977), p. 526. Most of the passage was formulated in a 1948 letter to V. S. Pritchett reproduced in *Graham Greene: A Life in Letters*, ed. Richard Greene (London: Little Brown, 2007), p. 155.

12 *May We Borrow Your Husband? And Other Comedies of the Sexual Life* (London: Vintage, 2000).

13 'Henry James: The Private Universe', in *Collected Essays* (London: Vintage, 1999), p. 22.

14 See Greene's 1968 essay on Philby, 'The Spy', in *Collected Essays*, pp. 310–14, and his coy comment in *A Sort of Life* (London: Vintage, 1999), p. 100, that his days at Oxford were comparable to Philby's and MacLean's at Cambridge.

15 *Ways of Escape*, p. 34.

16 Martin Green, *The English Novel in the Twentieth Century: The Doom of Empire* (London: Routledge & Kegan Paul, 1984), pp. 111–12; Elleke Boehmer,

Colonial and Postcolonial Literature: Migrant Metaphors (Oxford: Oxford University Press, 1995), p. 143.

17 Jon Thompson, *Fiction, Crime, and Empire: Clues to Modernity and Postmodernism* (Urbana and Chicago: University of Illinois Press, 1993), p. 86.

18 Paul O'Prey, ' "Taking Sides": Faith, Action, and Indifference in the Novels of Graham Greene', in *Graham Greene in Perspective: A Critical Symposium*, ed. Peter Erlebach and Thomas Michael Stein (Frankfurt am Main, Bern, New York, and Paris: Peter Lang, 1991), pp. 149–59, p. 151.

19 Anthony Burgess, 'Politics in the Novels of Graham Greene', *Journal of Contemporary History*, 2.2, Literature and Society (April 1967), 93–9, p. 95.

20 Allan Massie, *The Novel Today: A Critical Guide to the British Novel 1970–1989* (London and New York: Longman, 1990), p. 11.

21 Preface to *The Picture of Dorian Gray*, ed. Peter Ackroyd (London: Penguin, 1985), p. 3.

22 *A Sort of Life*, p. 85.

FURTHER READING

Adamson, Judith, *Graham Greene: The Dangerous Edge: Where Art and Politics Meet*, London, Macmillan, 1990

Baldridge, Cates, *Graham Greene's Fictions: The Virtues of Extremity*, Columbia, University of Missouri Press, 2000

Bosco, Mark, *Graham Greene's Catholic Imagination*, Oxford, Oxford University Press, 2005

Diemert, Brian, *Graham Greene's Thrillers and the 1930s*, Montreal, McGill-Queen's University Press, 1996

Erlebach, Peter, and Thomas Michael Stein (eds.), *Graham Greene in Perspective: A Critical Symposium*, Frankfurt am Main, Bern, New York, and Paris, Peter Lang, 1991

Evans, Robert O. (ed.), *Graham Greene: Some Critical Considerations*, Lexington, University of Kentucky Press, 1963

Hynes, Samuel (ed.), *Graham Greene: A Collection of Critical Essays*, Englewood Cliffs, NJ, Prentice-Hall, 1973

Massie, Allan, *The Novel Today: A Critical Guide to the British Novel 1970–1989*, London and New York, Longman, 1990

Meyers, Jeffrey, 'Graham Greene: The Decline of the Colonial Novel', in *Fiction and the Colonial Experience*, Totowa, NJ, Rowman & Littlefield, 1973

Sherry, Norman, *The Life of Graham Greene*, vol. I, *1904–1939*, London, Jonathan Cape, 1989

The Life of Graham Greene, vol. II, *1939–1955*, London, Jonathan Cape, 1994

The Life of Graham Greene, vol. III, *1955–1991*, London, Jonathan Cape, 2004

Sharrock, Roger, *Saints, Sinners and Comedians: The Novels of Graham Greene*, Tunbridge Wells, Burns and Oates, 1984

Sinyard, Neil, *Graham Greene: A Literary Life*, Houndmills, Basingstoke, and New York, Palgrave Macmillan, 2003

Smith, Grahame, *The Achievement of Graham Greene*, Brighton, Harvester, 1986

27

ROBERT MACFARLANE

William Golding

Discussing Henry James's ghost stories in December 1921, Virginia Woolf paused over James's use of the adjective 'unspeakable' at the eerie climax of 'The Turn of the Screw': 'The rooks stopped cawing in the golden sky, and the friendly evening hour lost for the unspeakable minute all its voice.' It was an unexpected adjective to encounter in the work of such a fastidiously garrulous writer, Woolf implied. But, she went on to suggest, unspeakability was in fact one of James's most important subjects. In his ghost stories, as in his novels, James was compelled by those moments when 'some unutterable obscenity has come to the surface': by those incidents or instants when – in Woolf's careful phrase – 'the significant overflows our powers of expressing it'. Readers shudder on encountering these narrative voids or superfluxes, she argued enigmatically, because they afford us a glimpse into 'the dark' that is 'perhaps, in ourselves'.[1]

William Golding (1911–93) and Henry James (1843–1916) could not, at the level of the sentence, be more different. James's sentences are prolonged, filigreed, and devoted – with their delays and recursions – to the subtle revision of implication. His favoured tense is the conditional, his natural mood the subjunctive. His prose cherishes the verb, which most often serves as a loom-end, sending sense shuttling back along a sentence in order to begin another, minutely altered, traverse.

Golding's sentences, by contrast, are declarative, often disdainful of the transitive, and frequently dispense with the etiquette of grammar. They are built out of what Golding industrially called the 'unit' of the adjective–noun combination.[2] Verbs exist most often as buffers upon which sentences must, judderingly, halt. To read James aloud requires a combination of memory and metronomy: recalling where the beat of sense falls, and how it is carried and adjusted between clauses. To read Golding aloud requires a laryngeal effort, an arduous voicing. His language can be – to borrow a phrase from the opening of *Pincher Martin* (1956) – 'hard in the throat and mouth as stones that hurt'.[3]

These strikingly dissimilar novelists, however, are alike in two significant ways. The first is their attraction to the free indirect style – the narrative mode which best allows the novel reader, as Golding put it, to 'thread in and out of a single mind and body, [to] live another life'.[4] The second is their commitment to writing about, or at least around, what James called the 'unspeakable' and what Golding called the 'indescribable'.

Both novelists, in that sense, should be considered mystics: James a social mystic, perhaps, and Golding a mystic of suffering – concerned as he repeatedly was with the perceptions of humans who have been brought to the outermost point of language by some collapse, catastrophe, or circumstantial pressure. Both are interested in characters who have – as James wrote of his child-character Maisie – 'more perceptions than they have terms to translate them'.[5] Dr Johnson famously chastised mystical and devotional writers, on the grounds that a person who had experienced the ineffable was under no compulsion to try to describe it. Golding took care to refute this bluff one-liner. 'It is our business', he wrote uncompromisingly in 1980 of the novelist's task, 'to describe the indescribable'.[6]

'Indescribable': Golding had used the same term five years previously in a review-essay entitled 'Cracked Youth and Age'. 'The Second World War', he observed:

> uncovered entirely different areas of indescribability. The horror of the brewed up tank, the burning plane, the crushed and sinking submarine – all that is difficult to describe but the job can be done. The experience of Hamburg, Belsen, Hiroshima and Dachau cannot be imagined. We have gone to war and beggered [*sic*] description all over again. Those experiences are like black holes in space. Nothing can get out to let us know what it was like inside. It was like what it was like and on the other hand it was like nothing whatsoever. We stand before a gap in history. We have invented a limit to literature.[7]

The passage is interestingly shifty in its tone: from the soldierly sturdiness of 'the job can be done' (a rolling-up of the sleeves, a Tommy-can-do attitude), to the invocation of Shakespeare's Cleopatra on her barge (a war-machine of a sort), to the astrophysics of the 'black holes in space' (a recurrent image in Golding's writing), and finally to the conceptual cave-in that occurs when Golding turns simile upon itself in order to acknowledge the occasional impossibility of likeness. The reader's attention is also drawn to that unexpected preposition 'before', in the penultimate quoted sentence. For Golding is writing in 1975, three decades after the end of the Second World War. The preposition we might expect in such a context is 'after' – 'We stand *after* a gap in history'. But Golding chooses 'before', and his choice compels us to imagine Golding as having turned backwards in time, peering over the abyss's rim, with the future invisibly behind him.

Golding was born in Cornwall in 1911. After studying natural sciences at Oxford University, he became a teacher; first at a Steiner school in London, then at a grammar school in Kent. In 1940, he joined the Royal Navy Volunteer Reserve; he subsequently spent several war years on active service. He served on board HMS *Galatea* in the North Atlantic, commanded minesweepers and rocket-ships, and took part in actions including the sinking of the *Bismarck* and the taking of Walcheren Island on the Dutch coast. Prior to experiencing combat, Golding remarked to his friend Jack Biles, he had 'believed in ... the perfectibility of man'; afterwards, he could see little but man's 'beastly potentialities'.[8] The Second World War brought about a rupture in Golding's personal ethics. It also, as he suggested in 'Cracked Youth and Age', brought about a rupture in the history of literature, even the history of language. Although his fictions alter dramatically in their settings – from the ancient Egyptian (*The Scorpion God*) to the Neanderthal (*The Inheritors*) to the medieval (*The Spire*) to the nineteenth century (*The Sea Trilogy*) to the roughly present-day (*Lord of the Flies*, *Free Fall*, *Pincher Martin*, *Darkness Visible*) – Golding seems to have possessed a powerful sense of himself as always writing out of a specific period in human history. The job that he set himself as a novelist was to gaze back into the metaphysical gap that the war had opened up – the 'black hole' – and to glimpse, or at least to gesture at, its 'indescribable' contents. Like James, then, he was concerned with scrying the 'dark ... in ourselves'.

In an important 1970 essay, Iris Murdoch proposed that twentieth-century novelists could be usefully sorted into the categories of 'Existentialists' and 'Mystics'. Existential novelists (Lawrence, Hemingway, Camus, Kingsley Amis), whose work had dominated the novel form from the 1920s onwards, specialised in strong-willed, self-interested, atheistic protagonists, men (they were usually men): godless adventurers with an atrophied sense of duty. However, Murdoch suggested, the events of the Second World War had produced a new generation of mystically minded writers, who were reacting both against the assumptions of the existential novel and against the atrocities of war. These writers – and here Murdoch named Muriel Spark, Graham Greene, Patrick White, Saul Bellow and Golding, as well as, implicitly, herself – were committed to exploring the non-rational, to describing the power of intuition over that of comprehension, and to approaching those subjects – God, the Good, Evil – which necessarily exceeded the representative powers of language. They attempted to 'express a religious consciousness without the trappings of religion'.[9]

Certainly, what joins Golding's very various novels is that each approaches or orbits moments of speechlessness. Again and again, as we will see, his characters reach what he once called the 'point ... where definition and explanation break down' (the phrase recalls Woolf's 'when ... the significant overflows our powers of expressing it'). At such instants, proposed Golding, language as we recognise it is no longer fit for purpose: 'We must call on a higher language ... We are at a height – or a depth – where the questions are not to be answered in words' (*MT*, 146).

But how can a novelist abandon language? How is it possible for a writer to make the wordless visible? One way to begin to answer these difficult questions is to examine closely some of the instants of breakthrough or breakdown in Golding's novels. For such instants offer points of entry into his surprisingly elaborate metaphysics. They also give some purchase on the concept of what a 'higher language' might be: a concept with which Golding was wrestling from the very start of his writing career.

'The vileness beyond all words'

The island on which *Lord of the Flies* (1954) occurs is tropical in two senses. Riotous with vegetable growth, it is also lush with emblem and image. Most of its images operate symbolically, which is to say that their correlate is unambiguous. The summoning conch is a shell, and also the labial mouth that bestows the right to speak upon its bearer. Simon is both dreamy young boy, and the novel's Christ-figure. Many of the children who occupy the island are, appropriately enough, unambiguous readers, for whom there is little or no free play between signifier and signified. This is true of Ralph, of Jack – and above all of Piggy, with his dutiful literalism, his insistence that vows be kept and laws adhered to, and his confidence in his interpretations. Only Simon – intuitive, non-prescriptive – accepts the variousness and uncertainty of life on the island; and he pays for his tolerance with his life.

There is a conventional critical reading of *Lord of the Flies*, which treats it much as Piggy treats the island: that is, as a stable symbolic system. This reading approaches the novel as a fable: 'an allegorical tale used to illustrate a moral precept or pragmatic truth', to borrow the *OED*'s definition, or – to borrow Golding's – a fictitious story picturing truth with a 'human lesson tucked away in it'. The lesson, in the case of *Lord of the Flies*, being that 'man is a fallen being ... gripped by original sin'.[10] In his lecture-essay 'Fable', Golding (who enjoyed, it should be noted, releasing red herrings and wild geese for his critics to chase) aligned his novel with the simple and prudential tradition of the classical fable, which emerges out of the Greek and runs through Aesop, Voltaire, Swift, and Bunyan.

There is, however, an alternative and more modern version of the fable form, which might be called the 'false fable'. False fables are structurally subversive of the classical tradition, in that they use a reader's expectation of fabular reliability to unsettle the notion of truth itself. An example might be *Moby-Dick*: Melville flirts throughout with various classically fabular readings of the ship, the crew, and the whale, but in the end overwhelms any single reading of the situation with hundreds of possible interpretations, presented from dozens of points of view. What appears at one point to be an easily decipherable 'moral tale' becomes an exercise in relativism.

Lord of the Flies is another false fable, but in contrast to *Moby-Dick* the fabular form is destroyed not by an excess of potential readings, but by the inclusion within the novel's apparently fabular system of an irreducible presence: a force which has no referent, which refuses to reduce to the role of symbol, either for the characters of the novel, or for its readers. This presence is the novel's heart of darkness and it shifts shape in the course of the novel between various avatars: the non-specific monster that haunts the island's interior; the Beast; the dead parachutist tugged winsomely by the wind; a sow's head on a stick; the Lord of the Flies; and, eventually, a vast darkness-containing mouth – or black hole – into which the novel implodes or is sucked.

Golding himself knew that he had created a novel which both assumed and exceeded the status of fable: a psalter with stitches by Hieronymus Bosch. He knew that his novel contained occasions when, as he put it, 'the fable splits at the seams', and he knew also that these occasions were the sources of the novel's uncanny power. 'The very moments', he wrote, 'when I felt the fable to come to its own life before me it may in fact have become something more valuable, so that where I thought it was failing, it was really succeeding.'[11]

What are these 'moments'? The most obvious splitting of the seams occurs when the novel's most supple interpreter, Simon, encounters the novel's most interpretation-resistant presence – its 'unspeakable minute' (James), its 'unutterable obscenity' (Woolf). Simon walks into a jungle grove to discover the sow's head roosting on its bloodied perch: an 'obscene thing' that 'grinned and dripped':

> There was the head grinning amusedly in the strange daylight ... A gift for the beast. Might not the beast come for it? The head, he thought, appeared to agree with him. Run away, said the head silently, go back to the others ... Go back, child, said the head silently.[12]

The novel has, to this point, been conscientious in its attribution of speech: quotation marks have served scrupulously to denote each speaker. In this passage, however, it is no longer clear who is speaking to whom, or more exactly who is *speaking* to whom. Is Simon involuntarily ventriloquising the head, with his thoughts being registered by free indirect speech? Or is the head in fact speaking 'silently' to him? Speech here has become disembodied, migrant.

Five pages further on comes Simon's final confrontation with the 'black ball' of the pig's head, which is by now fully animated. Trying to speak back to the head, Simon's mouth and tongue are described as becoming detached from his mind and skull. He is – to borrow another fine phrase from Woolf's essay on James – 'already half-way out of the body':[13]

> Simon's mouth laboured, brought forth audible words.
>
> 'Pig's head on a stick.'
>
> ...
>
> 'Come now', said the Lord of the Flies. 'Get back to the others and we'll forget the whole thing.
>
> Simon's head wobbled. His eyes were half-closed as though he were imitating the obscene thing on the stick. He knew that one of his times was coming on. The Lord of the Flies was expanding like a balloon.
>
> Simon found he was looking into a vast mouth. There was blackness within, a blackness that spread.
>
> Simon was inside the mouth. He fell down and lost consciousness.
>
> (*LF*, 158–9)

The word 'obscene' recurs here, and the context might remind us of its etymology, from the Latin *obscaeneus* meaning both 'against the presentable' and – less familiarly, but more appropriately – 'unrepresentable'. Again, the novel's punctuation registers the pressure of the indescribable upon utterance. A speech mark is missing from the Lord of the Flies' last words: '"Get back to the others and we'll forget the whole thing.' The omission is eloquent: all that follows is, by means of this covert lacuna, spoken by or out of the Lord himself. From that moment onwards, Simon is engulfed, and so is the novel. 'The mouth' operates as one of Golding's many 'black holes', into which sense is sucked, and out of which nothing conclusive can be made or taken. One of the several paradoxes of the scene is that a mouth – a site of articulation and speech – becomes the space within which structure is abolished. It is a trope that recurs in almost all of Golding's novels.

'The truth is', wrote Golding frankly in 1976, '*Lord of the Flies* has either no theme or all theme ... The theme defeats structuralism for it is an emotion. The theme of [the novel] is grief, sheer grief, grief, grief, grief' (*MT*, 162–3). There is an echo here of King Lear's fourfold howl as he comes on stage with dead Cordelia in his arms; and to his cry in the Quarto version as he kneels over her body: 'O, o, o, o' – four empty sets, or the typographic rendering of a row of anguished mouths.

'A terrible darkness'

Lord of the Flies implodes into one dark mouth; *Pincher Martin* (1956) issues out of another:

> He was struggling in every direction, he was the centre of the writhing and kicking knot of his own body. There was no up or down, no light and no air. He felt his mouth open of itself and the shrieked word burst out.
>
> 'Help!'
>
> When the air had gone with the shriek, water came in to fill its place – burning water, hard in the throat and mouth as stones that hurt. He hutched his body towards the place where air had been but now it was gone and there was nothing but black, choking welter. His body let loose its panic and his mouth strained open till the hinges of his jaws hurt. Water thrust in, down, without mercy. Air came with it for a moment so that he fought in what might have been the right direction. But water reclaimed him and spun so that knowledge of where the air might be was erased completely. Turbines were screaming in his ears and green sparks flew out from the centre like tracer. There was a piston engine too, racing out of gear and making the whole universe shake. Then for a moment there was air like a cold mask against his face and he bit into it. Air and water mixed, dragged down into his body like gravel. Muscles, nerves and blood, struggling lungs, a machine in the head, they worked for one moment in an ancient pattern. The lumps of hard water jerked in the gullet, the lips came together and parted, the tongue arched, the brain lit a neon track. (*PM*, 7–8)

Like Simon, Pincher is here 'half-way out of the body': unlike Simon, he is avid to claw back into it. The passage sets the tone and the pace for Golding's best novel, a fiction as experimental as at least the first of Beckett's *Molloy* trilogy (1951–3), with which it has several family resemblances including a taste for epistemological vaudeville. But where the *Molloy* novels describe a progress towards bodilessness and a sundered voice, *Pincher Martin* begins with sundered voice, which is then effortfully fused back to its body.

Reading the opening page of Golding's novel, you experience a bewilderment that is a version of Pincher's own panic. Orienting information does not so much drop out from this prose as barely exist (it recalls, in this respect, Conrad's telling of the collision of the *Patna* at the start of *Lord Jim*). The retrieval of continuous sense requires a rapid co-ordinative effort on the reader's part. There is a man. He is drowning – or is he being tortured? Past combat is evoked – 'tracer', 'turbines', 'machine', 'neon track'. But where are we now? Is this realm even earthly? For space operates bizarrely in the prose: surfaces and substances refuse to behave in recognisable ways. Air can be bitten. Water assumes the form of 'stones', 'gravel', 'lumps'. The readerly effect of this bewilderment is what Golding termed 'sympathetic kinaesthesia', which he glossed as 'identification with someone else's body movement' (*MT*, 104).

A slow resolve follows this initial chaos. It is gradually revealed that 'Pincher' is a lieutenant, who was serving on a cruiser in the North Atlantic when it was sunk by a torpedo attack. He has by miraculous chance been washed up on a mid-oceanic rock island, craggy, jagged, and pointy, which protrudes only a few metres above the sea at high tide. The first half of the novel describes, in a free indirect style, Pincher's gradual recovery of his senses, and his exploration of the skerrie that is both his saviour and his aggressor. Intricately, he maps and names the rock's topography. He itemises its shelters (one – a covered cleft), its possible food sources (few: sea anemones, seaweed, seals, seagulls), and its dangers (many). What is memorable about this section of the novel is the realisation – in the sense of 'the making real' – of the island, which is presented indisputably to us through Pincher's assiduous inventory of its features and interconnections.

It is the apparent reliability of this realisation that gives the novel's volte-face its shock. About forty pages before the novel's end, it becomes clear that this obsessively particularised island is imaginary: nothing more than an apparition of Pincher's mind, summoned up by means of a massive force of will and memory, as he is drowning. The recitation of the rock's details has been an attempt to build himself out of language a reality that might save him from physical death.

Pincher's desperate and diligent vision will not hold, however. Its internal consistency is not sufficient to resist the pressures either of memory or of immediate elemental circumstance. As in *Lord of the Flies*, there comes a point when the telling 'splits at the seams'. Pincher spots, unexpectedly, a crack in the side of his rock, which he cannot remember from his first mapping. Initially, indeed, he refuses to accept the crack's reality. Then, reluctantly, he lowers himself down the steep side of the skerrie, until 'the crack was only a foot from his face. Like all the rest of the cliff where the water could reach it was cemented with layers of barnacles and enigmatic growths. But the crack was wider. The whole stone had moved and skewed perhaps an eighth of an inch. Inside the crack was a terrible darkness' (*PM*, 124).

The 'terrible darkness' returns us to the 'blackness within' of the pig's mouth which consumes Simon. As in *Lord of the Flies*, Pincher's 'mouth' possesses dimensions incommensurate to its aperture, and as in *Lord of the Flies* the nature of the 'darkness' is not glossed. There are clues in the novel as to where in his life Pincher might have sourced the idea of the crack. The crack is, implicitly, the vulva of a girl he tried to rape in his pre-war life. More metaphysically, it is an embrasure that lets Pincher gaze onto his own deep indecency as a human being. It is, too, the sudden striking knowledge to Pincher that he will die: that he has cast himself up onto nothing more than a rock of words. But the crack is also one of Golding's 'black holes', an abyss whose meaning refuses to be specified. The reader is left to speculate and to project into that 'skewed' eighth-of-an-inch gap: 'the crack [that] was absolute, was utter, was three-times real' (*PM*, 200).

In the pages which follow the discovery of the 'crack', Pincher's carefully fashioned world begins to shiver into fragments. Each aspect of the island is revealed to be a transposition of some kind from his memory. Finally, the origin of the island as a whole is revealed. Exploring his injured mouth with his tongue, Pincher finds a diseased tooth: it is craggy, jagged and pointy ... He realises that the topography of his rock is identical to the topography of the tooth. He has, in two senses, invented the skerrie out of his own mouth – linguistically and dentally. This discovery prompts Pincher's final fragmentation, and during the novel's closing pages, his body and voice begin to shear away from his mind, in a reversal of the novel's opening: 'His mouth said things but he could not hear them so did not know what they were'; 'Far out from the centre, the mouth quacked on' (*PM*, 171, 173).

By this stage in the novel, we understand something of its fierce experimentalism. We have been listening not to the free indirect ramblings of a man lost at sea; but rather to a monologue, spoken by a single mouth, and occurring in something close to a non-space (the 'black, choking welter' of water). In this respect, *Pincher Martin* significantly antecedes Beckett's play *Not I* (1973). That play occurs in a pitch-black environment, through which strikes a single beam of light. The beam illuminates a female mouth, and the mouth utters a monologue of shattered and jumbled sentences. Gradually, the audience is able to sort and coalesce a narrative out of these shards. The woman has suffered a trauma of some kind and is compelled to revisit it continuously; but only in order to deny that she ever suffered the trauma: 'Not I'. Like Pincher, she shores up language in denial of experience.

Golding's failed visions

The mouth, the crack: again and again, Golding's novels are drawn, centripetally, towards a black maw of some kind. Tuami at the end of *The Inheritors* (1955) watches an infant's 'mouth ... opening and shutting', before gazing off at the 'line of darkness that curved away under the trees as the shore receded'.[14] Sammy Mountjoy in *Free Fall* (1959) lies with his 'mouth agape' in the 'uncompanioned darkness' of a POW camp interrogation cell, brought to recall and evaluate his appalling career as a human to that point.[15] Jocelin, at one of the many moments of crisis in *The Spire* (1964), looks down into the pit beneath the edifice and glimpses 'some form of life; that which ought not to be seen or touched, the darkness under the earth, turning, seething, coming to the boil': a sight that causes his 'mouth [to] strain open in sudden fright'.[16] Each of these novels, like *Lord of the Flies* and *Pincher Martin*, moves towards confrontation between the possibilities of articulation and the indescribability of experience or vision. In each, a different kind of 'higher language' is tried: hyperbolic, paradoxical, or minimal. *The Inheritors*, for example, experiments with a language that is absolved of simile: for most of the novel we exist, by means of free indirect style, within the minds of the Cro-Magnons Lok and Fa, who have not discovered comparison as a mode of thought – for they have no need of it, their whole world being perceived as a continuous expression of a nature deity called Oa. *The Spire* mainly concerns the perceptions of Brother Jocelin – priapic, hubristic, occasionally self-abasing – and dramatises several accesses of faith, in which the usual pathways of cognition are bypassed, and Jocelin finds himself 'knowing' something that cannot be either explained or even ascribed an origin. Eventually, however, Jocelin – like Simon and Pincher – vanishes into a 'devouring mouth': the novel's last word is 'tongue' (*S*, 220, 223). In both novels, as Frédéric Regard remarks during an excellent essay on obscenity and Golding, 'the unnameable, which is that which precipitates the collapse of rigid patterns of meaning, and the ineffable, which is that which requires secrecy, do not antagonize each other'.[17]

The issue of this long experiment in the articulation of 'the blackness within' was Golding's 1979 novel *Darkness Visible*. The book appeared twelve years after its predecessor, *The Pyramid* (1967), which was poorly received and did much to damage its author's reputation. The novel's title clearly alludes to Milton's description of hell in the first book of *Paradise Lost*: 'As one great furnace flamed, yet from those flames / No light, but rather darkness visible'.[18] But it can also be heard as something close to an imperative, addressed almost by Golding to himself: *make* the darkness visible.

Its justly celebrated opening pages describe not darkness but light: the luminous holocaust of a blitzed London, in the hours after a bombing raid. A fire-crew stands and watches a section of the East End burn, 'out of control' with 'shameful, inhuman light'.[19] Then – improbably, miraculously – a child emerges from the flames, walking forwards towards the disbelieving crew, who cannot imagine that any solid substance, let alone any life, can have survived the conflagration. This is Matty, orphaned and terribly scarred by the fire, and the rest of the novel tells his difficult story, as he tries to find a way to live.

Darkness Visible is, along with *The Spire*, Golding's most hopeful novel; it is certainly his most mystical. Golding chose to structure the book around a series of equivocal epiphanies – moments of fierce seeing, which often turn out to be mirages or false hopes – as well as the by now more familiar glimpses into fathomless dark. Its final violent pages are occupied with two such visions.

The first of these is experienced by a character called Sim Goodchild, during an informal séance presided over by Matty and shared with Goodchild's friend, Edwin:

> Edwin spoke above his head. Or not Edwin and not speech. Music. Song. It was a single note, golden, radiant, like no singer that ever was. There was, surely, no mere human breath that could sustain the note that spread ... widened, became, or was, precious range after range beyond experience, turning itself into pain and beyond pain, taking pain and pleasure and destroying them, being, becoming. It stopped for a while with promise of what was to come. It began, continued, ceased. It had been a word. That beginning, that change of state explosive and vital had been a consonant, and the realm of gold that grew from it a vowel lasting for an aeon; and the semi-vowel of the close was not an end since there was, there could be no end but only a re-adjustment so that the world of spirit could hide itself again, slowly, slowly fading from sight, reluctant as a lover to go and with the ineffable promise that it would love always and if asked would always come again. (*DV*, 232–3)

Describing the indescribable is always – remember Dr Johnson – a high-risk enterprise, necessarily condemned to make a virtue of failure. The confession of language's inadequacy, traditionally, becomes the surrogate content of the devotional text. Here, however, Golding fails even to sublimate failure. Woolf wrote admiringly in her essay on James's ghost stories of how he used the supernatural to 'draw out a harmony which would otherwise be inaudible', but also observed warningly that James's prolixity, decorum, and 'sentimentality' could cause a disastrous clotting of mood.[20] And there are times in his *œuvre* when Golding also seems to say too much, or presses language too eagerly into the gap he has created.

Certainly, Sim's auditory vision is one of Golding's least accomplished mystical moments: impoverished and clumsy in comparison with, for example, the astral visions of Charles Arrowsmith in Iris Murdoch's *The Sea, The Sea*, or Patrick White's *Riders in the Chariot*, when language achieves a liquidity, seeming to shuck off its habitual states and forms. Here, however, repetition – that most repeated of stylistic shorthands for ineffability – feels stale and awkward. The analogy of the lover is intrusive and superfluous, as are the echoes of Genesis and the allusion to the first line of Keats's 'On First Looking into Chapman's Homer' ('Much have I travell'd in the realms of gold'). The prose, which is meant to connote spontaneous growth and fade, feels worked and staccato. The overall effect is of a writer labouring to communicate the effortlessness of a mystical experience.

Shortly after this episode, the novel moves into its darkest and most accomplished pages. Matty, born out of fire, is consumed eventually by the same energy: burnt punitively to death for superstitious reasons. And the novel concludes – almost in repudiation of its title, and certainly in recapitulation of its opening – in a storm of light. The pederast-teacher Sebastian Pedigree, to whom Matty has been a lifelong goad, is sitting on a bench in rich sunshine, watching children at play in a park. He knows Matty to be dead. Suddenly, however, he glances along the park path to see Matty approaching him, wading through the sunshine as though 'waist deep in gold'. Watching Matty's advance:

> Sebastian Pedigree found he was not dreaming. For the golden immediacy of the wind altered at its heart and began first to drift upwards, then swirl upwards then rush upwards round Matty. The gold grew fierce and burned. Sebastian watched in terror as the man before him was consumed, melted, vanished like a guy in a bonfire; and the face was no longer two-tone but gold as the fire and stern and everywhere there was a sense of the peacock eyes of great feathers and the smile round the lips was loving and terrible. This being drew Sebastian towards him so that the terror of the golden lips jerked a cry out of him –
>
> 'Why? Why?'
>
> The face looming over him seemed to speak or sing but not in human speech.
>
> *Freedom.* (*DV*, 265)

Here Golding presents us with another lyric utterance that aspires to supersede speech, to exist in what he called the 'higher language'. But, unlike the botched account of Sim's ecstasy, this vision succeeds stylistically. The images and figures that do occur are surreal: the bonfire, the peacock eyes, the 'loving and terrible smile'. The parataxis of the third sentence – 'and … and … and' – serves to suspend sense, or rather to diffuse it. The syntax of the sentence beginning 'This being drew …' works to similar effect, for 'being', when we first encounter it, operates both as verb and noun. The causality of the ensuing sentence is also ambiguous: does the 'terror' belong to the lips or to Sebastian, as he is inhaled towards Matty's great golden mouth? Throughout the passage, uncertainty flourishes. Golding's grammar works to place the reader in a state of tolerated bewilderment, not dissimilar to the mystical experience itself. This uncertainty is sustained to the novel's close: in its final sentences, it is not clear whether this experience has left Pedigree dead or alive, refined or dross.

What Golding seems to be experimenting with here is a kind of metaphysical 'synaesthetic kinaesthesia'. He is trying to reproduce as a readerly experience an instant of experience where 'questions are not to be answered in words', and so *are not* answered in words. Instead, as Mark Kinkead-Weekes usefully puts it, the experience of the indescribable is left to 'develop in ... the reader, in the space between the lines, wordlessly, with the risk that the space will not fill, that vision may fail'.[21]

The mandate of the novel

'The sole *raison d'être* of a novel is to discover what only the novel can discover', wrote the Czech novelist Milan Kundera of his form. 'A novel that does not discover a hitherto unknown segment of existence is immoral.'[22] It is a severe attitude, close to a diktat, which at once limits and exalts the novel form. A novel, for Kundera, cannot merely achieve a version of what another cultural form might achieve. There must be some intelligence in a novel that is indigenous to the work; some aspect of it that is not fungible, that would not survive if the novel were disintegrated and then reassembled as essay, historical account, theoretical proposition, philosophical dialogue, poem, or indeed any other arrangement of words. To come to know something which can only come to be known in that exact form: this, for Kundera, is the novel's peculiar mandate – and its morality.

Such an idea is not particular to Kundera, of course. Different versions of it have been proposed throughout the history of the novel as a form. But the idea became notably present in twentieth-century discussions of the novel's abilities. One thinks of Beckett's tart response to an inquiry concerning the influence of existentialism on his work: 'I wouldn't have had any reason to write my novels if I could have expressed their subject in philosophic terms.'[23] Or of Marcel Proust's claim that certain insights about human emotions could only occur in the extended narrative of a novel, which, with its flexible temporality, was peerlessly suited to representing the complicated structure of emotional 'thoughts' – those experiences that Martha Nussbaum elegantly calls 'the heart's intermittences between recognition and denial of neediness'.[24] Iris Murdoch repeatedly declared that the novel's special capacity is its attention to the specific otherness of people. Or – a different register, this – there is D. H. Lawrence's bracingly arrogant assertion of the novelist's unique status. 'I consider myself superior to the saint, the scientist, the philosopher, and the poet, who are all great masters of different bits of man alive, but never get the whole hog.'[25]

The question of the novel's specialism as a form also preoccupied Golding, as this essay has implicitly discussed. He worried at the question throughout his writing life. The critic Bernard Bergonzi, writing in 1970, devised a famous epitaph for post-war British fiction. Coming after modernism, Bergonzi wrote, the post-war novelists 'inherited a form whose principal characteristic is novelty, or stylistic dynamism, and yet nearly everything possible to be achieved has already been achieved'.[26] He saw the British novel as living – like the post-war British state, with its sequence of economic crises – on finite and dwindling resources; and looking to America for help. Golding's career, however, bucks Bergonzi's analysis. For as we have seen, he perceived the novel not as a starved form, condemned to the rehashing of previous technique and content. By contrast, he saw it as a form which more than any other could approach – *had* to approach – the 'limit to literature' that had been established by the Second World War.

This is not to say that Golding did not feel the novel to be under threat. 'Story will always be with us', he concluded in his 1983 Laureate address following his receipt of the Nobel Prize for Literature in that year:

> but story in a physical book, in a sentence what the West means by 'a novel' – what of that? Certainly, if the form fails let it go. We have enough complications in life, in art, in literature without preserving dead forms fossilised, without cluttering ourselves with Byzantine sterilities. Yes, in that case, let the novel go. But what goes with it? Surely something of profound importance to the human spirit! A novel ensures that we can look before and after, take action at whatever pace we choose, read again and again, skip and go back. The story in a book is humble and serviceable, available, friendly, is not switched on and off but taken up and put down, lasts a lifetime.[27]

The allusion of the last sentence is clearly to television. *Lord of the Flies* was published in 1954, the same year that the daily news bulletin began on British television, and four years before the number of television-owning households came to exceed the number of wireless-owning households. Golding's writing career was nearly simultaneous with the rise of television as a cultural medium, and he was alert to the menace that this new distributor of information and narrative posed to the novel. His response was to concentrate on what he saw as the novel's two unique abilities. First, to depict and evoke the complexity of human interiority. And secondly, to gesture at those mystical instants when darkness becomes visible, when there is – Woolf's phrase once again – 'communication without obstacle'.[28]

Golding liked to tell a story about Blaise Pascal, who, like Golding himself, was a scientist by training, a mystic by inclination, and a writer by vocation. Pascal, he recounted, once 'had a mystical experience of such profundity and force, such intensity and height, that he was prepared to shape his life from it. Yet he knew he would not always feel so and therefore scrawled the hopelessly inadequate words, *feu*, *joie*, on a piece of paper which he had sewn into the lapel of his coat' (*MT*, 190). Like most favoured stories, this reveals as much about its teller as about its subject. We can hear in this description two of Golding's most charismatic traits: his scepticism about the worth of the writer's project, combined with his conviction of the need for verbal record. 'Prose limps after the blinding fact', Golding wrote in the same essay (*MT*, 200). Nevertheless, to Golding, prose's limping gait was better than a stance of silence, which to him was a form of surrender.

NOTE ON EDITIONS

Copyright in all of Golding's novels is held by Faber and Faber: their edition of each novel is presently definitive. There is, as yet, no scholarly edition of any of Golding's novels, save for the 2004 'Educational Edition' of *Lord of the Flies*, which includes an introduction by Mark Kinkead-Weekes, student notes, and an appendix containing the essay 'Fable' that began as a lecture given at UCLA (see below).

NOTES

1 Virginia Woolf, 'Henry James's Ghost Stories', in *Collected Essays*, 4 vols. (London: Hogarth Press), I, pp. 286–92, p. 292.
2 William Golding, *A Moving Target* (London: Faber and Faber, 1982), p. 148. Hereafter *MT*.
3 William Golding, *Pincher Martin* (London: Faber and Faber, 1956; reprinted 1962), p. 7. Hereafter *PM*.
4 William Golding, 'Nobel Prize Acceptance Speech', 7 December 1983. http://nobelprize.org/nobel_prizes/literature/laureates/1983/golding-lecture.html.
5 Henry James, 'Preface' to *What Maisie Knew* (London: Penguin, 1966), p. 3.
6 Golding, 'Belief and Creativity', in *MT*, pp. 185–202, p. 202.
7 Golding, 'Cracked Youth and Age', in *MT*, pp. 98–103, p. 102.
8 Jack I. Biles, *Talk: Conversations with William Golding* (New York: Harcourt, 1970), pp. 30, 38.
9 Iris Murdoch, 'Existentialists and Mystics', in *Existentialists and Mystics*, ed. Peter Conradi (London: Penguin, 1997), pp. 221–34, p. 225.
10 William Golding, 'Fable', in *The Hot Gates* (London: Faber and Faber, 1965), pp. 85–101, p. 85, p. 88.
11 *Ibid.*, pp. 99–100.
12 William Golding, *Lord of the Flies* (London: Faber and Faber, 1954), p. 151. Hereafter *LF.*
13 Woolf, 'Ghost Stories', p. 289.
14 William Golding, *The Inheritors* (London: Faber and Faber, 1955), pp. 229, 231.
15 William Golding, *Free Fall* (London: Faber and Faber, 1959), p. 170.
16 William Golding, *The Spire* (London: Faber and Faber, 1964), pp. 79, 82. Hereafter *S.*

17 Frédéric Regard, 'A Reappraisal of Golding's First Novel', in *Fingering Netsukes* (Saint-Étienne: Publications de l'Université de Saint-Étienne, 1995), p. 45.
18 John Milton, *Paradise Lost*, ed. Alastair Fowler (Harlow: Longman, 1968), Book 1, ll. 62–3.
19 William Golding, *Darkness Visible* (Faber and Faber: London, 1967), pp. 9, 11. Hereafter *DV*.
20 Woolf, 'Ghost Stories', p. 291.
21 Mark Kinkead-Weekes, 'The Visual and the Visionary in Golding', in *William Golding: The Man and His Books*, ed. John Carey (London: Faber and Faber, 1986), pp. 64–83, 76.
22 Milan Kundera, *The Art of the Novel* (London: Faber and Faber, 1988), p. 5.
23 Gabriel d'Aubarède, 'Waiting For Beckett', *Trace*, 42 (Summer 1961), p. 157. Translated by Christopher Waters from the original French in *Nouvelles Littéraires*, 16 February 1961.
24 Martha Nussbaum, *Upheavals of Thought* (Cambridge: Cambridge University Press, 2001), p. 236.
25 D. H. Lawrence, 'Why the Novel Matters', in *Selected Critical Writings* (Oxford: Oxford University Press, 1998), pp. 204–9, 206.
26 Bernard Bergonzi, *The Situation of the Novel* (Pittsburgh: University of Pittsburgh Press, 1971), p. 19.
27 William Golding, 'Nobel Prize Acceptance Speech', http://nobelprize.org/nobel_prizes/literature/laureates/1983/golding-lecture.html.
28 Woolf, 'Ghost Stories', p. 289.

FURTHER READING

Carey, John (ed.), *William Golding: The Man and His Books: A Tribute on His Seventy-Fifth Birthday*, London, Faber and Faber, 1986

Crawford, Paul, *Politics and History in William Golding: The World Turned Upside Down*, Columbia and London, University of Missouri Press, 2002

Fowler-Melville, Anne, *The Paradoxical Appletree: Character, Reality and Illusion in the Novels of William Golding*, Peterborough, Double AA Studios, 2001

Gekoski, R.A., and P.T. Grogan (eds.), *William Golding: A Bibliography*, London, André Deutsch, 1994

Kinkead-Weekes, Mark, and Ian Gregor, *William Golding: A Critical Study of the Novels*, 3rd edn, London, Faber and Faber, 2002

Mackay, Marina, and Lyndsey Stonebridge (eds.), *British Fiction after Modernism: The Novel at Mid-Century*, London, Palgrave Macmillan, 2007

Regard, Frédéric (ed.), *Fingering Netsukes: Selected Papers from the First International William Golding Conference*, Saint-Étienne, Publications de l'Université de Saint-Étienne, in association with Faber and Faber, 1995

Tiger, Virginia, *William Golding: The Dark Fields of Discovery*, London, Calder & Boyars, 1974

GUIDE TO FURTHER READING

Allott, Miriam, *Novelists on the Novel*, London, Routledge & Kegan Paul, 1959

Armstrong, Nancy, *Desire and Domestic Fiction: A Political History of the Novel*, New York and Oxford, Oxford University Press, 1987

Beer, Gillian, *Darwin's Plots: Evolutionary Narrative in Darwin, George Eliot and Nineteenth-Century Fiction*, 2nd edn, Cambridge, Cambridge University Press, 2000

Buckley, Jerome Hamilton, *Season of Youth: The Bildungsroman from Dickens to Golding*, Cambridge, MA, Harvard University Press, 1974

Booth, Wayne C. *The Rhetoric of Fiction*, 2nd edn, Harmondsworth, Penguin, 1991

The Company We Keep: An Ethics of Fiction, Berkeley, University of California Press, 1988

Brooks, Peter, *Reading for the Plot: Design and Intention in Narrative*, Oxford, Clarendon Press, 1984

Realist Vision, New Haven and London, Yale University Press, 2005

Cohn, Dorrit, *Transparent Minds: Narrative Modes of Presenting Consciousness in Fiction*, Princeton, Princeton University Press, 1978

David, Deirdre (ed.), *The Cambridge Companion to the Victorian Novel*, Cambridge, Cambridge University Press, 2001

Eagleton, Terry, *The English Novel*, Oxford, Blackwell, 2005

Ermarth, Elizabeth Deeds, *Realism and Consensus in the English Novel: Time, Space and Narrative*, Princeton, Princeton University Press, 1983

Gallagher, Catherine, *The Body Economic: Life, Death, and Sensation in Political Economy and the Victorian Novel*, Princeton, Princeton University Press, 2006

Garrett, Peter K. *The Victorian Multiplot Novel: Studies in Dialogical Form*, New Haven and London, Yale University Press, 1980

Gilbert, Sandra M. and Susan Gubar, *The Madwoman in the Attic: The Woman Writer and the Nineteenth-Century Literary Imagination*, 2nd edn, New Haven and London, Yale University Press, 2000

Hale, Dorothy J. (ed.), *The Novel: An Anthology of Criticism and Theory, 1900–2000*, Oxford, Blackwell, 2006

Hardy, Barbara, *Tellers and Listeners: The Narrative Imagination*, London, Athlone Press, 1975

Heyns, Michiel, *Expulsion and the Nineteenth-Century Novel: The Scapegoat in English Realist Fiction*, Oxford, Oxford University Press, 1994

Hunter, J. P., *Before Novels: The Cultural Contexts of Eighteenth-Century English Fiction*, New York, Norton, 1990

Kermode, Frank, *The Sense of an Ending: Studies in the Theory of Fiction* [1967], *with a New Epilogue*, Oxford, Oxford University Press, 2000

The Genesis of Secrecy: On the Interpretation of Narrative, Cambridge, MA, Harvard University Press, 1979

Kucich, John, *The Power of Lies: Transgression in Victorian Fiction*, Ithaca, NY, Cornell University Press, 1994

Leavis, F. R., *The Great Tradition: George Eliot, Henry James, Joseph Conrad*, London, Chatto & Windus, 1948

Levine, George, *The Realistic Imagination: English Fiction from Frankenstein to Lady Chatterley*, Chicago and London, Chicago University Press, 1981

Lodge, David, *Language of Fiction: Essays in Criticism and Verbal Analysis of the English Novel*, London, Routledge & Kegan Paul, 1966

McKeon, Michael, *The Origins of the English Novel 1660–1740*, Baltimore, Johns Hopkins University Press, 1987

McKeon, Michael (ed.), *Theory of the Novel: A Historical Approach*, Baltimore and London, Johns Hopkins Press, 2000

Miller, D. A., *Narrative and Its Discontents: Problems of Closure in the Traditional Novel*, Princeton, Princeton University Press, 1981

The Novel and the Police, Berkeley and London, University of California Press, 1988

Miller, J. Hillis, *The Form of Victorian Fiction: Thackeray, Dickens, Trollope, George Eliot, Meredith, and Hardy*, Notre Dame, University of Notre Dame Press, 1968

Fiction and Repetition: Seven English Novels, Oxford, Blackwell, 1982

Moretti, Franco (ed.), *The Novel*, 2 vols., Princeton, Princeton University Press, 2006

Palmer, Alan, *Fictional Minds*, Lincoln, NE, University of Nebraska Press, 2004

Parker, David, *Ethics, Theory and the Novel*, Cambridge and New York, Cambridge University Press, 1994

Parrinder, Patrick, *Nation and Novel: The English Novel from Its Origins to the Present Day*, Oxford, Oxford University Press, 2006

Reilly, Jim, *Shadowtime: History and Representation in Hardy, Conrad, and George Eliot*, London, Routledge, 1993

Richetti, John, *The English Novel in History, 1700–1780*, London, Routledge, 1999

Showalter, Elaine, *A Literature of Their Own: From Charlotte Brontë to Doris Lessing*, rev. edn, London, Virago, 1999

Spacks, Patrica Meyer, *Novel Beginnings: Experiments in Eighteenth-Century English Fiction*, New Haven, Yale University Press, 2006

Spencer, Jane, *The Rise of the Woman Novelist: From Aphra Behn to Jane Austen*, Oxford, Basil Blackwell, 1986

Stewart, Garrett, *Dear Reader: The Conscripted Audience in Nineteenth-Century British Fiction*, Baltimore and London, Johns Hopkins University Press, 1996

Sumner, Rosemary, *A Route to Modernism: Hardy, Lawrence, Woolf*, Basingstoke, Macmillan, 2000

Sutherland, John, *Victorian Novelists and Publishers*, London, Athlone Press, 1976

Warner, William, *Licensing Entertainment: The Elevation of Novel Reading in Britain, 1684–1750*, Berkeley, University of California Press, 1998

Watt, Ian, *The Rise of the Novel: Studies in Defoe, Richardson, and Fielding*, London, Chatto & Windus, 1957

Welsh, Alexander, *Strong Representations: Narrative and Circumstantial Evidence in England*, Baltimore, Johns Hopkins University Press, 1992

White, Allon, *The Uses of Obscurity: The Fiction of Early Modernism*, London, Routledge & Kegan Paul, 1981

Williams, Raymond, *The English Novel from Dickens to Lawrence*, London, Chatto & Windus, 1970

Woloch, Alex, *The One vs. the Many: Minor Characters and the Space of the Protagonist in the Novel*, Princeton and Oxford, Princeton University Press, 2003

Wood, James, *How Fiction Works*, London, Jonathan Cape, 2008

Zunshine, Lisa, *Why We Read Fiction: Theory of Mind and the Novel*, Columbus, Ohio State University Press, 2006

INDEX

Cambridge Companions To ...

AUTHORS

Edward Albee edited by Stephen J. Bottoms

Margaret Atwood edited by Coral Ann Howells

W. H. Auden edited by Stan Smith

Jane Austen edited by Edward Copeland *and* Juliet McMaster

Beckett edited by John Pilling

Aphra Behn edited by Derek Hughes *and* Janet Todd

Walter Benjamin edited by David S. Ferris

William Blake edited by Morris Eaves

Brecht edited by Peter Thomson and Glendyr Sacks (second edition)

The Brontës edited by Heather Glen

Frances Burney edited by Peter Sabor

Byron edited by Drummond Bone

Albert Camus edited by Edward J. Hughes

Willa Cather edited by Marilee Lindemann

Cervantes edited by Anthony J. Cascardi

Chaucer, second edition edited by Piero Boitani *and* Jill Mann

Chekhov edited by Vera Gottlieb and Paul Allain

Kate Chopin edited by Janet Beer

Coleridge edited by Lucy Newlyn

Wilkie Collins edited by Jenny Bourne Taylor

Joseph Conrad edited by J.H. Stape

Dante edited by Rachel Jacoff (second edition)

Daniel Defoe edited by John Richetti

Don DeLillo edited by John N. Duvall

Charles Dickens edited by John O. Jordan

Emily Dickinson edited by Wendy Martin

John Donne edited by Achsah Guibbory

Dostoevskii edited by W. J. Leatherbarrow

Theodore Dreiser edited by Leonard Cassuto *and* Claire Virginia Eby

John Dryden edited by Steven N. Zwicker

W. E. B. Du Bois edited by Shamoon Zamir

George Eliot edited by George Levine

T. S. Eliot edited by A. David Moody

Ralph Ellison edited by Ross Posnock

Ralph Waldo Emerson edited by Joel Porte and Saundra Morris

William Faulkner edited by Philip M. Weinstein

Henry Fielding edited by Claude Rawson

F. Scott Fitzgerald edited by Ruth Prigozy

Flaubert edited by Timothy Unwin

E. M. Forster edited by David Bradshaw

Benjamin Franklin edited by Carla Mulford

Brian Friel edited by Anthony Roche

Robert Frost edited by Robert Faggen

Elizabeth Gaskell edited by Jill L. Matus

Goethe edited by Lesley Sharpe

Günter Grass edited by Stuart Taberner

Thomas Hardy edited by Dale Kramer

David Hare edited by Richard Boon

Nathaniel Hawthorne edited by Richard Millington

Seamus Heaney edited by Bernard O'Donoghue

Ernest Hemingway edited by Scott Donaldson

Homer edited by Robert Fowler

Ibsen edited by James McFarlane

Henry James edited by Jonathan Freedman

Samuel Johnson edited by Greg Clingham

Ben Jonson edited by Richard Harp and Stanley Stewart

James Joyce edited by Derek Attridge (second edition)

Kafka edited by Julian Preece

Keats edited by Susan J. Wolfson

Lacan edited by Jean-Michel Rabaté

D. H. Lawrence edited by Anne Fernihough

Primo Levi edited by Robert Gordon

Lucretius edited by Stuart Gillespie and Philip Hardie

David Mamet edited by Christopher Bigsby

Thomas Mann edited by Ritchie Robertson

Christopher Marlowe edited by Patrick Cheney

Herman Melville edited by Robert S. Levine

Arthur Miller edited by Christopher Bigsby

Milton edited by Dennis Danielson (second edition)

Molière edited by David Bradby and Andrew Calder

Toni Morrison edited by Justine Tally

Nabokov edited by Julian W. Connolly

Eugene O'Neill edited by Michael Manheim

George Orwell edited by John Rodden

Ovid edited by Philip Hardie

Harold Pinter edited by Peter Raby (second edition)

Sylvia Plath edited by Jo Gill

Edgar Allan Poe edited by Kevin J. Hayes

Alexander Pope edited by Pat Rogers

Ezra Pound edited by Ira B. Nadel

Proust edited by Richard Bales

Pushkin edited by Andrew Kahn

Philip Roth edited by Timothy Parrish

Salman Rushdie edited by Abdulrazak Gurnah

Shakespeare edited by Margareta de Grazia and Stanley Wells

Shakespearean Comedy edited by Alexander Leggatt

Shakespeare on Film edited by Russell Jackson (second edition)

Shakespeare's History Plays edited by Michael Hattaway

Shakespeare's Last Plays edited by Catherine M. S. Alexander

Shakespeare's Poetry edited by Patrick Cheney

Shakespeare and Popular Culture edited by Robert Shaughnessy

Shakespeare on Stage edited by Stanley Wells and Sarah Stanton

Shakespearean Tragedy edited by Claire McEachern

George Bernard Shaw edited by Christopher Innes

Shelley edited by Timothy Morton

Mary Shelley edited by Esther Schor

Sam Shepard edited by Matthew C. Roudané

Spenser edited by Andrew Hadfield

Laurence Sterne edited by Thomas Keymer

Wallace Stevens edited by John N. Serio

Tom Stoppard edited by Katherine E. Kelly

Harriet Beecher Stowe edited by Cindy Weinstein

August Strindberg edited by Michael Robinson

Jonathan Swift edited by Christopher Fox

J. M. Synge edited by P. J. Mathews

Henry David Thoreau edited by Joel Myerson

Tolstoy edited by Donna Tussing Orwin

Mark Twain edited by Forrest G. Robinson

Virgil edited by Charles Martindale

Voltaire edited by Nicholas Cronk

Edith Wharton edited by Millicent Bell

Walt Whitman edited by Ezra Greenspan

Oscar Wilde edited by Peter Raby

Tennessee Williams edited by Matthew C. Roudané

August Wilson edited by Christopher Bigsby

Mary Wollstonecraft edited by Claudia L. Johnson

Virginia Woolf edited by Sue Roe and Susan Sellers

Wordsworth edited by Stephen Gill

W. B. Yeats edited by Marjorie Howes and John Kelly

Zola edited by Brian Nelson

TOPICS

The Actress edited by Maggie B. Gale *and* John Stokes

The African American Novel edited by Maryemma Graham

The African American Slave Narrative edited by Audrey A. Fisch

American Modernism edited by Walter Kalaidjian

American Realism and Naturalism edited by Donald Pizer

American Travel Writing edited by Alfred Bendixen *and* Judith Hamera

American Women Playwrights edited by Brenda Murphy

Arthurian Legend edited by Elizabeth Archibald and Ad Putter

Australian Literature edited by Elizabeth Webby

British Romanticism edited by Stuart Curran

British Romantic Poetry edited by James Chandler and Maureen N. McLane

British Theatre, 1730–1830, edited by Jane Moody and Daniel O'Quinn

Canadian Literature edited by Eva-Marie Kröller

The Classic Russian Novel edited by Malcolm V. Jones and Robin Feuer Miller

Contemporary Irish Poetry edited by Matthew Campbell

Crime Fiction edited by Martin Priestman

Early Modern Women's Writing edited by Laura Lunger Knoppers

The Eighteenth-Century Novel edited by John Richetti

Eighteenth-Century Poetry edited by John Sitter

English Literature, 1500–1600 edited by Arthur F. Kinney

English Literature, 1650–1740 edited by Steven N. Zwicker

English Literature, 1740–1830 edited by Thomas Keymer and Jon Mee

English Novelists edited by Adrian Poole

English Poets edited by Claude Rawson

English Poetry, Donne to Marvell edited by Thomas N. Corns

English Renaissance Drama, second edition edited by A.R. Braunmuller and Michael Hattaway

English Restoration Theatre edited by Deborah C. Payne Fisk

Feminist Literary Theory edited by Ellen Rooney

Fiction in the Romantic Period edited by Richard Maxwell and Katie Trumpener

The Fin de Siècle edited by Gail Marshall

The French Novel: from 1800 to the Present edited by Timothy Unwin

German Romanticism edited by Nicholas Saul

Gothic Fiction edited by Jerrold E. Hogle

The Greek and Roman Novel edited by Tim Whitmarsh

Greek and Roman Theatre edited by Marianne McDonald and J. Michael Walton

Greek Tragedy edited by P. E. Easterling

The Harlem Renaissance edited by George Hutchinson

The Irish Novel edited by John Wilson Foster

The Italian Novel edited by Peter Bondanella and Andrea Ciccarelli

Jewish American Literature edited by Hana Wirth-Nesher and Michael P. Kramer

The Latin American Novel edited by Efraín Kristal

The Literature of the First World War edited by Vincent Sherry

The Literature of World War II edited by Marina MacKay

Literature on Screen edited by Deborah Cartmell and Imelda Whelehan

Medieval English Literature edited by Larry Scanlon

Medieval English Theatre edited by Richard Beadle and Alan J. Fletcher (second edition)

Medieval French Literature edited by Simon Gaunt and Sarah Kay

Medieval Romance edited by Roberta L. Krueger

Medieval Women's Writing edited by Carolyn Dinshaw and David Wallace

Modern American Culture edited by Christopher Bigsby

Modern British Women Playwrights edited by Elaine Aston and Janelle Reinelt

Modern French Culture edited by Nicholas Hewitt

Modern German Culture edited by Eva Kolinsky and Wilfried van der Will

The Modern German Novel edited by Graham Bartram

Modern Irish Culture edited by Joe Cleary and Claire Connolly

Modernism edited by Michael Levenson

The Modernist Novel edited by Morag Shiach

Modernist Poetry edited by Alex Davis and Lee M. Jenkins

Modern Italian Culture edited by Zygmunt G. Baranski and Rebecca J. West

Modern Latin American Culture edited by John King

Modern Russian Culture edited by Nicholas Rzhevsky

Modern Spanish Culture edited by David T. Gies

Narrative edited by David Herman

Native American Literature edited by Joy Porter and Kenneth M. Roemer

Nineteenth-Century American Women's Writing edited by Dale M. Bauer and Philip Gould

Old English Literature edited by Malcolm Godden and Michael Lapidge

Performance Studies edited by Tracy C. Davis

Postcolonial Literary Studies edited by Neil Lazarus

Postmodernism edited by Steven Connor

Renaissance Humanism edited by Jill Kraye

Roman Satire edited by Kirk Freudenburg

The Spanish Novel: from 1600 to the Present edited by Harriet Turner and Adelaida López de Martínez

Travel Writing edited by Peter Hulme and Tim Youngs

Twentieth-Century Irish Drama edited by Shaun Richards

The Twentieth-Century English Novel edited by Robert L. Caserio

Twentieth-Century English Poetry edited by Neil Corcoran

Victorian and Edwardian Theatre edited by Kerry Powell

The Victorian Novel edited by Deirdre David

Victorian Poetry edited by Joseph Bristow

War Writing edited by Kate McLoughlin

Writing of the English Revolution edited by N. H. Keeble